New, Expa[...]ed 4th Edition

THE COMPLETE GUIDE TO SELF-PUBLISHING

TOM AND MARILYN ROSS

WRITER'S DIGEST BOOKS
CINCINNATI, OHIO
www.writersdigest.com

 Published by Writer's Digest Books, an imprint of F&W Publications, Inc., 1507 Dana Avenue, Cincinnati, Ohio 45207. (800) 289-0963. Fourth edition.

Visit our Web site at www.writersdigest.com for information on more resources for writers.

To receive a free weekly E-mail newsletter delivering tips and updates about writing and about Writer's Digest products, register directly at our Web site at http://newsletters.fwpublications.com.

06 05 04 03 02 5 4 3 2 1

Ross, Tom

The complete guide to self-publishing: everything you need to know to write, publish, promote and sell your own book / Tom and Marilyn Ross.—4th ed.

p. cm.

Includes bibliographical references and index.

ISBN 1-58297-091-2

1. Self-publishing—United States. 2. Self-publishing—Canada. I. Ross, Marilyn Heimberg. II. Title.

Z285.5.R67 2002

070.5′93′0973—dc21 2001046631

CIP

Edited by Donya Dickerson and David Tompkins

Designed by Sandy Conopeotis Kent

Cover by About Books, Inc.

Production coordinated by Mark Griffin and Kristen Heller

DEDICATION

This book is dedicated to self-publ
Franklins, Sam Clemenses, and
Paul Evans, M.J. Roses, and David Chi
Most of all, it's dedicated to you, ou
of tomorrow.

...ar throughout this book: Adobe Pagemaker, Adobe Pho-
...ger King, Corel Otabind, Cribari Wines, dBase, Dr. Halo III,
...mmatik, IBM, IndexIt, Jiffy, LaserJet, Lotus 1-2-3, Macintosh,
...pe, McDonald's, Microsoft Word, MSFrontPage, Multimate,
...peaking, Nestle, PalmPilot, Paradox, PC PaintBrush, Peachtree,
...cript, QuarkXPress, Right Writer, RightWriter, Rolodex, Source-
..., Total Word, Ventura Publisher, ViaVoice, West Bend, WordPerfect,
...s.

...onson, *The Writer Publisher* (11520 Bixby Hill Rd., Arcade, NY 14009), 1976, ...Press Collections," reprinted by permission of *Small Press*, March/April 1984, ...x Corp., 1984. Proofreading symbols, from *The Writer's Encyclopedia*, edited by ...k Polking, reprinted courtesy of Writer's Digest Books. Typography chart, from *The Children's Picture Book: How to Write It, How to Sell It*, by Ellen E.M. Roberts, designed by Hal Siegel, reprinted courtesy of Writer's Digest Books. "Publisher's Planning Kit" used by permission of Delta Lithograph Company, Van Nuys, California. The spine width and the dust jacket charts reprinted by permission of Sheridan Books, Chelsea, Michigan. Small portions of this book have previously appeared in the *SPAN Connection.* POD specification sheet reprinted with permission from DeHART's Printing Services Corporation. Baker & Taylor Forms reprinted with permission from Baker & Taylor, Inc. Book Sense 76 Independent Booksellers Recommendations reprinted with permission from Carl Lennertz.

ACKNOWLEDGMENTS

Thanks to our many clients, students, and SPAN members for the contributions they've made to this work. Without their thirst for information and their faith that we could quench this thirst, we wouldn't have been challenged to dig so deeply, to probe so many crannies, to look beyond the readily available answers for true solutions. Nor would we have had the motivation or the opportunity to test these findings and document the results.

We also wish to express special gratitude to our original editor, Carol Cartaino, whose editorial suggestions showed remarkable sensitivity and depth of knowledge. To the entire staff of Writer's Digest Books, we say a hearty, "Bravo." You are a unique group of caring and competent people. Julia, Jack, Richard, Stacie, Joanne, Jennifer, Katie, Budge, Donya, Deb, and all the others . . . thanks for being who and what you are.

Without the help of our wonderful staff, this mammoth revision could never have been completed on time. The revisions were bounteous and meticulous, the Internet research and fact checking a gargantuan task. Our deepest appreciation to Cathy, Deb, Kate, Anna, Orpha, and Lurina. What a team! We are also indebted to Gene Schwartz for his input on the Internet sections, Bear Kamoroff for his feedback on tax and business issues, T.J. and Cindy Walker for their fine-tuning of the Web chapter, and Gail Nottingham for her librarian's expertise. And Mary Barton and Marcy Claman were wonderfully helpful about the Canadian publishing scene.

Additionally, we wish to acknowledge the countless individuals, organizations, and companies who so generously offered ideas, information, review copies of books, and software. *The Complete Guide to Self-Publishing* grew out of people's experiences—our own and many others'. Sincerest thanks to all those who have gone before, from the pioneers who cut the trails to the engineers who paved the road, so that our travels might be easier.

ABOUT THE AUTHORS

Tom and Marilyn Ross—and their passion for self-publishing—have been featured in *The New York Times*, *Los Angeles Times*, *Denver Post*, *Chicago Tribune*, *The Wall Street Journal*, *Success*, *Entrepreneur*, *U.S. News & World Report*, and dozens of other national magazines and newspapers. After self-publishing six books, this husband and wife team began giving nationwide writing and publishing seminars to share what they had learned about the process. A flood of requests for individual guidance led to the creation of their consulting service, About Books, Inc. Since 1978, they have helped thousands of authors, entrepreneurs, professionals, corporations, and associations successfully self-publish.

Their companion book to the award-winning *Complete Guide to Self-Publishing* is *Jump Start Your Book Sales*, which continues to rack up rave reviews. And Marilyn's new *Shameless Marketing for Brazen Hussies* is raising eyebrows—and ringing cash registers—from coast to coast.

These busy professionals "preach what they practice" and continue to be in demand as speakers. They've been on the faculty of Folio's New York Face-to-Face conference, lectured at colleges and universities, and been invited to keynote and give seminars for regional writing, publishing, and speaking associations all across the United States and Canada.

Tom Ross has masterminded promotional campaigns that created extensive print, radio, and TV coverage, and opened doors for national book distribution. As a consultant, Tom specializes in helping clients with project analysis, editing, production, computerization, and developing nationwide book marketing campaigns. A recovering computer engineer, he is a respected leader in the publishing industry.

Marilyn Ross is the award-winning author of twelve nonfiction books, hundreds of articles, and a monthly newsletter. She has also served as a corporate director of marketing and owned and operated her own advertising/PR agency. She currently heads Communication Creativity—the Rosses' publishing imprint that produces their other books.

This busy pair also serve as senior associates of the prestigious Center for the New West, "a think tank that casts its visionary net over the vast economic and cultural landscape . . ." according to *The Christian Science Monitor*. They are both listed in the twenty-fourth edition of *Who's Who in the West*. And between them, this dynamic pair is also included in *Who's Who of American Women*, *The World Who's Who of Women*, *International Businessmen's Who's Who*, and *Men and Women of Distinction*.

Their writing careers are detailed in *The Working Press of the Nation*; *Who's Who in U.S. Writers, Editors & Poets*; *The International Authors and Writers Who's*

Who; and *Contemporary Authors*. Both also belong to the Authors Guild, the American Society of Journalists and Authors (ASJA), and the National Speakers Association.

In 1996, as a way to give back to an industry that has been good to them, they launched SPAN, a nonprofit trade association for authors, self-publishers, and independent presses. The Small Publishers Association of North America (SPAN) has become the second largest such organization in the world.

About Books, Inc. (ABI), the publishing and book marketing firm founded in 1979 by Marilyn and Tom, provides turnkey service to individuals and organizations that seek to successfully publish and promote their books. The Rosses handle all aspects of book editing, design, production, and marketing. Since ABI works strictly as a consultant, authors retain all rights to their work, own all copies of their books, and reap 100 percent of the profits. Marilyn and Tom have a proven track record of producing attractive books and result-getting promotion and publicity.

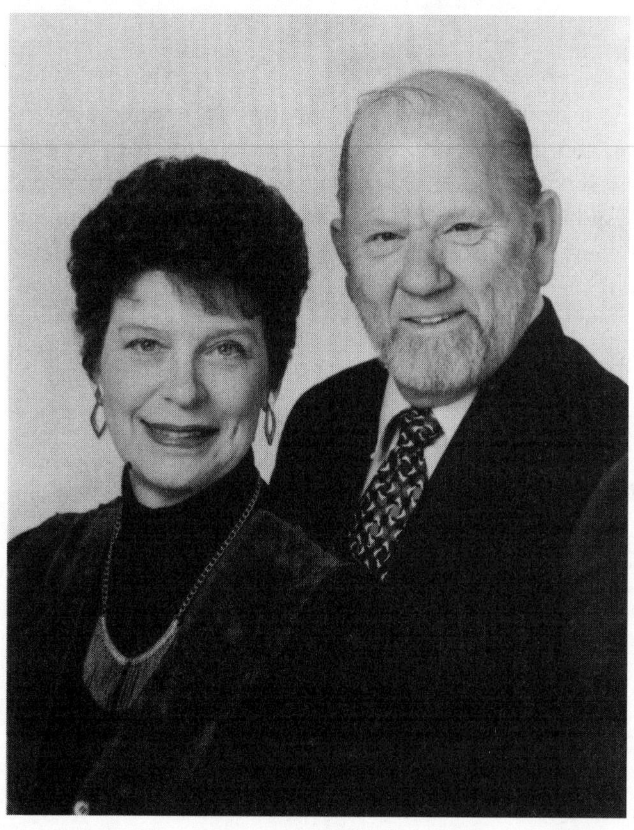

BOOKS BY MARILYN AND TOM ROSS

Jump Start Your Book Sales
Country Bound!
The Complete Guide to Self-Publishing
Marketing Your Books
How to Make Big Profits Publishing City and Regional Books
The Encyclopedia of Self-Publishing
Big Ideas for Small Service Businesses

Books by Marilyn Ross
Shameless Marketing for Brazen Hussies
Be Tough or Be Gone
National Directory of Newspaper Op-Ed Pages
Discover Your Roots
Creative Loafing

How to Contact the Authors
Tom and Marilyn Ross provide full consulting services for selected authors, businesses, associations, and nonprofit organizations nationwide. Requests for information about these services, as well as inquiries about their availability for speeches and seminars, should be directed to them at the address below. Readers of this book are also encouraged to contact the authors with comments and ideas for future editions.

Marilyn and Tom Ross, About Books, Inc.
425 Cedar St., P.O. Box 1500-G
Buena Vista, CO 81211-1500
Phone: (719) 395-2459, Fax: (719) 395-8374
Marilyn@About-Books.com
Web site: www.About-Books.com
Book information: www.SPANnet.org

Here's what people are saying about *The Complete Guide to Self-Publishing*:

"Marilyn and Tom have done it again with their new edition. Their book is still the most readable guide to self-publishing, and now it's loaded with up-to-date examples and current resources for e-publishing, on-demand publishing, and other forms of self-publishing. What a great resource!" —John Kremer, author, *1,001 Ways to Market Your Books*

"Besides telling how to write, publish, promote, and sell one's own book, the authors provide key names and addresses, book production guidance, sample sales letters, tips on business procedures, and suggestions on organizing and implementing a publicity campaign."

—*Publishers Weekly*

". . . a sound overview of self-publishing." —*Los Angeles Times*

"A good source of sound, detailed advice."

—Judith Appelbaum, author, *How to Get Happily Published*

"I have worn out two copies myself from constant use. This is THE most useful, authoritative guide for self-publishers, period." —Dan Kennedy, *No B.S. Marketing Letter*

"There's really nothing to self-publishing, except for about 6,000 little details, most of them covered in Tom and Marilyn's book."

—Bernard "Bear" Kamoroff, author, *Small Time Operator*

"Right after the book [*The Green Book—RVs Rated*] was published, I found your book at the local library. I was stunned. I read it from cover to cover twice in one week. I couldn't believe it. I had done almost everything wrong! I'm embarrassed to tell you about it. All was not lost, however. Your section on direct mailing triggered some ideas and I ran with it. It worked like a charm. I can't thank you enough for your knowledge, wisdom, and business savvy." —Connie Bernardo, publisher, Quill Publishing

"A handbook stuffed with essential information on how to get into print, and beyond. . . . The authors are fully prepared; they have self-published and successfully marketed several books. With realism and extraordinary thoroughness, every practical topic is covered: how to organize for research and writing; mastering the ISBN, ABI, and CIP formalities; developing necessary business procedures; finding the right printer and format; advertising and promoting (including some very inventive approaches); and pushing distribution. Under the rubric 'Other Alternatives' there are chapters on agents, conventional trade publishers, and vanity presses. Current lists of helpful organizations, reviewing media and syndicated columnists, bookstore chains, selected wholesalers, buyers of subsidiary rights, a bibliography, glossary, and index pack riches right up to the last page." —*Booklist*

"For those who are considering self-publishing their books, this newly revised and updated, comprehensive guide to the publishing process may be all they need."

—*The Bloomsbury Review*

"Zillions of times I have referred to your book. Thank you both for providing such a well-written, comprehensive guide to first-time publishers, like me. You helped me make a dream come true. I feel that your book is the best one on the market for self-publishers."

—Cassandra S. Clancy, author-publisher, Inky Press

"We've seen excellent guides devoted to various stages of self-publishing—writing and product development, or production, or promotion, or distribution—but this book contains all you need to know about *every* aspect in one volume." —*The Newsletter on Newsletters*

"If you've ever had the urge to write, publish, promote, and sell your own work, here's a fabulous book to guide you successfully through every step of the way. . . . It can save you thousands of dollars and be the difference between having a successful book or a flop."

—*Sid Asher's World*

"*The Complete Guide to Self-Publishing* is one of the, if not *the*, most valuable book in my library. I wish I had bought this book a long time ago. I would have understood much more about what I was trying to do." —Jennifer Rose, Recollections Publishing

"This is the best book I've seen on the subject. I felt a certain friendliness, kindness and compassion in it. Highest recommendation."

—John Paul Barrett, author, *How to Make a Book*

"Here's a practical work by a couple who have gone the standard route and have prepared a book full of hints on how to go about publishing your own book. The text offers sound advice on all the basic aspects of publishing." —*John Barkham Review*

"The Rosses are providing a primer, in a way, of how to get into the publishing business."

—*Canadian Author and Bookman*

". . . loaded with excellent practical advice, plus forms to fill out and models to follow. The authors are energetic yet irreverent, and their attitude is refreshing."

—*San Francisco Chronicle*

TABLE OF CONTENTS

LIST OF ILLUSTRATIONS

PREFACE

Self-publishing is a perfect example of the American dream. It is stimulating, demanding, and rewarding. For many it has proven to be the do-it-yourself way to fame and fortune.

This book evolved out of the nationwide writing and publishing seminars we gave in the late 1970s. During those workshops we were barraged with questions. What should I write about? How do we handle book production? What are the secrets for getting nationwide publicity and distribution? And people who couldn't attend our seminars wanted a guide to help them successfully navigate the risky waters of private publishing. These needs motivated us to write and self-publish *The Encyclopedia of Self-Publishing*. It was the forerunner of the first edition of *The Complete Guide to Self-Publishing*. This newly updated and greatly expanded fourth edition you're now reading also explores new venues for getting books to consumers, including the Internet, which has forever changed the face of publishing.

The Complete Guide to Self-Publishing has been researched not in the quiet halls of institutions, but in the bustle of the everyday marketplace. This isn't a book of fancy theory; it's a practical handbook of state-of-the-art specifics. We've used ourselves and our own books as guinea pigs, refining our craft and sharpening our expertise. We share many personal experiences in these pages and let you know what works . . . and what doesn't. It is not just our story but the story of many of our clients and students and more than a hundred other prosperous self-publishers. And this new edition is chock-full of Web sites to make your job easier and your results profitable.

Over the last several years, we've not only published our own titles but also served as consultants. Our company, About Books, Inc., has helped people and organizations from all over North America publish and promote their own books. We've dealt with all kinds of nonfiction, and with novels, poetry, children's books, family histories, and autobiographies. We've had the pleasure of working with some of the nicest people on the face of God's green earth. Although we haven't met many of these clients face-to-face, we feel a real kinship with them after helping give birth to their books.

No less real is the sadness we've felt for some self-published authors—authors who asked us to promote works that simply weren't marketable. The message was unclear or uninteresting, or the book itself amateurish and poorly produced. We had to say no far too often. We hope this book will help prevent authors from making these kinds of mistakes.

Done properly, self-publishing is an exciting and viable way to get your book into print. We hope this guide will show many thousands how to do just that.

* * *

P. S. Hi, ya'll. This is Tom. It seems only fair that I give credit where credit is due. As you may know, for years I've been active in the writing of this book. This fourth edition is different. As I enter into the winter of my life, my energies seem to be consumed by management responsibilities and SPAN. I just don't have the "go" anymore to burn the midnight oil writing.

Therefore, although I have edited every word and hopefully added some value, the research and writing has been done by my partner in all things—including business, writing, and life—my bride of twenty-four years, Marilyn.

I want to add my appreciation to yours. Marilyn, thanks for a brilliant work!

SHOULD YOU TAKE CONTROL OF YOUR OWN DESTINY?

The author, the professional, the entrepreneur—anyone who wants to control his or her own destiny will find this book's message of value. It unmasks the mystique of publishing and empowers you in new and well-paying ways. In fact, selling information in the form of a book or booklet is the ideal business because you have no direct competition and can do it from anywhere! You become an "infopreneur." Close encounters of a profitable kind become a distinct possibility.

Of course, creators of fiction and poetry have chosen to control their destiny since the days of Zane Grey, Virginia Woolf, and Walt Whitman. Today's midlist authors are joining their yesteryear colleagues in droves. Proven midlist authors, those who have written and published strong, well-received books through traditional New York publishing houses for years, are now finding the doors slammed shut. The warm welcome they once received has turned to a cold shoulder.

Talented, experienced writers are investigating do-it-yourself alternatives to getting their new books into print. Additionally, they're taking charge of their out-of-print works, serving as midwives to rebirth these books.

Let us identify the three routes to publishing and clarify some terminology. A person can be self-published, subsidy published, or commercially published.

Self-Publishing

Self-publishers are sometimes called micropublishers, private publishers, alternative publishers, independent publishers, or small presses (though usually the later two denote publishers of several titles). But whatever label they may wear, they are, in a word, "mavericks." And they are part of a larger whole known as the small-press movement—which, by the way, is growing at a breathtaking rate and has achieved not only respectability but extraordinary results.

Subsidy Publishing

So that no one is confused, let us briefly clarify what we mean by "vanity/subsidy" publishing. In subsidy publishing, the author gets only a royalty on each book sold—after paying the publisher to publish the book. The book may be stigmatized because book reviewers and bookstores usually avoid subsidy titles. Book sales are typically minimal. A new version of vanity publishing—electronic vanity publishing—has emerged over the last several years, however, and we will be taking a penetrating look at this process.

Commercial Publishing

Commercial, or trade, publishing houses are those that foot the publishing bill. The vast majority of these traditional publishers are located in New York City.

The industry has been transformed over the last two decades by mergers and consolidations. There are now five huge international conglomerates that account for 80 percent of all book revenues. They are Random House, Inc., Simon & Schuster, HarperCollins Publishers, Penguin Putnam Inc., and Warner Books/Little Brown. These conglomerate publishers have placed a much greater emphasis on the bottom line than was done in years past. In reaction many medium-sized houses have started around the country. They typically specialize in specific niche subject areas, such as gardening, health, cookbooks, parenting, novels, or regional travel guides.

Who Can Benefit From This Book?

Interestingly, the employees of these independent presses will find this book of great use. It opens exciting new vistas for new employees—giving them a quick overview of the industry. Even seasoned personnel discover within these pages answers to various questions, plus innovative marketing strategies often ignored in the rush to meet deadlines.

And because self-publishing is but a microcosm of the whole publishing industry, universities offering publishing courses will find *The Complete Guide to Self-Publishing* an unequaled textbook. So will printers and other suppliers who want to easily educate their potential customers without personally answering dozens of time-consuming questions.

Success is following your dream . . . without tripping over a nightmare. We show you how. Self-publishing is an exciting alternative to the millions of rejection slips unpublished authors collect each year. Repeated rejection can smother the hopes of ordinary men and women. But for the hearty, the courageous, it serves as a challenge. They decide to launch their own work. They become self-publishers. This book is for them.

It is also for entrepreneurs seeking to exploit their knowledge and create a dynamic new marketing tool and revenue stream. Here, they will discover proven methods for packaging and promoting ideas, concepts, experience, and skills. Authoring a book gives a businessperson fresh visibility and credibility—a reason to be "news." And it's an unequaled promotional piece; brochures are tossed—books, however, are saved on bookshelves.

The Complete Guide to Self-Publishing is also for doctors, other health care providers, ministers, educators, therapists, attorneys—any professional who wants to share knowledge or philosophies. Many men and women are opting to capitalize on their expertise in this way . . . and attract new patients and clients in the process.

And, of course, fiction writers and poets can use self-publishing as an alternative to the increasingly competitive world of commercial publishing.

Making a Career From Your Writing

A book is the ideal "product." Unlike a gadget or process that others can modify only slightly and pass off as their own, your book is protected by a copyright. You have 100 percent control. No one else can market an identical product. Another reason a book is preferable to an invention is that a patent has a limited life span; an author's copyright goes on and on. Fortunes have been amassed by average people who wrote books, booklets, or special reports, then merchandised them through direct marketing techniques. This guide shows you how to establish a publishing venture to sell your specialized information.

Writing an information-based book makes you an instant "expert." You are noted and quoted. People will pay for your expertise in other forms, too. Many authors begin by teaching courses on the subject, then graduate to paid speaking engagements and high-priced seminars or teleseminars. Often, an expensive newsletter follows to keep readers up-to-date on the subject. From there, consulting is a natural leap. A few consultants charge as much as $10,000 a day. Yes, properly orchestrated, a book can lead to a fascinating and lucrative career as an author-speaker-consultant. Each side of the triangle supports the other.

Associations, professional societies, churches, and other nonprofit entities will find this manual of great value. Such groups often discover that publishing books enhances their reputations, expands their spheres of influence, and is an effective fund-raising tool. For associations, books provide ideal forums for lobbying efforts.

A corporate history, a colorful CEO's story, or a how-to book related to a company's products or services can benefit that corporation. Many have found that such a publication stimulates business. A book helps establish corporate identity and attract investors. And many corporations find it makes sense to publish proprietary information previously used solely in-house. This product gives them a new revenue base.

Special Information for Canadians

We're pleased to say this revised fourth edition also contains information of use to our Canadian friends. Those who wish to self-publish in Canada can now find relevant information on copyright, ISBN, CIP, associations to join, plus specific marketing advice for successfully publishing in the provinces. Appendix C contains a list of Canadian resources. (Of course, much of this information will also be of use to United States' citizens who want to sell into the Canadian market.)

Using This Book When Working With Commercial Publishers

But what of authors anywhere in North America who currently have a book placed with a regular commercial publisher? Will this handbook be of any help to them? It's indispensable! It's imperative that authors take the initiative to help their books stand out from the herd.

Approximately 2 million different titles are currently in print. Two million! And there exists a sizable statistical gap about the number of books published each year. Most in this industry would say that about 50,000 new books come on the market each year. Yet with the advent of easy electronic publishing, we'd guess that closer to 100,000 new titles are being released annually. The discrepancy between the two figures is enormous. If the latter number is close, every author had better be extremely *proactive* in creating quality books and promoting the heck out of them! Otherwise he or she will never be separated from the cascading chatter of competition.

Unknown writers are hurt by the fact that a disproportionate chunk of advertising dollars is siphoned off for authors with established track records, celebrity status, and brand names. The policy of many mainstream publishers is to market one in every twenty books hard, take a few healthy swipes at one out of every three, and wait and see about the rest. This wait-and-see attitude is death to the average author's work. Happily, it needn't be. A book that is perceived as strong in the marketplace will command the necessary resources to become strong. That's where *you* can play an enormously vital role. This guide will give you the savvy and clout needed to leverage yourself and your book to a position of power.

This is vital to your success . . . every bit as important if you are published by one of the major commercial houses. Joni Evans, previously executive vice-president and publisher of Random House, revealed in an interview in *Lear's* magazine, "Only 10 percent of the books published by any house earn out their advances."

Do you realize what this really says? Nine out of ten books fail! All you'll ever receive is the advance. Imagine spending years of your life writing a wonderful book, then settling for a paltry advance of a few thousand dollars with the expectation that great things are just around the corner. And that's all you ever get. No wonder self-publishing is on the rise. If bigger was always better, dinosaurs would rule the earth. The good news is that to develop and successfully market a book, you don't have to visit a channeling medium or take a course in reading tea leaves.

For the author whose title has already languished to out-of-print status, this book offers tips on how to bolt from the trade publisher that has let your work languish. Books that were neglected through disinterest or blundering have later soared to great acclaim and profits through the efforts of their authors. Here, once you've recaptured the rights to your book, you'll learn how to republish and market it successfully . . . without being shackled to a big house's agenda.

Lastly, this guide is for people considering paying to have their books produced by subsidy (vanity) presses. We examine the realities of this form of publishing and offer thought-provoking comments on this controversial method of getting into print.

How to Use This Book

While certainly not a new field, self-publishing is becoming increasingly popular. The *Los Angeles Times* stated, "Self-publishing has become respectable and even fun" (not to mention a moneymaker for those who approach it properly). *Writer's Digest* magazine called it "the do-it-yourself way to success." No less than *U.S. News & World Report*, *The New York Times*, and CNNfn on the Web have featured recent stories about this growing phenomenon.

Self-publishing isn't a fad. It isn't a trend. It is a revolution! The Internet opens awesome new opportunities for authors and publishers, which we'll be exploring in depth. The information explosion is fully upon us. Good news, indeed, since how-to and self-help are the bread and butter of self-publishing.

Publishing is not an act of God; it is a series of actions. To receive the greatest benefit from the information contained in *The Complete Guide to Self-Publishing*, we suggest you first read the whole book *before* starting to apply any of it. Then, go back and take things one step at a time. This is the point when you'll be able to use the Self-Publishing Timetable on page 439. The timetable shows you each of the major steps you must take in the order they are taken. There is also a glossary of terms to define unfamiliar words, phrases, and acronyms.

To add a bit of variety and fun, each chapter concludes with Web Sites, Wisdom, and Whimsey. These sections provide snippets of insight, invaluable Internet resources, and a dose of humor to enliven your day.

For simplification, we'll be referring to a "book" throughout. If you're doing special reports, booklets, monographs, or chapbooks, please substitute the appropriate word. For additional clarity and ease, a list of resources and marketing contacts, a bibliography, and a comprehensive index are included.

To our knowledge, no other reference work contains so much detailed information for authors, publishers, and entrepreneurs . . . nor so many examples of stealth marketing strategies that work. We hope you find the reading interesting, the material helpful, and your endeavors profitable.

But doing a book is not just about money (though we believe wholeheartedly that there is absolutely nothing wrong with being well paid for your efforts).

Writing and publishing books is a trust, an honor. It gives us the opportunity to change lives—thousands, sometimes millions, of lives—to help people solve pressing personal problems, be more successful at work, or be richly entertained. It's about making the world a better place while creating books for social good, to inspire, to have fun, to cope more effectively. Authorship—and the publishing process that accompanies it—is an awesome responsibility accompanied by a wonderous privilege. True believers do it with spirit and with passionate commitment. May you join their ranks. To your success!

PART I

Today's Publishing Scene

1 *Your Portal to Self-Publishing: Enter Here*

Are you the type of person who wants to be behind the wheel rather than just go along for the ride? Then you have the right stuff—the stuff self-publishers are made of. Piloting a plane is much like driving a car, except that in flying, the operator's sights are set higher. So why don't you step into the cockpit, get your publication airborne, and pilot your work to success. The feeling is exhilarating, the rewards are great, and it is a lot simpler than it may seem. Not easy, mind you, but simple. Of course, as everyone who has gone before can tell you, the ride can sometimes get bumpy. Self-publishing, like flying, offers exciting highs and some worrisome bumps: the pleasures and pitfalls of the trade. Here, we examine the big picture in small publishing.

Success Stories From Yesterday and Today

Self-publishing—the act of privately producing and marketing your own work—is an American tradition as old as the thirteen colonies. Ben Franklin is credited as the first American to take this bold step. Tom Paine was another early American self-publisher. Since then, many famous men and women have first appeared on the literary scene through their own publishing efforts.

Fiction has often been successfully self-published. We might not have the marvelous story of *Huckleberry Finn* if Mark Twain hadn't become a self-publisher. The reception traditional publishers gave Zane Grey's first novel, *Betty Zane*, was as cool as the underside of a pillow. Consequently, he decided to produce it himself. Among others who have been successful through self-publishing are Anaïs Nin, Walt Whitman, Virginia Woolf, Gertrude Stein, Edgar Allan Poe, Mary Baker Eddy, even James Joyce with his classic *Ulysses*. Another name not normally associated with self-publishing is Carl Sandburg. Sandburg not only wrote poems but set them in type, rolled the presses, hand-pulled the galley proofs, and bound the books himself.

Can you guess what novel was printed in Florence, Italy? It was too controversial for its time, but D.H. Lawrence realized that the Italians couldn't read what they were printing, so that's where *Lady Chatterley's Lover* was first produced. And what of the Tarzan series? Think of the jungle drama that might never have been if Edgar Rice Burroughs hadn't taken matters into his own hands.

Some of the reference works that we value today were introduced years ago by their authors. This is how *Robert's Rules of Order* and, in 1855, *Bartlett's Familiar Quotations* came to be. Most writers are familiar with a small but superb book titled *The Elements of Style*. William Strunk, Jr. breathed life into it himself when he had it printed in the early 1900s as a text for his English classes at Cornell.

In 1969, when John Muir came out with his classic *How to Keep Your VW Alive*, he had no idea he was launching a publishing empire. On *VW*'s heels came more books from this prolific author. Though Muir has passed away, he left a legacy. John Muir Publications, Inc., spread its publishing wings to include titles in such diverse areas as travel, art, parenting, automotive, and even a young readers' series. It was recently acquired by a major publisher.

The phenomenally successful *What Color Is Your Parachute?* began its trek to best-seller status as a self-published book in 1970. Richard Nelson Bolles, an Episcopal clergyman, originally wrote it for other clergy contemplating a return to secular life. When Ten Speed Press took over this career-counseling handbook, Bolles was asked to make a few revisions to give the book broader appeal. Broad appeal is putting it mildly. *What Color Is Your Parachute?* has over 8 million copies in print, continues to sell at the rate of 1,000 copies daily, and is available in ten languages. It's been ordered in bulk by the Pentagon and General Electric and used as a textbook in countless classes.

Bolles has gone on to write several others. It was interesting to note, when we last spoke to Ten Speed's publicist, that Bolles's classic and another self-published book, Mollie Katzen's *Moosewood Cookbook*, were their two top-selling titles out of a field of approximately three hundred.

You may recognize a book that held sway as a sensational best-seller a decade or so ago: *The One Minute Manager*. One of the first business books to present practical management techniques in story form, this little book revolutionized how people learn. Authors Kenneth Blanchard, Ph.D., and Spencer Johnson, M.D., initially self-published the book to use in their seminars. Soliciting feedback from attendees, they revised it five times and sold 20,000 copies themselves before turning it over to a commercial publisher. The rest is history.

As we write this edition of *The Complete Guide to Self-Publishing*, Dr. Spencer Johnson's *Who Moved My Cheese?* is number one on the *Publishers Weekly* nonfiction best-seller list. (Not surprisingly, it has been there sixty-four weeks and carries a foreword by Kenneth Blanchard, Ph.D.) In spite of a mere 94 pages, this parable about change packs a mighty wallop. It takes place in a maze and involves four beings: two mice and two mouse-sized humans. There is nothing mouse-sized, however, about the success Johnson and Blanchard have accomplished. And it all began because of one little self-published book.

Vicki Lansky submitted her book *Feed Me! I'm Yours* to no fewer than forty-nine publishers before she and her then husband, Bruce, got fed up (no pun intended) and decided to publish it themselves. This little book is a guide to making fresh, pure baby food at home. It contains some two hundred recipes for sneaking nutrition into food for infants and toddlers.

Was the decision to self-publish wise? *Feed Me!* has sold over 2 million copies. Bantam bought the mass paperback rights, and Simon & Schuster and Meadowbrook sell the larger edition. Not too shabby for a book the trade publishers wouldn't initially touch. Next Lansky wrote *The Taming of the C.A.N.D.Y. Monster*, which headed *The New York Times* best-seller list for trade paperbacks.

Lansky now has a total of thirty books to her credit, about half of them given birth by her own publishing imprint, Minnetonka, Minnesota-based Book Peddlers. She also is a contributing editor to *FamilyCircle* magazine. In addition to selling to bookstores, she sells her products to catalogs, gift shops, and unique special markets. For instance, each year Lansky merchandises about 5,000 copies of one title, *Koko Bear's Big Earache*, to ear, nose, and throat specialists. It helps prepare youngsters for ear tube surgery. And her *Welcoming Your Second Baby* is a big hit with childbirth educators. Furthermore, when her original commercial publisher dropped the ball on her *Birthday Parties* book, she took it over and has 185,000 copies in print today.

Leadership Secrets of Attila the Hun was published by its author, Wess Roberts, who is a psychologist by training. He wanted to do a populist book that was funny and irreverent yet based on fundamentally sound business principles. Seventeen publishers rejected his efforts. He intended to just give it away to interested people. When Ross Perot ordered several hundred copies and Fortune 500 CEOs began sending Roberts laudatory letters, he knew he had something. So did a HarperCollins editor when an agent brought the book to his attention. Roberts got a $30,000 advance and now works as an author full-time. His book, which provides bite-sized nuggets of business information, is in twenty-two languages and has spun off a sequel, *Victory Secrets of Attila the Hun*.

Dr. William C. (Bill) Byham, the founder of Development Dimensions International, Inc., a Pittsburgh-headquartered consulting firm with global offices, wrote and published *Zapp! The Lightning of Empowerment* in 1988. The book was one of the first to cleverly combine the elements of a fable with a business management case study. *The Wall Street Journal* said Byham created a new genre. *Zapp!* was merchandised primarily in the few mega business bookstores in each city. Word of mouth led corporations to buy in bulk, resulting in the self-published version selling an impressive 275,000 copies.

"If I had it to do over I'd do exactly the same thing," comments Byham. By privately publishing the book, he was able to continuously improve it. The name of the hero was changed, two chapters were removed, and offensive references deleted. When he handed the reigns over to a commercial publisher, he ended up with a wonderful advance, plus unusual and especially practical contract terms. We discuss them in a later chapter.

Speaking of advances, we don't know of any self-published work that has topped the incredible results Richard Paul Evans achieved. He wrote a slim, intimate volume titled *The Christmas Box*, which dealt with twin tragedies in parenthood. He gave a few bound copies to family members. They were quickly shared with friends and passed along to other friends. Strangers started calling to say how much the book meant to them. Encouraged, Evans approached local publishers. They quickly rejected it.

So he and his wife risked their savings to self-publish 8,000 copies in August of 1993. It began selling in a scattering of Salt Lake City, Utah, bookstores where he lived. And those local ripples became a wave that swept America. Simon & Schuster ultimately offered him a $4.125 million contract for *The Christmas Box* and a sequel! His book has sold more than 7 million copies, has been translated into seventeen different languages, and made history when it became the only book to simultaneously hit the number one spot on both *The New York Times* hardcover and paperback best-seller lists. Next in the trilogy came *Timepiece*, then *The Letter*. These were followed by *The Locket*, *The Carousel*, and *The Looking Glass*. The list is sure to go on, as are the revenues.

Another self-publishing all-star, which garnered an $800,000 advance from Warner Books, is *The Celestine Prophecy*. This spiritual adventure parable taking place in Peru is by first-time author-publisher James Redfield. (The whole book sounds like a marvelous fairy tale, yet it's all true.) Redfield stoked his book to success by plunging full-time into the inspirational lecture circuit and giving away more than 1,500 copies in the first six months to generate word-of-mouth recommendations. Redfield and his wife published and sold over 100,000 copies, then came to the attention of several major publishers, "All promising us the moon," says Redfield. In 1994, *The Celestine Prophecy* was published in hardcover. By the close of the century, it had sold more than 4 million copies and had resided on *The New York Times* best-seller list for over three years! Interestingly, it has sold twice as many copies abroad as it has sold in the United States. Who would have guessed an unattractively packaged self-published story would touch so many lives and go on to become both a national and international best-seller?

Another self-published book captured the number ten spot on *The New York*

Times best-seller list. *On a Clear Day You Can See General Motors* was written and published by a freelance journalist, J. Patrick Wright. The book is a classical muckraking job in the Ralph Nader tradition. Press coverage and word of mouth in the business community put it on the best-seller list. But that was only the beginning of this self-published bonanza. Avon bought the paperback rights for a hefty $247,500; it was picked up by a Macmillan book club and by the Conservative Book Club; and Japanese translation rights were sold.

A book that was lodged firmly on the *Publishers Weekly* best-seller list when we revised this guide in 1989 was Louise Hay's *You Can Heal Your Life*. Hay has refused offers from several large publishers for mass-market paperback rights. Smart lady, that one. Sales just keep blossoming. From this grassroots beginning, she now has 150 books in print and 350 audiotapes. Hay House acquired one of its meditation tapes from no less than Dr. Bernie Siegel. This New Age publisher is definitely doing something right. Hay House has quintupled its sales over the last eight years.

One of the biggest contemporary self-publishing all-stars was Peter McWilliams and his Prelude Press, which he ran out of his home. McWilliams's track record is astonishing. He sold 3.5 million poetry books. Yes, we said poetry. He began selling his poems in high school. Best-seller status is nothing new to him. He experienced it with *How to Survive the Loss of a Love* (more than 2 million copies sold), *You Can't Afford the Luxury of a Negative Thought* (turned down by twenty trade publishers before he breathed life into it), and *Life 101* (another staple on *The New York Times* best-seller list). *Do It! Let's Get Off Our Buts* also hit number one on the *Times* list and his *Personal Computer Book* led a series of computer books that sold more than 1.6 million copies. It was rumored he was offered $1 million for his publishing company. He said no. Peter McWilliams died on June 14, 2000. He left a rich legacy for other self-publishers to follow.

Of more recent acclaim is a book whose author breathed life into it. A twenty-two-year-old recent college grad, Benjamin Kaplan, published *How to Go to College Almost for Free* in early 2000 and sold 15,000 copies the first few months it was out. Furthermore, he convinced Sallie Mae (no not a Southern belle but rather the organization best known for helping students fund college) to invest $250,000 in a twenty-city scholarship coaching tour, during which Kaplan also aggressively promoted his book.

When Chuck Ditlefsen started Cedco Publishing in 1978, he had no idea his company would end up on *Inc.* magazine's list of the five hundred fastest-growing companies in America. It all began with a self-published calendar. In the first year, he sold 16,000 copies of *Those Magnificent Trains*. The following year, sales mushroomed to 35,000 copies. Today Cedco has 225 calendars, 60 books, and 8 CD-ROMs on its list. Most of the San Rafael, California, company's products are the result of licensing deals with the Rolling Stones, *Star Wars*, Dilbert, Disney, and the representatives of Marilyn Monroe, James Dean, and Elvis Presley—which just goes to show you can come up with content in many different ways. Ditlefsen's advice? Emphasize quality, don't try to compete on price, sell what consumers want, and, "Do what you love, then you will do well."

The Rewards of Do-It-Yourself Publishing

Self-publishing offers the potential for huge profits. No longer do you have to be satisfied with the meager 5 to 15 percent royalty that commercial publishers dole out. For those who use creativity, persistence, and sound business sense, money is there to be made.

Self-publishing can be the road to independence. What motivates entrepreneurs to launch their own businesses? They want to be their own bosses. So said 82 percent of those surveyed in a recent study. More personal freedom was the second most important reason. Most people dream of becoming self-employed. You can turn that dream into reality. Here is a dynamic, proven way to shape your own destiny. It is an answer not only for city folks but for urban escapees seeking to prosper in paradise. (Do we ever know about *that*, living and working in a lovely Colorado mountain town of only two thousand.)

Becoming a self-publisher also provides a helpful tax shelter. After forming your own company and meeting certain requirements, you can write off a portion of your home and deduct some expenses related to writing and to marketing, such as automobile, travel, and entertainment costs. Always check current tax regulations and restrictions.

Another advantage is that you can begin your business on a part-time basis while keeping your day job. Why risk your livelihood until you've refined your publishing activities and worked out any bugs?

Want control over your work? In self-publishing, *you* guide every step. You'll have the cover you like, the typeface you choose, the title you want, the ads you decide to place. Your decision is final. Nothing is left in the hands of an editor or publicist who has dozens (or hundreds) of other books to worry about. You maintain absolute control over your own book. (Along with this advantage, however, comes the fact that you also get stuck *doing* everything.)

Privately publishing your work also gives you the advantage of speed. Big trade houses typically take from a year to a year and a half to get a book out. Self-publishers can do it in a fraction of that time. Zilpha Main, who self-published her book *Reaching Ninety—My Way*, commented when asked why she took that approach, "At my age, I can't wait for New York publishers to make up their minds." Most self-publishers agree. Peter McWilliams readily admitted he self-published "out of self-defense." Had he waited for Publishers' Row to get his book out, his phenomenal story would have had a very different ending.

We're finding many corporations are publishing books today. They have a different motivation. One of our past clients, Ralph Rosenberg, wrote us, "Your expert advice is paying off huge dividends for our small, nationwide consulting company. The book has become our calling card. It provides a great first introduction to our products and services. Often we are asked to provide follow up proposals." He and his partner coauthored a *Primer for Graphic Arts Profitability*. In less than two years, they went into a third printing.

Our company, About Books, Inc., does turnkey publishing for many entrepreneurs and professionals today who do books to position themselves as the leaders in their industries. Publishing books also gives these individuals a fresh reason to attract media attention and be a source of news. Once they've written books, they are perceived as instant "experts."

If your venture blossoms and the company expands by publishing others' work, you have fresh opportunities to join the growing small-press movement. You can set policy, serve as a spokesperson, and bring deserving writers to the public's attention. (See the later chapter "Enlarge Your Kingdom: Move Up to 'Small Press' Status.")

The publishing business is a constant flow of exciting events. You will never forget that supreme moment when you hold the first copy of your very own book, just off the press. Some people compare it to holding their first child. When the book starts making the rounds, things happen. There's a domino effect. One day you get your first fan letter (most likely read with blurry vision). Then a prestigious person gets wind of the book and requests an examination copy. Magazines and newspapers begin to review and mention it. Library orders start flowing in.

And, lo and behold, the biggies—those publishers that previously rejected your work—just may decide to reverse their decisions. Self-publishing can be the springboard to lucrative contracts with traditional publishers who were afraid to gamble before. Once the marketability of your book has been proven, they will be eager to take it off your hands. (We advise you on how to do this in the chapter "Bagging the Big Game: Selling Your Self-Published Book to Goliath Publishers.")

That's what happened to Roger Von Oech. After writing and publishing *A Whack on the Side of the Head*, which shows how to be a more creative thinker, he sold some 30,000 copies himself. Then he allowed Warner Books to get into the act. Says Von Oech, "It was a good deal for both of us." One of the things he negotiated into his contract was a commitment from Warner to spend $75,000 on promotion. Von Oech has traveled all over the United States promoting his book, speaking, and consulting.

In an interesting switch, Putnam picked up the rights to our clients' books, *Why Jenny Can't Lead* (Jinx Melia and Pauline Lyttle). The self-published paperback version sold 20,000 copies at $10.00 each. Then Putnam slapped a new title on it (*Breaking Into the Boardroom*), used the same interior pages we had prepared for these clients, and put it out as a hardcover for $14.95—after paying the authors a substantial advance, that is. It also went into mass paperback.

Stumbling Blocks to Avoid

Of course, like any business, self-publishing has some stumbling blocks you should be aware of.

Contrary to what Mama always said, you must become a braggart. You'll need to learn to toot your own horn. Since you—and you alone—will be promoting this book, it is up to you to tell anybody and everybody how great it is. (Later chapters will show you how to do this without revealing it is actually *you* doing the bragging.)

It is an investment, an investment in yourself. As in any business, you will require start-up capital. There must be enough money to print the book, send out review copies, do phone follow-up, sustain an advertising campaign, and so forth. How much depends on many variables. How long will your book be? Will it have photographs inside? Will the cover be full-color? Will you personally desktop publish it or have it professionally designed and typeset? How many copies will you print? Via what method? See what we mean? The costs vary drastically. You might skimp by on a few hundred dollars for a booklet on which you do most of the work yourself. On the other hand, you could spend over $35,000 on a coffee-table book with lots of color photographs.

Generally speaking, to produce a professional-quality book in the traditional way and promote it properly, you'll be in the range of $12,000 to $25,000 in today's marketplace. But be forewarned: Lack of market analysis, careful planning, budgeting, and persistence has caused some people to lose their investments. (Don't despair if your budget's as tight as fiddle strings. In chapter six, we'll be showing you thirty-two innovative ways to generate working capital.) And in today's world, books can be launched on a shoestring.

You should be willing to devote a substantial block of time to your publishing project. While this can be spread over a long period, there is no getting around the fact that to have a dynamite book, you must spend much time writing it, revising it, producing it, and promoting it.

The Many Hats of a Self-Publisher

A basic truth for most self-publishers is that they start out alone. That being the case, you will find yourself wearing many hats. Just because you may be an amateur doesn't mean the book you produce will be flawed. By studying and applying yourself, you can wear the various hats well. Many self-publishers never draw on outside help to do their books—and you can do it all yourself if you choose. We show you how to be all these people or how to find the best professionals to do the job for you.

- **Writer.** The basic foundation for your enterprise is writing. Study your craft and refine your product. Good, readable works sell much more readily than disorganized garble or lofty dissertations.
- **Editor.** If you're not lucky enough to have a qualified friend or relative to edit—one who knows the English language well and will be objective—hire a professional. This is the one area where it is so easy to miss the forest for the trees, overlook the same typo, lose your objectivity.
- **Designer/Artist.** Many books and book covers are self-illustrated or designed. Even if you decide to get professional freelance help, it would be foolhardy not to get somewhat involved personally.
- **Typesetter/Compositor.** When you use a computer to prepare camera-ready copy, you become a typesetter. More and more authors are opting to use desktop publishing software. We discuss the pros and cons of do-it-yourself typesetting in the chapter "Wow! Design and Typesetting."
- **Printer.** ands of books and booklets are created each year at copy shops. In this case, you are your own printer. Learn what will and will not provide crisp copies. Avoid wasted time creating masters or film that will not provide an acceptable end result. Make a wise decision between print on demand and traditional printing processes.
- **Financier/Accountant.** You are the chief accountant, bookkeeper, and company representative to your banker. You must keep good records for yourself and for the IRS.
- **Marketeer.** It doesn't matter how well all other hats fit if you don't wear this one well. Be imaginative and creative. Go ahead and slip into flamboyance when you don this hat. Shrewd promotion and sales strategies will do much to ensure your publishing project's success.
- **Shipper/Warehouser.** It doesn't do any good to get book orders unless you can fill and ship them. While this is a routine job, it takes time, space, and energy.
- **Legal adviser.** Many times attorneys collect sizable fees for answering

simple business questions. Take a good look at the question. The use of common sense and comparison to similar situations will often save a fee. There are instances, however, when you definitely need an attorney—if you've been accused of libel or copyright infringement, for instance.

- **Business manager.** This hat has been saved for the last but not because it's a low priority. Quite the opposite. You can do a fantastic job on all other aspects of the business and still lose your shirt if this hat isn't secured firmly on your noggin. In fact, a recent Small Business Administration study showed that 93 percent of the businesses that failed did so because of poor management practices. The job of business manager can be a piece of cake or an absolute nightmare—it's up to you. Managing a company is fun if you establish and adhere to operating procedures designed for that business.

Be prepared to fall and skin your knees occasionally. No one has all the answers; certainly not a new self-publisher. While we have compiled this reference to help you avoid mistakes, there will be times when you'll goof or when nothing seems to be going your way. Hang in there! Soon things will take a positive turn. As in anything, there are pitfalls, but there are also many pleasures. Move ahead with passion and conviction and you will succeed.

Identifying Your Motivation

Not everyone self-publishes for the same reason.

Most self-publishers probably choose this alternative for financial gain. They recognize that here is a potential for much greater returns than any other publishing avenue offers. Take Jim Everroad, for instance. Everroad was a high school gymnastic coach in Columbus, Indiana, before he published a 32-page booklet called *How to Flatten Your Stomach*. It sold a whopping 1.5 million copies and was number one on the best-seller list for so long that many thought it had taken up permanent residence. Then the ex-coach went on to endorse and market an exercise device called the Belly Burner, which was advertised on national television.

Bernard Kamoroff, CPA, having retired from his accounting practice, found himself seeking something to boost his self-esteem. He put together what has turned out to be the most popular small business guidebook ever published. (You need a copy!) *Small Time Operator: How to Start Your Own Business, Keep Your Books, Pay Your Taxes, and Stay Out of Trouble!* has sold well over 600,000 copies and gone into fifty-six printings. This little beauty grossed its owner $300,000 the first four years it was out. And it's an ideal ongoing moneymaker. Kamoroff updates it annually and has an extensive chain of distributors. Having attained his goal of creating a project that would give him purpose, he now spends the majority of his time playing. We share some of his secrets later in this book.

Literary contribution is an important facet of self-publishing. As trade publishers become more and more preoccupied with celebrity books and sure bets, good literary writers turn more and more to self-publishing. Here, they find an outlet for their novels, poetry, and literary nonfiction.

Many sensitive men and women are not concerned with making a profit. Instead, they need to see their work in print—to hold in their hands books with their names as authors. Some have spent arduous years submitting manuscripts and having them returned, cutting and rewriting and sending again, vainly trying to please an editor, any editor. Often those few who do sell find their work whittled and changed beyond recognition. Even more frustrated are those with a strong belief in their work, who have not been willing to alter it and have thus found themselves without a market. Often these are people who want to share their personal adventures, experiences, and feelings with generations to come. Or perhaps they are the more creative artists or poets whose work is too innovative to be appreciated by the regular markets.

Some people and organizations publish to espouse causes they feel strongly about. Many alternative publishers use their books to tout antiestablishment political views or to address issues such as abortion or gay rights.

We previously did a book for the National Buffalo Association. *Buffalo Management and Marketing* not only offers unique information about buffalo but also served as an effective national attention getter for the NBA. Through our book promotional efforts, we were able to get the organization's executive director on seven hundred radio stations, where she talked about the book, the association, and the benefits of eating buffalo meat.

Your book can have an impact on the lives of thousands, maybe even millions, of people. You have the opportunity to influence the thoughts and actions of your readers . . . to sow the seeds of hope, to motivate, to entertain, to inform. Your words are preserved for posterity.

To some, self-publishing is simply fun. They embark on kitchen-table publishing like kids with new toys. Their motive is simply to enjoy themselves. Alas, some end up making money, too.

Another less widely admitted reason for producing your own book is for ego gratification. It's downright satisfying to see your name emblazoned across the cover of a book. And your friends and associates immediately regard you as a celebrity. "Oh, he is an author," they whisper in reverent tones.

For those more practically minded, publishing your own book can be a springboard to other revenue-generating activities. Roger Von Oech says candidly that his book is great advertising for his consulting business. One of our clients who did a guide on how to find a mate, and who also happened to run a dating service, found his matchmaking appointment calendar overflowing when word of his new book got out.

Many authors discover paid lectures and seminar programs open to them once they've established their expertise between book covers. A surprising number of our About Books, Inc., current clients are Ph.D.'s, speakers, consultants, doctors, or other professionals. They've discovered that being an author gives them added visibility and credibility. It opens media doors and converts them into "newsmakers."

Whether your desire is to cart bags of money off to the bank or to etch a new line in the face of literary America, it's time to set some goals.

Setting Goals

Before you move ahead on your self-publishing venture, establish concrete goals. Over and over, it has been proven that those who take the time to think through and *write down* the desired results in terms of specific steps are the people who achieve success. Experts tell us that we can program our subconscious to help bring about something we genuinely want.

There are two things you must know to reach a goal. First, it must be clearly identified and quantified. Second, goals should be written and affirmed as though they already existed. To affirm something, you write and/or state it repeatedly, *sincerely believing it has already been accomplished.* You can do this even before you've written your book.

Your affirmation might go something like this: "I have sold five thousand copies of *My Story* as of January 1, 2003. Gross income from these sales is $45,000, and the net profit is $15,000." Or you might say, "I have written a book that is being very well received. It is helping hundreds of people every month." By expressing your desired outcome in the present tense, you condition your subconscious mind to accept it as fact. This method is taught by most success motivators.

Write your affirmation several times each morning and evening. Tack it up on the refrigerator, on the bathroom mirror, on your computer, on the car dashboard. Refer to it often. Repeat it aloud. Believe it! By planting this seed of positive expectancy, you condition yourself to move toward your goal swiftly and unswervingly.

To further promote positive goal setting, we'd recommend adding two books to your library: *Psycho-Cybernetics*, by Maxwell Maltz, and *Think and Grow Rich*, by Napoleon Hill. This type of reading helps form the goal-setting success habit needed to build a solid business foundation.

Now that you've set your overall goal, what steps will most effectively get you there? As we said earlier, it would be wise to read this whole guide before you map out the route that will best lead to your long-range destination. You may decide that catalog sales hold the key to success. Maybe selling to schools will get you there the fastest. Perhaps Internet exposure is your "open sesame." Which avenue you choose for self-publishing sales is up to you, so long as it brings you to the desired results.

What is important is that you lay out the course. Write the steps involved. Break down the overall process into easily digestible chunks. Chew on them. Spit out those that don't work. Take more generous bites of those that are satisfying. Set your goals, and plan carefully for a successful journey.

And as you embark into the universe of publishing, you will want to consider electronic publishing. That's our next topic.

Web Sites, Wisdom, and Whimsey

***A rotten review from an insufferable reviewer on Mark Twain's* The Adventures of Huckleberry Finn: "*A gross trifling with every fine feeling . . . Mr. Clemens has no reliable sense of propriety.*"**

* * *

"What is a best-seller?" we're often asked. There is no simple answer. Sure it's clear-cut when a book lands on one of the top three best-seller lists: *The New York Times*, *Publishers Weekly*, or *USA Today*. But there are dozens of other "best-seller" lists. Ingram has them, so do most other wholesalers. Amazon.com has lots of them for very definitive topics. *The Wall Street Journal* boasts one. Many newspapers run lists representing their geographic areas. Bookstores often have their own. *Entrepreneur* magazine has a business best-seller list . . . and it goes on and on. Books targeted as best-sellers have the shelf life of milk. For a brief period they are discussed, admired, recommended, touted, publicized. Then the window of opportunity is gone, and they usually slip into oblivion. Occasionally, books that are on the best-seller list in January end up in remainder bins in June. Surprisingly, a book can occasionally make a major best-seller list with maybe only 35,000 copies sold if the competition that week is very light. Yet other books that will never see a best-seller list might sell a million copies. They do it through direct mail or nontraditional speciality sales. So "best-sellers" come in many varieties and often don't appear on the official lists.

* * *

Find everything you need to know about online book clubs and book discussion groups. Good writers are typically avid readers. We glean knowledge of our craft as we subconsciously observe the work of other wordcrafters. Thus, Rachel's Compendium of Online Book Discussions, et al. may be of real interest to you. To my knowledge this is the most complete listing of such venues on the Net. This site is divided into several primary areas, which are more easily understood when you go there (www.his.com/~allegria/compend.html) than by an explanation, but I'll try. First, there is Online Book Clubs. In a Web-Enhanced Book Club, the participants read books on their own, then send their comments to a central Web location. Several such clubs are listed with direct links. They cover everything, including classic and contemporary fiction, mystery, science fiction, adventure, and general topics. Additionally, there are also E-mail-Oriented Book Clubs where lean and mean book discussions occur, and readers send comments to all participants. Many of these clubs are linked, as well. Then there is Chatting About Books. Using chat capabilities is an ideal way to exchange opinions with other readers. True to form, Rachel has several links here, as well. You can participate in one or more of these groups not only for sheer enjoyment but also to better understand the mind-set of readers in your genre.

* * *

Focus is power. Sometimes, it feels like life is a tug-of-war, and we are the rope. There is only so much sand in the hourglass. So who gets it? When you feel overwhelmed and frustrated, remember to take things one day at a time and stay focused. Focus is power under control.

* * *

Perhaps one of the reasons James Joyce chose to self-publish* Ulysses *was the following rejection: "We have read the chapters of Mr. Joyce's novel with great interest, and we wish we could offer to print it. But the length is an insuperable difficulty to us at present. We can get no one to help us, and at our rate of progress a book of 300 pages would take at least two years to produce." (Gosh, not a lot has changed in traditional publishing circles since 1922.)

* * *

Who is the most published author of all time? Would you believe it is the woman, who in 1949, penned a poem for a new invention called the "Doggie Bag"? The poem is still distributed to the tune of three million bags a year. This makes the queen of leftovers more published than even William Shakespeare.

* * *

Give the gift of a book! Flowers fade, but books are forever.

2 *Cyber Options Beyond Your Wildest Imagination*

The sands of publishing shifted dramatically in the last decade. The Internet opened unimaginable vistas for e-books, while Print on Demand (POD) transformed how some books are published. Other digital formats were also introduced. Along with all this change came a caravan of confusion. Many people confuse e-books, e-book readers, and POD. Others don't understand how these methods differ from other ways of digitally delivering information or from traditional publishing. Some folks fear that the demise of books as we know them is around the corner.

So we're riding in on our white horse (camel?) to try and put this jumble of terms and processes into perspective. For today, anyway. The only unquestionable aspect of this whole electronic publishing explosion is that no one knows for sure where it's headed—and few have the vision to know what may be possible in another ten years. It is ever evolving. We're sharing knowledge in totally new ways. The respected Forrester Research predicts that online book sales of digital books will represent a mere 14 percent by the year 2004. Others project far more aggressive numbers, so the thinking goes in both directions.

Let us begin to dissect the options by first covering conventional printing: This is where a self-publisher connects with a company that specializes in manufacturing quantities of books. Usual beginning print runs are 3,000 to 5,000 copies, although some people start with only 1,000 books. There are economies of scale: The more books you print, the cheaper each one becomes. (This method is covered in depth in chapter ten, "Affordable Book Manufacturing—the Printing Process.") In contrast, the cost to produce e-books and book-at-a-time POD printing remains the same no matter what the quantity.

Journeying Through the E-Book Jungle

It will take not only a sharp machete but considerable time and an astute tracker to find the buried treasure in e-books. The treasure is there all right. We just are not yet poised to take full advantage of this hoard of riches. At this juncture, the industry is suffering from a multiple of predators: (1) The devices on which one reads e-books are too expensive; (2) there are no formatting standards in how books are made available; (3) copyright infringement is an issue; and (4) content is limited and in some cases deplorable.

An April 2, 2001, story in *U.S. News & World Report* was headlined: "New E-Book devices don't threaten the printed word." The piece went on to say that so far the software-based digital texts, and the hardware devices dedicated to reading them, have failed to catch on with all but the most techie bibliophiles. Why is that? And will it change?

Reading Devices

One of the problems is the lack of consistency in reading devices; another is their high prices. According to Internet research firm Jupiter Media Metrix, fewer than 50,000 electronic reading devices have been sold in the United States. The research predicts this number will reach 1.9 million by 2005. But these figures are misleading because you can also read an e-book (albeit not as easily) on a handheld organizer known as a Personal Digital Assistant (PDA), such as a PalmPilot or Handspring Visor, which millions of Americans have. Of course, some e-books can also be displayed on a desktop or laptop computer (Imagine reading *War and Peace* that way!), or even printed out.

Says Dick Brass, VP for technology development at Microsoft, "This is like 1908 for cars. These are the worst devices we'll ever make and the most expensive. In a year they'll sell for $250 or $200. In five years they'll sell for $100 or be free if you buy five books or subscribe to *Time* magazine." Most industry experts believe reader prices must get in the neighborhood of $99 before their popularity will skyrocket.

Today's devices are tablet or slatelike objects typically weighing one to two pounds. The "pages" are turned with stylus taps or by repeatedly thumbing a button. Prices range from $299 for Gemstar's REB 1100 to a jumbo $699 for the Gemstar REB 1200 model. About to be launched as we write this is Franklin Electronic Publishers' eBookMan, to retail at $180. Positioned as an all-in-one gizmo, it will work as a personal organizer, play MP3 and digital books on tape, record memos, and store e-books. Though it features a stylus-touch screen operation à la PalmPilots, it's reported to be difficult to use and lacking in popular reading material.

Format Standards

E-books will not trounce p-books (print books) until the problem of competing formats is solved. The lack of a uniform reading platform is forcing publishers who want to go this route to make difficult choices about what format they will make their material available in. Right now it's like a marriage on the verge of divorce because of incompatibility. Now publishers will want to format their titles not only in PDF (Portable Document Format) for Acrobat but also in OEB (Open E-Book) for Microsoft Reader and Gemstar. Once this whole issue is solved and information can be shared, downloaded, and protected in a common format, companies such as Microsoft, Gemstar, and Franklin will have to compete for the quality of the device instead of the accessibility of the content.

One interesting survey conducted by www.NoSpine.net revealed that the majority of customers do *not* want special e-book reader formats like Microsoft Reader and Glassbook. Rather, they prefer standard formats, such as regular text Microsoft Word documents and Adobe PDF. Because of their comfort zone in using a word processing program regularly, it seems natural to them to buy a file in this format. They know how to change the type size, scroll down, search, even alter the font if they wish. And many have no qualms about printing out the material.

Security Against Copyright Infringement

As Stephen King found out, piracy on the Web can be big business. The first big e-book to be launched, his *Riding the Bullet*, had a single encryption key that was widely hacked and posted for free downloads. The protection of encryption software isn't always used—and doesn't always work when applied. Adobe's Content Server is a system that protects e-books in PDF format from being traded with other readers who haven't anted up for their copies. We're used to passing along a paperback to a friend. Some say that pass-along readership, such as magazines use to boost advertising revenue, should be viewed as a marketing opportunity. After all, free content has been around since the beginning of the printed word. Libraries, pass-along readership of books, and copy machines facilitate this. Many readers end up buying a book because it proves to be something they really want.

Some writers aren't concerned with piracy. But that may be because this technology is in its infancy and for many authors getting exposure is almost more important than garnering profits. We might be wise to learn from the music industry and the Napster situation where file sharing deprived many copyright owners of just compensation for their work. As our industry matures, losing out on large chunks of revenue because your book has been ripped off could become a grave concern. Forrester Research forecasts $1.5 *billion* lost to piracy over the next four years. If those figures are even close, digital rights management—how content is protected from unauthorized distribution—is a vital component of electronic books.

Content: What's Available and What's Needed

As we write this, there are only approximately twenty thousand e-book titles in existence. We suspect by the time you read this, that number will have at least quadrupled. Current offerings include best-selling releases from Mary Higgins Clark, David Baldacci, Suze Orman, Stephen Covey, and others. Or you can tap into fresh, innovative fiction by up-and-comers. Classics by Louisa May Alcott, Mark Twain, Willa Cather, and Edgar Rice Burroughs can titillate your literary palate, as can popular series, such as *Star Trek* and the various renditions of *Chicken Soup for the Soul*. Self-publishers are selling general nonfiction, technical works, and genre fiction from a multitude of sites.

What's most likely to work? If you have time-sensitive material, the Internet fits like a glove. Cliffs Notes now sells its popular college guides online. Imagine that it's midnight before a paper is due on *Moby Dick*. How much would a student fork over for the appropriate Cliffs Notes at that point? Clifton Keith Millegass started Cliffs Notes in his basement in 1958 with a $4,000 loan. In 1989, *Forbes* magazine reported his company was making $11 million a year.

Perhaps your potential buyers use computers extensively in their work. These are ideal candidates for e-books; they're used to the culture. Of course, a title dealing with any aspect of the Web is a natural. Those who must be constantly mobile are another likely market. Construction Trades Press creates electronic documents that can be used on location during construction jobs. Readers of romance and science fiction are voracious consumers. E-books priced to be disposable will attract this market in droves. Serious nonfiction readers, such as professionals seeking specific material, are another interesting niche as you can target them specifically on the Net.

Carrying one device loaded with ten, twenty, even forty titles has many advantages for students. Instead of hauling a backpack overflowing with heavy books, the student can simply carry a reader loaded with megs and megs of information. Some publishers see a strong school market as e-book availability widens. And a recent article in *The New York Times* noted that the library of the University of Texas had earmarked $1 million for digital materials.

The convenience factor also comes into play. Consumers can purchase a book on the Net and be able to start reading it within minutes . . . all without leaving home or paying any shipping or sales tax. Travelers can take several novels, guidebooks, or business reading in one handy package.

But beware of the e-book company you keep. When you place your books for sale on a Web site, you'll be sharing a publishing label with authors whose literary standards may not match yours. If books have amateurish, inappropriate titles, are riddled with typos, are poorly written, and were never touched by an editor's red pen, that reflects on you, as well. There is no quality control to determine what is print worthy. Sadly, many online books are vanity projects cobbled together by individuals who have made no effort to school themselves in the craft of writing.

John Feldcamp, president of Xlibris Corporation, said in Debbie Ridpath Ohi's *Writer's Online Marketplace*, "Let's be clear. Everybody who writes is going to publish what they write. This is not one of those things that is debatable anymore. . . . And it really doesn't matter whether you think this is a good thing or a bad thing for the world of books and publishing—it is going to happen regardless of what any of us thinks."

This statement reminds us of self-publishing twenty years ago. One of our concerns is how will the buying public discern which are the books of quality when certain online companies will pour any novice writer's unedited manuscript into a hard disk, wrap a standard cover around it, and call it published? We anticipate some sort of gatekeeper system will emerge where books will be vetted by reviewers or others who apply a set of standards.

Who is currently buying electronic books? we wonder. We were asked to host three Meet the Pros tables at a National Speakers Association annual workshop in March of 2001. We queried each of these groups about their participation in e-books. Of the twenty-seven people present—all well-educated, motivated individuals—not one had read an e-book. During research for this guide, we were visiting with a friend who frequently teaches community college classes on publishing. He has been asking the same question for months, and only two people had even seen an e-book reader!

The other part of this equation involves publicizing an e-book. First, it must overcome a prejudice of perceived lower quality, similar to the turnoff experienced by book reviewers of sloppy self-published books of two decades ago. Second, there is a demographic challenge: Few media people are equipped to read e-books! Will they not coincidentally assume audience interest to be low, as well? How receptive are primary review mediums? "We will review e-books when we get to the point when something is un-ignorable," said Chip McGrath, editor of *The New York Times Book Review*, at the e-Book World Conference and Exhibition in New York City during November 2000.

Opinions and Surveys

An informal survey of over 10 percent of the conferees at the above conference revealed some interesting numbers. Of those surveyed, 13 percent designated themselves authors, 19 percent print publishers, and 26 percent publishers of e-books or both mediums. The remaining 42 percent represented people in software areas and bookselling. So it was a book "insiders" crowd. In spite of this, 56 percent of the respondents admitted they had not bought an e-book in the past year. (In contrast, 72 percent anticipated doing so in the coming twelve months.)

The random cross section of fifty participants was evenly divided in opinions about the impending impact of e-books. Half saw them as evolutionary; the other half felt they would be as revolutionary as the invention of printing. Nearly a third said that security was paramount. While 54 percent felt optimistic that e-books would benefit every would-be writer, 13 percent thought best-selling authors would have the advantage. Concerning pricing, 45 percent picked prices of $10 or less as ideal, but 39 percent said the price should be determined by the economics involved, such as the costs and sales. Only 18 percent felt that new e-vendors would gradually overtake the major print publishers.

In assessing which publishing areas would be affected most by e-books in the next few years, the professional areas (legal, medical, etc.) ranked first. This group was followed closely by academic, then educational (school and college). General trade books were not seen as especially promising.

Getting Started in Electronic Publishing

Before electronic publishing can take you to the promised land, you need someone who knows the way. Victoria Rosenborg is that someone. She wrote *ePublishing for Dummies*, a $24.99 IDG book that has 342 large-sized pages plus a CD-ROM. It covers how to use the leading authoring tools to make e-books for PCs, for the leading dedicated reading devices, and for PDAs. We can't hope to give you a lesson here, but her book will provide you with the essential information to capitalize on this publishing venue.

Pricing E-Books

The price of electronic books is all over the place. Retail costs range from $3.00 to more than $24.95. They are delivered either by download or as an e-mail file attachment. Independent publishers who sell directly to their end customers often pass along some of the savings resulting from not needing an extensive inventory and having lower overall printing and distribution costs. Conversely, large conventional publishers don't do much discounting for the electronic format.

The Electronic Text Center offers its e-books for free; so do some other publishers, feeling this is a cost-effective loss-leader marketing tool. This practice, of course, is the exception. Most e-books tend to be a few dollars less than their traditional counterparts. Barnes & Noble has decreed the electronic books it publishes (yes, they're in the publishing business, too!) will run between $5.95 and $7.95. PublishingOnline.com suggests that publishers offer 40 percent off for pixel versus paper versions. The majority rationalize that something in the $4.50 to $5.50 range covers costs and isn't a daunting investment for the reader. This lower price may be your best bet.

On the other end of the spectrum are those who price their books higher than regular hardcovers because of added functions available. Rich media formats that support hyperlinks to URLs, audio, video, reader annotations, bookmarking, built-in dictionaries, not to mention search capabilities, can all now be part of a book—making the information more valuable than a p-book's contents could be.

Who Are the Players?

How can you find a good place to publish your e-book? That's a difficult question to answer. E-publishers tend to change as often as movie marquees. Here are some Web sites to check out: www.Booklocker.com, www.mightywords.com, www.BookZone.com, www.netLibrary.com, www.peanutpress.com, www.e-booknet.com, http://PublishingOnline.com, www.fictionwise.com, www.lightningsource.com, www.BookSurge.com, and http://iPublish.com. Go to their sites to examine the advantages of each and what their requirements are to self-publish on the Web. By the way, there is now a gray line between e-books and POD. Many vendors now do both, so check the suppliers we discuss in the Print on Demand section, too.

Stories From the Trenches

No discussion of e-books would be complete without addressing the daring steps horrormeister Stephen King took in the new millennium. King broke new ground on March 14, 2000, when his Philtrum Press and Simon & Schuster copublished *Riding the Bullet* exclusively on the Net. The phenomenal demand for the sixty-six-page novella had Web sites crashing like meteorites plummeting to earth. While the downloads were offered free in many quarters, consumers also lined up at netLibrary.com to willingly pay $2.50 for the book, which was made available in several formats suitable for various reading devices. King made history that day with 400,000 copies of the story ordered in the first twenty-four hours it was available. Compare that to his normal book launch of 30,000 to 75,000 copies the first day of sale.

Building on this success, King decided to bolt from S&S and self-publish another book, *The Plant* (about a carnivorous vine that takes over a publishing house), online in installments. Beginning in mid-July 2000, 152,132 King fans downloaded chapter one of the serialized book. Readers were asked to pay $1 on the honor system for each chapter, with the understanding the author would pull the project if too many people stole the book. Because he put it out *un*encrypted, which means hackers can steal it, theft was rampant. In spite of that, over 76 percent (116,200) of readers voluntarily paid the first $1 fee. When the second installment of the e-novel appeared, some loyal fans even paid extra so the story wouldn't vanish.

By then King, who had shelled out approximately $150,000 for ads in *PW* and *USA Today* plus technical and Web server fees, had already recouped his investment and was well on his way to being a profitable self-publisher. By the time the fifth installment was due, however, paying customers had dwindled to 46 percent and *The Plant* withered on the vine. Let it not be ignored, however, that King collected over half a million bucks in payments (not a bad return on a $150,000 investment) and contends he will return with more installments of the book.

We wouldn't be a bit surprised if he is joined by a whole cadre of best-selling authors who decide to take the do-it-yourself approach. Think about it: Why should the likes of James Patterson, Mitch Albom, Danielle Steel, Stephen Covey, Barbara Kingsolver, Jonathan Kellerman, Ken Follett, Spencer Johnson, Patricia Cornwell, and Tom Clancy continue to turn over huge amounts of revenue to their middlemen major publishers? They have the names and clout to drive fans to the Web and self-publish their own work! Comments Jason Epstein, cofounder of *The New York Review of Books* and a former Random House VP, "Once you are a brand-name author, why do you need a house to take all your profits?"

On the other hand, the Web could conceivably turn unknowns into name-brand authors. One of the earliest adopters, M.J. Rose, has been called the "poster girl" of e-publishing by *Time* magazine. Her self-published erotic e-novel, *Lip Service*, caught the attention of the Doubleday Direct Book Club and was the first e-book discovered online by the mainstream publishing industry. Her second novel, *In Fidelity*, is published by no less than Pocket Books.

Certain topics lend themselves ideally to e-books. Such was the case with *On*

Any Given Day, a book by Joe Martin and Ross Yockey about Lou Gehrig's disease. Since many victims of this disease can't turn a book's pages, e-book devices were a natural for this title.

John Oakes, publisher of Four Walls Eight Windows press has thirty titles in e-book format. He can see no immediate benefits for small publishers to use the Web. Of his press's titles, *God's Equation*, by Amir D. Aczel, is available both as a traditional hardcover distributed by Publishers Group West and as an e-book. While the hardcover version sold 1,500 copies, a grand total of only 121 e-books were moved.

On another front, Farrar, Straus and Giroux was one of the first publishers to produce both a p-book and an e-book for young adults. *Joey Pigza Loses Control*, by Jack Gantos, was designed to appeal to Internet-savvy kids, who were projected to be among the early adopters of the e-book format. While press response was enthusiastic, customer reaction was very quiet. Five of the author's books were put into e-format; fewer than 75 copies were sold. "We haven't found there is a developed audience for e-books yet," reports marketing VP Laurie Brown.

In our opinion, therein lies the problem. Just as there would be no developed audience for most traditionally published books without promotion, publicity, and established channels of distribution—we've taken a revolutionary technology and expected an "if we build it they will come" result. As John Moore of PublishingOnline noted, "Publishers must develop distribution and retail contacts in the e-world just as they have in the print world." Authors please take note: If you expect your e-book to succeed, you *must* devote time, energy, and resources to promoting it! Just putting it up on the Web is not the answer. Yet the Web provides an ideal opportunity for publicizing and selling e-books.

Are we against this technology? Never! It has great promise and will be a terrific complement to paper books. So keep informed. Participate. Just don't expect miracles for several years. People buy the medium as much as the message. As mainstream publishing companies begin to embrace e-books and publish material by today's top authors, more and more customers who once thought e-books were exclusively the domain of frustrated unpublished wanna-bes will discover that this view simply isn't true. E-books will steadily gain acceptance as the content matures, the formatting standardizes, and reading devices become affordable.

After all, cyber publishing isn't new. It's been around since the early 1970s when Michael Hart of the University of Illinois instituted Project Gutenberg. In the intervening years, more than 10,000 books have been downloaded free in digital format.

There are those who will never give up their sensory experience or the tactile feel of books to take to the beach, read in the tub, or curl up with in a comfy chair. To them, the printed word offers permanence and tradition. Digital text is fleeting, cold, impersonal. Others hunger for the high-tech interaction. The cutting edge. The instant, global availability of electronic books. Both have their place.

Exploring Print on Demand

There are several advantages to Print on Demand: You need no warehouse because there is no inventory to store. And there is flexibility: Suppose you decide you hate your title or cover? Change it! Hopefully, there is also an element of speed. If you're dealing with a timely topic, POD should get you books faster. Some vendors can turn out a book in two or three days; others promise two or three weeks. (This, however, is not always the case; we waited almost four months to get the companion book to this one, *Jump Start Your Book Sales*, into a POD format.)

POD is coming on strong. It's big enough to have its own topic-specific conventions with speakers from around the digital world; to sport its own magazine, *Print on Demand*; to have megacompanies like Barnes & Noble buy a large interest in iUniverse, and Random House to invest in Xlibris.

But to complicate matters, a close investigation of POD reveals it has two parallel avenues. Let's refer to them as "Burger King" and "McDonald's." In the Burger King ("have it your way") version, you are the publisher and you provide the POD printer with a print-ready book. Your book is camera-ready, has a professional cover, and has your own ISBN. The printer prepares multiple copies, usually ranging from 25 to 500. With the McDonald's approach, the printer typically controls the product and prints individual books as they are ordered.

The Burger King Approach

Some book printers who used to specialize in larger print runs are now doing short-run POD, either exclusively or in tandem with their previous work. There are many such printers to choose from; we list a few here. DeHART's Printing Services (www.deharts.com) can run as few as 25 copies or as many as 2,500. Other options are Network Printers (www.Network-Printers.com), Edwards Brothers (www.edwardsbrothers.com), B•O•D (Books on Demand, www.BOD.com), On Demand Machine Corporation (www.bookmachine.com), and First-Publish, Inc. (www.firstpublish.com).

So what will it cost you to ride the crest of this new wave? Prices vary enormously. Generally they are based on the length of your book (so much per page)

POD Specification Sheet

DeHART'S
PRINTING SERVICES CORPORATION

Preparing Your Files for Print

1. Proof your document carefully and make sure all necessary changes have been made before submitting your job.
2. Make sure you have all of the PostScript fonts that correspond with the screen fonts you have selected to use in your document.
3. Select an appropriate PostScript printer driver such as Adobe's PS Printer with the Xerox Docutech 6180 selected as the PPD.
4. Select "Print to File" or "File" as the destination of your document in the print dialog box.
5. Make sure all fonts and graphics are embedded into the PostScript file. This means that they must be written into the PostScript file by the application and print driver you are using.
6. Save your file(s) to a disk or other acceptable form of media. Send via FTP, email or physical media to DeHART's.
7. If you have any questions don't hesitate to contact your DeHART's Sales Representative.

Some Things to Supply with Your PostScript Files:

- A hard copy print out of the document.
- A previously printed sample.
- If multiple files are provided, a list of the order the files will be combined
- A pagination sheet.
- A print specification sheet.

Electronic File Checklist

Type of Media:
- ❑ Jaz
- ❑ FTP
- ❑ SyQuest Cartridge
  - ❑ 44 MB ❑ 88 MB ❑ EZ 135
- ❑ Zip Disk
- ❑ CD ROM
- ❑ Tar Tape
- ❑ MOD Disk
- ❑ Other:______________________

Platform:
- ❑ Macintosh
- ❑ Windows 95, 98, ME
- ❑ Windows NT
- ❑ SunOS/ UNIX / AIX

PDL Type:
- ❑ PostScript
- ❑ PCL
- ❑ PDF
- ❑ InterPress
- ❑ None (Source Files)

Application: ________________

Print Driver: ________________

Note: If source files are being supplied, **all** fonts (including fonts used in imported objects) and graphics (i.e.: EPS, Pict, tiff, GIF files) **must** accompany the source files. This will ensure that all elements of your files will print correctly. Also, if you are using Microsoft Word, and you have created a template for your document, make sure that you include a copy of the *.dot file.

3265 Scott Boulevard Santa Clara, CA 95054 408-982-9118 FAX 408-982-9912 www.deharts.com

One Print on Demand printer's guidelines for submitting a project. Reprinted with permission from DeHART's Printing Services Corporation.

plus a cost for the cover. Get quotes so you can compare costs, terms, and turnaround times. And ask where the normal price breaks fall. Here are a few guidelines: For a 250-page paperback book with a four-color cover, one POD printer charges $8.60 each for a quantity of 50, $5.13 each for 100, $4.49 each for 500, and $3.50 per book for 1,000. Hardcovers are considerably more, going for $15.87 apiece for 250, for instance, and $12.47 per book for 500.

We've heard of prices as low as $3.49 per book and as high as $20.00 and more. (POD is *not* your answer if you've written a 600-page romantic saga.) Be sure to determine both the interior price and the cover price. And ask about reprints. In virtually all cases, the price isn't likely to go down as it does in traditional printing. The hard reality is it's simply much more expensive per book to print in these small quantities.

Ideal Applications for POD

There are several instances where Burger King POD makes absolute sense. When only a few dozen or several hundred copies are needed, it's perfect for

- Family genealogies or church histories
- Autobiographies that will appeal only to family and friends
- Early copies of a book (galleys) that are needed to solicit advance blurbs, first serial/excerpt rights, etc.
- Authors seeking a conventional trade publisher who needs a "sample"
- When the budget is minuscule and market testing is needed to determine the best title/cover design/selling strategy
- Selling slow-moving backlist books that only move a few hundred copies each year
- Creating a short run of customized books for a specific market
- Established authors who want to break out of a genre and try a new passion
- Authors with out-of-print books who need a few copies for their loyal followers
- Speakers and teachers who need customized workbooks for seminars or classes
- Those wanting a few luxury hardcover first editions to be numbered, autographed

The McDonald's Version

In the McDonald's version of Print on Demand, books are first sold, then printed. These online companies set up your digital manuscript to be printed one book at a time, typically using a DocuTech, a technologically advanced photocopy machine. Covers, which can be full-color and laminated, are done the same way and then the book is conventionally bound. While paperbacks are more common, many companies can now do case-bound books with dust jackets as well. The publisher stores your book on a computer server in a compact format so it can easily be retrieved and a copy printed each time an order is received. Most of these online companies also offer fulfillment, thus they ship the book to the customer. You do not have to pick, pack, and ship the books. Your online publisher does that. And since this is an Internet venture, your work has global exposure.

There are some drawbacks to this method of getting into print. Because most Internet publishers only give bookstores 25 to 30 percent discounts and won't allow them to return books, it is not viable for the chains or independent bookstores to carry POD books. Because of this pricing and distribution structure, you are likely to be cut off from selling your books in normal bookstore and wholesaler channels. We predict circumstances will evolve to change this practice. POD printers are not set up to accept purchase orders, charge $3.50 for shipping, and don't offer advance reading copies—even more reasons why bookstores may be dissuaded from ordering POD books.

In rare instances, these obstacles have been overcome. One Xlibris author sold 3,000 copies of his novel in and around Boston. He was the consummate promoter, setting up appearances in over twenty stores, generating area media attention, and creating word-of-mouth buzz.

Be aware, however that with the McDonald's approach to POD—and with virtually all e-books—*you* are not the publisher. (There goes that control we wanted.) Typically, these companies issue one of their own ISBNs for your book. An ISBN is to a book what your Social Security number is to you. It's your ID in the world. Consequently, all orders and inquiries will go to them. They are also listed as the publisher of record in *Books In Print*.

Why would this matter? Let's take a few hypothetical situations: What if a book club discovers your book, loves it, and wants to adopt it for an alternate selection? The club will contact your Internet publisher who can't handle the deep discounts needed and thus has no financial stake in such a transaction. What do you think will happen? Zip. Zero. Nada. Suppose a corporation is interested in purchasing 1,000 copies of your book, contacts the publisher, but is turned off by the high cost of the books. You never hear about it. What if a distributor wants to take it on, but finds the economics aren't feasible? Tough luck. So think the decision through carefully as to whether or not to print with a POD.

The costs to create your book—and the royalties you are paid—vary widely. One of the major players is iUniverse, in which Barnes & Noble has a 29 percent stake. While iUniverse started out courting authors, for awhile it changed its business model and dropped authors and self-publishers in favor of larger fish. That has now changed according to Lynn Zingraf, general manager of author services. "We want to be a service to authors, to reach out and help them have control over their work and take advantage of POD technology," he told us.

As of June 18, 2001, B&N's Steve Riggio sent an open e-mail to the 7,000 authors who have paid iUniverse to print their books. It stated that the national chain welcomes any iUniverse author who can convince his or her local B&N community relations manager to hold an author event. There are certain stipulations for the New Writers Nights, which will be held once every three months or so. Since B&N stores do not stock iUniverse titles, authors must preorder books to sell, then remove them at the end of the event. The company one currently hears about most is Xlibris. In early 2001, however, Xlibris laid off ten people, then twenty—plus there have been policy changes, delays, and cost increases. As of March 1, 2001, the company's price schedule ranges from a core service of $200 to a premium option of $1,600. The standard mandatory retail price is $16 for a trade paperback and $25 for a hardcover. (Submission preparation guidelines appear on Xlibris's site.)

What do you make? On paperback, the author royalty is $1.60 on sales to bookstores, libraries, and resellers, and $4.00 for direct to consumer sales. For hardcovers, you get $2.50 for sales to bookstores, libraries, and resellers, and $6.25 on direct to consumer sales. Want to buy your own book for resale? A 25 percent discount applies. Thus, you pay 75 percent of the full retail price. Xlibris, like many other online companies, has also added e-book formatting to its product line. For information on both, visit www.xlibris.com.

Other sources you might want to check include www.PublishingOnline.com, www.lightningsource.com, and www.1stbooks.com. Do keep in mind that since the digital landscape changes so rapidly, you should consult current Web sites of any companies that interest you. Also read industry magazines and newsletters to find out about new firms that have hung out their virtual shingles.

Perhaps a discussion of contracts is appropriate here. If you are a trade-published author who has gotten your rights back and are a member of the 8,000-strong Authors Guild, you can bring your book back to life through the guild's on-demand program, Backinprint.com. This service gets your books listed at Amazon.com, at barnesandnoble.com, and with in-store databases at virtually every traditional bookstore, both chains and independents. To determine if you qualify for professional membership in the guild, contact the AG in New York at (212) 563-5904.

If you are preparing to sign a contract with a POD printer or for an e-book, study the agreement carefully. Here are a few things to watch for: You may not want to give the other party the *exclusive* right to sell your book; certainly that company's rights will apply only to the digital channel it represents. You also will want to hold the copyright. Ideally, you want to be able to set the retail price yourself. There should be a reasonable termination clause, usually one or three years.

Communicate with your designer/typesetter that your book will be printed with POD technology. There are some different settings and tweaks that may be needed if you are going this route. Once you've chosen your online publisher, obtain submission guidelines and formatting requirements. Submit a complete package; the clock doesn't start ticking until *all* your materials have arrived. Fill out all forms completely and include the needed files and their components (fonts, graphics, etc.).

Be sure your product fits the technology. POD is perfect for text-based books with limited black-and-white graphical elements. (No interior color!) Midrange finished page counts work best: 100 to 500 pages. Be aware, though, that this technology is an inexact science. While one company will do an excellent job, another will produce a book you could be ashamed of. The POD version of our *Jump Start Your Book Sales* had a cover far inferior to the offset print version. We've also seen paperback POD books in which the spine of the inside cover was smeared with unsightly glue. To help protect yourself, ask to see samples before you sign on and talk with colleagues to learn their experiences with various vendors.

Be aware that turning out a book is the end of the on-demand printer's or Internet publisher's responsibility. Once your manuscript is scanned, stored, and posted online, the publisher's job is done. Yours is just beginning! How will you sell your baby? How will people find your book? (Keep reading *all* the chapters in this book! Tons of strategies await you.)

More Adventures in Electronic Information Delivery

It's seldom acknowledged, rarely talked about. Yet it is the Cinderella of Internet publishing. A few self-publishers and small presses are doing it with extraordinary success. We might call this new model "multichannel publishing"—or, more realistically, "slice and dice." Think of your book as a car and the Internet as a chop shop. How can you divide and manipulate your content to create new revenue streams? The days when uttering the word *Web* sent people scurrying for the nearest broom are gone. Now you need to scurry for subject matter.

A new report from Forrester Research forecasts slow growth for both e-books and e-book readers. The report, however, predicts that strong sales of custom-printed trade books (those tailored to a specific company's needs) and digitized textbooks will force publishers to dramatically restructure their processes and technologies.

So let's multipurpose our core content and use the Net to provide customers with new options for getting our information! Instant updating, for instance, can yield a financial windfall. Dated material can be automatically and periodically refreshed, thus creating an ongoing market that can be easily reached via the Internet. Many professionals will pay dearly for current data—such as statistics, trend analysis, and demographics—that can be simply dispensed as an e-mail attachment.

When taking this approach, you can be ready for anything if the first thing you do when you introduce a new title is to archive it in a "platform neutral" format (such as XML) and use that version as your basic content resource where you make all your updates. This is the file you then convert into other e-book or p-book formats. Almost all the service providers mentioned in this chapter now offer an archiving service that is independent of whether they handle any other transactions with you. (Of course, they do that in the hope of having built such a good relationship with you they will get some of your other business.)

Why not make your material Web-centric by creating a parallel product line to profitably meet more needs in different ways? That's what Gordon Burgett did with his core book, *Standard Operating Procedures for All Dentists*. Normally, this 487-page three-ring binder with an easy-to-use disk sells for $325. It contains some 250 Standard Operating Procedures (SOPs) plus about 40 supporting forms.

But not every dentist can afford nor needs the whole 800-pound gorilla. And some want to access the information immediately. Enter the Internet. Burgett has reassembled the material, putting the forms with their appropriate SOPs and selling them electronically as stand-alone products. Dentists can now purchase specific subjects, such as scheduling, collections, or marketing and patient relations if that is their weak spot. Although he hasn't as yet aggressively marketed this product line, it adds about 10 percent to his sales. (To see his operation, go to www.sops.com.)

He also sells various reports plus a list of the one hundred best United States newspaper travel markets, which is updated annually. The high-tech delivery method? E-mail, which works ideally for short documents!

Janet Ruhl is the leading expert on computer consulting and computer careers. She has developed a Web site with lots of traffic (www.realrates.com) and sells three targeted information excerpts, each about 100 pages long. While many people cannot justify $30.00 or $40.00 for a book when they want information on only a single topic, there is little price resistence for the $14.95 excerpts. "The downloads are a great way of capturing this otherwise lost market," she reports. (All purchasers receive a coupon offer to buy the entire printed book. If they do that, the download is free.) Another way the Internet works for her is the immediacy factor. People often contact her just before a job interview or for guidance before signing a consulting contract. She can deliver the information in minutes, and the buyer comes across as a true authority. Ruhl stresses that you need to develop a site with lots of free information and generate considerable traffic before you try this. In her first five months, she sold 227 units at $14.95, a nice addition to her usual income.

Give you any ideas? Do you publish travel guides? Could you put your thumb into the vast archives of travel literature and pull out plums on specific topics (restaurants, bed and breakfasts, guided tours, etc.) to offer the reading public?

Christina Bultnick took a different approach. When she started Internet research in 1998 for clients seeking online recruiting sites, she realized there was a need for a directory of free sites that helped match job hunters with available employment. She filled this need with *The Recruiter's Bible*, which sells for $87. Since this type of tightly niched material, consisting of URLs and Web site reviews, has a very short shelf life, the information needed to be updated and expanded every thirty days. Bultnick does the book in QuarkXPress, has 100 copies printed each month at CopyMax (another form of POD), and puts them in personalized binders. By providing this timely, no-nonsense research, she sells out her stock each month. She also makes the updates available to previous book purchasers as a monthly subscription service. Pretty smart lady. Run the figures: 100 books each month at $87 and a cost of probably under $2,000. That's profitable self-publishing!

Or perhaps you have a wider vision like the folks at Winslow Press. One example of how they are using the Internet to change the face of publishing and give kids a blast from the past is their Dear Mr. President series. They have a patent pending on Interactive Footnotes and use a multitude of ways to empower youngsters and get them to love the reading experience. Their mission is to connect the magic of a book with the wonder of the Web. Each book has its own interactive Web pages for further exploration on its theme. There are links, games, a photo of Teddy Roosevelt as a Rough Rider that becomes a film, projects to make teddy bears and miners' clothing, an online tour of the White House, and much more. "Without the Internet it would have been only half the program," reports Lauren Wohl, VP of marketing. "This approach gives teachers the opportunity to integrate curriculum with current events."

Many authors and publishers use the Web to get direct feedback from readers. This can be a big benefit of this medium as you can test what works and get responses from buyers about what they like, and what you might need to add or modify before you print a large quantity in the traditional manner.

* * *

Will paper books disappear? Certainly not in our lifetimes. There are always alarmists who forecast dire circumstances: TV would replace radio, computers would put television out of business, VCRs would displace going to films, CD-ROMs would gobble up books. None of it happened.

Unquestionably, this digital terrain is moving under our feet. It's unbridled. Exciting. Unpredictable. What we say here is written in sand, not carved in stone. What you choose to do with it will infinitely shape your future. Now, in the next chapter, let us take an excursion into whether you should consider subsidy publishing.

Web Sites, Wisdom, and Whimsey

What's your intent? Whether you choose to print 500 copies or 5,000 depends on your ultimate goal. For example, Gordon Miller printed just 250 copies of his *Quit Your Job Often and Get Big Raises!* His goal? To grab the attention of a New York publisher. He not only sold Doubleday that book but signed a two-book contract for $220,000!

* * *

"Some people swear by e-books. I swear at them," said Matthew Rose in his November 27, 2000, feature in* The Wall Street Journal. *"If only I could have bought a can of New Book Smell, I might not have felt so lost."

* * *

Distributors move into e-books. Many of the master (exclusive) distributors have started to offer small-press publications in electronic format. Publishers Group West, National Book Publishing, and Independent Publishers Group (IPG) have all leaped onto the bandwagon. Says Mark Suchomel, IPG's president, "Our job is to make it possible for independent publishers and small presses to compete successfully in this emerging market with even the largest publishers."

* * *

Some major publications have begun to review e-books. If you want your electronic book to be considered for review by *Publishers Weekly*, e-mail e-forecasts@cahners.com for submission guidelines. For *Library Journal*, contact ebooks@j.cahners.com, and *ForeWord*'s guidelines are available at reviews@forewordmagazine.com.

* * *

E-books may be the future, but tree books are the present.

* * *

Prevent Internet copyright infringement. There are things you can do in self-defense to protect your site against unauthorized copying. CopySafe can guard text, images, even backgrounds from unauthorized use. Go to www.artistscope.com to learn about this watermark technology that places an invisible, permanent identification mark in images. When viewers go to a CopySafe page, they are free to browse but are not able to copy the material in any way. (This certainly doesn't work for all applications but may save some of your content from piracy.) Artistscope also has Secure Image Pro, which uses new encryption to support both Mac and PC platforms.

* * *

Free booklet awaits you. The *Reader's E-Book Primer: An Introduction and Guide to the World of Electronic Books* is 30 pages of basic and useful information for any author or publisher embarking on this venture. By Jamie Engle, it is updated frequently and can be downloaded from www.ebookconnections.com.

* * *

If bigger was always better, dinosaurs would rule the earth. Small is beautiful!

* * *

Questia seeks to build biggest online collection of books. With the college market as its target, this company is looking for books and reference materials that deal with the social sciences or humanities—topics such as art, economics, history, journalism, psychology, religion, or literature. If accepted (and there are rather selective criteria), Questia will "digitalize" your title to join the more than 40,000 books already offered on its site. Authors with rights to their books should contact the Collection Development Team via e-mail at collection_development @questia.com. Publishers need to e-mail the vice-president of publishing, Linda Cunningham, at publisher@questia.com. Good luck!

3 Subsidy Publishers: Another Alternative?

A subsidy publisher puts out books only when the author underwrites the entire venture. Vanity fare feeds the ego. That is not to insinuate that subsidy presses serve no purpose. Suppose you have no time or inclination to go the self-publishing route, yet have a book of poems you want to distribute to friends or relatives at Christmas? Or perhaps a beloved family member just died, and you want to preserve her writing for posterity. Maybe you've just finished tracing your ancestry and choose to distribute these genealogical findings to a wide circle of relatives. These circumstances, and any others where profit is *not* your motive, might be justification for subsidy publishing. Just remember that no traditional publisher *advertises* for manuscripts. When you see a headline such as "Manuscripts Wanted," it's always a tip-off that its source is a subsidy outfit.

What Does Subsidy Publishing Cost?

Just what kind of financial commitment are we looking at? According to various vanity presses, charges to "publish" your book can range from $4,000 to more than $30,000, depending on size and quantity.

When CBS's *60 Minutes* aired "So You Want to Write a Book," the show included an interview of the president of the biggest subsidy house in the country. He speculated that of the six hundred or so books his firm published in one year, twenty-five to thirty of the authors might make money on their books. That's a *failure* rate of 95 percent. Not very good odds.

What to Expect—and Not to Expect

The advertising copywriters hired by subsidy publishers are the best in the business. They could charm the lard off a hog. Brochures are cleverly worded to portray Utopia. Self-publishing successes are made to sound like subsidy accomplishments with statements such as, "It will probably surprise you to know that many prominent authors found it necessary to finance their entries into the literary world." You'll be led to believe that many dynamic leaders opt for this alternative. One promotional letter in our files reads, "Two of our authors, for example, are former Pulitzer Prize and Nobel Prize winners."

Another blurb says, "An Associated Press feature about the author and her book ran in hundreds of newspapers from coast to coast. Yes, imaginative and aggressive promotion paid off for the author of this book." Sounds like the publishers were really out beating the bushes to hype this book, doesn't it? Read it again. Nowhere does it say *they* generated this AP spread. It could very well have resulted from the author's own efforts. Further, they allude to outsmarting the conventional trade houses when telling how an obscure businessman, whose work was rejected nine times, published his book through them and achieved sales of almost 100,000 copies. These are *not* typical results. Instead, most subsidy-published authors never recoup their investments.

If you send your manuscript to a subsidy publisher, expect to receive a glowing letter in return. Flattery will be heaped upon you. You'll be praised for your flowing writing style, your choice of important subject matter, and/or your wisdom in contacting them. This letter will probably also imply that wealth and fame are just around the corner. There are those who say that subsidy publishers often praise writing that couldn't earn a passing grade in a junior high school English class. There is no question that quality control is missing in many of these publishing houses. They make their money up front when writers pay to have their books printed, reducing incentive for producing well-written material and, for that matter, for selling it.

A major drawback to subsidy publishing is the lack of promotion. Book reviewers shun these titles. You'll never see a review for one in *Kirkus* or *Publishers Weekly*. In fact, one major reviewer commented, "They come in four at a time, and when I see the imprint, I throw them immediately in the wastebasket. I wouldn't even give them away."

While the conventional trade publisher employs sales representatives or has developed a national chain of distribution, and the self-publisher seeks out specialized markets and uses creative publicity to generate attention and sales, the subsidy publisher does virtually none of these things. Oh, maybe he adds the book to his catalog and runs what is known in the industry as a "tombstone" ad (where oodles of titles are lumped together and read like a laundry list). If you're really lucky you get a fourteen-line ad all to yourself. That sounds nifty, doesn't it . . . until you realize that such an ad measures one column by one inch. Anticipating books to move from this kind of advertising would be like expecting a mechanic to overhaul a diesel rig with jeweler's tools.

Bookstores are not anxious to stock these titles. One subsidy published author received copies of invoices for a grand total of 64 books sold over a two-year period. In most cases, after paying thousands of dollars to print them, you don't own your books. You will be doled out a "royalty" on each copy sold. Alma Welch, author of *Always a Mimi*, learned this too late. "In order for me to acquire any books, even for promotion, I have to buy them," she laments.

How to Check a Subsidy Publisher's Credentials

But suppose you decide a subsidy house is your answer. How can you find out which is the straightest shooter? One thing you can do is write or call the Federal Trade Commission, 600 Pennsylvania Ave. NW, Washington, DC 20580, and request copies of complaints or decisions filed against any company you are considering. Read these over and come to your own conclusion. You might also ask your banker to get an up-to-date Dun & Bradstreet report on them to learn their business history.

Another smart move would be to contact the Better Business Bureau in the city where each is located. Be sure to inquire not only whether there are any unresolved complaints but also the nature of any previously settled problems. And talk to librarians and managers of your local bookstores to get their views about subsidy publishers. Another important source of information is the state attorney general's office. All these people can typically tell you about complaints against a publisher.

There are some pointed questions you should ask any subsidy publisher. Inquire what percentage of books published last year sold more than five hundred copies. Ask for a list of the bookstores that currently stock the publisher's titles. Request a catalog, and randomly choose two or three books from it. Ask your local bookstore to order them. (Don't just settle for the prescreened samples the publisher provides.) Do these look like "real" bookstore books? Are they well written? Free of typographical errors? Is the printing quality good? What about the covers? Are they striking, colorful, clean, and packed with promotional zingers? Were you able to get them in a timely way?

Something you might like to read is "Should You Pay to Have It Published?" This reprint is available for $1.50 from *Writer's Digest* "Paying for It" item # WRDSYPHP. Send to F&W Publications Products, P.O. Box 2031, Harlan, IA 51593. Include a #10 SASE with your request. Also carefully read over the checklist on page 46. It was prepared by Charles Aronson, author of *The Writer Publisher*, in which he tells of his dismaying subsidy publishing experiences.

Analyzing the Contract

As in any contract, there are certain phrases and conditions that may not be to your advantage. Watch for terminology that reads "up to" a given number.

Charles Aronson Checklist

CHECK LIST SUBSIDY PUBLICATION
(Check each item with your subsidy publisher before you sign his contract)

1. Insist on bids and quotations being in writing.
2. Insist on specific numbers, not "up to."
3. Obtain up-to-date Dun & Bradstreet report, and Author's League report.
4. Things publisher agrees to do, have in writing WHEN he will do them.
5. Term of contract must date from delivery of MARKETABLE copies.
6. How many subsidized titles did publisher issue last year?
7. How many subsidized titles sold over 500 copies last year?
8. Is the agreed retail price of the book comparable to others like it?
9. Get example book signed that your book will be as good as the example.
10. Have exact physical specifications stipulated. (Not less than 50-lb., inside paper, specific trimmed size, length of lines, lines per page, Smythe sewn, case bound hardcover, stamped cloth or morocco.)
11. There will be a dust jacket and it will be full four-color on cover.
12. There will be not less than 500 copies printed and bound—over and above specified complimentary copies and author's copies—in the house and ready for sale on official publication date.
13. There will be no less than enough page forms to produce 2000 copies of your book after publication date.
14. Publisher stipulates exactly when bound, salable books will be delivered.
15. Publisher stipulates the penalty he will pay to author for each day publisher is late beyond 30 working days past stipulated delivery day.
16. Author owns the page forms and can have them at termination, if he asks for them in writing at termination.
17. Author will receive 100 copies of his book on publication date, and these are over and above the 500 salable copies and all complimentary copies.
18. There will be no storage charge on books or forms.
19. Get a list of bookstores that stock this publisher's subsidized books.
20. How many book salesmen does publisher have, to actively sell your book?
21. Author can buy copies of his own book at 20% of retail.
22. Author gets 60% royalty on books publisher sells at retail.
23. On standard 40% discount sales to bookstores, author gets 40% royalty, publisher gets 20%; and this 2-2-1 ratio shall hold on all discount sales.
24. Publisher gives author copies of all sales accounted for each half year.
25. Author has complete and final O.K. of all editing and of page proofs.
26. Publisher will return to author all of author's manuscript and related material within 30 days of publication date, or forfeit $1,000.00.
27. "On an earlier page" will never be used in place of actual page number.
28. Author's name and address shall be on the book's dust jacket.

By consulting this checklist before signing an agreement with a subsidy publisher, you can be sure *your* best interests are served. Keep in mind, however, that asking such questions of a royalty-based pubilsher is not necessary.

29. Author should not use publisher's envelopes for author's direct mailing because publisher will get all the orders and author loses 20% of retail price that way.
30. Publisher supplies list of reviewers who will get complimentary review copies, to number not less than fifty, and review copies will be sent out within three weeks of publication date.
31. Publisher supplies list of major booksellers and libraries that will get complimentary examination copies, to number not less than twenty-five, and these examination copies will be mailed out within four weeks of publication date.
32. Book's promotional circular will be on slick paper, in four-colors, produced in a quantity not less than 5000, 2000 of which will be mailed out within four weeks of publication date; author to get the balance.
33. Publisher stipulates minimum column-inches of advertising that will be devoted solely to your book, naming the media said advertising will appear in, and that none of the ads will be "tombstone."
34. Publisher and author will use certified mail for important communications.
35. At termination, all rights, including subsidiary rights, revert to author.

You have to be especially careful with a subsidy publisher because he does not have to sell any copies of your book in order to make his profit; he already has his profit when you pay him to print and bind and promote your book.

Have your subsidy publisher comment on the above statement.

Reprinted by permission from *The Writer Publisher* by Charels N. Aronson, 11520 Bixby Hill Road, Arcade, NY 14009.

Instead, request that it say "not less than" that number. We are leery of statements that say publishers will "consider" doing something. That gives you no guarantee they will *actually* do it. These are all hedging statements that give you no real assurances.

Insist that specific production and delivery dates be stipulated. (And include a penalty clause that rapidly escalates if they aren't met. For instance, stipulate in the contract that for every fifteen days that delivery of the books goes beyond the promised date, 5 percent will be deducted from the cost of the publishing. You may not be able to get a subsidy publisher to agree to such a clause, but you can at least try.)

Be sure you know the exact number of *bound* books that will be available on the publication date. It is common practice to leave the majority of the books unbound and in flat sheets until they are needed (which is frequently never). Be aware that you will probably be assessed fees for storage of books, flat sheets, or promotional materials. Require that, upon termination of the agreement, all rights (including subsidiary rights) revert to the author. Before signing any contract, read the fine print carefully. Do not be carried away with the glamour of finally getting your book into print. Know *beforehand* what your situation will be if you agree to work with a subsidy publisher. You may want to hire an attorney who specializes in intellectual property/publishing to go over the contract.

We helped a client who signed a contract with a subsidy publisher to publish his book. This doctor had written a helpful guide about food allergies. It had genuine potential. We set him up with several distributors, developed supporting advertising fliers, ghostwrote articles for him in health magazines, and more. Now his dilemma is to work with and around the publisher until he gets the rights back, two long years after the publisher provides bound galleys.

While the author should be getting $4 (40 percent) on each of his $10 books that sell, there is a clause in the contract that hamstrings him. It reads, "On all sales made at a discount of more than 40 percent, the author's compensation shall be reduced by a percentage equal to the difference between 40 percent and the discount given." So now, because he's gotten behind his own book and made it sell, he is penalized and only given $3 per book (the distributors require a 50 percent discount), after he handed over many thousands of dollars to produce it.

His agreement stipulated that the publisher was required to have only four hundred bound copies available initially for publicity and sales. It says the publishing house will "print and bind from time to time sufficient copies of said Work to fill all bona fide orders." How promptly will this occur do you suppose . . . now that *the press* is footing the bill and not the author? Will the company support the demand the doctor may create? Furthermore, if he personally wants to purchase more than the fifty copies he got under the agreement terms, he gets only a 45 percent discount—after he paid to print them!

Working With Subsidy Publishers

Whether it's building a house or producing a book, production schedules can go haywire. If they do, somebody's work falls behind. See that it isn't yours. It's up to you to stay on top of the job and make sure that deadlines are met. (Remember that squeaky wheel.)

You can influence how much money you'll make. For one thing, insist that your name and address appear on the dust jacket or cover and on the copyright page inside the book. Then people who see the book can order it directly from you, instead of going through the subsidy publisher. There is another way you can steer more coins into your own coffers. Your publisher may encourage you to provide a mailing list of friends and relatives to whom it will send promotional material. Don't do it. Send to those people yourself! Why let the publisher collect the middleman commission? Recognize right away that if your subsidy-published book is going to sell, it will be primarily because *you* hustle it. For detailed ways to generate publicity and sales, study the forthcoming chapters.

Copublishing

In addition to the above, there are also several publishers who do both royalty and subsidy books. "Mum" is often the word on their subsidy activity, however, unless you happen to query them. These semisubsidy houses will then offer to do your book with you footing a large part of the bill. They don't necessarily turn out a product with any more merit than subsidy publishers do, so be cautious.

Sadly, the number of publishers seeking copublishing or cooperative arrangements with authors has increased in the past few years. We received a letter from a client who had entered into such an agreement with a subsidy publisher, agreeing to pay 50 percent of the total publishing costs. She was to get royalties of 40 percent on the *retail* price of the book. However, the publisher paid her only on the net amount. She took the company to court and received the following award: $17,000 in royalties, $20,000 in punitive damages, the return of the inventory of her book, and $255 in arbitration fees. Bravo!

Whenever a publisher suggests you share in the cost and get up to a 40 percent royalty, scrutinize the deal very carefully. How do you know the 50 percent you're supposed to pay is truly half of the total cost? The figures could be greatly inflated. And remember wholesalers and bookstores will need 40 to 55 percent discounts. Do the numbers make sense?

Subsidy publishing is sometimes the route taken for biographies, political stories, technical works, and business or industrial histories. University presses sometimes fall into this category, taking on a book if it is of excellent scientific or scholarly value. But university presses are by no means typical of subsidy publishers. As an arm of the educational institution, the university press has clout and respectability.

As we've noted, there are situations when subsidy publishing makes sense for certain people. If that is your case, fine. But remember caveat emptor—let the buyer beware. If you want value for your money and a credible, quality product, self-publishing probably makes more sense.

The first leg of your trip into that terrain has to do with developing a winning manuscript. Your book is your product. How can you assure that it is a good one?

Web Sites, Wisdom, and Whimsey

Remember—there's always hope.
The ark was built by amateurs, the* Titanic *by professionals.

* * *

***The Elements of Style* is available online.** Ever since William Strunk, Jr. breathed life into this slim volume to use in teaching his English classes at Cornell in the early 1900s, it has been a classic. That it is one of the all-time self-publishing success stories makes it even more of a treasure. His early rules are just as relevant today: Use the active voice, omit needless words, keep to one tense, etc. All his elementary rules of usage, principles of composition, matters of form, words and expressions commonly misused, and words commonly misspelled await you at www.bartleby.com/141/index.html. Enjoy!

* * *

Definition of a Dictionary:
A guide to the spelling of words,
which can be located if you know how to spell them.

* * *

Looking for a fast, free way to stay in touch with key contacts? Blue Mountain Arts has an extensive and delightful collection of computer cards and messages you can use to communicate with business and personal contacts. Under "Stay in Touch" there are business and thank-you cards. In other sections you'll find congratulations cards, motivational prints, cards slanted to certain interests and professions (computers, professionals, sports, teachers, etc.). And from a personal standpoint, you would be hard pressed not to find something appropriate here to send friends and loved ones. Go to http://bluemountain.com, and have a ball!

* * *

How do Americans use the Internet? A Harris Poll revealed that sending and receiving e-mail is by far the most common Web activity, with 89 percent of online Americans doing so at least sometimes. (Don't you just love those people who get back to you weeks later?) Second, with 68 percent, was to check on news, updates, weather, etc. To get information about a hobby or special interest took third place, with 67 percent. In hot pursuit was gathering information about products and services, doing research for work or school, and surfing to explore new and different sites (62 percent, 61 percent, and 60 percent, respectively).

The Net is definitely not going to replace typical education. The lowest use, at only 9 percent, was taking courses.

Learn how to avoid unscrupulous companies and people. The organization Science Fiction and Fantasy Writers of America, Inc., has established a real service for all writers. If you go to www.sfwa.org/beware, you'll discover a wealth of information to protect yourself. As they say, "There are sharks out there in the literary waters," and they don't pull any punches in telling you about the deceptions that abound. There is a whole section on subsidy and vanity publishers, that explains the pitfalls of this approach, lists names of some companies that have been in the news, and explains things to consider plus some warning signs.

PART II

Start-Up Considerations to Get You Off on the Right Foot

4 *Scoping Out a Marketable Subject*

As a self-publisher, you will go into business. The first and most important step any potential businessperson takes is to decide what product or service to offer customers. So, too, you must determine your "vehicle." Some forms of writing hold more promise for commercial success than others. You may dream of turning out a volume of poetry, writing a novel, or telling your life story. And you may feel a deep passion for your project. If making money is your primary goal, however, you could face an uphill climb. There are some tips that will help, though, and they are discussed in this chapter.

Whether you've already written your book, know what you are going to write about, or have yet to pick a subject, there are several steps you can take to help assure the salability of your manuscript. A marketable subject is vital both for commercial publication and for self-publishing. In this chapter, we'll explore how to choose a salable topic, how to tap into your personal storehouse of knowledge, and how to write about what you know. We'll look at doing cookbooks as fund-raisers and discuss ways to develop titles that hook readers. Writing novels, poetry, and other literary works for self-expression and the pure joy of it will also be covered.

Some books quickly establish phenomenal sales records and rocket to best-seller status, while others sit in warehouses awaiting unceremonious last rites. Why? There are two reasons: The winners are usually about hot, timely subjects, and they've been aggressively promoted.

Subject matter greatly influences your book's track record. Choosing a marketable topic is the first step toward the best-seller dream to which all authors cling (secretly or admittedly). But how do you know what's marketable?

Nonfiction tops the list. Americans are hungry for information. It can take the form of a book that shows how to do or make something or gives a formula for self-improvement. Books that show readers how to be wealthier, healthier, or sexier lead the pack.

But perhaps the thought of writing a whole book seems as ambitious to you as scaling Mount Everest. Then climb a smaller peak. You might prepare and sell a special report or a booklet, which we'll discuss in the next chapter.

Capitalizing on New Trends

Beyond the general hunger of Americans to be skinny, rich, and popular, certain specific topics are more salable than others. Catching the tide of current or anticipated trends is certainly one good way to find a salable topic. By staying alert, you can recognize a hidden need for information before others do. Bingo! A timely, marketable subject.

Such was the case of the first book about cooking in crock pots. The author attended a trade show and noticed that several manufacturers were introducing these new devices. Presto! The lights flashed. Would cooks need new recipes and guidance on how best to use their new cookware? You better believe they would. Since Mable Hoffman's *Crockery Cookery* came out in 1975, more than 3 million copies have been sold.

In 1978 when we wrote *The Encyclopedia of Self-Publishing*, the forerunner of this book, we stated, "An opportunity we see on the horizon is in the field of home computers." (We should have taken our own advice!) Adam Osborne and Peter McWilliams jumped on that bandwagon early, published how-to books, and made a mint. Osborne's *An Introduction to Microcomputers* sold out its first run of 20,000 in three months. It was adopted by dozens of universities as a text, and Osborne became the darling of the home computer industry. But today there is a glut of computer books. To be successful in this arena now, an author must find an ingenious approach to this constantly changing subject.

Take the advice of author Mark Van Doren: "Welcome all ideas and entertain them royally, for one of them may be king." Tune into hot topics. But be careful not to be trapped by a fad. When it comes to "fad-itis," no one is immune. The trick lies in determining the difference between a fad, which can be here today and gone tomorrow, and a genuine trend. Ignore the transient fads. Don't let a turkey gobble up your time and money.

There is keen interest in regional cookbooks, restaurant guides, and history books about specific areas. Niche publications—for kids, seniors, gays, singles, etc.—with a regional slant is another thriving category. In fact, we've had so many inquiries on how to do books about a specific geographic area that we wrote and published *How to Make Big Profits Publishing City and Regional Books.*

When devising a new product, you can give an old theme a new twist. That's what Tim and Nina Zagat did. They were part of a wine-tasting group that griped about there being no reliable source covering where to eat in the Big Apple. So, on a lark, they decided to gather and record their friends' opinions.

The *Zagat Survey* (pronounced "Zuh-GAT") began in 1979 as a mimeographed sheet. They now sell restaurant-goers' regional guides in forty-five cities. Their twist is that the patrons themselves rate and review the eateries by filling out surveys that the Zagats compile and publish.

Says Tim, "We tried to get a publisher, but they all turned us down." What a blessing; today they sell 75,000 copies a month! They also arrange special corporate-sponsored editions that companies can give to clients, license their data online, have a reservation system, use e-commerce, even sell restaurant-branded stuff such as Ruth's Chris Steak House knives. The books are available not only in English but also in Hebrew, French, and Japanese. And their scope now includes hotels, resorts, spas, airlines, and car rental companies. The family-owned firm won't disclose figures, but Tim admits it's been profitable (we bet!) since 1983.

How can you tell a genuine ongoing trend from a mere novelty? The best you can do is make a shrewd guess. Ask yourself if it's a single, freaky happening unrelated to anything else or an eruption into wide popularity of something of long-standing interest: fitness, maybe, or organically grown foods. Ask yourself if a lot of people are likely to still be interested in it in a year or two. Think whether other ideas in this field have tended to flash and die or whether they've lasted at least long enough for a book on the subject to be written, published, and find an interested readership. You can't really know for sure, but you can do your best to see that the star to which you've hitched your hopes isn't bright just because it's falling.

Now spirituality and religion are hot—in the workplace as well as the home. Of course the subject of money continues to peak peoples' interest: earning it, investing it, making it, saving it.

Americans continue to be caught up in diet and exercise. There are hundreds of books on these topics. It would make no sense to come out with another run-of-the-mill (pardon the pun) tome on jogging. If you are clever, however, you may find a new way to ride the wave of interest others have generated. That's what Kenneth Cooper did with *The New Aerobics*. Exercise has been popular through the ages.

Speaking of aging, books for people fifty and older are in great demand as the baby boomers mature. They seek titles on managing personal finances, volunteerism, aging gracefully, health and fitness, part-time self-employment, downsizing your budget, gardening, and more.

How many books on a subject are too many? Look closely at the competition. Do the existing books leave a gap your book could turn into a target? Remember, if your book is to stand out from the pack, it must have a fresh angle, a unique approach or information to persuade a prospective reader to buy it rather than one of the others. Ask a few bookstore buyers or managers how well your competition is selling. If it's one a month, maybe you ought to choose another project. If bookstores are reordering frequently and getting lots of requests, then maybe your book will do well, too.

When searching for a marketable subject, one trick is to look at what type of book is selling well, then take a different approach. As a takeoff on *Smart Women, Foolish Choices: Finding the Right Men, Avoiding the Wrong Ones* (Drs. Connell Cowan and Melvyn Kinder), Price Stern Sloan published a spoof entitled *Smart Women, Stupid Books: Stop Reading and Learn to Love Losers* (Lisa Ann Marsoli). The parody defines the problem (too many worthless men) and offers the solution (date them anyway). Since the latter title has gone out of print, however, it seemed to be the biggest loser.

For a self-publisher, it's important to select a specific, clearly defined market. Niches can equal riches. Write for dog lovers, organic gardeners, parents of disabled children, rather than everybody. By purposely ignoring big, general groups and targeting a select audience, you can find and penetrate your market.

Evaluate the possibilities carefully. People are willing to buy and own several cookbooks or gardening guides because these subjects are broad and of general interest. But how many books on hang gliding or training your pet gerbil to do tricks would *you* want to own? If one would be enough (or too much), your entry into an already crowded field could not be expected to do very well. Take these things into account and remember that your book's success isn't just dependent on how good a book it is; it'll depend on how many people need and want it. Don't let your enthusiasm for bringing out a complete guide to beekeeping blind you to the limited appeal of the subject.

Researching Potential Markets

Want to do stealth research to determine a marketable subject? Become a lurker! (This is not to be confused with a Peeping Tom.) Lurkers visit chat rooms, discussion groups, bulletin boards, or whatever you choose to call groups of people who deliberate online about specific topics. There are (take our word for it) several online groups devoted to your potential subject.

What you want to do is sign on so you can read the postings, then audit what is said to determine concerns and problems these people are having. When you see a pattern emerge, you've just learned about a need you might want to fill. Another idea is to take a more visible approach and actually ask the members to participate in a simple survey to help pinpoint their needs and wants.

While we're talking about online research, let's also address what type of e-books are most marketable. Certain types of fiction tend to do well: erotica,

Where to Find Online Chat Groups

Find them at the following places to name a few:

- http://chat.yahoo.com
- www.forumone.com
- www.theglobe.com
- www.topica.com

science fiction/fantasy, and horror, of course anything about computers or the Web is a natural. Tightly niched nonfiction—where you can find your audience online—is also strong.

As you climb the sheer cliffs of self-publishing, look for tiny crevices that have been passed over by the "big guys." You're a lot less likely to be outscaled by the competition if you define a small niche and address yourself to that audience. For instance, major trade publishers weren't inclined to do a children's guide to San Diego, but a private publisher tackled this topic very successfully.

Positioning for Profit

Positioning your product can give you extra sales clout. To "position" means to give your book a competitive edge by making it different or special in some way. Let's use cookies as an example. They are positioned in a multitude of ways: chewy, crunchy, nutritious, gourmet, like Grandma used to make, tiny, gigantic, etc.

In our seminars for writing and publishing organizations, we tell the story of *The Starving Students' Cookbook*. Its sales were lagging until the author, Dede Hall, decided to try packaging the book with an inexpensive skillet, shrink wrapping them together, and offering them in Price Clubs and Kmarts. When 150 sold in a test store the first two days, Hall knew she had a winning idea on her hands.

Another cookbook was positioned as a gift item by dressing it up with a scarlet ribbon and some cinnamon sticks, then placing it in the housewares and gift sections of department stores. By the way, while it languished at $5.95 in bookstores, it sold feverishly for $10.00 in department stores.

You can position your book in other ways, as well: We advised one client who was producing a nautical book to use water-resistant paper so boating enthusiasts could use his manual on the seas without fear of ruining it. One small press in California doubled its sales by adding a "workbook" to a self-help publication. And a Texas small publisher put out Nancy S. LeVick's *Your Housekeeper's Cook-*

book as a bilingual presentation giving recipes and menus in both English and Spanish, thus setting itself apart from other cookbooks and appealing to the fast-growing Hispanic population.

Secular versus nonsecular is another positioning approach. Perhaps you find too bountiful a harvest of books on your topic in the secular press. Perhaps you should consider giving it a religious spin. Today no subject is taboo for ecclesiastical books. Religious and spiritual titles deal with parenting, relationships, hobbies, travel, careers—and virtually every other subject including sex, abuse, homosexuality, and drugs.

Some publishers position their books by virtue of price. A $9.95 paperback edition may be slanted for bookstores or specialty retail outlets, while a $49.95 version (promoted as a *kit*—packaged in a three-ring binder, and perhaps containing a CD-ROM tucked in the binder pocket) is targeted for direct sales to the consumer. Creative, product-engineered strategies such as these, when used in the early stages, can pay big dividends later.

We might also learn a lesson from Hay House, which took a leap of faith and repackaged Louise Hay's *Heal Your Body*, in spite of the fact it had sold a whopping 3 million copies. "People don't necessarily have time to read through all 250 pages [of the original book]," reports Reid Tracy, Hay House's VP. So, instead of offering only the complex explanation, they radically changed how the content was presented and repackaged the information into a quick gift-book-type reference. The new look is inviting and fun, the results stunning. The original book continues to sell between 60,000 and 80,000 copies a year, and the new colorful hardcover version sells an additional 60,000 copies!

Write What You Know

Of course, you can also hook up to your own personal knowledge. Joe Karbo, the king of mail-order self-help books, commented before his death, "You bet your sweet patootie I've made a bundle sharing my information. And why not? I invested a lot more time and money in my 'education' than most doctors and lawyers."

There are things you can write about effectively and profitably even if you've never written anything in your life. No matter who you are, where you live, or how old you are, you know more about *something* than most folks, and therefore you possess special knowledge that other people will pay for. All you have to do is write what you know. People from all walks of life, not just professional writers, do it all the time.

A man who designed company symbols and did advertising layout wrote a book on logo design. He sells it as a "minicourse" and gets fifty bucks a crack for it. A young woman successfully sued her former employer for sex discrimination. Then she documented the steps taken and made her information available to help others fight similar injustices.

A businessman who holds exclusive import rights to a small water pump markets his booklet telling how to build ceramic fountains—which just happen to use his pump. A plastic surgeon does a book, complete with before and after photographs, on the wonders of cosmetic surgery. Both books boost their authors' overall incomes. A lesbian who has come out of the closet writes of her experiences and adjustments to publicly admitting her homosexuality.

Venus Andrecht cultivated an interest in herbs into a multichannel business that includes a career as an author and self-publisher, lecturer, expert on herbs, and entrepreneur extraordinaire. Her book *The Outrageous Herb Lady* is subtitled *How to Make a Mint in Selling and Multi-Level Marketing*. She sells it to her existing network of herb buyers, dealers, distributors, customers, clients, and students.

And that's just the tip of the iceberg. Each year thousands of people add substantially to their income by putting together a book or booklet, then merchandising it through direct-marketing techniques. We have one associate whose mailbox is full of orders each month as a result of a book she wrote after cruising the Caribbean for four months. Her cookbook for sailors gives practical boating hints, some two hundred galley-tested recipes for canned goods, and oodles of information on provisioning for long voyages.

But Shirley didn't stop there. She has gone on to write and publish other related books and even had a yacht delivery business for a while.

Another friend, a management consultant, is putting the final touches on a manuscript to show individuals how to develop their personal management potential. After tottering on the verge of bankruptcy, one man wrote a detailed report on his findings. Not only did he *not* go bankrupt, but by sharing the things he learned on the subject, he has sold more than 100,000 copies of the book. Many folks establish self-publishing businesses to provide healthy ongoing incomes during their retirement years.

Finding Your Interests

OK, you're convinced these people are making money selling their knowledge. "But what do I have to write about?" you ask. First grab a pad of paper and a pencil. Start listing your hobbies and interests. Write down the jobs you've had, and especially note any job functions or procedures that you particularly enjoyed or were good at. For instance, if you're in the field of credit and collection, you may be a very good skip tracer. Many small businesses would love to discover how they can crack down on customers who don't pay their bills—instead of shelling out 50 percent to a collection agency or, as often as not, writing deadbeats off as bad debt.

Now think about your successes. Have you won any honors or contests? Received special recognition for something? Do people always praise you for a characteristic or skill? That could contain the germ of a book, because if you are successful, you're better than most people, and thus you're an "expert" with information to sell. But know-how is worthless without "do-how." What's do-how? It's action. Synergy. Innovation. Persistence.

Also think about your failures. That's how our *Country Bound!: Trade Your Business Suit Blues for Blue Jean Dreams* was born. We moved from San Diego, California, to a town of five hundred people in central Colorado. What a disaster! We lost a huge amount of money, suffered unimaginable heartache, and learned a lot about ourselves we would never have known. This was in the early 1980s before it was "fashionable" to escape big cities for Small Town USA. When that trend emerged, we wanted to protect others from making the same mistakes. So we wrote a book and turned our crash into cash. It was not just about our experiences, but was also a how-to book to guide folks in carefully evaluating this life-altering decision, then offering practical suggestions on how to acclimate to rural America.

Before jumping into a book project, the smart people do their homework. Find out what books are already available on the subject and what they are titled. An impossible task? Not at all. Amazon.com is a terrific place to determine what's out there. Your local library is also ready to supply the answers. Look under all possible versions of your topic in the current *Subject Guide to Books In Print*; also check *Forthcoming Books In Print*. (See the example on page 62 to learn just how to interpret the listings.) You will want to photocopy the relevant pages for future use.

Look in the library for any titles that sound like they compete, request them from interlibrary loan, or purchase copies. Talk to key personnel at your favorite bookstore to determine their recommendations for the three best books on the subject. Get them and *study* them. What are their angles? What solutions are they offering? Can you think of better answers? What is missing? Your job is to go the extra inch, to *improve* on those books.

Alternatives for Entrepreneurial Types

Perhaps rather than writing a book in the typical sense, you may choose to bring together a collection of information that you edit into a consistent format and then publish. That's what a San Diego advertising man did. Gary Beals put out

Excerpt From *Books in Print*

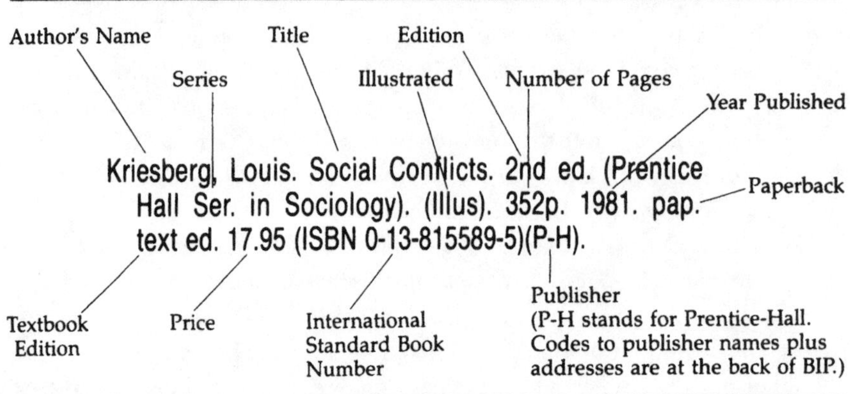

This is typical of the information booksellers, librarians, and others will find about your book in *Books in Print.*

the first edition of the *San Diego SourceBook*, which was a directory of country clubs, groups, local associations, organizations, and speakers. Beals didn't stop there, however. He capitalized on the fact that this sort of information quickly becomes obsolete. Soon there was a second edition, and a third. (One of the nice things about annual editions is that you can solicit standing orders from certain customers for each new volume.)

Since entrepreneurial blood pulses rapidly through Beals's veins, he decided other cities could also use such resources. This led to a network of more than a dozen directories across the nation. But Beals doesn't try to do them all. He sells or franchises given areas to other self-publishers who put out their own *SourceBooks*.

Directories can be big business. One of our previous students, Jacqueline Thompson, pulled together information on specialists in speech, dress, personal public relations, color, executive etiquette, and motivation. Then she put out the *Directory of Personal Image Consultants*. Thompson garnered plugs for her directory in *The Wall Street Journal*, *Publishers Weekly*, *Media Decisions*, *The New York Times*, *Signature*, and *Gentlemen's Quarterly*. Thompson, realizing she had a bull by the horns, immediately decided to make it an annual edition, thereby creating built-in obsolescence and an ongoing revenue base of previous customers. Directories have an added advantage. You not only reap financial rewards by selling the books but can also charge those listed a fee for being included, for a bold listing, and/or for advertising within the directory.

Cookbooks as Moneymakers

Cookbooks are another ideal independent publishing vehicle, both for individuals and for volunteer groups. They have flourished ever since 1742, when the early settlers in America started experimenting with ways to prepare the often-unfamiliar foods they found. The first one was published in Virginia and called *The Compleat Housewife, or, The Accomplished Gentlewoman's Companion.* Since that time thousands of cookbooks have sprouted. There are ethnic cookbooks and appliance cookbooks. In fact, two creative authors, Dale Darling and Julia Van Dyck, capitalized on the self-sufficiency craze and wrote *The Airtight Woodstove Cookbook.*

Pam Williams, the proprietor of a small chocolate shop, collaborated with Rita Morin to self-publish *Oh Truffles by Au Chocolat.* This pair of Vancouver, British Columbia, entrepreneurs sold out their first printing of 10,000 copies and worked out a deal with Stein and Day to release the Canadian book in the United States.

For many churches, temples, Junior Leagues, and other women's nonprofit organizations, sponsored cookbooks have established themselves as excellent moneymakers. Volunteers find this one of the easiest ways to earn a substantial sum in a short period of time.

The Baton Rouge Junior League put together a collection of lip-smackin' goodies and dubbed it *River Road Recipes.* This little fund-raising beauty earns profits of $100,000 to $150,000 a year! And the sequels, *River Road Recipes: A Second Helping* and *River Road Recipes III*, have also been tremendously successful. The classic *Charleston Recipes* has sold more than 650,000 copies over the years. In Washington, DC, the Congressional Club, made up of wives of government officials, self-publishes continuing editions of *The Congressional Club Cook Book.* It churns out $75,000 a year in earnings.

Did you know that the classic *Joy of Cooking* originated in 1931 with the First Unitarian Women's Alliance in St. Louis, Missouri? Scribner now owns the rights and sells more than 100,000 copies each year. *In the Beginning* is a taste-tempting collection of hors d'oeuvres that the ways and means committee of a Temple Sisterhood put together. Through aggressive marketing it has been reviewed in several hundred newspapers, has been merchandised successfully via direct mail, and was purchased by over fifty Waldenbooks stores.

Why are these cookbooks so successful? Because every cook who has a recipe included is an automatic salesperson! Of course, as in any venture, there are drawbacks. It is often difficult to work on such a project by committee. Fortunately, there are several valuable sources for help. Sara Pitzer's *How to Write a*

Cookbook and Get It Published is a treasure trove of sound advice. Look for it in your library. There are also two companies that specialize in printing cookbooks. Even if you decide not to use their services, write for general information. They are Cookbooks by Morris Press, 3212 E. Highway 30, Kearney, NE 68847, (800) 445-6621, www.morriscookbooks.com; and Cookbook Publishers, Inc., 10800 Lakeview Ave., P.O. Box 15920, Lenexa, KS 66285-5920, (800) 227-7282, www.cookbookpublishers.com.

A Case for Novels, Memoirs, and Poetry

You'll notice that the examples we've given are primarily how-to or self-help nonfiction. There is a good reason for that. Fiction writers have many obstacles to clear. If they depart from the "typical" novel, they're considered by the trade to be eccentric, arty, or simply unsalable. If it weren't for the small-press movement, few new and innovative books would see print.

Novels

When writing a novel, it's important to adhere to one of the several established genres: mystery, romance, science fiction/fantasy, thriller, or literary. Then you have a fan base for marketing purposes. Each of these genres has a "formula"; educate yourself before starting to write.

Those who come through like thoroughbreds frequently hitch their stories to current events, especially events they themselves were or are involved in. John Ehrlichman's *The Company* was inspired by Watergate. And the Egyptian attack on Yom Kippur served as the basis for *Three Weeks in October*, a tale by Yaël Dayan.

Dorothy Bryant, a Berkeley, California, woman who self-publishes her novels, began in 1971 by giving away her first novel, *The Comforter*, to generate word-of-mouth sales. (It apparently worked, as Random House now carries the book.) Dorothy admits that it is slow building an audience. But her books have achieved a measure of success. *Killing Wonder*, a literary murder mystery, was sold to a mass-paperback house. Lippincott previously published another of her works but let it go out of print. However, the company proved to be premature in measuring this novel for its literary casket. Not one to be daunted, Bryant got back the rights and reissued it herself. She sold more than 3,000 copies within the first year. *Ella Price's Journal*, which Bryant published under her Ata Books imprint, is doing well as a text in women's reentry programs. For another of her books, *Prisoners*, film rights have been optioned for a TV movie of the week.

Bryant's advice to self-publishing novelists is, "Put it through another edit." She feels the quality of writing can often be improved and uses literate friends to read and edit her work. It has been her experience that first-year sales will be around 3,000 books, tapering off to 700 to 1,000 per year thereafter.

Memoirs

Autobiography is another area appealing to self-publishers. And if you truly have lived through a unique experience, have rich historical fare to share, or were associated with a "name" person, writing an autobiography may be a prudent move. Otherwise, it can be an expensive ego trip. If you expect to recoup your investment, be sure your memoir will be of interest to the general public, not just to you, your relatives, and friends. *How to Write the Story of Your Life*, by Frank P. Thomas, offers helpful guidelines, as does *You Can Write a Memoir*, by Susan Carol Hauser.

I (Marilyn) wrote an "as told to" book about an adventurous modern cowboy who rode horseback and took a pack string from the Mexican border to Fairbanks, Alaska, in less than six months. Tom Davis's impressive forty-five-hundred-mile journey set several world records. *Be Tough or Be Gone* is his story. It was an excellent candidate for self-publishing, as he planned to duplicate the trip and peddle books along the way. While this title rolled off the presses, we were able to convince Ripley's Believe It or Not to feature Davis in a column syndicated to three hundred newspapers across the country. Of note is the fact that Davis tried to interest Ripley's in his adventure before we did a book—and had no luck whatsoever. Just another example of how a book gives you fresh credibility and visibility.

In another case, a trade-published author chose to breathe life into her book after Little, Brown and Company had let it die. *Snatched From Oblivion: A Cambridge Memoir* is a reminiscence of growing up in Cambridge, Massachusetts, in the early years of the twentieth century. It describes Cambridge characters, the local politics, college life, and a period and way of life that have virtually disappeared. Its author, Marian Cannon Schlesinger, decided to be in charge and do it herself when the hardback went out of print and the rights reverted to her. Only four months after publication, she had recouped three-quarters of her investment. More and more trade-published authors are electing to recapture their works and publish them themselves after they have been allowed to go out of print.

Poetry

It has been said of writing: "You don't choose it, it chooses you." Nowhere is this more true than for the poet. Poets are compelled to capture their expressive messages for the joy of it—and for the sadness of it. Although poetry is perhaps the most difficult thing to self-publish successfully, it can be done.

Not many people know that contemporary best-selling poet Rod McKuen originally published his own book of poems and sold 40,000 copies before his talent was recognized by Random House, which ultimately sold over a million copies of his *Listen to the Warm*.

A collection of poems can be gathered into a chapbook, which is a small paperbound book containing poems, ballads, tales, or political or religious tracts. In the chapter "Initiating a Nationwide Marketing Plan With Publicity Pizzazz," we investigate sources that review poetry and novels and look at some innovative ways of gleaning media attention for such literary works.

Titles That Hook Readers

Now that you've isolated your subject, how will you tempt potential readers to partake of this offering?

Christen it with a zesty title. A dynamic title—one that turns a sleeper into a keeper—will motivate people to sip the sparkling prose of your pages. There are no absolute rules or proven formulas for this. As soon as we say, "The best titles are brief: ideally two or three words, certainly no more than six," we're reminded of *Chicken Soup for the* ___________ *Soul*, which has to be one of the all-time best series titles. A close second is John Gray's *Men Are From Mars, Women Are From Venus*. Brief.

At least we'd all agree your title should be descriptive. Right? Then what about *Don't Make Me Stop This Car!* (Al Roker) or *Who Moved My Cheese?* (Spencer Johnson). The first, in case you didn't know, is about raising good kids; the second addresses change at work.

Well, then, humor. Should they be humorous? We could have *Beauty Secrets*, by Janet Reno, *Mike Tyson's Guide to Dating Etiquette*, *The Stripper's Guide to Woodworking*, *Things I Love Most About Bill*, by Hillary Clinton. Or what about *Spotted Owl Recipes*, by the Sierra Club?

Seriously, it usually works best to have a clear title over a catchy one. And ideally it should start with the two or three most relevant words, so when booksellers look it up on a database, they can immediately catch your drift. This will also help your book turn up more frequently in computer keyword searches.

When playing with titling, look at the power of numbers: 5 Ways to . . . , 7 Weeks to . . . , 21 Secrets for . . . , 101 Easy . . . , 307 Moneymaking Tips. It can go on and on. Studies show uneven numbers work best, by the way.

Another useful approach is to identify the three biggest problems your book solves. Become the reader and ask yourself, "What's in it for me?" or, "Why should I care?" Then cast these solutions in punchy, benefit terminology. Promise how you will change the reader's life.

Sometimes a play on words can have a dramatic effect. Capitalizing on the vastly popular *What Color Is Your Parachute?* Price Stern Sloan came out with *What Color Is Your Parody?* (Charlie Haas). The subtitle of the Jim Soules book about finding your perfect mate included *A Guide for* Two*getherness.*

Another way to stimulate ideas is to check magazine article titles to see what thought ticklers they provide. Also peruse the teaser phrases on magazine covers. Sometimes by substituting just a word, you have a grabber title. Look within your book itself for catchy phrases that might make a captivating title. Listen to songs and read poems to find a phrase you might turn. Toss around clichés and common sayings to see if a slight change of wording would yield an appealing title.

Just as there are guidelines for good titles, there are also some negatives to avoid. Stay away from trite titles, such as *All That Glitters Is Not Gold*, *Mother's Little Helper*, or *To Be or Not to Be*. Booooring! Profane or controversial titles usually spell disaster—you'll make some potential readers dislike your book on sight. And don't choose a title that gives misleading signals: Consider the monk who returned a copy of *From Here to Eternity* to the library, saying, "This isn't what I thought it would be."

Start jotting down some ideas. Don't be judgmental. Write down every idea that comes to mind. Let your thoughts hopscotch across all possibilities. Now use a thesaurus to find synonyms for likely candidates. Check any fuzzy definitions. Cast out those with no possible application. String the remainder together in various combinations. You may end up with ten or twenty possibilities. All the better. (Save all of these; they can probably be used for snappy chapter headings or subheads.)

Next, do some preliminary market research. Big corporations spend hundreds of thousands of dollars to test people's reactions. You can sample public opinion for free. Carry your list of suggested titles everywhere you go. Ask co-workers, relatives, neighbors, friends—even strangers—which they like best, and least, and why. Capitalize on every opportunity to discuss your potential titles. Keep accurate records of what folks say and additional suggestions they may make. You may want to seek feedback from an Internet discussion group devoted to your topic.

One caution: Be aware that feedback from friends and relatives will reflect your own opinions more than general public evaluations will. Why? We tend to surround ourselves with people of our own socioeconomic levels. This can be a real problem if, for example, you are a doctor writing a book for blue-collar workers and you only test the titles on your peers.

Especially if you're going after bookstore and mass distribution, a title with zap sells books. Here's a case in point: Two different newspaper ads told of new books. One was called *The Art of Courtship*; the other, *The Art of Kissing*. Which do you think sold best? *The Art of Kissing* outsold courtship by 60,500 to 17,500! Why? Kissing is fun; it's about a specific benefit we all like. Courtship is general and sounds like work. Then there was *The Squash Book*, which sold 1,500 copies. Yet when it became *The Zucchini Cookbook*, sales zoomed to 300,000 copies.

The right title is like the aroma from a French pastry shop: It creates instant hunger for the goodies within. We debated before calling Marilyn's latest book *Shameless Marketing for Brazen Hussies*. It indeed quickly tells what the book is about—and pinpoints whom it is for. But would the edgy title work? Ninety-five percent of entrepreneurial women who hear the title chuckle and show immediate interest. (The remaining 5 percent wouldn't be able to handle the inside, either.) Surprisingly, many men also like it. As Marilyn follows up on review copies, what has been interesting is that virtually every media person who received the book remembers it. That's a real plus. On the downside, we had hoped to sell quantities as a goodwill builder into companies who target female entrepreneurs. Corporate America, however, is ready for neither "shameless marketing" nor "brazen hussies."

As favored titles begin to emerge, play with them. See if by tossing two together you might mix in an appropriate subtitle. That's what happened with our book *Creative Loafing*. *A Shoestring Guide to New Leisure Fun* emerged as the ideal subtitle. This choice was painstakingly selected over numerous other candidates. *Creative Loafing* won over rivals such as *How to Be a Pleasure Pirate* and *The Joy of Just About Everything*. It was the victor because people perked up when they read or heard it. It was intriguing. It sounded like fun. "Boy, do I need that!" was a typical comment. Folks found the contrast of "creative" and "loafing" provocative. They wanted to know more.

A Shoestring Guide to New Leisure Fun was chosen because "shoestring" connotes free or cheap activities. "Guide" sounds less stuffy than "handbook" or "manual." "New" is always a selling word, and it suggested that these were unusual forms of entertainment. "Leisure fun" summarized the theme of the book.

Always subtitle your nonfiction books. There are two very good reasons. *Books In Print* and other important listing sources enter both the title and the subtitle, so you get more mileage out of your listing. It's like getting a brief sales message free. It also gives you more opportunity to describe the book. If you were looking to get a book on mail order, which would you buy: *Eureka!* or *Eureka! How to Build a Fortune in Mail Order*?

Titling Fiction

In titling fiction let's see what approaches some trade-published books can show us. Sometimes an object or living thing told about within the book lends itself to appropriate symbolism, to stand for the whole book. *The Thorn Birds* (Colleen

McCullough) and *Valley of the Dolls* (Jacqueline Susann) are examples of this method. Sometimes a new twist snaps a title into place. Mary Stewart's *Touch Not the Cat*, with its poetic switching of normal word order, communicates a sense of mysterious danger. If she had titled it *Don't Touch the Cat*, it would have lost that charm and mystery and sounded more like a children's story, or maybe even humor, like Jean Kerr's *Please Don't Eat the Daisies*. We wonder if the original title for *Lady Chatterley's Lover* would have doomed the book? Would many of that book's audience been attracted to a book titled *Tenderness*? And *Hurrah for the Red, White and Blue* was Fitzgerald's original name for *The Great Gatsby*. Fiction titles need to be appropriate to the genre and to resonate with promise.

Double-Check Your Title

Now it's time to recheck the photocopied pages of *Subject Guide to Books In Print* and *Forthcoming Books In Print*. Even though titles are not copyrightable, it is not to your advantage to publish a book that carries a name identical to that of another work. Why should you do a fantastic job promoting your book, then run the risk of customers getting the names confused and ordering the other one instead?

Another great source for title help is Amazon.com. Since it lists virtually every book in print, and some that aren't, reviewing this site can be a quick and easy way to do title and subtitle research. So can researching www.loc.gov, the Library of Congress site. Click on Search the Catalog, then Search LC Online Catalog Alternative, then Simple Search, and then enter the title or author's name and Submit Query.

Now that we've examined the ingredients that go into choosing a marketable subject and talked about ways to pinpoint an intriguing title, let's proceed to the actual development of your book.

Web Sites, Wisdom, and Whimsey

Scout for sales figures for competitive books. Typically, these are well-guarded numbers. There are a few sources, however, that can help inventive detectives pinpoint strong sellers. One is the issue of *Publishers Weekly* that lists books that sold more than 100,000 copies the previous year. It comes out in March and is chock-full of useful statistics for steadfast sleuths. Another resource is Amazon.com and its ranking of books. Some publishers' catalogs also state the sales figures on their strong backlist titles. Such reconnaissance can lead to profitable publishing decisions or save you from making a costly mistake.

* * *

Lack of money is no obstacle. Lack of an idea is an obstacle.

* * *

Should you get religion? Religion online, that is. *Religion BookLine* is a free e-mail newsletter from *Publishers Weekly*. Now you can receive the most up-to-date religious news, analysis, book reviews (give you any ideas?!), announcements, and mini-features. Says Daisy Maryles, coeditor of *RBL*, "This is really a very exciting opportunity. Anyone interested in books on spirituality and religion will benefit." Coeditor Lynn Garrett adds, "Not only will industry insiders find *RBL* useful and informative—so will everyone who is interested in these kinds of books, and today that's a lot of people." If you work in this area and need to keep abreast of insider offerings and opportunities, register today for your twice monthly personal subscription to *Religion BookLine* by visiting http://lists.cahners1.com/pwreligion.

Definition of an expert: a person who knows more and more about less and less.

* * *

Try this unique way to compile information. One clever gentleman registered as an "expert" (not the kind above) on various Web sites. He positioned himself as an authority on intellectual property and has answered about one hundred questions so far in that field. This put him in a strategic position to know what kinds of concerns the public has and gave him invaluable grist for his writing mill. He can simply compile the hundred or so questions and answers into some logical order, and presto he has a book.

* * *

It has been said that an autobiography is an obituary in serial form with the last installment missing.

* * *

Unique research site comes to writers' rescue. Gail and Pete Robertson have launched a most unusual free service called the Writers' Information Registry. While this site (www.pacificcoast.net/~gprobert/index.html) will be a godsend for novelists, nonfiction authors may also find its vast compendium of offbeat information useful. The registry is a vehicle for sharing your knowledge and expertise—and tapping into information from others around the globe. It's divided into four main sections. "Places" gives you contact individuals for far-flung locations you may not be able to personally visit yet need to mention for local flavor. There are folks willing to help all over the world: London, Montreal, Johannesburg, Munich, Copenhagen, Hong Kong, even Australia's Gold Coast . . . not to mention many U.S. cities. Under "Experiences" you can find out about chronic fatigue syndrome, being a kidnap victim, a near-drowning, a dog that serves the disabled, blindness, adopting older children, precognition, embezzling, diabetes, being wheelchair bound, and tons more. (Great possibilities here for interviews for nonfiction books.) And if you want your main character to be an avalanche rescuer, practice aikido, play the bagpipes, lay on hands, fly fish, breed and show horses, courier secret documents, work on a crab boat, or study Mayan archaeology, there are contacts for these and many other pursuits awaiting you in the "Activities" section. The newest category the Robertsons have added is a " 'Novel'ties Wish List." If you need information on a specific topic or concept, you can place a request. Have fun!

5 *Product Development: Writing Your Book or Booklet*

In this chapter, we'll investigate sources and tips for doing research for your book. We will also explain permission guidelines for using copyrighted materials. You'll learn the easy way to organize a book; how front and back matter can be powerful persuaders; and ways to "plant" editorial material for later sales clout. If you're looking for a quick, affordable profit center, be sure to read the section on doing booklets. And we'll advise you how to write tight, snappy text and offer techniques for editing your own book.

Treasures on the Web

Are you aware that millions of dollars' worth of free information awaits you? Much of what you need can be accessed on the Internet. If you're completely unfamiliar with computer research, get help from a librarian or friend or take a class. The speed of computer technology can trim months from your research schedule. This is an incredible way to leverage your knowledge and get plugged into a whole new universe of data: statistics, anecdotes, expert opinions, and much more. Once you've mastered the easy techniques, you can research globally right from home.

If you don't know a site's URL and are seeking it, or specialized information, the best search engine as we write this is considered to be www.google.com. Billed as the world's largest, it can get you access to over 1.3 billion Web pages. Just type in a few keywords, and you're on your way. Another strong resource is www.northernlight.com. Here you can ask questions as oblique as, Who won the 1979 Best Actress Oscar? and get answers. Have fun! While www.yahoo.com was previously considered the dominant Web directory, this once excellent search tool has fallen from our favor.

Another option for research is using what are called metasearch sites. For instance, at www.search.com you can gain entrance to eight hundred different search engines in tandem! Two other excellent metasearch resources are www.profusion.com and www.metacrawler.com.

Yet another fascinating option for gathering pertinent data for your book is to have relevant news stories delivered free on your e-mail each day! To get the latest on issues you're interested in, go to www.individual.com, where you can sign up to order e-mail delivery of news stories on over one thousand key topics. Each morning you'll find a custom-built list covering the topics you requested.

And in Your Library

You can locate the names and addresses of prospective buyers all over the country, command the free services of researchers to help you negotiate this maze of data, even pick up your phone and get immediate answers. This reservoir of information and services is located at your main branch public library. It's to your advantage to make optimum use of library facilities and personnel.

Chances are you're well acquainted with the main branch of your library, where the most current and extensive collection of reference material resides. If not, become friends. Find out about special departments and the names of the librarians in the sections you will most likely frequent. Get a library card so you can borrow material. When you're researching, always go armed with a roll of dimes for the copy machine.

Marilyn's favorite resource is the *Burrelle's Media Directory* set. Within its six volumes you'll find magazines and newsletters, daily newspapers, nondaily papers, TV and cable, plus radio. What more could you want?

Certain other periodical (magazine) indexes will be extremely beneficial. These can help you find out what has already been written on a subject, locate experts you may want to interview or have comment on your book, find articles that will give you more insight into a given subject, or help you get a feel for which magazines are prime candidates to review or sell your book. Unfortunately, not all periodicals are represented in one handy index. In fact, the amateur researcher can feel as frustrated as a robin hunting for worms in Astroturf. But there is help. *Ulrich's International Periodicals Directory* tells in which indexes any given periodical is logged. Another valuable resource is *The Standard Periodical Directory*.

The granddaddy of indexes is *Readers' Guide to Periodical Literature* with its references to magazines of greatest general interest. This is an invaluable source when you're researching a particular topic. There is a long string of specialized indexes, such as *Business Periodicals Index*, the *Applied Science and Technology Index*, and *Index Medicus*. To find out which one applies to your needs, check *Ulrich's* and talk with your librarian.

And don't overlook newspaper indexes for timely help. *The New York Times Index* comes out at two-week intervals and is consolidated annually. *The Wall Street Journal Index* catalogs corporate news in the first section and general news in the second. Frequently a date, location, or spelling of a name can be found in the index without ever seeing the complete news story. (Of course the Web is ideal for searching current news as well as archived articles.)

An additional suggestion is the *Encyclopedia of Associations*. Virtually every interest has a society, association, or group dedicated to it. Here is the place to track down technical "insider's" information, locate experts, find out what publications they publish, or perhaps rent mailing lists of their members. (In a later chapter, "Initiating a Nationwide Marketing Plan With Publicity Pizzazz," we'll show you how to build important association lists for publicizing and selling your book.) And don't overlook *Directories in Print*. It contains over ten thousand entries of business and industrial directories, professional and scientific rosters, and other lists. An easy subject index covers some three thousand topics.

The public library is not the only keeper of knowledge; university libraries are often more complete. In a school specializing in medicine, law, or business, the library is likely to be comprehensive in that area. And campus libraries' hours often include Sundays and more evenings than public libraries offer. The general public is typically allowed to use college and university library facilities. To check out material, however, you will probably need to become a "friend of the library." This friendship has a price; but the cost of a year's membership is usually modest, often $25 or less.

An exciting resource at universities is unpublished theses. You may find that a student has saved you weeks of research by writing a comprehensive thesis on the same or a similar topic. Find out what is available and what restrictions, if any, there are on its use.

There is yet another resource in addition to public and academic libraries. Across America numerous specialized collections exist. Some are part of large companies; others are maintained by associations. Still others are devoted to specific subjects, such as genealogy. Find out if there is a library dedicated to your topic, and contact the people in charge for assistance. The *Directory of Special Libraries and Information Centers* can point you in the right direction.

And even if you can't visit the collection in person, remember that you can lay your hands on almost any book in almost any library through the interlibrary loan system. Librarians have obtained books for us out of specialized libraries that would never loan parts of their collections to us as individuals. Just because a book isn't in your local library doesn't mean it is unobtainable.

Requesting Books From Publishers and the Government

Yet another avenue to obtain needed research materials is open to you. If approached professionally, many publishers will send you complimentary copies of their books relating to your subject. Remember that copy of the page you made from the *Subject Guide to Books In Print*? Drag it out again, and scan it for pertinent titles. Also look for reviews in newsletters and trade magazines devoted to your topic. We developed a form letter while researching this book, typed in the title we were requesting, added a couple of powerful enclosures to further establish our credibility, and made clear the subject of our work in progress.

Thousands of dollars' worth of books and reference texts were sent to us free because the publishers hoped we'd find them useful and that we'd mention them in our text or bibliography and give them some free advertising among readers specifically interested in the field. That kind of recommendation is worth money to any publisher, so the books weren't just sent for nothing: To the publishers, they were an investment in hopes of future sales. Since these books really did prove invaluable in providing information for this guide, we recommend many of them throughout the book and list them in the bibliography—just as the publishers had hoped.

You can also find a wealth of help in various government documents. As the country's largest publisher, the U.S. Government Printing Office issues a phenomenal amount of information. To find out what is available, go to www.access.gpo.gov or write the Superintendent of Documents, U.S. Government Printing Office, Washington, DC 20402. If your local library doesn't have the publication you need, it can probably be borrowed from one of the Federal Depository Libraries in your state. Ask the librarian.

The Telephone as a Research Tool

Additionally, you can secure information by simply letting your fingers do the walking. That's right. Call and ask for it. Suppose you're writing a mystery and need to know the specifics of a certain gun. Or perhaps you need the address of a wholesaler in a distant town? A helpful librarian can probably locate it in out-of-town telephone books. Want to know when and where the next meeting of BookExpo America is? The librarian can tell you. Whenever possible, use the phone to save time and money when doing research.

The telephone can serve you well for interviews and surveys also. After introducing yourself, it's a good idea to say, "I'd like to include your thoughts in my study of . . . ," and move right into the first question. Studies show this technique is better than requesting permission to ask questions; then you're more likely to be refused.

* * *

Whatever vehicle you use to obtain the information you need, be sure you are thorough and accurate. Rex Alan Smith observed that "faulty research is like a faulty septic tank. Sooner or later the evidence will surface and become embarrassing."

Permission Guidelines for Using Copyrighted Material

Now let's turn our attention to rights and permissions. Your research will no doubt turn up passages or comments from other published works that you would like to use. What are the rules?

First, let us discuss "fair use." Using material without the need to obtain permission is called fair use. *The Chicago Manual of Style* says that "quotations should not be so long that they diminish the value of the work from which they are taken." In the case of books, experts usually estimate you can use an aggregate of up to 300 words freely as long as it includes attribution. If you quote just a paragraph from a book and mention the author and title, you don't need to obtain permission. For magazine articles, 50 words is the maximum (that's assuming it isn't a 500-word filler). Brad Bunnin and Peter Beren, in their excellent *Author Law and Strategies*, say that straight news articles from newspapers (not features) of any length can be safely used after three months. This does not include any article that is syndicated, under a byline, or individually copyrighted. Photographs, artwork, and cartoons will also require the permission of the copyright holder.

Jack Heffron, editorial director at Writer's Digest Books, says, "BMI and ASCAP, the national organizations that handle permissions for written reprints on song lyrics, will need to be contacted directly. If possible quote only a line or two in your work, which will put your quote within fair use, and you won't need written permission." SESAC is another one, primarily for Canada. The cost to reprint songs is usually higher than for poems, but don't overlook negotiating.

One way to circumvent copyright problems is to paraphrase what was said. Ideas are not copyrightable—only the specific words used to express them. With all the mergers over the last decade, it's sometimes impossible to track down a copyright owner. If possible, we urge clients to avoid this hassle. The best rule is to use good common sense. Don't take from another writer something you would resent being used if you were the author.

Request to Quote Material

When in doubt, formally request permission to quote. Write the publisher stipulating the following in your request:

- The title and type of your book (i.e., nonfiction, novel, poetry)
- The estimated date of publication
- The title and author of the work you wish to quote
- The quoted work's publication date
- The page(s) in the original work on which the desired material is located
- The total number of words or lines of poetry or song lyrics you wish to use
- A transcript or photocopy of the exact quotation (or the first and last few words if lengthy)
- A statement about the right to use it in "any and all editions"
- A request for exactly how the copyright holder wishes the acknowledgment to read

Send a letter in duplicate to a work's creator, asking that the authorized holder sign and return the original giving you a release and keep the duplicate for his or her files. Including a stamped, self-addressed envelope is a prudent touch. Then be prepared to wait. And follow up. And wait. And follow up. Obtaining copyright permissions often takes several months, so handle your requests early in the creation process. If you have a large volume of permissions in the works, it would be wise to set up a control log so you know the status of each one. Also, code the letters in some way. For instance, note in a separate log the manuscript page(s) on which each piece of permissionable material will appear and from whom the permission will come, with the date you sent your original request. Then you'll find it simpler to integrate the material into your manuscript and check off the item as received when each permission comes. And if too much time passes and one or another of the permissions still hasn't come in, you'll easily notice the fact and begin follow-up.

Often a fee will be involved. If so, you must decide if the quote is worth the asking price. Charges range from a token ten dollars or so to several hundred dollars. These fees are frequently negotiable, however, so don't feel compelled to pay what is stated without trying to arrange a smaller amount. The copyright holder may charge you less if he feels it is for a publication with small distribution. (This is one of the few times to be humble.)

When you receive permission, pay attention to how the acknowledgment is requested. When this material appears in the book, you must cite the permission exactly as stipulated.

Sometimes the permission tables will be turned. Chances are after your book is out, publications, organizations, or individuals may want to reprint from it.

Request for Permission to Reprint Material

COMMUNICATION CREATIVITY
a colorado corporation

P.O. Box 909 • 425 Cedar Street • Buena Vista, CO 81211-0909
http://www.SPANnet.org/CC/ • e-mail: CC@spannet.org
(719) 395-8659 • Fax (719) 395-8374

RE: PERMISSION TO REPRINT MATERIAL

Dear ____________________:

My husband and I are writing a book tentatively titled THE COMPLETE GUIDE TO SELF-PUBLISHING, which Writer's Digest Books plans to publish in the spring of 1985. The book will retail for about $19.95.

We would like to request your permission to include the excerpt(s) as outlined below in any and all editions of our book. (And in any derivative or subsidiary works, including paperback and book club, and special editions for the handicapped, such as Braille, large type, and tapes, in all languages, and in the advertisement and promotion therefore nonexclusively throughout the world.)

We are looking forward to receiving your permission and giving your material greater exposure. Please indicate the acknowledgment you wish printed in the book.

For your convenience we've enclosed a duplicate copy of this letter and a stamped, self-addressed envelope. We thank you in advance for your cooperation and prompt response.

Sincerely,

Marilyn Ross

MATERIAL TO BE REPRINTED:

TITLE: ____________________

AUTHOR: ____________________

COPYRIGHT DATE & HOLDER: ____________________

PAGE ______, LINE ______ TO PAGE ______, LINE ______ .

I heareby designate that I am authorized to grant permission:

____________________ Date: ________

Acknowledgment to read: ____________________

It is important to get permission before using material belonging to others. Modify this sample letter to suit your needs.

This is good publicity. We generally say yes with two stipulations: (1) We limit the amount they can use (perhaps no more than three pages from an entire book), and (2) we require that they state where the material originated, such as *From Rags to Riches* copyright 2001 by Ima N. Fat City. Also insist a Web site and ordering phone number be included.

Of course, some things are not protected by copyright. They are considered to be in the public domain. Material goes into public domain if its original copyright was not renewed or if copyright protection has been exhausted.

Government publications are also typically in the public domain, but this can be a gray area. If you plan to use extensive sections verbatim, it is wise to have a copyright search performed. When you are using just portions, no permission is needed, but it's a good idea to cite the specific source. Also be aware that government publications often contain illustrations and other materials that are covered by individual copyrights. Read the fine print carefully.

The Easy Way to Organize a Nonfiction Book

When confronted with the task of organizing all your research, perhaps you feel a bit like the mosquito that wandered into the nudist colony. She knew exactly *what* to do, but *where* should she begin? Marilyn usually begins on the floor with Post-it Notes labeled with possible subject areas. The best approach is to sort through your ideas or research material like a deck of cards, dealing them out to the various subject areas fanned out around you alphabetically. Once they are in what appears to be the appropriate stack, look for the common denominators. When these patterns begin to emerge, you can often see the best way to order them. As you begin to group thoughts and materials, the book's skeleton takes shape.

Now use file folders to represent chapters, placing appropriate data in each folder. This way, you start to flesh out the book's skeleton. Review what you have gathered to see where you're rich with material—and what areas are thin and need further research, or perhaps reshuffling and combining of chapters.

Of course, this method won't work for everyone. Some people like to group their material into notebooks with section dividers. Still others prefer computer files. Just remember you must scan in all those articles, quotes, anecdotes, and so on. The upside of this is that they are already keyboarded when it comes to the actual writing.

We were once asked how long a chapter should be. Tom's answer? Long enough to reach from beginning to end. Seriously, there is no way to say ten pages or twenty pages. Organize the material carefully and make logical breaks. Some topics will naturally be more meaty than others. Of course, if you end up with one chapter out of all proportion in length to the rest, see if there isn't a natural break where it could be divided. Or combine meager information with another chapter. Once you've grouped material this way, refine it further into a working table of contents (the "outline" from your college days). Group like topics together, and consider a part one, part two, part three structure. Notice how this is done in our table of contents.

Getting Started

At this juncture we'd suggest you develop a mission statement just like businesses do. This is some twenty to forty words that capture the essence of your message. Who is this for? How will it assist them? What is its main thrust? Creating this now—and referring to it frequently during the writing process—will help you stay focused.

Determine who your audience is. Otherwise you'll be like a blindfolded fool with a dart. You can shoot, but the chances of hitting the target, not to mention the bull's eye, are slim to none. How old are your typical readers? Which gender? Where do they rank educationally and financially? What special interests, or problems, do they have? Get a firm picture of your readers, and write your book to them.

Next, write the introduction. This sets the stage for the whole book. A good introduction tells the scope of the work and details in what ways people will benefit from reading it. It further helps you think through the project and keeps you on target. You'll want to rework it after the book is written. Then work on the chapter you're most jazzed about. It doesn't matter if it's chapter three or chapter nine. Nonfiction books don't necessarily need to be written in chronological order; chapters are typically stand-alone units. By starting on the one that excites you the most, you get into the swing of writing. If you think of the chapters as a series of steps, each piece contributing to the whole, you'll have a finished book before you know it.

Now think about what you can provide to embellish or clarify your message. Should you include sidebars of relevant information? Checklists? Samples? Dos and don'ts? Also strive to have examples that are demographically correct. Include singles/couples, personal/professional, old/young, male/female. Don't favor or ignore any one group.

Some people already have the guts of a book and don't realize it. Have you written several articles on a similar subject? Do you do a regular column? Repackage that data and guess what? You have a book! Find the common denominators, write transitions, link the material, refresh obsolete facts or information, and you're in business.

We work with a lot of speakers who have a real advantage because they can simply use an audio- or videotape they already have produced for sale and transcribe it into a double-spaced document. (Or simply tape a speech and have it transcribed.) By reviewing and reworking this material, the shape of their books quickly emerges. To beef up their messages, they can simply hire research librarians for $15 to $20 an hour to find relevant articles and new statistics.

Perhaps you're a two-finger typist but feel sure you have a book inside you. What to do? Dictate it into your computer! If you can speak it, you can write it. There is speech-recognition software that allows you to talk into a microphone, even giving punctuation and formatting commands as you go. You can actually "train" your software to recognize your voice within a couple of hours. Since most of us can talk faster than we can type, this is an ideal method for developing a rough draft from your table of contents. The two main programs are NaturallySpeaking from Dragon Systems (www.dragonsys.com) and IBM's ViaVoice (www.ibm.com/viavoice).

Be sure you deliver value. People often comment how rich the information is in this book, how we seem to hold nothing back. And that's true. This is the *complete* guide to self-publishing. Our personal ethics mandate we make good on our promise to readers to "deliver the goods" rather than holding back particulars so we can repackage them into "Special Reports" and other documents for sale.

What length constitutes a book? It varies widely depending on whom you ask. The U.S. post office says you must have at least 8 pages to qualify. International postal standards dictate that 49 pages is the magic number, not counting the cover. Anything under that is deemed a pamphlet or periodical. The Library of Congress requires 50 to get an LCCN. We usually encourage at least 96 pages, depending on the subject matter. The bottom line is to give your reader genuine value.

Writing Tight, Snappy Copy

It has been said, "There are two things wrong with most writing. One is style; the other is content." The way a writer strings words together either grabs the reader by the scruff of the neck and shouts, "Read me," or hangs as limp and uninteresting as tattered sheets in a tenement window.

Let's examine the writing process and see how we can become better wordcrafters to improve our chances with readers . . . or editors. Here are some guidelines to help give your work momentum and sparkle. We've included a second list with some specific suggestions for novelists.

- **Communicate; don't try to impress.** There is a happy medium between reading so tough you need an IQ of 180 and material that is helpful only if you have difficulty falling asleep. The comfort zone of the average reader is about the eighth-grade level, so practice the old rule of KISS ("Keep it simple, sweetheart"). Studies show that eighth-grade readers can understand fairly easy sentences with an average of fourteen words. Remember, we said "average." You may have a two-word sentence and then a whopper. Just be sure it is basically a simple declarative sentence. If it becomes too long and unwieldy, break it in two. You can use such words as *and*, *but*, *additionally*, *yet*, *consequently*, *therefore*, or *accordingly* to divide sentences easily.

Use short words instead of long ones. For many writers who typically pride themselves on a strong, versatile vocabulary, this is difficult. Stickler three-, four-, and five-syllable words should be avoided. *Recondite* slows down most anyone; yet *family* and *company*—also three-syllable words—are totally acceptable. It comes down to using good judgment.

The late Robert Gunning, an American writer and editor, concocted a readability formula called a Fog Index to determine how difficult a given piece of writing was to read. The longer the sentences and the bigger the words, the higher the Fog Index. If you want to avoid "foggy writing" in which a reader may get lost between the punctuation marks, use common sense and keep your writing simple and direct.

- **Use the right word for the job.** Word choice is vitally important. Mark Twain observed, "The difference between the right word and the almost right word is the difference between lightning and the lightning bug." Are your words colorful? Specific? Descriptive? Don't have a man walk. Rather, let him amble, stride, stagger, or shuffle along. Avoid beginning most of your sentences with *the*. Try not to develop *I* trouble; overuse of *I* quickly bores the reader. Rephrase the sentence to do away with this repeated reference. Watch for repetition of words within close proximity. Using the same word over and over again (unless it's for emphasis) is a sloppy way of writing.
- **Avoid ambiguity.** Rewrite anything that is unclear. The story is told that FBI Director J. Edgar Hoover decided he didn't like the margin format used for a letter he had dictated to his secretary. So he scribbled "watch the borders" on it and gave it back to her. She dutifully retyped the letter and sent it off to the top FBI agents. For the next two weeks, dozens of agents were placed on special alert along the Canadian and Mexican borders. Think through any confusing areas. What do they mean? Could they be misinterpreted? Take the word *terminal*, for instance. It means entirely different things to a computer operator, an electrician, a bus driver, and a physician.
- **Keep a wary eye on overall language.** Foreign words and unfamiliar jargon confuse the reader. Likewise, "in vogue" terms date your manuscript and may appear ridiculous five years hence.

• **Guard against clichés.** These are the overused, trite bits and pieces of speech that are part of everyone's conversations. "Money hungry," "sly as a fox," and "grows by leaps and bounds" are all clichés. When we write, it's important to pare away worn phrases; replace them with more original phraseology. Clichés are a sign of lazy writing. Think of a fresh, new way of saying it.

• **Delete redundancies and needless words.** Why say, He stood up to make the announcement? (Have you ever seen anyone stand *down*?) Early pioneers should be simply *pioneers*; in the not too distant future = *soon*; due to the fact that = *because*; until such time as = *until*; combined together = *combined*. Get the idea? Watch your writing for conciseness. Have you pared away all unnecessary words? Eliminated repetition? Abolish words such as *very*, *really*, *just*, and other qualifiers that don't serve a definite purpose. And trim unnecessary *that*s like you would prune an overgrown tree.

Brevity is beautiful. Train yourself to shed the padding that comes from years of cranking out student papers. We've heard it said that if you run your pen through every other word you have written, you have no idea what vigor it will give your style.

• **Inject your writing with liveliness.** Use similes or metaphors to show comparisons. A simile uses *like* or *as*: His personality is as bland as oatmeal. A metaphor suggests resemblance: Her face blossomed with affection. Such additions help readers relate to what you've written.

• **Put more zip in your manuscript with analogies.** They help make or illustrate a point. An example of an analogy would be, Life is a hundred-yard dash, with birth the starting gun and death the tape.

• **Relate anecdotes, another important facet of nonfiction writing.** They are stories or examples that illustrate and clarify the points you wish to make. We've sprinkled anecdotes throughout this book.

• **Use the active voice to achieve readability.** In the active voice, the subject of the sentence *performs* the action rather than receiving it. Here's an example:

The active voice: The wind slammed the door shut.

The passive voice: The door was slammed shut by the wind.

How much more powerful is the active version. Here's a hint for spotting the passive voice: Look at the verb phrase. It will always include a form of the "to be" verb, such as *is*, *are*, *was*, or *is being*.

• **For additional horsepower, be specific!** Look for ways to support general statements with details. Think of your writing as a funnel. At the top is the general statement, then it narrows down to a specific incident. This targets the reader's attention toward one given example. Rather than saying the woods are full of trees, say the woods are full of aspen, spruce, and pine.

• **Transition smoothly.** This is another hallmark of good writing. Are there graceful bridges between sentences, paragraphs, and chapters? Some words and phrases that serve as transitional bridges are *still*, *on the other hand*, *another*, *next*, *however*, *of course*, *then*, *finally*, *but*, *yet*, *unfortunately*, *in short*, *once again*.

• **Be sensitive to sexism in writing.** The least whiff of sex discrimination is an immediate turnoff for most people. We certainly don't advocate such contortions as *shim*, *he/she*, *herim*, or *hisers*—all of which have actually been used in print. But we do feel you should be careful not to exclusively use discriminatory pronouns, such as *he* or *his*, when referring to both genders. One easy way around this is to use the plural form of *they* or *their* (but not with a singular verb form!). Or to alternate *she* and *he*. When dealing with work titles, there are many options: *Policeman* is *police officer*; *mailman* becomes *mail carrier*; *salesman* becomes *salesperson*. *Mankind* can be expressed as *humankind*. What is important is to maintain the dignity of all people by avoiding stereotypes.

• **Avoid bad taste of any kind.** Racist statements, gory photographs, sexual overtones, and other undesirable materials are bound to offend some readers. Don't preach religion in a nonreligious book, and keep your politics to yourself unless that's your theme. The one exception to this could be fiction, where you might use a touch of the above to characterize someone in the story. Of course, obscene or pornographic material will be objectionable to the vast majority. In every case it's important to consider your chosen audience, their mores and values, and edit or develop your material accordingly.

Tips for Writing Best-Seller-Quality Fiction

Besides all of the above, novel writers have additional challenges. First, know what kind of fiction you want to write. Will it be commercial or literary? Once you've determined that, read the kind of books you want to write so you gain a familiarity of style and audience expectations. Then consider these points:

• **Plot.** Developing a strong plot is the first ingredient of a good novel. Be sure it's believable and appropriate to the genre. A helpful book for novelists is Lawrence Block's *Writing the Novel*, which gives a good overview of fiction methods.

• **Premise/Theme.** Is your message clear? Can you summarize it in one simple sentence? (If not, the reader will surely be confused.) Focus on a single well-defined theme.

• **Dialogue.** Conversation adds depth to your characters and moves the story forward swiftly. But is it realistic? Do people really talk that way? In real life we use contractions in conversation, talk in incomplete sentences, and use slang. To see if your dialogue plays well, read it aloud.

- **Pacing.** Does the material move smoothly, or does it get bogged down like a car stuck in mud? Remember to alternate points of high and low action so the reader isn't kept at a constant peak.
- **Mood/Tone.** Is the mood appropriate to your theme? Are you consistent throughout? Starting a murder mystery with a humorous anecdote, for instance, would be misleading.
- **Tense/Point of view.** Are they the same throughout? If your book is in the present tense, don't accidentally wander into the past. Likewise, if your story originates out of Cathleen's head, to suddenly tell how John feels is to switch viewpoints. While many popular contemporary novelists do this, it is a tricky technique to accomplish. If you insist on trying this, what you might consider is devoting whole chapters to different characters and alternating them, as was done in *The Other Side of Midnight*, by Sidney Sheldon.
- **Settings.** Be sure you are familiar with your setting or are prepared to do extensive research so it will ring authentic. Establish the setting early so your reader can grasp what is happening. A conversation taking place in jail has very different overtones from one taking place at a picnic grounds or in bed.
- **Description.** Good description elevates a book from the pack. Here are two tricks that may help you create more powerful description. If you're talking about a place or a thing, consider giving it human characteristics. As Dick Perry says in *One Way to Write Your Novel*, "The hotel room had lost its youth. Its floors creaked with middle age. It had not bathed in years." Conversely, if you are describing people, give them the characteristics normally reserved for houses, streets, or things. Perry gives these examples: "She was, to children, a haunted house they dare not visit" and "Everyone else was an expressway, racing somewhere, full of purpose; she was a street labeled dead end."
- **Characterization.** Good characterization has been called the ability to create characters readers care about—ones who seem real, with qualities we can sympathize and identify with. But how does one achieve such people on paper? A vehicle we've found useful is the character sketch. In this sketch you detail every conceivable thing about each character. Not only such obvious points as sex, age, and physical description but the less tangible aspects, as well: mannerisms, education, philosophies, family background, religious history, political leanings, passions, and pet peeves. These are the things memorable characters are made of. Once *you* know your characters well, it's much easier to make them come alive for the reader.
- **Senses.** Appeal to the senses to further excite your reader. Let the aroma of paint, tar, freshly brewed coffee, or jasmine bring reality to your story. Allow the reader to hear locusts chirping, a trumpeter practicing, the crunch of dried leaves. Offer a taste of the delicate flavor of veal Oscar or soggy french fries

cooked in stale grease. Sit in a chair that's coarse and scratchy, or luxurious and soft. By appealing to the senses, you give your story mood, texture, and color.

* * *

Whether you're writing a novel or nonfiction book, you'll want a good up-to-date dictionary, such as *Webster's New World Dictionary* (computer versions of dictionaries are great!); a thesaurus (print version or one on your computer); and a copy of *The Chicago Manual of Style*, put out by the University of Chicago Press, or one of the other accepted style guides. (Of course, no personal library would be complete without a copy of this book *and* our *Jump Start Your Book Sales: A Money-Making Guide for Authors, Independent Publishers and Small Presses*. For full details go to www.SPANnet.org/cc/js or call (800) 331-8355 to order a copy.)

Front and Back Matter: Powerful Sales Persuaders

If your book is nonfiction, the main body of text will be enclosed not just by its covers but by "front and back matter," which can have a dramatic impact on your book's review potential and sales record. The front matter we discuss here includes such things as the foreword, preface, and introduction. Back matter is exactly what it says: material in the back of the book. It can include an appendix, biliography, glossary, index, and an order form.

Foreword

A foreword (notice it's spelled "foreword" not "forward") by an important person in the field of your book's focus can boost your book's sales considerably. Often it comes from the same authority you will ask to look over the completed manuscript for input in general. With a little polishing and expanding, this feedback may well provide a perfect foreword (assuming, of course, the authority liked your work).

Don Dible's *Up Your Own Organization* is an excellent example of using a name person to help promote a book. He had such favorable response from experts who reviewed his early manuscript that he ended up with *three* of them writing glowing commendations for his book. What a dilemma! Here's how he handled it: The book carried a foreword by William P. Lear, chairman of the board of Lear Motors Corporation; an introduction by Robert Townsend, who brought Avis Rent a Car to fame; and a preface by John L. Komives, director of

Booklets: A Quick, Affordable, and Profitable Way Into Print

If the idea of writing a whole book makes you as nervous as a mermaid in an alligator pond, relax. Or, on the other hand, if you want a "teaser" product to convince people to purchase your more inclusive and expensive book, read on.

Many people have made beaucoup bucks publishing booklets. Paulette Ensign is considered the "Booklet Queen." Her *110 Ideas for Organizing Your Business Life* has sold more than half a million copies in three languages and in various product formats. She hasn't spent a dime on advertising. Ensign believes in doing "tips" booklets: 101 ideas for . . . , 97 ways to . . . , 10 steps for . . . You get the idea. For full details and to get coaching from her, visit www.tipsbooklets.com.

Others who have succeeded royally in the booklet arena include Joan Stewart and Jeff Gitomer. Eric Gelb published *Budgeting at Your Finger Tips*. In volume, they cost him $0.55 each and that includes a color cover. He sells them at his speaking engagements, through retail channels, and especially in bulk to corporations, associations, and various organizations. Quantity sales is where the money is here. Many companies find booklets ideal goodwill giveaways for customers or use them internally with employees.

Booklets retail for $3, $4, or $5 each. Several savvy entrepreneurs give them away. Says Tom Antion, e-commerce expert, "Over the long run you'll build a stronger business model when you give away your basic material for free, hook your customers, and entice them to make more expensive purchases."

Finished booklets typically run 16 or 24 pages. They are either 5½″ × 8½″ or designed as 3½″ × 8½″ to fit in a #10 business envelope. This handy size streamlines order fulfillment and keeps postage costs reasonable.

Booklets also make ideal PR tools. Many magazines and newspapers will gladly give you space when you offer their readers free copies (request a stamped, self-addressed envelope, however, to cut down on your time and expenses). You can use this approach to build a mailing list as well as sell your more expensive product.

the Center for Venture Management. Being a good businessman, Dible splashed the names of these three gentlemen across the cover, as they had much greater recognition than he did.

Preface

Typically, you will write your own preface. It outlines your reasons for doing this book and helps establish your credibility. Reviewers frequently draw their material from the preface, so be sure you give them good ammunition. Let your warmth and personality come through. Reviewers and readers alike respond more favorably to a book if they like its author. You may also want to thank people in the acknowledgments and have a dedication.

Introduction

The introduction is where you lay the groundwork for the book and give any specific directions (such as "read the whole thing before attempting to implement any part of it"). It often falls in with the other front matter. We feel this is a mistake. Readers are likely to ignore it there and start reading with chapter one. List your introduction first in the table of contents, where people are sure to see it. Place it immediately before the first chapter. Maybe even call it something other than an "Introduction," such as "Should You Take Control of Your Own Destiny?" Sound familiar?

Appendix

An appendix is used for lists of sources of additional information or for quick-reference summaries. The inclusion of appendixes adds greatly to a book's overall usefulness. It can also have a more practical purpose. If your book is too skinny, adding a detailed appendix is an easy extender. One book we know of was stretched from 150 pages to more than 240 by adding a tremendous directory of additional reference material on the subject covered. This was turned to an advantage by promoting the fact that the book included a free directory of business information. Moreover, if your work has an extensive appendix, it may be accepted for listing in *Directories in Print*, as this guide has been.

Bibliography

Bibliographies or recommended reading sections are helpful additions for readers who want more information on your subject. You may want to list not only those publications from which you drew material but also other relevant works.

Glossary

Some nonfiction books can benefit from a glossary. When a reader comes across an unfamiliar term, it is comforting to be able to turn to the glossary for a quick explanation. Glossaries are also used later in the book's life, when a ready source for a technical definition is needed. We've had reviewers recommend publishing neophytes buy this book just for the glossary of terms.

Index

Indexes are to nonfiction books what butter is to bread. You can use the one without the other, but it's so much better with the added ingredient. And librarians are much more likely to purchase your book if it is indexed. They know that patrons prefer such books and that they are more useful to the library itself. If you hope to sell to educational markets, an index is almost mandatory. It's particularly helpful when you first use a book, as it allows you to quickly find answers to specific questions. Later, after you've retired the volume to your personal library, the need for an index emerges again when a reference on a specific point is wanted. That's one of the reasons we've tried to make the one in this book so complete.

Order Form

We believe every book should end with an order form. As a model, notice the one at the conclusion of this guide. We've received checks for as much as $300 from people who read one of our books, loved it, and bought multiple copies for their friends and loved ones. This makes it easy for people to do what you want them to do.

Planting Editorial Material for More Sales Clout

Before we leave the writing stage, let's talk a little about how you can introduce material into your book that will later serve as a sales or promotional hook.

Millions of books are sold each year on the basis of commercial tie-ins. For instance, if you have a book on gardening and mention the W. Atlee Burpee & Co. in a favorable way, you may be able to sell a special edition of the book to that company. (We'll be exploring this aspect of special sales in depth later.) Within reason, mention brand names or service companies. A bulk purchase will more likely be considered if you're specific.

Here's another way to get more mileage: Let's say you have a book on missing children. If you have only a couple of paragraphs on how teachers might prevent this problem, you'll be too limited to use it for promotional leverage. But if you expand your coverage to a full chapter, you'll have a whole new market base: the educational community.

Giving editorial space to specific geographic areas or points of interest can also provide valuable sales leads. In fiction, using interesting tidbits about a specific locale will give you a built-in marketing angle when it comes time to promote. Also consider name-dropping. People like to see their names in print. One book we know of included names, titles, and brief blurbs about the achievements and talents of some two thousand businesspeople. With a cover price of $24.95, can you imagine how fast the publisher's bank balance soared after all of these executives were approached about buying copies of a book that features them personally? This approach no doubt accounts for the success of various *Who's Who* directories.

So don't overlook the possibility of adding material at the writing stage that will help you downstream in the sales department. It could very well mean the difference between a publishing venture that loses money or one that prospers.

Editing Your Work

Your manuscript is finally written. You breathe a great sigh of relief. But hold on, you aren't finished yet. Never consider your book complete until you've spell-checked it on your computer. And if your computer has a grammar and style checking program, use it now to catch obvious flaws and flag overly long sentences, for example.

You also may have learned to type on a typewriter and thus put *two* spaces at the end of a sentence. In the computer age one space is preferable. Otherwise, it looks awkward when typeset. No problem, though. Simply do a search and replace, and change the two spaces to one.

Even the best writers can benefit from good editors working behind them. Editing is a special skill the average author doesn't perform well. And since, in spite of their expertise, editors are notoriously poorly paid, the expense of getting professional help for your work won't normally be too large. By the way, please, please don't submit an e-book without editing. Most sites will simply take what you give them and put it up. If our industry is to prosper, every author must take personal responsibility for presenting a quality product.

A poorly edited book is harder to read, harder to believe, and less likely to be reviewed. It is shameful to see a good book cut to ribbons by a reviewer because of poor grammar or spelling. In a recent review, while the plot of a particular book was praised, the reviewer noted, "Unfortunately, the reader also has to detour around some disasters in editing and proofreading."

Because authors know their subjects so well, they are usually too close to their material; objectivity is lost. A professional editor can help detect passages that are unclear, poorly organized, or overwritten. This is called content or creative editing. During a second reading your editor will do copyediting, whisking out grammar, spelling, usage, and punctuation errors. The job of an editor is to hone and polish your manuscript to a fine edge, *not* to impose her style on it.

Where do you find such folks? There are several options. Look in *Literary Market Place* under "Editorial Services," contact the Editorial Freelancers Association at www.the-efa.org or (212) 929-5400, or use the ASJA (American Society of Journalists and Authors) Writer Referral Service at www.asja.org/prowrite.php or (212) 398-1934. If you wish to hire help with editing—as well as retain complete services for design, production, and marketing for your book—you can also contact us at www.About-Books.com or (719) 395-2459.

Short of hiring a pro, which is best, enlist the help of several literate friends or associates to go over your work. It's a good idea to give them some instructions. Ask that they underline any misspelled or questionable words, circle unclear passages, and note rough transitions with a question mark. Also encourage them to jot any suggestions in the margins. Encourage them to be specific. Specific, constructive criticism is like surgery; it cuts out the malignancy and spares the rest of the body. Vague criticism is like chemotherapy; it causes the copy's hair to fall out and makes the whole thing look sick. Even best-selling authors use others to refine their work. James Michener says, "I invite four outside experts—a subject-matter scholar, editor, style arbiter on words, and a final checker—to tear it apart. . . ."

The following checklist will help you evaluate your finished work and pinpoint any potentially weak area:

- **Title.** Is it catchy? Short? Appropriate?
- **Opening.** Does it arouse interest and hook the reader?
- **Organization.** Do you tell readers what you're going to tell them, then tell them, and then tell them what you told them? Is the book logically presented? Have you used headings and subheads to help communicate your nonfiction message?
- **Credibility.** Is your manuscript built on a foundation of accurate information? Are the facts the most current available? Names and places spelled correctly? Figures right? Web site URLs accurate? Can the reader sniff the unmistakable aroma of authenticity in the pages? Have you avoided issues that could be too quickly dated?
- **Sentences.** Are their lengths varied? Their structure and meter? Mix 'em up, shrink 'em, stretch 'em, make 'em gallop, let 'em be languid. Just please don't let them go on forever.
- **Paragraph breaks.** Your manuscript needs frequent paragraph breaks. This is more appealing to the eye than long, long blocks of text.
- **Conclusion.** Does the book just stop, or is the package tied together and truly finished?
- **Spelling.** Pleez spel krecktly! Use your computer spell checker, check questionable words in the dictionary, or call the library for clarification.
- **Punctuation.** Does it clarify what is written? Give impact? Do you add zest by using varied types of punctuation, such as semicolons, colons, dashes, ellipses, parentheses, and quotation marks? Or do you simply stub your toe on a comma over and over again?
- **Grammar.** Is it correct yet alive? Be sure you haven't used plural nouns with singular verbs, and vice versa. Use common sense when applying the rules, and don't be inhibited by old forms that have become obsolete. For instance, in spite of what your stern English teacher taught you, starting a sentence with *and*

or *but* is acceptable practice today. Even slang has its place. Carl Sandburg observed that "slang is language that rolls up its sleeves, spits on its hands, and goes to work."

• **Consistency.** In preparing your book to be typeset, it is important that you observe uniformity. If you spell out *California* in chapter one, abbreviate it as *Calif.* in chapter six, and use *CA* in chapter eleven, you have no consistency. To avoid this problem, why not try a trick used by many professional editors? They establish a style sheet. It typically covers such things as abbreviations, how numbers will be expressed, and other points relevant to each manuscript. When we edit a book, we create a style sheet like the sample below. When we come across something that could be expressed more than one way, we enter our choice for how to express it on the sheet. Then when we run across the same thing, or a similar example, later in the manuscript, we can see how it appeared before. For more information on copyediting in general, we recommend *Copyediting: A Practical Guide*, by Karen Judd.

Style Sheet for Editing

ABCD	EFGH
IJKL	MNOP
QRST	UVWXYZ

Consistency is important in your manuscript. Decide on how you will handle the spelling of unusual words, and note other idiosyncracies in the appropriate alphabetical squares.

• **Presentation.** The physical appearance of your work is also important. You want a manuscript you can be proud to send out for advance comments or for editing. Dirty copy is likely to result in more errors and greater costs. And please don't get carried away trying to emphasize everything. Occasional italic is fine to stress a word or phrase. The overuse of *italic* and underlines and **bold** and CAPS—or worse, a combination of these—smacks of amateurism.

Each of us has an innate style of expression. The more we practice the writing craft, the more distinct that style becomes. Your style may develop to the point that people reading unbylined work will recognize it as yours because of your unique way of expressing yourself. Style wears many faces. It can be as simple as Ernest Hemingway or as complicated as William Faulkner; as lighthearted as Dave Barry or as profound as Jerzy Kosinski. The more you write, the more compelling your style will become. By practicing and using the guidelines in this section, you can turn a manuscript that is like a mild processed cheese into copy with the bite of sharp cheddar.

And to be sure that cheddar stays fresh and appealing, it's time to explore the intricacies of establishing your own publishing company—and generating that all-important working capital.

Web Sites, Wisdom, and Whimsey

A treasure trove for word mavens awaits you. At www.yourDictionary.com there are links to more than eight hundred dictionaries and thesauruses. Additionally, these references cover over 160 languages, ranging from Afrikaans to Yiddish. There's even a feature that lets you search 454 general and specialized English dictionaries simultaneously! At this site, you can find acronym dictionaries, synonym finders, thesauri, phrase dictionaries, quotation locators, lexicography and lexical databases, pronunciation and rhyming dictionaries, etymology, even some outright linguistic fun. While you can do deep research here, it's also easy to look up a word quickly. Simply enter it on the main page, and Merriam-Webster OnLine will come to your rescue with the quintessential virtual dictionary.

* * *

Getting the first draft finished is like pushing a peanut with your nose across a very dirty floor. —Joyce Carol Oates

* * *

There is a plethora of information for you at The Library of Congress. Visiting http://lcweb.loc.gov is almost like being there yourself. The many sections cover Collections and Services (catalogs, collections, and research services), American Memory (America's story in words, sounds, and pictures), Thomas (Congress at work), Exhibitions (an online gallery), The Library Today (news, events, and more), Copyright Office (forms and information). The library preserves a collection of more than 119 million items. The online catalog may be searched by name, title, subject, and call number. You can use keywords, commands, or a search form, and there are several advanced techniques to refine your searches.

* * *

William Safire was asked if sloppy communication was caused by ignorance or apathy. "I don't know and I don't care," he quipped.

* * *

Find expert answers to your every question. At www.AskMe.com, you can get great free answers to your questions—from real people. This site can be a godsend for an author researching obscure facts for a book or seeking an illusive statistic to include. A whopping 2.5 million people use AskMe.com each month. They inquire about everything from customs and traditions to weddings, health and wellness, labor unions, and scores of subjects in between. Whatever your interest or query, chances are this site can help.

* * *

"He writes so well he makes me feel like putting my quill back in my goose," said Fred Allen.

* * *

Metasearches yield greater results than normal search engines. A fascinating recent survey by an NEC Research Institute found that search engines can't keep pace with the Web's growth. Scientists concluded that the size of the World Wide Web has grown to 2.8 million public sites and over 800 million pages! That's up from 320 million pages estimated just a year ago. This mushrooming growth curve is outpacing the ability of search engines to index their content. Examining eleven search engines, the study found that no single engine indexed more than 16 percent of the Web. Yahoo got only 7.4 percent, Excite 5.6 percent, Lycos a mere 2.5 percent, for instance. Additionally, indexing of new or modified pages by just one major search engine can now take months. Still, 85 percent of surfers continue to use search engines to find information. To help fill the gap the next time you're seeking information, use one of the more comprehensive metasearch sites, the NEC experts advocate. Go to www.local.find.com or www.metacrawler.com.

* * *

Every novel should have a beginning, a muddle, and an end. —Peter De Vries

* * *

Use shortcuts with your word processing program. We've found a couple of innovative ways to use the thesaurus to save time. For instance, if you're unsure of which is correct, "effect" or "affect," don't take time to look it up in the dictionary. Simply type in one of the words, click on thesaurus, and see if the suggested alternative words fit your meaning. Unsure how to spell a word? Enter an easy synonym in your thesaurus, and chances are you'll immediately discover your sought-after word in the list of possibilities. And when you're writing a manuscript—or promotional materials—and need to find different words instead of overusing the same term, once again your program's thesaurus comes to the rescue. Can't locate just the right substitute? Try clicking on the most likely word, then bringing up synonyms for it.

* * *

When should you register the copyright for your book? First, let's clarify something. There are two aspects of copyright: the *notice* you put on a manuscript and the actual *registration* of the copyright. (Actually, your work is automatically copyright *protected* under Common Law the minute you create it; it just isn't copyright registered yet.) When you initially write a manuscript, put the following items in the notice: © (or the word *Copyright*), the current year, and the name of the copyright holder until the book comes off the press. Here's why: We're seeing a lot of manuscripts lately where the authors registered them with the copyright office in 2000, 1999, or even earlier. When the books are printed, they must technically carry those dates. Consequently, the books look old and can sometimes lose out on important reviews because of the antiquated copyright dates.

* * *

My spelling is Wobbly. It's good spelling but it Wobbles, and letters get in the wrong places. —A.A. Milne

* * *

Free directory of indexers is available. The American Society of Indexers (ASI) has published the *Indexer Locator*, a directory of two hundred ASI members who work freelance. The directory includes contact and background information for each person or company, as well as listings by subject specialty, type of material handled, and geographical location. Also included is "An Indexing Guide for Editors." To request your free copy, call ASI at (303) 463-2887, fax (303) 422-8894, e-mail info@asindexing.org, or go online to www.asindexing.org.

* * *

Why is abbreviation such a long word?

6 Establishing Your Publishing Company and Generating Capital

When you embark on a self-publishing journey, you also become a businessperson. This doesn't mean you must go out and rent office space or scale a mountain of red tape. But there are some questions to be answered and things you'll have to do to satisfy the local regulatory agencies. This chapter discusses business location (operating out of your own home and elsewhere), naming your company, how to form a legal business entity, licenses and permits, and your company image. Of special interest will be the section on ways to generate working capital.

The Ideal Business Location

Where are you going to operate? In the beginning, working out of your home usually makes the most sense. It helps keep down overhead. Ideally, you will have a bedroom or den that can be used as an office. If not, a corner of the garage or basement or even the kitchen table will suffice. Before starting, check with your local business licensing agencies to see if it is legal to operate from your home. Your local chamber of commerce can tell you whom to contact for this and other requirements for setting up a new business.

Get a post office box so your publishing company will have an address different from that of your home. You'll look more professional if you don't seem to be operating out of your basement or garage, even if that's really the case.

Of course, as your business grows and prospers, the office in home may become impractical. Most locales forbid employees or heavy pickup and delivery activities at businesses operated in residential areas. Consequently, if you are planning on starting out with one or more employees, it may be wise to rent commercial office space. Perhaps you can share an office at first to minimize expenses. Check the classified ads under "Office Space for Rent" to see what's available.

Naming Your Publishing Company

Notice that we refer to your venture as your "publishing company." The second point to consider is the right name for your new enterprise. It's prudent to tack the words *press*, *publishing company*, *books*, or *publishers* on the name to help eliminate any doubts about what you do.

Be wary of choosing a name that is too specific. While a company called Wildlife Publications would be fine for your first book on wildflowers of the Northwest, what happens when your second title, *How to Be a Good Stepparent*, is ready to be published? Likewise, geographic names can be limiting. Don't you agree that Tampa Bay Books sounds much less substantial than Windsong Books International? Your choice can also influence how easy it is to sell your company downstream and how receptive vendors are in letting you establish credit. Looking big has definite advantages.

If you want to spark your thinking about press names, try leafing through *Writer's Market*, *Novel & Short Story Writer's Market*, *Literary Market Place (LMP)*, and *Small Press Record of Books in Print* directory. So many names of existing small presses, conventional or unusual, are listed in these sources that one or another is likely to help you come up with a name that will be all your own.

Be sure you do *not* include any part of your own name in the company title. Why? Because you want to come across as an official publishing entity, not as a writer who publishes his own work. Including your personal handle would be a dead giveaway. John Martin publishing a book as Martin Press leaves little to the imagination. Neither does John Martin and Associates or John Martin Enterprises. It's also poor form to make the title of the book and the name of the publishing company identical. This shouts, "I'm a tiny, one-book publisher."

When you arrive at a name, always check in *LMP*, *Small Press Record of Books in Print*, and the publishers' section of *Books In Print* to avoid duplicating an existing publisher's name. (Duplication could cause numerous errors and missed sales.) Because so many new small presses have started over the last decade, it's tough to find an unused name. We advise clients to think about combining their children's names or considering a foreign word as a press name.

To use your new name legally, you'll probably need to file a fictitious name statement. In most locales this is done by paying a small fee and advertising on four consecutive weeks your intention to do business as (dba) XYZ Publishing Company. You'll receive instructions when you apply for your dba. (By the way, you can save money by looking for a little weekly neighborhood paper instead of inserting your notice in the major daily newspaper.)

Forming Your Business Entity

The third consideration is what type of business structure to use.

Sole Proprietorship

It is best to start as a sole proprietor, meaning you alone control the business. It is also the simplest to set up and operate. Profits or losses are considered part of your personal income. Funds can easily be transferred between personal and business accounts. The sole proprietorship allows flexibility for freewheeling operations. Over two-thirds of the businesses in America operate in this fashion.

Partnership

Occasionally writers team up as partners, or a self-publisher gets a financial backer and forms a partnership. Partnership agreements are usually somewhat complicated, and we recommend you have a written agreement that an attorney creates or reviews. This will assure that the agreement accomplishes your intent and protects all parties. Also be aware that in a partnership each person is completely responsible for the debts and obligations of the whole partnership, not just half of them. Additionally, your partner can make promises and incur debts about which you have no knowledge but for which you do have financial responsibility—a tricky business unless you know and trust the other person totally. A better solution could be to incorporate.

Corporation

As your business grows, it might be in your best interest to incorporate. In the beginning, however, the drawbacks will usually outweigh the advantages.

Drawbacks include more regulations from state and federal authorities. You will not be able to operate in the same freewheeling way that a sole proprietor often does. Social Security tax for yourself will be somewhat more, too. Unemployment taxes must be paid to the federal and state government covering yourself as an employee. Accounting procedures become more complicated, and personal and corporate funds cannot be intermixed. Your salary is watched closely by tax offices.

Advantages become significant after your business is established. You can set up and be included in employee benefits—such as insurance, tax-sheltered pension plans, profit sharing, and bonus plans. These are not available to the unincorporated owner-operator. Your personal assets cannot be attached by creditors.

If you decide to publish other authors, the corporate shield protects you against liability suits. The corporation can fully deduct medical insurance and charitable contributions, reducing the amount you personally spend. But you yourself are still allowed the standard deduction. You can also sell shares to help fund your publishing venture. Corporate shares are more attractive to investors than interest in unincorporated businesses. We'll be talking more about this shortly in the the section on generating working capital.

Authors could also consider an S Corporation. This provides the legal protection of a corporation but permits the profits or losses to flow directly through to the shareholders as though it were a partnership. A Limited Liability Company (LLC) has most of the advantages of the S Corporation and is more popular today.

A corporation has a permanency not available to sole proprietorships or partnerships. When a sole proprietor or partner dies, the business is legally dissolved and must be reorganized to continue. Should you decide to incorporate, remember that attorney fees are costly. Why not save several hundred dollars and do it yourself? A good guide is *Inc. Yourself*, by Judith H. McQuown.

A few publishers set up nonprofit corporations, a time-consuming and complicated process in some states that, among other advantages, can make it possible to get reduced postage rates and access to grant money. However, these are strictly regulated and closely watched by federal and state agencies, and you will require an attorney's assistance.

Legal Advice

If you need an attorney, check with your local Lawyer Referral Service, listed in the white pages of the telephone directory. This is a nationwide service that will refer you to an attorney who handles your type of legal question. You will typically receive a thirty-minute consultation for about $40. (Sometimes the session is even free.) If your consultation exceeds thirty minutes, the additional fee is usually negotiated. Before wasting your time or that of the attorney, be sure she specializes in literary work or can handle your general business questions.

Another time you may want legal advice is when you're negotiating with a trade publisher to sell reprint rights. There are many aspects of a book publishing contract that are flexible—if you're savvy enough to know how to effectively mediate certain clauses. An attorney or consultant who is conversant with publishing contracts and intellectual property rights will be less expensive than paying an agent 15 percent commission forever to evaluate/negotiate your contract.

Licenses and Permits

The fourth point you want to investigate is what licenses and permits are necessary. In most parts of the country the laws require people who operate businesses to have business licenses. Check with your chamber of commerce about new business start-up regulations.

If your state has sales tax or a similar form of taxation, you'll also need a resale permit. Here's a bit of advice: When you go to get your seller's permit, be a most *humble* person. If you tell the agents you're going to sell thousands of dollars' worth of books, they'll tell you to leave a hefty deposit against future taxes and report your taxes quarterly. On the other hand, if you meekly comment that you're going to print a couple of hundred books and sell them to friends, you'll probably duck the deposit completely and only have to report annually.

While you're there, be sure to get a sales tax chart so you know exactly what percent of tax to charge on all retail sales made in your state.

Your Company Image

Now that you have located, named, established, and licensed your new baby, it's time to send out birth announcements. You will want to get company letterhead, envelopes, mailing labels, and probably business cards before you start your announcement campaign. It makes good sense to get an Internet domain name established, as well, so you can include it on all your materials. (See the chapter "Using the Web to Rally 'Buzz' and Business.") Spend some time and thought on your letterhead design. You may want a distinctive logo. A logo is the company's special identifying mark or symbol. Perhaps your company name lends itself to a graphic. For instance, a flying bird, Pegasus, or even the Winged Victory would be a good logo for Winged Publications. Your local printer can steer you to a graphic artist who will be able to suggest an appropriate design for your letterhead, or go surfing on the Net for an artist. Remember that your stationery and business card make the first impression. Don't skimp here. Be sure they are uncluttered, professional looking, and printed on quality paper. Company image, like personal integrity, is of great value.

You will want to start building a good company credit rating immediately. To qualify for accounts with various suppliers, it may be necessary to use your personal credit history at first. But, in general, it's easier to establish business credit than personal credit. Of course, you should open a separate business checking account and pay commercial credit accounts promptly. In addition to building a solid company credit rating, prompt payment often allows you to take a percent discount.

We believe you'll profit by joining SPAN, the Small Publishers Association of North America. (Of course, we're prejudiced. We founded it.) But go see for yourself by visiting www.SPANnet.org. You can join by sending $95 to P.O. Box 1306, Buena Vista, CO 81211-1306. As a SPAN member, you team up with over thirteen hundred writers, self-publishers, and small presses who are committed "to advancing the image and profits of authors and independent publishers through education and marketing opportunities" (our mission). We publish a 24-page monthly newsletter that is the perfect ongoing complement to this book to keep you up to the minute on trends, news, and strategies. And there is an awesome annual three-day College and Trade Show where you'll learn more about marketing than you would ever imagine—and meet some of the nicest people on the face of this earth. The location of this trade show varies each year. Because our size gives us the clout to negotiate special prices, members also have access to freight discounts up to 60 percent, the cheapest price anywhere on *Publishers Weekly*, plus the ability to get credit card merchant status without paying any application fee . . . and the list goes on and on. There are currently twenty-three member benefits, including an online discussion group where you can become part of a publishing community and get your questions answered.

There are two other places you should contact now for information that will be helpful in establishing and managing your enterprise. The Small Business Administration offers a wealth of guidance; much of it is available for free. Call its toll-free number at (800) 827-5722 or go online to www.sba.gov.

The SBA has another arm, called SCORE, which could benefit you. It stands for Service Corps of Retired Executives and is made up of some very high-powered men and women, many of whom were corporate executives or successful small-business owners before their retirements. They will consult with you on-site free of charge, except for occasional out-of-pocket expenses, such as travel. Or you can access their e-mail counseling if you need help right away. They are dedicated to aiding in the formation, growth, and success of small businesses nationwide. While it is unlikely you'll find someone in your area who knows publishing, a SCORE volunteer can still be mighty helpful on general management practices or perhaps in helping create a direct-mail campaign.

SCORE's Web site (www.score.org) also sports a targeted, alphabetized Business Resource Index that's handier than a pocket on a shirt. A few of the things you can link to are amortized loan schedules that calculate monthly payments, associations, the AT&T Toll Free Internet Directory, an easy-to-follow, step-by-step business plan, access to a copyright search, even a listing by state of Internet Service Providers (ISPs) for hosting your Web site.

Thirty-Two Ways to Generate Working Capital

Going into publishing without adequate preparation is like trying to determine the nature of the ocean by studying a cup of water. You need "adventure" capital to make your dream come true. There are more ways to generate cash than there are instruments in an orchestra. Some, however, are more viable than others.

Many of the most visible options—banks, government programs, and venture capitalists—may be the *least* likely sources of business capital. Most new firms gain financial support in one of two ways: through their owners or via private investors. The role of the private investor is underestimated and undervalued because it is neither institutionalized nor documented.

How much money do you really need to get started? The amount may not be as much as you thought. According to a study done by the National Federation of Independent Business, one out of three new businesses start with $10,000 or less. The next most common capital investment amount is from $20,000 to $49,000. You'll probably fall in the $10,000 to $20,000 range. Examine the following money sources to decide which ones make sense for you. With a good book, a solid business/marketing plan, and your strong commitment, money is probably available.

1. If you're a home owner, an obvious money source is your home equity—four walls and a small fortune. For most of us, real estate has appreciated at a mind-boggling rate. These windfall profits can be perfect solutions for property owners in most large cities. Consider getting a second mortgage. Or, if you really intend to take publishing seriously, you may want to move to a smaller town where quality of life is better and living costs are less.

2. Have a passbook savings account, CDs, or annuities? Most people are tempted to use these to start new businesses. Don't. Once it's gone, it's gone. On the other hand, there's an old axiom that says, "Thems that got, gets." Never was this more true than when approaching your banker for a loan. If you have $7,000 in savings, there is little hassle in borrowing another $7,000. The lending institution probably won't even require your account as collateral. Now you have $7,000 of other people's money (OPM), plus your original $7,000 (less the amount of interest on the debt, of course). If you reverse the process, though—spending the $7,000, then trying to borrow that amount—you have about as much chance for success as the guy who went bear hunting with a switch.

3. There may be other assets you can use to capitalize your business. Do you receive rents from real estate or dividends from stock? What about royalties from a book, song, computer software, or invention? One acquaintance used her hefty divorce settlement to start a publishing company.

4. According to *The Boston Globe*, baby boomers may *inherit* the nest egg needed to start a business. Due to previous historic gains in the stock market, high real estate prices, and the growth of millions of family-owned businesses, many baby boomers can expect generous inheritances. The bounty amounts to an estimated $8 *trillion* in cash and other assets over the next ten years!

5. In the meantime, consider your credit cards. Many a creative financier has breathed life into a small business thanks to multiple MasterCards or VISAs. In fact, some folks plan years ahead to use this strategy. They amass as many cards as possible, use them regularly, and pay punctually. As a reward, the card companies keep raising the credit limits. We know of one person who borrowed almost $30,000 on his credit cards. The downside is interest rates for this money are exorbitant.

6. Building a good personal credit history will go a long way toward helping you in business. Borrowing increasingly larger amounts from your bank, S&L (savings and loan association), or credit union—and repaying promptly—is a good start. Business start-ups usually can't get unsecured loans. Usually the business owners must put up collateral—their homes, plus other personal resources. And most banks require your personal guarantee, sometimes even that of your spouse, if the collateral assets are jointly owned. Often your individual financial statement becomes the basis for the loan.

Be aware there are different levels of bank officers. While a regular loan officer at a branch may have a limit of $10,000, a senior loan officer at the main location can go much higher without requiring committee approval. Usually the higher you begin, the better your chances. If you dead-end at the local level, ask how to contact a regional investment bank specializing in financing small companies. There you'll gain access to a wide range of lenders and investors, including pension funds and insurance companies.

Money is expensive any way you look at it. There would be no problem if you were a Fortune 500 company and could borrow at the prime rate. But you're probably not. So bankers will expect to get several percent above prime as a precautionary way to hedge their bets and protect their banks' investors.

7. There are techniques for talking your way into money. One is to practice giving a twenty-minute presentation. Ideally, rehearse with a camcorder. Short of that, stand in front of a mirror and use an audiocassette recorder. Monitor your eye contact, comfort level, and voice projection. Dress conservatively for your interview. Bankers are known to be a restrained group. Don't inflate your numbers; it smacks of amateurism. Be sure to prepare an impressive dummy of your book. It's hard for investors to picture an intangible object. And have your marketing plan well thought out and on paper so the banker can see how the money will be repaid.

Put together the best possible sales pitch for your book. What makes it special? Why will people buy it? If you are not clear on these issues, you shouldn't be approaching a lender. Use third-party support (what someone else says about it). If the book is nonfiction, what problem does it solve? Don't overlook the approach of having your banker read it. If he thinks it's great, you're on your way.

8. An acquaintance of ours discovered another approach. Mike told his banker he wanted a loan to go into business. The bank refused him. Later Mike learned if he'd asked for a "home improvement" loan or a "vacation" loan, he would have achieved his aim. We don't recommend fibbing, but you be the judge.

9. Perhaps you have a vested interest in a retirement fund or pension plan. Such funds often allow loans at reasonable rates. Consider this as a revenue source.

10. At the last National Speakers Association workshop we attended, a woman told of getting an unusual birthday present. Her dad wrote her friends and family telling them about her upcoming birthday and that she wanted to do a book. Would they make a pledge? Indeed so. She received enough money to self-publish her book.

11. If you're a mature person, lump-sum retirement benefits may well pave the way to an exciting new enterprise. There are all sorts of annuities: 401(k)s, IRAs, Keogh Plans, plus a myriad of private and government pension plans.

12. Ex-executives laid off as a result of mergers and downsizing sometimes receive cash settlements called golden parachutes. These are meant to ease the bumpy ride back to employment. Instead, a golden parachute often aids the leap to freedom.

13. Life insurance is another funding option. Possibly a sizable chunk is lying there in cash value. Presto, magic! Such loans require no qualification and carry attractive interest rates. If you took out a policy before 1965, for instance, you can typically borrow an amount equal to the policy's cash value for about 6 percent interest.

14. But what if you've got lousy credit? One nontraditional answer for a small loan might be a pawn shop. Yes, you read right. You won't get big bucks here and the neighborhood may make you feel about as welcome as a furrier at an animal rights convention, yet if you need a thousand or so to bootstrap an idea, it's a possibility. Such items as stereo systems, expensive watches, diamond rings, sterling silver sets, musical instruments, guns, golf clubs, and family heirlooms are most likely to turn the most cash.

15. Some people get others to participate in their books, both literally and financially. They offer to include chapters from other writers—for a fee, of course. Several folks have raised enough revenue from this anthology approach to fund the whole project.

16. There are those who modify their W-4 forms to get the IRS to "lend" them withholding taxes. This can work if you make out a new form for your

employer early in the year. But understand the piper must be paid. If you underpay too much, you run the risk of healthy fines and penalties.

17. Another unorthodox seed money source is unemployment insurance. In Washington a while back they started a pilot program with five hundred unemployed applicants. Called the Self-Employment Demonstration Project, it lets jobless workers use their unemployment checks to start their own businesses—up to a maximum of $7,000. The aim was to reduce unemployment and boost small-business development. Put out feelers to see if any such program exists in your area.

18. In these days of troubled S&Ls, many authors-publishers turn to F&Fs: family and friends. In 65 percent of the cases, the start-up capital needed for a new business is obtained from personal savings, relatives, and friends. Yet many people shun approaching their relatives and friends. If you believe in your book enough to put yourself on the line, is it fair to *prevent* your loved ones from participating? Try to find family, neighbors, colleagues, and buddies who seem on your same wavelength. Sure some will give you a chilly reception. But you'll never know unless you ask.

19. Another popular source of start-up money is to find an *angel*. This term refers to a private venture capitalist not affiliated with any institution. Often these people are successful entrepreneurs who yearn to relive the thrill of the chase. Usually an angel won't require you to put up any collateral; rather she will want a piece of the action. In his book *Finding Private Venture Capital for Your Firm*, Robert Gaston estimates there are some 720,000 angels committing somewhere in the range of $56 billion annually.

So where do you find these heavenly investment cherubs? Go through your Rolodex. Ask around your professional community. Talk with lawyers, bankers, and CPAs. Search out people in your industry who have made money. Or visit one of the hundred or so venture capital clubs around the nation. You can get the *Directory of Venture Capital Clubs* by sending $9.95 to the International Venture Capital Institute, Inc., P.O. Box 1333, Stamford, CT 06904, (203) 323-3143. These groups hold regular informal meetings. Here guest speakers give presentations, angels hear your proposition, and lots of networking goes on. Some folks even find their angels by advertising in the "Business Opportunities" classified section in newspapers and business magazines. How much do they invest in a single deal? Twenty-one percent of them put in less than $10,000; 43 percent, less than $25,000; and 64 percent, less than $50,000.

Angels usually want returns of three to five times their investments in about five years. (They are not just financing your operation in return for a simple payback on the loan.) Angels are *investors*. They expect substantial ownership in companies and strong growth potential. That can present a problem. Some startups give away too large a slice of the pie and ultimately harm themselves.

20. What about using sympathetic suppliers as a form of short-term financing? A major vendor that will wait ninety days for payment may be just what you need. You might even entice a local printer into becoming your financier. In this case, the printer absorbs the printing costs in exchange for 15 to 20 percent of the sales.

21. If you're a super salesperson, you may be able to convince a banker to finance purchase orders for your product. (Bankers sometimes do this on receivables for established customers.) Here's how it worked for one person: When he got a purchase order, it went to his accountant, who verified that the order was accurate and the purchaser was creditworthy. Then the bank advanced him 40 percent of the value of the order. This equaled his production cost. When he billed the customer, he faxed a copy to the bank, which then sent another 40 percent. Finally, when the customer paid, the bank took its 80 percent of the bill, plus interest, and sent the business owner the rest—which was his profit. In effect, he pledged the purchase orders as collateral to gain short-term financing.

22. Grassroots peer-group lending programs are cropping up around the country to help low- and moderate-income individuals become self-employed. Many of these aim at home-based or garage-based entrepreneurs. One such alternative program is the Good Faith Fund in southeastern Arkansas. It makes small loans to anybody with an idea and four friends who also might need to borrow a modest amount. Borrowers—who require no collateral, work experience, or credit rating—can get from $500 to $5,000. It operates on the simple principle of people helping people and being responsible to one another and the fund. For information on this and other similar experiments in economic development, contact The Director, Good Faith Fund, 400 Main St., Suite 118, Pine Bluff, AR 71601, (501) 535-6233.

23. While the Small Business Administration is not always receptive to publishers, it has announced a new micro-loan program designed especially to help part-time or home-based businesses. These new SBA loans can run from a few hundred to several thousand dollars. Call (800) 827-5722 to locate the nearest SBA office and get more details, or go online to www.sba.gov/financing. After all, seed capital from Uncle Sam has financed many a fledgling business.

24. The United States Department of Agriculture (USDA) oversees about twenty-nine money programs. For example, the Business and Industrial Loan Program can help start almost any kind of business as long as it is in a town of fewer than fifty thousand people. The USDA wants to foster economic growth in rural areas. It guarantees loans up to 90 percent of the principal advanced, which local banks find very attractive. For more information, call (202) 720-4323 or check www.usda.gov.

25. To tap into a road map of more than nine thousand sources of free help, information, and money, get a copy of Matthew Lesko's sixth edition of *Government Giveaways for Entrepreneurs*. Some 150,000 businesses get funds from the government to start or expand businesses each year. You could be one of them.

26. You might also form a strategic partnership. That's what Bill and Sue Truax did for their book *The Blitz Call: A System for Fear-Free Prospecting and Making Cold Calls*. One of their existing training/consulting clients, Petro-Canada Products, underwrote all the publication costs. The print run was 6,000 and the company took 1,000. The two parties split the net proceeds fifty-fifty until the company is fully reimbursed for its costs for the first printing. Thereafter, Petro-Canada Products gets only 10 percent.

27. Does the idea of having bucks in advance reassure you? Perhaps selling advertising in your book should be considered. This works especially well for regional books. You can sell the inside front cover, inside back cover, plus quarter, half, or full interior pages. If you decide to run with this idea, put together an advertising rate sheet and realistic figures on how many books you expect to sell. You must be a good salesperson and have reassuring information if you expect potential advertisers to part with their cash. (We go into detail on how to do this in our *How to Make Big Profits Publishing City and Regional Books*. Check it out at www.SPANnet.org/cc.) This works ideally for certain kinds of books for which commercial product or service tie-ins coincide with the subject matter.

28. Another innovative way to generate working capital is to presell your book. We will cover this approach in more detail in later chapters. Briefly, you can do a prepublication special mailing to your personal mailing list—you know, friends and acquaintances, people who've given you their business cards, your holiday card list, fellow alumni, and any other similar groups whose snail mail or e-mail addresses you have. To special sales outlets or wholesalers, offer a generous discount for cash-in-advance early orders. Run mail-order ads that collect money for future book fulfillment. By using such tactics, some self-publishers earn enough to pay their printing bills before a single book has rolled off the press.

29. Subscribers could also be your answer. Years ago in England poets used this approach to cover the costs of printing books of their poems. More recently, it was employed by David McCann, an assistant director of foundation relations at Cornell University. McCann put together a collection of his poems, titled it *Keeping Time*, then put out a classy announcement offering subscriptions. Many of his family, friends, and colleagues were delighted to participate. For a nominal sum, their names were listed in the back of the book and they received an autographed copy upon publication. By using this patron approach, McCann was able to cover the majority of his self-publishing expenses. You might have three levels of participation: Platinum ($500), Gold ($250), and Silver ($100).

30. Attending a writers' colony or retreat may also be helpful. While it will not likely provide you with working capital, it may help get your book written. Such setups often supply free room and board, and sometimes a fellowship, which can help with book publishing expenses, to budding authors and artists. Stays range from as short as a week to several months. These retreats offer unencumbered time and valuable association with talented people in the same field. A good place to look for retreats is www.shawguides.com.

31. Grants can offer small presses (not necessarily self-publishers) another money source. The rest of this chapter discusses them. As a rule, they are designed either to support a general work in progress or to fund a particular literary-oriented or social consciousness project. In most cases the small press must either have nonprofit, incorporated status and an IRS tax exemption, or find a sponsoring organization to provide such a conduit. Grants, like ice cream, come in three main flavors: the national government, state governments, and private foundations and corporations.

The vanilla of grants is represented by the National Endowment for the Arts, the largest single resource of federal funding available. While past emphasis has been to support poetry projects, today there is a more balanced program. The NEA has been the road to print for poetry, fiction, creative prose, and contemporary creative literature. If your book has more literary merit than commercial appeal, this is a particularly intriguing funding source. To get more information, go online to http://arts.endow.gov/federal.html, call (202) 682-5400, or write the Literature Program at the NEA address in the sidebar. You will receive a booklet containing guidelines, application instructions, and an application form.

State funding is next in volume, the chocolate of grants. It is given via state arts councils. To get information on what is available and how to apply, contact the state arts council in your state capital.

Foundation and corporate fund-raising is the strawberry flavor of grants. It is extremely difficult, however, to determine who might have money available for your book. If you decide to pursue this course, talk to your librarian about listings of foundations and other private organizations that have grant money available for research. Sometimes you can be lucky and dovetail with a specific program that one of these foundations is concentrating on, such as an educational or ethnic-oriented project.

Another source of information is The Grantsmanship Center (www.tgci.com). It conducts workshops, employs a research staff, maintains a library, and publishes a magazine. The center's guide *Program Planning and Proposal Writing* gives clear, explicit guidance for the novice grant hunter. Creating a good proposal is over half the battle. This is one place where good writing skills pay off royally.

32. Lastly, for our friends to the north, there is a Canadian grant resource that may be helpful. The Canada Council for the Arts is the primary organization responsible for grants. It's almost impossible to qualify for it if your work is commercial, but perhaps simply giving the CCA a try would be worth it. Another place to look for suitable donors is the *Canadian Directory of Charitable Foundations and Granting Agencies*.

Funding Sources' Contact Information

The following is contact information for grant resource centers.

National Endowment for the Arts
1100 Pennsylvania Ave. NW
Washington, DC 20506

PEN American Center
568 Broadway
New York, NY 10012-3225

The Grantsmanship Center
1125 W. Sixth St., Fifth Floor
P.O. Box 17220
Los Angeles, CA 90017

Canada Council for the Arts
350 Albert St.
P.O. Box 1047
Ottawa, ON K1P 5V8 Canada

Going after grants is time-consuming hard work. But when you click, the rewards—like a big bowl of ice cream on a hot day—make it all worthwhile. There *is* money available for a good investment. Your role is to ferret it out.

The job of finding the right means to supply your working capital is only one of the many challenges of self-publishing. Now let's go on to investigate some of the others. In the next chapter we turn to understanding sound operating procedures so you keep the bucks flowing in the right direction.

Web Sites, Wisdom, and Whimsey

End the frustration: Quickly find a ZIP code! Simply surf over to www.usps.gov/ncsc, enter the city and state, and you'll have what you need. Such a handy resource when a customer leaves a book order on your voice mail but forgets his ZIP, or when someone incorrectly completes Web forms and forgets to add her ZIP code. There is also considerable information here about the ZIP + 4 coding and why it can help your mail reach its destination faster.

* * *

One self-publisher has the perfect answer. Stephen M. Gower, the author of eleven books, has come up with the ideal answer when someone happens to ask, "Is your book self-published?" His reply: "I am fortunate enough to own my own publishing company."

* * *

I never travel without my diary. One should always have something sensational to read in the train. —Oscar Wilde

* * *

Dynamite discussion groups for grants are online. By hopping over to http://groups.yahoo.com, you can search for two informative chat forums that deal specifically with grants and information for writers. Enter "fundsforwriters" in the search field to subscribe to the group that talks about grants, contests, sources of partnerships, and the like for writers making a living through their passion for words. By searching on "FFWJunior" you can join a smaller network that provides a weekly list of easier to achieve grants, awards, and other funding information.

* * *

Need to separate your business phone call expenses from personal ones? If you have a single phone line for both business and personal calls and want a quick way to differentiate one from the other, ask your phone company about a helpful free service. Called Call Organizer by Pacific Bell, there are similar functions available from other companies. All you do is set up a numeric code, then enter the code number when making a long-distance call. When the bill comes, it's divided into the codes. Don't answer a phone that serves for business with, "Hello." You are in business, so act like it. If you must use the same line for both business and personal purposes, answer, "Good morning/afternoon. How may we help you?" or something similar. Handling the phone well speaks to your professionalism overall.

* * *

Life is a grindstone: whether it grinds you down or polishes you up depends on what you do with it.

* * *

Want to know who *owns* a certain Web site? Suppose you need to contact the person or company that calls the shots at a particular domain but the site doesn't provide adequate contact information or the e-mailed personnel are unresponsive. Is all lost? Never! Simply go to www.allwhois.com and run a who's who search. Once you type in the Web address and click Search, Allwhois.com will list the name, address, and phone number of the folks who own and run the site in question. There is another site that can do this for you. At www.register.com, enter the URL, click Check It, then click on the link when it comes up. This will take you to information such as the administrator's name, company, address, phone, fax, and other particulars. It's an intriguing way to do behind-the-scenes research.

Consult the consummate guide to grants. *Grants and Awards Available to American Writers*, published by PEN American Center, contains more than 1,000 listings and 234 new awards. The recently completed twenty-first edition is thorough and affordable. Get information at www.pen.org.

7 *Mastering Operating Procedures*

This chapter is an overview of the essential operating procedures of your self-publishing venture: determining monthly expenses, order fulfillment, inventory control, and the secrets of proper pricing and discounts. We also explain tax deductions and offer shortcuts for conducting your business.

Your "How to Do It" Plan of Attack

It would be as irrational as trying to cross the Atlantic in a kayak to set up your business and expect it to run without operating procedures. More companies fail from aimless drifting than from any other reason. Make sure you have your destination (goals and objectives) firmly in mind and steer an unerring course. Goals and objectives provide the basis for generating your business plan. (See the earlier section on goal setting in chapter one.) Nothing, however, takes the place of action. This is our "how to do it" plan of attack.

Scheduling is the first consideration in developing a business plan. Create a detailed schedule of each task or event and when it must occur to reach your goal. Determine the whats that must be done and the whens. The Self-Publishing Timetable on page 439 will be helpful in doing this.

Next comes the who analysis. Decide which activities and events you will personally handle. Do you have helpers? What will they do? While such things as preparing labels or envelopes for a mailing list or packaging books for shipment can be delegated, you will personally want to handle the vital function of developing a nationwide marketing plan. Then consider which functions will be accomplished by outside suppliers, such as editors, designers, typesetters, and printers. When this step is completed, a who will be assigned to each what.

Now that the who, what, and when of the plan are integrated, it's time to consider feasibility. What is the probability of tasks reaching completion as outlined? Estimate how many hours each task will take. Then to be safe, double it.

Is the needed time between events available? Make the necessary adjustments to ensure that all steps are feasible. If you can realistically spend only twenty hours per week on your part-time publishing venture, don't schedule thirty hours. Perhaps some part-time help must be added. Or you may need to delay or stretch certain functions. Perhaps you'll take longer to write the book. You may even have to stall a while on some of the more imaginative promotional angles you want to try. Or, as many busy professionals do, hire consultants like us to relieve you of the burdens.

Be aware of schedules that create sudden needs for additional people. The fact that it takes one woman nine months to have a baby doesn't mean a nine-woman co-op can produce a baby in one month. When such scheduling inconsistencies occur, the plan may need to be revised. Review it thoroughly. Make any adjustments necessary to have the pieces fit together. All of the parts must add up to a whole. Perhaps you should reevaluate your goals. Are they too ambitious? A little tailoring will soon yield the desired, and achievable, result.

Determining Monthly Expenses

If these results could be achieved without regard to cost, the plan would be complete. But for most of us, part of the goal is to make a net profit. This means expenses must be determined and integrated into the plan. To ease the job of establishing cost factors for each task, figure out your monthly operating expenses (see sidebar on page 115). At this point do not include "cost of sales" (any money expended for production or sale of your book).

After arriving at a total of your recurring monthly expenses, it is simple to figure weekly or hourly overhead rates. (Weekly = 12 × monthly ÷ 52. Hourly = 12 × monthly ÷ 2080.) These figures must be added to cost of sales to arrive at actuals for each activity.

To develop your cost of sales, you must arrive at figures for

- Contract labor (editing, indexing, order fulfillment, etc.)
- Cover design
- Interior design and typesetting
- Shipping (ask your printer for estimated costs)

These items are considered cost of sales because money is spent (a) to create the product or (b) only when sales occur.

Combining all the cost and expense figures you developed gives you your profit and loss projection for the goal period. It's wise to project a minimum of two years. This will make any banker or financial backer feel more comfortable. It shows you have done your homework, know what is going on—and what will

Recurring Monthly Expenses

Be sure to include the following items in the recurring monthly expenses or overhead:

- Payroll, employees' total earnings (at the onset, this will probably be zero)
- Rent
- Office/operating supplies
- Taxes and licenses
- Auto expenses (gas, repairs, tires, insurance, parking fees)
- Interest
- Utilities
- Telephone
- Marketing expenses
- Insurance
- Equipment rental and repair
- Photocopying and printing
- Postage

Note: Money drawn from the business by the owner and payments for capital equipment purchased on credit are not considered expenses. These are listed as other payments. Even so, they should be included as part of monthly outlay for this exercise.

be going on—in your business. See the Profit and Loss Projection Chart for 2001 on page 116 as an example.

Let review the components of the business plan. You have identified and scheduled those activities that must occur so your goal can be accomplished. The doer has been named. Hours required to complete tasks have been estimated. Finally, costs were analyzed and applied. All that is needed now is to devise some method to monitor, control, and provide feedback on performance.

Bookkeeping

Bookkeeping provides this vital monitor of performance. "I'm definitely not a bookkeeper," you say? Neither were we. You will probably want to use one of the many computerized bookkeeping systems now on the market. Systems adequate for one-book self-publishers are inexpensive and available at office supply superstores and software discount houses.

One called Quicken would adequately take care of the *one*-book publisher but would soon be outgrown. For a couple hundred bucks, Peachtree Complete version 8 will fill your present needs as well as those of tomorrow. The only thing Peachtree does not do is compute royalties and sales commissions. If you are publishing only your own books and aren't taking royalties, there's no need to look further.

Profit and Loss Projection Chart

PROFIT AND LOSS PROJECTION
Fiscal 2001

GROSS SALES		
Books	*My Story*—Retail 2,500 @ 14.95	$37,375.00
	My Story—Wholesale 2,500 @ 6.73	16,825.00
Contract Labor	Editing 50 hrs @ 30/hr	1,500.00
	Keyboarding 36 hrs @ 20/hr	720.00
Total Sales		$56,420.00
COST OF SALES		
	Editing & Indexing	$1,814.00
	Cover Design	1,695.00
	Interior Design/Typesetting	2,173.00
	Manufacture	7,216.00
	Shipping	1,152.00
		$14,050.00
Gross Profit		$42,370.00
EXPENSES		
	Payroll	$4,800.00
	Rent	1,200.00
	Office/Operating Supplies	480.00
	Taxes & Licenses	300.00
	Auto Expenses	900.00
	Interest	1,500.00
	Utilities	240.00
	Telephone	900.00
	Marketing Expenses	8,500.00
	Insurance	500.00
	Equipment Rental & repair	360.00
	Photocopying & Printing	1,600.00
	Postage	1,800.00
Total Expenses		$23,080.00
Net Profit		$19,290.00
Loan Repayment		(2,400.00)
Capital Equipment Purchases		(2,500.00)
Owner Draw		(12,000.00)
Spendable Gain		$2,390.00

Create a forecast of the sales, cost of sales, and expenses for your project with a "P&L" Projection Chart.

With minimum time and effort, you will become an adequate bookkeeper. The most difficult thing will likely be the discipline to make entries daily. Daily entry is not an absolute requirement but will ease the task greatly. When entries are kept up-to-date, it's a simple matter to complete the monthly summary. This summary gives the information needed to compare what you planned to do with what you actually did. Take time to make this analysis to ensure you're on course.

Order Fulfillment

The term used for the entire order entry, invoicing, packing, and shipping process is "order fulfillment." Naturally, before you can fill orders, you must first determine where all those books will be stored. They certainly won't fit under the bed. Some options are your garage, the basement, a large closet, or renting space in a small storage facility. Or perhaps you have a friend with warehousing space in his business establishment. On average, 3,000 to 5,000 books will take up less than one-fourth of a single-car garage as you'll stack them about six cartons high. Be sure that wherever you warehouse them it's *dry*. Nothing would be more disastrous than to discover you had case after case of soggy books. You may also want to insure them by having a rider attached to your homeowner policy.

Let's examine the entire order fulfillment procedure step-by-step from the mailbox through invoicing and shipping.

Receiving Orders

There are basically two ways by which orders are received by self-publishers. One is face-to-face contact, wherein the product is presented, an order placed, and merchandise delivered in one call. If the delivery point is also the billing address, the invoice is left with the buyer. The second method is mail order or credit card calls. Mail call is a daily high for the self-publisher because it brings credit orders, orders with checks enclosed, and payments for previous credit orders. Imagine: money in your mailbox! Another version of this is orders you receive from the Internet.

The face-to-face sale need only be entered into the bookkeeping records after you return to the office. But mail-order sales involve more details.

Credit Approval Steps

The first step is credit approval. Frankly, we prefer not to deal with individual bookstores because it's a lot of paperwork and many pay very slowly. We've established relationships with six general wholesalers or distributors and refer trade orders to them. When individual bookstores contact us, our normal re-

Invoice

Communication Creativity
P O Box 909
425 Cedar Street
Buena Vista, CO 81211-0909

INVOICE

Printed on: 4/9/2001
Page: 1

INVOICE # 2678

Voice: 719-395-8659
Fax: 719-395-8374

Sold to:

INGRAM BOOK COMPANY
ACCOUNTS PAYABLE DEPT NO 605
ONE INGRAM BLVD - P O BOX 3006
LA VERGNE TN 37086-3650

Ship to:

INGRAM BOOK COMPANY
ONE INGRAM BLVD
LAVERGNE TN 37086-3650

ORDERED: 4/9/2001 SHIPPED: 4/11/2001 METHOD: US POST PO NUMBER: NQ0933AR

QTY	PRODUCT #	DESCRIPTION	PRICE	DISC%	DISC$	TOTAL
10	MTR33	BIG IDEAS FOR SMALL SRVC BUSINESS	15.95	55	8.77	71.80

NET 90 DAYS. THANK YOU FOR YOUR ORDER.

Sub-Total:	$71.80
Invoice Discount:	$0.00
Shipping:	$0.00
Sales Tax:	$0.00
Invoice Total:	$71.80
Amount Received:	
Amount Due:	**$71.80**

Invoices should be sent out monthly to collect monies due you.

sponse is, "We are not opening any new accounts at this time." Then we suggest they might put it on a credit card—done more by businesses these days—or use STOP (Single Title Order Plan), where they send a check for 20 percent off, and we absorb the shipping cost.

Some buyers need a pro forma invoice to allow them to pay in advance. This is simply the complete invoice, including all charges, sent for advance payment. Don't reduce inventory or ship until the payment is actually received.

Incidentally, there do exist swindlers who order books from small presses without having any intention of paying for them. They order in large quantities and then sell the books to used-book stores.

We once received an exciting first order for 420 books from an unknown distributor. It was typed on a standard purchase order form anyone can get at the dime store—the first warning. There was no listing for this distributor in *LMP*—the next red flag. When Marilyn called to check the company's credit references, I was given a bank reference that proved to be only three months old and already had experienced a bounced check. Furthermore, our records showed they had never received a review copy of the book, yet they wanted to place an initial order for 420 books. No way! Needless to say, we declined to ship to this source. Unfortunately, many other small publishers did not. This particular distributor filed for bankruptcy and was investigated for mail fraud. Still, there's no need to become paranoid: Businesslike caution will yield protection.

For the biggies, such as Barnes & Noble, Borders, and Waldenbooks, you may want to ship any amount. They aren't going out of business. It's easier to let a major wholesaler, such as Baker & Taylor, sell to the chains, however, and handle all the details.

Invoicing

Your invoices will be created by computer, via either Peachtree or another software program. A copy of the invoice also serves as a packing slip and mailing label when folded into a clear "invoice enclosed" envelope.

We photocopy the finished invoice for our records, attach it to the purchase order, then file it alphabetically. That's all there is to it. Of course, you could have an electronic file, but some feel more at ease with a paper trail.

Once a week, enter the order, including the invoice number, under the Accounts Receivable and Sales sections of the company books. Enter any face-to-face sales the same way. Create a Quantity Shipped column and record the number of copies that go out the door. Since you made careful count of your books and logged them when they arrived from the printer, your running inventory will let you know exactly how many copies you have on hand. Electronic accounting takes care of this, of course, as you enter the invoice.

Charging Sales Tax

State sales tax is collected when you make retail sales in your own state only. (Legislation before Congress aims to change this; so far it's been defeated.) Tax is *not* charged when bookstores and wholesalers purchase merchandise for resale purposes (get their resale numbers on file) or when books are shipped to individuals out of state. How much to charge, and how and when to hand these taxes over to the appropriate governmental agency will be explained when you apply for and obtain your resale number.

Shipping Procedures

On to the shipping desk . . . which may well be your kitchen table. Many books are shipped as Media Mail (the old fourth-class book rate: book post), which is an inexpensive way to disseminate information. The first pound costs $1.33, then it is $0.45 for each additional pound up to seven pounds. Be sure you rubber stamp "Media Mail" in the postage area. Even with recent increases, it remains the most economical method for shipping. Library Mail, cheaper yet, is available for books sent by a publisher to a school, college, museum, or library. These are not, however, the most reliable ways to get books to your customers. We often suggest UPS or FedEx Ground.

There are some rather odd requirements that apply to items shipped by Media Mail. To qualify, there must be eight pages of printed material. Another requirement is that a booklet be saddle stitched (stapled) in at least three places. A student in one of our recent seminars learned about this the hard way. Her book was assembled with two staples. She received a call from the postmaster informing her that her shipment of several dozen books did not qualify. She wound up at the main post office, stapler in hand, opening each package, adding a staple, and sealing the packages again.

Additionally, you cannot include general advertising in your book and get the benefit of this reduced rate. Only incidental announcements of books (fliers and catalog sheets) and order blanks may be included to comply with postal regulations. Although these requirements may seem nonsensical, compliance saves a hassle and costly unproductive hours. Questions? Call (800) ASK-USPS.

If you want to get books across the country quickly, Media Mail is *not* the best way. According to one study, it takes an average of twelve days. (One shipment took thirty-seven days.) UPS (United Parcel Service) typically takes eight days. Average cost per pound in this study (all costs have since risen) showed book post at $0.148, freight at $0.12, and UPS at $0.22. To speed things up somewhat, UPS two-day rush service is another option. Of course, if you're really in a hurry, there are Express Mail, Federal Express, UPS Next Day Air, and other overnight options, all of which probably cost more than the book itself.

Another intriguing alternative is the U.S. Postal Service's Priority Mail. For just $3.95 you can ship as much as you can fit (yes, even more than the specified two pounds) in the specified priority flat rate envelope. And the USPS even provides the envelopes free. Priority mail boxes are also free. The larger video boxes are ideal to ship 5½″ × 8½″ books. For details on the post office's shipping materials, see http://supplies.usps.gov.

Careful selection of shipping containers can cut your costs. As an example, we found that one copy of *Creative Loafing* shipped in a Jiffy bag weighed slightly over one pound. We started a campaign to find a shipping container that would drop weight under the one-pound mark. After some fancy spadework, the weight was reduced by using Sentinel brand shipping bags, which resulted in a savings of $0.18 per single-copy shipment. The bubble-type bags are usually your best bet. Shoreline Container and Packaging, (800) 628-1653, has good prices on shipping containers. An excellent mail-order catalog source for shipping bags—and office supplies—is Quill, (800) 789-1331.

For larger multiple-copy orders, use a sturdy box. You can find odd-lot boxes by checking in the yellow pages (the business-to-business yellow pages if your community has them) under "Boxes." We also save and recycle the boxes we get. It is wise to encourage full-case purchases since you can then use the cased books just as they came from the printer and avoid laborious unpacking and repacking. You can offer special discounts and do your best to sell the idea of ordering full cases when writing or talking to the buyers who are ordering many copies at a time.

We've been asked by students about insuring the books shipped out. This would be prohibitively expensive. Yes, when you send via Media Mail or Priority Mail, you will eventually lose some books, but it's cheaper in the long run than insuring every copy that's mailed. When going UPS, books are automatically insured up to $100 per package. And they can be tracked.

Packages can be carried to the post office counter for weighing and postage. But remember, time is valuable and standing in line is nonproductive, so you may want to invest in a scale that goes up to twenty-five pounds.

When individuals order a single book, they usually expect to pay a shipping and handling charge of around $4. Often the general public reads a review about a book that doesn't mention the shipping costs, however, so the consumer sends only the cost of the book. What do you do? We've found the simplest solution is to note it on the computer invoice. (Or send a money due form.) In most cases the person remits the additional amount.

By the way, pay close attention to these individual orders. Do they mention a publication or media appearance? Are they photocopies of a review? Often this is the *only* way you know a review has been printed somewhere. When you source orders this way, you learn what's working. Whenever we take a phone credit card order, we always ask where the customer heard about the book.

Individual foreign orders are a hassle. Frankly we discourage such business, suggesting the person order through Amazon.com. If you see sustained interest from a foreign country, contact a distributor there to carry your book.

You may have heard mention of the Canadian Goods and Services Tax or Harmonized Sales Tax (GST/HST) on books. For beginning self-publishers there is nothing to be concerned about if you ship into Canada. According to the GST recorded message, your total annual business income must exceed $30,000 before the tax applies and you need to register. Call (800) 267-5177 to receive a helpful guide called Doing Business in Canada—GST/HST Information for Non-Residents and to discuss your particular situation. To download Canada Customs and Revenue Agency GST/HST forms and documents and to file electronically, go to www.ccra-adrc.gc.ca.

Subcontracting the Whole Order Fulfillment Process

Suppose you don't want to fool with order fulfillment or have no room to warehouse your books. Maybe the whole idea of invoicing, inventory control, picking, packing, and shipping is about as appealing as an encounter with a black widow spider. Is there an alternative? Yes.

Money Due Form

COMMUNICATION CREATIVITY
a colorado corporation

P.O. Box 909
Buena Vista, Colorado 81211
(719) 395-8659

YOUR ATTENTION PLEASE

Thank you for your order. You overlooked the amount indicated below, however. So as not to hold up your order, we are shipping it anyway. Please return this note with the balance due listed below so we can clear your account.

Customer name: ______________________

Book(s) ordered: ______________________

___ Price change

___ Sales tax

___ Postage and handling fee

___ No discount on one-book orders (trade)

BALANCE DUE $__________

Remit to: Communication Creativity, P.O. Box 909, Buena Vista, Colorado 81211

PLEASE RETURN THIS NOTE WITH YOUR PAYMENT. WE APPRECIATE YOUR COOPERATION!

This simple form, which you complete and tuck in with the book ordered, will usually generate payment.

Commercial fulfillment firms relieve you of this responsibility—and also some of your profits. Some printers also provide this option. Fulfillment services work in one of two ways. The first of these is a drop shipment plan, under which you take all your own orders and deal with the financial and accounting aspects, but the subcontractor stores and ships your books. The second alternative is a more full-service method. The fulfillment center takes retail customer credit card orders over its own toll-free phone lines, plus collects orders that come through the mail, fax, e-mail, or your Web site. The center processes the credit card transactions and cashes the checks, then packages and ships your books. It also handles returns or damaged products and does the detailed accounting for you. In both cases you get a monthly report, a bill for services, and a check for your sales.

To find the names of fulfillment companies, look in the *LMP* under "Shipping Services." Some of the companies listed there will be strictly shippers; others specialize in complete fulfillment services. Read the ads. Be sure to compare apples to apples. There will be different charges for sending individual orders versus cases of books to wholesalers and bookstores. They may also assess a start-up fee, monthly warehouse charge, minimum monthly activity fee, etc. Using a fulfillment service will not increase your sales. The third party is merely shipping the books; you still must generate the orders.

Monthly Billings

File invoice copies in an accounts receivable file (an accordion-style alphabetical file works great), and you're finished with this order until monthly billing time. Monthly billings are used to jog credit buyers' memories. We recommend end-of-the-month reminders be sent to all credit customers owing over $6. Time your mailing to allow it to be in the customer's accounts payable file on the first of the month.

Most credit customers are happy to pay bills from invoices. You simply send a photocopy of the invoice from your accounts receivable file or your computer. However, a few demand monthly statements (an itemized list of all outstanding invoices, plus credits from any payments or returns during the billing period).

It makes sense to send copies of invoices in lieu of statements to any accounts that have no more than one or two unpaid purchases. However, for customers who have three or more orders per month, the monthly statement is preferable. An example of a monthly statement can be seen on page 125.

Hold a hard line with very slow-paying customers. It is a sad fact in the publishing industry that it isn't unusual for a bill to go 90 or 120 days without being paid. We suggest you take the following steps when a bill is 90 days past due (assuming it is large enough to warrant your time—perhaps over $20). Always remember that time is money. It's a lot smarter to spend fifteen minutes opening up a new sales channel than it is to devote that time to sending a collection letter for a $5 receivable.

On seriously delinquent accounts, call and discuss the problem with the accounts payable supervisor, the comptroller, or the store manager. If that doesn't shake loose some money, send a letter restating your standard credit terms and saying that discounts will be forfeited—that is, the buyer will be charged full list price—if the bill is not paid within 10 days. If payment is not received within that time limit, invoice the customer for the difference between the discounted price and the retail price. Or you can inform the buyer that you will begin charging the unpaid account 1½ percent interest per month. As a last resort, state that unless full payment is received promptly (perhaps within an additional 10 days), legal collection procedures will be initiated. But assuming you want your money, not a lawyer and a court hearing, this final threat should be reserved for a last resort.

If the account still ignores payment, notify the customer that the delinquency will now be reported to credit agencies and that small-claims or civil court action will be initiated unless response is immediate. If there is still no response, you have a nasty choice. Either carry through, or forget it and write off the sale. We've had very little success in getting judgments or financial satisfaction at this point. Sure, you can get an attorney to send a general collection letter or turn the account over to a collection agency, but don't expect much. That's the main reason we've tailored our operation to a cash basis whenever possible.

When a payment on account is received, enter it in your computer and match it to the invoice in the accounts receivable file. Once again, this paperwork can be handled on a weekly basis if preferred. Whew! The computer sure is easier. Let Peachtree do the work for you.

Returns

We all wish our books would completely "sell through"—meaning there would be no returns. But alas, it's an undeniable fact that a certain quantity of books shipped will be returned. Some wholesalers, chains, and bookstores will ask for a return authorization. If the request is within the time limit specified in your company's terms and conditions of sale (which we'll discuss later in this chapter), it should be approved.

In theory, returns are supposed to be in perfect, unblemished condition. In reality, many of them will have bent corners, stickers, scuffed covers, etc. Again,

Monthly Statement

Communication Creativity
P O Box 909
425 Cedar Street
Buena Vista, CO 81211-0909

Statement

Date: 3/31/2001
Page: 1

Voice: 719-395-8659
Fax: 719-395-8374

MIDWEST LIBRARY SERVICE
11443 ST CHARLES ROCK RD
BRIDGETON MO 63044-2789

A Finance Charge of 0% is applied to balances after each 0 day period.

Invoice Number	Date Shipped	Invoice Total	Amount Paid	Current Balance	Over 30 days	Over 60 days	Over 90 days	Over 120 days	Total Interest	Amount Due
2536	2/5/2001	19.95			19.95					19.95
2550	2/12/2001	19.95			19.95					19.95

Total Due: $39.90

(Please Return This Portion With Payment)

MIDWEST LIBRARY SERVICE
11443 ST CHARLES ROCK RD
BRIDGETON MO 63044-2789

Date: 3/31/2001

Amount Enclosed:

Please Disregard If Payment Has Been Made

Communication Creativity
P O Box 909
425 Cedar Street
Buena Vista, CO 81211-0909

A statement reflects all the monthly activity of a customer.

in theory, you should not have to refund money (or issue a credit if you publish several titles) when you receive a damaged book. In reality, if you want to continue doing business with the likes of Ingram and B&T, you'll accept damaged books.

All is not lost, however. Most individual consumers won't even notice minor blemishes; they're paying for information. So reserve the best of these books for them. Use the worst ones for review copies or donate them to a library. (Do be sure you show these books as coming back into inventory.)

Enter the credit for returns in the Sales section as a bracketed negative sale, that is (49.50), and the quantity as a negative, that is, (10), and as a separate line item in the Accounts Receivable section. Locate the original entry, and note "returned" and the quantity. Record the credit on the accounts receivable file invoice, and return the invoice to the system. In cases where you don't do ongoing business with the returning company, you will be expected to send a refund. Unlike large publishers, who can offer credit against other titles, you must ante up. Once again, your accounting program makes it easy.

Inventory Control

Inventory control can be very simple . . . or a source of frustration. Remember that one of the entries in the Sales section of the company books was a column entitled Quantity Shipped. Returns are also shown as negative entries in this column. That way you have at your fingertips complete information on shipments and returns—almost.

How about the freebie review and promotion copies you send out? By simply making a line entry showing "comp copy," date, to whom sent, and a tally in the Quantity Shipped column, however, you have a perfect inventory control. Recording every outgoing book provides a dependable cross-check on other records.

At the end of each month add any new quantities printed, subtract the net monthly shipments (shipped minus returns), and update the inventory sheet. For the publishing business, it makes sense to carry only one title per inventory page. And so we have simple, convenient inventory control as the last of the company operation procedures.

Secrets of Proper Pricing and Discounts

One of the dilemmas every publisher faces is how to price the book. Industry estimates say it should sell for anywhere from five to eight times the first-run production costs. Often a greater markup is established for mail-order titles, since people are willing to pay dearly for valuable information. Sometimes mail-order books, especially those based on business topics or how-to-get-rich ideas, are sold at ten, fifteen, even twenty times production costs. Joe Karbo openly stated that his $10.00 paperback cost him $0.50 to produce.

Peter McWilliams, whom you met previously, flogged the above formula until it surrendered in both directions. His hardcover edition of *How to Survive the Loss of Love* retailed for only $10, though he could have reasonably priced it at $18 to $20. He figured more people would buy it at the lower price. Conversely, he priced *Self-Publishing, Self Taught* (a 173-page paperback) at a whopping $95. Why? Because he wanted to attract the committed rather than the curious—who McWilliams said often feel you owe them a personalized response to any letter they write because they paid $10 for your book.

After much research and testing we have arrived at a *minimum* figure of five times first-run production costs to be profitable. The quantity of the first run should be what you are confident you can sell in one to two years. Otherwise, you have money tied up in inventory that would be better spent on marketing.

Using the recommended formula, here is a hypothetical example of how to price your book, based on a first run of 5,000 copies. Adjust the figures to fit your actual cost factors.

Cost of Sales

$1,814	Editing and Indexing
1,695	Cover Design
2,173	Interior Design and Typesetting
7,216	Manufacture
1,152	Shipping
$14,050	Total

The $14,050.00 divided by 5,000 books equals $2.81 per book. Multiplying by five yields a $14.05 suggested retail sales price. Take a tip from major retailers and set the price at $14.95.

As to the actual retail figure, Sears and Penneys proved that $9.95 is perceived as significantly cheaper than $10.00, $19.95 less than $20.00, and so on. The exception to this is a mail-order book, for which even numbers are less confusing to buyers. Occasionally there is rationale to price a book unusually, as Tab Books did with *The Log of Christopher Columbus*. It sold for $14.92 and served as a nice PR gimmick.

It should be noted that any equipment and software you purchase to produce your "one" book should be included in your costs. If you buy PageMaker and a LaserJet 4M (PostScript) printer to publish one book, your cost for design and typesetting is increased by about $2,500 above the cost of your time. Don't misunderstand "your cost" versus IRS deductions. You could not deduct $2,500 as an expense against one book.

We do want to reiterate that the five times formula is a guideline for establishing the *minimum* price at which you can make a profit and keep fiscally fit. If your market research (bookstore browsing and Amazon.com checking) proves that books of this type, length, and quality are all selling for $12.95 to $14.95, you should be in that range, as well. Surveys indicate that underpricing your product does not sell significantly more books. In fact, sometimes people are suspicious of a book that seems to be priced too low for its type and class.

Of course, there is another point that must be considered. What if your market research indicates the proposed retail price is too high? There are several alternatives:

- Reduce costs by seeking more competitive production bids.
- Reduce the size or downgrade the specifications of the book. Perhaps you can eliminate photographs, have a less costly cover, or use more economical paper stock. (Carefully study the chapters on production for other ways to cut costs.)
- Price the book at five times anyway. This probably won't hurt sales drastically if it's only a dollar more than similar books.
- Readjust your marketing efforts to sell more books directly to consumers for full retail price with fewer highly discounted copies going to wholesalers and distributors.
- Print more books. By going from 3,000 to 5,000, for instance, your unit cost will go down considerably and the formula immediately becomes more attractive.
- Price your book at less than five times cost of sales. This may make a profit improbable on the first press run.
- Get very aggressive about selling subsidiary rights. Most major publishers make a lot more money on such things as foreign rights sales, excerpts, audio, and mass market rights. They bank on revenue coming from these channels rather than sales of the actual printed book itself. (We cover these exciting options in chapter eighteen, "Tapping Into Lucrative Subsidiary Rights.")
- Don't publish the book. As harsh as this sounds, it is probably best if your goal is to make money. If, however, you are more interested in seeing your work in print and leaving your literary mark on posterity, then move ahead. Some

people and organizations have very valid motivations that have nothing to do with making a profit.

Your Dollar Breakdown

Where your book dollar goes on the first printing is demonstrated in the following breakdown:

50%	Marketing, promotion, and distribution costs, including industry discounts, complimentary copies, postage, printing, promotional materials, advertising, and phone follow-up
20%	Production costs, including editing, design, typesetting, printing, binding, freight
20%	Operating overhead
10%	Profit
100%	Total

This breakdown of your dollars spent is critical to your success as a self-publisher. By the way, the "profit" percentage will be much heftier on subsequent printings when all of the prepress production costs disappear and the higher initial marketing expenses are over with. This is where you really start making money! Moreover, if the book is going to be sold predominantly by mail order, there is no need to worry about discounting. If, however, your market includes bookstores, wholesalers, distributors, and schools, discounts will be necessary.

We're always saddened when people discover our book *after* they've printed and priced their books. Often they want us to help market it. Many times they've placed themselves in a no-win situation because there isn't room for the discounts the middlemen need.

Discounts

Establishing discounts becomes simple if the experiences of those gone before are used. In a nutshell, bookstores must buy at 40 percent off the list or selling price to make a profit. General wholesalers and distributors, which sell to libraries and bookstores, need 50 to 55 percent discounts. And exclusive (master) distributors expect 62 to 67 percent discounts. Wholesalers and distributors will tell *you* what they expect. Sometimes it's slightly negotiable if they feel you will really get behind the book with assertive national PR. They will also expect you to pay all shipping. While many publishers continue to give bookstores and wholesalers a discount on single-title orders, the trend is *not* to do so. We totally concur.

After reviewing dozens of schedules and doing considerable cost analysis, we have arrived at the following suggested bookstore discount schedule:

Quantity of Order	*Percent of Discount*
1	0
2–4 copies	20
5–99 copies	40
100 and up (in even case lots)	50

Many publishers, including ourselves, do not discount to libraries unless they buy five or more books. We have sold a lot of books to them all across the United States and Canada using this approach. It doesn't seem to hurt sales, as quantities are typically one or two copies at a time and thus not profitable when discounts are allowed. Schools are usually happy with what is termed a "short discount," meaning 20 percent off the retail price. This applies to college bookstores, as well.

There is another discount philosophy that is becoming increasingly popular. This is the "universal discount schedule." Discounts are based strictly on quantities regardless of whether the buyer is a bookstore or a wholesaler. Of course, discounts are only offered if certain conditions are met.

Ts and Cs

Terms and conditions are the absolute, cast-in-bronze parameters under which your company sells its product. Think them over carefully. Feel comfortable with them and stick to your policies. Here are suggested Ts and Cs:

- Invoices are due and payable in thirty days from the first of the next month after the date of the invoice.
- Discounts will be forfeited if accounts are not paid within ninety days of due date.
- Interest of 1½ percent per month will be charged on delinquent accounts.
- For orders of fifty dollars or more please supply the names of your three largest publisher accounts, plus one bank reference.
- Shipping charges will be added to all credit orders.
- Special-handling requests must be received in writing with the order.
- Special discounts or payment schedules are not available.
- Prices subject to change without notice.

You may be tempted to make special deals with certain customers to increase sales. Don't! Be aware that the Federal Trade Commission (FTC) insists that any "deal" you make with one customer must be offered to all *like* customers.

This means that if you sell 50 books at 50 percent discount to one bookstore, by law you must sell 50 books at the same discount to all bookstores. Don't trap yourself. But notice we said *like* customers. You'll no doubt have different discounts for catalog houses, corporate sales, or other categories of customers. And if the other party has a standard contract and the only way you can do business with that purchaser is to abide by its discount, this is acceptable.

You can legally increase discounts under certain circumstances, however, providing the buyer is willing to give up something in return. Tom has taken many orders for fewer than 5 books at a 40 percent discount. Contradictory? Not at all. Those sales were made at 40 percent off instead of 20 because of these modifications: Cash in advance (books were hand delivered at time of sale, thus eliminating shipping and handling costs) and no returns allowed. Tom had the money, and they had the books in a one-stop sale. Ten percent was allowed for payment in advance with no handling and an additional 10 percent for waiver of return privileges. You are also at liberty to arrange special prices for such things as premium sales, which we discuss in chapter nineteen, "Originating Extraordinary 'Out-of-the-Box' Opportunities."

Also be aware that distributors across the country will tell *you* what discounts they require to carry your book. In this case, it's all right to go above the 50 percent discount. For your planning purposes, the *average* discount given by publishers with annual sales of less than $100,000 is 38 percent, according to a Huenefeld Survey. This, of course, factors in many books sold at full retail price.

Return Policy

Return policies are an absolute requirement if you intend to deal with bookstores and wholesalers. After considerable research, we arrived at a one-year time limit for returns. The following states a return policy that protects the publisher and satisfies the customer:

> All unblemished books may be returned for credit or refund if received within one year of the original invoice date. A copy of the original invoice must be included with return shipment. Shipments must be returned prepaid to [your publishing company address]. Unblemished books are not torn, mutilated, scuffed, or defaced in any way.

Standard terms and conditions of sale can be established by taking the components in this section and putting them together as your "Standard Terms and Conditions of Sale" sheet, which you will send to distributors, wholesalers, and bookstore chains.

Taxes and Deductions

Of course, you'll be putting together a report for Uncle Sam annually. The items listed below can usually be claimed as tax deductions if they are business-related expenses. We suggest you consult a tax accountant or the IRS regarding your personal situation and current regulations. Two fine guides are *Small Time Operator: How to Start Your Own Business, Keep Your Books, Pay Your Taxes and Stay Out of Trouble* and *422 Tax Deductions for Businesses and Self-Employed Individuals*, both by Bernard Kamoroff and available online at www.Bellsprings.com.

- **Working from your home.** Some nice tax relief is available here. If you use one-half of your home solely for business purposes, you can deduct up to 50 percent of most of your home expenses. That includes a percentage of the cost of your home; gas and electric bills; water, sewer, or trash; and insurance. The amount of this deduction is restricted to the amount of taxable income your business would have had if this deduction were not taken. As with all deductions, be sure to keep good records. Save those receipts. Check with your tax consultant to be sure your deduction is OK.
- **Telephone.** The basic monthly charge for a home business telephone is *not* deductible if it is the only line into your home. (Especially if you have teenagers, it is wise to have a separate business number.) However, all business long-distance calls (keep a log) are deductible.
- **Office supplies.** Be sure to get receipts for printer toner, fax and copies, ink cartridges, pens, paper, file folders, and all other supplies you purchase. Also remember that stationery, business cards, printed forms, and promotional materials are deductible. And don't overlook the costs of duplicating. Those few copies every week add up to a chunk by the end of the year.
- **Postage.** This will be a considerable amount. Train yourself to always get a receipt at the post office or write a check.
- **Books, magazines, newsletters, newspapers.** Whenever you purchase a book for reference or a magazine for research, or subscribe to a newsletter or professional periodical (and virtually all printed matter you purchase falls into that category, right?), get a receipt so you can claim the expense. And don't forget to include your daily newspaper if you subscribe or get your news online. No self-respecting writer-publisher could be effective without keeping his finger on the pulse of book reviews, not to mention possible local and national publicity tie-ins.
- **Educational expenses.** Fees for seminars and classes related to your work are usually deductible, as are associated travel, meals (up to 50 percent), and lodging.

- **Dues.** Dues for the professional organizations you join that relate to writing or publishing are deductible. And if you attend lunch or dinner meetings of these organizations, get a receipt. They're partly deductible, too.
- **Travel and mileage.** Travel away from home for research, promotion, and speaking engagements is a legitimate expense. Travel for research must be capitalized, however, so you can't claim that expense until the research begins to pay off. Actually, this expense becomes part of the cost of your inventory and is expensed as you sell your books. (See "Major business purchases" below.) Of course, local travel is deductible, on the basis of either so much per mile or a percentage of the actual cost of operating your car. Keep odometer readings and/or receipts. And don't overlook parking lot fees and the change gobbled up by meters and toll roads.
- **Entertainment.** Be sure to claim 50 percent of any legitimate business meals. Note on the restaurant receipt the name of the person you're interviewing or the customer you're wooing. Don't abuse this category, or you may be selected for an audit.
- **Contract labor.** The fees paid any independent contractor are also deductible. If you have someone assist you with data entry, research, editing, envelope stuffing, and the like, be sure to keep records of how much you paid, to whom, and why.
- **Agent and consultant fees.** If you use the services of an agent or a publishing consulting service (preferably ours!), the fees paid are another deduction.
- **Major business purchases.** There are two ways of handling purchased items. Expensed items are deducted totally as a current-year expense. The IRS will raise an eyebrow if the small business tried to expense any fixtures, equipment, or furnishings costing more than profits. This will especially hold true if the business is showing a paper loss.

Many times it is advantageous to you, as well as mandatory because of IRS rules, to capitalize larger purchases. Such items as a computer, scanner, printer, modem, desk, chair, filing cabinet, tape recorder, and telephone answering machine would normally be capitalized and depreciated as five-year property (by IRS definition—property that has a useful life of more than four years and less than ten years). Here's an example of one advantage: If your current-year deductions reduce your taxable income to the point that you don't owe any tax, don't waste a valuable deduction by expensing it. By capitalizing the purchase, you will render it deductible as depreciation over several years. Usually it is not worth the paperwork to capitalize purchases under twenty dollars. The amount of expense election is a maximum of $24,000 less limitations as of 2001.

We do not purport to be tax experts. Consult the IRS office, a tax accountant, your computer program, or a lawyer if you have questions about these guidelines as applied to your case.

Miscellaneous Tips for a Smooth-Running Business

Have you noticed how things get away from some people like a slippery bar of soap? These folks never seem to have a handle on what they're doing. While we know you don't fall in this category, we'd like to offer a few suggestions regarding daily business transactions.

Time is money. Everything you can do to shortcut or save steps is important. When you get the mail, establish a habit of batching it for easy handling. You do this by dividing it into separate piles as you open it. Maybe setting up file folders labeled "orders," "payments," "inquiries," "correspondence," and "miscellaneous" would be useful. Another good idea is to create standard forms or checklists wherever possible. These needn't be fancy. The idea is to save yourself from having to sit down and compose a personalized letter. Another time-saver, if you do a lot of phone work, is to keep a file folder of quickie jobs on your desk. This might include such things as checks to be signed, ZIP codes to be looked up, or newsletters to read. When you're left hanging on hold during those calls, or routed through endless electronic mail destinations, you can whip out these random quickie jobs.

Speaking of telephones, did you know that if you live in the Rocky Mountain region or farther west, you may be able to save a whopping 60 percent on long-distance phone calls to the East Coast by placing your calls before 8:00 A.M.? It will be two or three hours later on the eastern seaboard. The reverse works for easterners wanting to call the West Coast. Calls placed after 5:00 P.M. are typically 40 percent off the normal rate. Also be aware that many big companies have toll-free numbers. To check, call (800) 555-1212 and tell the operator the desired company name and location, or get a toll-free number directory or look on the Web.

Using the telephone instead of writing letters often makes sense. Most calls are under $0.50 when you use our money-saving tips—and much quicker than typing a letter. The telephone can also be a handy fig leaf for shy people. If you're timid and hate the thought of approaching local bookstores in person, consider selling to them by telephone. E-mail, of course, is another option.

As your publishing venture becomes more sophisticated, there are several mechanical helpers you may want to acquire. A postage scale, photocopier, fax machine, and postage machine are laborsaving devices that are exceptionally wise purchases.

We can't imagine trotting to the post office, buying an adequate supply of stamps, and licking all those durn things. A postage machine is quick and easy. True, you must pay a monthly rental fee or make some similar arrangement for this convenience, but it's well worth it if you're doing any volume. Check with your closest Pitney Bowes sales and leasing office for costs and details. Postage scales are available at most office supply stores or through mail order. Get one that goes up to twenty-five pounds plus a baby model for mailings in ounces. (Use nine pennies to calibrate it correctly to one ounce.) Postage is available for purchase online now, too.

Our photocopy machine is a blessing. We use it to produce sales literature as well as for normal office procedures. Another useful device is a speaker phone. With one of these gizmos, you can do other things while talking on the phone, rather than being captive to the instrument. And, of course, having voice mail or an answering machine is a vital business strategy.

As your publishing venture grows, if you find yourself in a bind and need some people help, an intern may be the answer. Interns are students who serve as temporary part-time employees. They perform a variety of jobs, usually for a small hourly wage, although we've heard of rates from nothing to $10 an hour. We've also seen interns negotiate for payment based on the assignments they can use to build their portfolios and the numbers of hours they are available to work. Their primary rewards are the learning experience of working for an actual publisher and, often, course credit. You can probably locate an intern through your local college or high school placement office. University English departments are another place to prospect. Unless you really have your act together, however, don't expect to acquire such services, as these folks deserve to have bona fide training.

We've been fortunate with the interns who worked for us. Bill was a delightful person who contributed a great deal during his internship with us. He remained a friend after the period lapsed. Kathy was a bubbly young lady as enthralled with book publishing as a kid is with candy. After her intern stint, we hired her as a regular employee. She later went on to become an editor with Harcourt Brace Jovanovich. Ryan is a near genius we would welcome back anytime, even after all these years.

Our interns worked on specialized projects wherever possible. After being shown what to look for and given the proper reference materials, they did research for marketing plans. Another time they were responsible for proofreading manuscripts. Remember when you commit to using an intern that she will be around for only a few months. You must find the proper balance between giving enough training and giving too much, stealing time from your other important duties.

As we talk about business procedures, it is important to discuss one aspect that many self-publishers ignore. That is the area of revisions to your book. Most of us are so relieved to finally have that thing off the press and in print that we neglect to continue refining the product. As soon as you receive your printed book, you should set up a revision folder where you place updated material for future editions, new information you come across, or notes about obsolete material. It's also a good idea to take one book and designate it a correction copy. Note any overlooked typos that friends tactfully point out to you or other errors you belatedly discover. By doing these two things, going back to press will be less effort and more fun.

One other aspect of your publishing business (which will *not* be fun) is handling complaints. From time to time people will call or write to say they never received their books. Check back through your sales log to verify that you received and filled their orders. If a reasonable amount of time has elapsed, resend a book. It's cheaper than worrying about it.

The other form of complaint comes from someone who has received your book but is dissatisfied. If you've turned out a quality product, this will be a rarity. The secret to handling this type of complaint is to keep your cool, be especially gracious, and listen carefully. Find out exactly why the person is unhappy, then correct it. Goodwill is a cheap investment.

Four Rules That Will Almost Guarantee *You Success*

Before we move on from operating procedures, let us leave you with four tips that will help your business flourish in all areas:

1. Make it easy for people to do what you want them to do. This applies to individual consumers, trade customers, publicity people—everyone, everywhere. Remove the roadblocks, and you'll have better results.

We've had extraordinary success applying this rule. It got us a feature in *Modern Maturity*, which is the Big Daddy of magazines, with a colossal circulation of 22.5 million. The publication even included our toll-free order number for *Country Bound!* Here's how it happened: We scrutinized the magazine carefully to find a column that gives readers useful information. Then we wrote a piece on the five dos and the five don'ts about moving to a smaller town. We made it effortless, following the format in the magazine, adhering to the word count and other guidelines. All the editor's work disappeared; he was delighted. Such customizing can land you valuable magazine space as well.

2. Follow up. The squeaky wheel does indeed get the grease. It is constantly proven to us that we get results we never would have achieved because we continue to ask for the sale, stay visible, and be politely persistent about PR. There is a rule of seven in business. What this means is that people must hear about you seven times before they are moved to act. Calling a reviewer or a producer a couple of times then giving up is like ordering a beautiful steak dinner and walking out before it is served.

3. Apply the 80/20 rule. This says you'll get 80 percent of your results from 20 percent of your efforts or customers. In essence, it means determine what's working and focus on that priority. Don't waste time on marginal paybacks. Spend 80 percent of your time pursuing the most profitable 20 percent.

4. Ask for what you want. This is perhaps the simplest rule yet the most ignored. A person will usually accommodate your wishes, assuming they are reasonable, and you let the person *know* what it is you want. So often we neglect to communicate our desires. Want a pleased customer to write a customer review on Amazon.com and barnesandnoble.com? Ask for it! Want to speak at the next annual convention of an association that parallels the topic of your book? Request to be on the program. You get the idea. Please do it!

In the next chapter, let's turn our attention to some different guidelines and explore how certain early activities set the stage for your book to perform well.

Web Sites, Wisdom, and Whimsey

Get unlimited access to postage online—twenty-four hours a day, seven days a week. With www.stamps.com, you'll never run out of postage again. You can download free software, open an account, and start printing postage the same day. There are no start-up costs, reset fees, or additional hardware requirements. Now you can get the professional look of metered mail without the hassle of carting a postage machine to the post office, and the service fee is likely less than what you'd pay to lease a name-brand postage meter.

I love being a writer. What I can't stand is the paperwork. —Peter De Vries

* * *

Mailing/shipping rates escalate. The postal rates that went into effect January 7, 2001, and again in July 2001, are a blow to all publishers. Priority Mail flat rate envelopes jumped to $3.95, a whopping 16 percent increase. Because of its speed, this is the shipping method of choice by a majority of publishers. If you have a small book, however, are you aware there is a new one-pound Priority rate of $3.50? Book Rate, which also took a significant leap, is now called Media Mail. One pound costs $1.33. If you're not charging *at least* $4.00 for shipping and handling, you're probably losing money on each mailing transaction. Don't forget it isn't just the cost of delivery; often there is an envelope involved, always a label, and your time! First-Class Mail rose to $0.34, with each additional ounce costing $0.23. Postcards are now $0.21. These $0.20 pint-sized message boards can pack a mighty wallop. Use them whenever possible, as they also stand out from letters and packages. As is usually the case when a postal service rate hike occurs, FedEx and UPS are raising rates, as well. (By the way, standard procedure is that the *publisher* pays the actual shipping charges on orders to the trade: bookstores, wholesalers, distributors, libraries.)

* * *

Apply these collection tips if you're being stiffed. Have you tried all the normal ways of collecting a bill—to no avail? Consider going to small claims court in your area if the amount is small enough to stay within the bounds of this court . . . and large enough to make your time worthwhile. If the person or company who owes you doesn't show up (defaults), you get a judgment. Once you have this court judgment, you can roll into action and seize the defaulter's bank account! There are services (check the yellow pages in the debtor's locale) that can help you handle the details. Happy collecting!

* * *

I am being frank about myself in this book. I tell of my first mistake on page 850. —Henry Kissinger in his autobiography

* * *

Obtain unbiased book price comparisons on the Net. Deep discounting on the Web has become as commonplace as dandelions in a spring lawn. New best-sellers are being merchandised at 50 percent off retail. Now there is a site called www.PriceSCAN.com that looks at this fiercely competitive practice indulged in by heavyweights struggling to grab market share. What's interesting about this price comparison site is that it also includes the shipping costs, which can dramatically distort how much a book actually costs. In fact, because it doesn't invoice the customer if Book Rate shipping is used, an independent retailer (called 1bookstreet.com) bested Amazon.com, B&N, and Borders. This site has carved out a niche selling romance, mystery, cookbooks, and remainders—and offers customer service in spades.

Be more efficient! Something that will help you be more effective is a big wall calendar. We prefer the 24″ × 36″ plastic-laminated ones. You can write on them with erasable colored felt-tip markers and erase at will. It's a great way to organize yourself to keep appointments, record travel plans, meet deadlines and production schedules, and keep track of major sales follow-up.

8 *Must-Do Important Early Activities*

We live in an age of numbers. Just as you had to get a Social Security number when you snagged your first job, your book also needs to be given some numbers as identification tags. It is wise to begin the process of acquiring these early in your prepublishing activities. You'll also want to determine approximately how big your book is going to be. Another important facet of getting started is establishing your publication date. And once you've done these things, a whole raft of advance attention-getting publicity avenues are open to you. We discuss these in chapter eleven.

Preparing a Castoff

No, we're not talking about setting out to go sailing. This strange-sounding technical term refers to estimating the length of your finished book. The estimate can be rough at this stage, but it is important to determine approximate length. Obviously, if you have only enough money to publish a book of about 125 pages and your estimate adds up to 250 pages, you're in financial hot water before you start.

Another reason to begin getting a handle on how long your book will be is to have reasonably accurate information for printers when you request bids to determine your budget. You will also need to state an approximate length on the sales and promotional literature you'll soon be developing. Now that you know all the reasons for doing this, let's proceed with the methods. (We'll show you specifics as we go along, so don't panic if it sounds like Greek at first.)

Let us take a look at some hypothetical examples. Suppose your double-spaced manuscript is 285 pages long. You do a little preliminary scouting in a bookstore to find an attractive book to use as a model and decide on a page size, text image size, type style, and leading (all of which are explained in the next chapter). In most cases, one finished 6″×9″ book page equals about one and one-fourth (1.25) pages of a double-spaced manuscript if done in 12-point Times Roman with 1-inch margins. Now computing the text pages in your book is a snap.

Divide your total manuscript pages (285) by the 1.25 conversion ratio. The result indicates you will have 228 typeset text pages.

Now you must take into consideration several other elements that make up a complete book. Front matter (those pages that appear before the actual text begins) in this example will consume 8 pages. We will figure back matter to consist only of an index (10 pages) and your order form (2 pages). In good design, each chapter heading will take up about one-third page. For optimum design, you want each chapter to start on a recto (right-hand) page if you have the room. Figure half the chapters will fall wrong, so allow for a blank verso (left-hand) page for these and add that number of extra pages. Now consider interior artwork. Will there be any photographs, illustrations, tables, charts, or graphs? Allow for them. Your book has definitely grown, hasn't it? Here's how the example breaks down:

Manuscript pages	228
Front matter	8
Chapter headings (12)	4
Chapters not starting on recto pages (estimate half)	6
Interior artwork (four charts at a half page each)	2
Back matter	12
Total estimated pages	260

At this point, you have some decisions to make. If you're using traditional printing, it is much more economical to print books in what is known as even signatures. A signature is the number of pages a press can print on both sides of the paper in one pass. Most book manufacturers use presses with a 32-page signature capacity. If you divide the 260-page example by 32, it comes out to 8.125. This is a definite no-no as it will cost considerably more. There are 4 pages too many. You need to condense your book to an even eight signatures.

In the example, this is easy. The front matter includes a bastard title page, also known as the half-title page (2 pages you can do without). The back matter includes 10 pages of index, which, by reducing the type size by 2 points, will shrink to 8 pages. You have just shortened your book to the ideal even-signature configuration. You could have dropped additional pages by allowing chapter title pages to start on verso pages, which you would certainly want to do if it means saving the cost of going into an additional signature.

Assume for a moment that your calculations had come out to a total of 252 pages. You now know this is not good. What should you do? Perhaps you could add a 4-page preface or foreword. The example allots the dedication and acknowledgment 2 pages; you could very easily start each on a recto page and use up 2 additional pages. Each page of the table of contents could be started on a recto page, using up 2 more of your blank pages. You could elect to simply leave 2 blank pages at the front and back of the book. If you do leave blank pages, it usually looks better to divide them rather than leave them all in the back. In our opinion, 8 blank pages would be maximum, and even that looks somewhat tacky. We feel there are much better uses for your dollar than to pay for blank pages. We'll bet if you really make an effort, you can come up with a way to add up to 16 useful and meaningful pages to your book.

The following figures show why we try so hard to stay in even signatures (sigs). Comparative costs are shown for printing 3,000 paperback copies of even 32-page sigs as well as for additional 16-page, 8-page, and, worst of all, 4-page sigs:

224 pages	$5,805	7 even sigs
228 pages	$6,077	7 even sigs + 4-page sig
232 pages	$6,127	7 even sigs + 8-page sig
236 pages	$6,382	7 even sigs + 8-page sig + 4-page sig
240 pages	$6,236	7 even sigs + 16-page sig
244 pages	$6,492	7 even sigs + 16-page sig + 4-pg sig
248 pages	$6,543	7 even sigs + 16-page sig + 8-page sig
252 pages	$6,799	7 even sigs + 16-page sig + 8-page sig + 4-page sig
256 pages	$6,422	8 even sigs

Note that a full additional signature costs very little more than 12 extra pages (compare 236 pages with 256 pages). Compute the cost per page for the uneven signatures between 7 and 8. Amazing, isn't it, how *more* can cost *less*. It becomes very obvious how important your page count really is. Additional help on actual interior design is coming up in the next chapter. (Note that these parameters apply only to traditionally printed books; the page length doesn't matter for e-books or one-book-at-a-time POD books.)

Choosing the "Right" Publication Date

There is an idiosyncrasy about publication dates you should be aware of. It stands to reason when you indicate a pub date that you would write down the first day you anticipate having finished books in hand, right? Wrong! In this industry, strategic reviewers prefer to pass judgment *before* the official publication date. Sometimes complete first printings are sold out prior to the pub date. Yes, you can definitely sell books before this date. So tack three or four months onto the actual anticipated delivery date to give reviewers a good chance to supply you with free publicity. (Example: If you will have books on January 1, set the publication date as May 1.) You will want to forecast the date at this early stage because you'll need it to complete an Advance Book Information (ABI) form, which is explained later in this chapter.

Some other considerations come into play when choosing a publication date. Bear in mind that trade advertising is concentrated during those times of year when the sales force is making its effort to sell the forthcoming major publisher lists. That is in January and February, and again in June and July. Also remember that the time from Labor Day until shortly before the December holidays is rather chaotic as publishers vie for holiday gift dollars. Advertising and publicity (reviews especially) go hand in hand. If you can steer clear of these periods, you'll have a better chance of garnering publicity, as there simply won't be as much competition. Thus, December and January are especially good choices.

You might benefit by tying your pub date to some special event or day. A book on how to achieve success, wealth, and fame might well be launched on the birthday of Horatio Alger Jr., January 13. Mae Day, in honor of the ultra liberated Mae West, is August 17. Got a book on how to attract men? This would make a heck of a link. How do we know about such kooky things? It's all in a book called *Chase's Calendar of Events* (more about its marvels later).

Securing Your ISBN

One of those vital numbers we referred to at the beginning of this chapter is the ISBN, which stands for International Standard Book Number. This ten-digit numeral unmistakably identifies the title, edition, binding, and publisher of a given work. It is a mandatory sales tool, as it provides the basis for identifying books in all industrywide systems. Bookstores, wholesalers, and distributors keep track of books solely by the ISBN.

So how do you go about getting this little goody? Just request the necessary forms from R.R. Bowker Company, 121 Chanlon Rd., New Providence, NJ 07974, (877) 310-7333. Or you can log onto www.isbn.org, where you can complete the forms and pay the required $225 by credit card or download the application and mail it in.

You will receive a computer printout containing ten numbers that serve as your registry log. Assign a number to each title you publish. Bowker includes directions telling you where to place the number, which must appear inside and outside your book. Every version of the book must have a *separate* ISBN: hardcover, paperback, e-book, audio, and so on. Each new edition of the book that contains 30 percent or more changes should have a new ISBN. (If you anticipate

ISBN Application Form

isbn

International Standard ISO 2108

INTERNATIONAL STANDARD BOOK NUMBER--UNITED STATES AGENCY
International Standard Numbering System for the Information Industry
121 Chanlon Road, New Providence, New Jersey 07974
TEL: 877-310-7333 FAX: 908-665-2895 Email: isbn-san@bowker.com
R.R. Bowker, A division of Reed Elsevier Inc.

APPLICATION FOR AN ISBN PUBLISHER PREFIX

FOR AGENCY USE ONLY

SYMBOL: ____________

PREFIX: ____________

As per enclosed "Release Form" please mail log to:
About Books, Inc. / Cassidy Books
P.O. Box 1500
Buena Vista, CO 81211-1500
ATTN: Marilyn Ross

PLEASE PRINT OR TYPE:

Company/Publisher Name: Cassidy Books

Address: P.O. Box 9723, Denver, CO 80209-9723

Phone Number: 303-733-6216 Fax Number: 303-777-1868

Toll Free Number: 800-541-6544 Telex Number: ____________

E-MAIL: mwillis@amdevgrp.com Web Site: www.CassidyBooks.com

Fax-on-Demand: ____________ Toll Free Fax: ____________

If P.O. Box Indicated, Local Street Address is Required:
371 South Emerson Street, Denver, CO 80209-2213

Company Position: ____________ Phone Number: ____________

Name of Rights & and Permissions Contact: ____________

Title: ____________ Phone Number: ____________

Name of ISBN Coordinator/Contact: Marsha A. Willis

Title: ____________ Phone Number: ____________

Division or Subsidiary of: ____________

Imprints: ____________

PAYMENT: A NON-REFUNDABLE PROCESSING SERVICE CHARGE PRIORITY PROCESSING SURCHARGE $50

ISBN PREFIX BLOCK	REGULAR PROCESSING FEE	PRIORITY PROCESSING FEE
10 ISBNs	$225.00	$275.00
100 ISBNs	$800.00	$850.00
1,000 ISBNs	$1,200.00	$1,250.00
10,000 ISBNs	$3,000.00	-

Fee Waiver:
Applicants requesting a fee-waiver MUST provide a list of titles and formats along with 501(C3) and mission statement documents.
Failure to provide this title list will delay Agency processing.

X Check/Money Order enclosed. Make payable to "R. R. Bowker."

__ Charge: ____ American Express ____ Visa ____ Master Card

Card Holder Name: ____________

Account #: ____________ Expiration Date: ____________

Total amount enclosed ~~or charged~~: $225.00

Authorized signature: Marilyn Ross Date: 11/06/00

* **Note: Credit Cards are the preferred form of payment**

Every book must have an International Standard Book Number. Complete this form to obtain your prefix log.

ISBN Application Form, continued

PUBLISHING INFORMATION:

1. Indicate year you started publishing: 2001

2. Indicate what type of products you produce (circle):

(Books) Videos Spoken Words on Cassette/CD
Software Mixed Media

Other - Please specify: ______

3. Book Subject Area (circle):

o Children's
o Law
o Medical
o Religious
o Sci-Tech
xx Other - Please specify: Non-Fiction

DISTRIBUTION INFORMATION:

1. Do you distribute for, or are you distributed by, any other company?
Yes: ______ No: X. If yes, please provide full company name, address and ISBN Publisher Prefix (if any):

______
______
______

PROCESSING INFORMATION:

Your application for an ISBN Publisher Prefix will be processed ONLY if you include the following:

1. Completed application
2. Payment

*** Note: Credit Cards are the preferred form of payment**

The ISBN U.S. Agency will not provide an ISBN by telephone or fax. Processing time for an ISBN application is 10 business days (Saturdays and Sundays and holidays are not business days) from the date of our receipt of the completed form. This means that the application is inhouse for that length of time; ISBNs will be mailed to publishers after this processing period is completed (provided there are no problems with the application).

PRIORITY PROCESSING:

If you intend to ask the agency for a faster turn around time, a priority charge of $50. applies and must be added to the service charge fee. Priority service includes return, within 72 business hours of receipt, of your ISBN Publisher Prefix and ISBN log book (provided there are no problems with the application).

If you are requesting priority service and would like your ISBN log book e-mailed, please provide the e-mail address to where it should be sent: ______

Please Note: The priority service is either by e-mail or courier service, but NOT both.

WAIVING OF THE SERVICE CHARGE:

Your firm may apply for a waiver of the service charge if your firm has been granted a 501 (C3) charitable/philanthropic tax exemption status & your firm can supply a statement of your charitable/philanthropic mission. Your firm must supply documentation on BOTH to be eligible for a fee waiver. If you request a waiver of the service charge and require priority processing, a charge of $50.00 does apply.

Return the application and payment to:

ISBN U.S. Agency
R.R. Bowker
121 Chanlon Road
New Providence, NJ 07974
isbn-san@bowker.com

publishing several books, you may want to purchase the hundred-number log, which goes for $800. Ouch!)

Should you need to make corrections—publishing company name, address, phone, fax, e-mail, URL—you can either mail a revised form or go online to www.isbn.org/corrections, select Publishers/Distributors, Wholesalers of the United States, complete the Corrections Form, and submit it.

If you're publishing in Canada, to get the process started, call (819) 994-6872. The Canadian ISBN Agency is handled by the National Library of Canada, 395 Wellington St., Ottawa, Ontario K1A 0N4. The Web site is at www.nlc-bnc.ca.

The Bookland EAN Scanning Symbol

We're all familiar with the UPC symbol that has replaced price tags in grocery stores and mass merchandisers across the country. Publishers use a bar code identifier called a Bookland EAN scanning symbol. (EAN stands for European Article Number, the international product code standard through the world.) It must be printed on the lower half of cover four (the back cover) of your book. When ordering your Bookland EAN scanning symbol, here are a couple of tips to follow for the film master parameters. Magnification ranges from 80 percent to 200 percent, but the most common is 90 percent for a 2″ × 1⅛″ area. Use film positive or negative, or an electronic file (usually an eps file estension).

Current prices range from $10 to $30. Here are a couple of vendors we have used: Fotel Inc., (800) 834-4920, www.fotel.com, and General Graphics, (800) 887-5894, www.ggbarcode.com. You can view a bar code film master suppliers' list at www.isbn.org/standards/home/isbn/us/barcode.html.

The only cautions to use when designing with the Bookland EAN are as follows: Don't crowd the symbol; crop marks are provided to indicate necessary clearances. Crowding could result in a nonscannable symbol. The colors for the background can be white, yellow, or red. Don't try to overprint any shades of black, blue, or cyan, as the scanner can't differentiate the bar codes from the backgrounds. Print the bar codes in dark inks only (preferably black or dark blue—reflex blue, process blue, and cyan are also good). The bars must always be the darker color. Bar and space colors cannot be reversed. Of course, include your ISBN and the price of the book.

The All-Important ABI Form

Now that we've taken care of the ISBN, let's explore a way to generate orders before you even have a finished book in your hands. Bowker publishes a bimonthly print directory called *Forthcoming Books In Print* that is updated monthly to *Books In Print* on CD-ROM and daily for online *BIP* subscribers. It can be as helpful to you in generating orders as the yellow pages are to local businesses.

Bookland EAN Scanning Symbol

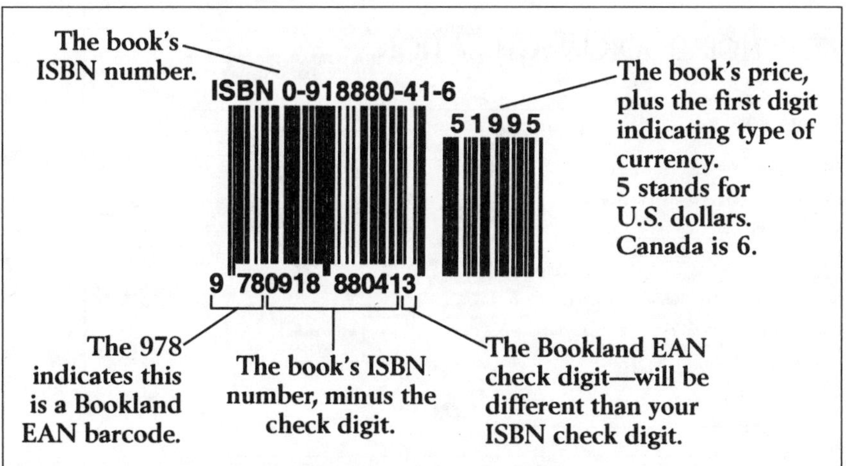

This symbol must appear on the lower right back cover of any book published. It contains information booksellers can scan.

And you can be included in it for nothing by completing the Advance Book Information (ABI) form.

When it reaches the publication date, your book will automatically proceed from *Forthcoming Books In Print* to the bound version of *Books In Print*, which is referred to by everybody who is anybody in the book business. The two-volume book version of *BIP* comes out in the fall each year, followed by a supplement in March. However, the CD-ROM format carries more weight with subscribers. This disk version is issued monthly and can be searched in various ways, including by date or by subject. The *BIP* database is also available online so that electronic subscribers throughout the country will have immediate access to the latest information on your title—if you've done your part. (By the way, you'll probably get a call asking you to advertise in *FBIP* and/or *BIP*. Don't waste your money. Bookstore and library personnel typically go to these reference books *after* they've already made a buying decision.)

You will receive an Advance Book Information form with your ISBN log, along with an instruction booklet that explains how to proceed. You can submit this form via the mail or online by going to www.bowkerlink.com.

New publishers can be included in *Books In Print* by signing up at www.bowker link.com. Click on Add/Update in Books In Print at top right on the home page, then hit the Register button and enter your publishing company name. A search here will reveal your publishing company name as a link, since you have already submitted it for an ISBN log. Click on your name to verify the complete name

Advance Book Information Form

PLEASE FILL IN AS MUCH INFORMATION AS POSSIBLE OR APPLICABLE *RETURN ENTIRE FORM* TO:

ADVANCE BOOK INFORMATION

R.R. BOWKER DATA COLLECTION CENTER
P.O. BOX 6000, OLDSMAR, FL 34677-6800

TITLE: The Ethan Chronicles
SUBTITLE: Requiem for a Life Stolen

Title Volume Number: 1
Is this a set? Yes☐ No☒ Number of Volumes: ______
Pub. Date: (MM/YY) 09 / 01
Copyright Date: (year) 2001
Pages: 352 Illustrated?: ☒YES ☐ NO
Status: ☐ Active ☐ On Demand ☐ Out-of-Print

PUBLISHER (Not Printer): Cassidy Books
ADDRESS: P.O. Box 9723
Denver, CO 80209-9723
PHONE: 303-733-6216 TOLL FREE: 800-541-6544
FAX: 303-777-1868 E-mail: mwillis@amdevgrp.com
Web site: www.CassidyBooks.com
IMPRINT (If other than company name): ______
DISTRIBUTOR (if other than publisher): ______
(If you distribute foreign books, please send us a copy of your documentation and indicate whether distribution is exclusive or non-exclusive. Currently, only exclusive distributors are included in the US portion of the BIP database.)

CONTRIBUTOR NAME (A=Author, E=Editor, I=Illustrator, P=Photographer, T=Translator):

Contributor Marsha A. Willis ☒A ☐E ☐I ☐P ☐T ☐Other ______ (check all that apply)
Contributor ______ ☐A ☐E ☐I ☐P ☐T ☐Other ______ (check all that apply)
Contributor ______ ☐A ☐E ☐I ☐P ☐T ☐Other ______ (check all that apply)

Series Title: ______
Series Subtitle: ______ Series Volume Number: ______
Edition Info.: ☐Reprint ☐ Revised ☐ Abridged ☐Large Type ☐ Unabridged ☐ Deluxe ☐ Other(specify) ______ Edition No. 1
E-Book File Format: ☐ASCII Text ☐ HTML ☐ MS Word ☐ PDF ☐ RTF ☐ Other(specify) ______
E-Book Edition Info.: ☐ Rocket ☐ SoftBook ☐ PalmPilot ☐ Millennium ☐ EveryBook ☐ Other(specify) ______
Audience: (children's books require grade levels) GRADES: ______ AGES: ______
☐Juvenile ☐Young Adult ☐College ☒Other (specify) Adult/General
Original Title: (if previously published & changed) ______
Translated Title: ______
Current Language (if other than English): ______ Original Language (if translated): ______
Publisher Order No.: ______ LCControl No.(LCCN): 00-136795
Point Size (LARGE TYPE BKS.): ______ Book Size: 6 x 9 Book Weight: ______

For ISBN Applicants: Fill out this form for each of your titles and return with your application. When your copy is returned to you with your ISBN log book, assign an ISBN to each title, enter it below, and return the form(s) to the R.R. Bowker Data Collection Center, Oldsmar, Florida. This will allow your title(s) to be listed in Books In Print or complete the ABI form online at www.bowker.com/titleforms/home/index.html.
ISBN Note: Write full 10-digit number in space below. The BIP system requires a separate ISBN for each edition and binding.

BINDING	ISBN	PRICE	*TYPE:	**CURRENCY	MARKET	
Hardcover: ☐ Trade ☐Textbk		$___.___			US___	CAN___
Paperback: ☒Trade ☐Textbk	0-9707194-3-4	$___.___		$14.95	US___	CAN___
☐Library Binding		$___.___			US___	CAN___
☐Mass Market		$___.___			US___	CAN___
☐E-Book		$___.___			US___	CAN___
☐Other: ______		$___.___			US___	CAN___

*Price type refers to invoice, retail, tentative, etc.
**Currency refers to US, Canadian, etc.

Type of Work: ☒Non-Fiction ☐Fiction ☐Poetry ☐Drama ☐Essay ☐Other ______
Subject Area: ☐ Children's (CB) ☐ Law(LB) ☐ Med(MB) ☐ Relig(RB) ☐ Sci-Tech(ST) ☒ Other Family

Description of Content: The book, based on a true story that gained national media coverage, documents a family's devastation and outrage at an impersonal system that sacrificed a loving, wholesome young man rather than take the steps necessary to stop an alienated kid from acting out his impulses.

The ABI form is very important as it triggers your inclusion in *Books In Print*.

Advance Book Information Form, continued

BISG MAJOR SUBJECTS

The Book Industry Study Group (BISG) has developed a list of **2800** subjects and subject codes. Known as the BISAC Subject Heading List, they are used to describe the subject contents of a book. Below you will find a list of **48 major BISAC categories.** If you are interested in using the full BISAC subject Headings List, you may write to BISG at 160 Fifth Ave., New York, NY 10010, or call 212-929-1393, or e-mail bill@bookinfo.org.

Please be advised that even if you use these headings, you should still complete the section above entitled "Description of Content" so that your book can be properly classified.

Please Indicate Appropriate Subject(s)

❑ANTIQUES & COLLECTIBLES
❑ARCHITECTURE
❑ART
❑BIOGRAPHY & AUTOBIOGRAPHY
❑BODY, MIND & SPIRIT (formerly OCCULTISM / PARAPSYCHOLOGY)
❑BUSINESS & ECONOMICS
❑COMPUTERS
❑COOKING
❑CRAFTS & HOBBIES
❑CURRENT EVENTS
❑DRAMA
❑EDUCATION
☒FAMILY & RELATIONSHIPS
❑FICTION
❑FOREIGN LANGUAGE STUDY
❑GAMES
❑GARDENING
❑HEALTH & FITNESS
❑HISTORY
❑HOUSE & HOME
❑HUMOR
❑JUVENILE FICTION
❑JUVENILE NONFICTION
❑LANGUAGE ARTS & DISCIPLINES
❑LAW
❑LITERARY CRITICISM & COLLECTIONS
❑MATHEMATICS
❑MEDICAL
❑MUSIC
❑NATURE
❑PERFORMING ARTS
❑PETS
❑PHILOSOPHY
❑PHOTOGRAPHY
❑POETRY
❑POLITICAL SCIENCE
❑PSYCHOLOGY & PSYCHIATRY
❑REFERENCE
❑RELIGION
❑SCIENCE
❑SELF-HELP
❑SOCIAL SCIENCE
❑SPORTS & RECREATION
❑STUDY AIDS
❑TECHNOLOGY
❑TRANSPORTATION
❑TRAVEL
❑TRUE CRIME

and address, then fill out the registration form. If you have misplaced your publisher record number, call Bowker's Editorial Department at (800) 521-8110, ext. 2881, who will supply it over the phone. Once you have chosen a user name identity online and submitted your form, Bowker will e-mail your password within three days. Wait another day for it to be activated. Then you can enter new titles, view your listings, or add and update your records to your heart's content.

Bowker will occasionally contact you to inquire if all information is correct on your checklist. Follow the above directions to double-check your listing. If you have questions, call customer service at (888) 269-5372, ext. 2881 (editorial).

When you need to make corrections—for example, change of title, subtitle, address, phone—you can make them at www.isbn.org/corrections. Select Books, then Books In Print, complete the Corrections Form, and submit it. Registration at these sites is free. You may also view your *Books In Print* titles for free at www.bowkerlink.com.

Before mailing the completed form, make several dozen copies. This is a concise presentation about your book that can be sent to select people as a prepublication attention getter (more about that soon).

Library of Congress Card Number

Books also need a Library of Congress catalog card number. It should appear on the copyright page of your book. This number allows subscribers to The Library of Congress catalog card service to order cards by number and eliminate a search fee. Approximately twenty thousand libraries belong. If you hope to sell to libraries, and it's a great market, you *must* have an LCCN.

Write for information and the Request for Library of Congress Preassigned Control Number. Contact Library of Congress, Cataloging in Publication Division, 101 Independence Ave. SE, Washington, DC 20540-4320, (202) 707-5000, or go online to http://pcn.loc.gov/pcn/pcn001.html for the preassigned control number.

Cataloging in Publication Program

Another useful numbering key allows libraries to shelve your book more speedily. It is called the Cataloging in Publication Program (CIP). This is not available to self-publishers, however—only to these who publish the works of others. Self-publishers can pay a fee to Quality Books, the major library supplier for independent presses, however, to get QB to create a special data block of information, termed Publisher's Cataloging in Publication (PCIP). You can call (800) 323-4241 for details, but we feel adding this to a book shouts "self-published!"

Unlike the United States, Canada encourages self-publishers to participate in the Canadian Cataloguing in Publication (CIP) Program. It is coordinated by the National Library and is divided by areas of jurisdiction. To get general information, call the CIP office Cataloguing Branch in Ottawa, Ontario, at (819) 994-6881.

An additional free listing can be obtained by contacting Dustbooks, at P.O. Box 100, Paradise, CA 95967, (800) 477-6110. This company logs titles for both small publishers and individuals. By contacting Len Fulton of Dustbooks for the proper forms, you can get your book entered in his *Small Press Record of Books in Print*, a junior version of *BIP*, and *International Directory of Little Magazines and Small Presses*.

Now that you've assigned your pub date, done a castoff to determine your book's length, pushed the right buttons to start the process for your ISBN, LCCN, ABI, and other listings, what's next? A very intriguing set of maneuvers . . .

Powerful Prepublication Attention Getters

There are several things you can do early on to draw attention to your work. Now it's time to explore what those strategies are and how to implement them.

LCCN Application Form

REQUEST FOR LIBRARY OF CONGRESS PREASSIGNED CONTROL NUMBER

NOTE: Control numbers cannot be preassigned to books which are already published. Works that receive a Library of Congress Preassigned Control Number are not eligible to receive Cataloging in Publication data for the same edition of the work.

Please type or print clearly. See instructions on verso of pink copy. Return white and yellow copies of this form to the Library of Congress. Retain pink copy for your records.

DATE: December 14, 2000

PUBLISHER'S NAME ON TITLE PAGE: Cassidy Books

YOUR NAME: Marilyn Ross PHONE NUMBER: 719-395-2459

The complete address to which the Preassigned Control Number should be sent. (This will be your return mailing label.)

About Books, Inc.
P.O. Box 1500
Buena Vista, CO 81211

FOR CIP OFFICE USE

Your Library of Congress Preassigned Control Number is:

Transcribe the informaiton in items 1-8 exactly in the form and order in which it will appear on the title or copyright pages of the printed book. Use only those abbreviations which will actually appear on these pages. **(Please attach a copy of the proposed title page, if available.)**

1. Author(s) Marsha A. Willis
2. Editor(s)
3. Title The Ethan Chronicles
4. Subtitle Requiem for a Life Stolen
5. Edition (exactly as printed in the publication, e.g. second edition, revised edition, etc.) First Printing
6. U.S. place of publication: City Denver State Colorado
7. Any copublisher(s) and place
8. Series title and numbering, exactly as printed in the publication
9. Approximate number of pages 352
10. ISBN (Hard cover) ISBN (Paperback) 0-9707194-3-4
11. Proposed date of publication: Month September Year 2001
12. Language of text, if other than English
13. Does (or will) the title in item 3 appear at periodic intervals, e.g. annually, quarterly, etc.? ☐ Yes ☒ No
14. Is this work intended principally for children or young adults? ☐ Yes ☒ No
15. Is this work paid for or subsidized in any part by the author(s), editor(s), or illustrator(s)? ☒ Yes ☐ No

Send the white and yellow copies of this form to: Library of Congress
Cataloging in Publication Division
101 Independence Avenue, SE
Washington, DC 20540-4320

1517 (2000/04)

LIBRARY OF CONGRESS COPY 1

Self-publishers should obtain a Library of Congress number for their books. This is the form to fill out in order to receive this number.

Get Blurbs—Those Golden Advance Comments

Schedule your book so you have some time between your completed edited manuscript and the beginning of the typesetting phase. Why? Because with imagination and research you can probably locate several noted people who may give your book an endorsement. These might be generally recognized experts on the book's subject, or people you notice either writing or being written about and quoted in the course of your research. Or they might be celebrities in *any* field who have a known interest in your subject.

Once you have their names, find out how to contact these people through Web search engines, listings in various Who's Whos, or the specialized references organized by profession, available at your public library. Look in a copy of *The Yearbook of Experts, Authorities and Spokespersons*. If you're tracking down authors, you can write them in care of their publishers, which are listed in the *LMP*. Have a few actors in mind? Contact the Screen Actors Guild (SAG) in Los Angeles at (323) 549-6737 or in New York at (212) 944-6797. Be prepared to stay on hold for a long time. Ask for the actor's agent or publicist. SAG is extremely busy and will give you only three contacts at a time.

And don't overlook asking friends or associates to refer you to someone they have a connection with. Contacts are very useful in promoting your book, both now and in all future stages. Ask your friends to write or call the people they are referring you to so your approach won't hit them cold.

Here is how you proceed: Send the endorsement candidate a riveting cover letter introducing your project (and mentioning the friend who referred you, if this is the case), your bio, a brief but powerful overview of the book, and some possible sample quotes. Explain why you feel this person would find the material interesting, and ask if he will look it over and share his comments. These are busy folks. If you hope to get their cooperation, be quick and direct. And it never hurts to stroke their egos. To facilitate their request for a copy of the book, include your e-mail address, any toll-free phone number, and an SASE. Whenever you want someone to do something for you, make it as *easy* for them as possible.

Following this line of thinking, craft several customized rough drafts upon which they can extrapolate. "What a great book" endorsements aren't as powerful as specifically slanted ones that each praise a different aspect of the book.

With the person's written permission, these favorable quotes become "advance comments." They can be splashed across your promotional materials like paints across canvas. If the people are superstars in the field, their comments on your cover or dust jacket can send sales skyrocketing.

But these blurbs don't come easy. Expect delays. Hesitancy. Nos. Now is the time to drag out your pleasant persistence. Stay in touch. Over and over and over again.

What if you've done a book on money management? Who could give a better endorsement than Suze Orman? Let's suppose you send Orman your package. She comes back showing interest. Get her a manuscript quick! Why not take it one step further and ask if she would consider doing a foreword? (In some cases it's easier to get cooperation if *you* volunteer to write it—subject to modification and approval, of course.) It can be as short as one or two pages, yet it can lend tremendous credibility to your project, so don't be backward about asking for a foreword. (And do spell it correctly!) Send everyone who provides an advance comment a gracious handwritten thank-you note. And be sure they each get an autographed copy when the books come off the press.

Does this work? Jacqueline Marcell self-published *Elder Rage, or, Take My Father . . . Please! How to Survive Caring for Aging Parents.* She was an unknown with lots of chutzpa. This lady ended up with forty celebrities endorsing her book, names you'll surely recognize: John Bradshaw, Phyllis Diller, Mark Victor Hansen, Art Linkletter, Regis Philbin, Betty Friedan, Dr. Harold Bloomfield, Leeza Gibbons, Dr. Bernie Siegel . . . the list goes on and on. And the media results were astounding, as well. Marcell was featured on CNN, and KNBC did a story that was picked up by its affiliates nationwide. The American Association of Retired Persons flew in its chief editor, and Marcell landed on the cover of the *AARP Bulletin*, which goes to millions of mature readers.

If the people you contact are experts, and sometimes even if they're not, they may comment in detail on ways the book should be different. If these remarks are useful and there is still time to make changes, go ahead and revise the manuscript. You've gotten a free expert reading! If it's too late for changes, reserve the suggestions for the revisions you'll do before another printing.

Try to Get Trade Announcements

There are four places where important fall and spring adult books of general national interest may be listed. They are *Publishers Weekly*, *Library Journal*, *Today's Librarian*, and *ForeWord*. It's wise to send them advance information about your book, as the more often people hear of it, the better. (This is not to say you'll be guaranteed a mention, as competition is fierce.) Here is where your duplicate ABI forms will come in handy. It's also a good idea to type out a brief blurb on your letterhead. It should include publisher, author, title, pub date, price, and binding information (hardback, paperback, or other). Also add about a ten-word description and tell what category the book falls in. Note your publicity and advertising plans.

It's easy to reach these magazines. The first two are published by the R.R. Bowker Company. Address your information to Spring (or Fall) Announcement Editor. *Publishers Weekly* comes out fifty-one times a year and serves the entire book publishing trade. Among its approximate 40,000 subscribers are the people you particularly want to reach: wholesalers, subsidiary rights managers, booksellers, and media personnel. *Library Journal* is a full-service publication for librarians, predominantly those serving adult needs and interests in public and college libraries. It is published twenty times a year and has about 26,000 subscribers. The remaining two, *Today's Librarian* and *ForeWord* magazine, both cater to the smaller independent press. Find info for them in Appendix E.

Contact Baker & Taylor

Baker & Taylor is one of the two largest wholesalers in the United States. It is education oriented and concentrates on serving the library market plus many bookstores. And it can mean big bucks for you. The first step any new publisher wanting to do business with B&T should take is to send advance book information (ye ole ABI form will do nicely) to the Publisher Contact Section. In turn, you will receive a New Title Information Form and a Vendor Profile Questionnaire requesting your terms, discounts, and returns policy.

Baker & Taylor maintains a master database of publishers' names and addresses and will add you to it once you've paid the $150 fee. (We've negotiated a waiver of this fee for SPAN members, however, so it more than pays for membership.) This database is used for placing special mail orders with publishers that the company doesn't regularly stock. B&T does not inventory new titles until a consistent demand pattern emerges. To activate things with them, write to the Publisher Contact Section, Baker & Taylor Company, P.O. Box 6885, 1120 U.S. Route 22 E., Bridgewater, NJ 08807-0885, call (908) 541-7000 or e-mail pubsvc@BTol.com and ask for the package of information for new publishers. (We'll be discussing this company in greater depth in chapter fifteen, "Milking the Standard Channels of Distribution.")

Exploit Your Subsidiary Rights

Although a whole chapter is devoted to this topic later, we want to briefly introduce it here, as there are strategic early maneuvers you may want to make. Some subsidiary rights—such as book clubs and first serialization or excerpt rights—should be pounced on as soon as possible. The reason is very simple. Subsidiary rights offer a substantial opportunity to maximize your income and get your book national exposure. The place to prospect for likely ones is *LMP*. Your ideal goal is to click with one or more book clubs at this infant stage. Then you can produce the book club copies at the same time as those you plan to sell yourself, greatly reducing the overall unit printing costs. The more books printed, the less cost to you per copy. If the arrangement is negotiated carefully, it can also yield "front money" to use for paying the printing bill. You can approach book clubs early with a clean manuscript.

Serial and excerpt rights apply to materials appearing in magazines and newspapers. When they come out *before* the publication of a book, they're called

Baker & Taylor Forms

BAKER & TAYLOR BOOKS VENDOR PROFILE QUESTIONNAIRE

1. PUBLISHER NAME: ______________________________

2. PUBLISHER ADDRESSES

HEADQUARTERS: ______________	MAIL ORDERS TO: ______________
TELEPHONE: ______________	TELEPHONE: ______________
TOLL-FREE: ______________	TOLL-FREE: ______________
FAX: ______________	FAX: ______________
CUSTOMER SERVICE: ______________	SEND RETURNS TO: (NO PO BOX) ______________
TELEPHONE: ______________	TELEPHONE: ______________
TOLL-FREE: ______________	TOLL-FREE: ______________
FAX: ______________	FAX: ______________

3. CONTACT NAME: ______________ E-MAIL: ______________

4. ISBN PREFIX: ______________ SAN NUMBER: ______________

5.

WHOLESALE DISCOUNT: (%)	FREIGHT PAID BY:	RETURNS POLICY:

6. PAYMENT TERMS: NET 90 DAYS

7. OTHER DISTRIBUTOR/WHOLESALER RELATIONSHIPS IN EFFECT. PLEASE INDICATE IF THIS IS AN EXCLUSIVE/ NON-EXCLUSIVE ARRANGEMENT. ______________

8. TYPE AND NUMBER OF TITLES YOU PUBLISH ANNUALLY:

BOOKS________ AUDIO________ SOFTWARE________ OTHER (please specify)________

9. WHAT IS YOUR INTENDED MARKET(S)/MARKETING PLAN? ______________

PREPARED BY: ______________ DATE: ______________

Please return completed form to:

Baker & Taylor
PO Box 6885
Bridgewater, NJ 08807-0885
Phone 908-541-7000

BAKER & TAYLOR USE ONLY

☐ F ☐ A ☐ PMA IMPRINT CODE________

☐ NF ☐ V ☐ SPAN DATE COMPLETED________

☐ PU ☐ Y ☐ TERMS

If you want the major wholesaler Baker & Taylor to carry your book, you need to complete their forms. Reprinted with permission from Baker & Taylor, Inc., 1120 US Highway 22, P.O. Box 6885, Bridgewater, NJ 08807. For the most recent information on Baker & Taylor's services, e-mail pubsvc@btol.com.

Baker & Taylor Forms, continued

BAKER & TAYLOR - TITLE INFORMATION SHEET

(ONLY ONE ISBN NUMBER PER SHEET)

ISBN________________________ **RETAIL PRICE**________________________

FULL TITLE / SUB-TITLE____

____

AUTHOR NAME (S)____

BINDING (Paper, Hardcover, Reinforced Library Binding, Cassette, Compact Disk, Other: ______________

PUBLISHING DATE (Month & Year)______________ # OF PAGES______________

PUBLISHER________________________ **IMPRINT**________________________

EDITION # ______________

EDITION DESCRIPTION (Reissue, Revised, Reprint, CD-ROM, Collector's or Limited) ______________

BOOK TYPE (Non-Fiction or Fiction)______________ **JUVENILE** (Yes or No) ______________

VOLUME # ______________ **NUMBER OF VOLUMES IN A SET**______________

DISCOUNT______________

RTM SUBJECT CATEGORY (see reverse side) ________________________

INITIAL PRINT RUN______________ **ADVERTISING BUDGET**______________

DESCRIPTION____

____

FOR BAKER & TAYLOR USE ONLY

BISAC SUBJECT CODE (S)____

VENDOR CODE______________**IMPRINT CODE** ______________**PRICE KEY**__________

PLEASE SEND TITLE SHEET TO:
Baker & Taylor Inc.
PO Box 6885
Bridgewater, NJ 08807-0885
Phone: (908) 541-7000

BAKER & TAYLOR USE ONLY

☐ F ☐ A ☐ PMA **IMPRINT CODE**__________

☐ NF ☐ V ☐ SPAN **DATE COMPLETED**______

☐ PU ☐ Y ☐ TERMS

"first" rights. That's what you're going after now. There is a list in Appendix E that will be helpful in your quest for possible serial/excerpt sales.

To approach book clubs, magazine editors, and newspaper editors, your ABI form once again comes into play. All you need is that, a copy of the table of contents, and a benefit-oriented, sizzling cover letter in which you briefly describe why their members/readers can't live without this book. Be sure to offer a no-obligation reading copy of your manuscript.

If you hear nothing within three weeks, send brief e-mails saying you're just checking to make sure they received your original correspondence and asking whether they wish to consider the book. Wait a week, then scan your list for the most promising prospects. Now's the time to get on the phone and see if you can activate a spark of interest.

If you get to the point where you have galleys (these are *not* kitchens on boats, but you'll "miss the boat" if you don't have them), send them instead of a manuscript: It looks more official. Likewise, use your news release and mock review after they are prepared. Remember, these editors are swamped with book proposals every day. If you want to be considered, stay in front of them until you've received a firm no. This advice goes for any important sale or promotional opportunity you are pursuing.

Before leaving this topic, realize that in major trade publishing houses, the subsidiary rights director would also be going after foreign sales and premium or sponsored editions at this point. We feel this is too sophisticated for self-publishers at this stage of their undertaking. These avenues are covered in later chapters.

Now let us move on to the actual creation of your book, the designing and typesetting of an incredibly attractive and useful volume.

Web Sites, Wisdom, and Whimsey

Turn strangers into friends who will blurb your book. When Marcia Yudkin was thinking about identifying possible endorsers for her book *Six Steps to Free Publicity*, she took a novel approach to secure testimonials. Believing that a request for a blurb can feel like an imposition from a stranger, she introduced herself earlier by interviewing the people she wanted and including their stories in the book. That made asking for, and getting, an endorsement a lot easier.

* * *

Learn what you need and don't need. A barrage of letters has gone out to publishers, distributors, and wholesalers advising them that they should purchase a SAN (Standard Address Number) from the U.S. SAN Agency, another arm of Bowker. The letter states in part, "It is a surprise to us to discover that your firm has no SAN. Possession of a SAN is one—certainly not the only—indicator that a firm is a full participant in the publisher-to-consumer business environment and in touch with many markets and suppliers. Conversely, lack of a SAN frequently is a sign that a firm either is just starting out in publishing or is just beginning to learn the ropes of the trade." Yet our publishing company, Communication Creativity, has been in business for twenty-three years and has had a SAN (which used to be free) from the beginning. Guess how many times we've been asked for it? Would you believe twice?!

* * *

Why won't bookworms eat the pages of cartoon books? Because they might choke from laughing too much.

* * *

New service protects your intellectual property online. In our present Digital Age, manipulating records is child's play. Now the world's first global registry featuring instant digital fingerprinting and time-stamped registration awaits you. If you're concerned about protecting works you publish online, or having your Web site infringed upon, this is a simple solution. FirstUse.com creates a tamper-proof audit trail to strengthen documentation, help resolve disputes quickly, and discourage theft. You can use it to establish ownership before you get a copyright, trademark, or patent. What's especially nice is that the first three transactions are free. This service is being used by fifty professions in fifty-three nations. In addition to publishers, Web and software developers, songwriters, photographers, and inventors are all taking advantage of this method for providing irrefutable proof of original creation. To participate and protect, go to www.FirstUse.com.

* * *

Need a UPC for your book? While every book must carry a Bookland EAN Scanning Symbol, if you hope to sell to mass merchandisers, such as Wal-Mart, Target, or grocery chains, you will also need a UPC. This is handled by the Uniform Code Council. You can reach the UCC in Ohio at (937) 435-3870 or online at www.uc-council.org. Ask about the "price point UPC with the ISBN add-on." You must apply for a manufacturer's number for your company, however, which runs at least $300, so be sure your book is at the right price point and size for this marketplace and that you can anticipate a real return on your investment before you take this step.

* * *

It has been said that every writer, without exception, is a masochist, a sadist, a peeping Tom (or Tomacina), an exhibitionist, a narcissist, and a depressed person constantly haunted by fears of unproductivity. Thank goodness. Now we know why we write!

* * *

Buy ISBN numbers online and complete ABI forms. If you're in a hurry, the Internet comes to the rescue. (Or if you want to know more about the International Standard Book Number [ISBN], go to the FAQs and find answers to questions you didn't even know to ask.) Stop by www.isbn.org/standards/home/isbn/us/isbn.qu.html. To complete an Advance Book Information form online, simply surf over to www.bowkerlink.com and click on Add/Update to register your title.

PART III

Creating a Quality Product That Attracts Buyers

9 *Wow! Design and Typesetting*

Before embarking on the printing of your book, there are several points to consider. What kind of a cover design should it have? What types of cover blurbs are most effective? How vital is good interior design, and how can it be achieved? What's the lowdown on desktop publishing? Are there secrets to good proofreading? How do you create an index?

The Importance of Good Cover Design

Let's talk about the cover design first. Book covers first appeared in second-century Egypt, created to protect valuable papyrus pages. Later, they were embellished, and beauty merged with practicality. Today, a book cover must advertise the author, showcase reviews, set a mood, and offer a glimpse of the book's content.

If you expect to market the majority of your books through retail venues, online, direct marketing, and other similar avenues, your cover is your billboard and it had better be good. Book browsers will only give a book a few seconds of consideration. It must wrench their attention away from thousands of other volumes.

In a bookstore, most books are shelved spine out, so this narrow strip is your first sales tool. Make it stand out with arresting color and compelling lettering. It should display the title, author, and publisher. Be sure it runs the right way and the type is as big as possible.

Next, book browsers look at the book's front. If it interests them, they'll turn to the back. If they're still intrigued, the front and back flaps—if there's a dust jacket—will receive their consideration.

The local bookstore offers a tremendous resource for cover analysis. Here you can look at the designs of best-sellers and books similar to yours. Do your homework well. Many self-published books look amateurish because of poor design.

Your cover must be distinctive. Peter McWilliams told of creating a cover for *The Personal Computer Book*: "All computer books had four-color covers with science fiction type artwork." When placed next to each other, they all blended together. So he took the opposite tack, using a white cover with clean black and blue type. *Time* magazine said it was "Like a beacon of simplicity, sanity and humor." Sometimes it pays to deliberately set yourself apart.

Make your cover capture the essence of the book. This can be accomplished through the use of type, dynamic copy, a photo, or an illustration. It should be consistent with the inside material and carefully slanted to the tastes of your potential readers. If you were doing a book of interest to attorneys, for instance, dignity rather than flamboyance would be the key. Don't confuse busyness with boldness. You want a dramatic cover, not one with meaningless clutter. The goal of a cover is to convince consumers the book will solve their problems, or—in the case of fiction—provide an entertaining read.

Be sure you don't get so caught up in the graphic presentation on your cover that the title text loses out. Your title should be number one when you take a quick glance at your cover. It should pop off the background and be large enough to read from a distance on a bookshelf or a display table. If you plan to do any one-color advertising, make sure your cover is readable and clear when it's converted to black and white. A red title on a black background could look dramatic, but once it's changed to shades of gray, you might just as well have black on black. Remember the Internet, too. What's that cover going to look like on Amazon.com when it's one-inch tall on someone's computer screen? Can the title be read at that size?

If you don't have genuine professional graphic arts experience, get in touch with a professional—someone who has done *book covers* before—and talk concepts and prices. Don't choose a person who specializes in logos or brochures. Such individuals aren't familiar with the intricacies of cover design. And be sure the person you choose has experience working with book manufacturers and knows how to prepare the final artwork or electronic files for a book printer. One place to look is in the *LMP* under the "Artists and Art Services" listings. Or try checking with nearby publishing houses. We located a couple of very talented local freelancers by calling the production department at the San Diego branch of Harcourt Brace Jovanovich and explaining our dilemma.

John and Tom, who worked as a team, came out, read the table of contents and a couple of sample chapters, then talked with us about the "feel" of Marilyn's book *Creative Loafing*. They also asked about our budget allocations. A few days later, they came with rough sketches in hand. That gave us a whole new dilemma. We liked elements from each! Tom had designed logolike lettering for the words *creative loafing* that immediately captured our fancy. Yet John had come up with a pair of whimsical-looking people participating in activities mentioned in the book, and we liked the human interest they lent. Back to the drawing boards they went and incorporated the best elements of *both* roughs into a final drawing that had us nodding eagerly.

Our financial agreement, by the way, was to pay them only when they came up with an acceptable design. We ended up with a bill of around $700. This price included the more costly processes of hand lettering and a custom illustration. Of course this was several years ago, and as time goes by, we gain a deeper appreciation for the bargain we received even then. In today's market, you can get a basic cover design for anywhere from $500 to $3,000, depending on the complexity, colors, and custom work involved.

Usually you will be working with only one artist. After a preliminary agreement on the flavor of the book, she will come back with a few rough or thumbnail sketches. From these, the two of you should be able to pull together the final cover. Be sure your contract with the cover designer is "work made for hire." You may want to acknowledge your cover designer's talents on your copyright page or in your acknowledgments, but you don't want your designer to own the rights to your cover design. You'll want copies of all the computer files when it's finished and to be confident that you own the rights to use the design for any purpose.

Cover Considerations

Covers create different effects. To develop an aura of mystery and romance, the classic gothic novel sports a frightened young woman hurrying from a castle or an old house with a solitary burning light in an upper window. To generate another feeling, the designers of the cover for Erich von Däniken's *Chariots of the Gods* used large three-dimensional block letters. Check the illustrations showing the covers on pages 165 and 166. On *Jump Start Your Book Sales*, the bold type intermingled with the lightning makes it look electrified—jump started. The font used on *Between Friends* feels friendly. The photos or graphics used should match the titles; they create the effect or mood that fits the book. You can look at *Coloring Outside the Lines* and know that this is a *fun* business book. Notice how the light seems to shine through the type as well as the hand in *Light at the End of the Carpal Tunnel.* If you could see it in color, it's a bright sunny yellow. If you're a speaker and your book will be used as promotion, you might want a photograph of yourself on the front, as on the cover of *Habits of Wealth*.

Letting Type Do the Job

Type by itself without illustrations is often appropriate, especially if the book is of a business or how-to nature. But even typefaces have different personalities, as we'll be explaining shortly, so take care to match your type choice to your

Book Covers

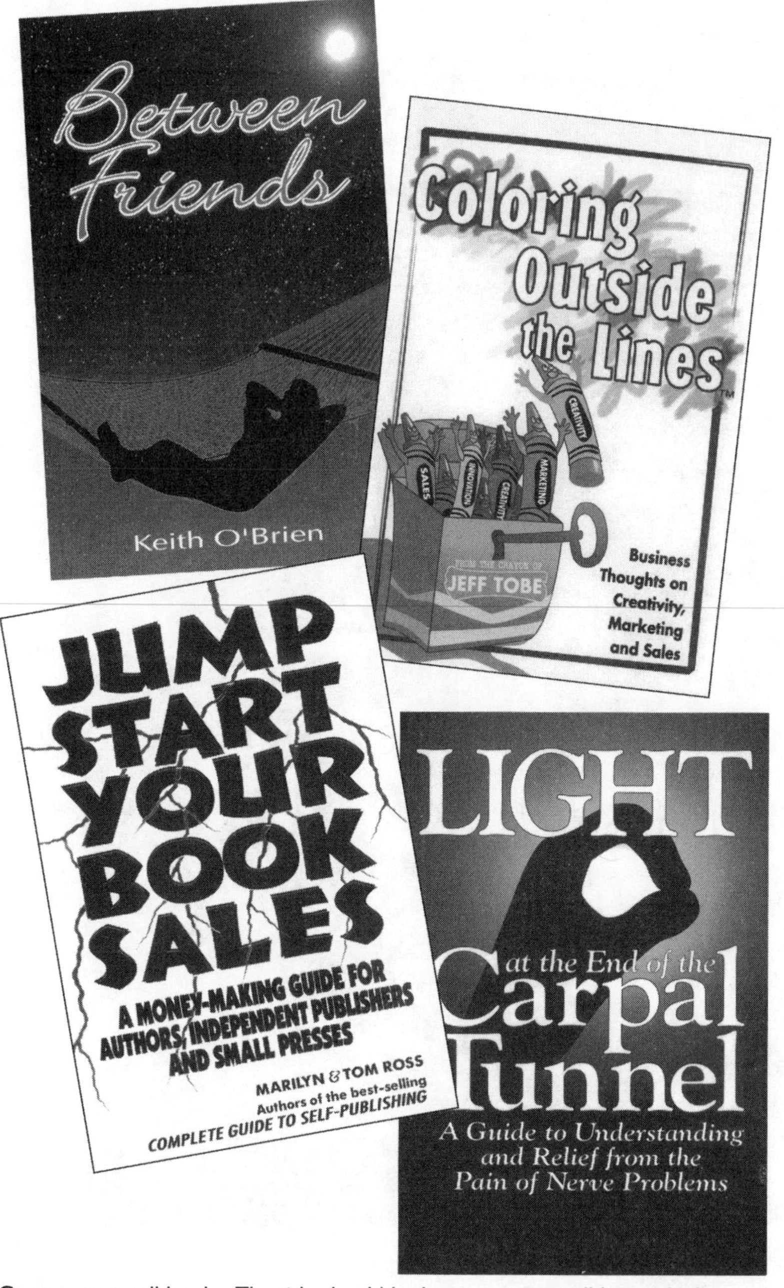

Great covers sell books. The title should be large so it can still be read when reduced on the Web.

Book Covers, continued

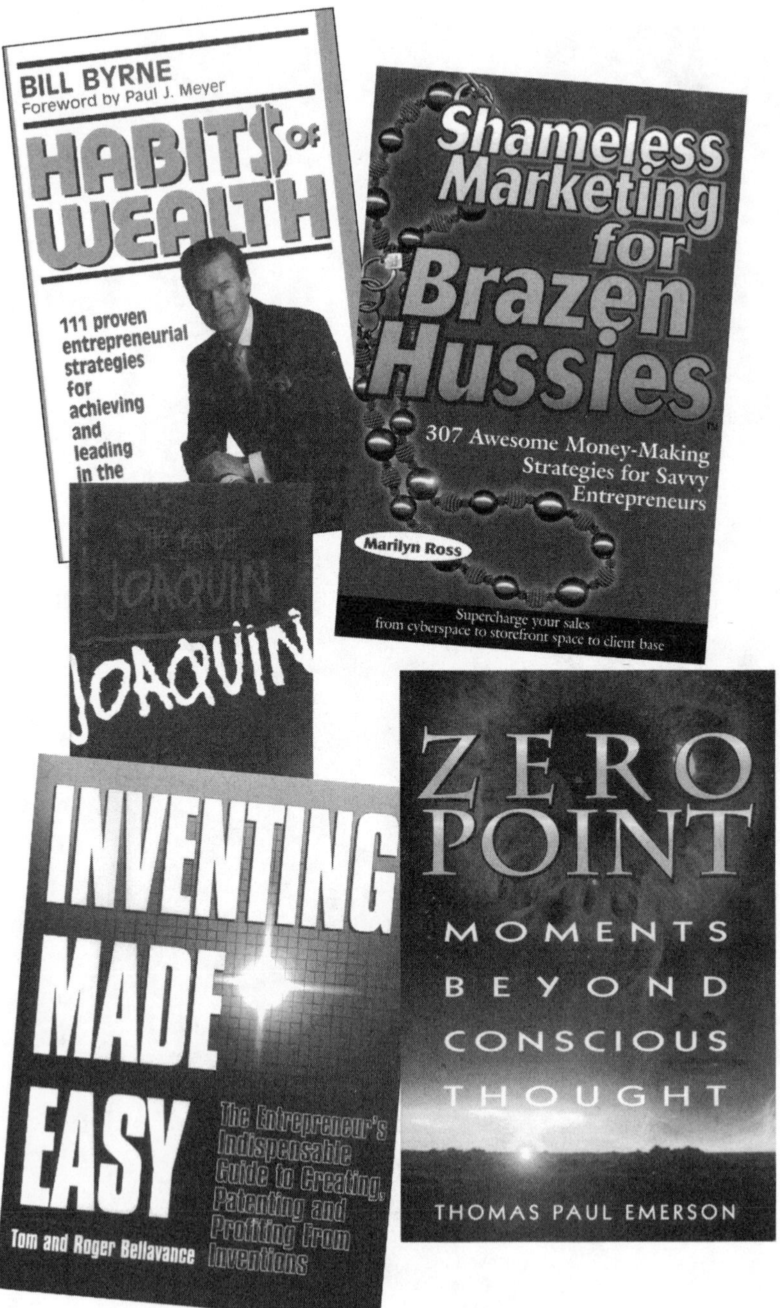

subject. Note how the typeface and design for *Shameless Marketing for Brazen Hussies* plays on the title implication. Even though it's a book for women, the title is bold and shameless as an entrepreneur must be. Can you feel the toughness and anger in *The Bandit Joaquin*? *Inventing Made Easy* has a cover that's clean and uncomplicated . . . easy. As different as these covers are, they have one thing in common: They all photograph extremely well. If you're using just type and plan a hardcover, you might want to consider going *without* a dust jacket and have the title stamped on the book cover itself. This technique was used for our original, self-published edition of *The Encyclopedia of Self-Publishing*. We chose a brown, leatherlike cover and stamped the type in gold. It was very elegant.

The Magic of Color

Color also plays a large role in book cover design. This is one place where one plus one does *not* equal two. It can equal three or even five or six! Why? Because a skilled designer uses one color of ink by itself, introduces another contrasting color by itself, then combines the two to create an additional color or two. Another color effect is created by reversing out the color and letting the white of the paper show.

The illusion of an additional color can be created by what is called a screen tint, a tone created by a regular pattern of tiny dots—the denser the dots, the darker the tone. The eye sees the screened tone as a tint of color. Often, type appears over the tinted area. Screen tints are expressed as percentages—10 percent being very light, 50 percent much darker. If you want to print over the screen tint with the same color, don't use more than a 30 percent screen. Twenty percent is usually a safer specification for best contrast. The pale yellow on the cover of this book is a screen tint of the darker yellow background color.

Screen tinting is an economical technique that will also give your promotional materials added appeal. If you count up the possibilities, you'll see you can get several colors while merely paying for a two-color job, and thereby reduce your printing costs.

Another treatment that gets a lot of mileage out of two colors and a black-and-white photo is called a duotone. In this process, two halftone negatives are made from one print. The darker and shadow tones usually are printed black, while the second color picks up the middle tones. Using black and brown is quite popular for producing expensive portrait prints.

Metallic Inks and Embossing Add Pizzazz

As the competition for the buyer's attention intensifies, the use of metallic inks on covers is a growing trend. You probably think of gold, silver, and copper, but in addition to these standards, you can get shiny metallic inks in just about every color you can think of. As you've probably noticed during your research, they are quite striking, especially if film laminated. However, you should consider a couple of things before specifying metallic ink.

First, the inks themselves are significantly more expensive than regular colored inks. Second, and more cost significant, a metallic ink cannot be printed along with other colors in one pass through the press. Metallic ink is much slower drying than other inks; therefore, it must be run through the press by itself, then set aside to dry before the other colors can be printed on the same surface. Regular inks are usually laid on in one press pass. As you can surmise, your printer is going to charge for the additional press pass for the metallic inks. A recent book we did for a client had a four-color cover, plus metallic gold as a fifth color. The additional charge for adding metallic gold was $940 for 5,000 copies.

Another treatment you may have seen in your research is foil-stamping. This will give a similar effect to using metallic inks except the foil makes it much flashier than using ink. Besides shiny solid colors, there are foils that give mirror effects, holographic patterns, and rainbow colors as you move them back and forth. Just like embossing, a customized die is created for the stamping, and it's a costly process. For *Jump Start Your Book Sales*, our companion to this book, the lightning on the cover is silver foil. We felt foil was necessary in this case to make it look like lightning and not cracks in a wall.

Embossing, in which certain words or elements are raised, is yet another option and especially effective for novels. A customized die must be created for the embossing process, and it is typically too expensive in the lower quantities most self-publishers print.

Understanding PMS Colors

In printing your color cover, you'll either be printing with PMS spot colors or four-color process. PMS? It stands for Pantone Matching System and is the standardized ink system that all printers use. Your computer software will even list Pantone colors for you to choose from. If you specify a PMS color number, you'll always know what you're getting—no surprises. Using PMS spot colors will also give you bolder, brighter colors than four-color process printing. If you're interested in finding out more, go to www.pantone.com. You can order color swatch books, screen tint books, and more. Be aware that inks print differently on coated and uncoated papers. If you have a PMS swatch book, you'll notice there are two sections showing you what the ink color will look like on both coated and uncoated paper. Uncoated paper absorbs more ink, so the colors will be somewhat muted.

When you choose a color photograph or full-color illustration for your cover, you must use what is called a four-color process printing. This is sometimes called a *full*-color process because from different combinations of the four prime colors (CMYK: cyan, magenta, yellow, and black), every possible color is created.

Looking at the overall cover project, four-color process is more costly. Some book printers prefer four-color process printing over using PMS inks because the majority of their work is full-color, and they don't have to wash up their press and change ink colors for your job. But coming back to your designer, a full-color cover design is going to cost more than a simpler two- or three-color cover. If your printer wants the final file as four-color process, it's a simple step for your designer to change the spot colors to process color.

Will full-color add substantially to buyer acceptance of your book? For something like a cookbook, a coffee-table book, or a travel guide for which a lush photograph will be a major factor in capturing the attention of your audience, it's definitely worth the cost. Again, if you're going to the luxury of a color photograph, make certain it fits the tone of your book. Check the photo collage on *Zero Point* (on page 166)—the sunrise, the eye, the girl's face. We think you will agree it fits the title and makes for a very dramatic cover. Imagine the impact in full-color. A cookbook showing the actual foods (in full-color) will definitely enhance its cover.

If you use a color photograph, there are additional costs for scanning it to a high-resolution image for color separation and any necessary color correction to the photo. When you're preparing your cover, it's best to have this scan done by a professional. If it's not done on a high-quality scanner at a very high resolution of dpi (dots per inch) or ppi (pixels per inch), your cover photo will look fuzzy. Talk to your printer about the resolution he recommends for his presses. There are many sources for stock photos now, especially on the Internet. Be sure they are royalty free and allow for commercial use before using one on your book.

Look for a company that does digital imaging or prepress work. Such a company will most likely have a drum-type scanner, which gives better quality than a normal flatbed scanner. Ask for a high-res scan for the printer and a low-res version to use in designing. Your designer will use the low-res file to work with, and your printer can swap it for the high-res scan before processing the file for printing. You'll want a match print, which is a proof for four-color process work. If you elect to go this route, be aware that a photo will never gain sharpness in the printing process. As a matter of fact, subtle tones in a photograph do not reproduce well. Be sure the image you start with is as sharp as possible.

Tips for Author Photos

A book cover usually includes the author's photo. On a dust-jacketed hardcover, we typically use the entire back for sales copy and put our photo and bio on the back flap. Paperbacks typically have the sales copy and an author photo and brief bio all on the back cover. If you want to reserve the entire back cover for sales copy, you can include the author photo within the book. You'll want a black-and-white glossy print (unless you're doing a full-color cover). Also, please realize that your author picture is for a different purpose than any photo you have ever had taken. It is to sell you as the expert. We asked an experienced trade book editor to tell us what's wrong with most of the hundreds of author photos she has seen.

> What is usually wrong with the author's picture? Usually a snapshot is submitted instead of a thoughtfully and professionally composed photo, which means all the things wrong you'd expect—cluttered (even stunningly cluttered) background, out-of-focus shot of the author in a plaid blouse standing in front of the lilac bush in the driveway. A picture not only unflattering but uninteresting. This doesn't mean it must or should be a plastic, perfectly-groomed-but-lifeless grinning studio shot. Yes, it would be more appropriate for a writer to be in an unusual setting or an unusual pose doing something that quintessentially says writer. It doesn't have to be sitting at the desk or in front of a typewriter—it's not only hard to get an uncluttered and interesting picture of same but that's pretty old hat by now. It could be irreverent or quirky or even slightly bizarre—but it *should* give you a good sense of the persona of the author and most of all be close-up enough that you can actually *see* the face. It should be a well-composed and effective photograph of good reproduction quality—which means it should probably be taken by a professional or a really good amateur photo bug.

Cover Finishes

For paperbacks, most publishers use a 10-point C1S (coated one side) stock. You can pay a little extra and get press varnish, liquid (UV cured) lamination, or film laminate—which will give even more durability, keeps your cover from curling, and gives greater reflective quality. This is a good idea because it enhances the colors and protects the book from soil and scuffing (especially important for bookstore sales). Film laminate also eliminates the need for shrink-wrapping, which is a pain and costs extra. We find it is nearly a wash cost-wise to film laminate, and using this process provides convenience and a sharper-looking cover.

There's been a recent popularity surge in using matte laminate finishes. These covers have lamination, but it's dull instead of glossy. Some publishers even mix the two, using a matte laminate on the background and glossy laminate on the title type, for example. These look great, but be careful. The matte laminate isn't as durable. It scuffs easily and starts to look bad, especially on a solid black or solid white background. If you want this type of finish, you might also consider shrink-wrapping the books for extra protection. To help gauge overall book or dust jacket dimensions, we've included visuals on page 173 that identify proper sizing.

If you're doing a booklet, consider a "self-cover." This simply means the cover stock will be the same as the interior pages and will be printed and saddle stitched right along with them. In some cases it makes sense to upgrade to a heavier, colored stock for more durability and a better appearance.

If your publication will be sold mainly through mail order, cover design takes on a different aspect. Color, a prime ingredient in bookstore sales, is not needed for mail order. What you want here is a cover that will photograph well so a picture of the book can be used in your advertisements (notice our previous samples). Choose large display type. If an illustration is included, make sure it uses strong lines that will photograph sharply and reduce well.

Determining the Dimensions

So now you've got a great design in mind. How do you determine the dimensions for the spine? In the earlier castoff you did, you figured out a close approximation of the number of pages in your book. Now you will need the final page count. The dimensions needed are developed as follows: First we must determine the bulk. To do this, divide the page count by the pages per inch (ppi) of the paper you are using. (Get this ppi from your printer.) For a paperback, the bulk equals the spine width. That's all there is to it.

For a hardcover with a dust jacket, you must add the amount in the "plus column" of the Spine Width Chart on page 174 to allow the jacket to wrap around the extra thickness of the hardcover boards. Let's assume we have a 320-page book that we're printing on 320-ppi hi bulk paper. Obviously our bulk equals 1 inch. But we need to add 7⁄16 inch from the Spine Width Chart to give us a total spine of 1 7⁄16 inches. It's important to get this spine width correct. The printer will usually check it, and if you're off, he'll send it back to you, delaying your printing job.

Whenever possible, design your cover or jacket so that one background color continues around the front, spine, back, and flaps. Especially for a hardcover book, the dust jackets may not be wrapped on the books just perfectly every time in manufacturing. With continuous color, it isn't as noticeable if the dust jacket slips a little one way or the other.

Next, let's look at the overall cover width. On a paperback book the front and back jacket width, or cover width, always equals the trim width. If your book is 5¼ inches wide, you'd multiply that by two and add it to the spine width. For you folks doing hardcovers, there is another step. The hardcover boards extend beyond the trimmed edge of the paper, and your dust jacket has flaps. Allow 3 to 3½ inches each for the front and back flaps, plus ⅜ inch for each hinge (where the jacket will wrap around the extended edges of your boards). If you're using a photo or illustration on your dust jacket, it should extend beyond the front to cover the entire ⅜-inch hinge area, as well.

As to height, for a paperback, the final trim height equals the trim height. So if your book is 8½ inches high, that's the cover height. On hardcovers, however, you must add ¼ inch to the dust jacket dimensions so it will extend over the boards on the top and bottom.

A final caution: If your book has bleeds (where the color or illustration goes clear to the edge of the paper) extend it ⅛ inch beyond your trimmed cover dimension on both the height and the width.

Cover Copy

Now that we've talked about the visual impact of your cover, let's discuss the copy that will appear on it. Cover blurbs are the sales message. To get an idea of what to say, study Avon and Bantam publications. These two publishers employ some of the nation's top copywriters. Read 'em. Study 'em. Imitate 'em.

Usually about twelve words work well on the front and about seventy-five on the back. They must have wallop! Zip! Punch! We find it amusing that many reviewers parrot the message that appears on the back and/or flaps of a book, sometimes without even changing a word. (Study the chapters on advertising and direct marketing for tips on powerful advertising copywriting.) Of course, you won't want to make any false claims in this, or any other, sales literature.

If you've garnered a foreword by an authority or celebrity, don't forget to splash the person's name on the front. This will give your book greater credibility and sales appeal. Some people have put ill-advised things on the cover, such as a dramatic label-like graphic proclaiming "Destined for #1 Best-seller," with "Destined for" in very tiny print. A better idea is to use a powerful advance comment you've received from a notable in the field or a prominent book critic.

Along with these cover blurbs you will want to develop material for the jacket flaps if you're doing a hardcover. The front flap should tantalize the prospective reader with more nice things about the book. The ISBN number should be printed in a small font at the top of the front flap. If you're going to list the price, this is a good place to put it. By placing it in the top right corner, it can

Dust Jacket Dimensions

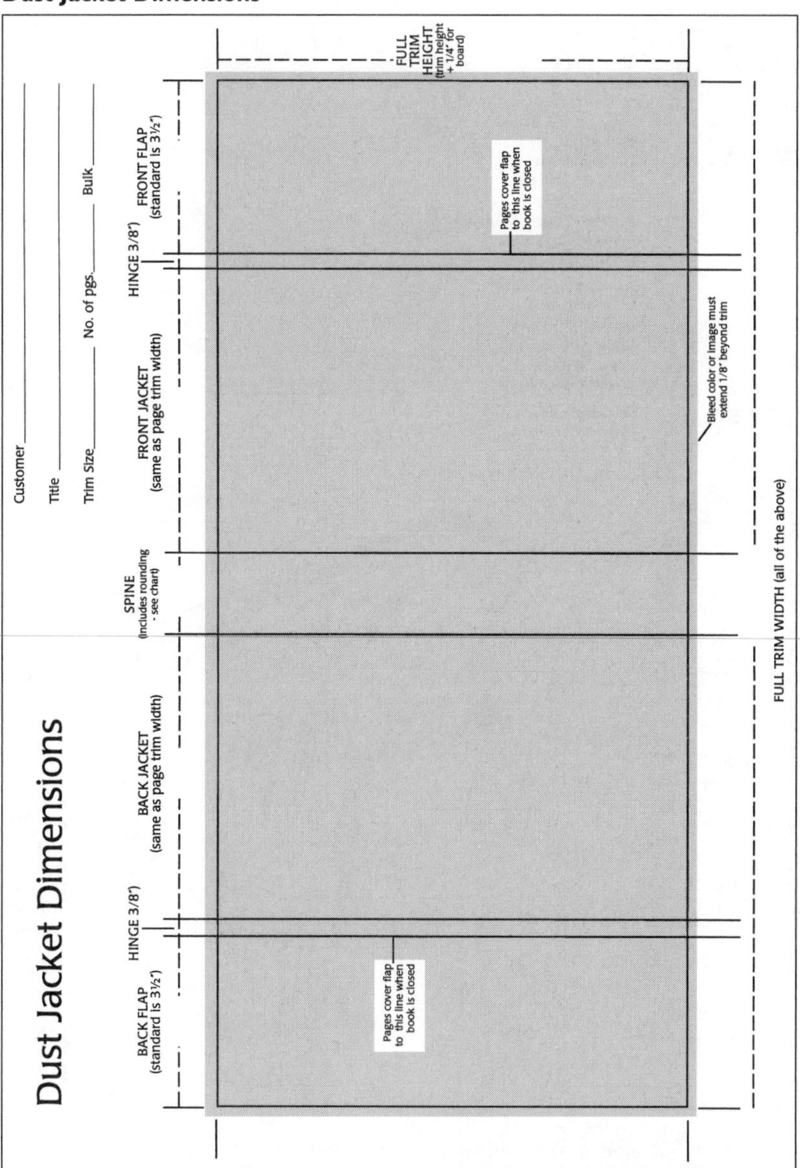

Hardcover books usually have dust jackets. It's vital they be designed to fit precisely.

Spine Width Chart

SPINE WIDTH CHART

THIS TABLE GIVES THE FINAL WIDTH OF THE SPINE (INCLUDING THE ROUNDING) OF NORMAL CASE-BOUND BOOKS MADE BY LITHOCRAFTERS.

Adjustments will have to be made in the case of extra-heavy binders' boards, a change of paper, or extra rounding.

(Not applicable to flat-back bindings.)

bulk	plus	total width
3/16	1/4	7/16
1/4	1/4	1/2
5/16	1/4	9/16
3/8	1/4	9/16
7/16	1/4	11/16
1/2	1/4	3/4
9/16	5/16	7/8
5/8	5/16	15/16
11/16	5/16	1"
3/4	3/8	1 1/8
13/16	3/8	1 3/16
7/8	3/8	1 1/4
15/16	3/8	1 5/16
1"	7/16	1 7/16
1 1/16	7/16	1 1/2
1 1/8	7/16	1 9/16
1 3/16	7/16	1 5/8
1 1/4	7/16	1 11/16
1 5/16	7/16	1 3/4
1 3/8	7/16	1 13/16
1 7/16	7/16	1 7/8
1 1/2	1/2	2"
1 9/16	1/2	2 1/16
1 5/8	1/2	2 1/8
1 11/16	1/2	2 3/16
1 3/4	1/2	2 1/4
1 13/16	1/2	2 5/16
1 7/8	1/2	2 3/8
1 15/16	1/2	2 7/16
2"	1/2	2 1/2

2" to 2 1/2 : add 9/16
2 1/2 to 3" : add 5/8

SPINE WIDTH
FLAP
HINGE
CASE HEIGHT
BULK

This chart shows the additional width needed for the spine roll on a hardcover book.

easily be cut off by someone giving the book as a gift. (For paperbacks place the price on the bottom of the back cover.)

There rages a controversy over whether or not to print the price on the book. On the yea side, bookstores in the United States much prefer that books be priced; otherwise, they must sticker each one. Those who say nay contend that pricing poses two problems: Canadian booksellers, who must charge more for you to make the same profit, resent having to up the printed price of the book. And if *you* decide to raise the price, this limits you considerably. (People *do* tear off those stickers and peer at what's underneath.) We recommend printing the price in the following format: $19.95 U.S.

If you anticipate strong Canadian sales, also include a Canadian price. An informal survey showed that major trade publishers charged from 35 to 48 percent more for books sold in Canada. At the current exchange rate, it's probably safe to use a 1.5 times markup. Thus if a book sold for $10 U.S., it would be $15 Canadian.

The back flap is best devoted to information about the author. Here's where your photo and bio appear. Toss away your humility. This must be an ego-puff piece. Study what is written about other authors and mold yours similarly. As an exercise, it's helpful to make a list of your accomplishments, honors, awards, degrees, experience, past writings, and organization memberships. This list will yield many ideas for developing your biography. Remember to slant your copy to the subject at hand. Make the information establish you as an authority on your subject.

To make ordering easy, include your publishing company name and address on the back flap of dust jackets or the back cover of paperbacks. And add one or two subject categories. This helps bookstore clerks shelve the book in the most appropriate section.

At this point you've got a smashing cover. What about the interior text? Are there design questions here, too? You bet there are.

Pieces of the Interior Puzzle

Trim Size

For economic reasons relating to the size of paper and printing presses, most books fall into the 5 3/16″ × 8¼″ to 6″ × 9″ size. A new size in the general range of 7″ × 9″ to 7″ × 10″ has also emerged. Think about the use for your book. If you want to include business letters or forms, 8½″ × 11″ might be more practical. Gift books often run 6″ × 4″ or 6″ × 4½″. If you choose to use an odd and unconventional trim size, be prepared to pay more and work closely with your printer.

You may wonder why we seem to avoid the 4″ × 7″ mass-market paperback size. Wouldn't that be cheaper yet, sez you? No, sez us, and we'll give you some good reasons why: Because of the high number of words-per-page, the high page count, and the low prices (usually $7 or $8), print quantities must be very high. Print runs for mass-market paperbacks often run around 100,000 copies.

But even more intimidating, jobbers and distributors typically rip off the covers when returns are due, thus you don't even have a book to resell. Avoid this size!

Paper

Another thing to think about is the paper used. While this is a design consideration, it also affects cover design because of spine width, and it has great bearing on your overall printing costs. Depending on the number of pages and the quantity of books printed, paper costs from 28 to 50 percent of the total printing bill! In the early seventies when we were getting started, a paper shortage existed and paper companies raised their prices every few weeks until they had almost doubled in two years. The real culprits are catalogs and newspaper supplements, which have proliferated in recent years. Since they use coated paper—and paper merchants can charge more for coated paper stock—many paper companies have stopped making book paper and switched to coated stock. The few merchants left who make book paper keep raising their prices à la the old supply-and-demand rationale.

Paper is chosen for its weight, opaqueness, and color. If you have a skinny book, use a "high bulk" paper and the book will appear fatter. You'll pay a little more for high bulk stock, but if it makes your book appear to be a better value and allows you to charge more for it, this stock is a wise investment. Remember that paper is measured by ppi (pages per inch). You'll usually be working with those in the 330 to 480 range. This is standard text paper for books with 120 to 400 pages. Most books are done on 50-, 55-, or 60-pound paper. Ask your printer for samples. Be aware, however, that a 60-pound paper from one printer may differ from a 60-pound paper from another. A better method for comparison is the ppi measurement. If you will be using photographs or artwork with heavy ink coverage, be sure the stock has good opacity so the material from the other side of the page doesn't show through. A paper's weight and its opacity don't necessarily correspond. To test it, place your art under the sample and observe how much you can see.

Unless you specify otherwise, your book will be printed on stark (blue white) white. Yet books on a natural or off-white stock that is easier on the eye are often favored by schools and libraries. Today virtually all papers are acid-free. This means your book will still be in good shape a century from now. Limited recycled paper stock is available at most printers. If you're producing a special deluxe edition—perhaps one that is numbered and hand-sewn—you may also want to upgrade to a more expensive paper stock. One other thing to remember about paper is that it has a definite grain, or direction, to it. Be sure your printer prints your book *with* the grain—meaning the grain runs parallel to the spine. Otherwise, the book will snap shut like a mousetrap. Most printers have "house"

Paper Bulk Chart

Bulk	1/16″	1/8″	3/16″	1/4″	5/16″	3/8″	7/16″	1/2″	9/16″	5/8″	11/16″	3/4″	13/16″	7/8″	15/16″
312 ppi	20	39	59	78	98	117	137	156	176	195	215	234	254	273	293
320 ppi	20	40	60	80	100	120	140	160	180	200	220	240	260	280	300
330 ppi	21	41	62	83	103	124	144	165	186	206	227	248	268	289	309
336 ppi	21	42	63	84	105	126	147	168	189	210	231	252	273	294	315
352 ppi	22	44	66	88	110	132	154	176	198	220	242	264	286	308	330
364 ppi	23	46	68	91	114	137	159	182	205	228	250	273	296	319	341
368 ppi	23	46	69	92	115	138	161	184	207	230	253	276	299	322	345
384 ppi	24	48	72	96	120	144	168	192	216	240	264	288	312	336	360
392 ppi	25	49	74	98	123	147	172	196	221	245	270	294	319	343	368
396 ppi	25	50	74	99	124	149	173	198	223	248	272	297	322	347	371
434 ppi	27	54	81	109	136	163	190	217	244	271	298	326	353	380	407
436 ppi	27	55	82	109	136	164	191	218	245	273	300	327	354	382	409
440 ppi	28	55	83	110	138	165	193	220	248	275	303	330	358	385	413
444 ppi	28	56	83	111	139	167	194	222	250	278	305	333	361	389	416
448 ppi	28	56	84	112	140	168	196	224	252	280	308	336	364	392	420
476 ppi	30	60	89	119	149	179	208	238	268	298	327	357	387	417	446
480 ppi	30	60	90	120	150	180	210	240	270	300	330	360	390	420	450

This chart shows the thickness of books depending on the pages per inch (ppi).

papers they regularly stock, and you'll get the best price by going with one of these.

Photographs

When using photographs inside a book, for best results work from 8″ × 10″ black-and-white glossies. However, 5″ × 7″ glossies will save some developing costs, are a little easier to work with, and will give results almost as good as the larger size. You can crop (omit from the printed photograph) edges of the picture to do away with unneeded or unwanted details or background. The best way to do this is to lightly mark the edges of the photo with a grease pencil indicating which parts of the photos are not to be used. Reducing or enlarging your photograph to fit the allocated space is easy. This process is called scaling. A photograph gets snappier when it's reduced; it can lose quality when it is enlarged. When a photograph is scanned, it's made into a halftone, a process that converts the picture into a pattern of tiny dots or pixels that, when printed, looks like the gray tones of a photograph.

One tip for ending up with quality photographs is to take instant pictures first. This helps you determine optimal lighting, balance, and other conditions. Another tip for good design is to place your photographs so they will have some white space around them. Don't crowd them or add any other graphic element.

The better a photo is, the better your halftone will be. But a good prepress or digital imaging specialist will be able to produce an adequate job from less than perfect pictures. We've done client books on city histories, for instance, where many of the photographs were priceless old gems of the horse and buggy era. Many were faded and had a matte rather than a glossy finish, and some were scratched. Nonetheless, the printed photographs turned out well. So don't despair if the photos you have to work from are less than ideal. Once a photo is scanned, software can be used to adjust the color levels and contrast. We've also worked from color photos and slides, converting them to black and white. When using photographs, key them to your manuscript by using the page number as the photo number. (If there's more than one to a page, go to a 91a, 91b, 91c tactic.) When numbering photos, do so very *lightly* on the back with a soft pencil or use a peel-off label on the back.

Photographs, and often illustrations and charts, require explanations. These are called cutlines or captions and should be brief but clear. Decide how you're going to approach this task, then be consistent. We find that making an artwork log is helpful. We list the number of the photo or art, then type the cutline beside it. This helps the typesetter and gives us a quick and complete reference list. It also gives a ready reference when preparing the list of illustrations for front matter.

As was mentioned earlier, using color photographs boosts the printing costs very quickly. There are ways, however, to minimize the costs. Careful planning by someone who knows what she is doing and can place the color between signatures might make it economically feasible for a self-publisher. Otherwise, it's probably off to Asia for printing.

Illustrations

Photographs are only one option for interior art design. You may be an artist yourself or want to include illustrations to amplify certain points. Illustrations help people understand information better. Many of us comprehend pictures more easily than words. These needn't be works of art per se; a simple sketch showing how to do something you're explaining can be a real aid to the reader.

If you're an amateur artist, don't cheapen your book with poor art. Professional artists are listed by fields of activity in the *LMP*. Look over their portfolios before you commission one. If you create the art, use black India ink for any drawings to be scanned, or use a computer graphic program if you have such skills. Avoid large blocks of ink, such as an all-black dog. (Why do you think old Spot is so popular?) When large expanses of ink are used, there's apt to be bleed-through to the reverse side of the page, with paper of average quality. The alternative is to go to a heavier, higher-quality, and more expensive grade of paper throughout the text.

A cardinal rule for interior art design is always to place the piece of art *after* your discussion of it. Have you ever tried to read a book where a diagram or illustration precedes the text that explains it? Distracting and confusing, at best.

And try not to bunch your art all in one place. Artwork breaks up page after page of text and gives your book texture and a sense of liveliness. If you want to add this touch by spending very little, consider clip art or click art. There are oodles of sources for CD-ROMs containing illustrations. But remember, the quality of the pieces is often reflected in the price. And be careful with the color aspect when using click art. Many of the illustrations will print in four-color process if left unaltered. But by selecting the image and designating black in the color palette, the art will print in shades of black ink, keeping your interior pages to one color.

Clip art is also a wonderful way to enliven your sales materials. And it's a cheap way to give a book of poetry fresh interest. Don't overlook illustrations in government publications, most of which can be freely reused. You may even find something in your local newspaper or the "junk mail" pile (assuming it isn't copyrighted).

Are there any special diagrams, charts, graphs, questionnaires, or exercises that could enhance your book? Consider an attractive approach for displaying them. If you're presenting technical information, be sure it's accurate. Nothing is more frustrating than to follow a plan for a woodworking project only to learn that the measurements are off.

Chapter Title Pages

Depending on your subject matter, a decorative touch on the chapter title pages might be nice. You could use clip art to suggest the chapter theme. Another frequently used visual device is a relevant quotation, or a bold horizontal line might work.

Your text for each new chapter typically begins about a third of the way down the page. Above it you have the chapter number, title, or both. For a nonfiction book, start each chapter on a recto (right-hand) page unless you're condensing to fit into even signatures. If you're also dividing your book into parts, each part title will ideally have a page to itself. Novels typically run page to page with chapters starting on both left- and right-hand pages.

Here again you have an opportunity to put typography to good use. For contrast you can use larger bold, italics, or a combination of both. Many book designers also add a second typeface for chapters, titles, subheads, or sub-subheads as long as it coordinates well with the text type.

Subheads

What about subheads? If you're doing a nonfiction book, these are not only helpful but for some subjects they're almost mandatory. Subheads allow the reader to scan and quickly find a topic. Think about how much less useful this book would be if there were only the main chapter titles without any subdivisions. In many cases sub-subheads are also helpful. We're using that technique right now. This will increase your typesetting costs a bit, but it will make your book more marketable and easier to use.

Image Size

Think about how much of the interior page you want covered with type. In a 5½″ × 8½″ book you might want an image size of 4″ × 7″. Be sure to leave plenty of blank room in the gutter—the space where facing pages come together. Although, you don't need to be concerned with leaving extra space in the gutter for binding considerations. Book manufacturers will take care of that. They know exactly how much space is needed for the particular types of book bindings. Don't have margins that are too skimpy. If you've ever picked up a mass-market paperback with barely a quarter inch of margin, you'll know what we mean. On the other hand, if your margins are too big, readers will feel you tried to stretch the book. The best test is to look at several volumes. You'll quickly gain a feel for what is pleasing.

In fact, a simple way to get a model of what you want overall is to go to a bookstore and buy one. Locate a book that has the layout, margins, feel, type, and so on you like. Then pattern yours after it. You'll want a dab more room at the bottom of the page than at the top for good visual balance. On page 181 is a sample page identifying where elements should go, and on page 182 is a *bad* example as well (one of those cases where a visual is worth a thousand words).

Remember, here is a place to expand or shrink the page count of your book. You can shrink the image size by deleting one pica or adding one line per page; either will result in the few pages' difference you might need to fit in even signatures.

Ink Color

Most books are printed in black ink. There is no set rule for this, however. A book of poetry or a cookbook might be more interesting if printed in brown, a lively green, or a rich blue, for instance. The cost is insignificant. But if your design requires that you use two (or more) ink colors, and if you believe that the increased cost will be justified, either aesthetically or by increased sales, then go ahead. Just be sure you calculate the higher cost in working out when your

Example of Page Design

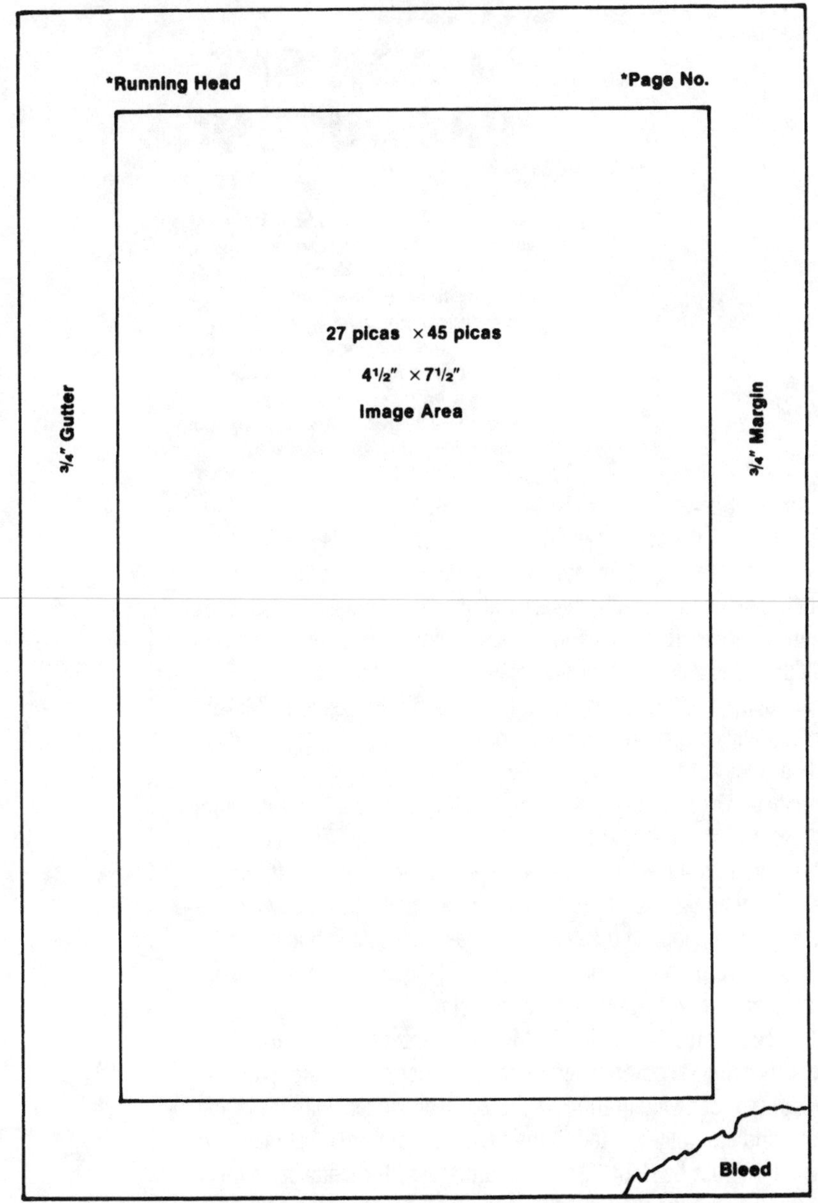

A dummy page showing image area for text, margins, running heads, and page number.

Example of Bad Page Design

8
DESIGN AND PRODUCTION

Before embarking on the printing of your book, there are several points to consider. What kind of a cover design should it have? What types of cover blurbs are most effective? How vital is good interior design and how can it be achieved? What's the lowdown on typesetting and pasteup? Are there secrets to good proofreading? How do you create an index?

The importance of good cover design

Let's talk about the cover design. If you expect to market the majority of your books through bookstores, your cover is your billboard and it had better be good. Book browsers will only give a book a few seconds of consideration. It must wrench their attention away from the hundreds or thousands of other volumes nearby. Since most books are shelved spine out, this narrow strip is your first sales tool. Make it stand out with arresting color and compelling lettering. It should display the title, author, and publisher.

Next, book browsers look at the book's front. If it interests them, they'll turn to the back. If they're still intrigued, the front and back flaps—if there's a dust jacket—will receive their consideration.

The local bookstore offers a tremendous resource for cover analysis. Here you can look at the designs of best-sellers and books similar to yours. Do your homework well. Many self-published books turn out looking amateurish because of poor design.

Your cover must be distinctive! Make it capture the essence of the book. This can be accomplished through the use of lettering, dynamic copy, a photo, or an illustration. It should be consistent with the inside material and carefully slanted to the tastes of your potential reader. If you were doing a book of interest to attorneys, for instance, dignity rather than flamboyance would be the key. Don't confuse busyness with boldness. You want a dramatic cover, not one with meaningless clutter.

Poor page design has narrow side margins and flows too high and low on the page.

book can be expected to break even (earn enough to cover expenses) and start making a profit.

Doing children's books in full color is enormously expensive. Consider instead treating them as coloring books or using just two interior colors.

Footnotes

Unless you are producing a scholarly work or a textbook, it is best to avoid footnotes. They distract the reader and increase the typesetting costs. When you must use them, place a number after the material to be annotated and give the explanation at the bottom of the same page with the same number. When there are a lot of references, it may be best to number them in the text, then include a consecutive list at the end of the chapter or book. These are endnotes. Your word processing or desktop publishing program will help immensely.

Front Matter

Just as a sandwich has a piece of bread on the top and bottom to hold the ingredients inside, a book has pages of front and back matter that sandwich the main text. While in most books front matter is either not numbered or numbered with roman numerals, we suggest using letters of the alphabet on your manuscript copy of the front matter for the sake of simplicity and clarity. If you want roman numerals on the finished book, the typesetter (who will know the difference between XVI and XIV) can put them in for you. If you want to mark either numbers or letters on the galleys, use a pencil with light, nonreproducing blue lead that won't photograph.

It is our opinion that front matter should be designed to fill all available pages without going over, thus keeping down printing and paper costs. Let's elaborate on that for a minute. Offset books are printed on large flat sheets or continuous roll paper with 4, 8, 16, or 32 pages to a side. Since these sheets are printed on both sides, books are ultimately made up of signatures that are twice these increments. Signatures most commonly consist of 16 or 32 pages. It is important that you be aware of these multiples and plan for them in your book. Ask your printer what size signatures her press provides.

If you envision a 64-page book, but find it is going to run 65 pages, you will be charged for another whole signature or for the manual labor required to cut out the unnecessary pages. So it makes sense and saves dollars to use all available space or to look for ways to trim your manuscript to avoid going into an additional signature. Perhaps you can change the size of the type image on the page, tighten up the line spacing, delete or reduce a photograph, or tighten chapter beginnings.

Here is how front matter lays out.

Page A. The half-title (also known as the bastard title) page consists only of the main title. The subtitle is omitted, as is the author's name.

Page B. The back (verso) of the half-title page is usually blank.

Page C. Your second page on the right (recto) will be the title page. It should include—you guessed it—the title, subtitle if any, author's full name, plus publishing house name and address. Also include the illustrator's, editor's, photographer's, and foreword writer's name if any of these people are well known or otherwise important to the book.

Page D. The copyright page (title page verso) is the back of the title page. It contains much vital information. See the sample on page 185. There is the © symbol (which secures world rights), the year, and your name as the copyright holder.

Speaking of copyright, here's a trade secret that was told to us by a top executive of a major New York publisher: When a book will roll off the press anytime after September 1, it is automatically assigned the *next year's* copyright date. Thus a book published September 15, 2001, would carry a 2002 copyright date. This prevents the "yearling effect" that is so prevalent in horse breeding—that on the first of January everything is a year older. We suggest all small publishers follow this example and give themselves sixteen months to promote the work as a new book instead of just four. Of course, this applies to books published in October, November, and December, as well. (We also checked with the copyright office and found that this is an acceptable practice and that you don't forfeit any protection.)

Also include the terms "All rights reserved" and "Printed and bound in the United States of America" (if it is), plus "First printing" and the year. You can secure copyright merely by publishing your book with a valid copyright notice. Registration with the copyright office just registers a copyright that already exists; this can be done at any reasonable time after the book has been published—even years later.

On the other hand, don't register your copyright too soon. We've seen people copyright their manuscripts while in the writing stage, though they aren't in a position to get the books printed for two years. Their books are then stuck with that two-year-old copyright date and, to reviewers and others in the industry, look old. (To obtain information on copyright in Canada, contact the Canadian Copyright Institute, 35 Spadina Rd., Toronto, Ontario M5R 2S9, www.web.net/~ccinst. And a free copyright kit is available from the Canadian Intellectual Property Office, Industry Canada, 50 Victoria St., Hull, Quebec K1A 0C9.)

The copyright page is also where you will list the Library of Congress Catalog Number, Cataloging in Publication data if applicable, and the ISBN. If there are a lot of trademarked names in the book, we prefer to list them here alphabeti-

Copyright Page

> © 2001 Robert K. Smith. Printed and bound in the United States of America. All rights reserved. No part of this book may be reproduced or transmitted in any form or by any means, electronic or mechanical, including photocopying, recording, or by an information storage and retrieval system—except by a reviewer who may quote brief passages in a review to be printed in a magazine, newspaper, or on the Web—without permission in writing from the publisher. For information, please contact My Publishing Company, 345 Sunshine Road, Suite 101, Buena Vista, CO 81211.
>
> Although the author and publisher have made every effort to ensure the accuracy and completeness of information contained in this book, we assume no responsibility for errors, inaccuracies, omissions, or any inconsistency herein. Any slights of people, places, or organizations are unintentional.
> First printing 2001
>
> ISBN 0-9706790-2-5
>
> LCCN 2001131124
>
> ATTENTION CORPORATIONS, UNIVERSITIES, COLLEGES, AND PROFESSIONAL ORGANIZATIONS: Quantity discounts are available on bulk purchases of this book for educational, gift purposes, or as premiums for increasing magazine subscriptions or renewals. Special books or book excerpts can also be created to fit specific needs. For information, please contact My Publishing Company, 345 Sunshine Road, Suite 101, Buena Vista, CO 81211; ph 710-395-6789.

Here are the elements we feel should appear on your copyright page. Note the disclaimer and the plug for bulk sales.

cally rather than have the symbol intrude on the reader's flow. If you want to place a disclaimer in the book, this is an appropriate spot. Here is a disclaimer we used for a client's book on a health subject:

> Although the authors and publisher have exhaustively researched all sources to ensure the accuracy and completeness of the information contained in this book, we assume no responsibility for errors, inaccuracies, omissions, or any inconsistency herein. Any slights of people or organizations are unintentional. Readers should use their own judgment or consult a holistic medical expert or their personal physicians for specific applications to their individual problems.

Notice the blurb at the bottom of the sample copyright page above. This kind of suggestive selling can open the door to lucrative bulk sales.

Page E. Here is a good location for the dedication or acknowledgment. You may also want to list any previous books you've written or list them on a separate page.

Page F. At this point you can put in the foreword, "note to the reader," or preface. The author's preface should follow any of the above. While many would also tuck the introduction here, we suggest it be placed as the first item following the table of contents. It's much more likely to be read there.

Page G. Now (or later if your previous entries run longer than our example) comes the table of contents. Begin on a recto page. Take pains in writing your table of contents. Many people make buying decisions by scanning this recap of a book's contents. Give it sizzle. Make sure it presents a thorough, enticing overview of the ingredients. You might study the table of contents of this book as a model. (Also be alert to leaving space for the appropriate page numbers, which must be added after the whole book is typeset and numbered.) If your book contains many illustrations, diagrams, or charts, you should create a list of illustrations. It typically falls on the page following the table of contents.

* * *

This concludes front matter. You may choose to spread things out a bit to have key elements on recto pages for easier reading. Just be aware that such luxurious designing might cause you to run over into another signature and boost the cost of the book. Of course, you can use this technique as an expander, filling out a few pages and thereby getting to an even signature. On the contrary, you can shrink your book by eliminating the half-title page and flipping some of the recto starts to verso starts—such as moving the table of contents from page XII to page XI—to prevent running over even signatures.

Back Matter

Now on to back matter. You may choose not to have all the things we'll be talking about, so just skip what doesn't apply. First there is the appendix (or appendices). If you have long lists of items, names and addresses, or material that intrudes upon the message, these are best saved for an appendix. This has two advantages: It makes the material easy to locate for quick reference, and it doesn't interfere with the flow of the book itself. Next comes the bibliography or recommended reading. A glossary, if included, follows. Then the index. Its purpose is to help the reader find information quickly and easily. In some manuals you also see an afterword, which is a personal message in which the author wishes the reader success and sometimes requests feedback for improving subsequent editions. Occasionally a colophon will appear at the end of the book. A colophon details the production facts about the book, such as the computer and word processing system used, type style, designer, typesetter, printer, kind of paper, binding, and so forth.

It's a good idea to include a final page with an order form for obtaining additional books. Place it so readers will not be snipping away part of the book when they cut it out, although most people will photocopy it. The last recto page is ideal.

Canadian author-publisher-speaker Dave Chilton believes in order forms in a big way. When we first advised him to add one to his already-successful Canadian book, *The Wealthy Barber*—which offers homespun advice about financial planning in a fictional barbershop setting—people laughed at him. Now he laughs all the way to the bank. "It went wonderfully well," reports Chilton. "A lot of people buy four or six copies at a time to give to friends. The other thing it did was plant the idea that you could buy the book in bulk. We've sold almost a quarter of a million in the corporate arena. Of course that's very lucrative; the margins are better, and the corporate sales lead to more bookstore sales."

Chilton is one of the most aggressive and prosperous authors we know. He took a whole year off from his speaking practice when his book first came out to devote his time exclusively to generating publicity and developing special sales. His entire focus was on making his book well known. Was he successful? Chilton sold 12,000 copies in the first two months. The book leaped onto Canada's best-seller list. Overwhelmed, he farmed out the bookstore, wholesale, library, and educational sales to Stoddard Publishing. But he retained control over special sales, bought books from Stoddard at slightly above cost, then remarketed them to the corporate sector.

Chilton ultimately negotiated a deal with Prima Publishing to handle the book in the United States. This guy is a quick study. He didn't ask for a big advance. Instead he insisted on an exclusive for special sales, a significant purchasing discount, and a contractual obligation for them to send him on tour. "I'll get the money later," he says. And he's right. Many self-publishers would be wise to follow his lead. A fat advance is a onetime shot in the arm. Retaining rights, getting a good discount, and demanding promotional support will usually lead to strong ongoing profits.

Another of his personal achievements was capturing the prime spot for the PBS TV Pledge Drive. Viewers all over the country have seen *The Wealthy Barber With David Chilton* on some 340 member stations in 150 top markets. (This is what really launched Leo Buscaglia, John Bradshaw, Les Brown, and others.)

"A lot of my success is attributed to *The Complete Guide to Self-Publishing*," he says. Ironically, Chilton bought the book on a lark. At the time, he wasn't even thinking of writing or self-publishing. "It seemed like a fun thing to do," he comments. It was. He relates getting his first book order and driving down to show it to his wife at work. "We got more excited about that first order than if we get an order for 6,000 books today," he relates. Yet the orders pour in. At the time we interviewed Chilton for this vignette, his book was selling at the rate of 25,000 copies a *month* and had sold more than 700,000 copies.

* * *

Turning your raw manuscript into an attractive book is a challenging and satisfying process. You can do the interior design yourself if you adhere to the tips we've offered so far and pay attention to the next section, or hire a professional graphic designer to do it. If you have only so much cash, we feel a pro can better serve you by creating the cover.

If you've decided to handle all the design functions yourself, there are two books we recommend you get: *Page Layout*, edited by Roger Walton, provides endless inspiration, and *How to Understand and Use Design and Layout*, by Alan Swann, works wonders for the novice trying to wade through technical details.

Page Design and Typesetting

Now let's look at the actual typesetting phase of publishing. When getting your book ready for printing, you can either prepare the text yourself or hire a graphic designer. While hiring a professional may seem expensive, it can be a lot less so than charging out and buying additional computer software and equipment to do the job yourself.

Desktop publishing isn't always the panacea it's touted to be. If you suspect you are a one-book person, it probably isn't prudent to spend large sums on a laser printer, necessary software, PostScript fonts, and possibly the scanner you'll need. Plus remember the learning curve involved. If, on the other hand, you foresee a continuum of books on the horizon, it might be a good investment. Also keep in mind the additional hardware requirements for the software programs—the more bells and whistles, the more hardware (memory and hard disk space) required.

Please remember that buying a page layout program will not automatically make you a book designer. It's been said that it used to be easy to spot a self-published book by its cover. That may no longer be true, since even the most inexperienced novice now recognizes the importance of cover design in projecting a professional image. Now, what separates a quality product from its poorly produced counterpart is usually interior design. Professionalism is evident, even on the page of a book.

Do-It-Yourself

You feel proficient on your computer, so you've decided to do your own interior page layout. There are some choices you'll need to make and necessary equipment to invest in if you don't already have it. The first thing you need to decide is how you'll be providing your finished book to your printer. We don't discuss working with a book printer until the next chapter, but you really need to be thinking about it at this point. Different companies have different requirements. Most book manufacturers today prefer receiving digital files of your finished book. Some do *everything* electronically and go straight to plate from your computer disk. If you really want to work with a specific company, and it's one that uses this technology, then sending camera-ready pages is out of the question. Others may charge you extra if you provide camera-ready copy instead of digital files.

Most book manufacturers will accept either PC or Macintosh files. They do, however, have rigid requirements on the types of software or final files they will take. The most common page layout programs they accept files from are Adobe PageMaker or QuarkXPress. There are more: Adobe InDesign and FrameMaker, Corel VENTURA and others. But be sure to talk to your printer ahead of time about compatibility. It's costly in both time and money to run into electronic file "bugs" after your book is at the printer. You've probably been using a word processing program, such as Microsoft Word or Corel WordPerfect, for your writing and editing. These word processing files can be imported directly into the page layout software file. The learning process on these page layout programs, however, is a big consideration.

The reason most printing companies won't take your final layout in a word processing program is that those programs won't hold a print driver. Have you ever opened a disk from someone else's computer and gotten a message that says the print driver (from the other person's computer) isn't found and will be replaced by yours? Then if you compare printed pages that person sent with what's on your computer screen, the document isn't paginating the same way. That's why.

Every print driver will space the type differently. Page layout programs will embed a print driver that you designate. So as long as another computer has the same driver installed, the pages will look exactly the same when the files are opened. So if you send a Word file to a book manufacturer, you could end up with a mess—extra pages, graphics in the wrong place—you get the idea. Which leads us to print drivers.

Your computer will need to be set up with PostScript print drivers in order to make the PostScript files necessary for your book printer. Your printer can tell you the PostScript driver he prefers you use for his particular equipment. If you have a non-PostScript printer, such as an ink-jet printer, installed on your computer, you probably don't have PostScript print drivers. If you have a PostScript laser printer, then you're part of the way there. If your book manufacturer requests a specific print driver, you can either find it on your computer operating system CD (like your Windows installation CD), get it from your book printer, or download it from the Internet.

If you don't have them already, you'll have to invest in PostScript fonts. The TrueType fonts that came free with your word processing program won't work here. Sending digital files to any printer requires PostScript fonts. The biggest provider of PostScript fonts is Adobe. You can purchase them online at www.Adobe.com. Each font package or family (for example, the regular, italic, bold, and bold italic make up a typical font family) will cost $100 or more.

If you plan to scan your own photos or graphics, you'll need a good-quality scanner. Flatbed scanners go from cheap to out-of-sight. Be sure you get a good one. It does make a difference in the quality of your graphics. For your interior graphics, you'll need to scan at a minimum of 300 ppi, and if you have photos or illustrations with a lot of detail, up to 600 ppi is better. Then of course you'll need the software to operate with your scanner. We use Adobe Photoshop, which is popular, but there are others on the market, as well. This software will enable you to adjust contrast and color levels (yes, even black-and-white photos and illustrations have color levels to adjust for a better-looking end result) and crop and size your art. A scanning tip: Always scan and adjust the size of your art or photo before you place it in your page layout program. If you adjust the size later, the dots or pixels will be distorted. For example, your 300-ppi photo scanned at 2 inches wide, then enlarged to 4 inches wide on your page, will end up being only 150 ppi. There are many file formats to choose from in saving your electronic scans. To get the best quality, you'll want to save them as .tif or .eps files.

Your printer is another consideration. A PostScript laser printer is the best, although it's pricier. Sure, you can get a color ink-jet printer for less than $100, but in most cases you'll get what you pay for. If you've decided not to provide digital files to your printer, your camera-ready pages must look great! A 600-ppi laser printer is a must in this case, because with every generation those pages go through, the quality will decrease. From your laser printers, your book printer will be shooting negatives, then burning plates. So you need to start with the best quality possible. By the way, to get even better solid blacks on your final camera-ready originals, see your office supply store for a ream of the smooth, bright white laser paper made by several paper manufacturers.

If you are providing digital files, your printer is not quite as important. You'll need an adequate printer to proof your pages and to provide a printout for your book manufacturer to go along with your files. You'll still want a printer good enough to give an accurate representation of what you're getting. And there's a big variance between printers. Recently we had a client who approved an initial cover proof printed from our cover designer's color printer. The sky was dark and brooding—a charcoal gray color. Right before going to the printer, we printed a final proof for the client's approval from the high-quality color printer in our office. The sky in the designer's electronic file was actually completely black, but his color printer didn't print it that way. The client wanted charcoal gray, so it was back to the drawing board.

Once you have everything you need, you can start on your book design. The decisions to be made about the type itself include style, size, and the white space around it. When designing fliers or ads, you can be daring with typefaces. In book design, however, the hallmark of good typography is *legibility*. It gets the job done without calling attention to itself. There are two major families of type: serifs and sans serifs. Serifs are much easier to read because they have little hooks on them that serve to hold the eye on the line. Readers have been trained to read body copy in serifs from the time they entered kindergarten. School books, newspapers, and most magazines are done in this family. Some common easy-to-read styles are Century, Times Roman, Bodoni, Garamond, Palatino, and Bookman. When you find a style that pleases you, stick with it rather than mixing faces. The place to introduce something different, such as a sans serif typeface, is in the chapter titles or subheads. Please limit the number of different fonts you use to two or three at the most. You don't want your book looking like a ransom note.

What about size? Point is one of the standard units of measurement used in typesetting. A point is approximately 1⁄72 inch. In other words, there are 72 points to an inch. The other standard unit of measurement is the pica. One pica equals 12 points, or (approximately) 1⁄6 inch. Line lengths for typeset copy are specified in picas. For instance, a line that measures 4 inches wide would be designated as 24 picas. Picas appear on the accompanying Typography Chart on pages 193 and 194.

The white space between lines is called line space or leading. It is typically the type size plus two. For example, 10/12 indicates 10-point type with 12-point leading. Its purpose is to make the lines of type spread apart enough that they do not strain the eye. For a more open look with additional white space, you can add another point or two of leading.

The higher the number of points, the larger the size. Most newspapers and magazines are done in 9- or 10-point type. On the Typography Chart you will see that 11 point is a nice, readable size (though it can vary from one style to another). The kind of book often dictates a size range. A children's book, for instance, will want larger type. And for goodness' sake, if you have a long book with few illustrations for relief, don't force the reader to plow through the whole thing in 9-point type! How condensed the typeface is will also have a bearing on how much you can get on a page. Some fonts really pack in the copy. If your book is running a bit too long, you can use a more condensed type that is still highly legible, and you'll save going into a new signature for just a page or two. For instance, Garamond is more condensed (has more characters to the inch) than Bodoni.

Now is a good time to refer back to your initial castoff. Will the typeface, point size, and leading you selected give the characters or words per page you calculated? If not, it is easy enough to adjust things to expand or shrink your book to size.

There are certain things you may want highlighted by the use of boldface or italics. Chapter headings and other important divisions should be done in boldface or with a different font. One book designer said that good interior design is like a football referee: It works best when you don't notice it. Just because your software can create lots of special effects doesn't mean you need to use them all in this one book. Make your book as easy as possible for your reader to use. If you're working on a novel, you'll want the text to flow smoothly with few interruptions. If you're designing a how-to book that the reader will refer back to again and again, you'll want to emphasize main points, use breakout charts for important information, or incorporate sidebars. Think about the end user of your book.

Since you're using your computer and software, your book will most likely be complete and finished as it looks on your monitor. However, if you've decided to provide camera-ready art to your printer, you forgo the scanning of photos and graphics. You can reserve space for your graphics or photos with a box, add the cutline under the box, and have your manufacturer shoot halftones of your photos to strip in. Another alternative is taking your photos or illustrations to a prepress or digital-imaging company for scanning to electronic file. If you decide to do pasteup of anything on your camera-ready pages, however, be aware that wax will almost certainly create a smear, so you're relegated to using rubber cement. Keep those pages clean!

Now you need to prepare the digital files for your printer. If your printer will accept your application files—the actual PageMaker, Quark, or whatever page layout files you've been working on—you need to be sure to include all the files, every font you've used, and every graphic or photo file you've imported. Book printers have said this is the biggest problem they run into. If you don't include each item,

Typography Chart

132

The Author's Guide to

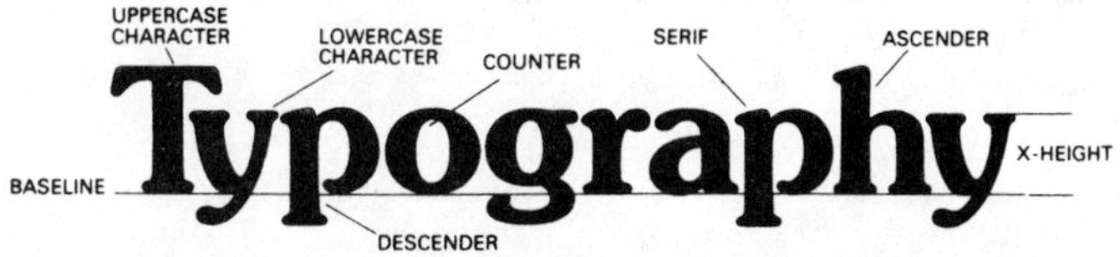

UPPERCASE CHARACTER
LOWERCASE CHARACTER
COUNTER
SERIF
ASCENDER
BASELINE
Typography
X-HEIGHT
DESCENDER

The words are yours and type is the medium used to convey these words to the reader. The right typeface can enhance your concepts and embellish the appearance of your book. It is the job of the designer to make those choices that would most effectively convey your meaning. To give you a sense of what the designer deals with, the following is a general description of the most used typographic terms:

Melior
Optima
Palatino
Serif Gothic
Bodoni
Caslon
Bauhaus Demi
Benquiat
Baskerville
Caledonia

Ascender—The part of a lowercase letter above the x-height

Baseline—The line on which the characters appear to stand

Characters—Individual letters, figures and punctuation marks

Counter—The enclosed or hollow part of a letter

Descender—The part of a lowercase letter that falls below the baseline

Em—A printer's unit of width measurement which is equal to the body size of the type in question. An 8-point em is 8 points; a 14-point em is 14 points, etc. It takes its name from the widest letter in any typeface: M.

Font—A complete alphabet: one typeface in one size

Italic—A type in which the forms slant to the right

Justify—To set a line to a desired measure

Leading—The spacing between lines (measured in points)

Letterspacing—The space between the letters in a word

Lowercase letters (l.c.)—The small letters

Pica—A unit used to measure the length of a line of type. One pica (0.166") consists of 12 points and six picas (72 pt.) equal one inch

Point—Used to measure the typesize—from the top of the ascender to the bottom of the descender plus space above and below to prevent the lines of type from touching. The point (0.1383") is the basic unit of printer's measurement.

This shows a few different type faces, defines some typographic terms, and gives examples of various sizes.

they'll have to hold your project up while they contact you and wait for the missing parts. These page layout files will be large, so your computer will need a CD writer, Zip drive, or some other way to transport the files to your printer.

Typography Chart, continued

133

Ragged right, ragged left—Unjustifed type that is allowed to run to various line lengths

Roman—A type in which all the letters are upright.

Sans serif—A typeface without serifs

Serif—The short strokes that project from the ends of the main body strokes of a typeface

Typeface—A specific design for a type alphabet

Type family—All the styles and sizes of a given type

Word spacing—The spacing between words in a line

Uppercase letters (u.c. or c.)—The capital letters or caps

x-height—The height of the lowercase x in a given typeface

Three commonly used faces shown in various sizes.

Baskerville	Times Roman	Univers
9/10 Once upon a time once upon a time once upon a time once upon a time once upon a time once upon a time once upon	9/10 Once upon a time once upon a time once upon a time once upon a time once upon a time once upon a time once upon a time once upon	9/10 Once upon a time on ce upon a time once upon a time once up on a time once upon a time once upon a time once upon a t
10/11 Once upon a time once upon a time once upon a time once upon a time once upon a time	10/11 Once upon a time on ce upon a time once upon a time once up on a time once upon a time once upon a	10/11 Once upon a time once upon a time once upon a time once upon a time once upon a time
11/12 Once upon a time once upon a time once upon a time once upon a time once upon a time once upon a time	11/12 Once upon a time o nce upon a time on ce upon a time onc e upon a time once upon a time once u pon a time once up	11/12 Once upon a time once upon a time once upon a time once upon a time once upon a time onceuponatime

A showing of 18 pt. Souvenir Roman (the face used for this book).

abcdefghijklmnopqrstuvwxyz1234567890
ABCDEFGHIJKLMNOPQRSTUVWXYZ$

Trade Gothic

Garamond

Century

Cooper Black

Univers

Korinna

Gill Sans

Helvetica

Tiffany

Times Roman

Futura

Some printers won't accept your application files or will charge you extra for processing them. In that case, you'll need to create PostScript files. In one way this is simpler, because the PostScript files embed your fonts and graphics within them, so you don't have to send so many pieces. The most common PostScript format right now is the .pdf file. We use Adobe PageMaker for our page layout, and this program easily creates .pdf files. Be sure you're creating a "print" .pdf file. Otherwise, you'll get a low-resolution "on screen" .pdf used on Web sites. It will look fine on your computer monitor but will print at a shocking 72 dpi. The word processing software companies say they are going to be coming out with new versions soon that will create .pdf files. This may change the page layout software requirement when it comes to book design.

Working With a Professional

Suppose you prefer to go the professional route all the way. Be sure to have a manuscript that's as clean as possible, edited, proofread, and finalized. Prepare a disk with the files named to clearly indicate what they are. Always keep the original on your computer or a disk for yourself, as well. Also print a hard copy for the designer to refer to. Strange things can happen when transferring files from one computer to another.

Step two is to shop. Compare. Negotiate. Find a designer you personally like and can work with, someone who is willing to take the time to explain things, hear your ideas, and advise. Ask for, and study, samples of her work. We mentioned this when talking about cover designers, but the same advice applies here. Just because someone has done graphic design, doesn't mean she is a book designer. There is specialized knowledge necessary in knowing how to design a book effectively and correctly. Look for a *book* designer.

Prices will fluctuate wildly. While one company will turn out work for $5 a page, the next wants $25. Of course, the condition of the manuscript you provide will have some bearing on your costs. Clean copy without much formatting done in your word processing program goes a long way toward getting a good deal. Elements such as different fonts and larger type sizes for your subheads should be added in typesetting not in your editing file.

Make sure you are comparing apples to apples, not apples to oranges, when getting bids. Every bid should be for the identical product. Do all include design, typesetting of running copy plus chapter heads, and running heads or feet? Do the bidders know how many graphics, photos or charts are included and how you'll be providing them? Does price include footnotes or endnotes if required? If designer A bids $12 a page but doesn't include page headers and B bids $16 a page but *does* include them, B may actually be more economical. Be sure you communicate to them the number of finished pages you're shooting for from your castoff. You also should be able to get electronic file specifications from your printer to pass on so designers know what's required as an end product.

One tip for trimming costs is to schedule your work during downtime. Although "downtime" is often used to refer to the period when equipment isn't usable because it's broken or being fixed, we're using it here to mean time when the designer's business is slow. Equipment is idle, but there's still a payroll to meet. Often the designer will settle for a smaller margin of profit under these circumstances. Unfortunately, the best competitive book designers seldom have a lull. In fact, make sure a lull is not due to poor quality. And, of course, being scheduled during idle time could cause your job to take longer, since you will be last priority. Discuss this with your designer.

When you've decided on a designer, the first step should be preparing style pages. You'll want to work with the designer on the overall style of your book before the complete book is formatted. What will the title page look like? The chapter start pages? How are the headers and footers going to be handled? What will subheads and sub-subheads be like? Your charts or graphics? Do you like the fonts the designer has chosen? Is the book readable? Does it give the feeling and look you envisioned? We always provide clients with samples of all these elements for their approval.

Once you're happy with these styles, the entire book will be formatted from your disk. If you'll have an index in your book, communicate this to the designer ahead of time so pages will be allowed for it. When the pages are laid out and you know where everything will be, you can work on your index, which we explain shortly.

Proofreading Procedures

When you get back the galleys (proof pages of the finished book), read with the eye of an eagle. Clearly mark any corrections you want, using accepted proofreader's marks (see page 197) and a red pen. Watch especially for transposed letters and omitted or duplicated words. When you find such a mistake, correct it and write "PE" in the margin, signifying printer's error (if, indeed, it was a printer's error). This way, *you* will not be charged for correcting the error. Should you find oodles of errors or a serious blunder, always request a corrected set of proofs to be sure the problems are rectified.

If there is something *you* want to change, make the change and mark it "AA," which stands for author's alteration. From here on, changes become expensive; this is *not* the time to do extensive rewriting. Each line you alter will cost from $1 to $2. Although that doesn't seem like much, some changes will bump the rest of the paragraph or even the entire page. Costs can escalate quickly when this happens.

It's a good idea to ask a friend, relative, or associate to cross-check the manuscript against the typeset copy with you. Typesetters who must rekey the manuscript have been known to omit whole paragraphs or repeat words. Far better to take some extra time now than suffer the heartbreak of catching major errors

Proofreader's Marks

Proofreader's Marks

Compliments of **Writer's Digest School**

MARK	EXPLANATION	(In margin.) EXAMPLE (In text.)	
ℓ	Take out character indicated.	ℓ	Your manuscript.
stet	Let it stay.	stet	Your manuscript.
#	Put in space.	#	Yourmanuscript.
⌒	Close up completely.		Writer's Di gest School.
tr	Transpose; change places.	tr	Yuor manuscript.
caps or ≡	Use capital letters.	caps	writer's digest school. writer's digest school.
lc	Use lower case letters.	lc	Your Manuscript.
bf or ~~~	Use bold face type.	bf	Writer's Digest School. Writer's Digest School.
ital or ___	Use italic type.	ital	Writer's Digest. Writer's Digest.
✓'	Put in apostrophe.	✓'	Writers Digest School.
⊙	Put in period.	⊙	Your manuscript
,/	Put in comma.	,/	Your manuscript
:/	Put in colon.	:/	Your manuscript
;/	Put in semicolon.	;/	Writer's Digest School
✓" ✓"	Put in quotation marks.	✓" ✓"	He said, Yes.
(?)	Question to author.	(?) No hyphen OK	Free lance writer.
=/	Put in hyphen.	=/	Free lance writer.
!	Put in exclamation.	!	This is great
?	Put in question mark.	?	Are you starting
(/)	Put in parenthesis.	(/)	Your first rough draft.
¶	Start paragraph.	¶	a writer. Learn to sell
‖	Even out lines.	‖	Writer's Digest and Writer's Digest School.
⊏	Move the line left.		Your manuscript.
⊐	Move the line right.		Your manuscript.
No ¶	No paragraph; run together.	No ¶	a writer. There are more needed
out, sc	Something missing, see copy.	out, sc	Writer's School.
spell out	Spell it out.	spell out	Your ms.

These are the main notations editors use to show changes to a manuscript.

when the completed book is in your hands. Errors in your finished book will flash like neon signs. To accomplish this double check, one person reads aloud while the other follows the text. Trade off occasionally so neither of you loses your voice.

Or you may want to have a professional proofreader do the job for you. This will help weed out any spelling or grammatical errors resulting from your own blind spots, plus errors the typesetter has reproduced. Proofreading will cost you, but your book will be the better for it. Your printer or typesetter may be able to give you a name.

However you do your proofreading, close scrutiny at this point will prepare a quality product. Of course your main proofreading was done before the manuscript was typeset. We still recommend, however, you carefully check it in case any computer gremlins have taken up residence in your project.

Now, review your pages with the following in mind: Is the book thoughtfully presented? Are the subject areas and subareas clearly marked? How about arty touches that make reading a pleasure? Do graphics provide a visual rest as well as adding helpful and stimulating information?

Watch for widows and orphans. No, we don't mean women who have lost their husbands or parentless children. A widow is the last line of a paragraph that appears alone at the top of a new page while the rest of the paragraph is on the bottom of the previous page. An orphan is the first line of a paragraph that appears alone at the bottom of a page while the rest of the paragraph is on the next page. You display a cleaner design if you let the page fall short or run long rather than allowing widows or orphans. Of course, your computer software can automatically accomplish this task, but check it.

Here are some other things to watch for:

- Check the bottom of each page against the beginning of the next page to be sure words or entire lines didn't accidentally get left out.
- Be sure all artwork, photographs, charts, or graphs are in appropriate places and have the necessary cutlines.
- Check the headers and footers on each page.
- In a nonfiction book, remember to leave blank pages if necessary so that chapters will start on recto pages (if you have enough pages for this lavish format).
- Check the page numbers on each page. (You count, but don't necessarily have to number, chapter title pages and full pages of illustrations.)
- Check that the page numbers in the table of contents are accurate.
- Photocopy your pages before sending them to the printer (always keep at least one set for your own reference).
- Now is the time to create your index.

Creating an Irresistible Index

An index increases a book's usefulness and salability. But how do you go about giving this mass of information shape and form? Indexing can be reasonably simple when approached logically. It is basically a series of decisions. And no one is more familiar with the material—or better equipped to make these decisions—than you. (Ironically, many trade publishing houses delegate this function to a freelance indexer, typically paid out of the author's royalties.)

In creating your index, work from a photocopy of the final book. First, think through the book; review your outline or the table of contents for a mind jog. You wouldn't want to slight any primary idea or philosophy. This is an intellectual, as well as clerical, task. Decide on the main concepts of your book. Consider how readers will use it. What questions will they have? What material may they wish to locate again? Look at the indexes in several books from your personal library to get a feel for format.

Virtually all the new page layout and word processing programs have powerful built-in indexing capabilities. Most allow you to create a concordance, which is a list of frequently appearing names, terms, or words. Then the indexing program automatically searches the entire book and lists each page number where the words appear. You also go through the text and mark the appropriate words. Then when you create the index it automatically adds the page numbers and creates an alphabetical list. This is a tremendous boon and saves laborious hours for frustrated authors.

Regardless of whether you're indexing by computer or manually, you get to read your book again. As you read, highlight the items to be indexed. By using different-colored highlighters, you can indicate the main entries and subentries. (If you are indexing manually, arm yourself with a horde of 3″ × 5″ cards and a file box with A–Z alphabetical file dividers.) Begin scanning on page one. Identify and mark subjects, proper names, charts, and so on and their page numbers. Write each on a *separate* file card if you're doing it manually. (No adjectives, folks; just the facts, please.) As you make a notation on a file card, place it behind the appropriate A–Z divider, then if you find the same subject on a later page, it will be easy to locate the card and add the new reference. Alphabetize entries strictly by the first word, disregarding *the*, *an*, *of*, and *a*.

Try to hit a happy medium: neither too general nor so nitpicky that the index ends up almost as long as the book. The American Society of Indexers contends there should be three to five pages of index for every hundred pages of text. A very useful Indexing Evaluation Checklist is available on ASI's Web site at www.asindexing.org/checklist.shtml.

Don't overlook cross-indexing. Suppose you have a cookbook with a recipe titled Marinated Fish Supreme. It should be listed under the *M*s and the *F*s ("Fish, recipes for"). Also consider "See" and "See also" cross-references. Use subentries generously. When there are several references to a general topic, it's convenient to enter the reference to general discussion first, then the specific features in alphabetical order:

Formal writing, 123–235
    mixed with informal, 132–33
    sentence structure of, 128
    when appropriate, 126–27

If you are using indexing on a word processing program, rather than in the final page layout program, you have some makeready to do. Go back through the book on your computer and repaginate it to match exactly your typeset pages. Now you simply follow the instructions for your index program. Happily, alphabetizing is done automatically.

Let's suppose you have a computer but no index program. You can still do a computerized index more easily than by hand. First, set up an A–Z format. Then enter all the highlighted data alphabetically. If you goof and put something in the wrong place, it's easy to electronically move it.

When you've finished categorizing the entire book, review each file card or your computer screen to make sure you haven't added fluff or meaningless words that shouldn't be indexed. Are the most obvious and helpful keywords used? Remember to think like a reader who's using the book. Further, to see if you've accomplished your aim, take a few random pages and look up the subjects they relate to in the index. Are they covered? Any cross-references missed the first time around? Are all the cards properly alphabetized? If so, all that remains is to type the 3″ × 5″ cards into page form, and you have an index ready to fire off to the typesetter.

If you're doing your own typesetting, use the index in this book as a guideline; design and format yours accordingly. Proofread it thoroughly.

You may decide to hire a professional indexer. Be sure you contract for the creation of your index as "work made for hire." This most likely won't become an issue, but that way you're sure you have complete rights to print and reprint your index, as well as electronic rights. The best way to locate an indexer is by contacting the American Society of Indexers, which will mail you a free copy of the *Indexer Locator*, a comprehensive list of indexers with experience or expertise in particular fields. You can also find it online at www.asindexing.org. An indexer will most likely charge you a project rate, but obviously it's going to be based on the number of pages in your book. When giving you a quote, the indexer will also be asking you about the size of the pages, type size used in your book, number of illustrations, and general layout of your book. You'll need to allow two to four weeks for indexing if you have a professional do it.

Of course, if your book is fiction or poetry, you can omit the indexing process and move right onto the book manufacturing, which is covered comprehensively in the next chapter.

Web Sites, Wisdom, and Whimsey

Test-drive the largest graphics resource on the Web. With more than 1.2 million downloadable images available, this site can undoubtably meet your every illustrative need. It has clip art, photographs, Web art, illustrations, woodcuts and engravings, images from the Masters, even a huge array of fonts. And you don't have to waste time surfing, as there is a lightning-fast search engine to find what you want. Here's the deal: You can get a free three-day trial offer with over 1 million images, sign up for the Standard Program that contains over 870,000 images and sells for $29.95 a year, or spring for the full meal deal with the Professional Package for $99.95 per year and get 1,212,898 images. It all happens at http://arttoday.com.

* * *

Well-done books are image makers not budget breakers.

* * *

Consider the Internet when designing book covers. It came to our attention recently that we need to be sure our cover titles are big and bold if we want them to work in cyberspace. When designing covers, assess whether the title will be readable when the book is reduced to the tiny size presented on most Web sites. When I thanked Carol Waugh for putting a photo of our *Jump Start Your Book Sales* on publishing attorney Lloyd Rich's home page, she commented that it was a colorful, easy-to-read addition. Be sure your covers translate well to a small Web graphic. And also use the Internet, especially Amazon.com, to view a multitude of cover treatments, and print those you especially like to use as possible prototypes.

* * *

The profession of book-writing makes horse racing seem like a solid, stable business. —John Steinbeck

* * *

Here's an opinion from a pro. Successful independent publisher Dominique Raccah, says, "You can reposition a book through cover design, the title, even the way you lay out the internal text. These are all ways of communicating what the content of the book is. They should all be aligned."

* * *

Need help? A good place for desktop publishing novices to start is www.dtp-aus.com/dtpstrt.html. The site has various tutorials so you can learn the terms and processes.

10 *Affordable Book Manufacturing—the Printing Process*

Book manufacturing, also known as printing, will be your largest expense. But paper stock can make a big difference in overall production cost. And the size and binding you choose affect it dramatically. So do many other variables. All of this might make you feel as exhausted and intimidated as someone competing in the Iron Man. No need to fret. By studying the following information and tips, you, too, can be a winner.

Traditional Book Manufacturing

If you've decided to use a traditional ink and paper printer, one of the first things you want to do is to seek a full-service book *manufacturer*, as opposed to regular printers who do offset printing. Why a book manufacturer? Because typical printers earn a living churning out forms, fliers, and stationery, whereas book manufacturers specialize in books. That means they have technical know-how for you to lean on, they buy paper by the carload, their prices are more competitive, and they handle binding as well as printing so you don't have to find a bindery, too. It is better to deal with one company, rather than subcontracting jobs to a lot of different ones who will never be able to agree who was at fault if something goes wrong. That's one reason many busy professionals use our turnkey service—to keep everything under one umbrella. A list of selected book manufacturers is included in Appendix D.

Another reason to go to a book manufacturer is that it will have a range of equipment and can choose the most efficient and cost-effective method to print your book. There are a number of variables that affect this choice:

- **Sheetfed press.** These are efficient for short runs of 1,000 to 5,000 copies of a book with illustrations. The sheets of paper are fed into the press rather like a copier.
- **Web press.** Mini-webs are efficient for 5,000 to 7,500 copies, webs for

10,000 and up of illustrated books. These are particularly good for books with high page counts. They use huge rolls of paper and run faster than a cheetah.

- **Cameron belt press.** There are a few book manufacturers around the country that have Cameron belt presses. This can slice a chunk off your printing bill if you're printing a large quantity—10,000 copies or more. Although this would *not* be a good choice if your book contains photographs or screens, because this particular press can't reproduce the sharp edges and tiny dot patterns they require. Another thing to be aware of with a Cameron belt press is that the 16- or 32-page signature rules no longer apply. Each trim size has a unique signature.

Something to keep in mind is that in the printing business more is less, meaning the more books you print, the less each one costs. That's because much of the expense revolves around the preparation of negatives and plates and the time involved in setting up the presses—called makeready time. It requires just as long to prepare to print 500 copies as it does 20,000.

As the quantity escalates, the unit price shrinks dramatically. At around 10,000 copies, however, the economy of scale dwindles. Makes it seem tempting to print the 10,000, doesn't it? Don't. That's a whopping order. As a rule of thumb, never print more than you know you can use in a year or two. Run 3,000 to 5,000 copies first. Five thousand puts you in a better position to get five times the cost. You can always reprint after the book proves itself. In fact, poets and others may want to print 1,000 or less initially. This reduces the risks and capital outlay required.

While you're still working on the book, it's a good idea to get a rough estimate of what the book would cost to produce. It will help you determine expenses and set the book's retail price. A useful publication is *Getting It Printed*, by Mark Beach, Ph.D., and Eric Kenly, M.S. In addition, Sheridan Books offers a free book preparation guide called *Get Ready . . . Get Set . . . Go!* You can get a copy by calling (734) 475-9145. And Thomson-Shore, Inc. makes available a complimentary newsletter called *Printer's Ink* that is helpful to publishers. The phone is (734) 426-3939.

One last word of advice: In your planning, be sure to allow enough time for your book manufacturing. It's not like getting business cards printed with a two-day turnaround. Some companies are faster than others, and the time will vary depending on how busy they are when your book comes in, but generally, a paperback book will take from four to six weeks, and a hardcover book from six to eight weeks with a traditional book manufacturer. (Then you'd better add another week for shipping.) If you need books on a specific date, don't expect your printer to make up for your falling behind schedule. More rush means more chance for mistakes. Use those weeks of waiting wisely. It's the perfect time to launch your marketing plan.

Print on Demand

If you've decided to use Print on Demand (POD), be sure of what you're going to get. (See the Exploring Print on Demand section in chapter two.) Some companies are actually printing with ink, like a traditional book manufacturer, but their equipment allows them to print short runs economically. They may be using less-expensive paper plates on the press instead of metal. These paper plates don't do the best job with photo halftones. Other companies are doing digital printing, so what you're actually getting on your interior pages is toner on paper, like a huge laser printer. Their salespeople will tell you, "Each page on your two hundredth copy will be as crisp and clear as your first copy, because the image is coming straight from your computer file every time." If you have photos in your book, they'll look great! But will the toner hold up over time and constant use as well as ink, in a library, for example? This is still a fairly new technology, so time will tell.

Examine your quotes carefully. You may have to do some thinking, planning, and figuring to determine who's *really* giving you the best price. Some will give you a flat fee price per book no matter how many you order. Other companies work like traditional printers. You'll get a better price per book if you can order 200 instead of 25. So how many books will you really need? Depending on your subject matter, you may be thinking one-book-at-a-time sales to family and friends. But on the other hand, are you going to need copies to send reviewers? Send sample copies of your book to drum up interest in your seminars? That's all coming out of your pocket. What if you make a sale of 100 or 200 books? How much will it cost with the printer you choose, and will you be able to offer a decent discount? You'll need to do some dreaming to make a wise decision. Digital printing is generally more expensive than short-run offset in quantities over 500.

Your book must be submitted electronically. Your POD printer may work with you if you have graphics or photos that need to be scanned and placed, but this will add to the cost. Because of the technology used and the quick turnaround, the printer will also require that your cover be prepared as four-color process. Your cover will most likely be stripped up and printed along with several other covers. If you've specified PMS inks in your cover design, they will need to be converted to process color before your final files are prepared for the printer. Check on the printer's requirements for file submission and follow those rules. If you don't, the quick turnaround you're expecting won't happen.

Quotes, Proofs, Galleys, and Other Details

Whether you decide to go with a traditional book manufacturer or POD, some of the steps in the process are the same. Find two or three vendors whom you like working with, and who seem in line cost-wise, and ask for a price *quote*. Unlike the estimate, a quote is a firm commitment to print your book at the stated price. It is guaranteed for a given length of time, usually thirty or sixty days (although you should push for ninety). When you're giving your page count, include all the pages—front matter plus text plus back matter. Even your blank pages count. As in typesetting, be sure you're comparing apples to apples. Are the paper weights the same? Do the vendors understand how you will be providing the final layout? What's the turnaround time? How are they handling the shipping? A request for printing price quote form (RFQ) is shown. Many printers will have their own forms for you to fill out or the process can be done online.

We recently conducted an interesting experiment. We contacted three dozen of the top book manufacturers for price quotes. To make a long story short, the results were quite amazing. The prices ranged from a low of $3,532 to a high of $6,914—almost twice as much. We had not been dealing with the vendor who offered the lowest price, but since the company had a good reputation, we decided to try it for the next book we published. What a mistake. That one printing job entailed more problems than we've had for all our other jobs combined. Moral of the story: Don't automatically choose the cheapest.

Consider quality, too. Request a couple of samples of similar jobs. Examine these carefully. Look at the paper, ink, and binding planned for your job. One self-publisher suggests you interview the high bidders simply to get in practice for working with those on the low end to whom you'll finally give your business. If you have any reason to doubt a company, check it out with the Better Business Bureau and have your bank run a Dun & Bradstreet rating on it. Also ask for referrals from other jobs the company has done—and check them out. Unless you live in the relatively few areas where manufacturers are clustered, you'll probably get better price and service from an out-of-town firm. However, being personally involved with the job would make communication easier, perhaps help you avoid mistakes, and teach you more about the printing process, so that is another consideration.

Ask about downtime to shave costs. But beware. Even under normal conditions, getting your book printed happens about as fast as getting your teeth straightened. To wait for downtime may delay the process beyond a hint of practicality. It's always a good idea to pad a vendor's promised delivery date anyway. You never know when the binder may break down or some other unexpected delay may happen.

Request for Quote

about books inc.

p.o. box 1500 • 425 cedar street • buena vista, co 81211-1500
(719) 395-2459 • fax: (719) 395-8374 • e-mail: ABI@about-books.com

Request for Quote ABI contact person: ______________

NOTE: Quote must be received within 48 hours to be considered. All information must be provided. Please fax completed quotes to Tom Ross at (719) 395-8374 or e-mail tomross@about-books.com. If you have questions, call (719) 395-2459.

Date of request: ______________ Author: ______________

Trim size: ______________ Title: ______________

❑ Softcover ❑ Hardcover Quantities: ______________

BOOK INTERIOR: Number of pages:________ + / - ________'s Proof requested:________

❑ Camera-ready copy ❑ Electronic files ❑ Negatives furnished

Halftones________ Strip-ins________ Stock color:________ Weight:________

Bleeds:________ Press:________ Ink color(s):________ PPI: < ________

BOOK COVER / DUST JACKET: Ink colors:________ Proof requested:________

❑ Camera-ready art ❑ Electronic files ❑ Negatives furnished

Stock:________ Lamination: Lay-Flat film

Hardcover binding: ❑ Adhesive case bind ❑ Additional to Smyth sew ❑ Other________

Use Kivar 7 cloth, regular color and finish over .088" binder boards; 80# plain endsheets; rounded and backed; headbands and footbands; stamp spine with 1 impression imitation gold foil; 10 square inches with manufacturer furnished dies; wrap dust jackets

Softcover binding: ❑ Perfect bound ❑ Layflat binding ❑ Other________

Terms: Net 60

Packing: Bulk pack in plain single wall cartons on pallets.

Shipping: FOB point of manufacturing. Manufacturer's zip code:________

Weight per thousand:________

*** * * * * * This information is neccessary for quote to be considered.**

Other: ❑ Quantity extra covers/dust jackets (printed on 80# enamel with lamination):________

❑ Quantity bound galleys:________ (Folded and gathered signatures, perfect bound with 65# cover printing black, 1 side. Camera-ready art will be provided for the cover.)

Specials: ______________

The form About Books, Inc. uses when approaching printers for client bids.

It is important to get your book manufacturing agreement in writing. Printing and binding costs can loom like the national debt to a self-publisher, yet the beginner hesitates to identify specifications, tending to operate with vague verbal agreements.

Always insist on approving proofs before your book is printed. Depending on your printer and how you've provided the final book, you'll get either bluelines or laser proofs. There's a wide variety of types of color proofs for your cover. Be sure to find out if you need to check if the color is accurate or if you're just checking for type and placement of elements. Mischievous printer gremlins have a way of sneaking into your perfect work somewhere between the typesetting phase and the time when the pages roll off the press, even if you've provided electronic files.

Check for errors in pagination, meaning out-of-order or missing pages (as page 33 was in our *Creative Loafing*). Be sure the margins are correct and the text is positioned as you specified. Also watch for misplacement of illustrations or photos, correct bar code, crooked pages, light spots, blurry type or illustrations, and any missing elements. Additionally, there may be broken fonts where individual letters didn't print well—or specs or dust on the page. Always double-check your ISBN number with your R.R. Bowker paperwork. On the cover proof, check for color registration (colors are fitting together correctly) and that the color is close to what you expected to see. Be aware that digital color proofs, even from a printer, are rarely perfect.

We can't emphasize enough to be careful at this proofing stage. This is your last check before the presses roll. Be aware that author changes are expensive at this point, so this isn't the time to be editing or proofreading your book. But if a mistake gets by here, the fact is, it's your responsibility, not the printer's. You'll be required to sign off on a proofing form giving your OK to proceed with the printing. If you end up with an "Oh, no!" after the books are printed, your printer will have your signature on that piece of paper, and the Printing Industries of America guidelines behind them.

Covers for Promotion

While we're talking about printing, let us make a suggestion that can save you a lot of money on promotional materials. While the book manufacturer is printing your book, have him do what is called an overrun—an additional quantity—of the cover or dust jacket. Because the press is already set up and running, all you actually pay for is the paper. We just ordered a five-hundred-piece overrun on a four-color cover and paid a paltry $95. What a bargain for full-color sales literature! And for a few bucks more you can have the flaps trimmed off (assuming it's a dust jacket), and you have a dynamic brochure. To get added mileage, have your neighborhood printer put your table of contents and ordering information on the reverse side. Olé! You're ready to do business. In some cases you can even negotiate with your printer to do the covers early—and thus your overrun of sales materials—so you have very professional-looking advance promotional materials. If you're doing a paperback, have the overrun done on 80-pound enamel paper rather than the stiff cover stock, unless you want it for an oversized postcard.

Overrun of Cover

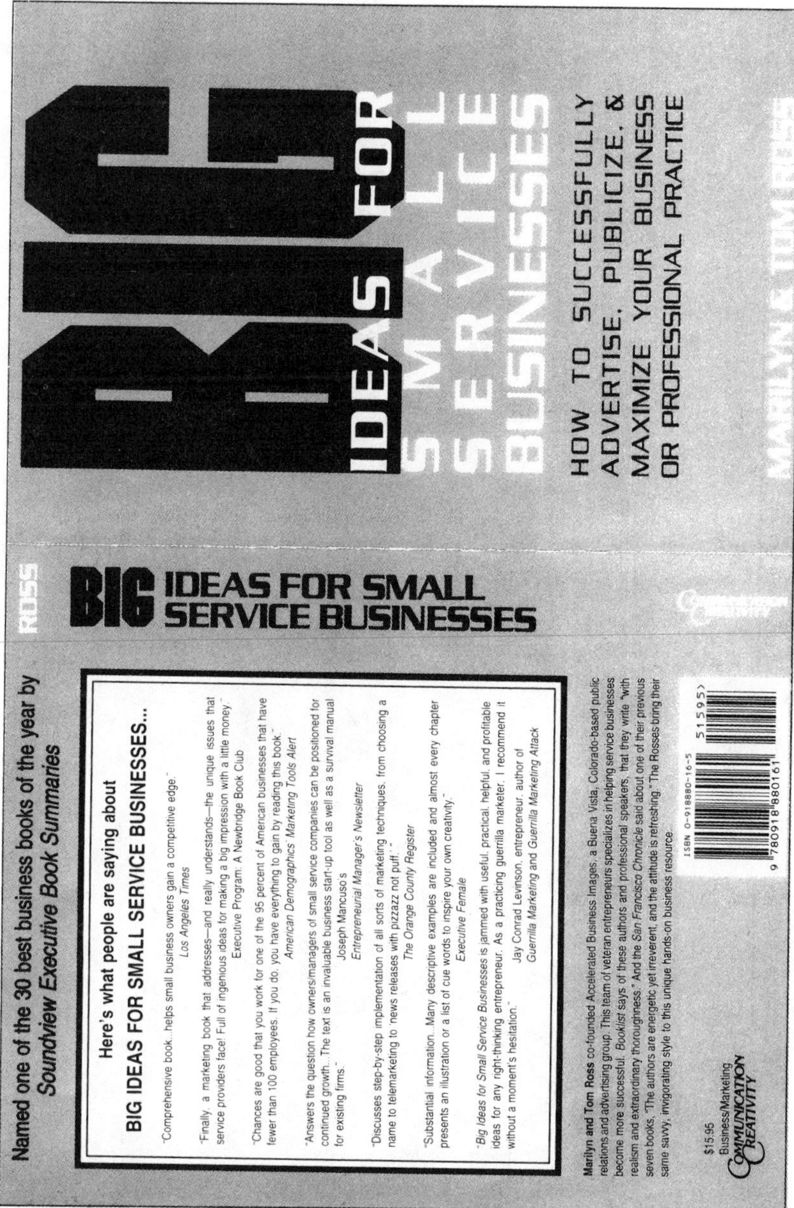

You can use overruns of covers as powerful customer brochures.

Overrun of Cover, continued

Here Are 283 Proven Strategies to Boost Your Profits!

Dream of increased profits?
Afraid an effective marketing campaign costs too much money?
At a loss for innovative ways to promote your business or practice?

Big Ideas for Small Service Businesses shows how to successfully publicize, advertise, and maximize your business or professional practice. More than 283 fact-filled, easy-to-read sections to get your business started on the right foot—or give your existing firm new direction in the mid '90s. What sets this book apart from others is that it shows you how to truly separate yourself from the humdrum herd. Then it describes ways to spotlight these distinctly diverse traits, promote your originality, and pocket the proceeds. Best of all, *Big Ideas for Small Service Businesses* gives you the tools for doing it all economically—often for free! Get your copy today. You'll discover how to . . .

- Develop the right business image
- Design brochures with "Aye" appeal
- Do quick and easy market research
- Cultivate testimonials and referral business
- Write ad copy that generates big results
- Use your business card as a mini-billboard
- Have a brainstorming partner to fuel your imagination
- Create news releases that get printed
- Plan a dynamic special event
- Successfully mix business with pleasure
- Generate free radio and TV exposure
- Develop a "presence" as *the* expert in your field
- Locate resources and suppliers to save time and money
- Sample Marketing Plan, News Release, Client Survey, etc.

(See over for exciting comments about this new book)

ORDER TODAY

Call credit card orders to (800) 331-8355

or fax your credit card order to (719) 395-8374

NO RISK . . . MONEY BACK GUARANTEE!

ASK ABOUT OUR QUANTITY DISCOUNTS

Title:	*Big Ideas for Small Service Businesses*
Authors:	Marilyn and Tom Ross
ISBN/LCCN:	0-918880-16-5 * 93-27219
Format:	6" x 9" trade paperback
Retail price:	$15.95 plus $3 shipping
Publisher:	Communication Creativity, Box 1500, Buena Vista, CO 81211

ORDER FORM

YES, I want to be more successful and reap more profits! Please send ____ copies of *Big Ideas for Small Service Businesses* at $15.95 each, plus $3 per book shipping. (Colorado residents add $1.12 state sales tax.) Canadian orders must be accompanied by a postal money order in U.S. funds.

Name ____________________ Phone ____________

Company ______________________________

Address ______________________________

City/State/Zip ______________________________

____My check/money order is enclosed • Bill my____VISA____MC

Acct# ______________ Expires ____ Signature____________

Here's my check or money order, made out to Communication Creativity, for $ _________.

Mail to: Communication Creativity, Box 1500, Buena Vista, CO, 81211.

Review Copies

And if you didn't get extra galleys from the typesetter or photocopy your pages before sending them for manufacturing, let your printer know that you'll want bound galleys. Even if you're printing your book with a traditional book manufacturer, you may want to look into POD for your galleys. One self-publisher we talked to recently was able to get twenty galleys cheaper from a separate POD printer than from his book printer. You'll want galleys to send to prime book reviewers who appreciate having an advance opportunity to screen new titles. (More about that later.)

Shrink-Wrapping

Talking about covers, there is an option called shrink-wrapping that you may want to get on your books, if you haven't followed our advice and your cover isn't film laminated. It's a clear plastic protective covering. If your cover has heavy ink coverage in a dark tone, or a very light-colored background, chances are the books will be scuffed during shipping if they aren't film laminated or shrink-wrapped. This can be done individually or in lots of three or five and will cost only a few pennies per book. A good investment, considering no one wants to buy a book with a beat-up cover. We favor the film lamination protection and convenience, however.

Shipping Concerns

Another detail you may want to work out is to have your printer drop-ship cases of books directly to your major customers. This saves you having to pay for the books to be shipped to you, just to reship them. One other point some folks negotiate is that the negatives and halftones for their jobs be considered their property and returned to them when the work is completed. (Some manufacturers are testy about this.) Be sure to specify that materials for printing the cover or dust jacket, as well as the dies for stamping the hardcover boards, be included. In some cases, the text printing and the cover printing and binding are done by different vendors, so don't assume your requirement for negatives and halftones will automatically include all the cover printing materials.

Something else you have to work out with your printer is what form the books will arrive in. Larger publishers often take their books banded on skids, which results in a stack of books almost five feet tall. You want to have your printer ship your books cartoned (how many to a box depends on how big your books are) and on skids.

By the way, when you get your printing bill, don't be surprised if there is an entry for X number of additional books at X price. There is an industry standard that says a printer may print overs and unders, meaning a 10 percent variance either way. Inevitably, it's always over, so be prepared to come up with a little more on your printing bill. Oh, and don't forget to figure in shipping costs, which will be extra. FOB (freight on board) means you pay the freight from the printer's plant. Printers will give you a general estimate of freight costs, so be sure to ask for this when you request a price quote. It often runs into several hundred dollars. Your books will probably come on an eighteen-wheeler tractor trailer. Be prepared to have help unloading all those lovely cases of books.

Printing in Color

Before we leave the area of printing, there is one other option we want to mention. There are those who specialize in children's books or coffee-table books with full-color spreads. These printers usually do their color separation and four-color printing in Asia—primarily Hong Kong, China, Singapore, Indonesia, South Korea, and Thailand. The advantage of this arrangement is simple: No American manufacturer can compete with Asian labor prices. There are disadvantages: Communication can be a real bugaboo. Be sure you are working with a reliable print broker based in the United States who speaks and understands English well. In addition to your manufacturing time, you have to add the time and cost of overseas ocean or air shipping and check into the United States import technicalities. Most jobs take three to four months from start to finish. Check these printers out ahead of time. Ask for references and past clients you can talk to. *Publishers Weekly* typically runs a large article about printing in Asia in a summer issue, and overseas printers advertise in this issue.

Binding Options

One of the major decisions in book production is the binding. Should it be a hard or soft cover? Are the traditional sewn or glued spines the best, or will saddle stitching (stapling), wire, or plastic comb binding be more suitable? There are many factors that will help you make this decision.

Think about how the book will be used. If it is a sourcebook that readers will be in and out of many times, hardcover (frequently referred to as cloth or casebound) is more durable. A collection of photographs designed as a coffee-table book would definitely be hardcover.

The Cadillac of hardcover bindings is Smythe sewn. In this technique thread is used to stitch the signatures before they are glued into the cover. While the most expensive, it is the sturdiest and also allows the book to be opened flat, which is a definite plus. For a top-quality book, spend a little extra and get headbands and footbands. They are little reinforcing strips of

Basic Choices for Binding Styles

- Hardcover Smythe sewn (with or without a dust jacket)
- Hardcover adhesive bound (with or without a dust jacket)
- Hardcover with an imprinted four-color cover (called a litho case)
- Softcover (perfect bound)
- Softcover Otabound, or lay-flat, binding
- GBC bound (cookbook-style plastic binding)
- Wire-O bound (spiral plastic-coated wire)
- Saddle-stitch booklet (not more than 96 pages)

cloth added to the top and bottom of the book, which help it to stay together through rough use.

Perfect, or adhesive, binding is another method—and currently the most popular. In this process, the signatures are collated, run through hot adhesive, then affixed to the cover. It is frequently used because it gives a spine surface area and is the least expensive of quality bindings. Your local phone directory, many hardcover books, paperbacks, and some magazines are bound this way.

With book prices escalating so rapidly, softcover (often called paperback) books are accepted most places today. While libraries have traditionally preferred hardcovers, they are becoming more accepting of paperbacks all the time. The educational field has also come around. In fact, many schools prefer softcovers to keep prices down. They typically cost about $1.25 to $1.50 a book less to manufacture than their fancier sisters—plus they weigh less, thus saving postage and freight costs.

But if you seek to impress reviewers, you may want to stick with hardcover. In years past, many reviewers tagged paperbacks with a stigma that goes back to the days when they were all reprints. Hardcover books are considered more prestigious and are simply taken more seriously by old-line critics. Speakers and consultants are often wise to print in hardcover as they will use their books as "calling cards" to reach key executives in corporations and associations they wish to impress. A personally autographed hardcover book has a better chance of getting past gatekeepers.

Happily, you don't have to go strictly one way or the other. What some people do is bind the majority of their books in paperback and do the remainder in hardcover. This is called a split run. How do you avoid guessing wrong and running out of the softcover edition while still having oodles of hardcovers left—or vice versa? You can't. Some publishers elect to bind only half of the split run and leave the other half as flat sheets stored on pallets at the manufacturer's or the bindery until they determine which version book buyers want. Or you may want to come out in hardcover first, with the idea of launching a paperback edition the following year after sales for the more costly version have peaked.

Do you need a book that lies flat? This is ideal for cookbooks and workbooks where people will be writing inside a lot. Otabind is a process that achieves this more economically than plastic comb binding. Not all printers offer this option, and it will cost more per book than perfect binding.

By the way, when we refer to paperbacks, we are talking about the larger trade paperback, not the small 4″ × 7″ mass-market paperback. As we mentioned earlier, to be profitable, the latter has to be printed in quantities of 100,000 or more. Mass-market paperbacks also involve a very impractical distribution system for a small publisher.

While we're talking about bindings, be aware that you have further options. The least expensive method, which will work for monographs and booklets, is to use staples. You can staple one corner of a report or through the fold on a small booklet. A more ideal method is to saddle stitch them. This horsey-sounding term simply means to staple two or three times where the fold is located. It requires a special machine. It should not be used for a book of more than 96 pages, and the disadvantage is that your book won't have a spine when it's on a bookshelf.

If your work is a manual to which readers may want to add pages or if you are starting a series of some sort, a three-ring binder with a silk-screened cover might be best. Many office supply sources sell plain binders with clear plastic fronts under which can be slipped a printed cover page. (Libraries hate material presented in notebooks, however, because patrons "appropriate" favorite pages.) A cookbook might be most usable with a spiral comb binding that allows it to be laid flat or folded back to the chosen recipe. In that case, do print the title of the book on the comb binding or bookstores will shun you.

Hand-sewn binding might be your choice if you have a special literary work. You will need access to a binder or a letterpress and someone to show you the ropes—pardon us, the threads. With a little practice you should be able to turn out a couple of dozen books in an hour's time.

Checking Your Delivery

There are a few things you should do when you get your books from the printer. First count the cartons, multiply that by the number of books per carton, and make sure your total figure matches that on the freight company's paperwork. Next, sample random cartons to determine the books are not damaged or bound wrong—like upside down. Now celebrate! It's been a long time coming. Right? We congratulate you!

If boxes are damaged, you'll need to file a claim with the freight company. Should there be problems with the printing, send a letter detailing the problem and a sample book to your printer immediately.

Don't forget to recover all your original artwork, cover art (plus all materials and dies, if a hardcover), camera-ready copy or disks, and if possible, the negatives and halftones for your job. Store all of these in a safe, dry place.

Copyright Registration

The function of copyright is to protect your writing so others may not use your work for their purposes. It does for the printed word what a patent does for an object. To be valid, your copyright notice must contain three elements: the symbol © or the word *copyright*, the year of first publication, and the name of the owner of the copyright, for example, copyright 2001 John Jones.

On January 1, 1978, new statutes went into effect. The copyright term now lasts for the life of the author, plus fifty years after death. Another important change is that manuscripts are now protected by copyright *before* they are published. Form TX and Short Form TX, which cover "nondramatic literary work," are used for fiction and nonfiction books, short stories, essays, articles in serials, computer programs, poetry, periodicals, textbooks, reference works, directories, catalogs, compilations of information, and advertising copy.

The Short Form TX is used for a living author who is the only author of the work and the sole owner of the copyright. If you are publishing under a pseudonym, there is more than one author of the work, or if a business organization is the copyright claimant, use the regular Form TX.

Both forms can be obtained from the Library of Congress, Copyright Office, 101 Independence Ave. SE, Washington, DC 20559-6000, (202) 707-3000. They come replete with instructions, so we won't duplicate them here. To register an unpublished work, you deposit one complete copy, the filled-in form, and a check or money order for $30 made payable to the Register of Copyrights. To register a published work, send two copies of your book plus the other items. We suggest that you wait to register a book until it is actually printed so you don't have an old copyright date.

Be wary of publishers or online establishments that insist on copyrighting your book in *their* names. This is not standard practice and should be avoided. While we're on the subject, any copyrights (and all royalties due you from contracts with trade publishers) should be provided for in your will. Ownership of a copyright can be passed on to your heirs just like a piece of real estate. If your book is selling well, these funds can be a meaningful part of your estate. Be sure

Copyright Short Form TX

FEE CHANGES
Fees are effective through June 30, 2002. After that date, check the Copyright Office Website at www.loc.gov/copyright or call (202) 707-3000 for current fee information.

SHORT FORM TX
For a Nondramatic Literary Work
UNITED STATES COPYRIGHT OFFICE

Registration Number

TX TXU

Effective Date of Registration

Application Received

Examined By

Deposit Received
One Two

Correspondence ❑

Fee Received

TYPE OR PRINT IN BLACK INK. DO NOT WRITE ABOVE THIS LINE.

Title of This Work: Alternative title or title of larger work in which this work was published:	**1**	The Ethan Chronicles
Name and Address of Author and Owner of the Copyright: Nationality or domicile: Phone, fax, and email:	**2**	Marsha A. Willis Cassidy Books P.O. Box 9723 Denver, CO 80209-9723 Phone (303) 733-6216 Fax (303) 777-1868 Email mwillis@amdevgrp.com
Year of Creation:	**3**	2001
***If work has been published,* Date and Nation of Publication:**	**4**	a. Date September (Month) 29 (Day) 2001 (Year) *(Month, day, and year all required)* b. Nation U.S.A.
Type of Authorship in This Work: Check all that this author created.	**5**	☒ Text (includes fiction, nonfiction, poetry, computer programs, etc.) ☒ Illustrations ☒ Photographs ❑ Compilation of terms or data
Signature: Registration cannot be completed without a signature.	**6**	*I certify that the statements made by me in this application are correct to the best of my knowledge.** Check one: ❑ Author ☒ Authorized agent X [signature] 05/29/01
OPTIONAL **Name and Address of Person to Contact for Rights and Permissions:** Phone, fax, and email:	**7**	☒ Check here if same as #2 above Phone ( ) Fax ( ) Email

8 Certificate will be mailed in window envelope to this address:

Name ▼ About Books, Inc.
Number/Street/Apt ▼ P.O. BOX 1500
City/State/ZIP ▼ Buena Vista, CO 81211

Complete this space only if you currently hold a Deposit Account in the Copyright Office.

9 Deposit Account #
Name

DO NOT WRITE HERE Page 1 of ____ pages

*17 U.S.C. § 506(e): Any person who knowingly makes a false representation of a material fact in the application for copyright registration provided for by section 409, or in any written statement filed in connection with the application, shall be fined not more than $2,500.

June 1999—100,000
WEB REV: June 1999

PRINTED ON RECYCLED PAPER

☆U.S. GOVERNMENT PRINTING OFFICE: 1999-454-879/53

This is the form used to actually register your book with the copyright office.

to spell out how proceeds are to be divided among the beneficiaries.

Now that you've taken the steps to produce a first-class book, let's move ahead into the chapter that deals with creating publicity with pizzazz and find out how to give it a fitting send-off.

Copyright Short Form TX, continued

Instructions for Short Form TX

For nondramatic literary works, including fiction and nonfiction, books, short stories, poems, collections of poetry, essays, articles in serials, and computer programs

USE THIS FORM IF—

1. You are the **only** author and copyright owner of this work, *and*
2. The work was **not** made for hire, *and*
3. The work is completely new (does not contain a substantial amount of material that has been previously published or registered or is in the public domain).

If any of the above does not apply, you must use standard Form TX.
NOTE: Short Form TX is not appropriate for an anonymous author who does not wish to reveal his or her identity.

HOW TO COMPLETE SHORT FORM TX

- Type or print in black ink.
- Be clear and legible. (Your certificate of registration will be copied from your form.)
- Give only the information requested.

NOTE: You may use a continuation sheet (Form __/CON) to list individual titles in a collection. Complete Space A and list the individual titles under Space C on the back page. Space B is not applicable to short forms.

1 Title of This Work

You must give a title. If there is no title, state "UNTITLED." If you are registering an unpublished collection, give the collection title you want to appear in our records (for example: "Joan's Poems, Volume 1"). Alternative title: If the work is known by two titles, you also may give the second title. If the work has been published as part of a larger work (including a periodical), give the title of that larger work in addition to the title of the contribution.

2 Name and Address of Author and Owner of the Copyright

Give your name and mailing address. You may include your pseudonym followed by "pseud." Also, give the nation of which you are a citizen or where you have your domicile (i.e., permanent residence).

Please give daytime phone and fax numbers and email address, if available.

3 Year of Creation

Give the latest year in which you completed the work you are registering at this time. A work is "created" when it is written down, stored in a computer, or otherwise "fixed" in a tangible form.

4 Publication

If the work has been published (i.e., if copies have been distributed to the public), give the complete date of publication (month, day, and year) and the nation where the publication first took place.

5 Type of Authorship in This Work

Check the box or boxes that describe your authorship in the copy you are sending with the application. For example, if you are registering a story and are planning to add illustrations later, check only the box for "text."

A "compilation" of terms or of data is a selection, coordination, or arrangement of such information into a chart, directory, or other form. A compilation of previously published or public domain material must be registered using a standard Form TX.

6 Signature of Author

Sign the application in black ink and check the appropriate box. The person signing the application should be the author or his/her authorized agent.

7 Person to Contact for Rights and Permissions

This space is optional. You may give the name and address of the person or organization to contact for permission to use the work. You may also provide phone, fax, or email information.

8 Certificate Will Be Mailed

This space must be completed. Your certificate of registration will be mailed in a window envelope to this address. Also, if the Copyright Office needs to contact you, we will write to this address.

9 Deposit Account

Complete this space only if you currently maintain a deposit account in the Copyright Office.

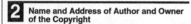

MAIL WITH THE FORM

- A $30 (effective through June 30, 2002) filing fee in the form of a check or money order *(**no cash**)* payable to "Register of Copyrights," **and**
- One or two copies of the work. If the work is unpublished, send one copy. If published, send two copies of the best published edition. (If first published outside the U.S., send one copy either as first published or of the best edition.) **Note:** Inquire about special requirements for works first published before 1978. Copies submitted become the property of the U.S. Government.

Mail everything **(application form, copy or copies, and fee)** ***in one package*** to:

Library of Congress
Copyright Office
101 Independence Avenue, S.E.
Washington, D.C. 20559-6000

QUESTIONS? Call (202) 707-3000 [TTY: (202) 707-6737] between 8:30 a.m. and 5:00 p.m. eastern time, Monday through Friday. For forms and informational circulars, call (202) 707-9100 24 hours a day, 7 days a week, or download them from the Internet at www.loc.gov/copyright. Selected informational circulars but not forms are available from Fax-on-Demand at (202) 707-2600.

PRIVACY ACT ADVISORY STATEMENT Required by the Privacy Act of 1974 (P.L. 93-579)

The authority for requesting this information is title 17 U.S.C., secs. 409 and 410. Furnishing the requested information is voluntary. But if the information is not furnished, it may be necessary to delay or refuse registration and you may not be entitled to certain relief, remedies, and benefits provided in chapters 4 and 5 of title 17 U.S.C.

The principal uses of the requested information are the establishment and maintenance of a public record and the examination of the application for compliance with the registration requirements of the copyright law.

Other routine uses include public inspection and copying, preparation of public indexes, preparation of public catalogs of copyright registrations, and preparation of search reports upon request.

NOTE: No other advisory statement will be given in connection with this application. Please keep this statement and refer to it if we communicate with you regarding this application.

Web Sites, Wisdom, and Whimsey

Hear ye, hear ye . . . want to print overseas? Did you know that federal law requires you to print this fact in your books? It must be placed on the copyright page. For full details go to the U.S. Customs Web site at www.customs.ustreas

.gov. Once there, click on Importing & Exporting. Then, under Other Commercial Importing Information, click on Marking Country of Origin.

* * *

Printers smell the ink so long they sometimes go weird on us.

* * *

Do your pages bleed? No, we're not talking red blood. A bleed is when an image or type runs right up to the edge or off the edge of your page. This is one of the questions you'll get from your printer. Most printers want ¼ inch of white space inside your trim lines. If you go closer, it's a bleed. This can get expensive on your interior pages. On your cover, you'll usually have a color or image bleed, but many printers require any text to be ¼ inch away from the trim line there, as well.

* * *

Specify residential delivery. Are you having your book shipment delivered to your home? Let your printer know you need residential delivery specified to the trucking company. You can also request inside delivery if you don't have a muscular friend to help unload your boxes of books, which will probably weigh about 35 to 40 pounds each. The cost is based on the weight of the shipment and presently runs about $3.50 to $4.00 per hundred pounds. Depending on your situation, it may be worth it. Otherwise, all the truck driver is obligated to do is unload the skid of boxes off his truck. If you don't arrange for these things in advance and ask the shipper (your printer) to put it on the bill of lading, you may have to jump through some hoops once that truck pulls up.

* * *

More things can go wrong in the printing industry than in the space program.

* * *

Gain more shipping wisdom. Shipping costs are a lot like an author's alterations to an edited manuscript. Nobody is happy about the costs, nobody makes money on it, and it can be a source of contention if the cost comes as a surprise in the end. Normally book manufacturers (or print brokers, such as we are) will give you a price for shipping in the beginning. That assumes that *all* the books will go to one destination. If you decide, however, to have a third of them sent to your Uncle in Padauk, two cases mailed to you, and the rest shipped to your fulfillment house, the overall shipping costs are going to go up. The more you divide a shipment, the more costly it becomes, so factor that into your thinking.

* * *

Follow the printer's directions! You kind of wonder about people's ability to comply with instructions when you see folks in the grocery store in the "ten items or less lane" with fifteen or twenty items in their basket.

* * *

Apply these miscellaneous book tips for more protection and sales. One of our colleagues always has his books shrink-wrapped in quantities of five or ten. Besides protecting the contents, when clients want to buy several copies, he tells them the books come in packs of five or ten. Often they bump their order up to the next packaged size—ten rather than eight, for instance. He also insists on keeping the skids the books are shipped on to elevate the product from the floor and provide for airflow underneath. (This also allows those of you who live in buggy climates to spray under the cartons for pest control.)

PART IV

Killer PR: The Great Equalizer

11 *Initiating a Nationwide Marketing Plan With Publicity Pizzazz*

Publicity and promotion are very similar. Both are the exposure a product or service receives for which you make no payment. But a rough way of distinguishing between them might be that promotion is what you, the author, do; publicity is what, if you're shrewd at promoting, you'll get from the media as a result. Promotion is giving the book a push from behind; publicity is a pull from the front, from the world you're trying to reach. It's making a splash without much cash. Both are vital. And we'll be exploring them, plus other ways to generate killer PR, in this entire part of the book.

Developing a POW! Marketing Plan

Of all the hats you wear as an author, the marketing fedora probably itches the most. The way to secure reviews, get your book mentioned in nonreviewing publications, and generally light a fire that will ignite word-of-mouth recommendations is to create a nationwide marketing plan. It's actually a very doable thing. We'll show you how.

Your plan will include not only national book reviewers but any publication targeted to your audience, syndicated columnists, newsletter editors, book club editors, and excerpt rights buyers. It will also pinpoint selected distributors, wholesalers, bookstores, and libraries. And if you're smart, you'll add to your list selected radio and TV programs, associations that may buy in bulk, special retail outlets, catalogs, and various innovative ideas for moving books.

Don't overlook regional magazines and newspapers. It's fun to be a hero or heroine in your own hometown. Some publications serve specific geographic areas that target groups, such as New Agers, businesspersons, seniors, or women. If you have a book slanted to any of these audiences and you ignore the regional media, you're cheating yourself. Also consider alternative newspapers around the country if you have a controversial or exposé title aimed at a hip young audience. And what about civic, social, fraternal, and alumni associations to which you belong? They like to highlight the accomplishments of members. When you prepare your marketing plan, you pull together every conceivable source—both general and specialized—that may talk about or buy your book.

Developing a mailing list of the reviewers you want to court is one of your first priorities. Tailor your list to potential contacts whose editorial slant matches your type of book. Being specific will save significantly on promotional material and postage costs. It will also avoid tempting a lot of folks who wouldn't seriously consider reviewing your book to request a free copy anyway.

Building Your List

If you publish a general interest book, you should at least contact the Selected Book Review Sources listed in Appendix E. An additional list can be harvested in *LMP*. Here you can locate magazine and newspaper review editors, plus radio and TV review sources. Two excellent newsletters to help you in various aspects are John Kremer's *Book Marketing Update* and the *SPAN Connection*.

Build by researching thoroughly and selectively. In the main library, you will find several directories that provide marvelous aids for developing specifically targeted rosters. Many of them are also on the Internet. (Check out www.newstips.org/MRC2.) Do be aware that directories are out of date before the ink is dry or the CD-ROM is burned. Before you send a pitch letter, it's best to call and verify contact names.

The *Gale Directory of Publications in Broadcast Media* is a four-volume set revised annually and indexed by state. It includes regional markets, networks, and syndicates. *The Standard Periodical Directory* is an essential reference work. It lists more than seventy-five thousand North American periodicals. *Ulrich's International Periodicals Directory* offers an excellent source of magazines of the entire world. This directory is broken down by subject and cross-referenced, allowing you to be quite selective. It also notes in which periodicals book reviews are regularly used.

The Working Press of the Nation (WPN) offers a comprehensive rundown of names and addresses and is user-friendly. This three-volume directory covers newspapers, magazines, and Internet publications, plus radio and television. Our copy also includes feature writers, photographers, and professional speakers. Research here will net a list covering the important reviewers in both print and electronic media who would typically be interested in your title. The *Newspaper Directory* of *WPN* not only lists reviewers' names for all daily papers but additionally gives special interest papers, religious newspapers, and ethnic papers. This is an ideal place to prospect for syndicated columnists, as they are cross-referenced by subject area.

In addition, you might want to consult Gebbie's *All-in-One Media Directory*. It is a comprehensive resource that lists radio, TV, newspapers, trade and consumer magazines, news syndicates, and more. Much of this information is available free on the Web at www.gebbie.com.

A few miscellaneous recommendations: To reach newsletter editors, check out *The Oxbridge Directory of Newsletters*. It contains over 20,000 newsletters and is a vital source for this growing, influential medium. You can find scads of magazines for potential publicity in *Writer's Market*. And many PR professionals swear by the Bacon directories, while we use the *Burrelle's Media Directory* set a lot.

There is another work that is most helpful: The *Encyclopedia of Associations* is a fat and expensive reference set listing almost eighteen thousand organizations covering thousands of subjects. Since associations can play an important role in your marketing mix, be sure to investigate this reference.

Of course, for book clubs, wholesalers, distributors, and many other valuable contacts, there is nothing like *Literary Market Place*. It gives you the who's where information on publishing industry resources. Be sure you are working from a current edition, and purchase your own desk copy if possible.

For a directory of Canadian print and broadcast media, the 2001 edition of *Media Names and Numbers* has just come out. It includes more than six thousand entries and sells for $89.95 GST. Get information by calling (416) 964-7799 in Toronto or going online to www.sources.com.

Facts of Publishing Life

It is a fact in the publishing industry that books perceived as strong by reviewers, booksellers, readers, and publishers will command the necessary resources and space to make them strong. This axiom is every bit as important to self-published authors as it is to those who are trade published. It is the policy in major trade publishing houses to allot a minuscule publicity and advertising budget to most books. After that tiny allotment—and only then—will the ones that show promise command greater energy and money commitments. Consequently, *all authors* should realize it's a "publicize or perish" game and get behind their own books.

Publicity and promotion are the great equalizers for the little publisher or the unheralded writer. By knowing what buttons to push, you can generate thousands of dollars worth of free publicity—all sizzle, no fizzle. Two excellent titles on generating publicity are our *Jump Start Your Book Sales* and *1001 Ways to Market Your Books*, by John Kremer. Both can be ordered at (800) 331-8355 or online at www.SPANnet.org/cc.

Getting Reviewed

Every day millions of potential book buyers turn to the book review pages of their local newspapers to see what interests them. Thousands of people in the book industry also study reviews and book listings in newspapers and magazines.

Thus book reviewers have a tremendous impact on publishers and writers. They decide which few of the some two hundred titles published in any given day will be reviewed. Book reviews are often regarded as the most persuasive book-buying influence of all. Much of the available review space gets gobbled up by celebrities with virtually guaranteed best-sellers and the huge trade publishers who woo the most important reviewers and editors and spend thousands of dollars in advertising each month.

In spite of these facts, it isn't hard to get a fair share of publicity from book reviewers if you astutely organize your promotional efforts. You will probably be very frustrated if you concentrate all efforts on *The New York Times*, *Publishers Weekly*, *Library Journal*, *The Christian Science Monitor*, *Time*, or other prestigious mass-circulation review media. Go after less-in-demand sources.

Of course, you shouldn't automatically eliminate these choice plums, either. *Publishers Weekly* does capsule forecast reviews of about 5,500 of the approximately 53,000 books published each year. The big houses hover around their editorial and book review staffs like seagulls around a garbage scow. Yet our *Creative Loafing* was reviewed. *Country Bound!* was touted in both *Library Journal* and *Booklist*, and *Jump Start Your Book Sales* scored in *Publishers Weekly* in 2000. Need we say more?

Self-publishers who have followed the points in this guide and who are willing to search for the review media whose editorial interests most closely match their books will get reviews and a resulting boost in sales. The secret is to romance your prime media with a planned and persistent campaign.

Best of all, this valuable review space or electronic media time doesn't cost you a cent. In print media, however, the ad sales department may attempt to convince you to place advertising. Be aware that any review medium with credibility does not decide which titles it will critique on the basis of an advertising commitment. Resist the overzealous salesperson who implies that an ad will influence editorial decisions—and gushes about how wonderful your book is.

We also disagree with the philosophy some review publications are adopting in which they charge a fee for reviews.

Perhaps a word should be said here about the fine art of "review pruning." Just as you cut away the dead wood of trees and bushes so new growth can flourish, so, too, you will excerpt quotable bits of praise from longer reviews. The sheer limitations of space require that material be condensed. In fact, Amazon.com limits reviews to a mere twenty words! Naturally, as you do this encapsulation, you want to ignore the less desirable phrases while highlighting the especially complimentary gems. Realize as you do this, however, that to change the actual intention of a review by taking words out of context is flagrantly wrong. Be ethical in your review pruning. In case you're wondering, by their very nature reviews are quotable, in whole or in part, without permission.

There's an adage that says "There's no bad publicity." It's true, too. When the Disney family tried to discredit a highly critical biography of Walt, all they did was send orders for the book skyrocketing. Their "damage control document" resulted in more than one hundred front-page newspaper stories. Keep this in mind if you have a controversial book. Sometimes you can twist fate and parlay bad press into an advantage by facing it head-on and exploiting it.

One other point: Don't ever refuse to provide a review copy if the request seems valid. We've known of publishers, both large and small, that made statements such as, "We've sent out our allotment of review copies." This is ludicrous! Reviews, inclusion in bibliographies, and mentions in other books continue to sell our books year after year. Just because a title is on the backlist is no reason to clamp down on complimentary review copies. Just the opposite is true.

And don't think a magazine or newspaper is unsuitable because it doesn't run formal book reviews. Many have sections that tell of newsy items or new products of interest to their readers. These mentions can be golden. So can ones in newsletters. In fact, a five-line blurb in *John Naisbitt's Trend Letter* opened useful doors for us. The fact that it mentioned *Country Bound!* and us as urban-to-rural movement experts caught the eye of an editor at *Entrepreneur* magazine. She wrote a story about us and complemented it with a color photograph. This kind of ripple is one of the marvelous consequences about this business. One thing leads to another in an ever-widening universe of publicity and book sales. We've sold many books because *The Complete Guide to Self-Publishing* was mentioned in articles about do-it-yourself publishing in *U.S. News & World Report*, *Kiwanis*, *Changing Times* (now *Kiplinger's Personal Finance Magazine*), *The New York Times*, and others.

By the way, seldom will newspapers or magazines send you tear sheets—copies of what appears about you. Typically you'll learn of such coverage because orders come in or someone phones as a result of the coverage. Then call the editor or reporter and request a copy.

Mention in Magazine

TIP SHEET

ried, divorced or what. Are there children? Does the spouse work?

√If there are battles going on within the business and they're known to the public, you can't ignore them. But, you can deal with them in a positive way:

> Fazlin's first attempt at starting his own company was a joint venture with another larger firm, which has since gone out of business, and "philosophical differences" forced him to leave after less than two years.

Usually, investigative reporting is not expected in writing business profiles. Most of the editors for whom I've done these profiles wanted very little in the way of controversy and prefer "chamber of commerce" journalism; affirmative and upbeat with the problems getting little space.

The beauty of business profiles is that they are easy to resell to other magazines. In 1983, I wrote about a 25-year-old Venice, Florida, millionaire who sold his chain of six computer stores to start his own software company. In the last four years, I've sold the story to 11 different magazines. Net pay; $3,650 for two interviews and several phone call updates.

—*Lary Crews*

8 CITY/REGIONAL BOOK IDEAS AND 1 SOURCE OF INFORMATION

Include city and regional books—those aimed at a specific geographic area—among the beneficiaries of the computer revolution. In *How-to-Make Big Profits Publishing City and Regional Books* (Communication Creativity, Box 213, Saguache, Colorado 81149-0213; $14.95 paperback), authors Marilyn and Tom Ross explain how even a small personal computer puts these books into the individual writer's reach. They also analyze the market often overlooked by large publishers, and suggest these eight types of city/regional books:

√*Travel and tourist guides* introduce visitors to an area.

√*Consumer books* serve as shopping guides for residents.

√*Activity guides* detail recreational opportunities.

√*Nature field guides* explore a region's flora and fauna.

√*Special-interest titles*, such as *The Greatest Honky-Tonks in Texas* or *Single in Portland*, appeal to specific segments of the population.

√*Historical books*.

√*Regional cookbooks*.

√*Photography books*.

There are other possible regional subjects that defy categorization, say the authors—everything from trivia books to anthologies collecting works of regional writers.

A dark cover with bold type shows up well when a photo is included with reviews.

While we cover Internet marketing extensively in chapter twelve, it's interesting to note that at least one author, and we suspect countless others, is taking a new approach to book reviews. Wayne F. Perkins, who wrote and published *How to Hypnotize Yourself Without Losing Your Mind* as an e-book, found it financially prohibitive to send out the needed 300 to 500 review copies usually required to assure a top-selling book. So when he gets requests from book reviewers his response is: "It sounds like you are excited and wish to read my book right away. Why wait for the old-fashioned next-day courier when you can read it online right now? I will give you the unique Internet address of my book or send it to you as an e-mail attachment that you can view in the Adobe Acrobat Reader."

He goes on to offer a free Adobe Acrobat Viewer if needed and says he'll call tomorrow to answer any questions. This turns out to be a great qualifier and weeds out those who really wanted books as a gift for a friend.

Of course, reviews are just the tip of the marketing iceberg. In chapter thirteen, "Provocative Promotional Strategies," we'll be talking about loads more PR print opportunities. Some of the other ways to get your book noticed include author interviews or profiles that compel readers to buy books as they lend a personal angle to a writer's story. We'll also address features, which can utilize your book as a lens through which to examine a particular topic. And excerpts draw attention to new titles by offering an enticing sample of what the whole book holds in store for its potential readers. We'll also show you how op-ed essays can focus attention on your work.

Advance Activities

After you've developed your nationwide marketing plan, study the list of sources and determine which are more apt to give your book the best boost. These are your prime contacts.

Galleys should be sent to your list of prime reviewers as soon as you have the material in hand. We recommend that galley review packages be shipped by Priority Mail or a courier service, such as UPS or FedEx. If yours is a general interest book with nationwide appeal, use the list Where to Send Galleys we provide in Appendix E. If it is a specialized or regional book, add select prime review sources based on the publications you have culled from research. Invest in a phone call to get the correct editor's name.

Some publishers go to great lengths to make their galleys stand out from the crowd. For *The Butcher's Theater*, a novel by Jonathan Kellerman, Bantam had a letter opener (aka knife) piercing the cover of the bound galley. Said marketing director Matthew Shear, "Buyers receive a tremendous number of advance bound galleys of upcoming books, and a key marketing challenge is to get them to pay attention to our book and hopefully to read it." Give you any ideas?

Sending actual review copies is more than just mailing books. This is a *promotional effort*. Make it good. In addition to the book itself, each review shipment should include at least a news release (the hows and whys of which we'll be explaining shortly) and an acknowledgment form (see illustration on page 229). Since a galley has no regular cover, add a color photocopy of your cover art if available. Be sure to include a galley title page containing all the important facts about the book. To help you construct this, we've included a sample on page 231. This can also become the galley cover. Share your planned advertising and publicity campaigns; if you've set up an author tour, don't keep it a secret.

We're amazed at how many trade publishers neglect to ship any promotional material with their review books. Most complimentary copies we receive at Communication Creativity have no promotional literature with them whatsoever. Sometimes we don't even know how much the book sells for.

Always follow up on prime review copies. This can be done by letter, telephone, or e-mail. Some editors of major publications reportedly are so busy that phone calls from publishers are annoying. We haven't found this to be typical. If approached in a sincere and businesslike manner, most reviewers are quite congenial. The best way to jog them without being offensive is to inquire if they

Acknowledgment Form

★★★★★ **Here is Your Pre-Publication Review Copy** ★★★★★

Shameless Marketing for Brazen Hussies™
307 Awesome Money-Making Strategies for Savvy Entrepreneurs

by Marilyn Ross

Price: $19.95
Publication date: November 2000
382-page 6 x 9 original trade paperback
ISBN 0-918880-44-0 • LCCN 00-030334

Communication Creativity
POB 909, 425 Cedar Street, Buena Vista, CO 81211
Phone 719-395-8659

PLEASE RETURN THIS FORM

- ☐ We expect to review this book in: ______________________ on approximately: _________, 20__.
- ☐ We are considering the following subsidiary rights on this title: ______________________
- ☐ We are considering stocking/adopting this title.
- ☐ Please send a photo of the book.
- ☐ Please send a photo of the author.
- ☐ Sorry, we didn't find this book suitable for our needs.

Name ______________________
Job Title ______________________
Publication/Organization ______________________
Address ______________________
City/State/Zip ______________________

Send to: Communication Creativity
POB 909, 425 Cedar Street, Buena Vista, CO 81211

Two tear sheets of any printed review or advance notice of electronic media coverage will be appreciated.

This form, sent out with each review copy, provides the reviewer with necessary data—and sometimes prompts a reply back to you.

received the review copy and offer some bit of news. Remember, as we pointed out earlier, using your telephone before 8:00 A.M. and after 5:00 P.M. saves money, so look where reviewers are located, then try to schedule your calls to catch them during your cheaper time zone.

But what of all the other sources left on the marketing plan that were not deemed as "prime"? Contact all of them about a month before you have finished books in-house.

The letter should be brief and enticing. To be famous, you must be shameless. Tell reviewers what the book is about, when the publication date is, and why it will be of interest to their audiences (fills an immediate need or solves a current problem). Explain your promotional and advertising plans and any special qualifications of the author. We also add something else: a mock book review. This is simply a review that *you* write. We have ours typeset so it appears to have been clipped from a newspaper or magazine. This strategy has one big advantage. Many reviewers are too busy to read your book carefully. A mock review makes it easy for them. They can simply print the review intact or pull passages from it.

Of course, reviewers aren't your only targets. Why not offer a special early sales inducement to wholesalers, distributors, and bookstores? Major publishers use this ploy all the time. You could offer one book free with every five ordered before the official publication date, for instance.

Requests for review copies are filled just like standard book orders. When you receive the request it is a good idea to create a control card (or use a software contact management program, such as ACT! or GoldMine), noting the person's name, publication or medium, address, phone, e-mail, and the date the book was sent, for easy reference and future follow-up.

Include promotional materials with the review copy. If it's for a prime reviewer (the sources listed in Appendix E under Where to Send Finished Books), send the package fast: either First-Class or UPS. If it's *not* for a prime reviewer, ship via Media Mail or Priority Mail.

Regardless of how thorough your investigation has been, you will probably get requests from unknown people asking for review copies. Log these in and send them a book. Chances are their interest is legitimate.

Some reviewers tell us they appreciate a good black-and-white photograph of the book or the author. You can get extra impact this way. Sometimes photos will be used to dress dull review pages. They are even occasionally used with just a caption when a review is not forthcoming. So be sure to include a cutline below your photo that includes your name and the title of the book. And you might take a tip from veteran California publicist Irwin Zucker: Whenever possible he has his picture taken with celebrities. The most recent we saw was of him schmoozing with gossip columnist Liz Smith, whose book, *Natural Blonde*, was

Galley Cover

UNCORRECTED PROOF
FOR LIMITED DISTRIBUTION

Jump Start Your Book Sales

A Money-Making Guide for Authors, Independent Publishers and Small Presses

by Marilyn & Tom Ross

Category:	Writing/Publishing
ISBN:	0-918880-41-6
CIP:	99-11466
Pub Date:	July 1999
Price:	19.95
Pages:	352
Trim Size:	6 x 9
Binding:	Softcover
Illustrated:	71 illustrations
Backmatter:	Appendixes, bibliography, index
Rights:	Ann Markham
Editor:	Tammy "Sue" Collier
Distributed by:	Writer's Digest Books/ F&W Publishing
Publisher:	Communication Creativity POB 909 Buena Vista, CO 81211 719-395-8659

When sending galleys for prepub reviews, we recommend creating this attachment for the cover.

on the best-seller list. You never know where things go once they get started. One of our clients wrote to say his picture and article in a local newspaper resulted in a photographer seeing him and wanting to pose him for a brochure she is doing! Talk about author celebrity.

Of course, if you plan to merchandise your book via direct marketing, a photo of the book is a must. To make your product stand out, use a contrasting background and don't go in for a lot of busyness. A simple shot is all that's required. Today most publications can scan the book cover if they want a color photograph.

If you are going to supply photos, it's a good idea to have them made in the 3″×4″ size, as these will fit in a #10 envelope. Here's a tip that will more than save you the cost of this book: Contact Jemtech Photo Service, Inc., at (412) 621-0331 or visit its Web site at www.jemtechphoto.com.

Of course, editors of specialized media are not as deluged with attention from publishers as are book reviewers for periodicals. A phone call or a lunch, if it is convenient for you, can make your name and written material mean a great deal to such folks. And if your book is highly specialized, they could do you more good than the mass media.

Like all promotion, communication with reviewers is playing the odds. It reduces to a matter of percentages. But if you proceed in a planned, persistent, friendly manner, the amount of free publicity it yields can have a substantial impact on your book sales. And it can go on for years and years as new review sources emerge or editors change at existing publications.

Special Literary Publicity Opportunities

The person with a book of poetry or fiction or an avant-garde literary work faces a unique challenge. While most nonfiction lends itself to publicity quite readily, the novelist and poet must be more creative. Often this is doubly difficult, as these talented people are not the assertive, business-minded types with few qualms about self-promotion.

To make this campaign less painful, we've included a list in Appendix E titled Literary Review Sources. If you use it as the foundation for your promotional efforts, you'll be off to a good start. Poets will find the annual *Poet's Market* a wonderful resource, and fiction writers can look for marketing outlets in the *Novel & Short Story Writer's Market*.

Another place to prospect is the *Directory of Literary Magazines*. Prepared by the Coordinating Council of Literary Magazines, it has complete information on more than five hundred U.S. and foreign magazines that publish poetry, fiction, and essays. This little jewel can be ordered for about $15 by calling (212) 741-9110. One of the most beneficial organizations you could get in touch with

Letter to Reviewer

Date

Dear Reviewer:

The work week shrinks. Companies grant earlier retirement. Our life span increases. Most people reel from the one-two punch of lots of spare time . . . and too little money. Unfortunately, Americans have never been shown how to constructively cope with leisure. Creative Loafing fills that void! In addition to being a lively trade book, it is a suggested text for leisure, retirement and gerontology studies.

This exciting newcomer offers a shoestring guide to new leisure fun that contains hundreds of ideas for free spare time activities. An unusual source book, it includes special quizzes and exercises designed to steer the reader towards pastimes that will be personally enriching.

The publication date for Creative Loafing is October 1, 1978. The book will be launched by "Creative Loafing Days", a gala Leisure Fair. Held in San Diego, the author's home town, this event will feature many of the unique activities discussed in the book. This title has been allocated a generous advertising budget. A nationwide author tour is scheduled to begin in September.

After you've enjoyed looking over the enclosed material, simply complete and return the reply card. We will see that you promptly receive a copy of Creative Loafing to read for yourself!

Yours truly,

Tom Mulvane

Tom Mulvane
Marketing Director

TM:et
Enclosures

A cover letter to reviewers allows you to customize your pitch and tout the newest developments.

is Poets & Writer's, Inc., an information center for the U.S. literary community. It publishes *Poets & Writers Magazine*, puts out several reference and sourcebooks and audiotapes, helps to sponsor workshops and readings by poets and fiction writers, and serves as a general information resource. Phone (212) 226-3586 or visit www.pw.org.

Suppose you have a book for a culturally elite audience or a work of interest primarily to a specialized or minority group. One of the most important things you can do is substantiate why you wrote the book. A tome decrying nuclear buildup will be more widely received if the world knows it was written by a nuclear physicist. A political novel, written by a political scientist, carries more weight than the same book written by a biology teacher. So if you have specific qualifications that bear on your book, for heaven's sake *flaunt 'em*.

Also don't keep the general subject matter of your novel a secret. Often this can be tapped for a promotional tie-in to a current event, local angle, or human interest aspect. (By the way, don't feel you can do this only when your book first comes out. Always be on the lookout for newsworthy angles.) Suppose you've done a novel with detailed background information on hunting. The National Rifle Association might review it in its publications and promote it to its membership. Similarly, if immigrants' experiences at Ellis Island are featured in your novel, there might have been some potential tie-in with the renovation of the Statue of Liberty or the museum about immigrants.

Publicity for Fiction Writers and Poets

Sometimes novelists have to use what has been called the "side door" method for getting attention. This provides alternative angles to the press that framework the book and author from a perspective not immediately apparent. Are there parallels between the author's life and the novel that could be used as media hooks to reinforce credibility? Maybe your book addresses an issue of specific concern to a professional organization, foundation, or special interest group that would benefit from copromotion? Do any of your plotlines deal with subjects in the news? Can you make a topic edgier, come from the opposite direction, be an advocate—or a rebel? As the author of *The Christmas Box* did, look beyond the obvious. Richard Paul Evans comments, "Luckily, I had a story behind my book [his mother's losing a child] that made it interesting to the press."

Poets can also slant their work to certain target audiences. Just as Chaucer's bawdy stories in verse entertain many literate people, and the folksy verse of James Whitcomb Riley appeals to Midwestern farmers and rural people, so, too, might your poetry find a home with a specific segment of the populace. If crass commercialism doesn't grate against your creativity too much, see if there is a segment of the market that your material will particularly interest.

Any award you may have won, along with literary merit, is a good way to promote fiction and poetry. If you live in Alaska, Arizona, California, Colorado, Idaho, Montana, Nevada, New Mexico, Oregon, Utah, Washington, or Wyoming, another possibility awaits you. The Western States Book Awards are presented annually to outstanding authors and publishers of fiction, creative nonfiction, and poetry who work in the West. Among other things, the awards are designed to increase sales and critical attention nationally for fine literary works from the West. For information write the Western States Arts Federation, 1543 Champa St., Suite 220, Denver, CO 80202, call (303) 629-1166, or sign up at www.westaf.org. Information on general book awards can be found in the *LMP*. Many organizations and publications dole out various honors or sponsor assorted awards.

These are some ideas to help you develop your own specialized nationwide marketing plan. Literary works *can* be financially, as well as creatively, rewarding if you're willing to take the steps to make that happen.

Writing Effective News Releases

A major step toward generating free publicity is effective and timely news releases. They are relatively simple yet enormously productive. Jack Erbe, publisher of *The Fifty Billion Dollar Directory*, told us of generating 1,350 requests for information about his book from a news release. And 245 of those free leads were converted into firm orders for his high-ticket marketing guide.

By the way, we refer to them as "news" releases rather than "press" releases for a very good reason: Electronic media do not necessarily consider themselves press, so why run the risk of offending them?

A news release is essentially a short news piece. It should tell the story *behind* the book, not just the story *of* the book. These brief news stories that publicists churn out by the thousands are often the lifeblood of harried newspaper and magazine editors who want to keep their readers abreast of what's new but don't have the editorial staff to cover such things themselves. It is estimated that fully three-fourths of what you see in print is a result of news releases. Be sure to always include a name and full contact info.

Start with a provocative headline. (Some headlines have twice the interest of the products or events they promote.) Weird may work here. A recent release started with "Go to Bed Between the Lions." Especially with the popularity of the movie *Gladiator*, this provoked considerable curiosity. But, rather than being gruesome, it was done in the spirit of childish whimsey. A home fashions company had licensed the rights to develop a line of sheets based on the PBS children's program *Between the Lions*. With some clever wordsmithing, the company captured the attention of even jaded journalists.

News releases present a challenge. One never knows how much of the text will be used. Editors cut releases to fit available space. Since this is the case, it is prudent to get the five *W*s—who, what, where, when, and why—solidly covered in the first or second paragraph. Although some editors rewrite the release, most will not. But they will keep cutting material from the bottom until it fits the space. If the points are strewn over four pages, they'll probably just throw the entire release in the trash.

This medium demands tight, snappy copy to be effective. Start out with a provocative statement, startling statistic, or arresting question to grab attention. After covering the five *W*s, add supportive information in order of importance. As in all promotional writing, state a problem or concern with which the editor and readers can identify. Your book offers the solution. (In the case of fiction, an intriguing synopsis can be the attention getter, or tie into current events if possible.) Do *not* rave about how good the book is. Such fluff hits the round file. Instead, develop the problem and offer a new solution.

Include the author's credentials for writing this book. These should be condensed into one power-packed paragraph. You can adapt or use the author bio you wrote for the cover. Don't be alarmed if your name is not a household word. A little imagination and brainstorming will soon disclose supportive information about your qualifications. Certainly you are qualified—you wrote the book.

Last comes information as to where your book may be acquired. Include the name and address of the publishing company (code it), the retail price, and any shipping charges. Also list your Web site. While some editors feel this is too salesy and will cut it, others will let it ride. Look over our sample news release. A release should never be more than two double-spaced typed pages. One page is even better (we sometimes "cheat" and do it at 1½ line spacing to make it fit). Be sure to include *all* pertinent book statistics: the title, subtitle, author, price, ISBN, LCCN, pub date, number of pages, trim size, binding, number of illustrations, and any back matter. Put it all in a little block at the beginning or end of the written text.

Of course with the Information Age, you can customize your news release with a few flicks of computer keys. Enter a new headline and modify the first and last paragraphs, and you can spin out versions tailored to several different niche markets.

The presentation is important. Print your release on your publishing company letterhead or on plain paper so it can be duplicated on letterhead. Then have it reproduced at your neighborhood print shop. Send news releases to

News Release

P.O. Box 909 • 425 Cedar Street • Buena Vista, CO 81211-0909
http://www.SPANnet.org/CC/ • e-mail: CC@spannet.org
(719) 395-8659 • Fax (719) 395-8374

News Release News Release News Release

FOR IMMEDIATE RELEASE
Contact: Ann Markham
days: 719-395-8659, eves: 719-395-2227
e-mail: Ann@BrazenHussiesNetwork.com

Women Business Owners Wage a Revolution

Sassy lassies are starting new companies at twice the rate of macho males. This isn't a fad. It isn't a trend. It's a revolution. According to statistics released by the Business Women's Network, it's estimated that by 2005, fully 50 percent of all American businesses will be owned by women, thus significantly increasing the growth rate of new enterprises. This is a gender bender of huge proportions and far-reaching ramifications.

"These entrepreneurial women will change the face of business," predicts Marilyn Ross, author of the new book *Shameless Marketing for Brazen Hussies*™. "Woman is blessed with a nurturing nature. We're intuitive, good listeners, and well organized. Plus we think holistically, are as tenacious as pit bulls, and can use our sensuality as a powerful agent for change in the marketplace."

Ross contends that as stewards of their own talents and gifts, women are possibility thinkers. To fully succeed in today's competitive and complicated business environment they must be clever. Gutsy. Dedicated. Technologically savvy. Service oriented. "We can have just as much 'juice' as the guys and play hardball to the max," she says. "We just do it differently."

Shameless Marketing for Brazen Hussies™: *307 Awesome Money-Making Strategies for Savvy Entrepreneurs* has 20 informative, inspirational, irreverent chapters to help female entrepreneurs kick butt. The material covers everything from generating free publicity (then truly *capitalizing* on it) to advertising on the cheap—from forming strategic alliances to unveiling nontraditional sales channels. Dozens of helpful Web sites put this guide on the cutting edge, and personal stories of successful female entrepreneurs encourage as they edify. The book shows women how to be risk takers. Rule breakers. Rainmakers.

As of 1999, there were 9.1 million women-owned businesses in the U.S. employing over 27.5 million people and generating $3.6 trillion in sales. Yet women traditionally make less in their ventures than do men. Ross is out to change that. "We must develop a marketing mind-set that capitalizes on our femininity; one that allows estrogen and entrepreneurship to mix—and create excellence."

Shameless Marketing for Brazen Hussies™ can be ordered from Communication Creativity, POB 909, Buena Vista, CO 81211; call credit card orders toll-free to 800-331-8355; or fax 719-395-8374. The price is $19.95 plus $4 shipping/handling. For more details visit http://www. BrazenHussiesNetwork.com.

The news release is your constant workhorse. By changing the title and first paragraph you customize it for different target markets.

News Release, continued

About the Author: Marilyn Ross, dubbed a "trend tracker" by *Entrepreneur* magazine, has written 12 previous books. Soundview Executive Book Summaries selected one to be among the 30 best business books of the year; another was picked up by Quality Paperback Book Club. Marilyn lives what she writes. Bitten early by the entrepreneurial bug, she made and sold potholders door-to-door at 9, managed in women's ready to wear at 18, and was the first woman night manager ever hired by the Mervyn's Department Store Chain. Marilyn has headed her own advertising/PR agency, owned and operated a hotel and restaurant, and co-founded a nonprofit trade association. A provocative and in-demand professional speaker, she has been a consultant and leader in the publishing industry since 1978.

Book Statistics

Title:	*Shameless Marketing for Brazen Hussies™*
Subtitle:	*307 Awesome Money-Making Strategies for Savvy Entrepreneurs*
Author:	Marilyn Ross
ISBN:	0-918880-44-0
Category:	Business/Marketing
Length:	382 pages
Retail price:	$19.95
Binding:	6" x 9" trade paperback
Illustrations:	Original whimsical line art
Additions:	Sidebars, checklists, Web sites, extensive appendices of resources

magazines, newspapers, and newsletters that reach groups that would have a natural interest in your book. Always be sure to cover your hometown thoroughly. And don't overlook wholesalers, bookstores, catalogs, and radio and TV stations.

Some clever PR people also include a clipsheet of reproducible artwork—such as illustrations from the book, the cover, logos, or other camera-ready art. By providing the media with easily reproduced art to illustrate the news story, you heighten your chances of getting coverage.

Submitting news releases should be a saturation campaign. The more that go out, the better your chances. Most will wind up in the round file. But those that are used are like a third-party endorsement of your book. If a large metropolitan daily newspaper publishes your release, hundreds of thousands of people are reached. A few such victories will outweigh the cost of paper and postage manyfold. Exposure for you and your book is the goal. The more often people hear or see the name, the more apt they are to buy the book.

We know an assertive publisher who sends out a fresh release every month. He ties into current workplace statistics and trends and relates them to his business book. His news release hit rate is awesome, and the media consistently calls him when they need an expert to quote.

The window of opportunity big publishers see is a maximum of six months: three before the book comes off the press and three after. Then they're off to publicizing the next season's books. Smart authors realize their window of opportunity is virtually forever! They constantly nurture their books. (The real money in publishing is in backlist books anyway.) Bernard "Bear" Kamoroff solicits new reviews every single year for his *Small Time Operator*. That's one of the main reasons the book has sold 600,000 copies. Writer's Digest Books bought the rights to *The Complete Guide to Self-Publishing* in 1984, and it's been in print ever since. It may have gone the way of many other titles if we didn't help them keep fanning the PR fire year after year.

But maybe your news releases are falling on deaf ears. Try a different kind of promotional material. We've found postcards to be very effective. We put a colorful photo of the book on one side and a brief but salesy message on the other. Study the sample to see what we mean.

These postcards offer a myriad of possibilities: They make ideal low-key follow-up reminders, can be used to answer a quick question about the book,

Marketing Postcard

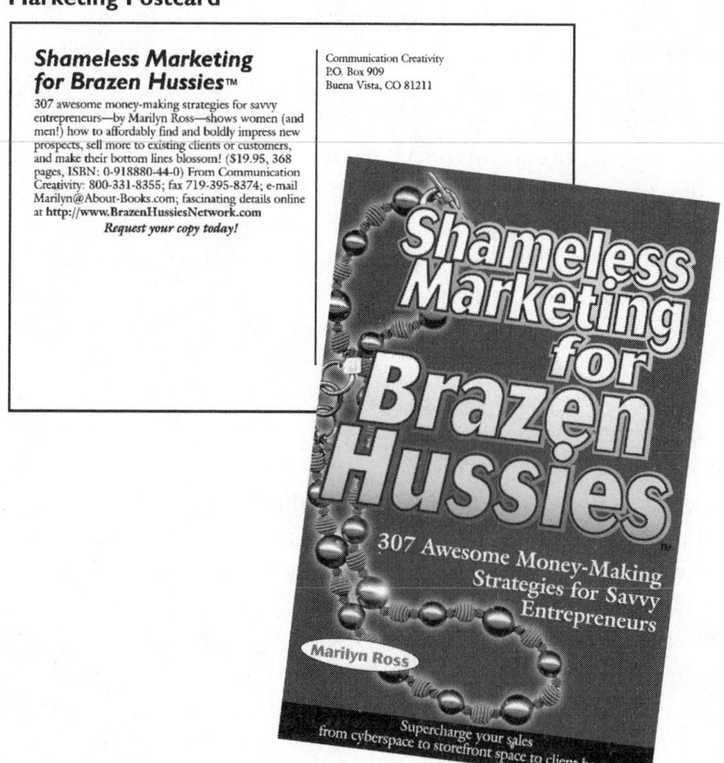
Shameless Marketing for Brazen Hussies™
307 awesome money-making strategies for savvy entrepreneurs—by Marilyn Ross—shows women (and men!) how to affordably find and boldly impress new prospects, sell more to existing clients or customers, and make their bottom lines blossom! ($19.95, 368 pages, ISBN: 0-918880-44-0) From Communication Creativity: 800-331-8355; fax 719-395-8374; e-mail Marilyn@About-Books.com; fascinating details online at http://www.BrazenHussiesNetwork.com
Request your copy today!
Communication Creativity
P.O. Box 909
Buena Vista, CO 81211
Shameless Marketing for Brazen Hussies
307 Awesome Money-Making Strategies for Savvy Entrepreneurs
Marilyn Ross
Supercharge your sales from cyberspace to storefront space to client base

Postcards are affordable and effective—plus they can be used in a multitude of ways.

are perfect to alert bookstores about author media plans for their area, and are great for thank-yous. They can save you bundles of money. In one campaign we sent them *instead* of expensive media kits. We had a rubber stamp made that read "This is a great book! Did you receive my package?" and stamped it in green ink, signed it "Ann," and waited while *they called us* for a change. To think it's only $0.21 to send such a mighty motivator! See a list of affordable postcard printers in Appendix F.

Where to Obtain Free Listings

Another way to take advantage of sales-boosting free publicity is to avail your book, your company, and yourself of the various listings in the industry. These listings fall into three basic categories: book, author, and publishing company.

The top-line listing is, of course, *Books In Print*. Assuming you processed the Advanced Book Information (ABI) form as previously directed, your book will automatically progress from *Forthcoming Books In Print* into *Books In Print*. This comprehensive index catalogs by author, by title, and (if nonfiction) by subject. If your book is for children, grade levels K through 12, you'll also be listed in *Children's Books In Print*.

You will also want to send a copy of the ABI form and book as soon as possible to The Library of Congress, Washington, DC 20541. This serves as a means of getting your title on public record in the *National Union Catalog*.

That should cover everything, you say? Not quite. We certainly wouldn't want to overlook the annual *Small Press Record of Books in Print*. To have your titles included here, request an application from Dustbooks, P.O. Box 100, Paradise, CA 95967, (800) 477-6110.

The above represent the major listings for your book. We do recommend you study the Bowker catalog that we suggested should be in your library. Are there other specialized publications in which you might be included?

Author listings are a good way to boost credibility and increase prestige. These are also important to you for future writing assignments and speaking engagements. Certainly they are worth more than the slight effort required to fill out the necessary questionnaires.

Contemporary Authors (Gale Group, 27500 Drake Rd., Farmington Hills, MI 48331, www.galegroup.com) is published several times a year and contains over forty-two thousand sketches. In addition to biographies of major living literary figures, it lists the first-time novelist, the provocative essayist, the new poet, and other writers beginning their careers. The prerequisites for inclusion are that a person be published by a recognized house (not a subsidy press) and that the subject be on the popular, not scientific or technical, level. Both adult and juvenile writers are covered. Drop Gale a line on your company letterhead and request author entry forms. And December Press publishes *Who's Who in U.S. Writers, Editors and Poets*. Contact this press at P.O. Box 302, Highland Park, IL 60035, http://pma-online.org.

Are you a poet or novelist? Then you will want to be included in *A Directory of American Poets and Fiction Writers*. For information write Poets & Writers, Inc., 72 Spring St., New York, NY 10012. There are many other specialized directories. To get a feel for others in which you might appear, ask your reference librarian to steer you to where such volumes are kept or look in the *Directories in Print*.

Company listings help to establish the credibility and image of a publisher. Dustbooks' *International Directory of Little Magazines and Small Presses* will be glad to know of your existence. Write Len Fulton, the editor-publisher, at P.O. Box 100, Paradise, CA 95967. Another place to get a free listing for your publishing house is in the *Publishers Directory*. This reference is also put out by Gale Group, (800) 877-GALE. When you are up to three or more titles annually, your company can be included in *LMP* and *Writer's Market*.

If your book is appropriate to be sold in college bookstores, write for a listing in *The Book Buyer's Manual*, published by the National Association of College Stores. The association can be reached at (440) 775-7777 or online at www.nacscorp.com. You may also qualify for a product release blurb in *College Store Executive*, which is the national news and merchandising magazine of the college store industry. Send a one-hundred-word description of your title, including a photo of your cover and where the book is available, to *College Store Executive*, managing editor, 825 Old Country Rd., P.O. Box 1500, Westbury, NY 11590. You can find out more about the magazine at www.ebmpubs.com.

For our friends to the north, there is *The Book Trade in Canada*, *Canadian Books in Print*, and *Canadian Publishers Directory* (published by Quill & Quire) and its primary review magazine, *Quill & Quire*. Contact info for all these appears in Appendix C, Canadian Resources.

Now let us investigate the magic of using the Internet to open lucrative national and global doors.

Web Sites, Wisdom, and Whimsey

Swiftly access current information on major magazines. It all waits for you at www.PubList.com. You can do a quick title search and go directly to a link to the publication you're seeking. Or, if you'd like to browse more leisurely to seek publications for review or feature prospects, try any of these subjects: Arts & Humanities, Business & Economics, Computers & Technology, Education,

Entertainment & Leisure, Health & Medical Sciences, Law & Political Science, Reference, Sciences & Mathematics, or Social Sciences. The 150,000-title database also has information on foreign magazines, newsletters, and journals.

* * *

Use this cheap new source for finding syndicated columnists. The beauty of locking in with a syndicated columnist is that your information doesn't go out to the readers of only one newspaper or magazine; it goes out to dozens, often hundreds, of individual outlets. We received over five hundred full-price orders from one review that was syndicated all over the country. The new edition of *Editor & Publisher's Syndicated Directory* is off the press and still only an astounding $8.50. There are over three thousand features listed in seventy-two different subject classifications. Topics run the gamut from food and wine to pets, religion to travel, beauty to consumerism, health to retirement—and lots in between. This is not your typical directory; it's chock-full of cumbersome ad pages you must cope with. But take a few minutes to learn how the book works. It can return your investment hundreds of times over. Order it on your credit card by calling (888) 612-7095.

* * *

Writing a book is an adventure: it begins as an amusement, then it becomes a mistress, then a master, and finally a tyrant. —Sir Winston Churchill

* * *

Are you involved with children's and young adult books? Then visit *The Horn Book*'s site at www.hbook.com. Features include *The Horn Book*'s Children's Classics, all revised, updated, and available free for downloading; the Parents' Page, with recommended reading lists, articles, and excerpts to help parents with book selection; and the For Authors & Illustrators page, replete with advice and information for aspiring children's book writers and illustrators. You can also preview the next issue, plus find out who won the Boston Globe–Horn Book Awards. And if you're a creative marketer, chances are good you can weave some information about your titles into the fabric of this site.

* * *

Children's books sought by often visited Web site. Carol Hurst's Children's Literature Site overflows with a collection of reviews of books for kids, ideas of ways to use them, plus curriculum areas and professional topics for educators. The site carries about 250 reviews, plus annotations about other titles and listings of the Newbery and Caldecott Awards. With approximately 180,000 hits per month, this is a well-visited niche site. Site hosts discuss books in such basic subject areas as language arts, math, history, science, and literature. More obscure topics covered include trains, oceans, quilts, bullies, farms, and more. You can also subscribe to a free monthly newsletter here. Visit www.carolhurst.com, then send review copies (finished books preferred) to Carol Hurst at Consultants, 41 Colony Dr., Westfield, MA 01085, or e-mail her at carol@carolhurst.com.

* * *

In the* Anthenaeum *the following was said of Herman Melville's* Moby Dick: . . . *"an ill-compounded mixture of romance and matter of fact. . . . Mr. Melville has to thank himself only if his errors and his heroics are flung aside by the general reader as so much trash belonging to the worst school of Bedlam literature—since he seems not so much unable to learn as disdainful of learning the craft of an artist." How astute that reviewer was!

* * *

Visit robust site about alternatives in print and media. Casey Hill is a self-described "information junkie"—and it shows on his site at www.NewPages.com. Billed as the portal of independents, it offers news, information, and guides to a fascinating collection of literary and alternative periodicals. A resourceful author or publisher can use this site to find unusual review opportunities, such as *African American Review*, *American Letters & Commentary* (eclectic literary magazine), and *The Advocate* (gay and lesbian). Also used here are links to alternative news weeklies, which can provide a terrific forum for features on edgy books/topics appealing to a hip, young audience. Additionally, by clicking on NewPages Resource Library, you'll find Web sites featuring books and publishing information that could take you a week to investigate. And for the most current buzz, check out the Weblog daily links to items on the Internet of interest to publishers, writers, booksellers, librarians, and readers. If you're into more nontraditional publishing, it's indeed a site to bookmark!

* * *

Calling all science fiction and fantasy buffs, authors, and publishers. At www.sfsite.com you'll find perhaps the most complete SF novel site in cyberspace. It's packed with reviews (get yours on there, too!), author biographies, Q&As with authors, plus author and fan Web sites. There is also a link to newsgroups if you're looking for more, such as Anne Rice's works, or *Babylon 5*. Furthermore, there is a section for small presses publishing in this genre, complete with links to their sites.

* * *

A "classic" has been called a book which people praise . . . and don't read.

* * *

Make a PR killing in small community "giveaway" newspapers! Throughout North America, about three thousand community papers are distributed free of charge to a community base. While some of these publications serve only five thousand people, others produce more than five million copies weekly. Virtually all of these are run with small staffs and budgets as tight as fiddle strings. They welcome interesting stories, reviews, and photographs. Many of these papers belong to the Association of Free Community Papers, which maintains a site at www.afcp.org. Once at the site, you can click to your heart's content: Do an online search of freebie newspapers in your area, or reach much broader and access the entire AFCP member listings. The detailed format includes not only the usual address, phone, and fax but many more particulars. This can be an excellent source for placing stories across the land.

* * *

A man applying for a job in the news office at the University of Texas Southwestern Medical Center at Dallas informed his prospective employer that he was especially good at "offensive public relations." Needless to say, he didn't get the job.

* * *

Take advantage of this Internet review site. Dubbed the boox review—after the wise, bold, and beautiful Booxie Hatton—this site bills itself as "just a little bit different." It exists to promote good books, and the service is 100 percent free. It covers adult fiction, adult nonfiction, children's titles, and poetry. Based on the volume of reviews, things appear to just be getting off the ground, so this may be a superb opportunity to get your book reviewed. Simply go to www.thebooxreview.com and click on Contact Us to get info on where to send your book for review. You may send either galleys or the final bound version.

Are you overlooking an opportunity right under your nose? If you are employed outside of your own publishing company, look into any publications put out by your employer and see if you might be the subject of an article. Short articles about you, or by you, appearing in a company newsletter add clout to your reputation on the job and give you another piece of PR for your media kit.

12 *Using the Web to Rally "Buzz" and Business*

The Internet is vital to your success, whether you have an e-book, are using POD, or have a traditionally produced book. It can be used in a multitude of ways, which we discuss here, and it *must* be part of your marketing mix. The proportion of American adults with Internet access grew to 56 percent from 47 percent during the second half of 2000. We are on the precipice of reaching critical mass, and this tool is ideal for niche players such as self-publishers.

In this chapter, we explore how to put bytes in your bark. While we don't pretend to be Web-profit prophets, we've been active in this arena ourselves for five years and have marvelous input from dozens of other successful e-commerce merchants. So get ready to learn how to create a dynamite Web site and market your books effectively in cyberspace.

Creating a Web Site That's a Surfer Magnet

What's lovely about the Net is that a tiny publisher can look as imposing as a big one. As in a brick-and-mortar business, the first step in an e-commerce business is to decide on a name.

Domain Names

On the Internet it's called a domain name. The most ideal situation is for it to match your publishing company name. Wondering if a certain domain name is taken? Of course, you can enter the URL and see if anything comes up. But just because there is no active Web site doesn't mean the name is available. Now there's an easy way to check. If you're brainstorming names, go to www.namestorm.com and type in the name you're considering. This is a free service to help brainstorm product and company names. You supply the creativity; the site supplies the grunt work. The Namestormers will instantly search available domains, even suggest related terms. Two cheap sources for domain name registrations are www.godaddy.com and www.000domains.com.

It used to be that most domain names ended in .com, some in .net, some in .edu, and others in .gov. Now we have more space in the domain name system—call it the Net's real estate. Seven new top-level domain extensions have been approved by ICANN, the organization that governs domains. While dot.com will probably always be king, now you can opt for .biz, .info, .pro, .coop, .museum, .aero, and .name. Preregistration sites, including www.PreRegisterYourDomains.com, have been taking applications. It's like trying to pick the most satisfying flavor of ice cream on a hot summer day.

Site Hosts

At this point it's time to find someone to host your site. Since companies who specialize in Web services often provide a whole suite of options, this could be your designer or an ISP (Internet Service Provider) that you will need to help you connect to the Internet and get an e-mail account. There are several free or very reasonable alternatives. If you choose frugality, however, there will be limitations. Read the small print. If your budget is minuscule, check out the following: www.DellHost.com, www.BizLand.com, or www.Bigstep.com. If you subscribe to a commercial ISP, such as CompuServe or AOL (America Online), you can access free site space. AOL, for instance, gives you two megabytes for each screen name you have, and you can have up to five screen names.

Content

The next step in your Web site development is to decide on the content. Just as you wrote a table of contents or outline for your nonfiction book, do the same for your site. (To get an idea of this, visit www.About-Books.com and click on Site map.) What will you include? Certainly a photo of the book, a sales-oriented description (perhaps book cover copy or your news release), a chapter excerpt or synopsis, information about the author, reviews and reader comments as they arrive, a schedule of your upcoming book signings and speeches, perhaps even a section for the media and a list of statistics or interesting facts that relate to your topic. Naturally, you'll provide several ways to order the book: via the Web on a secure server, over your toll-free phone number, by fax, and by mail. Some search engines require that retail establishments offer a money-back guarantee. But that's no problem because you've written a fantastic book. To get ideas, go site seeing. Check out what your competitors are doing.

What will bring visitors back to your site, however, is constantly changing content. Create a daily, weekly or biweekly tip to entice them to return. (For nonfiction it can be a snippet pulled from the book; you don't have to reinvent the wheel.) Novelists might want to present a writing hint. Another way to keep them coming is to put your URL on *everything*—not just in obvious places, such as on your stationery, business cards, and mailing labels, but also on customer bills, newsletters, receipts, fliers, ads, and so on.

John Kremer, author of *1001 Ways to Market Your Book* and the newsletter called *Book Marketing Update*, reports doing $1,500 in three days in orders for books, reports, and newsletters directly or indirectly as a result of the Web. He suggests creating a Hall of Fame to list deserving people related to your book. And look for links or listings you can feature. If you write a travel book, what resources could you include on your site? Kremer recommends hotel chains, airlines, cruise lines, theme parks, railroads, rental car agencies, and other sources of information. Of course, you're going to request a link *back* to your site. Right?

Site Design

Now it's time to design that site. Doing it yourself, although cost-effective, may be false economy. It's kind of like editing your own book or designing your own cover. Most writers aren't professionals in those areas—and it shows. If you insist on taking the do-it-yourself route, here are three Web sites with great online tutorials: www.WebDeveloper.com, www.Builder.com, and www.WebReview.com. You can probably do an OK job with MSFrontPage 2000 or Macromedia Dreamweaver. Someone who will do a spectacular job, and also offers sophisticated marketing help, is Dr. Ralph F. Wilson. Visit his site at www.wilsonweb.com. Under any circumstances, you want to have design input. Here are a few things you should know:

- It's important your pages load quickly. Eight seconds is the longest people will wait before they begin to get edgy. The Web has spawned a new kind of fury, a seething, silent kind that results in shoppers dismissing you with a keystroke. We might call it Web rage. If you incorporate many graphics or animations, it will take longer for the user to download your material. Don't forget some of them have dinosaur computers and slow Internet access. Keep it simple and quick.
- Unless your target audience is kids, forget about anything that blinks, spins, or otherwise moves just for show. Adults want meat, and they want it quick.
- Put important stuff at the top of your home page. "Ninety percent of people reading a Web page don't scroll down," notes the director of the International Informatics Institute. Grab their attention fast.
- Your material should be chatty and friendly. Keep sentences and paragraphs short. Introduce subheads. Use bullets.
- Work with your designer to create a logical navigation path. Always have

a way to get back to the "home" page on every page. When the site is designed, try navigating it yourself. Can you get around rationally and easily? On the Internet, tempers have a low simmering point, and competition is just a click away.

- Consider who will maintain the site. It's ideal for you to handle such maintenance as changing text, including a picture, adding a new page. But that means you have to learn the language (HTML) by taking a class or reading a book.
- Stay away from sound or audio files that load automatically. This can anger people. Also avoid anything that requires a plug-in (or third-party download) to work.

Getting Positioned for Traffic

Search Engines

The skinny on search engines changes faster than the colors on a chameleon. What we write today could be obsolete by the time you read it—and that applies to anything about the Internet—but here goes: According to e-business consultant Ralph F. Wilson, who also edits the free e-newsletter *Doctor Ebiz*, "Search engines are the number one and least expensive way to get traffic for a small company." While you cannot control if they will list you, or in what order, it's mandatory you get your site registered with the major search engines; 81 percent of visitors find sites by search engines.

You can get your Web site listed free with the top nine search engines by going to www.uxn.com/search_engines.html. All you do is enter your URL and press Go, and it will be submitted to the following engines: AltaVista, Direct Hit, Excite, Fast, Google, HotBot, Lycos, and Northern Light. This is a really good deal because many of the lesser known search engines actually search these! Also check out www.jimtools.com, which has a SearchEngineSubmitter that goes to forty-six major engines. Another option is to pay $59 a year to www.submitit.com to send your site to up to four hundred search engines. A great portal for tutorials and tools about how to get better placement and traffic is located at www.virtualpromote.com.

You notice Yahoo!, which is the oldest major site directory, having launched clear back in 1994, wasn't included. That is because it isn't technically a search engine that uses automated "spiders" or "crawlers" to find pages. Yahoo!, LookSmart, and Open Directory Project are actually manually managed online directories. Yahoo!, for instance, employs about 150 editors to categorize the Web. They are the secret to people finding things easily on Yahoo!. You must register there individually by going to www.yahoo.com. As you may have guessed, since humans do all the work, this slows things down. Some people have waited as long as six months to get registered. Want to get quick consideration? Yahoo!, LookSmart, and a few others allow you to pay a fee (around $199) to jump to the head of the line.

By the way, you can find specific submission guidelines for most search engines or directories on their home pages. Sometimes doing individual submissions makes a big difference, rather than depending on mass-production automated techniques. You want to resubmit your URL every couple of months to keep the listings fresh. This also helps improve your ranking in the search results. Someone once quipped, "The Internet is an interesting beast because it's almost like being in a new business every six months."

Getting the most from a search engine requires a bit of savvy. If you really want to learn the subtleties of how to get yourself ranked high in the top sites, visit www.SearchEngineWatch.com. On the home page is posted an article (with links to many more fascinating articles) called "Search Engine Submission Tips." It will explain keywords and meta tags and give you insider tips on how to improve your placement.

Links

The second most popular way for visitors to find your site is through links. One study shows they represent 59 percent of the traffic. Not only do links bring people from other sites to yours, they also impress search engines, many of which use link popularity as one measure of the importance of a site. Let's look at an example of how a small press could find appropriate links. Matilija Press has a book titled *The Mainland Luau: How to Capture the Flavor of Hawaii in Your Own Backyard.* Webmistress Virginia Lawrence suggests looking for Hawaiian sites, cooking sites, exotic food sites, travel sites, even pork sites.

Once you've identified possible online partners, review their sites to see if they include links, and note exactly where your book fits best. If they have no pages with links, move on. Next, e-mail the Webmaster a congratulations for the site, introducing your book and stating why it would be a good match, and suggesting precisely where the link should appear. (Don't be surprised to receive a request for a reciprocal link on your site.) Strategic linking is a time-consuming task, but it can bring a lot more potential buyers to your site.

Many people ask us if they should advertise on the Web. Generally, our answer is no. But there are exceptions. (You knew that was coming, right?) Banner ads, which were enormously popular a couple of years ago, have fallen out of favor; most small businesses didn't find them cost-effective. On the other hand, a classified ad in an e-zine or e-newsletter that is targeted directly to your audience could be a terrific buy.

Pay for Position

You also have another intriguing option: *buying* top positioning on search engines. Places like www.GoTo.com and www.FindWhat.com auction off placement. With less popular search terms, you may only have to bid $0.05 or $0.10 a click-through for each person who comes to your site. If this small investment in pay-for-placement puts you in the number one, two, or three spot, you're in hog heaven. One nice aspect of this form of advertising is it is very fast. You can usually be up and running in two or three days, and you can put a cap on it so your costs don't go beyond your budget. It can be an inexpensive way to funnel interested prospects to your site. More and more search engines are also going to paid listings. You can run up a bill here quickly, however, so proceed with caution.

Using Internet PR to Start a "Buzz"

Word of mouth, at 56 percent, is the third best way for visitors to find your Web site. It can encompass a myriad of tactics ranging from chat rooms to electronic news releases, from giving away free copies of e-books to employing sophisticated e-mail campaigns.

Viral Marketing

Viral marketing—old-fashioned word-of-mouth operating at Internet speed—is a mighty weapon. Statistics show that between 5 and 15 percent of those receiving viral messages click through or follow the links. This guerrilla strategy took root with the movie buzz about the independently produced *The Blair Witch Project*. Viral marketing encourages loyal customers and friends to spread the word about you and your book to their friends, acquaintances, business colleagues, and family. So the message gets forwarded several times over.

Says M.J. Rose, "It's about building a fan base and getting readers buzzing about you." A book you should read is by Rose and Angela Adair-Hoy. *How to Publish and Promote Online* not only details their Internet success stories but has contributions from many other accomplished writers and publishers.

Chat Groups

Building community is a big part of word of mouth. Ignite consumer networks, then get out of the way and let them talk. Let interested people market you to each other. You can do this via participation in chat groups (also called forums, newsgroups, listserves, discussion groups, and bulletin boards). The point is, there are groups on the Net that care about your subject, and you should be part of them. To find out what is available, go to http://chat.yahoo.com, or www.topica.com. While overt advertising is frowned upon, you should have the title of your book as part of your signature (more about that later), plus you can offer free lists, quizzes, and other bits of intriguing information to entice people to your site. And when you show your expertise by answering relevant questions, you start to build a real presence in the group.

Writer Marcia Yudkin tells an interesting story about one gentleman who found the material for a book on his listserv. Scott Ringwelski had adopted a Siberian husky from the pound. Finding the dog difficult to work with, he began airing his frustrations to subscribers on Sibernet, a group of husky owners. After seventeen tales of woe, he wondered if anyone was reading. Actually, some ten thousand people worldwide were following his stories like a weekly soap opera. He ultimately crafted seventy-eight tales into a book and found his list mates some of the best customers. "Some folks on my list are looking to obtain up to 20 copies," he reports.

You might also take part in a virtual chat tour. Instead of spending a bundle to traipse around the country, you simply hold chats online. Top sites for such activities are www.yahoo.com, www.iVillage.com, and www.TalkCity.com. Online chats allow you to speak directly to your readers.

One Woman's Approach to Marketing on the Web

Let Marilyn share how she approached using the Net to market *Shameless Marketing for Brazen Hussies.* First, she amassed a list of hundreds of sites targeted to working women, women, marketing, PR, sales, entrepreneurs, and small businesses that might want to promote or sell the book. Then she created a spreadsheet to capture the information needed when visiting those sites. It included researching the following: Did they do reviews? Did they sell books? (Directly or through Amazon or some other affiliate program?) Did they include links? Did they post useful articles by a variety of writers? (Good excerpt potential there!) Did they have e-newsletters—where they might sell, review, or mention the book, plus do an interview with Marilyn? She captured full contact information, even though she knew that e-mail would be the most appropriate approach for an Internet-based company. Now she was ready to hit the e-trail.

Electronic News Releases

Just as news releases open PR doors in the traditional world, they can accomplish remarkable things on the World Wide Web. But there is a *big* difference, and you need to learn how to craft releases that are appealing to busy online journalists. That means cut, cut, cut. Think of your release as a teaser. Once you have their interest, it's a simple thing to point them to your Web site where full details await. (Don't use attachments, however, and know that journalists hate wading through too much stuff and needing to scroll down a release to find the meat.) State your point in a lead paragraph of no more than forty words. Have one or two more short paragraphs that elaborate, be sure your full contact info is at the top or the bottom, then quit! Writing tight is tough. It was Mark Twain who observed, "If I had more time I would have written less." To get the hang of how to pitch a story so succinctly, study the home page of *The New York Times*.

You may decide to use an e-mail pitch letter or memo rather than a news release format. Weave in benefits frequently and put your call to action at the top, in the middle, and at the end. As with the press release, intensify and condense. You can track and test what works in online marketing just as you can in direct mail. Simply give your e-mail promo a unique URL. Unlike direct marketing, however, the results here are quick. Rather than waiting three months to know what works, you have the final order—or request for a review copy—within three days.

Free Books

Giving away books is another excellent way to generate a buzz online. When Seth Godin wanted to publish *Unleashing the IdeaVirus*, he planned to give away e-copies. But his publisher, Simon & Schuster, felt that if he gave his book away for free it would devalue it, reports Godin. So he passed on the sizable advance, opting to self-publish.

Six weeks after releasing the free e-book on the Web, over 200,000 people had downloaded it. When the hardcover went on sale for $40 each, the 26,000-copy print run sold out in only three weeks. Every copy was sold over the Internet; not a single book went through a brick-and-mortar store. (Godin felt that if the e-book and the hardcover had been available simultaneously, he would have sold even more copies of the print book.)

If this approach feels entirely too daring for you, use a modified strategy: Give away e-copies of books you've written that have gone out of print or a collection of short stories to promote your novel, or offer half the chapters of your nonfiction book free to get readers interested and talking. Your goal is to lift your book from obscurity.

E-Mail Newsletters and E-Zines

E-mail newsletters and e-zines are other ways to generate attention. To promote her self-published books, Angela Adair-Hoy created a free e-newsletter for writers that featured freelance job listings and new paying markets. Her e-mag subsequently generated sales for her main products: books on how to make more money writing. "I quickly noticed that the more subscribers I attracted, the higher my income was," Adair-Hoy reports. She also discovered that when she

A Creative Way E-mail Can Be Used Effectively

Book Birth Announcement
(and a not so subtle plea for your unabashed support!)

HELP . . . again to recreate the book sales BUZZ. Once again, I am coming to you for HELP . . . to launch *The Confidence Factor—Cosmic Gooses Lay Golden Eggs.*

Endorsements have been received from Chicken Soup's Jack Canfield, businessguru Tom Peters, best-selling author Susan RoAne, activist Sarah Weddington and *Washington Post* columnist Judy Mann—just to mention a few. Judy Mann wrote a wonderful column on April 4th recommending the book.

Eleven years ago, the original "baby" was born . . . *The Confidence Factor—How Self-Esteem Can Change Your Life.* It has consistently been my most popular speech since 1990.

Mile High Press is the publisher and the publishing date is May 1. The cover (and contents) are terrific—all 170 pages of it; feedback from readers excellent—they love the quick read. Procter & Gamble is using it in the promotion of the new Downy Wrinkle Releaser (because of the book, I'm its national spokesperson).

Books are rarely in the store . . . so I need your help in calling your favorite bookstores and requesting it—(it's posted on Amazon.com and bn.com). Ask any author, and she or he will tell you that publishing is odd—we often wonder if publishers really want to sell books. We authors do know that, we all can make the difference by getting the word out!

We are mounting a media campaign for papers, magazines, radio, TV and the Internet that will cover several months. But it's my friends, family and colleagues that help the most. You make that difference.

Frankly, I need your support again. "How to Create the Buzz" hints:

- If you know of anyone in the media, a producer, a writer, an affiliate with any paper, radio show, TV show . . . or Internet site—please let me know. They can go to my Web site www.Briles.com for lots of info and can call me at (800) 594-0800 or my cell at (303) 885-2207.
- If you are comfortable with connecting me with your acquaintances, I would be eternally grateful. The media coverage contributes to sales and that contributes to my speaking gigs and that sells books, books which create more gigs. It's a great circle to get caught in!
- If you know of anyone in the media, a producer, a writer, an affiliate with any paper, radio show, or if you pass by a bookstore . . . could you inquire about my book? You don't have to buy it . . . but asking for it creates the groundswell . . . and they probably don't have it . . . yet. Tell the bookseller you know me, etc. If the book is there, face it out—they sell better this way. My Web site has a link to Amazon.com, but I am a big supporter of local and independent bookstores. Go to www.Briles.com—on it you will find the Table of Contents and the first chapter. In fact, you can find the Table of Contents and first chapter for most of my books there—all free for downloading.

• If you have a chance, please tell your friends, colleagues and family. It's the perfect gift for anyone you know who has hit a few potholes in and outside of work—also for new grads. No matter how confident you are—you can always learn new things in rebounding when you hit the potholes of life—i.e., the legendary leader of GE at the age of 68 discovered the Internet when his wife booted up the GE Web site and he learned that people were saying he was a jerk. That weekend, he bought a typing course, learned how to type and thinks the Internet is HOT! Confident old dogs learn new tricks. His support of using the Internet saved GE $100 million in travel related expenses!

• Go to the Internet sites of Amazon.com and bn.com and post glowing reviews. Ordering from those sites would also make my day!

• Ask your local libraries to order it so that it's carried on the community shelves for all.

• If you live in the Denver, Colorado, area, I will have a book signing and reading at the Tattered Cover Book Store in LoDo at 5:30 P.M. on Thursday, May 31. The TC is one of the most influential bookstores in America. Your presence would mean so much.

The original *The Confidence Factor* sold over 250,000 copies—this one is all new (it was the most popular title to use—the subtitle is different.) It's also written for MEN and women—different from my first book on confidence. Your help and support are so special, essential and very appreciated!

Please feel free to forward/fax this to anyone in your circle and address book—the more, the better! Why not go global?! Thank you so much. With great, great appreciation, Judith (who wants to sell more books and get off the road!).

P. S. If you see any articles with my book or me quoted, would you please mail them to me? Dr. Judith Briles, www.Briles.com, (800) 594-0800. Best-selling and Award Winning Speaker, Author & Spokesperson.

Dr. Judith Briles, Speaker—Author—Spokesperson
DrJBriles@aol.com—Judith@Briles.com—www.Briles.com
800-594-0800—303-885-2207—Cell—303-627-9184 Fax

The Confidence Factor
Creating Confidence Out of Chaos
Zapping Conflict in the Workplace
Smart Money Moves
Thriving with Change

bumped her free e-mag to weekly, the profits jumped accordingly. Today she makes about $5,000 each month from her publishing company, which is located in her bedroom.

As you can see, e-mail can play a huge role in your Internet success. In the year 2000, Americans sent 610 billion e-mails! An essential element of a Web-based marketing campaign is to collect as many of these online addresses from your Web visitors as possible. This is often done by offering a free newsletter, special report, chapter, or related small gift. With their permission, you can then periodically e-mail these people about specials, new books, exciting reviews, Internet chats scheduled, and other promotional events.

You can even use what is called an autoresponder (also called autobots or mailbots) to automatically answer e-mail within minutes using a response you prepare. It functions twenty-four hours a day, seven days a week, so you can concentrate on other aspects of your business. This definitely puts the "calm" in dot.com and can be quite effective. Author Wayne Perkins gets a book sale from approximately one out of every four requests he receives. Autoresponders are often free; check with your Webmaster. If that isn't the case for you, the following sites perform this service for no charge: www.SendFree.com, www.GetResponse.com, and www.FastFacts.net.

Before leaving e-mail, we want to address the signature issue. Of course, you've figured out by now you're living in the Dark Ages if you don't have e-mail. But if you don't have a carefully crafted signature, you are also missing an opportunity. This should include full contact information for you, plus the title of your book, and one brief benefit-oriented sentence or offer of free information. (Try to keep your signature under six lines.) You may want different signatures for different occasions. Get in the habit of adding your signature when you initiate an e-mail or reply to one. Always use it in newsgroups when you post something.

Eight Ingenious Ways to Use Amazon.com to Your *Advantage*

Does it make sense to capitalize on every possible means to influence those who visit the earth's biggest bookstore? You bet! Every day thousands of book buyers go to Amazon.com to select from its 4.7 million titles.

These eight zealous ideas won't cost you a cent. Yet they help level the playing field, making your books more outstanding than the competition. No matter whether you are an author or a publisher, you can apply creativity to bend the consumer's will to *your* liking.

1. **Write customer reviews of other books and plug your titles.** Reviews beget sales. There are ways to insert information about your own book as you review worthy competing titles: You can compare the two books, sign off as the author of *XYZ*, even list yourself as the reviewer at the beginning (Jane Doe,

author of the *Enervating Entertainer*). Partway down each book's page is a section called Customer Reviews. Click on Write an online review and do your thing.

2. **Use Amazon's best-seller list for detective work.** Wondering just what *is* your competition and how you stack up? You can search via general subjects, such as business, parenting, and gardening, or more specific topics, such as woodworking, zoology, and astronomy. Then ask that the books be sorted by Bestselling. Bingo. You have insider information about what else is available on your topic and how each ranks.

Of course, another benefit of having this data is, if you're in the top ten or so, you can legitimately say you have a best-selling book. (And how would publishers with obscure titles on coin collecting or witchcraft, for instance, ever be able to make such a statement otherwise?)

3. **Turn Amazon into a PR tracking tool.** Suppose you're doing media blitzes in four different areas, or perhaps you're scheduled to be on a big syndicated radio program or a major TV show. Would you like to get a sense of how well it went? Here's how: Go online ahead of time and see where your book is ranked overall in sales. This ranking number is shown just below the picture of your cover. (For instance, our *Jump Start Your Book Sales* is currently number 3,649 out of all the books they sell.)

Then wait a few hours or a day and check your online sales ranking. You'll be able to see immediately if there is a big blip in sales activity. And on the overall Bestsellers list, in the left column is a link called Top Movers & Shakers. By clicking on this you can find out the biggest Amazon.com gainers over the past twenty-four hours.

4. **Garner scads of customer reviews for your books . . . and capture library sales.** Having a couple of dozen or more consumer reviews on your site is "a good thing," as Martha Stewart would say. It's virtual worldwide word of mouth. How do you get them? Ask! When someone e-mails us with kudos, writes a thank-you letter, or expresses appreciation for our books over the phone, we try to remember to ask if they would do us a favor. Then we request that they go to Amazon.com and barnesandnoble.com and write a brief customer review for the book. Does it work? Says Amazon spokesman Paul Capelli, "We know from our feedback that they are an important way that people decide on what to buy."

Not only do these reviews hold powerful sway over customers surfing Amazon's site, they also impact another important audience: librarians. A library purchasing study conducted by the American Library Association and the Association of American Publishers revealed a startling statistic: Forty-five percent of the respondents rated Amazon.com as a "highly effective" source for book reviews! Because many libraries, especially small rural public facilities, are budget challenged, most can't afford to subscribe to expensive review journals. They admitted to using this free resource to make purchasing decisions.

5. **Get your books into the hands of Amazon's own key reviewers.** The editorial team at Amazon.com organizes feature presentations and welcomes promotional materials and review copies. To ensure that your request is processed in the most efficient manner, and to increase your chances of actually getting reviewed, make sure that you indicate which of Amazon's categories best represents your book. To see a list of these categories, go to Browse and select Books, then select Browse Subjects. After you've determined which category your title falls under, make sure you include that information on your mailing label and mail your materials for review to Editorial Department, [Relevant Category], Amazon.com, P.O. Box 81226, Seattle, WA 98108-1226. The toll-free phone number is (800) 570-1454. If you're lucky, Amazon editors may decide to review your book themselves.

6. **Investigate Purchase Circles.** Purchase Circles are highly specialized best-seller lists covering what people are buying around the world, in your hometown, at various companies, for the government, even at your alma mater. There are thousands of such lists. Find these lists by selecting Purchase Circles in the Special Features menu. The lists can then be organized by geography, government, organizations (nonprofits, professional), companies A–Z, or education A–Z.

Perhaps you want to conduct a regional marketing campaign and need to research what is moving in New York versus Los Angeles versus Chicago versus Houston. Go to the Geography category, click on United States, then the city. Likewise, you can see what books certain corporations are buying and if your new title might fit in. Or check out what books are hot at what institutions of higher learning.

Worked imaginatively, these circles can provide a wealth of insider information. And, once again, if you find your own book leading the pack at one of these circles, you can proclaim it a best-seller.

7. **Participate in discussion boards.** Have an opinion to voice? A question to pose to readers? A book that needs promoting? As of this writing there are fifteen discussion boards about books. The easiest way to locate them is to go to http://Amazon.remarq.com/Amazon. Here you'll find topics under Authors' Corner, Women In Mystery, Science Fiction & Fantasy, Romance, plus such nonfiction areas as Health, Fitness & Diet, Politics & Current Affairs, and Travel. Editors are also seeking topics for new boards, so suggest away.

8. **Hand-sell your books by enhancing your page.** Amazon is wonderful about allowing authors (and publishers) to create many promotional features that literally hand-sell your products to their customers. Be sure you have the

following on your book's detail page (which can go on almost indefinitely):

- Book cover photo (There is currently a $15 charge to include a color photo. One tip: If you send your cover as an FTP, the art will go up in twenty-four hours rather than taking weeks to appear when e-mailed or sent on a disk.)
- Table of contents
- Interior book spreads
- Reviews from established review venues (This includes advance blurbs from notables, and reviews from such publications as *Publishers Weekly*, *Library Journal*, *Booklist*, *Kirkus*, *Choice*, *The Bloomsbury Review*, *The New York Times*, *The Village Voice*, and *ForeWord*.)
- Reviews from customers
- Excerpts (The whole first chapter is often a good choice.)
- A synopsis, if your book is fiction
- Jacket or back cover copy
- Author comments
- Publisher comments
- Author self-interview
- Author biography

For full details on how to submit information to Amazon's catalog and join their Amazon.com Advantage program, go to their Books home page, scroll down until you see Publisher Resources on the right side. You'll want to click on the Publishers' Guide just below it. This will take you to a page that touts the Advantage program. If you look along the left side, there is a list of options. We suggest you Click on Complete Instructions and Rules (Do you feel a bit like Hansel and Gretel following bread crumbs?), then download this information so you have a printed copy of the guidelines in front of you.

The major benefit of the Advantage program is that it assures your book will show availability within 24 hours. While there is no charge to join, they require a 55 percent discount and you pay freight. For some authors and small publishers this works ideally; others prefer to have Amazon purchase from a major wholesaler such as Baker & Taylor.

To add to all your book goodies we discussed in the bulleted list above, you want to go back to the page titled Welcome to Amazon.com Bookseller Services and look in the left column. When you click on the appropriate term, you'll find directions for Cover Art, Interior Art, Descriptive Text, and Content Form. This isn't brain surgery, just tedious. Please set aside a day to embellish your Amazon.com home page. Add persuasive content, and pursue the ideas in this section. It can pay off in big dividends. Happy sales!

After reading this chapter you should get the idea that the Internet provides an unparalleled vehicle for creating promotional buzz—and selling thousands of dollars worth of books. Have at it: There's unlimited shelf space in cyberspace.

Of course, your marketing needn't end there. There are many more innovative promotional strategies—many we *guarantee* you've never thought of—awaiting you in the next chapter.

Web Sites, Wisdom, and Whimsey

Access a profit-making accumulation of Internet booksellers. The following is a list of the more prominent Internet booksellers. Here we give you not only their Web addresses, but also directions on getting to their individual book pages: Amazon.com, click on Books under the Browse menu; barnesandnoble.com, select Bookstore from home page; Borders.com, select Books heading; BUY.com, select United States, then Go, then Books; Booksamillion.com, select Books from the home page; Fatbrain.com (a barnesandnoble.com company), make a selection from the Shop our Bookstores menu; Wal-Mart.com, select Books from the home page; Gohastings.com, select Books from the home page; VarsityBooks.com, search, browse and buy textbooks; BookBuyer.com, loads up to its Books section; WordsWorth.com, brings you to its independent bookseller site; AlphaCraze.com, select Books from the home page; Powells.com, brings you to Powell's books; and one of our favorite bookstores, Tattered Cover, has a site, www.TatteredCover.com.

* * *

Make your Web site address and e-mail easier to read. Although the rule of thumb is up to the .com, .net., .edu, or .org, you can use capitals in your Web address or e-mail. Thus, when citing your domain name (not individual pages), rather than saying www.joeblowpublishers.com, use www.JoeBlowPublishers.com for better identification. Likewise, for easy-to-read e-mail, make it Joe@JoeBlowPublishers.com.

* * *

This is not a novel to be tossed aside lightly. It should be thrown with great force. —Dorothy Parker

* * *

New discussion group is called I-Content. Savvy entrepreneur and marketing expert Marcia Yudkin is moderating a new discussion group about how to make creativity pay off on the Internet. Sign up for your free subscription at www.audettemedia.com/lists/icontent/summary.html.

* * *

Need to make corrections on your Amazon.com book page? No big deal. Just send an e-mail to book-typos@amazon.com. Be sure to include the ISBN of the book, plus your name and phone number so you can be contacted if there are questions.

* * *

Take lessons on the links. No, we're not going to give you golf instruction. Rather, we want you to know about a site that can be used innovatively to boost your Web site placement in search engines. At www.LinkPopularity.com you can access free information about where your site is linked. Link prominence can dramatically increase traffic to your site. Many of the major search engines are now factoring link popularity into their relevancy algorithms. Consequently, increasing the number of links to your site can actually improve your rankings! To discover how many links you have (and what they are) on three top search engines—AltaVista, HotBot, and Google—all you do is plug in your URL at LinkPopularity.com and up come the statistics! Why not be creative with this available information and check out the link status of your *competition*? This is an easy way to find additional sites that might link to you!

* * *

When you depend on the Web to find an expert, you don't have to kiss a million frogs to find a prince.

* * *

Does it pay to have your book featured online? *Up Your Service*, by Ron Kaufman, appeared on an Internet best-seller list for Asia. As a result, he was offered a contract for global rights by Hyperion, which proposed a $75,000 advance with $25,000 committed to promotion.

* * *

Discover how to work smarter with e-mail. If you want to use e-mail to push your business to the max, there's an online "course" by Paul Krupin that covers the subject in detail. There are sections on Writing Business Quality E-Mail, Replying, Forwarding, Attaching Files, Managing Your Mailbox, Closing The Sale With E-Mail, even Protecting You and Your Company From Liability. It's a good investment of twenty minutes of your time. Find this resource at http://emailtothemax.com.

* * *

A lifeline exists for those confused by acronyms used in chat groups. Does it baffle you when people communicate (we use the term loosely) on the Web with things like AFAIR, BTW, or TBYB? There is a whole shorthand vocabulary that some folks delight in using when they get online. If you would like a list of these various chat acronyms, go to www.computeruser.com/resources/dictionary/chat.html. We'd suggest you download it to your printer for reference. Don't be surprised, however, if the first few pages are virtually blank; the high-tech dictionary will soon start rolling out.

* * *

If it weren't for the last minute, nothing would ever get done.

* * *

There is a cheap source of additional domain names. At only $13.50 per year, now you can afford to establish multiple new domain names that provide additional doorways to your Web site. You might want to do one for Your Name.com, one for TheTitleofYourBook.com, and others with key words that lead to your subject. Or perhaps create .net and .org extensions for your present Web site URL as future insurance. It all happens at www.000domains.com. You can use the site's Bulk Registration form to look up and register multiple domains at once, making the process a piece of cake. New names are being registered at the rate of more than ten thousand a day, so act now if this is a strategy you want to take.

* * *

New Internet search engine for book Web sites is launched. Looking for a free way to generate more online exposure? Then mosey over to www.SeekBOO

KS.com where you can get your book Web site listed. Dedicated exclusively to book sites, this unique search engine lets consumers look for books within specific subject categories, then be linked to your Web site for more in-depth information. SeekBOOKS.com rotates the order of the book site descriptions within search categories, so each has the chance to be number one. The search engine also offers affordable advertising. Additionally, SeekBOOKS.com produces a free newsletter called *Authors Online* that is full of useful tips. In talking with CEO Doug DeGroot, he explained that this search engine also has a radio show on one of the major satellite networks that interviews authors and has audio on its Web site that publishers or authors can buy into.

E-mail, e-mail, and more e-mail is the order of the day. Even though you probably use e-mail on a regular basis, at http://everythingemail.net/index.html there are many practical tips that may help alleviate some confusion or make your e-mail more productive. There are links to e-mail programs, autoresponders, forwarding services, e-mail list search engines, and other e-mail assistance. There is also an online bulletin board forum to discuss issues and questions on the topic.

13 *Provocative Promotional Strategies*

Promotional activities provide free and fun ways to get exposure. Here we explore how to get lots more print coverage. And we'll investigate the world of radio and TV, giving you pointers on generating interviews, then telling what to do when you're a guest. You'll also read about various other creative and low-budget promotional vehicles.

Getting Newspaper Coverage off *the Book Pages*

Did you know there are 1,730 newspapers published daily in the United States? They have a combined circulation of nearly sixty-two million people. Reviews, as we discussed earlier, are only one way of using them. Throughout the year, newspapers put together special supplements, which can be another bonanza. These are topic specific: seniors, health, automobiles, gardening, college, investment, and others. Find out what's planned for your major daily.

Lifestyle or Trends sections, known in the old days as the "Women's Pages," are often a good bet. Other more specialized sections (Business, Religion, Sports) may also welcome you, depending on the subject of your book. Frankly, you're usually better off in special sections. It takes a true book lover to digest the book review pages, but all kinds of folks read the other sections. Gardeners, for instance, will have their noses buried (no pun intended) in the gardening section but would seldom discover your book about organic gardening if it were discussed only in the book pages.

Let's say you have a book on child raising. Every major newspaper has an education writer or editor. Articles in this section are read by both parents and teachers. Author David Cole suggests you target the papers with circulations over 100,000 (there will probably be about one hundred of them) and send a series of short three-hundred-word articles extracted from your book for one-time use. Make sure you include how-to tips and provide illustrations if possible.

Surely you have looked with awe and maybe envy at full-page spreads about authors and their books, complete with numerous photographs. Worth a lot? Bet your sweet bippy it is! Don't buy into the idea that only famous best-selling authors get that kind of coverage. 'Tain't so.

William Zimmerman would testify to that. He's had spreads in *The Washington Post*, *BusinessWeek*, and *The New York Times*. Zimmerman, founder of Guarionex Press, which published his *How to Tape Instant Oral Biographies*, comments, "I've shown how you can leverage no money and gain a lot of national attention and sales." The *Times* feature about him prompted two thousand inquiries replete with countless orders for his book.

The successful author-publisher has staying power. Tenacity. Persistence. Bill Gordon, author of *The Ultimate Hollywood Tour Book*, pitched no less than thirteen different reporters at the *Los Angeles Times* before he got one to do a story. It first appeared in the Orange County section, then hit all the metro pages a week later.

Print media offers the enterprising writer-publisher a bumper crop of opportunities for promotion. Don't ignore the rich harvest small independent newspapers can provide. They, too, can be of assistance to your campaign. Alert them to newsworthy activities. Press releases to hometown papers about author tours filter into coverage in columns or feature stories. Consider contacting the media in any town where you've previously lived.

Don't forget the wire services. Should you be fortunate enough to lock into one of them, your book could skyrocket to stardom virtually overnight. If you live in a major city, check the phone book for local editorial offices. Otherwise, contact The Associated Press (AP) at 50 Rockefeller Plaza, New York, NY 10020, (212) 621-1500; United Press International (UPI) at 1510 H St., NW, Washington, DC 20005, (202) 898-8000; and Reuters at 1700 Broadway, New York, NY 10019, (212) 603-3300.

Hitchhike on Current News

One of the best ways to get into the news is to hitchhike with another item of current interest. When President George W. Bush put Linda Chavez up for Secretary of Labor, the controversy heated up when it came out she had had an illegal alien living in her home, doing miscellaneous chores, and had given the woman money. Kathy Fitzgerald Sherman, author of *A Housekeeper Is Cheaper Than a Divorce: Why You* Can *Afford to Hire Help and How to Get It*, jumped on this issue.

Perhaps your book solves a problem that has just hit the headlines. Such was the case of one clever author who had written a book on how to stop snoring. One day his newspaper vigil uncovered an obscure two-liner about a pending divorce. It seems the poor harried wife could no longer tolerate her snoring spouse. A long-distance call to the presiding judge, a couple of bottles of booze, and an overnighted book resulted in a front-page spread with pictures. The judge felt this book could save the marriage. Picked up by the wire services, the word spread swiftly, and the book went into four printings.

This is one story of many that confirm the value of a "news peg" and the hitchhiking principle. With a bit of inventive brainstorming, we bet you can think of lots of ways to link your book with news items. As we write this, for instance, the story of the adoption battle over the twin girls brokered over the Internet continues to dominate the airwaves. What a built-in peg for several books: It's a natural for a guidebook or true story about adoption. A novel centering around the birth mother could find a home here. So would a book about the ethics of the Internet.

To tie in with a breaking news story, you, of course, have to know about it. If you're serious about attracting more than your share of print, radio, TV, and Internet coverage, you must read the newspaper first thing every morning. Marilyn has bookmarked the home page for *The Washington Post*. You can read it free online by going to www.washingtonpost.com.

To add verve and flair to your promotional campaign, you might consult *Chase's Calendar of Events* to see if there is a special day, week, or month you can hitchhike with. This directory offers 736 pages of imaginative PR angles. It is a day-by-day resource of holidays; historical anniversaries; fairs and festivals; and special days, weeks, and months. It lists more than twelve thousand entries of national or broad regional interest. Besides normal contact info, this hefty edition also contains e-mail addresses and Web sites—and is fully indexed by category and locale. It's a great reference for tagging your promotions to a special time.

Got a book on mystery writing? Don't overlook August 13. That's the birthday of Alfred Hitchcock—and that's just the sort of kooky thing the wire services pick up. Have you written a career guide for nurses? Perhaps you can tie in with National Nurses Week in May.

Greg Godek, who wrote and self-published *1001 Ways to Be Romantic* and its sequel, *1001 More Ways to Be Romantic*, uses Romance Awareness Month (August) to his advantage. He appeared on *Donahue* to conduct a romance seminar—and pushed his books onto Walden's and Ingram's best-seller lists. In 2001, he was a guest on the *Today* show. Of course, he always has a busy January and February because he ties his books in with Valentine's Day celebrations. It definitely works.

And Nolo Press, an assertive California publisher of legal self-help books, laid down the law by combining with KFI radio to sponsor L.A. Law Day. The event drew more than three thousand people to hear several Nolo authors speak on legal issues. In addition to local media coverage, the event garnered them a photo and blurb in *PW*—thus drawing bookstore attention to their imprint.

Finding the Niches

Cross promotion to niche markets can help you get a leg up as well. Carol Lea Benjamin's mystery novel *Lady Vanishes* stars a PI named Rachel Alexander and her sleuthing pit bull, Dash. In this case, the PR strategy passed over the main character in favor of the dog. Thus there were excerpts, reviews, and interviews in such canine media as *The Bark* magazine and the American Kennel Club's *Bloodlines* magazine.

And the angles for clever novelists are never ending. For Glynn Marsh Adam's mystery titled *Dive Deep and Deadly*, there was a review in the National Association for Cave Diving publication and the author appeared at the National Speleological Conference. Consequently, orders are coming in not so much from bookstores but from shops that sell cave diving equipment!

In another astute match, jazz drummer-author Bill Moody's book *Bird Lives!* was launched at the Jazz Bakery, a musical club in Los Angeles. The event was so successful, the club continues to sell Moody's book. Another publicist successfully courts travel writers and travel agencies for Ann Livesay's *The Madman of Mount Everest* and *The Chala Project*, which is about rafting down the Colorado River.

Plan your initial publicity for the print media to coincide with the publication date of your book. Let the press know you will be available for interviews during this period of time. Oh yes, there is definitely a technique for letting the press know. Here is one that has proven extremely successful for us. Create an Available for Interview announcement, like the one on page 268. This needs to be a power-packed fact sheet about the book and the author. Ideally, this package should go out under a name other than your own, such as your pseudonym. This makes it more credible when the book and author are lauded.

Take a look at the example. Now start brainstorming. Focus clearly on *your* book's premise. Think of as many short punchy zingers about the book as possible. Cover the what and why thoroughly. Boil down your ideas, combining and eliminating, until you have four or five strong points. Don't forget the material on your book cover as a resource.

Now let's work on promoting the author. You're an expert . . . you wrote the book . . . so establish that fact beyond doubt. As you can see, half of the grabbers about the author feature qualifications and credits. Give a strong logical reason why the author wrote this book, stressing the writer's credibility for tackling this subject. Go through the same exercise for pruning your "about the author" comments into their most productive form as you did for the book. Brainstorm, write a bunch,

Available for Interview Sheet

Available for Interview

Marilyn Ross: author, speaker, expert, trend tracker

Women Waging a Revolution

■ Women are starting new companies at twice the rate of men. This isn't a fad. It isn't a trend. It's a revolution. According to statistics released by the Business Women's Network, it's estimated that by 2005, fully 50% of all American businesses will be owned by women. As of 1999, there were 360,300 women-owned firms in the Los Angeles metropolitan area, representing 39% of all businesses. This is a gender bender of huge proportions and far-reaching ramifications for all consumers.

■ The expert to talk about this is Marilyn Ross, author of *Shameless Marketing for Brazen Hussies™*. "These entrepreneurial women will change the face of business," predicts Ross. "Woman is blessed with a nurturing nature. We're intuitive, good listeners, and well organized. Plus we think holistically and are as tenacious as pit bulls. Add these qualities to our natural intelligence and business savvy, and you have a powerful agent for change in the marketplace that will dramatically impact consumers."

■ Ross contends that as stewards of their own talents and gifts, women are possibility thinkers. To fully succeed in today's competitive and complicated business environment they must be clever. Gutsy. Dedicated. Technologically savvy. Service oriented. "We can have just as much 'juice' as the guys and play hardball to the max," she says. "We just do it differently."

■ *Shameless Marketing for Brazen Hussies™: 307 Awesome Money-Making Strategies for Savvy Entrepreneurs* has 20 informative, inspirational, irreverent chapters to help any entrepreneur—man or woman—kick butt. As Jay Conrad Levinson (author of the *Guerrilla Marketing* series) says, "Your book is fun to read, shockingly incisive, and extremely enlightening—whatever your gender."

■ Ross can address everything from generating free publicity (then truly *capitalizing* on it) to advertising on the cheap—from forming strategic alliances to unveiling nontraditional sales channels. She can also inspire those who dream of starting a business of their own...show them how to be risk takers. Rule breakers. Rainmakers.

About the Author/Expert: Marilyn Ross is an experienced, articulate, provocative media guest and professional speaker. Dubbed a "trend tracker" by *Entrepreneur* magazine, she has written 12 previous books. Soundview Executive Book Summaries selected one to be among the 30 best business books of the year; another was picked up by Quality Paperback Book Club.

This dynamic woman has been noted and quoted in publications across the land: *The Wall Street Journal, U.S. News & World Report, The Los Angeles Times,* and *The New York Times* have all written about her and her work. Additionally, she has been featured twice on NPR's All Things Considered, cn scores of other radio stations, and on dozens of TV shows from coast to coast. Recently Marilyn was also spotlighted in a lead story on CNN financial news on the Internet.

Marilyn lives what she writes and talks about. Bitten early by the entrepreneurial bug, she made and sold potholders door-to-door at age 9, managed in women's ready-to-wear at 18, and was the first woman night manager ever hired by the Mervyn's department store chain. Marilyn has headed her own advertising/PR agency, owned and operated a hotel and restaurant, and cofounded a nonprofit trade association. She has been a consultant and leader in the publishing industry since 1978.

Marilyn Ross will be in Los Angeles Oct. 23-26. To book her, Call 719-395-8659, fax 719-395-8374, or email Ann@about-books.com. Contact us for faxed material, request a book/media kit, or visit www.BrazenHussiesNetwork.com for further details.

Create a power-packed sheet for the media that will encourage them to want to interview you.

cut, condense, improve—until three or four emerge as the pick of the crop.

This kind of media approach, which included a news release and the dust jacket promotion piece, produced as many as seven interviews in one day during our *Creative Loafing* tour. That was almost too much, even for Marilyn. We suggest that four or five per day produce less stress and better interviews.

Be sure to get the Available for Interview material to editors in plenty of time to accommodate their scheduling. (And indicate specific dates you are available even if the notice is going only to your hometown paper.) For newspapers and weekly magazines, allow four to six weeks minimum. Four to six months is a normal lead time for monthly magazines. Allow a couple of weeks for your information to filter down to the proper desk, then follow up by phone. Find out if the package was received and the reaction. In the case of newspapers, if the recipient doesn't exhibit much enthusiasm, ask if she could suggest a different reporter in another department who might find the information more appropriate. Then you can contact the new person, say that so-and-so suggested you call, and go into your spiel. Interested editors will request a copy of your book.

Of course, it doesn't end there. Smaller community newspapers dot every urban area, targeting information to those in the communities they serve. Their readers are usually very loyal. And there's a profusion of weekly newspapers published in small towns, as well. Also don't overlook the college presses. These bright young reporters may give you valuable space if your message fits their audiences. What an overall windfall for the assertive promoter!

Publications for Fiction Writers

If you're a novelist, don't overlook fanzines that specialize in your genre. As the word implies, these are fan magazines. They represent every fiction category: romance, science fiction, horror, fantasy, mystery, and westerns. This is an excellent way to build a loyal readership because they are devoured by readers who love each of these kinds of books. In addition to reviews, fanzines do author profiles, run Q&A articles, have What's New sections, and accept paid advertising. (This is one of the few places it might make sense to advertise: in your genre fanzine.) You learn about these magazines by participating in the various organizations (Sisters in Crime, Romance Writers of America, Western Writers of America, for example) that deal with your genre.

* * *

With imaginative PR—and a lot of persistence—you should fill your interview calendar nicely. Keep notes in your contact management software, a database, or on some sort of control cards. Don't be surprised if the interviewer hasn't read your book. Such is the case the majority of the time. And don't overlook the possible advantage of inviting an editor to be your guest at breakfast or lunch. This may be just the touch that convinces him to interview you. There may be, as the proverb says, no such thing as a free lunch—but one that results in a story is better than free!

Recycle, Recycle, Recycle

We can't emphasize enough the value of print media exposure. You get a one-two punch here. First, you get space that would cost thousands of dollars if you had to buy it. Second, most of what is printed becomes support material that can be used as sales aids and promotional literature. Reprints of articles are dynamite. It isn't *you* saying you're good; it's the impartial publication. (Who cares if its circulation is smaller than your neighborhood?) Get it out there! Recycling a feature story or review can be more valuable than publishing it the first time. The media like to climb on a moving bandwagon. If they see you are already getting exposure, they are more likely to want to do a story.

You want to send these reprints to *everybody*! Get copies in the hands of wholesalers or distributors you're wooing, to major bookstores or Web sites you hope will carry your book, to electronic producers you are pursuing, to your banker, to any investors, to board of director members. What's interesting is that this publicity may well have been generated from one of your news releases. So now you send a news release about the news . . . to trade journals in your book's industry, to associations to which you belong for their Member News sections, and so on. If in doubt, send it. It may even be appropriate for a direct-marketing package you are preparing for consumers.

After we've amassed several reviews, we condense them and put together a sort of "here's what people are saying" flier, such as the sample sheet on page 271 titled Reviews about *Jump Start Your Book Sales*. While the writers of most reviews expect them to be reprinted by their very nature, feature stories and author profiles are often copyrighted, and may require reprint fees; check into this before doing any major duplicating.

More Creative Print Angles for Writers on a Budget

For self-publishers with budgets tighter than shrink-to-fit jeans, there are several intriguing ways to stir the pot. None of these costs more than money for postage or gasoline, yet they can yield dramatic results.

Review Sheet

Reviews about *Jump Start Your Book Sales*

"Demonstrates how energetic authors and publicists can increase revenue by carefully planning a book's marketing strategy on TV, on the Net, in bookstores, through 'buzz,' etc. A particularly helpful section teaches writers how to actually *sell* their books at those ubiquitous author readings. 71 illustrations. Writer's Digest Book Club selection."

—***Publishers Weekly***, July 26, 1999

"Their [Rosses'] advice is up-to-date, specific, and practical, whether the topic is generating publicity, cracking nontraditional markets (home-shopping networks, for example), or 'muscling your way into traditional channels' (wholesalers, the library market, educational sales)...This guide is an essential reference."

—***Booklist***, July 1999

"Marilyn and Tom Ross help inspire those who want to sell more books. I highly recommend that you purchase *Jump Start Your Book Sales.* It's a steal at the low price of $19.95."

—***Independent Publisher***, Nov/Dec 1999

"A very good new book. You'll find lots of nuts-and-bolts ideas on getting publicity, opening distribution channels, selling online and more."

—***Book Marketing Update***, April 30, 1999

"The information the Rosses have packed into this twenty-five chapter book comes not only from the experience gained in marketing their own books for many years, but from what has been learned from the give-and-take sessions of their highly respected seminars. *Jump Start* has suggestions for selling to bookstores, libraries, non–traditional markets, premium and incentive sales. Throughout every chapter the reader comes upon a treasury of insider tips and tricks of the trade. The many sidebars liberally sprinkled through the text provide concrete contact and lead information.... This is a book for serious people interested in making a serious attempt not to have their books wallow in the basement."

—***ForeWord***, September 1999

Communication Creativity, 719-395-8659, POB 909, Buena Vista, CO 81211-0909

For more information, visit our Web site at http://www.SPANnet.org/cc/js

Once you begin to generate reviews, pull them together into one impressive sheet.

One idea is to provide magazines with freebie chapters. Editors are always interested in receiving well-written pieces relevant to their publications' audiences—especially if they don't have to pay for them. Be sure to study the magazines' and newsletters' formats. Look for such things as the length of pieces, if they use an anecdotal approach, and whether their styles are casual or formal, elementary or sophisticated. In your cover letter, indicate you have written a book and are willing to provide selected chapters without any cost to them. Include some of your promotional materials so the editors can taste the flavor of your message, and refer them to your Web site. Also state that at the end of the excerpt you expect a reference to the book and full ordering information.

Since your book is on computer, you can go one better. Take a chapter, or a subhead section, alter it slightly, toss in an introduction, plop on a little conclusion, and you have a fresh article. We've done this several times and made some big bucks. We did a piece about self-publishing for *Science of Mind* magazine.

The results were astounding. Because of a meaty paragraph at the end of that article, we sold over $4,000 in products! We did a similar thing with *Pace* magazine, taking a chapter from *Big Ideas for Small Service Businesses*. It brought in over $12,000—certainly more than any freelance article we've sold! This kind of win-win partnership with a magazine benefits everyone.

If you don't want to turn over actual parts of your book, write a short piece on the subject in general. We did this about self-publishing for *Southwest Airlines Magazine*, *The Toastmaster* magazine, the Women in Communication trade journal, and several others. Of course, we always insist on a bio that gives specific ordering information for our book.

Quizzes, tips, lists of dos and don'ts—they are easy to create and editors love them. We offer them on a complimentary basis as long as full ordering information is included. That's the trade-off. On page 273 you'll find the piece we did on "5 Money-Making Tips for Business Owners." By the way, this type of material also works well as a giveaway when you're on the radio. By offering it for an SASE, you help listeners and sell more books. Naturally, you'll include a sales brochure about the book when you mail the giveaway.

A Toronto-based couple has a tip for Heloise: Graham and Rosemary Haley use tips to promote their book of household advice called *Haley's Hints*. Columns of their tips run free in Canadian newspapers, and they recently offered them to *The National Enquirer*, which plans to run them on a regular basis. Last we heard, they were also in negotiation with Amazon.com to create a free Haley's Hints on that site, complete with a link to their book. Additionally, the Haleys have created almost three hundred two-minute TV tip ideas, which are offered throughout the world. A lot of people put them in as filler material between shows. We have no way of knowing if this tip approach is the reason, but this self-published book has topped 300,000 copies sold.

We've had good luck using Letters to the Editor in strategic publications. (You do subscribe to the trade journals relevant to your subject area, don't you?) When a *PW* columnist talked about reissues of regional titles in her "West Watch" column, we took this as an invitation to promote our *How to Make Big*

Free "Tips" Article

AVAILABLE FREE FOR REPRINT

5 Money-Making Tips for Business Owners

by Marilyn Ross, Award-Winning Colorado Author

Marketing is the crucial ingredient for any business, whether you're a newcomer or a veteran entrepreneur. It's required constantly—and forever. Yet where do you find the time? Here are just five of the 307 guaranteed strategies from the bold new book, *Shameless Marketing for Brazen Hussies*. Use these ideas to supercharge your sales from cyberspace to storefront space to client base.

- **Form strategic alliances.** Think about who is already reaching your client or customer base, then forge a win/win partnership with them. Why spend thousands of dollars and countless hours reinventing the wheel when you can team up with other companies, organizations, Web sites, and individuals to build market share?

- **Create a reason to be "news."** Free publicity is the lifeblood of many enterprising entrepreneurs. You can do many things to catch the attention of the media: Conduct a survey. Hold a contest. Present an award. Comment on a timely controversial issue. A simple news release about your imaginative endeavors can open doors to print, radio, TV, and the Internet.

- **Recycle your media exposure.** Often what you do with your publicity *afterward* is more important than the original publicity itself! When you get print exposure, include copies in client proposals; send it to your banker, venture capitalists, or angels you're wooing; impress your current customers by mailing it to them; put reprints out on the counter; frame and mat a copy for your wall. Leverage your PR by spreading it everywhere!

- **Cultivate testimonials and referrals.** It's always more impressive when someone other than yourself says you're good. When people compliment you, do you ask that they put it in writing on their letterhead? Sharing this with prospects is powerful stuff. And do you encourage current and past clients or customers to recommend you to their friends, loved ones, colleagues, neighbors (enemies)? A satisfied customer can be your best salesperson. Tap into this remarkable river of revenue.

- **Brand yourself to stand apart from the herd.** In today's competitive environment, we need to seek ways to differentiate ourselves and our companies. Branding is the act of creating specific impressions that contribute to overall attitude among a target group of prospects. Build an image that is uniquely you. Martha Stewart did it. So have Madonna and Oprah. Create your distinctive brand with imagination and uniformity: in colors, signage and logos, value offered, customer expectations.

###

Provided the following credit is given, you are welcome to reprint this article for free.

"Excerpted from *Shameless Marketing for Brazen Hussies: 307 Awesome Money-Making Strategies for Savvy Entrepreneurs* © 2000 Marilyn Ross. Used with permission of Communication Creativity. All rights reserved. Order from 1-800-331-8355 or visit http://www.BrazenHussiesNetwork.com."

Note: This "Tips" article can be produced via e-mail or on disc for your convenience.
Contact: Ann Markham, 719-395-8659

Giving away articles is terrific PR. A short "tips" piece will appeal to both traditional print publications and Web sites.

Profits Publishing City & Regional Books. Marilyn's Letter to the Editor ran a full column and talked about doing new area books, of course mentioning our title in the process. We were able to directly trace several orders to this source.

A cousin to this is the op-ed essay. These pieces usually run about 750 words and are placed opposite a newspaper's editorial page. Many papers pay for them. The essay is a forum to showcase the idea or industry behind your book and typically carries the title at the end of the piece.

One of our clients has succeeded in syndicating a column. It's being offered to the more than one hundred gay publications across the country. The title? "The Straight Poop." Creating a column might work for you, too. Monthly is easier than weekly. It quickly becomes a chore to think up new topics and crank out 500 to 750 words of copy every week. The beauty of this approach is after awhile you can put out another book . . . of your columns!

Start Locally, Grow Nationally

Many self-publishers don't have the budget to be all things to all people in all places. There is nothing wrong with starting in your immediate area, then letting things ripple out from there. We say this with two caveats: Don't overlook sending galleys to the major national reviewers initially; if you miss this window of opportunity, it slams shut permanently. Also line up a few national wholesalers/ distributors. You never know when your local promotion will catch fire in a big way and you need to be ready.

Because it wasn't practical for Brenda Ponichtera to extend her efforts financially much beyond her own region, she focused on local bookstores, media, and signings for *Quick and Healthy*, her book of recipes and ideas for people who don't have time to cook healthy meals. Instead of being a detriment, this approach proved to be beneficial because it helped her establish credibility with chains such as Barnes & Noble and Waldenbooks. Having seen how successful her promotion was in the Northwest, they were more receptive to carrying books nationally. Apparently the strategy worked in spades. Ponichtera has two books out and has sold nearly 600,000 copies.

Richard Côté is a South Carolina author-publisher who launched *Mary's World: Love, War and Family Ties in Nineteenth-century Charleston* in November of 2000. His strategy for this scholarly biography was to use concentric circles, starting out where it was cheap and easy. That meant phase one covered a twenty-five-mile radius around Charleston, South Carolina. He wanted to totally saturate sales in the hometown market—and take advantage of possible Christmas sales—so he set out to personally stock every major Charleston bookseller in the first two days after the book arrived.

Phase two took in coastal South Carolina, while phase three encompassed the rest of the state. From there he moved to all of the former Confederate States of America, and finally to the whole nation. And when you're taking the "big

Local Bookstore Strategies

Richard Côté used four strategies we feel are brilliant:

1. Although he had called and gotten initial stocking orders over the phone, he automatically arrived with a larger order. Since the book has lots of visual and emotional appeal, seldom did he have to take back any inventory.
2. He signed every book and had the bookstores affix a "Signed by Author" sticker to each one.
3. He asked that the books be displayed in three different locations in the stores: under New Arrivals, in the Local Author section, and by the cash register.
4. He gave each store two 11″ × 17″ color mini-posters and suggested one be taped on the front door. Most agreed. (These were copies of the book's cover and were made for $1.79 each at Office Depot.)

fish in a little pond" approach, don't overlook regional magazines for your area, such as *Los Angeles Magazine*, *Palm Beach Life*, and *New York* magazine. Many give special feature consideration to local authors.

Generating Radio and Television Interviews

You are unique indeed if, at some time in your life, you have not visualized yourself as an idol of the film industry or its smaller sister, TV. Some of you may have even accompanied Captain Midnight or The Lone Ranger in daring capers across the radio waves. Well, your time has arrived. Come along now and let's make you a star!

Putting together a radio and television promotion campaign is much the same as dealing with print media. In fact, we can use the identical Available for Interview promo package. Be aware of one difference, however: In electronic media, formats and personnel change as often as bed linen. It's a pressure-cooker world, making radio and TV mobile career fields. As personalities move on, often the shows they chaired disappear.

Television, being the most prestigious of promotional media, many times presents the largest challenge to your imaginative publicity campaign. Always contact TV stations in main metropolitan areas at least eight weeks before your availability date. Major network shows will require even longer lead times. Call the producers' offices to find out how far ahead their guests are booked, and ask the names of the producers or guest coordinators, the correct spellings, and their e-mail addresses.

We recommend both the front- and backdoor approaches to television in the big cities, meaning you send one package to the general program director and another to the producer of any specific show you wish to be on. Of course, follow up on both if you haven't heard anything in a couple of weeks. As with all promotion, tenacity and repetition may turn the key. Then perhaps one day you'll utter the seven words every author wants to be able to say: "It's nice to be here again, Oprah."

Tips for TV

The best TV plums are the *The Oprah Winfrey Show*, *Today*, *Good Morning America*, and *Rosie*. Needless to say, it wouldn't hurt if Jay Leno, David Letterman, or Larry King took a personal interest, either. If you're on the show any length of time, Oprah moves buyers to bookstores like lemmings to water.

Before you hope to crack one of these babies, get lots of media experience under your belt. Always bring a videotape and have stations tape you each time you're on the air. This will cost you a little, but rest assured that the producers of the above-mentioned shows aren't about to let an amateur on the air. You'll have to prove you're worthy of their precious airtime.

One of the tricks of the trade a very successful publicist shared with us is that she scours *TV Guide* cover to cover. It tells what guests are being featured on which shows and helps you see a pattern emerge for certain producers. Something else she does is read the entertainment trades (*Variety*, *Hollywood Reporter*, *Broadcasting & Cable*). Here she learns about new shows and staff changes, picks up on trends, and gleans other information that gives her a heads-up on media opportunities. If you're really serious about TV, you might want to follow her lead.

As we advised you earlier, *make it easy* for people to do what you want them to do. Think about putting together a show or segment yourself. If you can provide a panel of experts (yourself included, of course), this takes a big burden off the producer's shoulders. What authorities do you know who can complement what you have to say—or take the opposite tack?

As soon as you've made contact with the proper person at the TV station, start keeping notes. This will be of immense help in preparing for the interview. Think about the subject matter of your book and how it could be made interesting to television audiences. Offer any suggestions to vary the normal interview format. Think visually. One author we represented, who had done a book on nutrition, prepared a food demonstration on the air. If you've written about camping and hiking, you might give a demo on how to pack a backpack. Have a book on flower arranging? It's a natural for a demonstration. Did you author a romance? Perhaps you can concoct a segment on decorating a wedding on the cheap.

After the interview is scheduled, ask questions. Find out what the host wants to cover. Suggest areas that "your author" wants to touch on. You may get insights into the personality of the host and some hint as to the slant needed to put yourself and your book in the best light.

If the thought of being grilled by a TV interviewer scares your socks off, don't be dismayed. This is common with many authors. The world of television studios, cameras, bright lights, and people rushing everywhere can be a bit overwhelming. (One way to become more at ease is to muster up your bravado and join Toastmasters.) Watching or listening to the shows you'll be on gives you a higher comfort level, as you'll know what to expect. Role-playing with friends and family is also excellent training. Be prepared to summarize your book in one clear, tantalizing sentence.

By having a clearly defined agenda you wish to explore, you'll cut through apprehension like a hot knife through butter. Make specific notes of the things you want to cover. Prepare three or four key points. Then work on brief, punchy statements to explain them. These are called sound bites and the media loves them. Have anecdotes to support them. People adore stories. Some interviewees even go so far as to type out a list of questions to provide interviewers. (Notice our examples on pages 278 and 279: The first is a sample of what you might send to the media. The second is for our internal use; it gives the questions and the points we want to develop under those questions.)

Anticipate in advance the questions you're likely to get, and don't dodge the difficult ones. Then you won't be surprised when you're thrown a zinger. Train yourself to expect the unexpected. Remember, you're the expert. You know your subject backward and forward. Rehearse your answers and comments to build your self-confidence. The key to successful interviewing is organization; it's what keeps you focused. Want to know exactly how you'll look and sound? Use a camcorder.

When dressing for TV, avoid distracting plaids and busy stripes. Keep it simple. Women shouldn't wear glittering or jangly jewelry. Take your notes, any visuals you plan to use, two copies of the book, and a duplicate promo package along. Plan to arrive about a half hour early. You'll be put in what is called the Green Room. (Don't ask us why; we've never been in one painted green yet.) This is where TV guests wait. It's a cushy holding pen (sometimes) with coffee, snacks, and—you guessed it—other guests. Therein lies a danger. Don't get so animated and excited explaining about your book to a guest that you lose all your pizzazz for the actual interview! Ask someone for a glass of water if you feel tense. Take several deep breaths. Before airtime, study your notes, psyche out probable questions, and rehearse your answers. Most times, you will be the better prepared of the two of you involved in the interview.

With this kind of groundwork you're bound to have a good interviewing

Media Sheet to Mail

Give Your Listeners Tools for Entrepreneurial Success!

WHO: Marilyn and Tom Ross, authors, lecturers, marketing experts

WHAT: *Big Ideas for Small Service Businesses*

WHEN: Anytime by appointment

WHERE: National interviews by phone; personal appearances in key U.S. cities

WHY: To provide your audience with stimulating guests who offer provocative marketing solutions for small businesses

To make your job easier, here are some sample questions . . .

- ☐ Why don't you encourage entrepreneurs and professionals to spend large amounts for advertising?
- ☐ In the book you talk about using business cards as mini-billboards. Elaborate on that.
- ☐ What led you to write *Big Ideas for Small Service Businesses*?
- ☐ What types of businesses are included in the service sector?
- ☐ How important is "positioning?"
- ☐ How can an individual or small firm generate free radio and TV exposure?
- ☐ How can a small firm implement an effective marketing campaign on a limited budget?
- ☐ What are some more ways a company can prospect without spending money?
- ☐ How can our listeners get access to your *Big Ideas for Small Service Businesses* program? By calling 1-800-331-8355.

P.O. Box 909, 425 Cedar Street, Buena Vista, CO 81211-0909 • (719) 395-8659

What the media receives to prompt them to interview you.

presence. This is the quality every TV person wants: someone who is relaxed but not sloppy; informed but not overbearing; vivacious but not silly. During the actual interview, ignore the camera and crew. Concentrate your attention

Media Question Sheet With Answers

P.O. Box 909 • 425 Cedar Street • Buena Vista, CO 81211-0909
http://www.SPANnet.org/CC/ • e-mail: CC@spannet.org
(719) 395-8659 • Fax (719) 395-8374

Media Questions for Marilyn Ross, author of
Shameless Marketing for Brazen Hussies™

▪ **You state in *Shameless Marketing for Brazen Hussies™* that twice as many women as men are starting new businesses. To what do you attribute this trend?**

A) Glass ceiling . . . women make 75¢ on the dollar compared to men (a lifetime loss of $420,000).
B) Women today are more skilled and knowledgeable...many entrepreneurs come from the ranks of managers.
C) They want to control their own destiny.

▪ **Why are women beginning to have an edge on success?**

A) Customer expectations. We're not selling garments or tires, dentistry or consulting services . . . we're selling customer satisfaction.
B) Women excel here. We're the nurturers. We're learning to capitalize on this innate characteristic to build stronger businesses.
C) First it was the Industrial Revolution. Then the Technological Revolution. Now we have a backlash: The People Revolution. Customers want a caring experience. In general, women simply deal with people more pleasantly and effectively.
D) More women than men are going to college. By 2003 the gap will widen to 5.2 million women attending compared to 4.1 million men.

▪ **What one thing can any business owner do to grow his or her company the fastest?**

A) Form strategic partnerships with companies, organizations, and individuals who already have your customer base.
B) These affinity programs could be neighborhood businesses that refer overflow (for a 5%-10% referral fee or reciprocity); Web sites that form strategic alliances; traditional professionals or national merchant collaborations, etc.

▪ **How important is the Web?**

A) In most cases, vital. It gives your company a global marketplace 24/7.
B) Need 4 ingredients to be successful, however: Good site design, high search engine placement/links, ease in ordering, outstanding customer service.

▪ **What are the 4 rules that almost guarantee success for business owners?**

A) Ask for what you want.
B) Make it easy for people to do what you want.
C) Apply the 80/20 rule.
D) Follow up, follow up, follow, up.

▪ **How can our audience get *Shameless Marketing for Brazen Hussies™*?**

A) Order online at www.BrazenHussiesNetwork.com.
B) Call toll-free 800-331-8355.

To make their job easier, prepare a list of questions for the media. (You will provide them only the bulleted bold questions.) This is to show *you* the answers as well.

on the person interviewing you. Resist the urge to fiddle with the mike, a handkerchief, or any other object. Don't slouch. Keep your voice lively and assured. Smile. Be friendly and enthusiastic.

Letty Cottin Pogrebin, president of the Authors Guild, recommends, "Find out in advance how long your segment will be. . . . Don't let other guests dominate the microphones and use up your time slot. Interrupt if you have to. You're not there to win an etiquette prize, you're there to hook people on your book so they'll want to run right out and buy it."

Do speak in human terms; don't get mired in a bunch of statistics. Brief, clipped, precise answers are better than rambling replies. Suppose you get a question that requires you to pause and gather your thoughts? Don't panic. A trick we've used to stall for think time is either to repeat the query or to say, "That's a good question." Reply positively to negative questions. Explain what your book is, not what it is not. Mention the title instead of referring to your work as "it" or "the book." And be ready to plug your book if the host happens to forget. If you're doing a seminar or appearing to autograph books, mention this. "Show and tell" goes on in broadcasting as well as in kindergarten.

Some stations will flash information on the screen if you've made prior arrangements for your phone number or Web site to be shown. The words trail along the bottom of the screen and reinforce what you say.

After the interview there's still one vital detail to handle. If you made a good impression, the audience is going to want to know where to buy your book and how to contact you. Be sure you've brought several media reminder cards telling all ordering information about the book and how to reach you. One of these cards should be left with the host, one with the talent coordinator or producer, and one with the station's receptionist. (She often gets calls asking about guests.) Some broadcasters have information centers that handle inquiries. Ask if this station has such a thing, and be sure the staff knows where your book can be purchased. Send a thank-you note to the producer and the interviewer. They gave you valuable exposure, and you may want their cooperation again. This will help them remember you.

And we hasten to add that the things we're discussing here are not the sole domain of the self-publisher. All authors can and should become involved in the promotion of their books. It makes all the difference.

Take Callan Pinckney, for instance. When her *Callanetics* was launched by Morrow, it sold a respectable 10,000 copies, then went back to press for another 5,000. But interest waned and books went unsold. Not one to give up easily, Pinckney arranged media visits to southern cities, then wangled her way onto a Chicago television show. Within an hour of her appearance, Kroch's & Brentano's received some 400 orders. That was the firing pin that shot her book into best-seller status. With 182,000 copies in print, the paperback rights were sold to Avon for a reported $187,000 guarantee—all because an author took an interest in her own book.

Timing can also have bearing on your success. Television networks conduct regular rating sweeps in February, May, and November. These are *bad* times for you. The local program producers will be seeking blockbuster guests to pull in greater viewing audiences and boost their ratings.

Getting on TV News

One thing in television that should not be underestimated is the power of a short news spot. News falls into two types: hard, which covers matters of local, national, and international consequence; and soft, the kinds of human interest features that people find fascinating. An author is more likely to fit in the latter. As we discussed earlier, you can also "use news to make news" by packaging your subject matter with something else of current note.

Perhaps you can create some news. Can you do a survey or study on a topic of timely interest that relates to your book? Joan Stewart, editor-publisher of *The Publicity Hound*, tells of etiquette expert Marjabelle Young Stewart who has used this technique for twenty-five years! This author-speaker travels a great deal in her work and surveys people, creating lists of the "most mannerly cities." When she releases the results to the media, they go nuts. The media and their audiences are curious about how their areas fared. Her surveys have been reported by hundreds of media outlets throughout the United States, including on CNN and in *Time* magazine, *The New York Times*, *The Washington Post*, and countless business journals. What a clever way for Stewart to create national publicity.

News time is precious time. Learn to zero in on the essence of your story quickly. Use those sound bites! You may only have seventy-five to ninety seconds in which to pack your punch. But think of all the thirty- and sixty-second commercials that sell millions of dollars' worth of products and services each year. (And the sponsors have to pay for those.)

We were once booked for a taped news slot on a popular station in Phoenix. Because we were usually well on our way to the next stop, or the programs were live, we typically missed seeing them. So imagine our surprise when we walked into our hotel room, flipped on the TV, and heard the anchorman say that the station would be talking about *Creative Loafing* later. Then a full-screen shot of the book appeared. Needless to say, we were glued to the set, afraid to blink for fear we would miss the anticipated few-second spot.

What transpired left us a little breathless. A thirty-second clip from the prerecorded fifteen-minute interview had Marilyn introduce the subject and the book.

Then for five minutes we were entranced by film clips from the station's news file showing people participating in activities suggested as pastimes in the book. These were interspersed with narrated close-ups of the front cover. Another thirty seconds of Marilyn's prerecorded interview closed the segment.

Six minutes of prime TV time, including a long plug by a local news celebrity. Who could have guessed that such a gem would be aired on the six o'clock news on the most popular network TV station in town? Do you have any idea of the value of such exposure? We don't know of many publishers who could afford to buy that kind of coverage. The great equalizer struck! And it can strike for you, too.

Our point, of course, is that a minute or two of prime-time news coverage can have greater impact than a half-hour midmorning talk show. We believe, however, that any TV coverage can have significant impact on bookstore purchasing decisions. We book 'em all. Since TV is so influential, competition for available time is fierce, especially with all the celebrity authors out stumping these days. With imagination, a creative approach, and tenacity, you may be able to land some good shows.

Going National

As you work with major media in the large markets, another dimension may be added. You may be asked for an exclusive. That means you will appear on that TV show, on that radio station, or in that paper *only*. (Or *first*.) Don't take exclusivity lightly. Be sure what you're getting is worth the concession. Look at such things as audience size or circulation, prime-time exposure, the prestige of the program or paper, and the enthusiasm of the people involved. Then be grateful they feel you are important enough to warrant such a request.

Don't expect to start out with *Oprah*, *Rosie*, *Good Morning America* or *Today*. You must prove yourself first. Get several important local interviews under your belt before tackling a major network or syndicated show. Conversely, you will find that once you've booked a major program, the rest are much easier. Here again, start at home and fan out according to the appeal of your book and the availability of travel funds. Use the news peg idea to open doors. If you piggyback on a hot news item, tight schedules can miraculously get shifted to make way for airing timely material.

Want an original ploy to seize the attention of producers? One small publisher we know gathered thousands of names on a petition saying how fascinating he would be on the air. Then he *faxed* it to major producers. Can you imagine the commotion when page after page—virtually a scroll—came rolling in? Everyone was talking about it . . . and the author. Perhaps a more practical tip is to encourage friends and relatives to write producers suggesting you as a guest.

Of course, the other ingredient needed for any successful media campaign is to get books into the stores. Beverly Nye was being taped for *Morning Exchange* where she showed a copy of her book. Before the program was aired, she scanned the yellow pages under "Book Dealers, Retail" to gather a list of sales outlets. She organized them by area, called to learn the names of buyers, then hit the streets. She and her son peddled a lot of books—in threes and fives and tens. The day after she hit the airwaves, Cleveland, Ohio, was in a turmoil. Walden's on the west side sold a thousand books. Customers kept coming in and requesting *A Family Raised on Sunshine* for weeks afterward.

Beverly Nye took to the media, and they to her, like the proverbial duck to water. A year later she had her own syndicated radio series on which she gave homemaking tips. Radio stations across the country carried her sixty-five-show package, paid her royalties, and plugged her books. By then she had written *A Family Raised on Rainbows*. Of course, not all of us feel about a camera and a microphone as Nye does.

Ratcheting Up Your Radio Exposure

Radio programming is not normally scheduled as far in advance as television, so your mailings can go out as little as four weeks in advance. We find results are better, however, with six to eight weeks advance mailings. Your material should be addressed to the producer of an individual show. Call ahead and get the name (and correct spelling) of whoever books the guests. After a couple of weeks follow up by phone or e-mail. Be politely persistent.

Radio shows come in several types, and hosts come in various degrees of preparedness. Some interviewers will not have bothered to read the book and will depend strictly on you and the cover blurbs. Others pride themselves on being up on their subjects and will chat at length about specific passages in the book. Most of the same tips we offered earlier work for radio. The one thing to remember here is that your voice must do all the work. A smile is important; it *does* carry over a microphone.

The creme deluxe is National Public Radio. NPR likes to learn of a book early and do a wide range of topics from fiction to cookbooks, economic intrigue to issue-based nonfiction, sports to history. *The New York Times* has said of NPR, "An interview or a review on any of the three main programs—'Morning Edition,' 'All Things Considered,' and 'Weekend Edition'—practically assures a rise in sales." *Fresh Air* is another key show. You can reach National Public Radio at 635 Massachusetts Ave. NW, Washington DC 20001-3753, (202) 513-2000, fax (202) 513-3329, www.npr.org.

Talk radio has become huge. Shows aired during early morning and late afternoon drive times—when folks are traveling to and from work—are the first choice, with midday programs being good for some audiences. Of course, a lot depends on the host. Some have tremendous listening audiences even during bad hours because they are talented, dynamic, or controversial.

Several cases come to mind where the host was so high on *Creative Loafing* that the whole program became a fantastic third-party endorsement of the book: just one long commercial from an enthusiastic radio personality. Imagine for a moment what a *thirty-minute commercial* is worth. But it didn't cost one red cent. The beauty of publicity demonstrated again.

If you're going to be on a show for a half hour or more and there are audience call-ins, it's a good idea to have a friend or two primed to phone in and get the ball rolling. One client who coauthored a regional biography spun such good stories and so enlivened the radio listeners that about fifty of them came to the bookstore when he was doing a signing.

In addition to promoting a local author signing, many writers give their toll-free numbers or Web URLs for ordering books. Radio hosts are very gracious about allowing this. Howard Gregory, the author of *Battered Husbands*, uses radio interviews to stimulate orders for his wholesalers. He encourages listeners to read his book free by going to their local libraries and requesting that they order it. As a result, Baker & Taylor has upped its typical one- and two-book orders to fifteen at a time.

While we're talking about radio, there is another option available if you shudder at trotting from station to station to do your thing. Many radio programs will interview you via long-distance telephone call. These are termed phoners. This is a great way to get free national exposure. Most of the media directories previously mentioned state whether specific shows do phone interviews.

Joe and Judy Sabah wrote and published a book titled *How to Get the Job You Really Want—and Get Employers to Call You*. They decided they didn't want to fool with bookstore sales, waiting an average of 104 days to collect their money. So they took to talk radio. And it took to them, too. Ninety-five percent of their books sold this way. Our good friend Joe told us of moving 23,750 copies via radio without ever leaving his home. His phoners brought in more than $376,500! Not bad pay for a little one-book publisher.

Joe has gone on to write and publish a great new guide titled *How to Get on Radio Talk Shows All Across America Without Leaving Your Home or Office*. He also sells a database of 970 up-to-date radio shows. For information call (800) 945-2488. His advice to newcomers? "Commit yourself to doing at least twenty shows or don't even begin. It's a learning experience. The first dozen or so times you may stink. But you'll learn what works and what doesn't. You'll refine your spiel and start selling books."

Something else you may want to consider is an ad in *Radio-TV Interview Report* put out by Bradley Communications Corp. For a free report on *30 Ways to Sell Your Book Through Radio-TV Talk Shows*—plus a complimentary audiocassette on *How to Make Sales on Radio and TV Talk Programs*—simply call (800) 989-1400, extension 743.

By the way, pay attention to the commercials while you're on the air. When we were interviewed on the *Paul Gonzales Show* recently, an ad came on the air promoting books via For the People Bookstore. When the interview ended, we called and pitched *Country Bound!* The result? The store bought the book not only for radio commercials but also to put in its Christmas catalog. And the bookstore already reordered.

How to Handle Hostile Hosts

If you do enough radio, you're bound to encounter an openly hostile host. These nasty individuals don't really present much of a challenge if you refuse to rise to their bait. Just laugh off their barbs, say something like, "Opinions are like belly buttons, we all have one," and maneuver the discussion back to your own comfort zone and your book. If the interviewer persists, direct the conversation to neutral ground, something about your research habits, the writing process, or what led you to become a writer.

Going After PSAs

One other aspect of radio that could be very meaningful to some of you is public service announcements, better known as PSAs. If you are a nonprofit organization—via structure, not happenstance—you are eligible for *free* airtime. This is a terrific boon to churches with cookbooks to peddle and nonprofit associations that have produced books about their aims. The Federal Communications Commission says that all stations must allocate a certain portion of their time to these PSAs. What they usually amount to is unpaid commercials. This free time goes to those bold enough to seek it. So if you qualify, get your share.

Speaking of getting your share, if radio plays a big role in your marketing mix, be sure to get a copy of our *Jump Start Your Books Sales*. We devote a whole chapter to the topic: "Radio Interviews: How to Be Hip and Shoot From the Lip." (More details at www.SPANnet.org/cc/js.)

By the way, *never pay* for radio interview time. We often get calls from hucksters who want us to "host" a show . . . and line up our own sponsors and advertisers to offset the fee the hucksters intend to charge us. No way!

More Promotional Tactics to Create Momentum

Developing a support system of your peers also makes sense. Networking with other authors and small publishers provides mental stimulation, emotional comfort, and a source for getting your questions answered. Find a writing group or publishing association in your area, or organize one if none exists. The collective promotional ideas will amaze you. You may also find someone willing to serve as an informal mentor, guiding you toward greater heights in this exciting venture.

Capitalizing on contacts is a surefire way to expand awareness of your book. Alert friends, relatives, acquaintances, and business associates about your "new baby." They may know someone who produces a local TV show or be able to put you in touch with an organization that would be interested in making bulk purchases. There is a "six degrees of separation" rule that connects all of us. That means anyone you would care to meet is only six people away from you. Start asking who knows whom!

But don't stop there. Tell the main newspaper in the city of your birth that a native son or daughter made good. If your parents, children, or brothers and sisters have influence in their hometowns, see if you can ride on their names to get mention in newspaper columns or maybe even feature stories or author profiles by telephone.

Anything you can do to get people talking about your book is like money in the bank. The most baffling and elusive element in a book's success is word of mouth. Statistics from a Gallup Poll bring this point quickly into focus: When asked why they bought fiction, 4 percent of the respondents said it was because of ads in magazines and newspapers; book reviews fared only slightly better. By contrast, 27 percent bought because they were familiar with the author and 26 percent because a friend or relative recommended the book. Powerful testimony to word of mouth. Said the former president of B. Dalton in an interview in *The New York Times*, "I would probably rate the most effective techniques for selling books as being the individual telling a friend, reviews, and the author's ability to appear on talk shows."

Sometimes you can turn adversity into opportunity. When the Wall Street crash struck, the financial community mourned the loss of a fortune. Meanwhile, the publishing community dreamed of a fortune to be made. Publishers across the land reached into their backlists and dusted off titles having to do with the stock market and investing. Headlines capitalized on the crash. Simon & Schuster's new ad campaign shouted, "Brilliantly plausible . . . horrendously disturbing . . . and starting to come true." It's the old story: If life gives you a lemon, make lemonade!

Our friend Raleigh Pinskey suggests you donate products to charity auctions. It's a "giving to get" philosophy that builds title recognition and goodwill. Learn about such possibilities by checking the social section or calendar listings of your local newspaper for charity events, association happenings, service organizations' auctions, children's events, businessmen/businesswomen meetings, and the like.

All you do is call the RSVP number and offer your book for the auction, a raffle, a gift table, a goody bag, or what have you. Charitable donations always reflect positively on the givers.

Teaming Up With Organizations to Fund-Raise

How about promoting your book as the ideal fund-raising tool? There may be groups of youths, seniors, or church folks who would love to help you sell copies for a percentage of the receipts. Anytime you can ally yourself with others who will serve as your sales force for a small percentage, it is worth serious consideration.

One of our previous clients, Margaret Malsam, sold 225 copies of her *Meditations for Today's Married Christians* at the National Theresian Convention of Chicago, then donated $375 to the organization. She offers prudent advice for dealing with nonprofits: "Don't say, 'I will give you 50 percent off.' Instead say, 'I will donate $5 for every $10 book purchased.' "

This works just as well for backlist titles as for new books. Diane Pfeifer has been selling her *Angel Cookbook* as a fund-raiser for years. Catholic organizations are a perfect match with recipes such as Dominus Vo-Biscuits and In Excelsis Mayo. She sells a minimum of 300 at a time on a nonreturnable basis and collects 60 percent of the retail price. People apparently talk about the book, as she reports getting a ton of reorders at full price.

Forging creative partnerships can add up to big numbers. Waldman House sold 10,000 copies of Tom Hegg's *A Memory of Christmas Tea* in one day—and generated enormous publicity—by teaming with the Good Samaritan Society, which operates nursing homes, assisted living centers, and senior care facilities in twenty-six states. The event was a nationwide Remember Me Day on which guests were encouraged to visit the residents, share a cup of tea, enjoy a reading of the book live via satellite, and receive packages of tea, tea recipes, and cookies. Waldman House was in seventh heaven as they had 250 facility administrators around the country doing PR for them.

There's yet another way you can creatively merchandise your book. How about trading it for things you want? Many small publishers barter with each other. Perhaps someone has published a book, newsletter, or magazine you would enjoy. Offer to exchange a copy of your book for another's. This can be carried even further to bartering a quantity of books with vendors for items or services.

Look around for other possibilities. If you or your spouse is employed in a large company, it may have a newsletter that mentions employee happenings. (If you have written your book while working for someone else, be sure the boss knows of this accomplishment and that mention of it lands in your personnel file.) Your college alumni newspaper is another place for publicity. And don't overlook any associations or organizations to which you belong. The more times your name and the name of your book get out, the better.

Using Reader Testimonials

How about testimonials? These are fan letters you receive or comments that people make about your book. Letters and e-mails from readers will become one of your most priceless treasures. While we all hope to make money from our writing, there is no greater gift than a heartfelt thank-you from a reader who tells you your book made a real difference in her life. (Marilyn received two such e-mails while doing this revision. They were just the spark she needed to keep up with the eighty-hour weeks.) There is nothing like knowing that your work significantly contributed to the life of another person. These devoted fans are usually delighted you would want to use their comments. (You might also want to request that they go to Amazon.com and barnesandnoble.com and write a glowing customer review. Hint, hint.)

Of course, you don't have to meekly wait for such lovely accolades. You can solicit them! Whenever someone tells you he enjoyed your book, sends a laudatory e-mail, or pens a brief note, capitalize on it. Make up a comment card similar to the example on page 289, explaining that you are interested in using comments from satisfied readers to tell others about this new book. To encourage a high return, include an SASE. We have used this system with great success, gaining "quotable quotes" not only from appreciative readers but also from television personalities, radio producers, legislators, doctors, journalists, and educators.

The Benefits of Events and Awards

To corral even more exposure, launch your book with a special publication date splash. One way to do this is to create an event that is newsworthy. For instance, if your book is about photography, schedule an exhibition to coincide with the publication date and invite cultural editors from the local press.

Or you might team up with a local worthy cause as we did. We introduced *Creative Loafing* by putting on a fund-raiser for the Aerospace Museum and Hall of Fame Recovery Fund in San Diego. It was called (appropriately enough) Creative Loafing Days. This gala event was a weekend in Balboa Park during which activities in the book were depicted. We had jousting matches, magic shows, a frog-jumping jamboree, poetry readings, fiddlers, archery demonstrations, fencing, puppet shows, and more.

Since we were working with a nonprofit organization, free radio public service announcements (PSAs) were available to us, and we got coverage in many local

Comment Card

Dear Reader,

Thank you for your kind words about ______________________________.
We are interested in using comments from satisfied readers to tell others about this exciting book. May we share your views as excerpted below with others? . . . Or feel free to write anything additional!

____

____

____

____

Yes, I agree that my comments may be used for national publicity and advertising. I understand that I will not receive any payment or compensation for this permission. My name or initials (circle your preference), as well as the city and state in which I reside, and my occupation may also be used.

SIGNATURE ______________________________________

DATE________________ OCCUPATION ______________________

NAME ____

ADDRESS ____

CITY/STATE/ZIP __________________________________

E-MAIL__________________________ PHONE ________________

Thank you! Please return this form in the enclosed self-addressed and stamped envelope.

By soliciting testimonials from your readers, you'll soon have pages of favorable comments to share with prospective buyers.

newspapers, not to mention landing on the evening news of all three network TV stations! It was a tremendous amount of work, but the net result was a $5,000 donation to the Aerospace Museum and incredible local name identification for our book.

Another way to draw attention to yourself is to sponsor an award that ties in with your title. You get free publicity when you announce the contest—and again when you declare the winner(s). In addition, it's a fun and legitimate way to educate people about your subject. Sourcebooks did this for one of its titles, *My Cat's Not Fat, He's Just Big-Boned*. The publisher designed a clever Show Us Your Fat Cat contest and worked with over one hundred independent retailers. Each participating store that purchased a prepack of eight books received entry forms and low-cost promotional materials for a fat-cat beauty contest. Customers brought in photos of their own cats, and the winner received a bag of cat food and a signed lithograph by the book's author and *Sylvia* cartoon strip creator, Nicole Hollander. To further capitalize on the contest, Sourcebooks arranged for Hollander to do an event with the winning bookstore, giving the booksellers extra incentive to push the contest and the book.

Publishers occasionally use gimmicks to draw attention to their wares. Here are three examples. Maybe these stories will ignite a fiery idea for you. Parenting Press, the publisher of Elizabeth Crary's *Pick Up Your Socks*, a children's book, sent one sock with her media kit. A self-defense book was promoted with one chopstick (said to be a useful weapon in a pinch). By separating what is usually a pair, both situations played on the unusual. And M. Evans, publisher of *The I-Like-My-Beer Diet* (written by physician Martin P. Lipp), gave retailers a gimmicky liquid enticement. Interested booksellers were offered galleys of the book and a *free case of beer* if they were willing to test the diet. One bookseller was quick to commend Evans on this "civilized method of bribery."

These are just some ideas for developing creative promotion. No doubt you can dream up others, or adapt some of the above strategies, to give your own promotional campaign zest. Now let's address the nuances of autographing yourself to success.

Web Sites, Wisdom, and Whimsey

Sometimes I think I understand everything, then I regain consciousness.

* * *

Doing mysteries or romance novels? Then you need to know about www.themysteryreader.com and www.theromancereader.com. While both these sites are targeted toward fans, they offer new reviews, features, archives, and freebies (goodies from authors, etc.) that may provide promotional venues for you.

* * *

Try this innovative way to use TV. When Brad Herzog appeared as a contestant on *Who Wants to Be a Millionaire?* he happened to mention his book *States of Mind*. Boy, what a door opener! Not only did it spur sales, the plug also helped him sell the paperback rights to Pocket Books. Let's see now, how smart do we have to be, and how many calls do we have to make to get on that show . . .

* * *

Maximize your biz-ability with vis-ability. Raleigh Pinskey has a Web site full of outstanding free articles on how to promote and prosper. You'll find ways to target your market, develop name recognition, explore media leads, market effectively online, and much more. She also has a free e-zine to which you can subscribe. Find it all at http://promoteyourself.com.

* * *

At last, an unprintable book that is fit to read! —Ezra Pound

* * *

National reputation can be built through talk radio. One of the tools to help you achieve this goal awaits at www.rronline.com. This is the site of *Radio & Records*' Web pages. Buried here is a wonderfully complete list of radio stations, all divided by format. You want classic rock? Got you covered. Would your readers prefer classical, oldies, or smooth jazz? It's here, too. So is country, Spanish-language stations, even NPR selections. Click on your choice, then click on the stations within that category to go directly to their individual sites.

* * *

Today's consumers want CNN timing and MTV pizzazz.

* * *

Capture those illusive Web site awards. Web site awards yield recognition, credibility—and additional visitors. Now there is a tool that not only leads you to the over eight hundred awards sites around the world but helps you apply and track your activities, as well! Go to http://websiteawards.xe.net. You'll find specific, usable suggestions on how to prepare your site, then how to apply for awards. If you want good advice, listen to the experts. An index of articles written by leading authorities in the field of awards offers more valuable insights.

* * *

"What's your book about?" This is a question you'll hear over and over again from reviewers, booksellers, consumers, friends, the media. You need to create a succinct response that elicits intrigue and appeal. This is called a book handle. It need only be twenty to thirty words, but it must capture the essence of your book and make people think, "I want (need) that!" This book handle will be useful in a multitude of ways, so craft it carefully.

14 *Turning Book Signings Into Stellar Events*

A good book-signing author has been called a cross between a politician and a carnival barker. We couldn't agree more. You may want to suggest an autographing . . . then again, if you value your time, you may not. For an unknown author, book signings do little more than give an ego boost. They are a cherished idea that seldom sells books on the spot. But like everything, there are exceptions to this rule—especially if you apply the techniques contained here! Then you can have a high-impact, low-cost event.

What to Expect

You're not likely to go from book signing to bestsellerdom. Yet we placed a nice front-page newspaper story about one of our clients that noted he would be available to autograph copies of his book at a local bookstore, and before the session was over, the author had signed eighty books! A more normal scene involves long leisurely talks with bookstore personnel, complete with their apologetic comments about, "Where is everybody?"

Book signings actually accomplish three main things: (1) They introduce you to the public and generate PR for your book in advance via posters, newspaper ads, calendar listings, and a blurb in the store newsletter; (2) they provide a venue for you to meet fans and sign books the day of the event; and (3) they give you an opportunity to get to know store personnel and help them understand why they should sell your book after you leave. A well-kept secret is the actual signing is usually the *least* effective of the three parts!

There is one way you can enhance the chances of your signing being a success: Don't make it a signing! Make it an "event." Give people value, a reason to come out, by offering a mini-seminar on your subject. Attendees are given a few precious tidbits, then provided a tempting glimpse into the rest of the materials covered in the book. For novelists and poets, a reading is often the answer. Choose a dramatic section of the book and practice it aloud at home. Or you might choose to talk about how or why you write. In any case, you do more than passively sign books; you create an event.

Of course, how you handle this event will make an enormous difference. Mark Victor Hansen and Jack Canfield are the masters of book signings. They discovered a very successful approach to getting people to buy books. First, they usually do signings in malls and position themselves at a table just *outside* the bookstore. Then they simply hand each shopper a copy of *Chicken Soup for the Soul* and request, "Would you please take thirty seconds to read one story on page 24? A whopping 90 percent of passerbys read it—and more than 70 percent buy the book on the spot. Admittedly, this is an ideal gift book with 101 stand-alone stories that lend themselves to this kind of treatment, but it's also a heck of a way to maximize book sales.

Then there's the true story of a Texan who heard Jeanne Horn, author of *Hidden Treasure*, mention on the *Today* show that she would be autographing books that same afternoon at Brentano's in New York. This Dallas tycoon jumped in his private plane, flew to New York, rushed into Brentano's, and bought an autographed copy to present to his wife as a Valentine's Day gift.

What to Do Before Your Book Signing

Of course, first you have to schedule your signing. Simply look on the Web for particulars or call the store and find out who schedules authors for signings. While Borders used to have a CRC (Community Relations Coordinator) in every store, it has now gone to a more centralized approach where one person handles several outlets. At independent booksellers, you will usually speak with the owner or manager. It's a good idea to work several months out. Popular independents can be booked as much as five months in advance.

Call before you mail information, and always ask, "Am I catching you at a good time?" If people are on deadline, their attention spans will be scattered. Should individuals say that your book doesn't fit the profile of their customers, ask whom they would suggest you contact. This worked well for us in Los Angeles, where there are so many Barnes & Nobles, some of which were a much better fit for our business book than others.

Find out if the bookstore already has your book in stock. Chances are it won't, so offer to send a reading copy with promotional material. (Stamp it "Review Copy" so it won't be sold.) Follow up in about a week to be sure it arrived and to set up a signing/mini-seminar time. Let the coordinator guide you about time of day. Most stores prefer weekday evenings, but certain topics in certain locations work better in the afternoon or even on a weekend. Things that you'd never think to consider, such as parking availability, can kill a signing. Determine whether the store will order stock from its headquarters or a wholesaler/distributor of if you should bring copies of the book. Be sure the staff has everything needed to place the order!

Also ask if the store has a media list you might use. While this has never worked well for us—employees either claim not to have one or provide a list so out of date it's worthless—some authors find this helpful in locating newspapers, radio, and TV to contact. At least inquire what is the best radio station for promoting books.

Now think about what you can do to support the overall signing effort:

- What kind of invitation list can you put together? Go to your database and locate fans, friends, and colleagues within a fifty-mile radius.
- You probably printed postcards already, so simply send them with a note about the date and time, store location, and a personal "Hope you can make it" message. Plan for the postcards to arrive about a week before the event. (Sometimes the store will do this for you. When Marilyn did a Professional Pursuits Program for the Tattered Cover Bookstore recently, the staff requested one hundred names on labels and sent out the cards themselves.)
- Go to Kinko's or Office Depot and have your book cover enlarged in color to an 11″ × 17″ poster, laminated and put on a stand-up easel back. This works well for signings and also to take along when you speak. You might want to add a little sign that says "Today only! Meet the Author!"
- It's also fun to wear a badge. (And while signings can be a lot of work, they should also be fun!) You can get your book cover made into a miniature badge, or simply create one that says "Author" and your name.
- Now the writer in you gets to pull into high gear. There are several things you should write: (1) a brief news release with the signing specifics, which you provide to the coordinator for the store newsletter; (2) three or four thirty-second punchy, benefit-oriented announcements that the coordinator will (should) read the evening of your engagement encouraging people to come hear you; (3) a short bio of less than a minute that the coordinator can use to introduce you before you speak; (4) a sales flier to hand out at the store, which will contain a photo of the cover, a paragraph explaining why potential readers *must* have this book, bullet points, a brief author bio, plus store contact information (and your phone and Web site URL).

It would be wise to think about any places you could post a similar version of this flier. Author Patricia Bragg, for instance, had a mini-seminar on health and fitness scheduled for Santa Barbara, so she posted fliers in all the area health food stores. The bookstore was packed, and readers kept her for almost four hours!

• Go to your book's page on Amazon.com. Then go to the Customer Reviews section and print the reviews. Staple them together and write "Desk Copy . . . please don't take" on the front. The last one we made up for *Shameless Marketing for Brazen Hussies* showed twelve reviews and a five-star rating. This is good third-party endorsement and can keep one person busy reading while you're visiting with someone else. You just hand the reviews to a prospective buyer and say something like, "Here's what other readers are saying about my book." Then shut up!

Preparation for a Successful Experience

Plan on getting there at least a half hour early and staying late, late, late if things are going well. Of course, you'll want to take the items we mentioned above that were made for the signing. It's easier to designate a box, backpack, or suitcase and permanently keep your book signing materials all together if you plan on doing much of this. Here are some other things to take:

• Two pens (of the same color and ones that are comfortable to your hand).

• A bottle of water in case the organizer forgets or you run out.

• Extra books. What a terrible problem if the event goes like gang busters and the bookstore hasn't ordered enough books.

• A sign-up sheet so people can leave you information for your database. There are many reasons to gather the names of interested readers.

• Some 3″ × 5″ index cards so individuals who don't carry business cards can write you a message and leave their information. (Of course, *you* will bring business cards.)

Actions to Take While You're in the Store

What should you expect? One store will treat you like royalty; another will barely acknowledge your presence. It all depends on the person in charge. If said person is disinterested and lackadaisical, *you* take charge!

• Your first concern is where in the store you are located. You don't want to be situated just inside the door. People will automatically think you're either seeking blood donations, doing fund-raising, or trying to sign up voters. Nor do you want to be banished to some dark corner. You want to be where the action is: near the customer service center or in the line of sight when people enter the store.

• Remember we said one of the primary reasons for a signing is to get to know the store personnel and help them become excited about selling your book after you leave. Now is the time. Ask the organizer to pull store personnel together for about five minutes. Have a good pitch ready and deliver it with passion. This overview, when done effectively, will get the staff recommending your book for months to come.

- Hand over the announcements you've written, and suggest one be broadcast over the PA system now and the others shortly. Don't hesitate to remind the staff later if they forget.
- If you are selling the books directly, ask for cash payment or that the bill be paid by credit card, or at least get a purchase order.
- Prepare your table. You may want to bring a colorful tablecloth and a few balloons. Put up your poster. Some authors even bring a few books gift wrapped with the thought they will make impulse gift buys. Get your pens and water ready.
- Never, never just sit in the chair that's put behind your table! If no one is around your area, cruise the store. Pay particular attention to the section where your book would be shelved. Approach people there, telling them you are the author of ____________ and you'll be doing a mini-seminar shortly.
- *Hand people books.* This is very important. In retailing it is vital to get the merchandise into the hands of the prospective customer. That significantly increases the chances of them buying. Be friendly and open. Some people feel authors are unapproachable. This is the most "up close and personal" opportunity you'll ever have with your readers. Enjoy them!
- Your actual presentation should run twenty to thirty minutes. It's best to have it be interactive. Three or four times, when you talk about a specific concept or character, ask listeners to turn to that page. This involvement is a good sales strategy. Always invite questions afterward, and don't be surprised if they are slow to start. When that happens we usually say, "One of the questions I'm frequently asked is . . ." This sort of breaks the ice. Of course, end by saying you'll be happy to personally autograph a book for them or their friends.
- What if only a couple of people show up? Forget the formal presentation and sit down with them individually, discover their needs, and explain how the book will help them. Sometimes impressive things come out of what appears to be a flop. We had such a situation when only one woman showed up. During the conversation Marilyn discovered the bookstore customer was a founding member of a large businesswomen's organization that brings in speakers on a regular basis. It ended up being a very lucrative signing, though a total failure in the traditional sense. If people stay away in droves, don't complain to the staff and stalk around with a long face. Sometimes you win; sometimes you lose.

Other Useful Advice

Remember to say thank-you afterward—even if the experience was as unpleasant as visiting your deaf uncle Norman who has both halitosis and body odor. A brief handwritten note goes a long way. Also make notes for yourself about the store location, personnel, and attitude for future reference.

One other thought we'd like to toss in is that you consider combining with other complementary area authors and create a more flamboyant event by having a panel discussion. If you asked two other mystery novelists from your local Sisters in Crime group to join you, there could be great synergy as you all shared how you research methods to "dispose of" your characters, for instance. Or three business writers might discuss the subject overall—one talking about raising working capital, another about marketing, and a third about hiring good employees. By using this "rising tide lifts all boats" philosophy, you create more of a critical mass.

We have another idea to share with you regarding autographed copies. Why not personally sign several copies you leave with the store and request they be stickered with "Autographed Copy"? (These are seldom returned.) If a customer is debating between two books, they're sure to choose the autographed one. And they make nice gift items. Additionally, suggest the store feature copies in the window, especially at your hometown store, and in the Local Author section. And while you're there, be sure the employees shelve the book in the proper section—and face out! This can make a big difference. Many bookstore buyers browse the Self-Help section diligently, for instance.

People like autographed editions in their personal libraries, and sometimes will buy your book as a gift if you'll autograph it. This brings up a point that is often overlooked by authors. What will you say in your signed note? Think this through before you ever get books off the press. Devise a short standard generic comment, such as the one Marilyn used for *Creative Loafing*: "May you find new adventures in these pages. Enjoy." Naturally, you'll vary it for special people and circumstances. Sign on the top of the title page. Always autograph for a person by name. And verify the spelling; there are as many Jons as there are Johns these days. If you expect to be swamped with sales, sign just your name ahead of time. Then all you have to do is personalize it with the buyer's name, a couple of words, and the date.

Also read chapter twenty, "Seminars, Classes, and Trade Shows can Multiply Your Profits." There is a lot of commonality between signings and speaking.

Less Common Venues for Signings

Bookstores, though usually thought of as the primary places for signings, are not necessarily the only game in town. In fact, libraries are desirable locations, as well. At a recent American Library Association meeting, Francine Fialkoff, editor of *Library Journal*, pointed out that libraries are attractive venues for author appearances, bring in large audiences, and sell many copies of the authors' books.

Schools should not be overlooked, either, if you have a book appealing to children or college students. What about considering the other end of the age spectrum? Senior centers often sponsor events and would love to have a real-live author in attendance.

And what about churches? New Thought churches, such as Unity, Science of Mind, and Religious Science, often sponsor authors to give brief presentations for love offerings—then allow them to sign books afterward. Other options are museums, hospitals, even shelters. Anywhere people gather is a possibility and may prove more successful because of its distinctiveness.

Patricia Rust has a children's book, *The King of Skittledeedoo*, which is about a king who must become literate in order to save his kingdom. She has popularized it by traveling to different states and giving readings and signings to children in the state mansions! After all, literacy is a hot topic with virtually every governor.

And what about supermarkets? Yes, right in front of the produce section, where people have to walk by you. Says Richard Côté, author of *Mary's World: Love, War and Family Ties in Nineteenth-century Charleston*, "I sold as many books at a supermarket signing (at a 40 percent discount) as I did in major, high-volume chain stores (where he had to give a 55 percent discount)." Your customer profile must match the typical supermarket shopper, but that's not hard. And chances are there are a lot more grocery stores than there are freestanding bookstores in your area. Additionally, Côté found that supermarkets paid him in cash, right on the spot.

Now let's go from the imaginative to the proven. These are the places publishers have been selling books for eons—in bookstores, through wholesalers and distributors, to libraries, and schools. You need to know about these standard channels of distribution.

Web Sites, Wisdom, and Whimsey

List your signings and book events on NetRead. This site is a hub for book publishing, marketing tools, how-to guidance, news, and business listings. You can submit a free listing to its calendar, EventCaster, by going to www.NetRead.com/calendar, clicking on the Add an event link in the left column, and registering so you can add and edit events. On the login page, click on the Registration form link. Then enter your e-mail address and password (twice) and click the Submit Registration button. Finally, fill out the Add an Event form. Online calendars require about two weeks advance notice; newspapers prefer three weeks, so post all events as early as possible for maximum exposure. NetRead automatically submits your information to major online event calendars and to newspapers around the country. You can even enter an entire author tour at one sitting and NetRead will send the events to the right places at the right time!

* * *

Largest reading in the history of books draws crowd of twelve thousand. The Toronto SkyDome was the scene of the International Festival of Authors, where J.K. Rowling—creator of the phenomenally popular Harry Potter series—read to an audience of more than twelve thousand. She admitted to being terrified as well as delighted. In keeping with the tone of the books, magicians mingled with audience members and loudspeaker announcements evoked images of a fantasy world.

* * *

Author "rides the rails" on unusual book tour. Linda Watanabe McFerrin, a veteran novelist and travel writer, has conjured up a unique author tour. She bought a thirty-day unlimited Amtrak train pass and set out on a month-long Book Passage by Rail tour. She promoted *The Hand of Buddha*, her new collection of short stories, conducted autographings, and held a traveling workshop titled How to Turn Life Into Literature. McFerrin showed how personal experiences can be channeled into writing, demonstrating various story forms and detailing markets for publication. "My fiction is grounded in real experience," she explains. "I go into communities and share ideas and knowledge rather than teaching." She wants to slow things down, thus the train travel. The tour started at Bluestockings Women's Bookstore in New York City. Then she worked her way across the country, hitting independents that included Chapters in Washington, DC, Quail Ridge Books in Raleigh, North Carolina, Tattered Cover in Denver, Colorado, and ending at Sam Weller's Books in Salt Lake City, Utah. No doubt she also garnered substantial publicity with her unorthodox method of book promotion.

* * *

There's no business that's not show business.

✶ ✶ ✶

Book tour purposely *avoids* all the big cities! When Lawrence Block, the author of some 50 books, decided to promote his new E.P. Dutton mystery, *The Burglar in the Rye*, he convinced his publisher to set up a tour of second- and third-tier cities, rather than the usual major markets. "Everyone was surprised that I chose Spokane and not Seattle, Peoria and not Chicago," reports Block. "I drew two to three times better in those places than I ever did in the large cities." His rationale that at any given time in any of the large markets too many writers are competing for audiences at readings and signings definitely panned out. Give you any ideas?

✶ ✶ ✶

The nice thing about living in a small town like we do is that when you don't know what you're doing, someone else does.

✶ ✶ ✶

New book signing twist gives "paws" for reflection. New Sage Press of Troutdale, Oregon, hit upon a doggone good way to promote its latest title, *Unforgettable Mutts: Pure of Heart Not of Breed.* The publisher organized "pawtographings" at bookstores around the country. Some of the unusual mutts featured in the book appeared for the signings. (Truth be told, a human rubber-stamps the paw prints.) Author Karen Derrico came up with the idea to have the critters appear in her place in cities where she was unavailable. The ploy seems to attract both pet lovers and animal rights people. At one store nearly one hundred folks turned out for a signing where Keller, a Chihuahua born without eyes, gave his paw of approval to eighty copies purchased in just one hour. Think about your titles: Is there any such hook possible that would save you from traipsing all across the country . . . and provide a unique media angle with both bark and bite?

PART V

Selling Books the Usual Ways

15 *Milking the Standard Channels of Distribution*

There are several proven methods for selling more books. In the following pages, we investigate selling to bookstores and reaching wholesalers and distributors. We'll also explore tapping into the lucrative library market, going after educational opportunities, and using sales reps.

If your main aim in life is to see your book emblazoned on best-seller lists, then this chapter holds valuable information. These lists are compiled from sales figures reported by individual bookstores, bookstore chains, wholesalers, and distributors. There are several, and they often disagree. *Publishers Weekly*, *The New York Times*, *USA Today*, and *The Wall Street Journal* are the most well known. Many regional lists exist for an area's most popular titles, as do ones put out by the chains, independents, and wholesalers. On the *PW* or *NYT* list, one book might sell a mere 5,000 copies yet hit the lists on a slow week—or another sell hundreds of thousands and stay there for months on end. The term "best-seller" is as fickle as a lover with several sweethearts. It's not like the record business where you must sell a million copies to have a platinum record. A publisher with five books, for instance, might even dub the one with the most sales her "best-seller."

But be aware many books that never see a best-seller list are immensely profitable. In fact, only 48 percent of books are sold via traditional bookstore channels! Some books have moved millions of units through direct marketing or other venues yet never hit a list.

Getting Your "Baby" Into Bookstores

Bookstores base their decision on whether to carry a book on one question: Will it sell? They want to know what you'll be doing to create customer demand.

They are often hesitant to deal with a one-book publisher. Too much paperwork, they say. Yet you can make inroads.

Today the two biggest chains are Barnes & Noble, Inc. and Borders. In Canada, Chapters has bought out SmithBooks, and the Coles Book Stores chain—and has itself merged with Indigo.

When you deal with Barnes & Noble (B&N), you're also dealing with B. Dalton and other familiar names. Full contact information, and directions for submitting, are contained in the Appendix E. Besides a book, also include a copy of your news release, your mock review, and specific details about your publicity and review *plans*. Chains want to go through a distributor or wholesaler (such as Baker & Taylor or Bookpeople) rather than buying directly from self-publishers. We discuss how to work with these intermediaries shortly.

We live in an age of elephantiasis. Superstores now dot every city of any size, offering lots of space and tons of books. This is the fastest-growing trend in book retailing. They sport 20,000 to 40,000 square feet of space and carry about 150,000 titles. Most offer refreshments, entertainment, and discounts from 10 to 40 percent. The biggest and boldest, Barnes & Noble, had seventeen superstores in 1989, 240 by 1994, and 569 on February 3, 2001, plus 339 B. Dalton stores. And the chain plans to open 40 superstores in 2001. The list of these book supermarkets goes on and on. Borders has about 240 superstores and plans on opening another 35. Then there are Books-A-Million, Waldenbooks (part of Borders Group, Inc.), and others. Of course, by the time you read this, the ownership and names of some will no doubt have changed.

The chains have lots of room for small press titles. Don't overlook them. B&N, for instance went from the top ten publishers representing 76 percent of their sales, to a market share of only 46 percent three years later.

Superstores are taking a toll. The nation's oldest continuously operated independent bookstore, Huntington's in Hartford, Connecticut, closed its doors in May of 1993 citing competition from chain superstores for its demise. It was the forerunner of many to come. The American Booksellers Association (ABA) had a membership of 5,100 independent bookstores in 1993. By 2001, they were down to less than 3,500.

To combat this decline, the ABA instituted a five-prong program called Book Sense that seems to be stemming the tide. Independent booksellers (indies) are competing in ways that provide good opportunities for small publishers, such as category specialization (children's; travel; gay and lesbian; feminist; African American; mystery; science fiction; mind, body, spirit; scholarly; business and technical; even college. It's possible to rent mailing lists from the ABA for each of these specialties if you publish in one of these areas. Many independents have also been instrumental in fostering self-publishing successes.

Many of the smaller chains operate in specific geographic areas. This can be ideal for you because their main offices will be close by. We learned of one that wasn't at all close, however, and ended up selling them a quantity of Tom Davis's client book, *Be Tough or Be Gone*. We discovered Alaska's Book Cache (unfortunately now defunct) independent chain by reading *Publishers Weekly*. (See what gems you can pick up there.) A long-distance introductory phone call and a sample book, plus promo materials, had the chain hooked. You see, part of the book takes place in Alaska, so there was a definite geographic tie-in that caught the attention of Book Cache buyers.

There are two methods to catch the attention of local bookstores. The first is setting up an appointment. That way you don't arrive to find the person you must see has the day off. If, however, you prefer cold calling (going unannounced), plan your visit just after opening or around 3:30 P.M. These are the least busy times, and the buyer won't likely be out to lunch or dinner. Be sure to determine whom you should be talking with. Ask for the store manager or the hardcover or paperback buyer. It is useless to give your pitch to a friendly salesperson only to learn he has no authority to make purchasing decisions.

You may hear the comment, "Oh, we can only take your books on consignment." Very tempting. We suggest you usually resist. Why? For several reasons. Put yourself in management's position. If you have two books to sell—one of which you've already paid out hard cash to acquire and the other you have on consignment—which one will you push? Exactly. If your books don't move, the burden to go back and pick them up is all on you. In addition, as a small-business person, you can hardly afford to have large blocks of inventory tied up unproductively. By holding a hard line on bookstore consignment, we had stores end up handing over cash to purchase books. Of course, you will be expected to offer a 40 percent discount and give return privileges as noted previously.

Another dodge you will frequently encounter when you call on a branch of one of the chains is that individual stores aren't allowed to make purchases. "Everything must go through the central office," you'll be told. Not always. Sometimes the local manager has authority to purchase books independently, either through you or a wholesaler. But it's up to you to convince the manager to exercise that authority.

How do you do this? Be prepared. Have a strong *book handle* ready. One good method for developing a presentation is to put together a loose-leaf binder with such things as a copy of the dust jacket or cover, a prepublication announcement, newspaper interviews, advance comments, reviews, Standard Terms and Conditions, and discount information. You might also wish to make a list of the highlights, the chief points that you think will be most effective in capturing the sale and that you want to be sure you don't forget to mention. Go armed with extra sales literature and an adequate supply of books.

If you aren't used to selling, it's a good idea to role-play with a friend before confronting a potential buyer. Get comfortable with your sales presentation and the use of your sales aids. Buyers are especially interested in your advertising and promotional plans, since this is what will motivate people to come in and ask for the book. They are also interested in author affiliations or qualifications, if the author is a native son or daughter, and if there are any regional or local tie-ins. Experience has shown us that it works better to make your sales presentation and then offer a copy of the book. If you hand over the book as soon as you walk in, the buyer will be so busy thumbing through it, she won't hear what you say.

Now ask for the order. But give your prospective buyer a choice. The best choice is between something and something rather than between something and nothing. You could say, "Would you prefer to order five copies or would eight meet your needs better?" Be sure to get the purchase order number and collect the cash or put it on a credit card. If you have any point-of-purchase sales items, leave them. With certain titles it also makes sense to discuss with the store manager where he intends to place the book. A title that principally deals with nutrition, for instance, could inadvertently be shelved with diet books, where many of those most concerned with its contents might never think to look. Better to place it in Health.

Follow-up is an important part of building business relationships. Make up a card or use your contact management software on which pertinent information can be recorded. Do this for unsuccessful sales calls, as well, and remember to note the manager's reason for not buying or any other remarks. You may figure out how to overcome these objections later.

Stay in touch. Drop a note with a copy of any favorable reviews. Develop self-awareness. Check back to see if the store's inventory needs replenishing. If the book is hard to find in the store, suggest how it might be displayed to better advantage.

Previous self-publishing superstar Peter McWilliams recommended getting a statement from stores where your book has a good track record. But avoid generic testimonials, such as, "____________ sells well in our store." This doesn't really say anything. Compare your results to something else. "It's a matter of relative sales," said McWilliams. "Outsells every other title we carry in the recovery section" has teeth. So does "One of the best-selling books we carry. Sells as well as Robert James Waller." Of course, include the store's name and location. This kind of endorsement is reassuring to other stores considering carrying your title.

Larger publishers publish books for certain seasons. Though a few have gone to three seasons, most stick with spring and fall. Spring titles have pub dates from about January 15 to the end of May, while fall books go from June to October. Sales reps are busy advancing books (selling them before they come off the press) so they can have what is called a good "sell in" before the book is ever available.

When working with bookstores, Lady Luck is more apt to be on your side if your contacts are made before the summer season and again in early fall. Timing is important. In the fall, buyers stock up anticipating the holiday barrage of customers. June is their second busiest period, with graduation gifts, Father's Day, and summer vacation reading accounting for extra business. Are college bookstores your target? Remember, they replenish stock just before each new term starts.

If your book is specialized—on becoming a born-again Christian, for example, or a children's story—it might be wise to look into renting a mailing list of specific stores that handle such reading matter. Bowker rents lists of religious bookstores, museum and art bookstores, and outlets that specialize in metaphysics, children's books, or black studies, to name a few. (For details call (800) 323-4958 or go online to www.cahnerslists.com.)

Now let's weigh the advantages of going after the major bookstore chains. Once you've cracked the resistance of a chain, it's open sesame for getting books into many of its stores. Naturally, you can't afford the staff of salespeople that biggies such as HarperCollins put into the field. Nor can you pay for full-page ads in *Publishers Weekly*. But you don't have to sneak into bookstores under the cover of darkness, either. You can sell to this strategic market by mail and by phone. In a recent study of a dozen chain buyers, 38 percent said they learned about new titles from publishers' direct-mail promotions—certainly a vehicle available to self-publishers.

If you want to have an impact on these chains with their centralized buying power, get in front of them and stay there. Use the list of major bookstore chains we provide in Appendix E, or look in the *American Book Trade Directory* to create your own list. Determine who the proper buyer is and woo that person. The chains buy by category or have a general small-press buyer. Send a copy of your powerful marketing plan, prepublication announcements, press release, dust jacket (or cover), advance blurbs, or letters from strategic people. Offer a complimentary copy of the book as soon as it comes off the press. Some small publishers have generously scattered reading copies of their books to store personnel, who got so excited about the book they became walking, talking advertisements—another example of the power of word of mouth. Not a bad idea for certain kinds of books.

It surely worked for us. One of the things the ABA Book Sense program encourages publishers to do is make available free advance reading copies (ARCs) to independent booksellers. This is called the Advance Access Program. Monthly, The ABA e-mails indies with news of galleys or ARCs that are being offered to encourage the stores to carry and recommend the books. Stores e-mail you directly with requests; you'll typically give away 25 to 50 copies. We offered up to 100 (the maximum allowed), feeling the more bookstores we could satiate, the better.

Almost eighty stores requested copies of *Shameless Marketing for Brazen Hussies.* We immediately acknowledged each request by e-mail to start building a relationship. Then we sent the books and a short letter thanking the bookstores for their interest and suggesting they recommend the book to customers—and to Carl, senior marketing consultant, for the Book Sense 76 Independent Bookseller Recommendations list. Here's how that works: Every two months, thousands of independent booksellers passionately nominate their favorite new books from a great array of publishers. From these, 76 eclectic and diverse books of quality are chosen. Typically, only 20 percent are from smaller presses. We're pleased to tell you our book was included in the January/February 2001 list, the only business book to make the cut! This "best bets" broadsheet is not only distributed at every indie store but widely circulated in other venues, as well. It carries a lot of weight. As a result, we were contacted by a new wholesaler, asked by several bookstores to do signings if we came to their areas, and approached by a major publisher interested in purchasing rights to the book!

This can happen to you, too. To prime the pump, send an e-mail to Carl Lennertz at carl@booksense.com with the following information *in this order*: title, author, publisher, subject, category, number of free copies available, plus a maximum two-sentence description. End with your e-mail address. That's it. Period. Do *not* stipulate "title," author," and such. Put this all in one paragraph so it can easily be cut and pasted into a larger message. Then give it about three weeks before the requests come in.

Giving away books definitely builds buzz. Remember Charles Frazier's 1997 book, *Cold Mountain*? It sold 1.6 million copies in hardcover, and much of the success came from an extensive seeding program. Atlantic Monthly Press sent 4,000 advance copies to selected hubs, such as booksellers, other authors, even salespeople of competing publishing houses—all chosen for their roles in helping people decide what to read. Free comp copies can yield overwhelming sales.

Back to the subject of chains, we do have one reservation. Let's take a hypothetical situation. Suppose you produce a timely good-quality book and do an exceptional job of convincing a buyer from a major chain to take it on. The chain buys a few hundred that it sells out quickly, so the buyer comes back with

Book Sense 76 Independent Booksellers Recommendations

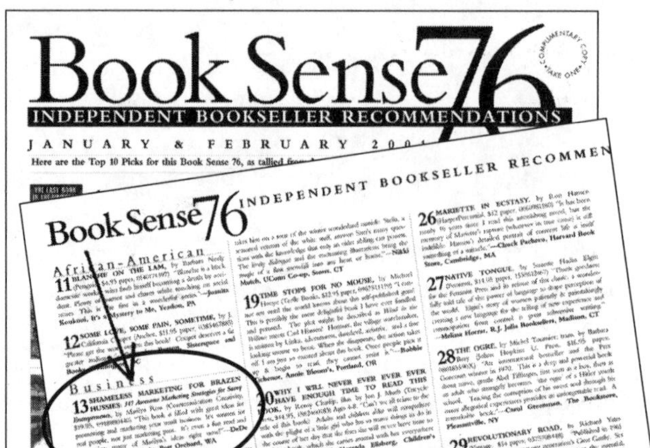
Book Sense 76
INDEPENDENT BOOKSELLER RECOMMENDATIONS
JANUARY & FEBRUARY
Book Sense 76 INDEPENDENT BOOKSELLER RECOMMEN
African-American
Business
Why 76?
1776 · Independence · Independents

Making the Book Sense 76 Independent Booksellers Recommendation list is a real coup for a self-publisher. It can happen to you if you woo independent bookstores. Reprinted with permission from Carl Lennertz.

an order for 2,000 copies. You're elated. You've sold all your first print run, so you scurry back to the manufacturer and order 5,000 more copies.

Then the world crashes. The chain says the book is not moving and wants to return it. Meanwhile, the company has paid you—but now expects a refund. And there is the printing bill for the second run to cope with. Get the picture? To survive in this business, small-business owners must be leery of putting all their eggs in one basket, especially when the basket can be upended any minute.

Let's talk more about returns, that nasty seven-letter word of publishing. There are those who tell us, "I'm not taking back any returns." OK, then don't expect to play in the bookstore or wholesaler/distributor arena. You are trying to drive against traffic on a one-way street. None of us likes returns—and that's one reason we spend so much time in *The Complete Guide to Self-Publishing* talking about nontraditional venues for selling books.

As we write this, Canadian publishers are reeling from astronomical return rates, some as high as 50 percent. The government has given the green light for Chapters Inc.—which has 71 superstores and 220 traditional stores—to merge with former rival Indigo Books & Music. As part of the merger, Chapters must adopt a Code of Conduct that should go a long way in addressing some of the problems plaguing the Canadian publishing industry, including unmanageable return rates and long delays in payments. Pegasus Wholesale, one of Canada's main wholesalers, was bought by Chapters and may be caught in difficult transitional times, as well.

The Publishers Marketing Association (PMA) released a white paper on the subject of returns in March of 2001. Returns for the book business as a whole amount to $7.1 billion annually. Small publishers account for $1.95 billion of that. Unfortunately, due to high-profile bankruptcies, such as those of Crown Books, Wallace's Bookstores, and the Bibelot chain, returns rose significantly during the first part of 2001. Industry leaders are seeking remedies to lessen the flow of red ink, but solutions don't come easy.

Today, various small publishers and associations tout mailings to bookstores. Their fees range from a couple of hundred dollars to five or six hundred (plus the cost to prepare and print your flier or ad). The problem with such mailings is you get lost in the crowd. It's been our experience, and that of most with whom we've talked, that paying to be part of such a cooperative mailing program isn't cost-effective.

Reaching Wholesalers and Distributors

If you want wide distribution, wholesalers and distributors must be romanced. While the terms "wholesaler" and "distributor" are frequently used interchangeably, there is a difference. Wholesalers have no sales reps; they simply fill your book orders and actually buy your book outright. Distributors work on a consignment basis, paying you for sales ninety days after they have been made. For your convenience we've included a selected list in Appendix E. You woo both of these groups much as you do the chain buyer. (Some self-publishers choose to place their books exclusively with master distributors. We address that subject shortly.)

But before you seek outlets across the country to plant your products in, make sure your own backyard is tended. Check the yellow pages or call a local bookstore to find out who the local wholesaler is. Set up an appointment and do a good selling job. But don't feel you are finished when the wholesaler accepts your book. That doesn't mean it will push your book; it simply means the company will stock it. Fortunately, you can influence how well the product moves.

Find out who services local accounts and stocks bookstore shelves. Then climb on your campaign wagon and let them know about your book. In our case we learned the truck drivers for San Diego Periodical Distributors held weekly meetings at 7:30 A.M. All it took was a request, and we were invited to be present at the next session. Guess who went armed with promotional materials, a convincing spiel, books, and a variety of yummy donuts? It's very important to PR these people, who wield much more clout than normal truck drivers. Many bookstores place great weight on their opinions and give them carte blanche to stock shelves as they see fit.

Wholesalers will want to see your Standard Terms and Conditions, as well as your book. There is no sense in their getting excited about a title if you have structured your discounts in such a way as to make it impossible for them to do business with you. Most will expect discounts in the 50 to 55 percent range and return privileges.

Baker & Taylor

Baker & Taylor is to book sales what KFC is to chicken. The country's oldest and largest library wholesaler, over the last few years B&T has dramatically increased its sales to bookstores, as well. There are branches in Reno, Nevada; Momence, Illinois; Commerce, Georgia; and Bridgewater, New Jersey. The wholesaler's file system lists more than 1.4 million titles. An earlier chapter detailed how to get started working with B&T's Publisher Contact Section. To get on its database, B&T now requires a $125 fee to establish new vendors (SPAN Members don't have to pay this, however) and aggressively courts small publishers.

Creative Loafing was stocked in three of the centers and on computer in the fourth. That didn't happen by accident. First, we found out who had authority for buying hardcover nonfiction books. (Today, Baker & Taylor buys according to publishing company name.) It's the same treatment again—stay in front of your contact. Keep sharing good reviews, letters, important media appearances, and so forth. Be aware, however, that B&T is "order driven." That means it won't start ordering from you on a stocking basis until it sees a swell of orders from libraries and bookstores.

There is another form of leverage you can use to encourage B&T to stock your book. The different centers will automatically trickle in mail orders for one, two, three books. These special orders are in response to requests from their customers. Audit these orders. When a center begins to place frequent tiny orders, you have marvelous ammunition to suggest that B&T select you for its Final Approval Program. The reason you want this is so that your book will become part of its bibliographic journal, *Directions*, and be afforded valuable exposure to the thousands of accounts the company serves. The initial order will be from zero to one hundred copies—but bigger things are just around the corner. If you do it right, the prepublication stocking order can be as much as five hundred copies.

Once Baker & Taylor actually stocks your title, there are several things you can do to stimulate sales, including advertise in *Forecast*, *Directions*, or *Book Alert*.

A point of interest: B&T will carry your books even if you choose not to help push them by buying special advertising.

Ingram

Just as KFC's success attracted Boston Chicken, Picnic 'n Chicken, and other contenders, there are more large book wholesalers. Headquartered outside of Nashville, Tennessee, and with five regional distribution centers, Ingram is another huge wholesaler. Its forte is fast delivery of popular books to bookstores.

As of BookExpo America 2001, however, Ingram announced it is no longer dealing directly with publishers of less than ten titles. The reason for this new business model in Ingram's words is "to offer more accessible, economical, and effective options for their [small presses] publishing and distribution." Many tiny independent presses have been negligent in doing publicity and creating consumer demand for their titles, thus suffering huge returns at Ingram's hands.

Under the new program, you will need to go through a distributor or other supplier that already has a relationship with this wholesaler. Ingram has picked Biblio Distribution, a new division formed by National Book Network, as its preferred exclusive distribution partner for small presses with ongoing publishing programs (no one-book self-publishers). While National Book Network has an extensive outside sales force, initial Biblio participants will not get the benefit of this. One person is slated to call on the major national accounts; then Biblio will have an in-house sales staff to help sell titles by maintaining an online catalog site.

Those who want to reach the print-on-demand channel are being referred to Ingram's subsidiary Lightning Source. Individuals are also being encouraged to go with Xlibris, which prints with Lightning Source. It's a tidy package. While Ingram is diligent in trying to steer people to its partners, it says publishers can work with any supplier that has a relationship with Ingram. Then, in effect, they can say Ingram carries their books.

Quality Books Inc.

Quality Books can be a tremendous asset to self-publishers whose books pass its high standards. It is a jobber and direct-sales company dealing primarily with libraries. We feel so strongly about the value of this distributor for self-publishers that we have included its description of the "ideal book," which can be found on page 314. Use it as a checklist when developing your product.

QBI's sales efforts include twenty-five salespeople; contracts, bids, standing orders, and approval plans with most of the largest library systems in the United States; plus exhibits at some fifty state, regional, and national library conventions. With a customer base of ten thousand active accounts, QBI specializes in work-

Quality Book's "Ideal Book" Requirements

- Adult and *selected* children's nonfiction
- Timely subject matter
- New copyright date—must be the current year
- Well organized
    - Includes an index and table of contents
    - Same title on cover, spine, and title page
    - Readily accessible information
    - No "fill in the blanks" workbooks
- Sample copy or galley proofs prior to official publication date
- Book not exposed to the library market
- Publisher's primary market outside of the library market
- Subject coverage "fills a gap"—book clearly differentiated from others in its field
- Cover and title effective and clear in conveying the book's purpose *at a glance*
- Book bound durably and functionally

ing with small presses that do fewer than ten new titles a year. To be considered, get general information and the Book Information Form by calling (800) 323-4241 or going to www.quality-books.com.

For books that are selected, Quality Books offers four consignment stocking arrangements ranging from a 55 to 65 percent discount. You can ship in even cartons, the company is nice to work with, and it pays promptly. QBI will want thirty sales aids in the form of covers or damaged copies of books to use for promotion.

Another company that does a conscientious job of getting smaller publishers into libraries is Unique Books, Inc., which has twenty-one reps and handles about three thousand titles. Call (800) 533-5446.

There are hundreds of other wholesalers in addition to those mentioned here, some reputable and fast paying, others not. You will begin to recognize them as you receive special orders. As we suggested with B&T, if any outlet sends repeat orders and pays promptly, contact its buyer about carrying your book in regular stock.

We've had brushes with many distributors, some less than pleasant. One outfit didn't pay us, wouldn't return the unsold books upon request, and had the gall—*six months* after the order was delivered—to say we had short-shipped. It was only after a letter threatening to write the American Booksellers Association and the Better Business Bureau that we got paid and our unsold inventory was returned.

It should be obvious that you must evaluate every distributor before entering into any agreement. One of the first things you want to know is the discount requirements. Most will expect a 55 percent discount, the right to return inventory for up to a year, and for you to pay freight.

As you work with book chains, one or more are bound to ask, "Who is your Vendor of Record?" What they want you to do is designate one wholesaler or distributor as your VOR: the place where returns are funneled through.

Bookpeople

Bookpeople, headquartered in Berkeley, California, caters to small publishers and specialty stores. Many of its accounts are outlets for titles on health and fitness, spiritual awareness, alternative lifestyles, women's issues, gay and lesbian subjects, plus literature and poetry. Contrary to popular belief, it is not just a regional distributor. Fifteen percent of its business comes from foreign booksellers.

The giant of the nonexclusive distributors, Bookpeople doubled its size by moving into a 31,000-square-foot facility. More changes are taking shape. Bookpeople wants to become more service oriented, telling booksellers, "This is what we can do for you."

Specialty Distributors

New Leaf Distributing Company was started in 1975 with a lot of idealism, a strong vision, and little else. It has experienced great growth since then. Its specialized subject areas are holistic health, self-reliant lifestyle, and New Age spirituality and metaphysics. We especially enjoy working with this outfit, as there is never a wait or a hassle for payment. Along with the monthly sales report, New Leaf sends a postdated check for the money owed. You simply wait until the appropriate time rolls around, then cash your check.

"Waiting for the appropriate time" brings a story to mind. A number of years ago we took on clients Elizabeth and Elton Baker, who wrote and published a title called *The UnCook Book*. Our marketing research turned up a wholesaler called Nutri-Books (a dba of Royal Publications, Inc.), which specialized in health-related titles. Since our book dealt with eating raw food, this company seemed a natural. Its buyer didn't agree. We were sent a polite letter declining the book and saying the company was already carrying several volumes on raw foods and sales were soft. But since we knew Nutri-Books was our "open sesame" to the lucrative health food store market, we didn't give up.

It was a case of the old 80/20 rule, which says 80 percent of your business will come from 20 percent of your customers. Every time we got a favorable review, someone wrote a letter commending the book, or a big purchase order arrived, a copy was fired off to the buyer. This went on for several months.

Finally—in desperation to shut us up perhaps—a purchase order arrived for one case. Pretty soon another purchase order arrived. Then another.

The UnCook Book (now revised and titled *The Gourmet UnCook Book*) is still one of Nutri-Books' biggest sellers. Thousands of copies have been merchandised through this one source, and it has gone into eight printings. The moral of the story is if you have a gut feeling that a book is really right for certain outfits, but they say no, don't give up. Polite persistence does pay off. The other thing that paid off for us was designing and printing fifteen thousand fliers, which were provided to this wholesaler free of charge. In turn, Nutri-Books enclosed them with every mailing that went out. This helped keep the book in front of potential buyers and reminded them it was a strong seller.

Another kind of specialized wholesaler is the one that deals regionally. These are usually small firms with a sales rep or two who beat the bushes aggressively. We used to deal with Gordons Books in Denver (which was by no means small). When we chatted years back with buyer Robert Hobson, he commented how few authors or publishers kept them abreast of breaking reviews or other noteworthy publicity. Take a tip from this good advice: Keep your wholesalers and distributors informed. That way they can do a better job of stocking stores and making sales for you. (See the ad flier on page 318, which is a sample of what goes out to all distributors/wholesalers, chain buyers, and prime media on a regular basis.) Another regional wholesaler is Beyda and Associates, a Los Angeles jobber of children's books. There are surely one or two such companies in your area. Look for them in the yellow pages or in *LMP.*

And then there are what is often referred to as jobbers. These distributors serve mass merchandisers, such as supermarkets, Kmart, Target, 7-Eleven stores, and wholesale clubs. While they typically deal only with mass-market paperbacks, sometimes you can make inroads here. Tom Davis had his *Be Tough or Be Gone* in all the area Safeway stores. It sold so well that newsstand distributors in other parts of Colorado and Wyoming took it on, too. If you do connect here, be sure the jobbers understand that any returned books must be *intact and resalable.* (They are used to simply ripping the covers off mass-market paperbacks and returning just those covers to major publishing houses for credit.)

One more bit of advice is to believe in yourself and your product enough to see that you get fair treatment. We had a frustrating experience with our first book, *Discover Your Roots.* Since it was released a few months after Alex Haley's television spectacular, the book was extremely timely. We stopped by a distributor with one of the first copies off the presses and left it for the buyer, who wasn't in at the time. Realizing it would take a while for reading, we didn't attempt further contact for a couple of weeks. But then our repeated phone calls got no further than a secretary.

Pitch Letter to Wholesaler

Dan Nidess, Merchandising Manager
Nutri-Books Corporation
P. O. Box 5793
Denver, CO 80217

Dear Mr. Nidess:

You remember The UNcook Book? Its goose is far from cooked!

Thought you'd be interested in these recent developments:

- Favorable review in Health Food Business magazine
- Nationally syndicated column devoted totally to the book, due to break April 5th
- Samples of orders coming to us that could be coming to NutriBooks

You indicated your mind was never set in concrete when we chatted on the phone a while back. This book is really beginning to take off. We are continuing to support it with ongoing promotion and media coverage, such as a Houston blitz the end of this month and a Northwest author's tour scheduled for this summer.

Why don't you give The UNcook Book a try? It really is different from other books on raw food!

Cordially,

Marilyn Ross

Marilyn Ross

MR:bb
Enclosures

415 Fourth Street, P. O. Box 213, Saguache, Colorado 81149-0213 303-665-2504

Be tenacious if you feel a specialized wholesaler should carry your title and they refuse.

Flier for Distributors/Wholesalers

To____________________________________ Fax____________________

From Ann Markham, Communication Creativity
Happy New Year!

The latest happenings about . . .

✓ **BookSense 76, the independent bookseller recommendations list, has selected *Shameless Marketing for Brazen Hussies* for January & February 2001.** Placed at #13 out of 76, it is the only business book represented. "This book is filled with great ideas for promoting and marketing your small business. It's written for read people, not just marketing pros. It's even fun to read and I'm using many of Marilyn's ideas right now!" said DeDe Teeters of Armchair Books in Port Orchard, WA.

✓ Best-selling author Jay Conrad Levinson (the *Guerrilla Marketing* series) named author Marilyn Ross to "The Guerrilla Marketing Hall of Fame."

✓ Marilyn was interviewed for a marketing story in *Working Woman* magazine, which is scheduled to break in January or February.

✓ *La Opinion*, the largest Spanish Language Daily Newspaper in the U.S., ran an article and two photographs November 14th.

✓ *Home Business Journal* will be excerpting and reviewing the book in their January/February issue.

✓ A review is forthcoming in *Mail Order Digest.*

✓ Book signings/mini-seminars are scheduled at Barnes & Noble and Borders in the San Francisco area for early March.

✓ The Web site Asian Women in Business has posted an excerpt.

✓ The *Denver Business Journal* has a piece scheduled.

✓ *Success* magazine has a two-page story with photos scheduled for the March issue.

We anticipate many more reviews, excerpts, author interviews, book signings/mini-seminars, Internet activity, etc. We will keep you posted. If I can be of any help, please ask!

Ann Markham, Director of Marketing for Communication Creativity
phone 719-395-8659, fax 719-395-8374, e-mail Ann@BrazenHussiesNetwork.com

Keep your wholesalers, distributors, and sales reps informed! A one-sheet monthly fax—or whenever something big is about to break—does the trick.

Finally, after six weeks, we were able to get through to the buyer herself, who casually informed us it would be another four weeks or so before she could evaluate the book and make a decision. That was like telling a jockey he could work in the stables but couldn't ride a horse. Our patience was gone. A letter politely explaining the situation was in the mail to the general manager that night. Two days later the buyer called, set an immediate appointment, and subsequently ordered one hundred books.

Understanding Exclusive (Master) Distribution

There are self-publishers and small presses that swear by their exclusive (master) distributors—and others who feel like they have shot themselves in the foot with such arrangements. They tell horror stories of being left holding the (empty) bag when their distributors went out of business. Everyone agrees, however, this form of getting books sold has really come into its own in the last ten years.

When you sign with an exclusive distributor, it handles all sales to the trade: bookstores, wholesalers, other nonexclusive distributors, and often libraries. Many offer toll-free numbers and take credit cards to facilitate consumer orders that result from author radio interviews and other publicity. This distributor advertises your book in its catalog, exhibits the book at BEA and other conventions, and has from twenty-two to twenty-nine sales reps who tout your books on their travels across the country.

The company also handles shipping, billing, and taking payments, plus handling collections, returns, and customer service. For this, the distributor expects a discount of 62 to 67 percent off the retail price. (Do remember that distributors must pass along discounts ranging from 40 to 55 percent to their accounts, so it's certainly not all profit.) Some who take the lower amount expect you to chip in for catalog ads and BEA booth rental, so it about evens out. Most remit your payment ninety days after the month in which the books are sold, minus returns. Your job is to create a demand for the book. They depend on you for the publicity that drives buyers into bookstores.

Like publishers, they vary in size, quality, business practices, and ethics. Publishers Group West (PGW) is the major player, having established itself decades ago. Because of its reputation, and the fact it often has a title on national bestseller lists, PGW isn't receptive to taking on one-book neophytes. Other prominent exclusive distributors include Independent Publishers Group (IPG), Login Publishers Consortium (LPC Group), Partners Book Distributing, Inc., National Book Network (and its Biblio Distribution for very small presses), BookWorld Services, Inc., Associated Publishers Group (APG), Midpoint Trade, and Consortium Book Sales.

Whether you can get one of them to accept you—and whether you care to accept one of them—is dependent on several factors. Ron Smith of BookWorld is very sensitive to book covers. "We lose more orders because of bad or weak cover design, by far, than from any other cause. And we reject more publishers for this reason than any other," he explains. Independent Publishers Group's Curt Matthews laments he must turn down many new publishers because they don't work far enough in advance. He (and each of his colleagues) needs sample covers and sales materials many months in advance. "It comes as a terrible shock to most new publishers that so much work has to be done long before their books are printed," says Matthews.

A primary reason exclusive distribution is attractive is that often it's the way into the likes of Ingram, Barnes & Noble, and Borders for a new publisher. Exclusive distribution should increase your trade sales considerably. According to a PMA survey of its members who had gone with an exclusive distributor, the average title sold about 2,800 copies for a value of $25,000. Going this route also frees you from many time-consuming jobs, including filling orders, doing billing, collecting on invoices, and handling customer service. Because of this, it may actually be cheaper to use an exclusive distributor.

Here are some questions to ask:

- How accessible is the management?
- How many books does the distributor typically sell of your type?
- Are payments prompt?
- Are there any unforeseen expenses in working with the company?
- For how long is the contract?

We also suggest you do a financial background check. You need to be as aware of this working partner's financial state as you would be of an acute toothache. Additionally, determine how the organization plans to handle returns. A few automatically withhold a hefty percentage of the money due. And if you're having trouble getting credit card merchant status, choosing an exclusive distributor that offers this service could be important. Give the distributor only the trade and *non*exclusive rights to such markets as gift shops, book clubs, and foreign sales.

Once you've signed a contract, keep your distributor in the information loop. These operations all have sales conferences around the first week in May and the first week in December. Be sure you've provided a copy of your marketing plan so its obvious you're dedicated to creating demand for your title. And whenever you're scheduled for national media or an important review breaks, inform the distributor immediately so it can get the word out to bookstores and wholesalers.

Wholesalers and distributors come in all sizes, shapes, and dispositions. Some are a delight to work with. Others make you want to get out your horse whip. But they spell $-a-l-e-s for your book and should be wooed into your camp.

Tapping the Lucrative Library Market

There are approximately 15,000 public libraries in the United States. Their purchasing power—combined with academic and special libraries—represents a growing $2 billion business. Library patrons number in the millions each day. Would you believe that our country has approximately 103,000 libraries, including elementary, high school, college, armed forces, public, and special libraries? Yes, library sales can be to the self-publisher what the salmon spawning season is to a fisherman.

In fact, some books reach the break-even point—or climb into profitable status—on library sales alone. Bear Kamoroff told us this about his *Small Time Operator*: "Three-fourths of the people who call to order the book saw it first in the library." In fact, he even *gives away* copies to libraries because it more than comes back to him in patrons who want to purchase a personal copy. We have many people call our publishing company's order line, (800) 331-8355, to get a personal copy, having previously discovered the book in a library.

Why are libraries so great? First of all, we recommend that library sales be at the full retail price for orders under five copies because many of them are single-copy orders. (Or you might offer a freebie. Our friend Carol Waugh tells of extending a free tote bag for every order over $100 and finding it worked exceedingly well.) Second, unlike bookstores, libraries involve no return hassle. Only in rare instances will a library refuse a book it has ordered. And third, some buy in nice quantities. Here's a sampling of orders we've received: The San Diego County Library bought thirty-five copies. The City of Chicago stocked its branches with twenty-eight copies. Fairfax Public Library ordered twenty-three, and the Nassau Library System purchased twelve. Not too shabby, eh? And we've gotten smaller orders from virtually every state in the Union.

Although recent citizen mandates for less governmental spending have tightened library purse strings, this remains an ideal market for the small press. William Lofquist, the publishing industry's statistician at the Commerce Department in Washington, estimates it at about 10 percent of the entire book market.

Start your campaign by contacting the proper person in the local library system. Call the main branch and ask who is in charge of acquisitions (meaning ordering) for your type of book (children's literature, reference, business, adult fiction, etc.). This information can also be found in the *American Library Directory*. It's probably just as well to approach the acquirers as the *author* rather than the publisher, since librarians enjoy supporting local authors. You can do this by mail (see sample letter on page 323), or you can approach them in person. Send or leave a complimentary copy of the book to be circulated, plus plenty of promotional material. Potential library books are displayed for branch librarians to examine and order. Consequently, it may be a couple of months before you actually receive a purchase order.

Be sure you cover all local bases. In San Diego, for instance, the city and county are two separate entities. We received generous orders from both. Investigate the structure in your hometown so as not to neglect a nice sale.

Now that you've tapped the local resources, where to next? The whole country is your oyster! Librarians are very review driven. This means they put a lot of stock in the primary review media. For that reason you would be wise not to approach them until a favorable review has appeared in one or more of the following: *Library Journal*, *Booklist*, *Publishers Weekly*, *Kirkus Reviews*, *Today's Librarian*, *Wilson Library Bulletin*, *School Library Journal* (if it is a work for children or young adults), or *Choice* (if a work slanted to college or research libraries). These publications carry great weight with librarians. Once one of these sources has praised your book, library orders will begin to trickle in with no effort on your part. But don't be discouraged if you miss these; there are still dozens of smaller publications librarians respect and that can give your book credibility. And don't overlook Internet reviews; librarians, bless their hearts, are information junkies.

Speaking of reviews and libraries, we must tell you of our dear colleague Jim Cox. He heads the Midwest Book Review, which specializes in reviewing small-press titles. He publishes five monthly library newsletters for community and academic library systems in California, Wisconsin, and the upper Midwest; produces *Bookwatch*, a weekly TV program; produces an Internet Bookwatch; and does who knows what else. This man is a true friend of the self-publisher who turns out quality books, and his reviews are welcomed and respected. Reach him at James A. Cox, Editor-in-Chief, Midwest Book Review, 278 Orchard Dr., Oregon, WI 53575. His e-mail is mwbookrevw@aol.com.

Another friend of the independent publisher is a new magazine on the horizon titled *Today's Librarian*. In 2000 it reviewed more than 450 books with a driving mission of bringing public librarians news of smaller publishers' best offerings. (See contact information in Appendix E.) One of our clients, Lorraine Peoples, the author of *You Can Teach Someone to Read*, was thrilled to discover her book made *Today's Librarian*'s first annual Best of Short Takes 2000.

Fortunately, libraries are interested in books other than best-sellers. They seek titles of good quality that fill a well-defined patron need. Collection development depends on the goals of the local institution and the needs of the commu-

Library Follow-Up Letter

Arthur E. Murray, County Librarian
San Diego County Library
5555 Overland Avenue, Building 15
San Diego, CA 92123

Dear Mr. Murray:

With "Roots" due to be re-run on television in January and the paperback edition of the book expected to be released soon, the interest in family history continues to mushroom.

Why not take this opportunity to expose the users of San Diego County libraries to the excitement of tracing their own roots? Our book, DISCOVER YOUR ROOTS, is an easy guide for climbing your family tree. It has been praised by the GENEALOGICAL HELPER (copy of review enclosed). This is the "Bible" of genealogists, and theirs is a high commendation for a book to receive.

I am hopeful that you have had a chance to review the copy we sent you previously and that it is making the rounds of other librarians. We have already filled a large order for the city libraries, and I hope we can do the same for residents who live in the county. By the way, the author is a local woman who is actively involved in speaking to various local groups.

We look forward to answering any questions for you and to filling your order promptly. Thank you for your interest in continuing to bring helpful and interesting reading materials to San Diego County residents.

Sincerely,

Ann Markham

Ann Markham
Marketing Director

AM:111
Encl.

Persistence pays off! Stay in touch and romance potential big opportunities.

nity. For instance, if your book deals with African American Studies or a topic of interest to Hispanics, you'd be wise to contact libraries located in areas with these high ethnic populations. Likewise, a book of gay or lesbian interest will go well in cities with large homosexual contingencies.

Reviews

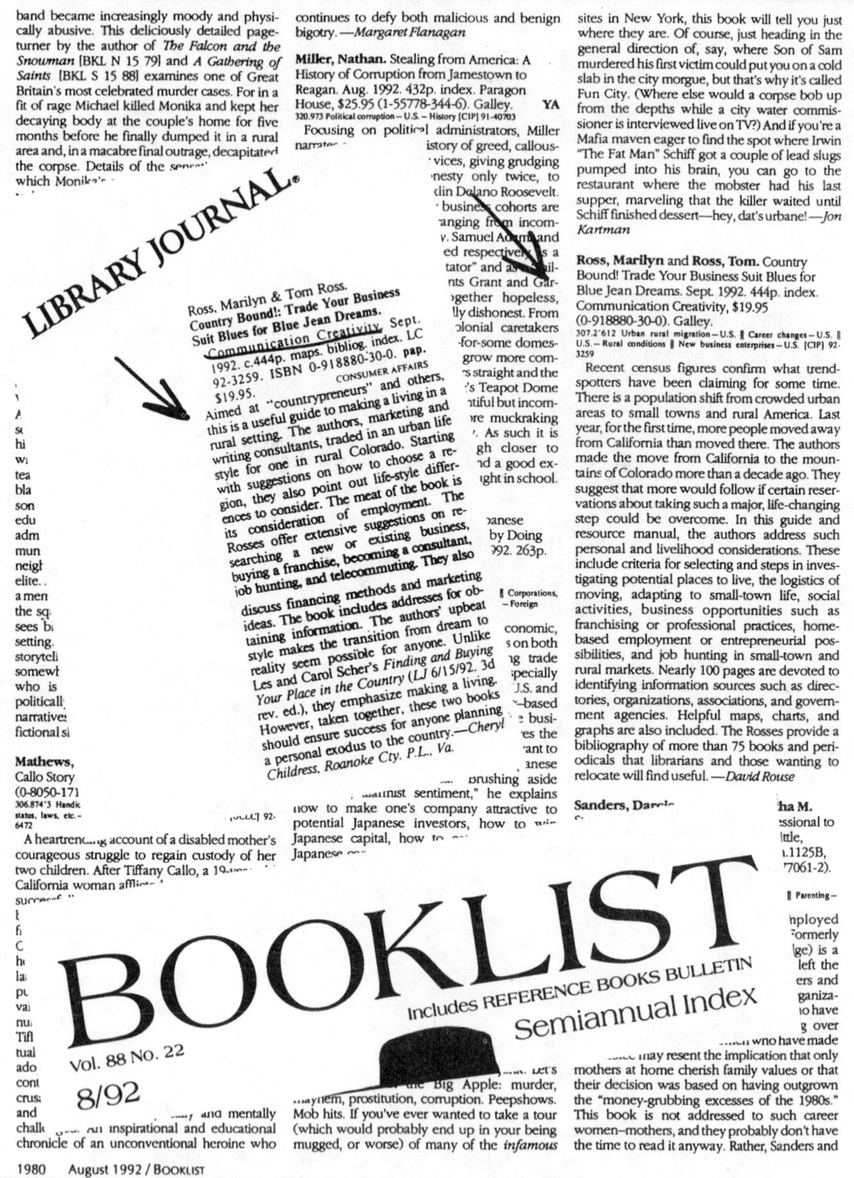

band became increasingly moody and physically abusive. This deliciously detailed page-turner by the author of *The Falcon and the Snowman* [BKL N 15 79] and *A Gathering of Saints* [BKL S 15 88] examines one of Great Britain's most celebrated murder cases. For in a fit of rage Michael killed Monika and kept her decaying body at the couple's home for five months before he finally dumped it in a rural area and, in a macabre final outrage, decapitated the corpse. Details of the sens... which Monika's ...

Mathews, ... Callo Story ... (0-8050-171... 306.874'3 Handic... status, laws, etc.– 6472 ... [OCLC] 92-

A heartrending account of a disabled mother's courageous struggle to regain custody of her two children. After Tiffany Callo, a 19-... California woman afflic... ... and mentally chall... An inspirational and educational chronicle of an unconventional heroine who continues to defy both malicious and benign bigotry. —*Margaret Flanagan*

Miller, Nathan. Stealing from America: A History of Corruption from Jamestown to Reagan. Aug. 1992. 432p. index. Paragon House, $25.95 (1-55778-344-6). Galley. **YA**
320.973 Political corruption – U.S. – History [CIP] 91-40703

Focusing on political administrators, Miller narrates ... istory of greed, callous... vices, giving grudging ... nesty only twice, to ... klin Delano Roosevelt. ...

LIBRARY JOURNAL®

Ross, Marilyn & Tom Ross. **Country Bound!: Trade Your Business Suit Blues for Blue Jean Dreams.** Communication Creativity. Sept. 1992. c.444p. maps. bibliog. index. LC 92-3259. ISBN 0-918880-30-0. **pap.** $19.95. CONSUMER AFFAIRS

Aimed at "countrypreneurs" and others, this is a useful guide to making a living in a rural setting. The authors, marketing and writing consultants, traded in an urban life style for one in rural Colorado. Starting with suggestions on how to choose a region, they also point out life-style differences to consider. The meat of the book is its consideration of employment. The Rosses offer extensive suggestions on researching a new or existing business, buying a franchise, becoming a consultant, job hunting, and telecommuting. They also discuss financing methods and marketing ideas. The book includes addresses for obtaining information. The authors' upbeat style makes the transition from dream to reality seem possible for anyone. Unlike Les and Carol Scher's *Finding and Buying Your Place in the Country* (LJ 6/15/92. 3d rev. ed.), they emphasize making a living. However, taken together, these two books should ensure success for anyone planning a personal exodus to the country.—*Cheryl Childress, Roanoke Cty. P.L., Va.*

... brushing aside ... nationalist sentiment," he explains how to make one's company attractive to potential Japanese investors, how to wi... Japanese capital, how to ... Japanese ...

... Let's ... the Big Apple: murder, mayhem, prostitution, corruption. Peepshows. Mob hits. If you've ever wanted to take a tour (which would probably end up in your being mugged, or worse) of many of the *infamous* sites in New York, this book will tell you just where they are. Of course, just heading in the general direction of, say, where Son of Sam murdered his first victim could put you on a cold slab in the city morgue, but that's why it's called Fun City. (Where else would a corpse bob up from the depths while a city water commissioner is interviewed live on TV?) And if you're a Mafia maven eager to find the spot where Irwin "The Fat Man" Schiff got a couple of lead slugs pumped into his brain, you can go to the restaurant where the mobster had his last supper, marveling that the killer waited until Schiff finished dessert—hey, dat's urbane! —*Jon Kartman*

Ross, Marilyn and **Ross, Tom.** Country Bound! Trade Your Business Suit Blues for Blue Jean Dreams. Sept. 1992. 444p. index. Communication Creativity, $19.95 (0-918880-30-0). Galley.
307.2'612 Urban rural migration – U.S. ‖ Career changes – U.S. ‖ U.S. – Rural conditions ‖ New business enterprises – U.S. [CIP] 92-3259

Recent census figures confirm what trend-spotters have been claiming for some time. There is a population shift from crowded urban areas to small towns and rural America. Last year, for the first time, more people moved away from California than moved there. The authors made the move from California to the mountains of Colorado more than a decade ago. They suggest that more would follow if certain reservations about taking such a major, life-changing step could be overcome. In this guide and resource manual, the authors address such personal and livelihood considerations. These include criteria for selecting and steps in investigating potential places to live, the logistics of moving, adapting to small-town life, social activities, business opportunities such as franchising or professional practices, home-based employment or entrepreneurial possibilities, and job hunting in small-town and rural markets. Nearly 100 pages are devoted to identifying information sources such as directories, organizations, associations, and government agencies. Helpful maps, charts, and graphs are also included. The Rosses provide a bibliography of more than 75 books and periodicals that librarians and those wanting to relocate will find useful. —*David Rouse*

Sanders, Darc... ... ha M. ... ssional to ... ttle, ... 1125B, ... 7061-2). ... Parenting – ... mployed ... Formerly ... lge) is a ... left the ... ers and ... ganiza- ... o have ... g over ... en who have made ... may resent the implication that only mothers at home cherish family values or that their decision was based on having outgrown the "money-grubbing excesses of the 1980s." This book is not addressed to such career women–mothers, and they probably don't have the time to read it anyway. Rather, Sanders and

BOOKLIST
Includes REFERENCE BOOKS BULLETIN
Semiannual Index
Vol. 88 No. 22
8/92

1980 August 1992 / BOOKLIST

Share your reviews in major media. Others want to climb on a moving bandwagon.

Sources Librarians Use to Buy Books

According to a study conducted by *Library Journal*, this is what prompts librarians to buy books (they add up to more than 100 percent because librarians rely on more than one method):

Reviews in trade journals	96%
Patron requests	89%
Best-seller lists	74%
Consumer media	68%
Publishers' catalogs	65%
Wholesaler/distributor catalogs	56%
Word of mouth	54%

Librarians aren't moved by hyperbole. They want to see significant reviews, a table of contents, a typical entry for a directory or reference book. They also need all the book's vital statistics, such as ISBN, LCCN, year of publication, binding info, and grade levels for children's books. And they'll appreciate a listing of distributors and wholesalers that carry your title. Talk about your book in terms of circulation and the patrons who will use it. Be sure to tell if it includes annotations, footnotes, a bibliography, or other academic qualities that will serve as resources. If you don't know the buyer's name, addressing the "Acquisition Librarian" works fine. Early on in your development process, consider getting advice from librarians. You might form an editorial advisory committee or an informal focus group to help you identify library needs or spot flaws in your book.

Ordering often goes in cycles. Certain periods during the year will yield a better response than others. The best time to contact libraries is probably just before the end of their fiscal years (June 30 or December 31), as they may be in a hurry to use up unappropriated funds. (Or they can sit on the information until just after those dates when they have fresh sources of money at their disposal.) If you're making multiple contacts, get the first to them early in June or December, with the second thirty to forty-five days later.

There are other ways to influence librarians, too. Exhibiting your book at the American Library Association Convention or midwinter conference, or specific annual state conferences, may make sense. There are also subject-specific library conferences that could yield tremendous sales for a niche book.

And don't forget libraries as a means of promoting your book. As we discuss, they are author-friendly and many sponsor readings or seminars—with books sold in tandem. Check with the public relations department in larger libraries.

By the way, ask your friends and relatives to help you by requesting your book at their local libraries. Most libraries keep track of such requests. Demand may result in their acquiring the title to meet the groundswell of requests. A good way to further spread the word about your book is to rent a mailing list. You can get information on prices and quantities available from the R.R. Bowker Company, which breaks its lists down according to the size of a library's appropriation budget, or contact the American Library Association at (800) 545-2433 and ask for the Mailing List Department. As an example, you can rent a list of 337 law and political sciences sections, 290 women's studies sections, or 823 science and technology sections.

To capture the attention of librarians, send excerpts—or the complete review, if it is short—from the strategic publications mentioned above. Also include other testimonials and advance comments, and highlight any timely tie-in. Make ordering easy by providing an order form, which you have coded so you can keep track of results. Because library ordering tends to be a slow, bureaucratic process, there is no real advantage for the mailing to go out First-Class. Bulk postage will cut costs and probably not reduce results.

You might also consider asking another publisher to advertise piggyback with you. For the same amount of postage, you include the other's promotional material. We invited an associate to include a catalog sheet in our mailing at no cost to her. The arrangement was we would get 40 percent on all orders received, and she would take care of the fulfillment. That way we didn't spend anything additional and she had no initial cash outlay; yet both parties stood to benefit. It worked beautifully. We received enough orders for her book to cover all but a couple dollars of the entire mailing cost. This included list rental, printing, envelopes, and postage. The mailing was put out by manual labor, and since part of the deal was that our friend helped stuff and seal envelopes, we had fun in the process.

A discussion of libraries wouldn't be complete without explaining that there are about as many kinds of them as there are flavors of ice cream. For example, one intriguing possibility is military libraries.

Another library market that is often ignored is churches and synagogues. *Publishers Weekly* has noted that conservative estimates place the number at around fifty thousand church and synagogue libraries. And many carry inspirational and self-help books, as well as religious titles. While some stock only a few dozen books, other collections number in the thousands and have generous annual budgets. You can reach them by contacting the Church and Synagogue Library Association, P.O. Box 19357, Portland, OR 97280-0357, (503) 244-6919, www.worldaccessnet.com/~csla. Most have journals that carry advertisements, one of the best bargains around if this is a prime target for you.

Various specialized libraries may lead to further profit. Business, corporation, and technical library lists are available from Bowker. If you have a book about forestry, there are 1,361 libraries interested in the general field in which it falls. Is your tome a discussion of art? Then rent the art and architecture libraries list. And if you've done a book about easy ways to play the banjo, perhaps the almost five hundred music libraries would like to hear about it. Don't overlook the possibility that there may be a group of libraries ideally suited to your specific subject matter. An excellent manual on the craft of writing for libraries and educational institutions is Nat Bodian's *Copywriter's Handbook: A Practical Guide for Advertising and Promotion of Specialized and Scholarly Books and Journals.*

And we can't leave this subject without telling you of a new book with the unusual title of *i-Tips 2000*. Written by three savvy experts in the field, Kathryn Kleibacker, Linda Winter, and Carol Ann Waugh, it is subtitled *The Insiders' Guide to School and Library Marketing*. Here you'll find seldom-seen advice for effective product development, plus marketing strategies for libraries, K–12 education, even home school markets. And it is very Internet oriented because 98 percent of librarians and educators have access to the Internet through their institutions. Check it out at www.internet-monitor.com.

There are also school and college libraries that buy everything from juvenile storybooks to university reference works. It's a good idea to approach them with a double-barreled mailing targeted to both the librarian and the appropriate department head. Let's explore this potential further.

Going After Educational Sales

Schools cover an amazing range of possibilities: day care centers, K–12, adult education and community colleges, four-year institutions, universities, special education programs, even home schooling and vocational programs. They all have potential as large-scale buyers. Orders will not pop into your office, however. They will dawdle in. Promotional material sent now may result in an order six months or a year downstream. But that order could be for dozens, hundreds, even thousands of books. And it isn't necessarily a one-shot thing. Reorders are likely to roll in each new semester. Another reason this is an attractive market is that most sales are made on a "short discount," meaning that you only allow 20 percent off the retail price.

Perhaps you're thinking, "My book wouldn't sell to schools; it's not a textbook." You may be in for a nice surprise. The wide variety of titles that are appropriate in today's academic circles is amazing. For instance, the General Books Department of Harcourt Brace Jovanovich promoted the following for college use: *Hitler's Secret Service* (history and civilization), *Of Love and Lust* (psychology), *All Our Children* (sociology), *Zen Catholicism* (philosophy and religion), *The Company She Keeps* (women's studies), and the novels *The Voyage Out* and *Jacob's Room*. And because self-publishing is merely a microcosm of trade publishing, the book you're reading sometimes serves as a text for university classes on publishing.

To help educators appreciate why your book would be appropriate, stress any benefits that make it more likely for adoption. These might include chapters arranged a certain way to make it easier to teach, inclusion of exercises and quizzes, or review questions at the end of each chapter.

Even if your work is not suitable as a text, it may be used as related material for course planning. Such books are called supplemental texts. We were fortunate in introducing *Discover Your Roots* to the San Diego Unified School District. This contact netted us ongoing sales, as various junior and senior highs picked up the book as a supplementary text in history classes. Supplemental texts also find a fertile field in continuing education. Adult learning programs cover a lot of unlikely subjects, some of which may dovetail with your book.

Call the Board of Education at the nearest large city to determine who is in charge of curriculum for the subject area of your book. In our case the curriculum consultant was impressed with the examination copy we provided and invited us to supply him with a quantity of fliers to distribute to schools in the district. Needless to say, we were happy to cooperate.

Here again, the specialized mailing list is the perfect means of reaching your target market. Two main firms offer detailed breakdowns of faculty. One is QED (Quality Education Data). Its catalog offers a quick reference guide to the entire education market, and QED has both mailing lists and database services. For instance, with its new educator e-mail marketing service, you can have your message delivered to the desktops of such educators as pre-K teachers, guidance counselors, athletics coaches, plus teachers who cover English, fine arts and music, math, science, social studies, you name it. Reach QED at (800) 525-5811 or online at www.qeddata.com. The other company you want to check out is Market Data Retrieval, which has four areas covering K–12, colleges, libraries, and day care. Call (800) 333-8802 or visit www.schooldata.com. Consider renting a small subset to test your mailing's effectiveness before rolling out with the larger list.

The resourceful author-publisher, however, may be able to come up with a list using more creative tactics. Try calling the State Board of Education (usually in the capital) and ask for its publication department. Many times the BOE will sell you a list of schools on labels or send you a book with a list that you can type from. Sometimes these lists are free, other times $10, and in one case, a publisher got a wonderful CD with fifteen thousand school names for $100.

The best time to mail to colleges is the beginning of summer for the fall semester and prior to October for the winter semester. Educators will expect to receive an examination copy on which they can base a decision. That doesn't mean you automatically have to send books to everyone. Prepare a mailing piece and, as part of the qualification to receive a complimentary copy, require that the following information be provided:

- Title and nature of course
- Estimated number of students
- College upper or lower division course (Freshman and sophomore classes are larger and thus more profitable.)
- Starting date of the class
- Approximate date of "adoption" decision (Kids, pets, and books are adopted.)
- Source of the decision—person, committee, department (If committee or department, then also PR the faculty members.)

Because you can still end up giving away sizable quantities of examination copies in this way, some publishers indicate that they expect the books to be returned if they are not adopted. Or specify that a book can be retained for the instructor's personal library by paying the regular price minus a 20 percent "professional" discount. If you take either of these stands, be prepared to send out a lot of statements for unreturned books—with very poor results. Even so, educational sales can boost your earnings.

Of course, mailing to educators is only one way of reaching them. Most areas of teaching have focused teacher associations. And what do you suppose these associations have? Journals and conferences! Submit your book for review, mention, or excerpting in their journals—and track down information for attending and/or exhibiting at their conferences.

Something else not to overlook is the home school market. This craze is growing steadily, and every household needs books. There is a great directory from Bluestocking Press that leads you to 165 catalogs, 125 conferences, 85 stores, 195 newsletters/magazines, 160 reviewers, and tons more called *The Home School Market Guide*. If this is your niche, order it by calling (800) 959-8586.

Did you know there is a company that does book fairs for schoolteachers? It's called Reading's Fun/Books Are Fun. The company buys hardcover books in huge volume—sometimes 50,000 or 75,000 units. Should this perk up your ears, send a sample book and pitch letter to Book Buyer, Reading's Fun/Books Are Fun, 1680 Highway I, Fairfield, IA 52556. For more details, call (641) 472-8301.

Before we leave this subject, be aware that college bookstores may be interested in your book even if it is not adopted as a text or supplemental text. To get a feel for the kinds of books and merchandise they carry, send your ad agency rate letter to the *College Store Executive*, Executive Business Media, Inc., 825 Old

Country Rd., P.O. Box 1500, Westbury, NY 11590. Browsing in the bookstore of your own local college or university will also be most revealing.

Using Commissioned Sales Reps

Commissioned sales reps are independent salespeople who represent a given number of titles in a specific geographic area. They introduce new titles, take orders, straighten and restock bookstore shelves, and generally service the accounts for you. In return, they expect a minimum of 10 percent of retail sales and 5 percent on wholesale accounts.

Your position in the rep's bag is very important. This means where your book falls in the sequence of presentation to the bookstore buyer. (The earlier the better; later the buyer gets tired, interrupted, or disinterested—or the budget depleted.) Your chances of having good positioning increase with your number of titles and your marketing commitment.

Most reps will also want a protected territory or all the "ledger accounts," which is another way of saying an exclusive. That means that on all books sold to the trade in their territories, they receive a commission, whether you sell the books or they do. Several small presses that have tried sales reps have abandoned the practice. Uncollectible billings is one big problem. The rep gets a commission, but downstream you may get returned books, on which you already forked over 5 or 10 percent. In spite of these warnings, if you want to try to line up a commissioned sales rep (which isn't easy for a self-publisher), talk to successful small presses. Reps also sometimes advertise in *Publishers Weekly* for new titles to represent.

Sales and ads often go together like bread and butter. If you want to know when to advertise, how to develop a dynamite ad, and all the other nuances of this topic, read on!

Web Sites, Wisdom, and Whimsey

Want to reach 150,000 K–6 grade teachers and educational professionals? The *Learning Resource Guide*, published biannually in January and August, seeks information on products appropriate for this audience. Send relevant books to Anne Laura Credi at The Education Center, 3515 W. Market St., Suite 200, Greensboro, NC 27403, phone (336) 854-0309, fax (336) 547-1587.

* * *

Take a course on telemarketing to libraries. Bill Child has been very successful selling his products to libraries. Consequently he has created a course on how to telemarket to this medium that includes a list of resources that help publishers and authors find appropriate libraries. For a free fact sheet on the five points used to determine if your product is right for the market, contact Child at (888) 513-3400, or e-mail bchild@island.net.

* * *

Booksellers voice opinions on best marketing strategies. A recent survey of 150 independents and 150 chain stores, conducted by BookExpo America and *Publishers Weekly*, revealed interesting facts. The booksellers themselves have found the two most valuable strategies for selling a new title are the author tour and reading copies. Of the indies surveyed, 69 percent selected the author tour as the most desired; 71 percent of the chains chose this approach. For advance reading copies, the percentages were 62 for indies and 49 for chains. While most independent publishers can't afford to mount an extensive author tour, providing free reading copies of a new title to perhaps fifty to one hundred stores is a viable and obviously savvy alternative. This "right from the horse's mouth" input can be invaluable when planning your PR/marketing campaign and budget.

* * *

I know of one sales rep who is so good he could convince the Pope to go to the Methodist church.

* * *

Library budgets rise. This was the upbeat message of the recent American Library Association midwinter meeting. "This is the best time for library budgets that I have seen in my twenty-five years in the business," commented Larry Price, executive vice-president of Ingram Library Services. Some believe it parallels the LBJ years when tons of federal money was funneled to libraries. *Library Journal* also says overall public library budgets are up 6.5 percent. And those facilities serving populations of one million or more are enjoying increases of 14.1 percent over last year.

* * *

Excellent librarian-finding source is on the Web. If you're looking for links to academic libraries, public libraries, state libraries, regional consortia, special and school libraries, or national libraries and library organizations, have we got a doozie for you! Go to http://sunsite.berkeley.edu/Libweb. There are also avenues here for Canada, Europe, Africa and the Middle East, Australia and New Zealand, Mexico, and other locations. Other links can take you on a wonderful journey into more marketing havens.

* * *

Do you publish books appropriate for colleges? Then you'll want to know about the National Association of College Stores site at www.NACS.org. If you're doing textbooks, works that might be used as supplemental texts, or general titles of interest to the college bound, it will behoove you to consider marketing to college stores. By accessing NACS's Browse by Category, then selecting appropriate keywords, you can get a good idea of what books college stores currently carry.

This association publishes the *Directory of Colleges and College Stores*, considered to be the industry's telephone books for reaching this market. It lists colleges and universities plus the stores serving those campuses. Store listings include buyer name, address, phone, fax, and e-mail address. While this huge reference volume costs nonmembers $475, NACS members can receive one free copy. You might want to consider becoming an Associate Member if this is a primary market for you. Details online at Become a Member.

* * *

I never read a book before reviewing it—it prejudices a man so. —Sydney Smith

* * *

Do you market products to schools and libraries? Then surf over to www.internet-monitor.com. This site provides those targeting educational facilities and libraries with valuable information for investing their marketing dollars wisely. When we visited, the Today's Tip was a checklist to make your Web site educator-friendly. Additionally, there are articles on how curriculum standards impact product development, the home school market, state adoptions, ten ideas to improve your next catalog, and how to select responsive mailing lists for the educational market. And a click on Marketing Resources leads you to statistics, trends, funding, facts and figures; educational, library, and trade book magazine and review resources; conferences and associations; mailing lists and Internet databases; Internet discussion groups, mail lists, and newsgroups; plus e-commerce, e-books, and on-demand publishing. And the final crème de la crème is a section dubbed Internet Marketing Gateway that promises to lower your marketing costs and increase your responses with nifty ideas as well as tried-and-true strategies.

Are you a growing independent publisher looking for a literary distributor? The sole remaining one in the country has doubled its warehouse space and accepts quality fiction, poetry, and cultural studies. For details contact Small Press Distribution, Inc. at (510) 524-1668.

16 *Crafting Ads That Reel in Results*

You could have one of the greatest book ideas of the century, but if no one knows about it, you're not likely to sell many books. So how do you remove the cloak of secrecy? Advertising is one way. It can indeed be a mystical business that sometimes seems to border on the supernatural. How else can we explain why a one-word change in a classified ad can resurrect it from the graveyard and make it a winner? Or conversely, how an ad can die because of a wee change? None of us will ever know all of the answers all the time. The marketing genius John Wanamaker summed it up when he stated, "I know that half the money I spend on advertising is wasted. I just don't know *which* half."

Frankly, we advise you *not* to plunk down large sums for ads. It's usually like pouring money down a rat hole. We hear more sob stories from people who spent more than a thousand dollars on an ad and sold four or five books than we do anything else. Besides there's an old merchandising axiom that says you always publicize before you advertise. Why? Because once the ad has broken, it's no longer fresh news. That said, let us proceed.

The Trade Publishers' Approach

In an article in the *Authors Guild Bulletin*, Robert A. Carter explains why trade publishers advertise books:

- To help sell an individual title to the trade
- To help sell an individual title to consumers
- To help sell subsidiary rights
- To impress authors and agents
- To establish an image for the house

After studying these reasons, it soon becomes obvious why self-publishers must take a different approach. Even though the first and third reasons are of concern to self-publishing, the only item that really counts for us is the second one. But let's probe deeper into the advertising practices of trade publishers, as there are lessons to be learned. Fact: Their overall advertising and promotion budget is typically placed at a percent of the expected sales of the first printing. Unless you've got a blockbuster book, 'tain't much. (This is the major reason it is so important for trade-published authors to be aggressive in promoting their own books.)

And even then, advertising is often ineffectual. Some trade publishers admit it doesn't get people out to buy a book. One publishing executive quipped, "A lot of advertisements are for the author, his mother, and his agent."

When publishers are pushing a book to the trade, that means booksellers, wholesalers, and libraries. The medium used most often is *Publishers Weekly*. When you realize that a single page in *PW* goes for $6,535, it becomes apparent that the average budget will quickly be wiped out at that rate. An intensive sales campaign might also include *American Bookseller*, a monthly journal of the American Booksellers Association, plus *Library Journal*, *Booklist*, *Choice*, and selected wholesalers' publications.

But the big guns come out when Publishers' Row wants to convince the general reading public they should buy a book. The medium most frequently used for that is *The New York Times Book Review*. Would you believe one page costs $29,030? (Of course, major publishers negotiate better long-term contracts.) Other favored publications are *The New York Review of Books* (especially if it's a scholarly work), *The New Yorker*, *The Washington Post*, *The Wall Street Journal*, the *Los Angeles Times*, *The Christian Science Monitor*, *USA Today*, *Time*, and *Newsweek*.

But if a book is a flop, not even a fortune can turn it into a best-seller. Wealthy businessman Jack Dreyfus spent about $2 million of his own money promoting his book with full-page ads in newspapers and magazines around the country. In spite of his outlandish spending spree, *A Remarkable Medicine Has Been Overlooked* was itself overlooked by millions. Another businessman's crusade, *The Trimtab Factor*, died a similar death in spite of the $1 million spent by the author, Harold Willens, to boost it to stardom.

Needless to say, that kind of ad program is simply out of the league of most self-publishers. But that doesn't mean you can't have effective advertising. Quite the contrary. Much of the success of any advertising effort depends on the basics: the development of sales materials with pizzazz, an effective means to determine who should receive these materials, and a repetitive campaign.

Developing Sales Materials With Punch

A punch is quick and to the point, right? Start noticing ads that grab your attention. Betcha it isn't just the full-page spread or the full-minute spot on radio or TV. It doesn't take a full-course meal to whet the appetite. A short well-done ad pulls much better than a long ineffective one. The key is not length but rather quality and repetition. You'll get more bang for your buck by investing in twelve identical small ads than from one large, full-page spread. Most people give you only a few seconds to set the hook. Boiled down to basics, it becomes: Stay in front of your prospects. If you keep in front of them with punchy sales material, you will make sales. We've included some examples on the following pages.

Some of your sales material can be created in parallel with the jacket or cover by printing an overrun as we discussed previously. Note our sample Book Spec Sheet, which is simply a one-page flier telling about the book. It plays an important role in promoting to libraries, bookstores, wholesalers, and educational systems. It's straightforward, low-key, to the point, and quickly communicates the message. Notice how all the information any trade account could need is included. Put a salesy cover letter, a book cover, and copies of reviews with it and you have a powerful package. This trade-oriented Book Spec Sheet is different, however, from a flier directed to *consumers*. The consumer promo flier starts out much more salesy, has a "you" approach expressed in a benefit way, and contains an order form (see example on page 337).

Use your imagination and those beautiful third-party accolades that drift in from reviewers, columnists, educators, experts, and media personalities. We sought and received permission to reprint a nationally syndicated column by Jack Smith that lauded one of our books. A lot of extra mileage can be gained from use of this type of material in your sales kit. We paid $50 for permission to reprint this copyrighted material, and it was money well spent. How about the letter from Claude Pepper, chairman of the House of Representatives Select Committee on Aging? We rest our case for third-party testimonials.

Now let's review some basic rules about effective sales material.

- **Sell the sizzle, not the steak.** If you've been around salespeople at all, surely you've heard this well-worn phrase. Tell folks what the book does for them. What problem will it solve? Will it make them healthier, wealthier, skinnier, sexier? People don't buy books to make this a better world or to support your family. They buy books to make their own lives easier, happier, more successful, or to give them an edge in this competitive world.
- **Stress *benefits* rather than features.** Here is an example of what we mean: A feature of a book is that it "shows how to go job hunting in Chicago." But expressing this as a benefit, we could say "discover how to find high-paying, hidden jobs in Chicago." See how much more powerful the second statement is? It relates to the needs of the potential book buyer. Always give your sales

Book Spec Sheet for the Trade

P.O. Box 909 • 425 Cedar Street • Buena Vista, CO 81211-0909
http://www.SPANnet.org/CC/ • e-mail: CC@spannet.org
(719) 395-8659 • Fax (719) 395-8374

Book Spec Sheet

Jump Start Your Books Sales: A Money-Making Guide for Authors, Independent Publishers and Small Presses by Marilyn and Tom Ross, authors of the classic best-seller, *The Complete Guide to Self-Publishing*. You can turn yourself into a marketing master and make tens of thousands of extra dollars with the ideas in this book! Discover how to get your books into catalogs, rack up lucrative bulk premium sales, and do author signings and radio interviews that get outrageous results. Find the secret to generating lots of free publicity, then master how to *really* capitalize on it. Add to that insider information on how to make the Internet a fabulous sales generator, penetrate libraries, sell to book clubs, get onto QVC Home Shopping Network—and you can't do without this guide. For less than 6¢ a day, you can turn the next year into a wealth-building bonanza!

Title:	Jump Start Your Book Sales
Subtitle:	A Money-Making Guide for Authors, Independent Publishers and Small Presses
Authors:	Marilyn and Tom Ross
ISBN:	0-918880-41-6
Available:	August 1999
Retail price:	$19.95
Illustrations:	whimsical illustrations, quotations, checklists, sample forms
Web sites:	scores of Internet resources
Category:	Publishing/Marketing
Trim size:	6" x 9"
Length:	368 pages
Binding:	trade paperback
Cover:	4 colors, title embossed, "lightening" in iridescent silver foil, film laminated Designed to be unusual enough to be placed face out, photographs well for catalogs
Print run:	11,000
Distributed by:	Writer's Digest Books/F&W
Ads/PR:	$20,000 budget, 8-city author tour/signings, national radio phoners, excerpts in major trade journals, book club sale, extensive ongoing reviews/features
Endorsements:	Clarissa Pinkola Estes (*Women Who Run with the Wolves*—2 years on *The NYT* best-seller list), Judith Appelbaum, Dan Poynter, Paul and Sarah Edward, many more

Wholesalers, distributors, chain buyers, etc., will appreciate a one-sheet with all pertinent information in a single place.

Consumer Sales Flier

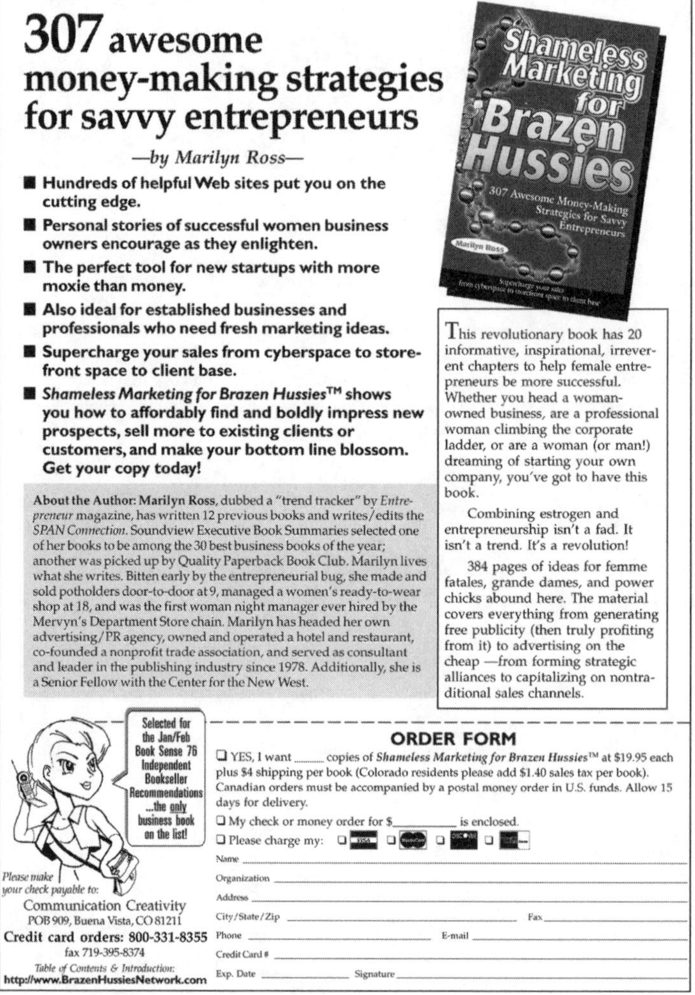
307 awesome money-making strategies for savvy entrepreneurs
—by Marilyn Ross—
■ Hundreds of helpful Web sites put you on the cutting edge.
■ Personal stories of successful women business owners encourage as they enlighten.
■ The perfect tool for new startups with more moxie than money.
■ Also ideal for established businesses and professionals who need fresh marketing ideas.
■ Supercharge your sales from cyberspace to storefront space to client base.
■ Shameless Marketing for Brazen Hussies™ shows you how to affordably find and boldly impress new prospects, sell more to existing clients or customers, and make your bottom line blossom. Get your copy today!
Shameless Marketing for Brazen Hussies
307 Awesome Money-Making Strategies for Savvy Entrepreneurs
Marilyn Ross
About the Author: Marilyn Ross, dubbed a "trend tracker" by Entrepreneur magazine, has written 12 previous books and writes/edits the SPAN Connection. Soundview Executive Book Summaries selected one of her books to be among the 30 best business books of the year; another was picked up by Quality Paperback Book Club. Marilyn lives what she writes. Bitten early by the entrepreneurial bug, she made and sold potholders door-to-door at 9, managed a women's ready-to-wear shop at 18, and was the first woman night manager ever hired by the Mervyn's Department Store chain. Marilyn has headed her own advertising/PR agency, owned and operated a hotel and restaurant, co-founded a nonprofit trade association, and served as consultant and leader in the publishing industry since 1978. Additionally, she is a Senior Fellow with the Center for the New West.
This revolutionary book has 20 informative, inspirational, irreverent chapters to help female entrepreneurs be more successful. Whether you head a woman-owned business, are a professional woman climbing the corporate ladder, or are a woman (or man!) dreaming of starting your own company, you've got to have this book.
Combining estrogen and entrepreneurship isn't a fad. It isn't a trend. It's a revolution!
384 pages of ideas for femme fatales, grande dames, and power chicks abound here. The material covers everything from generating free publicity (then truly profiting from it) to advertising on the cheap —from forming strategic alliances to capitalizing on nontraditional sales channels.
Selected for the Jan/Feb Book Sense 76 Independent Bookseller Recommendations ...the only business book on the list!
Please make your check payable to:
Communication Creativity
POB 909, Buena Vista, CO 81211
Credit card orders: 800-331-8355
fax 719-395-8374
Table of Contents & Introduction:
http://www.BrazenHussiesNetwork.com
ORDER FORM
❑ YES, I want ____ copies of Shameless Marketing for Brazen Hussies™ at $19.95 each plus $4 shipping per book (Colorado residents please add $1.40 sales tax per book). Canadian orders must be accompanied by a postal money order in U.S. funds. Allow 15 days for delivery.
❑ My check or money order for $________ is enclosed.
❑ Please charge my: ❑ ❑ ❑ ❑
Name
Organization
Address
City/State/Zip
Fax
Phone
E-mail
Credit Card #
Exp. Date
Signature

An attractive flyer slanted to consumers can be mailed, passed out, and used in many ways.

material the Benefits Test: Are you highlighting the specific advantages the reader will derive from buying your book?

• **Don't assume that more is better.** Many times we have the urge to keep hammering away, lapsing into verbosity trying to make the point. Today's prospective buyer loses interest quickly. Like a crop duster, you need to swoop in, deliver your payload, and pull up before you hit the trees.

• **Make your message obvious through organization of the material.**

Publicity Letter

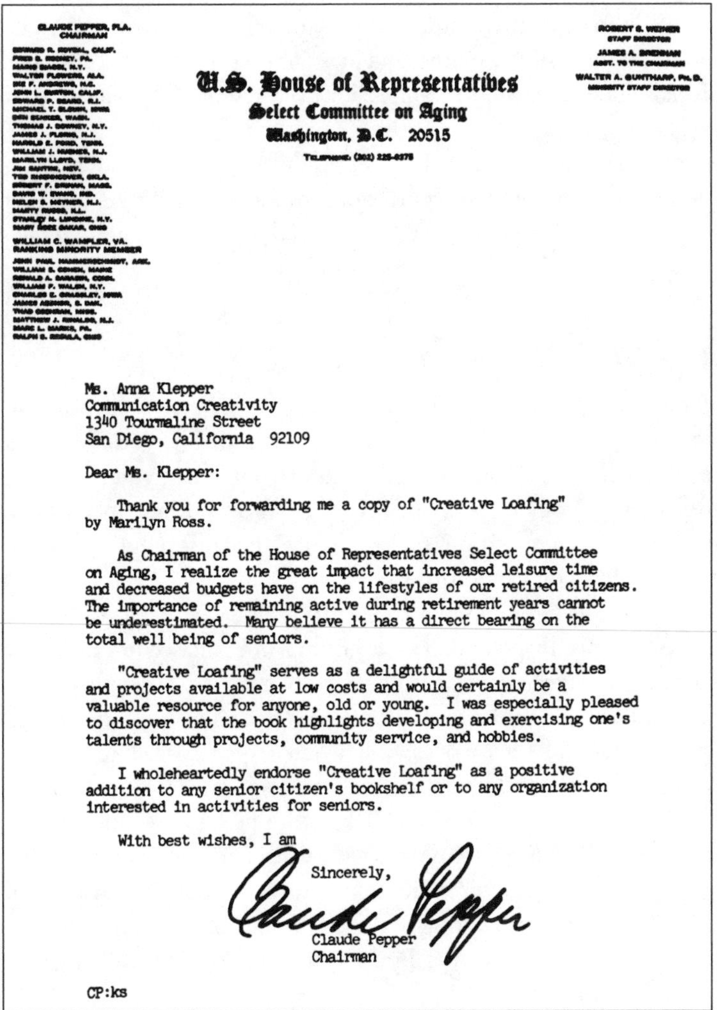

CLAUDE PEPPER, FLA.
CHAIRMAN

WILLIAM C. WAMPLER, VA.
RANKING MINORITY MEMBER

U.S. House of Representatives
Select Committee on Aging
Washington, D.C. 20515

ROBERT S. WEINER
STAFF DIRECTOR
JAMES A. BRENNAN
ASST. TO THE CHAIRMAN
WALTER A. GUNTHARP, PH.D.
MINORITY STAFF DIRECTOR

Ms. Anna Klepper
Communication Creativity
1340 Tourmaline Street
San Diego, California 92109

Dear Ms. Klepper:

Thank you for forwarding me a copy of "Creative Loafing" by Marilyn Ross.

As Chairman of the House of Representatives Select Committee on Aging, I realize the great impact that increased leisure time and decreased budgets have on the lifestyles of our retired citizens. The importance of remaining active during retirement years cannot be underestimated. Many believe it has a direct bearing on the total well being of seniors.

"Creative Loafing" serves as a delightful guide of activities and projects available at low costs and would certainly be a valuable resource for anyone, old or young. I was especially pleased to discover that the book highlights developing and exercising one's talents through projects, community service, and hobbies.

I wholeheartedly endorse "Creative Loafing" as a positive addition to any senior citizen's bookshelf or to any organization interested in activities for seniors.

With best wishes, I am

Sincerely,

Claude Pepper
Chairman

CP:ks

Solicit testimonial letters from prominent people who can influence others to buy your book.

The way you use folds, layout, type, artwork, and color can all bring your message into sharp focus. Make it easy to understand what's going on. Compel the reader to feel this was written just for her. That's effective communication.

- **Keep your budget low to start.** Lean toward the less expensive options for creating your material. Start off with a flier in one color of ink (not black). Use standard colors of plain bond paper. To save on postage, print on the lightest weight paper that won't bleed through.

• **Increase your odds by offering prospects several choices.** Use the piggyback principle. Team up with another self-publisher or two (locate them by checking with librarians, bookstores, online, and in writers' and publishers' groups), and include materials about their books, while they do the same for yours.

If you adhere to these rules, many of the eerie mists shrouding advertising will be lifted. Don't forget that repetition is more important than size, but that quality is the first consideration. Shoddy sales material will make potential customers assume your book will be shoddy, too—and pass it by.

Advertising to Target Audiences

If you, as a small publisher, try to compete with the biggies in overall advertising, you will look like a mouse in the shadow of a lion. If, however, you identify a specialized core audience who would be interested in your book, you can come on with a mighty roar of your own. That's why it's so important to produce niche books that appeal to a specific target audience. Because your sphere of influence is much smaller, you can afford to *dominate* it.

This is often done on a geographical basis. Perhaps you have a regional history or a guidebook to restaurants. By pounding away just in San Francisco or exclusively in Houston, for instance, you can develop high visibility and reap dramatic results.

Advertising in a specialized trade journal or newsletter can be a good way to reach a given target market. This works well when trying to sell to specific professional groups, such as accountants, attorneys, or educators. We contacted health professionals for Elizabeth and Elton Baker who had a book appropriate for this audience. *The UnCook Book* we mentioned earlier ended up being carried in the offices of many physicians, chiropractors, dentists, and nutritionists. You, too, can find a niche of highly susceptible buyers. Whenever you can influence one person to influence many, your sales figures take quantum leaps.

Point-of-Purchase (POP) Sales Aids

Point-of-purchase is a strange-sounding description that refers to stands, racks, and PR aids you can make available to bookstores or other retail outlets to help promote your book to consumers. They earn you prime display space. Some chains now charge to put them out, however. Bookmarks are one example of POP aids and are especially advantageous when perched right next to the cash register, thus reminding people about your book and stimulating impulse buying.

One enterprising author got himself top billing next to the cash register with a poster on an easel. How did he manage that? On the reverse side of his poster, visible to the cashiers, was a description of how to identify a counterfeit bill. It was to the store manager's advantage to keep that information handy. When doing promotional posters, normally it's a good idea to have them printed on *both* sides. When they are placed in a window, you get double exposure.

One other possibility for point-of-purchase aids is to provide free counter display stands to the retailers with quantity purchases of five or more books. These holders help prevent a book being shelved spine out with other titles and getting lost in the shuffle. This is a smart move if you plan on placing your book in specialty stores and other nonbookstore outlets (an especially lucrative sales approach we'll explore in detail in chapter nineteen, "Originating Extraordinary 'Out-of-the-Box' Opportunities." While in theory providing a counter display will help keep your book well positioned, the rack could end up being used for someone else's title unless the stand is identified with a header card advertising *your* book. To locate suppliers who can provide these stands, look in Appendix F under Point-of-Purchase (POP) Suppliers. A field trip to independent bookstores or specialty outlets may be in order first, however, to determine who will use such displays.

Downstream, when your reviews are breaking and consumers are coming into bookstores to order your book, you may want to invest in some in-store promotions. Done in tandem with other publicity, this can increase the momentum and take your book to a new plateau. It can also break the bank if you're not careful. Trade publishers pay from $3,500 to $10,000 for chain front-of-the-store placement on a table of hardcovers for two weeks! Other options include $10,000 for a month of end caps (displays at the end of a shelf), or $2,500 for participation in a program such as B&N's Discover New Writers, which brings with it inclusion for two weeks in a prominently placed special display rack.

Co-Op Advertising

Now let us take a minute to explain what is known as co-op advertising. This is an arrangement whereby the publisher and a bookstore divide the cost of a newspaper or magazine ad, with the publisher picking up the biggest part. The ad appears under the sponsorship of the bookstore and lists its name and address. While on the surface that may sound appealing, it can be deadly. You see, FTC regulations say that if you honor such an arrangement with even one bookstore, you are mandated to do so with *any other store that wants to participate*. Such a practice could break a self-publisher in no time. That is why we suggest you leave this to the biggies. Co-op ads certainly have their place in the industry, but they are not good ammunition for the small publisher to use. Besides, your ad budget will do you a lot more good spent in other ways in which you don't have to split the profits.

Innovative Advertising Maneuvers

There are many imaginative advertising pursuits you can use to enhance your sales position.

Prepublication

Selling prepublication copies of your book—taking orders before the books are printed—has several advantages. One obvious plus is that it helps generate cash to pay your printing bill. Another is that you get a feel for how receptive the public is to your book. Of course, it gives you a head start on your full advertising campaign and gets people talking about your title before it is even released. If you're promoting through the mail, be sure to state clearly that people are purchasing the book for future delivery. About four months ahead is the longest realistic lead time. Indicate the projected delivery date, and make it generous to avoid hassles with postal regulations. We did this very successfully when we first brought out *The Encyclopedia of Self-Publishing* (the forerunner to this book), and you can, too.

Gimmicks

It never hurts to dream up some odd little thing to draw attention to your book. One way to beef up awareness is to have buttons made. Ours said, "I practice Creative Loafing." They're great attention getters and conversation pieces. They also made nice giveaways to bookstore personnel and others who helped promote the title. You can even carry it a step further and have a personalized T-shirt silk-screened, which you—or others—can wear to promote the book. There are many companies that manufacture specialty items, for example, personalized notepads or pens. One way to see that your book stays in a buyer's mind is to have notepads printed up sporting the title. Give or send them to prime accounts and use them to woo large prospective buyers.

Order Form

Don't overlook the order form at the end of your book as an ad medium. It can be one of your best salespeople. Readers often want additional copies for friends, relatives, or colleagues; or people borrow the book, then want copies themselves. The order form makes extra sales easy.

Here are a few tips regarding this piece: Always compute the tax yourself for sales within your state, and express it as an exact amount rather than a percentage the customer must figure out. Be sure to request adequate shipping and handling. We find $4 suffices for most books. Remember, you have not only postage but also a mailing container, label, and your time involved. It's a good idea to include a statement similar to "Check your local bookstore or order directly from us." This helps reassure bookstores.

It's also wise to offer VISA and MasterCard options on the order form (and on your other sales literature, of course). Banks are sometimes reluctant to give new small businesses credit card merchant privileges, however. SPAN has negotiated a good deal for members and also absorbs the $125 application fee.

There are companies that will rent you a portion of a toll-free number, accept orders over the phone, even write up credit card sales. With this kind of coverage you can widely advertise the phone number. Once again, you've made it *easy* to buy. Be cautious in signing up with such service bureaus, however. You'll need heavy credit card sales to offset their setup fees, ongoing monthly charges, and individual processing fees. By the way, unless you can obtain merchant status, there is little point in getting a toll-free number. Credit cards and toll-free numbers go together like clowns and circuses.

But suppose you've already printed your book and didn't include an order form? Don't despair. Have some labels printed as an order form, and affix them to the inside back cover. People will photocopy them. Mission accomplished.

Bounce-Backs

Another possible advertising approach is called a bounce-back promotion. It works best when you have more than one product or are working with another writer-publisher. This is a merchandising trick used by virtually every retailer who ships products to customers. When an order is filled, a flier or catalog sheet is included offering an additional item—in your case another book. Thus, a bounce-back is an order received as a direct result of a promotional offer enclosed with a product shipment. The welcome windfalls from this kind of merchandising are typically 5 to 15 percent. For a "free ride," you can have a big impact on overall sales by using this strategy.

Telemarketing

What about using your telephone for advertising? Telephone solicitations to select markets can be very effective. If you want to reach feed stores, marinas, or florists, for instance, you can first prospect in the yellow pages for a list, then cover a lot of territory in a few hours on the phone. As in print advertising, think through what benefits your book offers. Jot down a few notes or develop a script until you become relaxed at this type of sale. Using the phone is also wise for follow-up on accounts you've already opened face-to-face.

Inbound telemarketing is a further possibility. Many wholesalers and distributors do phone sales to bookstore personnel who call in to purchase books. You can pay your distributors to pitch your title. They'll ask something like, "Would you like to hear our feature titles for this week?" When the customer says yes, he hears a thirty-second spiel about from one to six books. The bookstore buyer can then add the additional purchases to his order. You can sign up for a week of this advertising. If you have a big publicity event or interview coming up, this may be a cost-effective way of promoting it and getting books into stores.

Another good idea for the aggressive small publisher is sending postcards to bookstore buyers.

Card Packs

Merchandising through direct-response card packs is a possibility if you have a high-ticket, professionally oriented book. Titles geared to engineers, accountants, doctors, and executives, for instance, are all prospects. Card packs are packages of anywhere from ten to fifty business reply postcards stacked and polysealed, then mailed to a carefully targeted list. When asked about card packs, a librarian at Syracuse University remarked to one book marketer, "They are wonderful. The professors bring in the cards and say, 'Please order this book.' " They only work, however, for specialized high-ticket products.

Holiday Catalogs

In some cases—for a certain type of book that is already doing well—a Christmas catalog can be the best place to put your advertising dollar. First, you must have a title suited for this kind of advertising—a gift book or what's called a perennial (something of popular appeal that sells in all seasons and is as good today as it was last year or will be next year). You must also have a fat budget. While you may find a catalog that will accept a one-unit ad (about one-tenth of a page) for $500 or $600, it's more likely the price tag will be in the thousands. Of those who have tried it, however, at least one reports a gross dollar return of six to one.

B. Dalton's 40-page Christmas catalog appeared in *People* magazine, and the American Booksellers Association ran its first catalog as an insert in *Time*. Waldenbooks elected to distribute its catalog in its stores and via direct mail, continuing a practice begun over a century ago when Aaron Montgomery Ward sent a one-page list of 163 general merchandise items—such things as bonnets, boots, and blankets—to Midwest farmers and their families. Mail-order catalogs have been big business ever since.

If you're tempted to try and crack this medium, you need to start about February by writing to book catalog companies and requesting their deadlines, costs, and circulation figures. Some have a circulation of 300,000; others go as high as 5 million. Naturally, ad space is more costly for the latter. Be prepared to meet some resistance. They're used to dealing only with trade publishers and may fear you won't be able to supply the demand their catalogs may generate. Such a problem! Seriously, though, you must have the cash resources to print a lot of books in a hurry if things click.

Mail Order Classified Ads That Sell

Trying to start an advertising program without knowledge of ad strategies could be likened to becoming a gourmet Italian chef without using oregano or basil. Unlike those herbs, however, ads can either stand on their own merit or be used to enhance your overall campaign. Let's sample this wonder ingredient and see what makes it so popular.

From the publisher's vantage point, there are five important keys to succeeding in this marketplace: product suitability, reader profile identification (demographics and psychographics), media analysis, the ad itself, and timing. Let's examine these points.

Product Suitability

Not every book works for a one-title mail-order campaign. Bookstore shoppers go browsing with the idea that they'll buy books when they find the right ones. The ad buyer typically has no thought of purchasing until motivated by you. Whereas the browser may shop for several minutes, the ad peruser is won or lost in seconds.

What triggers this almost instantaneous urge to own? Usually it's an offer that promises to improve the quality, pleasure, or results of life. Remember, we talked about people wanting to be safer, healthier, more attractive, sexier, more loved, smarter, and richer? Does your book tell readers how to get a job, find a mate, or make more money? In other words, does it solve a problem or offer something most people need or want? If your title fits into one of these slots, it may have advertising potential.

Pinpointing Your Potential Customers

OK, you've determined your book is ideal for mail order. Now analyze it from a reader-appeal standpoint. In this hypothetical exercise it is imperative that you describe your reader as precisely as possible. One way to do this is to create a reader profile sheet. Establish categories of people. Within each category, list as many characteristics as possible. Rank each one on a scale as a percentage of potential readers. Example: After street-corner surveys, asking relatives and friends, and considerable soul-searching, you have concluded that only 20 percent of your readers will be men. It therefore follows that 80 percent will be women. Such deduction!

So forget men and follow your female profile. Your research has determined that 90 percent of your readers are single women between the ages of eighteen and forty and that 80 percent of these work. Therefore, your prime customers are single working women between eighteen and forty. You have just charted the demographics of your readers.

As you can see, armed with this information, you know whom you are trying to reach. Now it must be determined which medium is the most likely vehicle for your message. Be observant and talk to people (especially eighteen- to forty-year-old female workers). Find out what they read. Go to the library for additional research.

Doing Media Analysis

In the library, you will find several volumes from Standard Rate and Data Services, Inc. (SRDS). The volume we need for this analysis is called *Consumer Magazine Advertising Source*. Here a wealth of information about magazine publications will be unveiled: rates, editorial slant, and so forth.

When you are analyzing in which publication to buy space, try to stick with those that have *audited* circulation figures. This means the figures have been checked and that X number of people do indeed subscribe to the magazine. If there is reference to just "circulation," a magazine often includes not only the primary recipient of the magazine but also the two, three, or four other family members who might also look through it. While it appears that this publication may be a better place for your ad, it actually represents a smaller overall purchasing readership. Referring back to our example, it would appear from our research that *Cosmopolitan*, *Working Woman*, and *Today's Secretary* would be prime targets for your ad.

If you plan on putting ads in newspapers, SRDS's *Newspaper Rates and Data* is your source. And if you have published a technical or professional book, look in *Business Publication Rates and Data*.

After perusing SRDS for likely candidates, write to those on your list, asking for a media kit and three recent sample issues. Once the prospective publications have sent you their literature, you're ready to select the most suitable media.

Of course, don't overlook ads on the Internet. You can find many newsletters and e-zines targeted to your specific audience. Running classifieds here (and referring them to your Web site for more info and ordering) can be quite effective. This is an especially good advertising venue for e-books. Here are some

Web sites you can check for locating e-zines and placing online ads: www.EzineAdvertising.com, www.Ezine-Universe.com, and www.freezineweb.com.

Developing Your Ad

Having identified the audience for your book and the media vehicle to reach that audience, it is now time to create an ad. We subscribe to the philosophy of "start small and test, *test*, *TEST!*" Not every idea will work. You run an idea up the flagpole and wait to see if people salute it. If nobody does, you haul it down. Pronto. Even Joe Karbo's full-page newspaper extravaganzas plugging *The Lazy Man's Way to Riches* didn't start full blown. He followed the rules and began small.

A modest-sized classified ad is usually the best way to begin. We know people who plunked down thousands of dollars for a full-page ad and only sold a half-dozen books. Tread softly here.

An ad is a sales tool. It must be designed to sell. In spite of this, two out of three classified advertisers use copy that is watered down and ineffective. A word, the turn of a phrase, or a benefit properly described makes all the difference in the number of inquiries or sales your ad pulls.

Don't try to shorten your copy so much that it loses its punch. Agreed, longer ads cost more. But will a ten-word ad that costs $40 and sells three books be cheaper than a twenty-word $80 ad that sells a hundred books? Give yourself enough room to use persuasive words and action verbs in the ad. Write from a benefit perspective. What problem do the potential readers have that your book will solve? What's in it for them?

Let's dissect a few ads that appeared in the *Globe*. How about the following headline: "Seaweed recipes, $3." Would that move you to action? Hardly. Why not embellish it as one advertiser does: "Delicious seaweed recipes! Nutritional, economical! $3." Notice the implied health and money-saving benefits?

Don't expect an ad like the following to make profits: "Pound cake recipe, $1.00." Instead, sell it with "Absolutely delicious pound cake. You will beam with pride when they ask who made the cake. Send $1." This ad is personalized for the reader and uses an action verb to create involvement: "You will beam with pride."

How about this for selling the sizzle: "Want money? Hate work? Lazy ways to big money explained in full. Send $2." This has pulled a whale of a lot of two-dollar responses. The "you" in the ad is very evident. Do *you* want money? Do *you* hate work?

Someone with little knowledge of advertising principles might put together nursery item headlines like these: "Plum Trees," "Strawberry Plants," "XX-6

The Twelve Most Persuasive Words

According to Yale University researchers, the twelve most persuasive words in the English language are

- save
- discover
- safety
- health
- you
- guarantee
- love
- easy
- money
- proven
- results
- new

In addition to these, here are some more winning words from a list of one hundred famous headlines that were profitable: *your*, *who*, *now*, *people*, *want*, and *why*. We also find that *how to* and *free* pull well. Integrating these words with action verbs helps create compelling, selling copy.

Plant Food." The advertising pro senses the dullness of these heads and brings them to life. "Pick delicious plums from your own trees." "Plump luscious strawberries that grow bigger than hens' eggs." "Now—watch your plants grow healthier, faster, without danger of fertilizer burn. Use XX-6."

Need we say more? Classified ads can work only if the copy is crisp and clear. Sell the *benefits* of your book. Describe its qualities in terms of the reader's desires and needs. The greatest secret in advertising is to keep it human. Remember that your potential buyers aren't just statistics. They are people with hopes and emotions, ideas and prejudices, dreams and needs. Get those people involved.

Timing

If you were selling skis, you'd want your ads to appear just before the first snowflakes. Your book may have a less obvious seasonal tie-in, but there may be one. Time your ads to take advantage of a reader's increased interest either in the subject of your book or in books in general. For instance, summers are generally a bad time unless you have a great novel: Your potential customers are outdoors or on vacation, not reading magazines or thinking about ordering books. If the subject of your book has to do with summer activities—a vacation guide, for instance—run your ads in the spring when readers are just beginning to think about such things. Interestingly enough, gardening books, such as seed and plant catalogs, do better in the wintertime, when people are stuck indoors and like to poke through bright, summery photographs of flowers, anticipating winter's end and making plans for warmer weather.

If your book is a cold weather item—a cookbook on baked goods, or a how-to book on knitting or ways to winterize one's house to save energy, for instance—then fall is a good time to advertise. If the book is about making gift items, or if it's a likely candidate for being given as a gift, plan to place ads enough in advance of Christmas to allow time for orders to come in and for the book to be shipped and received by the beginning of December. Your customer may, in turn, want to mail it someplace else, so leave time for this. Early October might be a good time for such an ad to hit.

Or your book may be related to some other specific date—a holiday or an upcoming or annual event likely to be in the news. As in the case of Christmas, keep this event in mind in planning when your ad should appear.

Always think from the customer's point of view: Time your ad to run when there's likely to be the most interest in your book and its subject. This will help you get the best response for your advertising dollar.

Tracking Results

Recognize that you will be testing for two major things: which wording is most effective and which publication generates the most inquiries. A well-worded ad may pull beautifully in *Popular Mechanics* yet fail dismally in *Sports Afield*. If you want to be even more definitive, you can try running under different classifications, such as "personals," "books," or "of interest to all."

We recommend starting with a single insertion of your ad. Don't respond to the urges from media salespeople to save money by running several consecutive ads. Sure you will save due to a frequency discount, but what good is that if your ad is not pulling the required 2.2 times the cost of advertising? This is a simple formula proven by scores of advertisers who have gone before you.

To track results you must code each ad. Include a different department number for each variable you use. Go slow . . . *TEST.* Measure effectiveness, then build up in frequency and/or size. Here is an ad for *Creative Loafing* that did well. "DISCOVER CREATIVE LOAFING . . . New book shares hundreds of money-saving ideas for having fun and meeting people . . . Free details . . . Leisure MW93D, 5644 La Jolla Boulevard, La Jolla, CA 92037." Note the "Leisure MW93D." The MW93D is a code to indicate where and when the ad was run and which of several ads it was. The code tells us the ad appeared in *Moneysworth*, August 1993, and it started with "Discover." If you use a P.O. Box, consider affixing a code to it. Our Box 909 could become Box 909B, which would represent a specific ad in a specific publication.

Notice also that our ad initiates a two-step approach to getting a sale. It offers "Free details" instead of asking for the sale. Most mail-order experts agree that a small classified will not usually be effective for items costing more than $10 if you ask directly for money. So use the two-step approach and offer to send more details. When these inquiries are received, you shift to the direct-marketing approach covered in the next chapter. However, let's not be hasty about leaving this discussion on testing and tracking results.

The question to be answered as soon as possible is, How many sales will this ad pull? If you are advertising in a monthly periodical, it could take six months to get 96 percent of the final results.

Obviously, you could hardly organize a mail-order campaign if forced to wait that long before the next ad could be placed. On the other hand, it would be foolhardy to repeat a dud. It becomes apparent that some method of predicting results must be used to allow an ad to be repeated or changed long before all results are in. To partially solve this problem, mail-order merchants have developed a system for forecasting advertising responses (see sidebar below).

Industry experts warn that prediction charts provide only rough estimates and not accurate projections. Responses fluctuate widely depending on price, type of product, timing, ad medium, ad size, and other factors. Most agree that the longer you can hold off before predicting, the more accurate the prediction will be. As soon as possible, you should create a chart for your own product based on actual results. However, since we must have a forecast before results can be tallied, let's use this chart for predicting sales. Elapsed times are calculated from the date of the receipt of your first order—not the day the ad appears. Percentage figures indicate the proportion of the total response.

Response Recap

Elapsed Time	Dailies	Weeklies	Monthlies	Direct Mail
1 week	50–70%	35–40%	7–10%	33–52%
2 weeks	78–95%	60–65%	18–33%	60–65%
4 weeks	93–99%	79–81%	25–65%	89–90%
2 months	97–100%	89–90%	57–83%	96%
6 months		99%	90–96%	99%

Using the Response Recap table, an advertiser receiving 20 orders during the first week of response from an ad in a monthly publication would estimate her total to be 200–286 orders. At the end of the second week, if 15 more orders are received, she revises the forecast to 106–194. At the end of the fourth week, if 75 orders have been received, the forecast is now 115–300. Two months yielded 95 total orders, and the forecast is now 114–167. As can be seen by looking at this example, the chart allows a tremendous range that could be forecast at the end of the fourth week. We favor the conservative approach. Continuing our example, we would have used 200 as our projection at the end of week one, revised it to 106 at the end of week two, and then done our forecasting to determine if it will pay off.

Let's assume our ad cost \$300.00, and we are selling a book for \$9.95. If we add \$200.00 for postage and processing, we compute our return as $106 \times \$9.95 \div \$500.00 = 2.109$ times cost. That's close enough to the 2.2 factor to have us insert the ad a second time.

Graduating to Display Ads

Once we have proven the suitability of our book for mail order, pinpointed appropriate media, and developed an approach theme in classifieds—we are prepared to increase our ad size and/or frequency. Let's assume we have outgrown classifieds and are ready for display advertising. Again exercise caution. Start small, code, test, and measure. It wouldn't be prudent to jump from classified to full-page ads.

You may want to start out with "hemorrhoid ads." These are little scatter ads—perhaps only one-twelfth of a page. They got their less-than-decorous name because someone once ran the following ad.

Display Ad

HEMORRHOIDS?

Cured in 15 days

or your money back!

free details

P.O. Box 0000, Somewhere, USA

800-ALL-GONE

(800-255-4663)

Small display ads, that address a problem experienced by many people, can reel in the orders.

It was a to-the-point, effective ad. If you were plagued by these pesky things, your attention was riveted to the ad. Naturally, this kind of brief ad will work only for certain subjects. But if you can tell your story in a one-, two-, or three-word grabbing headline, it could lead to identifying hundreds of thousands of potential buyers.

On a more conventional level, one thing you can do is go with publications that have split runs. That means they publish regional editions, and you can test different ads in the same magazine or newspaper in different regions to see which one pulls best. *The Wall Street Journal*, for example, publishes a Western Edition, a Southwestern Edition, and so forth. Rather than biting the bullet and paying the high costs to run a nationwide ad for your business-oriented book, you might test an advertisement in one of the regional editions.

There is also a possibility of picking up what is known as remnant space (same thing as leftover pieces of fabric). This happens when another advertiser takes some, but not all, regions, or there is unsold ad space left and the publication deadline looms. The oddball leftover space can be bought for 25 to 50 percent below rate card price. Ask advertising sales representatives if they offer remnant space.

Designing Winning Display Ads

Let's take a look at some ground rules for creating effective display copy. Four elements are essential for effective display ads. They are strategy, media selection, design, and copy. Media selection has been covered previously. The strategy as defined here is to sell direct to the consumer. For the self-publisher it doesn't make sense to run ads directing people to bookstores; the majority of them won't stock your book.

The physical layout and visual effect of your ad is the tool for getting the attention of the reader. There are a couple of ways to stand out on a busy page of competing ads. One is by using what is called a reverse. That means the background of your ad is black with white lettering, instead of the usual black lettering on a white background. Another ploy is to use a heavy or decorative border around your ad to separate it from the others. Don't get too busy. Lots of white space, that area where there is no printing, gives a freer, more attractive appearance. Your layout should also help the reader understand your message as quickly as possible by guiding the eye through the ad.

Choice of type is important. While headlines should not focus attention on the design itself, they must command attention. Choose a display type that is punchy and bold enough to stand out on the page. As we said earlier, typefaces have personalities just like people. Consider different display typefaces. Some are fun, some sophisticated, some old-fashioned, some dramatic. Windsor Outline is

Reverses and Screens

Garamond Light Cond.	12 on 18 leading	15% black background
Garamond Light Cond.	12 on 18 leading	no background
Garamond Book Cond.	12 on 18 leading	30% black background
Garamond Book Cond.	12 on 18 leading	no background
Garamond Bold	12 on 18 leading	60% black background
Garamond Bold	12 on 18 leading	no background
Garamond Ultra Cond.	**12 on 18 leading**	**75% black background**
Garamond Ultra Cond.	**12 on 18 leading**	**no background**
Garamond Ultra Cond.	**12 on 18 leading**	**100% black background**

By using reverses and screens, you give your promotional materials visual variety and appeal.

as different from Hollywood as Blippo Bold is from Computer. Look at a display type chart and you'll see what we mean. The order coupon and body copy of the ad should be easy to read. Avoid condensed faces and don't use a type size so tiny readers must examine it with a magnifying glass. It's best to not intermingle a lot of different fonts. Use variations of one family instead, such as Garamond bold, Garamond italic, and Garamond roman to give variety and emphasis. (Never use large amounts of italic, however; it's hard on the eye in big doses, as are sentences in all capital letters.)

Another school of thought suggests that ads shouldn't look like ads. Advocates of this approach use straight copy to simulate editorial matter. (These are called advertorials.) When this is done the magazine typically prints "Advertisement" in small letters above or below the ad.

Writing Compelling Ad Copy

Copywriting gives vent to creative expression. Crisp copy that straightforwardly describes the benefits of a product is hard to beat. The trick remains to use persuasive, compelling words that move the reader quickly to action.

You may also want to tailor your ads to different audiences. This is considered market segmentation and can often be done by simply changing the headline. What an underused but powerful concept. Let's say you have a book on how to set up an appliance repair shop in your home. One market is the entrepreneur-type magazines; a second is the trade journals for the appliance field, such as *Appliance Service News*. For the prospective entrepreneur you might use a headline such as "Make Thousands Every Month Without Ever Leaving Your

Home." In the appliance trade journal, which is read by people who possess some technical skill, you could try "Become Your Own Boss: Turn Your Talents Into Big Dollars." By creating ads with different appeals, you will incur slightly higher production costs, but you can double your responses . . . and it's the bottom line that counts.

Design and copy must be coordinated so they complement each other. You can't pull together a good ad by closeting the designer and the copywriter separately, then pasting together the results. Many successful book ads consist of visuals of the book (either photographs or illustrations) supported by copy about the contents and an order coupon. Don't forget your jacket copy for ideas. As the ad size grows, copy can be expanded to offer the author's credentials, reviews, testimonials, and additional supportive material about the book.

We advise our students and clients to become pack rats. Get copies of as many magazines as possible. Start reading mail-order ads for books. Study them. Clip, emulate, paraphrase. Soon you will have a solid feel for an effective presentation. Of course, you may decide to get assistance in this process. You can locate advertising consultants in *LMP* who specialize in working with the book trade, or contact a reputable local ad agency through the yellow pages. A fascinating book on the subject is *Which Ad Pulled Best?* by Philip Ward Burton and Scott C. Purvis. It details fifty case histories on how to write ads that work. Regardless of how your ad is created, to be profitable it should pass the following tests:

- Can you conservatively project a return of 2.2 times the cost?
- Does the ad have a grabber to get the reader's attention—or will it be lost in the twelve thousand promotional appeals people are bombarded with daily?
- Will the ad clear the split-second interest test? Once you've caught readers' eyes, you have only six seconds to get them to nibble. The majority will be lost here. They are still subconsciously resisting the urge to read your ad. The most compelling reason people should be interested in what you are selling must be stated in very few words. The words must be immediately obvious to the reader whose eye your ad momentarily caught.
- Even after the ad passes this test, your catch is still a long way from the boat. The copy must be organized to lead the reader smoothly through your message. Any confusion will try the reader's patience and cause attention to wander. Layout, typography, and illustrations help avoid breaking reader attention.
- Once readers have nibbled, is the product presented forcefully enough to cause them to want to strike? Here copywriting takes over. It should give the reader the clearest, crispest, most appealing concept of the book you're trying to sell. Flamboyant adjectives or cute copy seldom help—and may even detract from credibility. A straightforward overview, or even the table of contents if

space permits, is a good backbone for your message. As we've said before, stress the benefits to the readers. Solve their problems. Make your point strongly and quickly.

• Do you adequately overcome suspicions and objections? Unfortunately, this is a snag that brings many trollers up short. Let's face it: People are suspicious of sales pitches and will use this as their final objection against buying. One of the quickest ways to dispel suspicion is by using testimonials, particularly from people who are well known or who are in positions of trust. Of course, excerpting select reviews is a powerful persuader, too. If you can't come up with quotes or reviews, describe reassuring author credentials. Offering a money-back guarantee will further crumble buyer resistance.

One successful self-publisher we know has a very straightforward return policy for mail-order customers: "Our return policy on books is remarkably simple: If you don't like the book, for any reason, drop us a note and we'll give you a full refund. You don't even have to return the book; just pass it along to someone who might like it, or donate it to your local library."

• Is it easy for the reader to respond? Have you called for action? Are you clear as to exactly what's to be done? Including an order coupon simplifies the reader's response. Make sure instructions are complete. Offer the option of putting the purchase on a credit card. Now the hook is set.

Some Final Thoughts . . .

When you enter into the world of display advertising, you should capitalize on the cumulative impact of repetitive insertions. All things being equal, it will yield better results to run four one-quarter pages repeated four times in the same media than to pop for a one-shot full-page spread.

As you've probably gathered by now, we're not heavy advocates of a big ad budget. But that doesn't mean there aren't occasions where display ads make a lot of sense. To help boost *Shameless Marketing for Brazen Hussies* with independent booksellers, for instance, we took out ads in the Spotlight section of *BookSelling This Week.* It cost us less than $400 for four ads, which repeatedly reached some nine thousand readers. (Call Bernadette Sabatino at (800) 637-0037. Tell her Marilyn Ross sent you.)

We also ran a small display ad in a special section for Independent Publishers in *The New York Times Review of Books*. Frankly, we didn't expect this to sell books. We merely wanted to have a legitimate reason to say the book had been featured in *NYTBR*. If you have a wholesaler or distributor who is doing a good job, consider reinforcing that by advertising in the company's catalog. Put your money where it will do the most good.

And if you publish a tightly niched book—something for bonsai lovers, Siamese cat breeders, people suffering from an obscure disease—advertising in the newsletters and journals targeted to that specific group could be very profitable. One tip: Try to get a glowing review *first*, then quote the review in your ad. Then it is the publication, with all its credibility with readers, saying the book is good, not you.

Let's examine positioning for a moment. This refers to where the ad appears. If you're willing to spring for a big ad, inside front covers and outside back covers get a lot of reader attention. But you also pay extra. Whenever possible, try to have ads placed on a right-hand page in the top half of the page ("above the fold," as they say in the newspaper business)—they will be more noticeable there. If you're using a coupon, stipulate that it must not back up to another coupon. (Otherwise, people can ruin your ad while cutting up the other one.)

And while you're negotiating with the space sales representative, ask whether you can get editorial coverage, as well. This means the publication would write a little feature story on you or your book. Some magazines have a policy against such practices; others will gladly comply, especially if you provide suggested copy for the piece.

Once you've developed a selling ad and have pinpointed magazines and newspapers that pull well, it's time to set up a contract. If you run in a magazine three, six, or twelve times, you'll get a reduced rate over single insertions. With newspapers you do this on a bulk-rate basis, committing to use so many inches of display space over a year's time. Opt for the *least* space available. If you go over that, the lesser rate is automatically granted. But if you don't use up enough space, at the end of the year you'll be short-rated. That means you will be billed for the difference between your contract rate and the regular price.

Remember that successful advertising is saying it again. And again. And again. With the guidance here, you should never have to suffer from advertising anorexia. Now let's move onto a close cousin to the wonders of advertising, that is, the marvels of direct marketing.

Web Sites, Wisdom, and Whimsey

Let's have some fun! What Victor Borge was to music, Richard Lederer is to words. His Web site is wonderfully woven for wordaholics. If you are heels over head (as well as head over heels) in love with words, feast here on puns about the English language. As he observes, only in our lingo can one drive in a parkway and park in a driveway. Furthermore, your *nose* can run and your *feet* can smell. Go to http://pobox.com/~verbivore and enjoy!

* * *

Here's a sophisticated Internet site for those looking to take their Web marketing to the next level. At www.clickz.com you can brush up on building links, cultivate e-mail marketing, pursue affiliate marketing, discover cross-media strategies, optimize search engine usage, you name it. In addition to an abundance of current articles, there is also a plethora of savvy advice in the archives.

* * *

Wanting to grow your online business? Then take a look at www.AdvertisingTips.net. It offers a bundle of free tools and resources to help you become more e-commerce savvy. You can also subscribe to a free e-zine called *Answers* that gives you daily advice and answers your questions in easy-to-understand language. Anyone can use these tips to increase their traffic and sales.

* * *

Writing the perfect ad is as easy as getting cats to march in a parade.

* * *

Newspaper advertising is on the grow. It went up by 5.1 percent in 2000; overall national advertising grew by 13.7 percent to $7.7 billion, and classified advertising went up 5.1 percent to $19.6 billion. There's definitely some money being spent here!

* * *

Are numbers manipulatable? You bet. There is more than one way of saying things: Someone could be 6' tall or 5' 12" tall.

* * *

Free industry e-newsletter is available for the asking. If you want to keep track of breaking industry and books news from the majors, *PW Daily* delivers. For a free subscription, go to www.publishersweekly.com and sign up.

17 *Direct Marketing Smarts*

Often the best approach is the direct approach . . . direct marketing, that is. As the name implies, this is a strategy wherein you mail sales literature to the prospective buyer. According to statistics, 19.6 percent—or almost one-fifth—of everything sold is now sold by direct marketing.

An American Tradition

There are now, always have been, and always will be consumers (yep, book buyers) who buy through the mail whenever possible. No, these aren't necessarily country folk; many live in the hearts of major cities. They just prefer to shop from the comfort of their armchairs. We would therefore be remiss if we didn't suggest ways you can take advantage of this lucrative opportunity. In fact, a Huenefeld Survey reported that the publishers with the briskest growth rates—a hefty 20 percent increase—were those using direct marketing for professional, vocational, and scholarly books.

One factor is crucial to success in single-title direct marketing campaigns: price. Individual books must be at *least* $49.95 to be viable. Ask yourself this question: Is the book priced so that the sale will yield a return of 2.2 times the cost of the mailing? This is the simplest formula. Forget percentages. It used to be that 2 percent was considered a good response. If you're selling BMWs that's true; for a $20.00 book it can kill you.

Since most of us don't publish $50.00 books, is all lost? Not at all. You can carry products from other publishers, as well. That's what Leigh Cohn of Gurze Books does. He sends out a whopping 225,000 copies of his *Eating Disorders Resource Catalogue* and makes money every year. Cohn has another secret: He charges for advertising in his catalog! The latest catalog contains twenty-three ads, which cover the costs for design, printing, and mailing—with a nice profit left over. Another ploy Gurze Books uses is encouraging professionals—therapists, dietitians, social workers, hospitals, and treatment centers—to request the catalog in quantity to pass along to their patients or clients. It's a lot cheaper to send one hundred catalogs to one place, than to mail one hundred individual ones. And the professionals often recommend specific books from the catalog.

Be aware that direct-response marketing creates what has been dubbed an "echo effect." This means there's a secondary effect that reverberates through all the other ways books are sold. The cumulative results can be very powerful. Direct mail can impact library sales, book club orders, distributors and wholesalers, Internet purchases, corporate purchases, and consumer telephone orders. In some cases, tests showed that echo sales were a whopping six to twenty times more than the directly traceable orders.

A direct-mail campaign has three crucial areas: the offer, the package, and the list.

The Offer

The offer has to do with what you're selling. Of course, for you it will be a book or books. Pricing has a lot to do with your offer. Will you give a discount? Free shipping? Is there a time limit? How about a money-back guarantee? Will a free gift be included? Is there a deluxe alternative—such as a limited, numbered, and autographed edition? These are all offer considerations. Be sure they are obvious and that they don't expire too fast.

The Package

Direct-mail packages usually consist of an outer envelope, sales letter, brochure, order form, and business reply envelope (BRE). Begin saving the so-called junk mail you receive. Study it. There are marvelous lessons to be learned here.

Your Outer Envelope

Your first challenge is to get recipients to open the envelope. If you fail here, it doesn't matter what's inside. There are different schools of thought on which strategy works best.

Many experts say you should use a teaser message. We just received a package that said "Inside—Valuable TIME & MONEY-SAVERS for the Overworked, Understaffed Editor!" It was obviously what some people call junk mail, but it did an effective job of appealing to a need, offering a benefit, and arousing our curiosity. We opened it.

Some experts feel that impressing people is most effective. They go for elegant simplicity, using an expensive envelope paper stock and appearing dignified and businesslike. Mail that looks important or official will often get opened.

Still others contend you're better off with a blind envelope that gives no clue as to the contents. With this approach, you either leave off the return address entirely or use just a street address or post office box with a person's name rather than any business identification. You hand address it and use a pretty postage stamp rather than a postage machine.

Sales Letter

When it comes to sales letters, more is better. A two-page letter will out-pull a one pager; often four pages is even stronger. Start off with a benefit-laden headline. Do your very best writing here—or hire a professional copywriter. This is an important document and must be carefully honed.

To create an effective sales letter, you need a plan. To develop this plan, assemble information. This doesn't need to be reams of information, but it is an important step. There are three things to keep in mind when writing your sales letter: the objective of the letter, who your prospect is, and the important characteristics, features, and benefits of your book.

Use the following checklist for developing your sales letter:

- Does the headline or first sentence attract attention by promising the most important benefit of your book?
- Is interest built quickly by enlarging on the promise?
- Do you constantly stress benefits, benefits, benefits?
- Have you appealed to the emotions to arouse a desire to possess?
- Have you emphasized the unique features of your offer? (Maybe this is the only way the book is available, or you're offering it at a reduced price, adding a little gift as an incentive to buy, or personally autographing copies.)
- Is one central idea emphasized so strongly that it avoids confusion?
- Have you included believable testimonials and reviews?
- Do you offer a guarantee?
- Is your letter organized so it's easy to read? Paragraphs should be short, especially the first two.
- Have you closed with a final call to action indicating exactly what you're offering, the price, how it will be shipped, and why the prospect should respond now?
- Have you included a postscript? This is one of the most read portions of any letter. Our eyes automatically turn to the P.S. Repeat your main sales feature in brief, make a special offer, or drop in a personal line to support the reader's decision: "If Brand X isn't everything we say it is, just return it and we'll cheerfully refund your money!"

Keep your letter open and airy looking. If possible, run it in two colors; this adds a personalized touch. Use colored ink for the letterhead, for your personal signature, and to underline main points or put a short handwritten note in the margin.

Brochure

While some direct-mail packages contain giant four-color brochures, such elaborateness is not necessary to sell books. Yours can be a small, two-color affair, or an overrun of your cover with sales copy on the reverse side works well. The important element is the selling job. As in your letter, creative copywriting is vitally important here. It must snap, crackle, pop. Be sure it is targeted to the market you're trying to reach. Dramatize and expand upon your book. Cite reviews or testimonials. If it is packed with sizzle, you might reproduce the table of contents. Be sure you tell a complete story and move the reader to action.

The Order Form

It has been said that the order form is "the moment of truth." Many prospects make a final decision on whether to buy after reading it. Therein lies a message: Don't forget to sell on the order form! It should begin with a benefit headline, such as "Secrets of How to Live Longer Revealed in New Book."

The order form offers another controversy among experts. One school says neat, specific, nonconfusing ones are best. The other side claims busy, cluttered, important-looking forms do better.

We feel the order form should make it clear to the customer exactly what needs to be done to get the desired books. Surprisingly, many buyers go straight from the headline that hits their "buy button" to the order form. If you get your prospect to the order blank, you surely don't want to lose the sale now. State the exact amount of state sales tax to be included, not a percentage the buyer must compute. A money-back guarantee is especially reassuring to a potential buyer. It assures there is no risk. If your book is good, seldom will the guarantee be invoked, but the very fact that this option exists will make some sales for you. (A trick of the trade: The longer the guarantee period, the less it will be used. People feel they have all the time in the world and forget about it.)

Clearly state the terms. If you're selling to individuals, we recommend that it be by check with the order or as a credit card sale (no CODs). When selling to stores, schools, or libraries, state your standard terms, which are covered in an earlier chapter. If this offer is multititle (for more than one book) and includes low-dollar items, you may need to specify a minimum order. If you feel that would hurt sales, at least make sure you can't lose money on any single-copy order.

Business Reply Mail (BRM)

A self-addressed reply envelope will increase response to your direct-mail offer. We do not feel that "no postage necessary" business reply mail (BRM) is worth the extra money, however. As with many of the variables in direct marketing, this can be determined only by testing your offer. The post office requires that the business reply envelope be imprinted per USPS specifications. There is a $125.00 annual permit fee and a charge of $0.35 plus First-Class postage for each return. Your main post office can supply you with full details.

Finding Your Market

To find a suitable list for your book, consult SRDS's *Direct Mail List Rates and Data*. Here you'll discover detailed information on who rents what lists. You'll also find firms that will be happy to help. Good ones are Infocore, Market Data Retrieval, Hippo Direct, Pacific Lists, and American List Counsel. These list brokers do not charge you a fee (they are compensated by the owners of the lists), but they also don't want to waste time with someone who is thinking very small. Use them if you're serious about direct mail; they can provide names for almost any category imaginable, and most are very skilled at what they do. When your list broker proposes a choice of lists, do comparison shopping. Ask the broker how each list is compiled, who the actual people on the list are, how frequently it is updated, and how often each person on the list buys. Also ask how often it is rented; avoid ones that are overmailed.

In the educational field you can pinpoint decision makers in science, vocational education, computer-assisted instruction, music, and every other curriculum area. Within the business community you can rent a list of 1,261 steamship companies, 14,946 appraisers, 21,141 psychologists, 39,176 CPAs, 3,679 dairy farmers, or 2,923 communication consultants, just to mention a few.

Calls to R.R. Bowker Company to rent lists, are referred to Cahners Business Lists. Because Cahners has a 250,000-name database to rely on, the information is updated monthly and thus is current. Here you can get lists for such specific library groups as religious libraries by religious affiliation, government libraries, and law libraries. And if you have a business book, Cahners has 651 bookstores that specialize in business books, not to mention 326 bookstores that sell travel books and 297 that carry primarily music books, to name a few. You can reach Cahners' mailing list department by calling (800) 323-4958 or going to www.cahnerslists.com. PCS Mailing List Company can put you in touch with lists for doctors, CPAs, dentists, attorneys, and many other groups. Reach this company at (800) 532-LIST (5478), or visit www.pcslist.com.

The Fine Points of Mailing Lists

Getting the right list is so important! Mailing lists come in three types. There is the occupant list, which includes every household in a given geographic area. Then there is the compiled list, derived from phone books and other directories. Finally there is the response list, made up of people who have already bought related products. For your purposes a response list is best. It will also be more costly, as it targets your potential buyers most precisely.

List rental fees range from $70 to $150 per thousand names. Give the list broker your reader profile and all the information you can about your book, so she can match it with the best list for maximum results. The broker will work with you. Most list owners require prior approval of your material before they will rent their lists. It is understood that a list is rented for *onetime* use only and may not be photocopied. Notice we are saying *rent*. Seldom do you buy a list.

Be wary of ordering mailing lists at prices that seem *too* low. There are fly-by-night outfits offering cheap lists that tend to be "dirty" (you will get a lot of returns because the addresses are no longer good or because the list contains duplicates). In the long run it'll cost you more to use a cheap list and have a lot of mail come back than to pay more to begin with for a relatively clean list of correct and current names and addresses.

Again the message: *Go slow*. Rent an initial list of 5,000 names. Your broker can supply these by what is called nth name selection. For example, if the list you are interested in has 100,000 names and you want 10,000 names, you would request that your test order be made up of every 100th name from the list. This gives you a good random sample and avoids misleading results. Don't ever fall into the trap of expecting a list that is terrific for Los Angeles to give the same results in New York. It may, but again it may not. In this case New York may only be half as good as Los Angeles. (We know, folks—it happened to us.)

Do a careful analysis of any planned mailing to make sure it will give you a minimum return of 2.2 times the money you spend. (Include costs of design, printing, mailing list rental, postage, and mail processing.) If your mailing pulls 1 to 2 percent of the list, will the return equal 2.2 times the cost? If not, reconsider.

More Strategy

Timing plays an important role in your direct-response success. Some months are much better than others. January and February are the all-stars; June, July, and August are bad months for mailing because people go on vacation. If you're promoting a Christmas item, October or early November is when your literature should hit the mailboxes. It's also a good idea to avoid having your mailing reach the customer on Monday or just after a holiday. There's too much other mail competing for attention then.

For large mailings you will want to cut postage costs to the minimum. To do this, use third-class bulk-rate mail (you may know this as Standard Mail). A Presort Standard costs $125 for a one-time application fee, plus $125 per year. Getting one will save you considerable dollars if you anticipate doing much mailing. Present bulk rates are $0.23 or $0.25 cents per piece for profit organizations, depending on how finely they're sorted. The post office requires special ZIP code sorting and bundling. Minimum quantity per mailing is two hundred identical units. If you plan on using the mail a lot, the U.S. Postal Service publishes a free monthly newsletter. You can subscribe by writing *Mailers Companion*, Address Quality, U.S. Postal Service, 6060 Primacy Pkwy., Suite 201, Memphis, TN 38188-0001, or by faxing (901) 681-4582. Read more at www.usps.com.

Another idea is to ask your local postal worker for last year's ZIP code directory when the new one comes out. You'll need one for the office, and this is an easy way to get a freebie if you have established good relations with that person.

After thinking about the hassle of sticking on labels, stuffing, sorting, and trips to the post office, you may decide to use a mail fulfillment house (listed in your local yellow pages) to take care of the whole thing for you.

When renting mailing lists, if you intend to use a mail fulfillment house to do the actual mailing for you, consult the business about what it needs. Your labeling choices will include such options as gummed, four-up, three-up, pressure-sensitive, heat-sensitive, and Cheshire. The mail fulfillment house will explain which of these it requires.

Now your mailing is out. Figure all your costs and get ready to track results. (See the Response Recap sidebar in the previous chapter on ads.) It is important to remember that you are testing two things: the mailing piece and the list. If your returns are at least 2.2 times the cost, expand your program. Test other lists. Try improved mailing pieces. Keep testing and keep tracking. If you proceed as suggested, you will risk little and have much to gain.

Another way to create a mailing list is from the inquiries drawn by an ad. The names of people who've inquired become your own mailing list. Keep it updated and add the names of customers. Although you can only use a rented list once, when someone responds, that name is then yours to use forever. Keep a permanent record of customers and prospects. Companies that do a lot of direct marketing find their computer databases are their most treasured tools for list maintenance.

By the way, if you're involved in direct marketing, you can get a complimentary subscription to the magazine *Target Marketing* by writing 332 Eighth Ave.,

18th Floor, New York, NY 10001. The sophisticated publisher using this method of moving books can also get a free subscription to both *DM News* and *iMarketing News* by calling (847) 588-0675 to obtain qualification forms, or by going online at www.dmnews.com or www.imarketingnews.com.

As the years go by, you will find your list of names is a viable source for additional income. It can be rented to others. Clean the list periodically by adding "Return service requested" to the outer envelope. Then any undeliverable First-Class Mail will be returned free of charge, and you can update your names and addresses accordingly. It's also a good idea to "seed" your own list with an address of your own so you'll know immediately if someone uses it in an unauthorized way.

Direct marketing can be tailored to nearly any budget. Success depends primarily on imagination, common sense, and diligence in following the rules. Many fortunes have been made starting with minimal investments in this field. An excellent reference for those especially serious about this subject is *Successful Direct Marketing Methods*, by Bob Stone.

According to the FTC's 30-Day Rule regarding shipping of merchandise, orders received both through the mail and over the phone must be shipped within thirty days of receipt of the order. Delay notices offering to cancel the order and refund payment if the buyer wishes (should you not be able to meet that deadline) can be provided by phone, or First-Class or Standard Mail. This could be important information if you're planning on preselling your book before it comes off the press.

Success Story

Joe Karbo, who was teetering on the brink of personal bankruptcy when he started promoting *The Lazy Man's Way to Riches* in 1973, was certified to have a net worth of more than $1 million before his death at age fifty-five. Karbo would receive most people's vote as the top mail-order self-publisher of the twentieth century. He had an innate knowledge of human behavior and a unique talent as a wordsmith. His full-page ads were splashed across newspapers and magazines from coast to coast. The same ad, featuring small type and big hype, ran for seven years with no changes, then he graduated to a new larger ad that boosted sales even more. That's the only way the book was sold—no public relations, no 800 numbers, no credit cards, and no bookstores. His publication sold more than 3 million copies.

From this example of direct-marketing success, it's obvious that your book could be made a best-seller . . . without its ever seeing a bookstore shelf. Another way to garner big bucks is by selling various rights to your book. Hold onto your hat; that's what we examine in the next chapter.

Web Sites, Wisdom, and Whimsey

Here's a tip for inexpensive printing of brochures or catalogs. Often small weekly newspapers print other jobs during their light days. Since they already have the presses and personnel, they like to keep them busy. With careful planning you might be able to fit that slot and save a bundle. You might also inquire about using the printer's bulk mail permit and addressing, labeling, and mailing services to get even more efficiency out of the process.

* * *

What can we learn from best-selling authors Sue Grafton and Orson Scott Card? Lots! These two famous novelists have turned the Web into a tool to communicate with readers, support bookstores, and sell more books. At www.SueGrafton.com you'll not only find out she has cats named Emma and Molly, but that she can also make a killer cheesecake. Scores of savvy authors are creating personal sites on the Internet. They are setting up chat rooms and e-mail lists to visit electronically with their fans, adding biographies, trivia, and general information about their books. Grafton's three-year-old site also features author tour information, first chapters, and an opportunity to write the author. "She gets a ton of e-mail," says a Henry Holt representative, "and seems to enjoy answering it." (What a smart marketing move!) Her site sends out a periodic e-mail to about five thousand readers and plans to add RealAudio recordings of Grafton reading from her books. Science fiction fans of Orson Scott Card, author of such best-sellers as *Ender's Game* and *Ender's Shadow*, can find him online at www.hatrack.com. He takes advantage of his captive Web audience to indulge in personal reviews of other books—even offers opinions on cheeses, potato chips, and lightbulbs! In addition to most of the bells and whistles Grafton employs, Card also uses his site to cross-promote film adaptions of his novels and get advice and feedback from his fans. Booksellers are encouraged to use both sites to help increase their own sales. This can be done via links or by taking certain information to add to their own bookstore Web sites. Time-crunched publishers don't have the inclination to develop interesting sites for their authors—even the celebrity ones. Thus, by extrapolating some of the strategies outlined above, all authors can develop compelling Web sites to market directly to their audiences. Go for it!

* * *

Your direct-marketing package must stand out like a black fly on vanilla ice cream.

* * *

Mail, lists, discussion groups, and chat rooms abound. There are Internet mailing lists on virtually every topic where people communicate on a regular basis. Have you tuned in to those that relate to the subject of your latest book? It's a wonderful way to psyche out what people interested in the topic are thinking, to learn their concerns, and to subtly promote your own title. But how do you locate these sometimes evasive groups of people? Go to http://List-Universe.com. Here you discover a roster of over ninety thousand mailing lists. Some may have as few as a dozen participants; other have thousands of subscribers. And if you're thinking of starting a list of your own, this is a gold mine of tips, articles, and promotional ideas.

* * *

Seeking free mailing list research? Then go to http://hrdirect.net. This is a site run by direct-mail consultants who state they can "find any mailing list in the world you are looking for." Whether you want a proven response list or a specialized compiled list, they can help. Because they work with a lot of publishers, you can easily find names ideally suited for specific titles: home-based working moms (5,002 names), theological book service catalog buyers (12,297), or addiction recovery book buyers (37,558), for instance. And if *you* have several thousand names on your own in-house list, HR Direct can also arrange to rent them and generate some quick cash. Click on Mailing List Revenues to find an article on how to make money with your mailing list. You can also subscribe to the consultants' free monthly e-mail newsletter by clicking on (you guessed it) Free Newsletter.

* * *

Make your copy lively and real. Said Carl Sandburg, "Slang is a language that rolls up its sleeves, spits on its hands and goes to work."

* * *

Use these clues to uncover better direct mail. Use "hot spots" in direct-mail packages that automatically attract readers' attention. Photo captions, for instance, always get read, so don't let a picture speak for itself. The signature line draws notice; print it in a different color so it appears to be handwritten. The P.S., even thought it is at the end of the letter, is one of the first things people read. Make it a Wow!

18 *Tapping Into Lucrative Subsidiary Rights*

When you sell subsidiary rights you allow someone else to repackage your information in another format. Major publishers often make more money from various subsidiary rights than they do from selling the book itself! You can exploit some of these rights, too, and the beauty is it is all "found" money.

In this chapter, we will concentrate on how to sell your book in "pieces" to magazines and newspapers. We'll also look at tapping into book clubs and merchandising mass-market and trade paperback reprint rights to a major publisher. Foreign rights will be examined, as will some other ways to turn your printed word into positive cash flow.

What Are Subsidiary Rights?

In trade publishing the *primary* sale is the actual sale or licensing providing for the initial publication of the book itself. *Subsidiary rights* (sub rights) follow and embrace all other rights. Perhaps an easier way to think of them would be as additional spin-off sales that allow someone else to reproduce and disseminate your material in a different form. This encompasses—but is not limited to—such things as selling the mass-market or trade paperback rights to your book, selling the right to produce your book in motion-picture form, and selling the right to excerpt part of a book for a magazine article.

It can be a dramatic avenue to profit, often producing greater revenue than the book itself. Selling subsidiary rights has another distinct advantage: It helps demonstrate your credibility. A book club that purchases a book or a respected national magazine that serializes it, for example, is in effect endorsing the book. This endorsement can be used in sales materials to influence other sub rights buyers, not to mention wholesalers, and other profitable outlets.

While such rights are more likely to be negotiated by large trade houses or literary agents, self-publishers should nonetheless seek out any possibilities that might be to their advantage. And there are several. In our high-tech world, new ones have emerged. Today there are CD-ROMs, computerized databases, and other electronic forms of disseminating information.

A most informative book on this overall subject was recently written by Thomas Woll. *Selling Subsidiary Rights: An Insider's Guide* is chock-full of detailed information, plus sample agreements, contracts, and forms to make your sub rights conquests much easier. Another way to educate yourself, and gain a sense of the fair value of rights, is to subscribe to the free e-mail newsletter *Deal Lunch*. Find out more about it at www.publisherslunch.com.

Selling Your Book in "Pieces"

Selling first and second serial rights will not bring you megabucks. Oh sure, *Woman's Day* paid $200,000 for Rose Kennedy's memoirs. And *The National Enquirer* has been known to shell out $150,000 for a celebrity book. But that was "the good old days," your name probably isn't a household word, and those huge numbers certainly are not the norm. You're more likely to get anywhere from a few hundred dollars to around $2,500. If you have something really juicy, the rate could go up to $7,500. What these rights *will* do is give you tremendous exposure and increased sales.

First serial rights are those that appear *before* the official publication date rolls around. They are the most coveted. Just be sure to plan around the date when the material will appear in the periodical. Since some first serial agreements prohibit you from publishing the book until a number of months have elapsed, you don't want to sign something that will hold up your pub date. Occasionally, a whole book will be serialized in installments in a single magazine, as was Norman Mailer's *An American Dream*. More often, a serialization contract will give the periodical the right to excerpt a stated maximum number of words or a specific portion of the work, such as a chapter.

Magazines, newspapers, and newspaper syndicates will expect exclusives for the material they select. In some cases this is easy. When Patricia Breinen, of Holt, Rinehart and Winston, started peddling *Love Medicine* (Louise Erdrich), she realized it could be easily divvied up between several takers. This was possible because the book—a saga of two American Indian families—was written like a series of short stories, each story (chapter) concerning a member of one of the families at a critical moment in life. Breinen really outdid herself, however, and set a precedent by securing *ten* first serial sales. She sold parts of the book to *The Atlantic*, *Ms.*, *The Kenyon Review*, *Chicago* (two excerpts), *Mother Jones*, *The Mississippi Review*, *North American Review*, *North Dakota Quarterly*, and *New En-*

gland Review. Perhaps you have a book with chapters that will stand on their own, as well.

Locating subsidiary rights buyers can be as tough as finding your way home in a blizzard. First, check the list provided in Appendix E. You will want to augment it by looking in the most recent *Writer's Market* for additional possibilities. Here's a well-kept secret: Those magazines in *WM* that will consider book excerpts say so the first thing under the section called "Nonfiction" in their individual descriptions. Another option is to read magazines that match your prospective audience and see if there are comments at the ends of the articles saying "Reprinted permission of . . . " or something similar to indicate they have used portions from new books.

Put together a sales package consisting of a letter, news release, and dust jackets if you have them. Be prepared to send a copy of your manuscript or galleys to those who indicate interest.

One way to beef up your chances of making a sale is to preselect material to suggest to each magazine. Again, you're making it *easy* to buy. When you tailor the material to the individual needs of each—by recommending that particular attention be paid to a specific chapter or to a certain block of pages—you show that you respect the editor's busy schedule and understand the slant of the publication, and are offering something that will interest the readers of that publication. And it usually pays big dividends. We sold a small excerpt to *The National Enquirer* for one client, who pocketed an extra $300 from the transaction. The *Star* took two installments of another book we represented, giving the author access to seven million readers. (In spite of the reputation of these publications, both excerpts were from very tame how-to books.) *New Woman* magazine excerpted two other books of clients, *Woman* magazine took second serial rights to another one, as did *Vogue*.

Second serial rights take place anytime *after* the official publication date. While not considered such plums, they still have the potential of bringing your book to the attention of millions of new readers. And you can approach these reprint opportunities at a more leisurely pace when the hubbub of initial publication activities has passed. The going rate is half or less of first-rights payments.

We've had excellent results selling secondary rights for our own books. *Income Opportunities* magazine took a chapter, "Finding a Rural Job: Gutsy Strategies Mother Never Told You," from *Country Bound!* and made us several hundred dollars richer. (See why we told you earlier to create unusual, stand-alone chapters?) While the readers of *Income Opportunities* aren't necessarily gung ho to move to the boonies, many of them needed to know about job prospecting in smaller towns.

More recently, I took a different approach with *Shameless Marketing for Brazen*

Hussies. I went through the entire book, section by section, and pinpointed the topics, then gave each a descriptive title and noted the word length. Then we grouped the "proposed articles" into logical main headings—business start-up tips, advertising, PR/promotions, miscellaneous business topics, sales, and the Internet—and created a faxable list to send to targeted magazines. Already two home business-type publications have bought excerpts, and we've only just begun. (See the first page of the Suggested Excerpt Offerings on page 373 to get the idea.)

One of the best excerpt markets is *Reader's Digest*. Though it's tough to crack, several self-published books have been featured in long excerpts. Approach this publication with a query letter containing a brief description of your book, why you are an authority, and a short overview of the chapters that contain relevant material. As you know, the *Digest* is heavy on pieces about fitness, health, finance, parenting, and other personal service topics. Contact information is in Appendix E.

Trade-published authors can often get permission from their publishers to pursue second serial rights—and keep *all* the revenue they generate. This is just one more way *any author* can impact book sales by following the guidelines offered in these pages. Before you proceed, however, get written permission for these rights to revert back to you.

When you sell your book in pieces, there is one very important stipulation you should insist upon. At the beginning or end of the excerpt, you want the entire copyright notice to be printed. It is also vital that readers be given ordering information about your book. Include at least the following: book title, author, and publisher. Also try to include a phone number and your Web site.

Usually, the magazine or newspaper will have a standard agreement it uses to consummate the sale. Read it carefully and ask that the above provisions be included if there is any doubt of that happening. If there is no contract, as was the case with one of the serial rights sales we made, create a letter of your own to outline the specifics.

Tapping Into Book Clubs

Placing a book with one or more book clubs will afford you both visibility and prestige. Another plus is the echo effect that a book club's publicity often creates. This means that people will hear about your title through their book clubs, but may actually purchase it in a bookstore, through your direct-mail campaign, or on the Internet.

What's the money picture like? You could receive as little as $600 or as much as $200,000. Realistically, it will most likely be in the $2,000 to $3,000 range. The two best known in the book club world are Book-of-the-Month Club

Suggested Excerpt Offerings

To:______________________________ **From:**____________

(5 pages) **fax: 719-395-8**

Looking for Information-Packed Articles/Sidebars/Book Excerpts?

Writer Marilyn Ross has been dubbed a "trend tracker" by *Entrepreneur* magazine. Author of 13 books, Soundview Executive Book Summaries selected one to be among the 30 best business books of the year. Additionally, she just won the "Evvie" Award for best business book of 1999. A freelance writer and editor of a monthly 24-page newsletter, she is a member of ASJA and the Authors Guild, and serves on the Editorial Advisory Board for *ForeWord* magazine. Her work has appeared in *Modern Maturity, Complete Woman, Essence, NFIB's Independent Business, Executive Female, Publishers Weekly, Nation's Business, Home Office Computing, Catholic Digest, Science of Mind Magazine, Westways, Southwest Airlines Magazine*, etc. Now her expertise is available to your readers via her articles—or an interview you may choose to conduct.

Marilyn's most recent title, ***Shameless Marketing for Brazen Hussies***™, contains 307 awesome money-making strategies for savvy entrepreneurs. Says Jay Conrad Levinson (author of the *Guerrilla Marketing* series), "It's fun to read, shockingly incisive, and extremely enlightening—whatever your gender." Supercharge your readers' sales from cyberspace, to storefront space, to client base. Twenty informative and inspirational chapters show how to affordably find and boldly impress new prospects, sell more to existing clients or customers, and make bank accounts blossom.

The articles below have been excerpted from this book and can be provided via email or on disk. They cover PR/Promotions, Advertising, Sales, the Internet, Business Startup Tips, plus Miscellaneous Business Topics. Photos of the author and book are available on request. (For more information on *Shameless Marketing for Brazen Hussies*™, go to http://www.BrazenHussiesNetwork.com.) To discuss using one or more of Marilyn's articles, call her at 719-395-8659 or email Marilyn@about-books.com.

Page	**Title/Topic**	**Approx. Word Length**	**Additional Sidebar Available?**
	BUSINESS STARTUP TIPS		
L/35-39	**Brainstorming to Flood Your Mind With Creativity**	1051	Yes
	Tips for Encouraging Innovative Thinking (sidebar)	306	
	Don't just compete—create! Techniques to help you be an innovator, plus tips for unleashing your muse.		
L/50-54	**The Name of the Game**	1447	Yes
	Naming Notions (sidebar)	94	
	A company's name can open fantastic doors . . . or do nothing. Includes examples of what works—and what doesn't—plus creative approaches for developing an outstanding business moniker.		
L/8-17	**Quick and Easy Market Research**	1785	No
	Who is your customer and what does he or she want? What's your competition? Answer these and many other important questions with the research strategies outlined here.		
M/17-21	**"Positioning" Yourself for Profits**	1581	No
	Don't fight for market share. Find ways to create your USP (unique selling proposition), then interpret it for your customers/clients.		

We make it easy for magazines and newsletters to run excerpts from the book by breaking it down into article-sized bites.

(BOMC) and The Literary Guild. But there has been enormous change in this industry over the last five to seven years. Book clubs have lost members to online booksellers and chains that offer generous discounts on best-sellers. Therefore, consolidation has become the name of the game. BOMC and Doubleday merged a couple of years ago, and the new company, Bookspan, has under its umbrella BOMC, The Literary Guild, Quality Paperback Book Club, and Doubleday Select. (As you'll see by looking in Appendix E under Book Clubs, there are many genres represented under each of these clubs.)

The medium-sized and smaller clubs—of which there are some 150—pay in the $5,000 to $10,000 range for a main selection, and from a few hundred to a few thousand dollars for an alternate. The clubs work on an "advance against royalty" basis; their royalties vary from a low of 6 percent to a high of 10 percent of the club price. (This royalty will be halved on books they offer at greatly reduced premium prices.) While negotiation always plays a role, normal advances are one-half of the club's total expected royalties. So you can guesstimate; figure on eventually ending up with a total revenue of approximately double what the advance is. As we recommend in all cases, don't accept an offer over the phone. Ask that it be submitted in writing so you can mull over all the points and use it for leverage to solicit other bids.

There are many niche clubs that serve specific audiences. For instance, there is the Movie & Entertainment Book Club, Conservative Book Club, Teen Age Book Club, Writer's Digest Book Club, Spiritual Book Associates, Rodale's Organic Gardening Book Club, Metaphysical Book Club, The Military Book Club, and scads more. This is but a sample of those listed in *LMP*.

As we mentioned in a previous chapter, you want to contact book clubs early in the book creation process—six months before the pub date if possible. Most will even work from a manuscript. All prefer to see a book at least in the galley stage. The reason for this is simple: The biggest clubs will print their own editions, but over 80 percent of the time, book clubs simply tag along on the publisher's print run, thus commanding a better unit cost for all involved.

Approach all likely candidates simultaneously with a letter describing the book and giving background information on the author. Also note any illustrative material that will be included. Spell out your publicity and marketing plans. Should you already have your covers, include one of them. Since you probably won't be that far along, at least send a color copy of the jacket design. Most club editorial judging boards meet every three weeks to review the current crop of books. If yours has been in the pipeline for a month and you haven't heard anything, call, write, or e-mail to determine the status. This is too important a subsidiary rights sale to let it slide through your fingers for want of basic sales follow-up.

Licensing Paperback Reprint Rights

Necessity may be the mother of invention, but ambition is definitely the father. And it's a wise writer-publisher who is ambitious when it comes to selling either mass-market or trade paperback rights to his book. This will most likely be the largest sale for a self-publisher. It often rakes in far more than the original book itself does, providing the gravy that makes the difference between profit and loss.

It's an intriguing phenomenon that many writers who initially find trade publishers' doors closed to them are opting to self-publish strictly as a stepping stone. They realize that self-publishing can bring them forcefully to the attention of the conventional publishing community with highly profitable, fame-producing results. The self-publisher's formula is to write the book, publish the book, make the book a success, then sell the book. And it's being done time after time.

It works one of two ways: Either a trade publisher comes knocking on your door with an offer, after perhaps learning of your book or meeting you at the BEA, or you solicit bids from publishers, accepting the most promising offer.

In regular commercial publishing circles, a hardcover house "auctions" reprint rights to the paperback publisher that promises to pay the highest guarantee against royalties. It is usually for a seven-year term. Often this auction takes place informally over the phone. Price is based on demand. The subsidiary rights director might negotiate vigorously, trying to get somebody up from $25,000 to $30,000; then a couple more biggies show interest and the amount leaps to $125,000 overnight.

Auctions are normally reserved for bigger books, and they receive advances to match. New American Library forked over $250,000 for a nonfiction work, *Women Like Us* (Liz Roman Gallese), and also picked up *The 100 Best Companies to Work for in America* (Robert Levering, Milton Moskowitz, Michael Katz) for $357,500. Not all reprint sales go this high. Century paid $38,000 for the rights to *Amateur City* (Katherine Forrest), a police procedural featuring a lesbian police detective. Pocket Books handed over $51,000 for *An Interrupted Life* (Etty Hillesum), which tells of a young Dutch Jewish woman killed by the Nazis. A Civil War novel, *Unto This Hour* (Tom Wicker), was auctioned to Berkley for $66,000. Auctions, however, are typically the ploy of the trade publisher.

For a self-published book you must first prove it can be a success in the marketplace. Then it is usually offered to one or several trade houses on a less structured basis than books that come under the auctioneer's hammer. There is no question, however, that reprint sales have swept many authors to national acclaim and healthy bank accounts.

Take the case of Kathy Coon, who originally published *The Dog Intelligence Test* in her garage. She was so swamped with orders from pet owners across the country that it was impossible for her to fill all of the orders. Avon quickly solved that problem by purchasing the rights to her book and capitalizing further by sending her around the United States on an author tour.

Bill Byrne, the author of *Habits of Wealth*, is the ultimate entrepreneur. His companies used to span food service, personal development, and magazine publishing. Now he's added book publishing to his list of accomplishments. Byrne has a lot of moxie. He *turned down* a five-figure offer from a conventional publisher, deciding he wanted to call his own shots. His elegant-looking hardcover helped win him a spot on the cover of *Fortune* magazine, the sale of rights for a three-video series based on the book's concept, and a $50,000 advance for paperback rights. That's quite a coup. Only 6 to 7 percent of business hardcovers ever go into paperback. "Looking at the full landscape, I couldn't have expected it to have come out better," he told us. Byrne is also pleased his book has made an impact on people's lives, that it has made a difference. Putnam Berkley came out with a press run of 75,000 copies of *Habits of Wealth*. In a compliment to us (we edited, designed, and typeset the original version of the book), the new publisher made only slight modifications to the cover and left the interior unchanged.

Making Money on Foreign and Translation Rights

The sale of foreign and translation rights may be practical if you have a book of universal interest. This is not so difficult for fiction, as the range of human emotions is no different in China or France, for instance, than in the United States. For nonfiction works there is more to consider. First, it will help if your book has a good track record in the United States. Next, ask yourself if there is any reason the book would not be of value or interest to folks in other countries.

A guide on how to homestead your house, thus protecting it from creditors, would be useless to someone in a foreign land where the laws are different. Yet a handbook describing how to cope with male menopause might be just as helpful to people in one country as in another. Your subject matter will dictate whether this subsidiary right is worth considering. It must have universal appeal to "travel." Homeopathic health is very hot now.

R.R. Bowker publishes *International Literary Market Place*, which covers some 160 countries, giving you virtually any information you could conceivably need. Here you can find agents who have representation abroad or who affiliate with a foreign literary agency.

The main stomping ground for setting up foreign and translation rights is the Frankfurt Book Fair in Germany, held each year in October. Subjects especially popular there recently were business, spirituality, self-help, health, and parenting. The London Book Fair has grown significantly and is now the big spring event. It is attended by British publishers as well as Spanish, Italian, and French houses. This is your primary market if you are targeting English-speaking publishers and don't want to fool with the issues surrounding translations. For illustrated children's books, the Bologna Book Fair, held in November in Bologna, Italy, is the place to be. Children's books are a key licensing and merchandise category in Europe these days, and this is the place to connect with the right parties.

Foreign rights are sold to publishers in English-speaking nations. You may sell an edition of perhaps 1,000 bound books from your own print run or 1,000 unfinished books, which the buyer will have bound in the country of purchase. The alternative is simply to sell reproduction rights. Then the purchaser can make any minor changes and produce a new edition using your electronic files. This is the preferred approach.

In this case the royalty is generally somewhere between 7 and 10 percent of the book's selling price. While most publishers use literary agents to negotiate such transactions, doing it yourself could provide a nice tax-deductible trip abroad. One word of caution on foreign rights sales, though: Insist on seeing a blueline of the book to be sure everything is OK before it rolls off the presses.

Translation rights for major languages—such as Spanish, German, French, Arabic, Chinese, and Japanese—usually bring at least $1,000 in an advance against royalties of 5 to 10 percent. Foreign publishers often request a two-month option period in which to consider a book. They prefer books of under 200 pages. When a deal is consummated, all you have to do is supply a couple of copies of the book and any photographs or illustrations. They handle all the details of the translation, printing, and distribution. While no one is likely to line up at your door with offers to purchase foreign or translation rights, they present just one more way to make additional money from your book project.

Other Ways to Profit From Sub Spin-Offs

Television and film rights may also hold promise for your title, especially if it is fiction. Film and television producers buy "properties" (makes your book sound like a piece of real estate, doesn't it?). Most often they purchase "options" that give them the right to hold the property for six months to two years while they try to arrange for financing to produce it or sell the idea to an independent TV packager, network, or sponsor.

Today you're not likely to get rich off options. The going option rate for unknown authors is from $500 to $5,000. Options are usually all there is, however. In an estimated 90 percent of the cases, they are never exercised for the big bucks waiting. But you could be in that other 10 percent!

Merchandising rights, especially for children's books and novels, can be very lucrative. In this situation, you license the content of your book for use on various products. Perhaps your book has memorable characters or a distinctive logo people would want to wear or feature on merchandise. You've surely noticed all the items related to the Harry Potter book series. The toys, stationery, pajamas, and dozens of other related things are all licenses for merchandise rights. Martha Stewart and Kathie Lee are other well-known examples. Both have clothing lines connected with their names, not to mention a bundle of other merchandise.

First you must target the universe of possible buyers within various product categories, then contact the specific companies within those lines. Besides what we mentioned above, some of the things you can license are calendars, gift wrap, greeting cards, mugs, jewelry, stickers, even board games.

And going back to *Reader's Digest*, what about condensation rights? The *Digest*, and a few other markets, condenses books into shorter versions. You might also consider whether audio rights is something you should pursue, although this is usually out of the realm of the self-publisher.

Electronic rights can be exciting because the universe of potential buyers is virtually infinite. Given the rapidly changing demands of the industry, not to mention the technology itself, you almost need someone with practical knowledge and industry experience—a sub rights person dedicated to the electronic marketplace. If this area intrigues you, be sure and read Thomas Woll's chapter on selling electronic rights in *Selling Subsidiary Rights*.

The Internet has not only opened fascinating doors for selling your rights to Web sites and other online entities, it has also given us a new way to prospect for sub rights sales. There is a company (www.rightsworld.com) that provides a venue for selling your rights online. Here you can make available all the rights we've been discussing above for all the world to see! Yup, it gives you global reach. Rightsworld.com offers a year-around 24/7 auction marketplace for the exchange of intellectual property in the publishing industry. This new central source for learning about available rights appeals to agents, film scouts, major trade publishers seeking new books, plus foreign rights buyers from all over the globe. Normally, Rightsworld.com charges a listing fee of $19.95 per title. But we have gotten a waiver of that fee for SPAN members. (Check out the Small Publishers Association of North America at www.SPANnet.org.)

Sub rights can boost your book into national acclaim and give your bank account a nice influx of cash. It makes sense to pursue these various options for found money to augment the actual book copies you will sell. In the next chapter, you'll discover a myriad of "out-of-the-box" strategies to turn your words into wealth.

Web Sites, Wisdom, and Whimsey

Doubleday Direct launches online book club. At www.booksonline.com, Doubleday has created a Web site that brings together more than thirty special interest and professional clubs. And the book club goliath expects to add up to a dozen more. This is a wonderful site to peruse for possible book club sales of your titles. The clubs cover a wide range from mystery to military, science fiction to sports. And don't overlook the more general Doubleday Book Club, which is slanted toward women and chock-full of romances, how-to's, and more. It's easy to see current offerings, and decide what area to pitch, when you scan the categories available. After you've done your homework, send a manuscript (preferably) or a finished book plus promotional material to Acquiring Editor, [name of book club], Bookspan, 1540 Broadway, 16th Floor, New York, NY10036. Go for it!

* * *

The greatest magnifying glasses in the world are a man's own eyes when they look upon his first book.

* * *

A bonanza awaits in licensing merchandise rights. According to the 1999 Industry Annual Report from *License!* magazine, retail sales of licensed merchandise from art and publishing totaled a gigantic $17.3 billion. What a market! As a category, art and publishing includes nonfiction books, novels, magazines, and art. Here's a breakdown of who licenses these rights: apparel companies:10 percent; toys and games: almost 20 percent; housewares: about 15 percent; hardware: around 15 percent; soft home goods: about 11 percent; music and video: about 12 percent; stationery: approximately 6 percent; and miscellaneous: around 8 percent.

* * *

Is selling reprint rights a good strategy? Sometimes, yes; sometimes, no. John Kremer tells of licensing the rights to his *Mail Order Selling Made Easier* to John Wiley & Sons. Wiley retitled the book as *The Complete Direct Marketing Sourcebook* and within two-and-one-half years had sold fewer copies than Kremer sold in six months. For him it was still a worthwhile sale as it came with a nice advance and he wasn't interested in promoting the book any longer himself. We've had similar experiences. We published *Country Bound!*, sold 10,000 copies, then allowed a trade publisher to take over the rights for a nice five-figure advance. They let it die. (That kind of treatment, like buying a goose, can get you down.) We now have the rights back again! (We're just waiting for another back-to-small-town-USA surge to revise and relaunch it.)

* * *

Here's another approach for added revenue. Vicki Lansky, owner of Book Peddlers, wrote and published a small book titled *Baking Soda: Over 500 Fabulous, Fun and Frugal Uses You've Probably Never Thought Of.* And what she did with it, most of us would never have thought of. Lansky put together a deal with a direct-mail marketer who licensed nonexclusive rights to reprint quantities of the book to support ads he runs in many national publications. He pays her $0.80 for each copy he sells, and she merchandises the book as usual. This has helped her reach 225,000 copies sold!

PART VI

Nontraditional Venues for Generating More Sales

19 *Originating Extraordinary "Out-of-the-Box" Opportunities*

Looking at innovative ways to increase sales and enlarge your marketing base? This is the place! We'll explore specialty retail outlets *other than* bookstores. And we'll talk about premiums and merchandise tie-ins, catalog opportunities, and more maverick ways to help you attract buyers to your book like bears to a honey pot. You'll also hear from two authors who have parlayed their books into company spokesperson jobs.

Creative Thinking Pays

Be a creative thinker. Only then will you come up with additional paths for merchandising your book. One of the smartest things you can do is forge strategic alliances with other companies, organizations, and people who *already have your customer base*. We've dubbed this partnering process "LinkThink." It can mean the difference between bare subsistence and astonishing abundance.

We might take a lesson from geese. They fly in a V formation for a specific reason: As each bird flaps its wings, it creates an uplift for the bird immediately following. Thus, the whole flock adds 71 percent greater flying range than if each bird flew on its own. People who share a common direction can get where they are going more quickly and easily traveling on the thrust of one another, too.

A good way to trigger these new strategic partnership ideas is to play the "what if" game. Ask what if—then finish with some out-of-the-ordinary idea, situation, or condition. This allows you to probe aspects thought to be impractical and impossible, things that lie outside the usual boundaries. Not all of your brainstorms will be successful. So what? Keep at it. If one idea isn't a hit, try something else. Babe Ruth and Hank Aaron struck out many times, but that's not what they're remembered for.

Other Retail Outlets Will Carry Your Product

There are numerous places besides bookstores where your product will sell. Major publishers call these "special sales." No, it's not as glamorous as normal trade sales. But do you want dazzle or dollars? If you sometimes feel the only way you'll ever get your cup to runneth over is to start using smaller cups, listen up!

The Book Industry Study Group released a study titled *The Sale of Books Through Non-Bookstore Retailers*. Because it costs $650, not many people have had access to it. This unique compendium of facts shows that one out of every four books purchased by consumers today is bought in nonbookstore outlets. Such places as home-improvement centers, drugstores, discount stores, grocery stores, gift shops, liquor stores, even auto supply outlets are prime candidates. The study says, "While there are 20,000 bookstores in the United States, there is probably ten times this number of nonbookstore retail outlets also selling books." What a bonanza waits here. Think about your subject matter, then play with various connecting possibilities as you play LinkThink. Here are some equations of subject matter to retail outlets to get your brain perking:

- Gardening—nurseries, garden centers, florists, botanical gardens, landscapers
- Hiking—sporting goods stores, camping equipment dealers, climbing centers
- Parenting—baby shops, toy stores
- Crafts—hobby shops, quilting outlets
- Nutrition—health food stores, vegetarian restaurants
- Wardrobe coordination—dress shops, fabric stores, cosmetic MLM (multilevel marketing) salespeople
- Art book—museums, artist supply stores, galleries
- Hair or skin care—beauty shops, beauty supply stores

An interesting article in *Publishers Weekly* a while back was titled "Books Wherever You Look: The Mall as Market Microcosm." It went on to detail that based on a directory of the two hundred stores in a shopping mall, which included two bookstore chain outlets, at least twenty-five other outlets carried books. They included The Nature Company, Williams-Sonoma, Smith & Hawken, FAO Schwarz, Crate & Barrel, Gamesmanship, Rand McNally, Port O'Call, Metropolitan Museum of Art, Successories, and Learningsmith. The books' topics ranged from children's titles to gardening guides, travel to cooking, inspirational to gift, art to chess, animals to astronomy. The opportunities abounded.

Once you've figured out some logical matches, get to work. That's what the sales director, Dennis Hayes, of The Crossing Press did for *The World in Your Kitchen* (Troth Wells), a collection of vegetarian recipes from Africa, Asia, and Latin America. Can you guess who placed an $80,000 order? Pier 1 Imports. This retailer bought for its nine hundred stores in the United States and Canada. Realizing the viability of special sales, this publisher also sold 18,000 copies of the book *Espresso!* (Shea Sturdivant, Steve Terracin) to the DēLonghi Espresso Company, which packages it as an add-on or sells it side by side with products.

Nick Lyons places fly-fishing books in sporting goods stores. A title on Jewish weddings flourishes in synagogues, bridal shops, florists, and caterers. Down East Books sells its titles in fish stores (a Maine seafood cookbook) and dive shops (a book featuring full-color photographs of marine life).

Carol Fenster, Ph.D., publishes a series of Special Diet cookbooks for people with allergies, asthma, and other illnesses. She finds a ready market in targeted grocery stores, such as Whole Foods Market, Wild Oats, and Alfalfa's. Her books are also recommended by local physicians (including allergists and ear, nose, and throat specialists), nutritionists, and naturopaths. Not one to let grass grow under her feet (unless it is amaranth, quinoa, or teff), she is also working with the Department of Agriculture, Cooperative Extension Service, and several groups interested not only in nutrition but also in promoting alternative grains used in the book. These organizations refer interested callers to her and promote the books in their publications.

Consider various professionals as resellers for your book. A lady you met previously published a book titled *Vicki Lansky's Divorce Book for Parents*. She purposely priced it at only $5.99 and sells it by the carton (100 books) for $3.00 each to lawyers, therapists, mediators, and other professionals. They give or sell it to their clients to help children cope with divorce and its aftermath. It must be working. Lansky has peddled 120,000 copies so far.

We used to sell the Bakers' *UnCook Book*, a recipe book for raw foods, to various alternative health care professionals. When you're selling to professionals or teachers or into smaller nontraditional markets, it's a good idea to establish a discount schedule for quantity purchases. (See the sample on page 385.) We encourage people to buy in case lots as it makes shipping much faster and easier. We also expect them to prepay and cover the shipping costs since the discounts are generous. To make it easy, we accept credit cards on these bulk orders.

On another note, a collection of recipes from street fairs called *Street Food* (Rose Grant) sells well in gourmet shops. "The book trade didn't know how to

Discount Schedule for Quantity Purchases

P.O. Box 909 • 425 Cedar Street • Buena Vista, CO 81211-0909
http://www.SPANnet.org/CC/ • e-mail: CC@spannet.org
(719) 395-8659 • Fax (719) 395-8374

DISCOUNT SCHEDULE FOR QUANTITY PURCHASES OF

JUMP START YOUR BOOK SALES: A MONEY-MAKING GUIDE FOR AUTHORS, INDEPENDENT PUBLISHERS AND SMALL PRESSES

Below is information on bulk quantity discounts for *Jump Start Your Book Sales,* which retails for $19.95. We are only able to provide these generous discounts on a nonreturnable basis when payment accompanies your order. You may charge the books to your VISA or MasterCard (1-800-331-8355) or send us a check or money order to the address below. We will ship your books within 48 hours. Thank you for your order!

10 copies	40% discount	$119.70
	UPS shipping	12.00
	TOTAL	$131.70
26 copies (1 case)	50% discount	$259.35
	UPS shipping	21.00
	TOTAL	$280.35
52 copies (2 cases)	52% discount	$497.95
	UPS shipping	42.00
	TOTAL	$539.95
104 copies (4 cases)	54% discount	$954.41
	UPS shipping	84.00
	TOTAL	$1,038.41
Larger orders	Quoted individually	

Individuals, associations, and others may want to buy quantities of your book. Create a discount schedule centered around even cases that are easy to ship.

respond to it," explains Hayes. "Should they put it in the cooking section? In travel?"

The possibilities are endless. And sometimes very unusual. Within the first few hours of the book's availability, the Pink Pony Cafe—a baseball hangout in Scottsdale, Arizona—sold fifteen copies of David Falkner's *The Short Season: The Hard Work and High Times of Baseball in the Spring.*

Expanding to Specialized Wholesale Suppliers

Now move this concept to the next level. Once you have established a few good accounts among nonbookstore outlets—and once the books are moving regularly—ask the store managers what *wholesale suppliers* they deal with. By contacting a specific wholesaler and explaining your new product is "a real moneymaker for Joe at XYZ," you can convince the supplier that this is a lucrative bandwagon onto which he wants to climb. Do whatever it takes to convince him: Bulldoze, charm, cajole. This is too big an opportunity to let it slip by. Once convinced, the wholesaler will represent you to all similar outlets within his territory. Presto! You've expanded your business by adding a whole new sales force—at no cost to you!

These wholesalers will need guidance. They usually haven't carried books before and will require encouragement and a simple plan for handling your title. Why not prepackage a few books and put them in an attractive point-of-purchase display stand? Supplying such displays, and whatever other attention getters you can think of—posters made from blow-ups of your cover, easel-style advertising for a counter, maybe even just a colorful mylar balloon to tie to the display stand—is particularly important in selling to stores whose main business is not books. Offer your new business partner easy guidelines for reordering. You might even coach the sales reps or sponsor in-store events, such as signings, demonstrations, slide shows, or lectures for certain strong accounts.

Why is this such a hot idea? You have suddenly acquired a nationwide group of sales reps! And these wholesalers are accustomed to a 50 percent discount, and they're *not* used to being able to return merchandise! Does this make sense or does this make sense?

Premium Books and Merchandise Tie-Ins

If we're to have large-scale successes, we must think *big*. That point was solidly brought home to us by our children one year. At Christmas, Marilyn used to bake batches and batches of cookies. And most years our four teenagers got into trouble because they'd sneak in and snitch them off the cookie sheets before they had even cooled, leaving telltale empty spots. One Christmas the sheets went untouched. We secretly rejoiced that the kids had finally outgrown their holiday mischief. It wasn't until weeks later while cleaning the garage, that we learned the truth. There, stuck in a corner, was an empty cookie sheet. They had solved their problem by thinking big—taking the *whole sheet*—which we never missed.

Sales that are anything but meager can be generated if your title lends itself to the premium market. And most do. Premium books (also called sponsored) are given away—or sold at a fraction of their normal cost—to promote business goodwill. A book is a perfect choice because it has keepsake value; people don't throw them away. They become consumer giveaways or motivational items for salespeople and dealers.

Banks and savings and loans dole out calendars or books to entice new customers into establishing accounts. Other frequent premium buyers are insurance companies, food companies, investment brokers, pharmaceutical companies, manufacturers of various products, network marketing companies, even newspapers and magazines that want to beef up their subscriber lists. And you can sell and resell your book as a premium. All that is required is that exclusivity be assured for a given type of business in a specific geographic area if requested. For instance, if you were selling a premium edition to savings and loans, exclusivity would mean that no other bank or S&L in the city (or county, depending on the bank's range) would be offering the book.

We're talking about quantity here: 5,000, 10,000, 20,000 books at one swat. Of course, since the volume is so large, premium buyers expect (and rightly so) that you give them a very good deal. Even though you make much less per book, when you multiply the amount by 20,000 it adds up quickly. Plan on doing a customized promotional cover that includes the institution's name. The CEO may also want to write a brief foreword (which could replace the bastard title page). Perhaps the purchaser will add discount coupons in the back or package it with another product. This kind of personalization is what makes books such perfect premium items.

Approach prospective premium buyers with a well-thought-out sales package of your promotional materials. If these prospects show interest, send them each a sample color cover and a galley if the book isn't off the press yet. Ideally, arrangements should be done far enough in advance of your print date so the extra books can be manufactured at the same time, allowing you to benefit from the reduced price of the larger print run. But with a first book this may not be possible, you may need reviews and other post-printing aids to convince premium buyers that your book is worthy. But it can't hurt to try earlier, and if you've been careful to back off before a buyer can give you a definite no, you can always reopen negotiations later when you have a finished book in hand and wonderful reviews to share. And at that point, you can either arrange for a new run of appropriately personalized covers or perhaps order a classy gold sticker imprinted with the customer's logo or slogan that can be affixed to the regular cover.

Or, as a self-publisher, you can provide customized editions! It's possible to manipulate the contents any way you can imagine—or your customers can request. Suggest retitling the book to include the buyer's name, such as *The XYZ*

Company Guide to . . . (*How to Talk to Your Cat,* by Jean Craighead George, became *The Meow Mix Guide to Cat Talk.*) Perhaps you'll condense it into a booklet; this is especially practical if it's long and only part applies. You could even do a series of smaller versions as a set. Or you might customize it in other ways: produce bilingual editions; create different versions of a kid's book for Blacks, Asians, or Hispanics; or slant the work to women, retirees, or those who live in a certain geographic area. Get the idea?

Suppose you want to find national wholesalers in a field allied to your book that might be persuaded to take on your title as a merchandise tie-in. What do you do? Happily, there is a set of books that will lead you to just the right manufacturing matches. It is called the *Thomas Register of American Manufacturers* and has some 80,000 headings covering more than 1.5 million sources. Because it is arranged alphabetically by product, this gigantic address book will help you track down virtually any American manufacturer. It's available in any major library and on the Internet. Think about what other products go to the market you're trying to reach, then determine specific manufacturers in *Thomas Register.*

That's what Marcella Smith, of St. Martin's Press, did. She sold Alfred Glossbrenner's *The Complete Handbook of Personal Computer Communications* to Hayes Microcomputer Products, Inc. The company purchased tens of thousands to promote sales of its modems. What would you do with a book called *The Best of Everything*? If you were smart, you might contact Sylvania, as its Superset nineteen-inch color TV was voted "the best in its field." That's precisely what St. Martin's did . . . and sold Sylvania a premium edition of this book of lists.

Dutton found a great premium home for A.A. Milne's children's book *Winnie-the-Pooh*. Dutton sold it to Lever Brothers, which was the manufacturer of Mrs. Butterworth's syrup. Bottles of the pancake syrup featured a promotion telling consumers they could buy the book for half price with a proof-of-purchase label from Mrs. Butterworth's syrup. While the initial order was small, Lever Brothers forecasted selling 40,000 to 80,000 books. Prentice-Hall does a lot of premiums as corporate gifts and for internal sales and learning tools. They recently did customized books for B.F. Goodrich, Getty Oil, and Manufacturers Hanover.

Better Homes and Gardens' special sales division has gone into premiums in a big way. Mike Peterson, of BH&G, told us of selling 2 *million* booklets to the Nestlé Company for its *"Best You Can Bake" Chocolate Desserts.* BH&G extracted appropriate recipes from another book, packaged them in the familiar red-and-white-plaid cover of the BH&G cookbook, tucked in some Nestlé advertising, and scored a supersale. Copies of the 32-page booklet were given free to purchasers of Nestlé Toll House Morsels. BH&G has put together similar little books with other companies. *Best Wok Recipes* was sold to West Bend; and Cribari wines gives complimentary copies of *Holiday Get-Together Recipes*.

But do you have to be a major publisher to tap into these deals? Absolutely not! Our friend Kim Gosselin got started in premiums when a pharmaceutical company agreed to buy 15,000 copies of her *Taking Diabetes to School*, a story she self-published to help kids understand what it's like to go through the illness on a daily basis, as her son does. Kim is a very astute businesswomen and realized she had a tiger by the tail. Her publishing company, JayJo Books, now has some twenty titles in print and has sold more than 1.5 million copies to date. Premium sales within the pharmaceutical and medical industries make up about 75 percent of her business. Her most profound piece of advice? "Follow up, follow up, follow up, follow up, follow up!"

Want to sell 350,000 copies of one book in four months? Follow the lead of Katherine Glover and her company, INTI Publishing. She specializes in selling books to network marketing companies. This is the MLM of old days and refers to such companies as Amway, Avon, and Discovery Toys. Top distributors often sponsor their own book clubs and buy thousands of books at a time. They seek classic personal growth–type books in the $9.95 to $12.95 range and typically under 200 pages. Discounts run between 60 and 75 percent, and they pay net thirty.

Of course, few sales run into these high numbers. But that's OK; part of the fun is finding the matches. One author suggested certain wines as appropriate accompaniments with each of fifty soup recipes. A group of affiliated wineries bought 400 copies of the cookbooks at just below retail price. And this same publishing house took another creative tack: It dedicated the book to the memory of a great soup-making grandmother whose family still owned a local wine and spirits shop. As a result, the family bought 200 copies to sell in their store.

Is your title *Play the Harmonica in Three Easy Lessons*? What a natural for a harmonica manufacturer. They cling together like brand-new dollar bills. A banana cookbook might interest Chiquita. If your message is about thwarting computer crime, contact computer manufacturers and suggest a mutual arrangement. Have a product that deals with being a better parent? You can reach a large number of pediatricians through distributors of medical supplies. They can be found in the *Hayes Directory of Physician and Hospital Supply Houses* or the *Directory of Medical Products Distributors*. Depending on your subject area, you might also look in the local yellow pages or contact trade and professional associations for names of suppliers.

Various service businesses also yield opportunities for book sales. Let's suppose you have a book on how to interview effectively. Jeff Herman had just such a challenge with *Getting Hired: Everything You Need to Know About Resumes,*

Interviews and Job Hunting Strategies (Edward Rogers). While *Time* magazine gave away a few thousand copies, he wasn't willing to stop there. Herman saw the book as a natural for college audiences. Who targets this market? Beer companies. So he solicited them for bids. His gusto resulted in Adolph Coors purchasing no less than 164,750 copies!

One of our students, Dennis Stricker, had good luck selling his booklet titled *Locks: How They Work and How to Pick Them* to—can you guess?—police departments. (Interesting correlation, that one.) Another unlikely alliance is Westphalia Press's *Tom's Remembrance* (Rebecca O'Hanlon Nunn). The press sold 1,000 copies of this title to the state funeral directors association. The association gave it to customers as "a salve for the soul." Writer's Digest Books worked with the Polaroid Corporation to carry one of WD's titles, *How to Create Super Slide Shows* (E. Burt Close), as a promotion for Polaroid's instant slide film system. Almost any book has premium potential if you are clever enough to determine where the fit is.

Hitting the Catalog Jackpot

There are more than fifteen thousand printed catalogs in existence. Thousands more tempt surfers on the Internet. Getting your books in them isn't easy. Catalogers won't chase you. It works the other way around. Smart authors and publishers are in hot pursuit of them.

There is a place for your book in catalogs. You can find a catalog for every category of interest you can imagine. Catalogs range from expensive gift and gadget books, such as the one Neiman Marcus puts out, to ones covering more everyday fare, such as Miles Kimball, Lillian Vernon, and Walter Drake. There are also specialized catalogs for electronics, collectibles, clothing, gardening, appliances, hardware, food, you name it. If you have a book on boating, try Goldberg's Marine catalog. Want to place your title dealing with crafts? Maybe Lee Ward would be interested. And Brookstone, famous for its hard-to-find tools, just might cotton to your career guide on blacksmithing.

Industry statistics reveal that 56.6 percent of all adults bought from a catalog in a recent twelve-month period. In the year 2000, consumers buying via catalog spent $60.9 billion. Additionally, $38.9 billion was shelled out by businesses buying through catalogs. That means catalog sales accounted for almost $100 billion in sales. The following list illustrates why you can't afford to ignore this marketing channel.

Three Important Lists: A Plan to Sell More Books With Less Risk

1. Virtually all catalogs buy nonreturnable. No more risk.

2. Most pay in thirty days. This unheard of practice in the publishing industry is as refreshing as a cold beer on a hot day.

3. They buy over and over and over again. Once you've made the sales, they'll purchase your book for as long as their catalogs remain in print (sometimes for several years). And if your title is a good seller, they'll put it in their next catalogs, and their next.

4. Rarely do they require exclusivity. You can place the same book in many different catalogs.

5. They usually pay the freight. This frees up your capital for more important things.

6. You get free exposure to hundreds of thousands, sometimes millions, of consumers.

7. Backlist is welcome. Catalogs couldn't care less if your book is two, three, or more years old—as long as the information is still fresh.

Finding the Best Catalogs for Your Book

There are many directories that list catalogs, which are typically grouped according to subject matter. Most are quite expensive; you probably want to look at them in a public or university library before considering a purchase. Here are some to investigate:

1. *The Directory of Mail Order Catalogs* (lists over 7,000 general catalogs)
2. *Directory of Business to Business Catalogs* (contains 6,000 business catalogs)
3. *Mail Order Business Directory* (lists 10,000 catalogs and mail-order firms)
4. *The Directory of Overseas Catalogs* (contains information on over 1,300 mail order catalog companies from around the world)
5. *National Directory of Catalogs* (9,000 mail-order catalogs)
6. *The Catalog of Catalogs*

The last on the list is our favorite: a very affordable directory ($25.95 versus the more than $100 for most of the others). Although it is designed with consumers in mind, you can use it handily to track down possibilities in some 900 subject areas. In a resource the size of a hefty phone book, the publisher covers more than 15,000 catalogs in all. This is a superb place for market research. You can order it by calling (800) 331-8355. We're impressed by the detail of this reference's organization, the affordability, and the scope.

Striking Gold on the Yellow Brick Road

Here are some guidelines on the actual process for catalog sales:

1. Sit down with one of the directories listed above and pinpoint likely catalogs that might carry your book.

2. Call and request a copy (most have toll-free numbers and will gladly provide a free copy).

3. Study it. Consume it. Think about it. Relate it to your product(s).

4. If it looks promising, call again. This time you want the buyer's name (get the spelling, too), address, direct phone number, fax, and e-mail. Request any available submission forms or guidelines.

5. Complete the form if applicable; write a benefit-oriented sales letter that emphasizes why the catalog's customers need your book and that cites specific examples from the company's current offerings that relate to the book. Include your Catalog Information Sheet (see example on page 393), a book cover or photo, and important testimonials or reviews. It is also wise for you to write a catalog blurb in that catalog's style. Bingo—you've just made the buyer's job that much easier. Most publishers agree it's better not to send the book at this stage. Follow up two weeks later with a phone call. Find out when the decision-making committee will meet. Offer to send a sample book.

6. At the designated time send the book (along with copies of all the previous PR materials). Then follow up two weeks after the committee was to meet if you haven't heard anything. (If the answer is no, try to find out the objection so you can overcome it at the next round of meetings.)

7. Don't get discouraged. Be tenacious.

Most catalogers will want to do a test first. This usually involves a purchase of a few dozen copies to as many as a thousand for a huge catalog.

When we published *Country Bound!* a few years back, we were sure it was a natural for *Mother Earth News*, which had a self-contained catalog in its magazine. But we could never catch the decision maker, let alone get to yes. Finally, on our fifth call, we reached the woman, gave her our pitch, and were promptly put on hold. She came back a couple of minutes later saying, "You know, you're right. I just pulled your book off the bookshelf, and it is right for our readers." Then she gave us a purchase order for several cases. We sold to *MEN* month after month, year after year thereafter.

Additional Catalog Details

If the book passes the catalog's test, the rollout order can mean a few hundred copies, or as many as 50,000. Subsequent orders for major catalogs may end up being your biggest revenue producer. Timing can be important. For holiday catalogs, you must catch them very early in the year.

Most independent publishers give catalogs a 50 percent discount. Larger catalogers will send you a product submission packet and their contracts with required discounts and terms. Don't be surprised if they want 80 percent off the

Catalog Information Sheet

CATALOG INFORMATION SHEET

TITLE: ***Country Bound!™ Trade Your Business Suit Blues for Blue Jean Dreams™***
AUTHORS: Marilyn and Tom Ross
SUGGESTED RETAIL: $19.95
ISBN: 0-918880-30-0, LCCN 92-3259
PUBLISHER: Communication Creativity
BINDING: 6" x 9" trade paperback
PAGES: 433
WEIGHT: 1 and 1/4 pounds
SHIPPING INFORMATION: FOB Buena Vista, CO
TERMS: to well-rated accounts: 2% 10 days, EOM/Net 30. Others, payment with order.

About the authors:

The authors live what they write about in *Country Bound!™*. In 1980 they left the southern California area for a tiny Colorado mountain town. They share their experiences with wit and candor, telling readers what *not* to do as much as what to do. Tom and Marilyn have collaborated on six previous books. The most recent, *Big Marketing Ideas for Small Service Businesses*, was tapped as one of the 30 best business books of 1990 by Soundview Executive Book Summaries.

Brief description of book:

At last there's a book that helps you achieve your vision of escaping the big city, earn a good living in the country—and have better quality of life. Hundreds of practical thought-provoking ideas you can use immediately to prosper in paradise. Readers discover ways to turn avocational pastimes into regular paychecks—telecommute to their present jobs—set up an "information age" home-based business—buy an existing rural enterprise—or create their dream job in the country. Dozens of quizzes, maps, tables, graphs, and checklists to make relocating easier and more fun. *Country Bound!™* is a cross between a friendly chat and a unique reference book. It shows you how to regain control of your life, to launch new adventures. Now you can swap yesterday's frustrations for tomorrow's serenity—easily, quickly, and profitably.

DISCOUNT SCHEDULE:

Quantity	Discount	Price Each
10 units	40%	$11.97
28 units (1 case)	44%	$11.17
56 units (2 cases)	47%	$10.57
84 units (3 cases)	49%	$10.17
1 gross (144 units)	55%	$ 8.98
2 - 5 gross (288 to 720 units)	60%	$ 7.98
6 - 10 gross (864 to 1440 units)	65%	$ 6.98
11 - 19 gross (1584 to 2736 units)	70%	$ 5.99
20 or more gross (2880 units and up)	80%	$ 3.99

Glossy photo and sample product available on request (no charge). Call Ann at 1-800-331-8355.

P.O. Box 909, 425 Cedar Street, Buena Vista, CO 81211-0909 • (719) 395-8659

Specialty catalogs are a wonderful place to sell books; they already have your customer base. Develop a one-sheet to make it easy for them.

retail price. If you've priced your book properly, you can give them that on orders of several thousand and still make a profit.

It's important, once you've negotiated a catalog sale, that you be able to supply books. Communicate with the catalog buyer about when to send additional stock.

If your book really takes off, you must be prepared to turn a reprint within four to five weeks.

Where on the Web can you find information about catalogs? Go to www.Yahoo.com and just type in "catalog." Also go directly to the following sites and do searches for topic-specific catalogs:

- Buyer's Index (www.buyersindex.com)
- CatalogLink (http://cataloglink.com)
- Catalog-Mart (http://catalog.savvy.com)
- The Catalog Site (www.catalogsite.com)

If you're really serious about making a commitment to this marketing strategy, it's wise to read the trade journal of the industry, *Catalog Age*. If it's not available in your library, you can get subscription information by calling (800) 775-3777, or check out the journal online at www.catalogagemag.com. You can access selected stories from the current issue, check the archives, or do a keyword search. Other good publications for those interested in this area are *Target Marketing*, *DM News*, and *Direct Marketing*.

Become a Paid Spokesperson?

Maybe yes; probably no. Being a paid spokesperson takes a certain kind of person. But since getting bucks for your clucks can be sooooo rewarding, we want to address it here. Media spokespersons are hired by companies and organizations to add credibility to consumer products or services being promoted through publicity campaigns. Spokespersons must be topic experts with credentials to back their expertise. The pay is typically from $2,000 to $5,000 a day, plus expenses.

Dr. Judith Briles, our friend you met in a previous chapter, recently signed a deal with Procter & Gamble to be the spokesperson for its new Downy Wrinkle Releaser. (It's for fabric, not faces.) This came as a result of Judith's new book, *The Confidence Factor*. P&G was looking for a woman who knew something about the topic and how appearance could be a factor in creating confidence, someone who could speak and had written on the subject. Bingo! Judith matched this need to a T. She's doing a ten-city tour; P&G sets up all the media and covers travel, hotel, meals, and a hefty daily rate.

Advises Judith, "Sponsorships and touchy-feely books don't usually work. If you have a how-to/practical book, you have more of a chance. For a self-publisher it's critical that your book has a classy feel to it. Spend the extra money to create it; it's your calling card." If she were to prospect for a sponsorship position on her own and go directly to the corporation, she would contact the brand manager or VP of marketing. When working through the PR agency, you must first find out which firm represents which product, then make a direct pitch to the account executive of that product line.

This is not Judith's first encounter with sponsorships. It's actually her third. She just renewed a contract with First USA bank and WingspanBank.com, which tie everything in with her *10 Smart Money Moves for Women*. Sounds like she practices what she preaches.

Another friend, Sandra Beckwith, works with The Soap and Detergent Association (SDA). Its PR agency developed a survey on housework and found that women who work outside the home are still doing far more than their share, thus causing tension between couples. Sandy authored *Why Can't a Man Be More Like a Woman?* a humorous look at what makes men different from women. She writes and speaks about the lighter side of gender differences. Because she had the credentials to explain the survey results, offer tips on how women could get more help around the house, and suggest to men simple steps they could take to help, she was the ideal spokesperson for SDA. This association contracted with her for three months and a range of media-related services, including travel to New York City and other locations for in-person interviews. She received valuable on-camera media training and also did telephone interviews from her office. Spokespersons' duties can range from participating in a satellite media tour to appearing on national television shows, from doing "phoners" to online chats. The responsibilities are varied, the pay exceptional, the exposure incredible.

More Maverick Sales Opportunities

"To boldly go where no man has gone before," *Star Trek* used to challenge. And why not? The person clever enough to use imaginative ways to command attention or to expand sales is like cream . . . always rising to the top.

Another merchandising possibility hides in very unlikely places and is therefore frequently overlooked. **National parks and monuments** could be ideal sites for your book. A book called *Bear Attack* has sold more than 68,000 copies to concessionaires in national parks. One of the places we wanted *Discover Your Roots* to be carried was the Cabrillo National Monument in San Diego. Why? Because it is the most popular historical site in the United States, frequented by people from every state and dozens of foreign countries. Nice exposure for a book. Well, *DYR* didn't make it. Even though it dealt with history, it had nothing to do with the monument itself. That bit of information was filed away for future reference.

When Marilyn was writing *Creative Loafing*, she decided to include national monuments as a leisure activity. Guess which specific one was used as an anecdote? (And guess which one agreed to carry the book? That's right, Cabrillo National Monument.) The gift shops at these spots typically order like bookstores and expect a 40 percent discount. This kind of sensitivity to your market can be used to your advantage in editorial ways, too. Just like The Babe and Hank, we were determined, and consequently we profited from our mistakes.

Museums may be another location to place books; virtually all of them have gift shops. They sell books on animals, art, history, science, nature, sports, transportation, and more, plus an array of children's books. You can reach the Museum Store Association, Inc. at (303) 504-9223, or look in *The Official Museum Directory*, a compendium of detailed descriptions on the focus and offerings of each museum.

National associations offer more rich veins to be mined. Go to the library and snuggle up with a copy of the *Encyclopedia of Associations*. No matter what your book is about, there is an association of people who would be interested in it. Joining forces with nonprofits creates win/win coalitions. That's what Pegine Echevarria, MSW, found out when she wrote *For All Our Daughters: How Mentoring Helps Young Women and Girls Master the Art of Growing Up*. She forged an alliance with Girl Scouts of the USA to use it as the association's mentoring handbook. (And Smith Barney has given it to five hundred financial consultants.)

Find out who the key players in an association are. Call and get the names of the executive director and the board chairperson. While you're at it, also find out about the organization's journal or newsletter, annual meeting, and availability of a mailing list. Inquire whether the business has a speakers bureau, and whether the company's internal structure has any subgroups or special interest committees. Follow up on each of these inquiries for bulk book sales, reviews, endorsements, speaking engagements, exhibits, listings in bibliographies or recommended reading lists, piggybacking on mailings to members, and so on. By applying out-of-the-box thinking, associations can be worked a myriad of ways.

What about **auctions**? You can sell your books through Internet auction sites. They take a percentage of what you sell plus a fee for placing your book online. Check out www.eBay.com.

One way to move books is to **hawk them personally**. The author of *A War Ends* sold his $8.95 novel door-to-door. Fortunately for him, a reporter for a Los Angeles newspaper lived behind one of those doors. The reporter was so impressed with this unusual approach to bookselling that he wrote a story. Subsequent publicity focused a national spotlight on the author.

Gary Provost, who wrote and published *The Dorchester Gas Tank*, a book of offbeat humor, contends that the secret of selling self-published books is eyeball-to-eyeball contact with people. In the early days of his career, you could find him around the Boston Public Library, City Hall, subway stations, or any busy place almost every morning. He toted a suitcase full of books, a poster, and the knowledge that he was earning his living solely as a writer-publisher. Back then, Provost peddled between twenty and twenty-five books each day he worked.

While you may choose not to become this directly involved in selling, there is still a message here. Always carry books with you! As you meet new people and circulate in new places, fresh opportunities materialize. We've sold books to a gas station jockey who saw a copy in the car and to strangers waiting in line next to us. Keep your book visible and yourself verbal.

Speaking of visible, **use your eyes** to open new horizons. Marilyn noticed a Dell Purse Book in the market one day and picked up a copy to scan the publisher's list of titles in this series. There was nothing on genealogy. A letter proposing that Dell excerpt portions of our *Discover Your Roots* was soon on its way. But the publisher wasn't interested in *Discover Your Roots*. It was interested, however, in contracting with Marilyn to write *another* book on genealogy for Dell. It was a quick and simple assignment, as all the research was complete. Two weeks later we were $700 richer.

In case you're wondering, we did give serious consideration to the question, Will a purse book detract from our book sales? The answer came out no. Our prime buyers were libraries, schools, and individuals who frequent bookstores—not the same audience who impulsively picks up a mini book at the grocery store.

Another nice spin-off for *DYR* occurred. We approached the Boy Scouts and the Girl Scouts to see if either would want to use it as a reference book for genealogy. The *Girl Scout Leader* ended up suggesting that tracing your roots would be a stimulating activity and gave our book top billing in a list of recommended resources. Many times being included in bibliographies leads to sales. If you become aware of one for your subject matter (and it does not already mention your book), write and request to be considered in the next revision.

A new trend has taken hold in homes and bookstores from coast to coast. This is where monthly **book club meetings** are held where from eight to eighteen participants discuss that month's book. These avid readers enjoy the critique sessions—where authors occasionally appear. (Give you any ideas?) According to publishing industry sources, books can be "made" by little brush fires of enthusiasm breaking out in living rooms, bookstores, and libraries around the country. Virginia Valentine, fiction buyer at the Tattered Cover in Denver, advises 125 such groups.

One other way we found to move individual copies of books is to **set up drop-ship arrangements**. In this situation someone else—perhaps a newsletter editor, organization, or magazine—advertises or recommends your book at full retail price. When the promoter receives orders, it deducts a percentage and sends you the order plus a check and a mailing label. You ship the book directly to the customer. Discounts usually range from 30 to 50 percent. Only books of $10 or more are practical to merchandise this way, however.

Having written a book and become an expert, there may be another track open to you. Have you ever thought of **becoming a consultant**? This is simply another way of selling information, only instead of relying on the written word, you work in person—or via e-mail, UPS, FedEx, fax, phone, or teleseminars. While this isn't applicable to all authors and books, it may be a service that will open new horizons for you. Orchestrating a consulting service is challenging and fun. It can also be very profitable.

As an expert, other opportunities sometimes arise—especially if you've groomed your business to attract them. While promoting *Country Bound!* we learned of the Center for the New West. The *Chicago Tribune* calls it "A Denver-based think tank that advocates innovative approaches to solving economic problems." During an intensive meeting with several of the institute's staff, President Phil Burgess invited us to become Senior Fellows of the Center. He felt our *Country Bound!* message complemented the center's thrust. (Burgess coined the term "lone eagle" to denote a professional who uses modern communications technology to live and work virtually anywhere.) Our affiliation as Senior Fellows with the Center for the New West gives us additional credibility.

The Junior League of Houston also believes in strategic alliances . . . with a different spin, however. The group teamed with the city's largest grocery store chain, Randalls, to promote the League's cookbook, *Stop and Smell the Rosemary*. The grocery chain received a tasteful thank-you in the front of the book—and the ladies received marketing valued at $57,000 in return! It consisted of more than a half-million grocery bags with a recipe and order phone number, radio tag lines, ads in the *Houston Chronicle* and the grocer's circular, plus in-store promotions to sell the book.

One mystery author had a Volvo automobile play a large role in the book's story. This led to the book being displayed and sold in Volvo dealerships.

As you can see, there are dozens of innovative strategies for making money on your book. Perhaps you will want to play with one of the ideas we've presented here. Or maybe you will simply use these concepts to trigger something else. In either event, it will be an exciting adventure as you reach farther out into the world and shape your own destiny.

Another possible outlet for growth awaits in the fields of speaking and trade shows. Let's go on now to the next chapter and discover how to dip your toe in these plentiful waters.

Web Sites, Wisdom, and Whimsey

Associations have enormous potential. Seven out of ten people belong to an association. But where do you find out about these organizations? Well, you could head to the library and consult the three-volume *Encyclopedia of Associations*. (It's too expensive for most publishers to consider purchasing.) Another alternative is the *National Trade and Professional Associations of the United States*. It covers 7,500 associations, professional societies, and labor unions—and is indexed in several helpful ways. You can also go online and do a search by entering the subject you want plus the keyword "association." Happy prospecting.

* * *

Be perpetually prepared to pitch. Do you carry product samples, plus brochures or catalogs in your briefcase, purse, or trunk? If not, start now. Be ready to pitch your book, show it off, and make a sale anytime, anywhere, to anyone! Also make it easy for consumers to buy. To simplify the sales process, offer your customers various payment options. When you accept credit cards or offer layaway or time-payment programs on expensive books or kits, you remove a barrier to making a purchase. This also lets customers take advantage of specials on seasonal books even if they don't have the available funds.

* * *

Sometimes you can't win for losing: The tycoon Andrew Carnegie financed a promotion to spell all words phonetically. His opponents then started spelling his name Androo Karnage.

* * *

Looking to place your book in catalogs? Then you'll be interested in this Web portal that works like a catalog department store. It has about 700 catalogs listed with automatic links to their sites. Another 2,000 are included with good contact information but no links. By going to www.CatalogCity.com, you can quickly access Harry and David, Neiman Marcus, and Hammacher Schlemmer, not to mention thousands of others. Product categories include books (yes!), cars, clothing, computers, entertainment, food and drink, gardening, health and beauty, hobbies and crafts, home, home office and small business, kids' place, lifestyles, music, pets, sports, and travel. A search here can yield many catalogs that might carry your book.

∗ ∗ ∗

Reach National Park Visitor Centers. The National Park Service has an extensive Web site, ParkNet, at www.nps.gov. It includes a park index. By clicking on Visit Your Parks, you can then search by theme. To experiment, we entered "airplanes" and "marine life." Both come up with many links to potential sales outlets. Surf over and see what you can come up with. Since regional and state park locations are also identified, this would be an ideal source to pinpoint places to merchandise field guides and other appropriately targeted regional titles.

∗ ∗ ∗

Premium sales are big sales. When approaching a possible buyer, think of yourself as such a terrific salesperson you could sell* Brides *magazine to Zsa Zsa Gabor.

∗ ∗ ∗

Consider these facts from the gift book segment. A recently conducted study by the NPD Group, a market research company specializing in consumer purchasing and behavior, found that almost half of all books bought as gifts are purchased during the fall: 44 percent were bought in September, October, or November. (It seems by December much gift book buying is already finished.) Wonder what the average amount paid for a gift book was? According to the study, $14.09 when bought at a chain bookstore.

∗ ∗ ∗

Think out of the box. What you lack in money you can make up for with moxie.

20 *Seminars, Classes, and Trade Shows Can Multiply Your Profits*

The meek may inherit the earth, but they don't sell many books. The lecture circuit is a natural for certain authors. Here we look at lectures and readings, talk about seminars and classes, and discuss how to develop a free author tour. We also peek behind the scenes at trade shows and book fairs—and explore how they can help you sell more products.

Giving Talks and Seminars

As an author you are an expert on your subject. People will be anxious to hear your opinions or of your work. Giving lectures and readings is one way to promote a book. It's gratifying for the ego, lets you meet interesting folks, and—when done selectively—sells books.

Any writer can find speaking engagements at church groups, the Y, PTAs, civic groups, libraries, women's clubs, professional organizations, adult educational institutions, or senior centers. You might also consider giving in-store demonstrations if your subject matter lends itself to a commercial tie-in. Constantly have your antenna out for possibilities to plant yourself in the midst of potential customers. The more specialized, the better. Sometimes, these contacts take a long time to develop, but when they ripen, look out!

Early in the history of our book on leisure, we decided it would make an ideal reference for retirement planning. Since this is the bailiwick of Action for Independent Maturity, we shot promotional letters, phone calls, and copies of the book off to the group's headquarters. To make a long story short, Marilyn was asked to serve as a resource authority on "meaningful use of leisure" at a regional conference. Since representatives from many Fortune 500 companies were there to learn how to organize preretirement planning programs in their firms, it was a perfect source of leads for bulk sales.

To maximize your exposure, here are a few dos and don'ts. If sales are your goal, it's a waste of time to talk about a specific subject (organic gardening) with a small general audience (the XYZ auxiliary). The few who would be passionately interested in your topic aren't worth the effort.

Be selective and accept only those engagements for highly specialized audiences or large groups where there is more likelihood that a reasonable number of sales will be generated. For instance, Marilyn spoke at a retreat for recreation majors, presenting a special education session for the California and Pacific Southwest Recreation and Park Conference. She also addressed a large audience at a College of the Emeriti lecture series.

Two of her invitations arrived out of the blue from people who had read *Creative Loafing* or had heard about her through our publicity campaign. One was instigated by a discreet phone call placed to the conference coordinator, alerting her to an authority in the field of leisure who could make a contribution to the delegates' insights. Marilyn received a complimentary pass to the conference (allowing her to mingle with the three thousand attendees anytime during the four days). The engagement was accepted on the condition that our book be displayed and sold, and promotional materials be made available.

Be sure to go armed with sales materials whenever you speak. Fliers with self-contained order blanks work well. If you are donating your time, don't hesitate to pass out literature, or at the very least have it available at tables. Some authors even manage to get fliers tucked into the next membership mailing. Naturally, you will have a case of books with you—and lots more in your vehicle. Display several of them. If you accept credit cards, don't forget to take the machine, order slips, and table sign. Of course, you'll need to take some change along. To avoid the difficulty of making loose change, many authors figure any sales tax (if selling in their home states), then round off to the nearest dollar to keep things simple. Some authors give a small discount—perhaps 10 percent—to induce immediate sales. In any event, be sure to weave into your presentation that *personally autographed* books will be available afterward. It's also wise to show the book a couple of times as you speak.

Before talking, find out what kind of turf you will be playing on. Who will the audience be: men or women? What is their average age? Educational level? Will it be a cozy group of two dozen or an auditorium of seven hundred? Also, give the setup person the arrangements input from your end. Do you want a blackboard or flip chart? Slide projector? Would a wireless lavaliere mike give you more freedom for delivering your message? Professional speakers usually provide the persons introducing them with written introductions. This makes sure your credits are given correctly and starts you off with the expert status you deserve.

After the talk, ask the introducer to announce something like, "The speaker will be in the back of the room to autograph books." This reminder is a good sales stimulator. People who have enjoyed your talk will want to take something of you home, and your book satisfies that desire. Appropriately enough, this is known as "back of the room sales." Many authors have sold thousands of books this way; some professional speakers make more from their back of the room sales than they do from their lecture fees!

Establishing good communication at the early stages with your sponsor and the person introducing you yields a smooth presentation. Make each occasion a performance. Soon your fame will spread, and paid engagements will be coming your way. (Not to mention hordes of single-copy book sales.)

If you feel more comfortable in a classroom setting, you're in luck. There are adult learning centers all over the United States and Canada seeking experts (you!) on an expansive range of topics. Find out who schedules classes at your local community colleges or universities and what they pay. There are many privately owned extended studies or adult education facilities, as well. These folks are especially open to your selling books at your classes. Check the yellow pages to locate nearby possibilities.

Schools and libraries sometimes have budgets and enjoy bringing in speaker-authors. Vicki Cobb specializes in children's books and does many fun school performances designed to get kids interested in science. She has used her Web site to increase her lecture bookings by 30 percent over the past five years, not to mention driving sales for her sixty-plus books. "An author's appearance," says Cobb "makes books come alive." It shows kids that authors are real people and gets the youth motivated to read.

Ann Cooper, with whom we shared the platform when we spoke to the Society of Children's Book Writers & Illustrators, gave a wonderful taste of what she does in schools. Cooper, who has spoken to groups of only eight clear up to full auditoriums, feels the schools value what you do more if you ask for a fee. She applies a "Robin Hood" formula, charging less for schools in less affluent neighborhoods. Her fees range from $100 to $150 for a performance, or sometimes she does three classrooms in a day and charges $300. This dynamic lady has written a Wonder Series of books for children ages eight to twelve that offers a wild variety of activities kids can enjoy as they explore the natural history and folklore of such critters as bats, owls, and eagles. Her other books are for younger readers (grades K–4) and deal with ecosystems, including the forest, seashore, and desert.

Her most popular performance is about bats, and she comes in full regalia.

Cooper arrives with an entourage of puppets, props, and costumes that entrance the youngsters. Many times the teachers will presell the books for her. But she doesn't want any child to feel left out, so for those whose parents don't buy books, she signs a bookmark for them.

Because library patrons are automatically book lovers, they make fantastic audiences, too. And you'd be surprised at how many libraries have budgets to bring in authors. Once you've made positive connections, find out if they will allow you to sell your own books, or will bring in a retail bookstore, or will have their Friends of the Library do it as fund-raisers. (You, of course, prefer the first option.)

One tip a library guest lecturer suggested to us was to inquire if the library intended to videotape the program. If the answer is yes, you're in luck. You want a second master of that tape and permission to use it as a promotional tool and to sell it (in markets that don't compete with the library). Also keep this in mind for any speaking engagement. It's a perfect way to get a new product for nothing!

Gail Savitz, author of *The Kidney Stones Handbook*, tells of doing a forty-five-minute talk for a public library that turned into a one-and-a-half hour marathon with an extremely active Q&A session. Sixty people attended and many flooded the back of the room sale table when it was over. To help with promotion, the librarian made fliers on official letterhead and had them available at the checkout desk of two libraries for a month before the event.

A wonderful training ground for the novice is Toastmasters International. It has more than six thousand clubs around the country where you can get over your jitters. Call (949) 858-8255 or go online to www.Toastmasters.org.

If you're serious about joining the ranks of those paid to speak, join the National Speakers Association (NSA) as soon as you're eligible. It has three dynamite meetings a year where you can learn more in a couple of days than you'd ever imagine. NSA also has a monthly magazine, educational audio/CD-ROM program, and regional chapters. The dues are high—and so are the rewards for the dedicated. Contact NSA at 1500 S. Priest Dr., Tempe, AZ 85281, (480) 968-2552, www.nsaspeaker.org.

If your talk is of interest to the business community or has an important local news angle, you may be able to get even more mileage. Professional lecturers often provide the media with copies of their speeches. These should be typed, double-spaced, word-for-word texts of your addresses. (No, you don't have to stick to it exactly when you actually talk—in fact, please don't. The text is a guide, not a shackle.) Be sure your name, phone number, Web site, and the name of the group you are addressing, plus the date and time of the talk, appear on the first page of all copies. It's a nice touch to also include a head-shot photograph, biographical sketch, and news summary (a brief paragraph giving the basic facts of who, where, what, and why) of your talk.

Many who are getting rich giving seminars have their "pulling power" because of books. The key to getting students is often a successful book. One Chicago author earned more than $2 million during a five-year span talking about his book's subject: real estate. And 130,000 people have attended Albert Lowry's lectures. He's the author of *How You Can Become Financially Independent by Investing in Real Estate*.

Readings for the Literary Inclined

If you are a poet or novelist, there are many prime candidates for sharing your message through readings. All sorts of places sponsor such events. You could give a reading at a library, community center, church, or bookstore. University programs also sponsor such activities, as do museums and literary coffeehouses and bars.

Poets & Writers, in conjunction with the Literature Program of the New York State Council on the Arts, serves as a clearinghouse for such events in New York State. In one year the organization was instrumental in 471 writers receiving over $200,000 in fees from readings and workshops.

Bruce Sievers is billed as "An American in love with his country." Sievers is a poet who has produced patriotic booklets and tapes. He is also a showman. If a nonprofit organization pays his travel and hotel expenses, he will put on a presentation free of charge in exchange for the right to sell his materials. And sell them he does. Sievers makes $200,000 a year merchandising his poetry this way.

Be sure there are quantities of books in the local bookstores. We often hear horror stories from writers published by the major trade houses. Many times when they give special lectures or appear for the media, there are no books available in the stores. This is self-defeating.

How to Develop a Free Author Tour

We have to be honest with you: It's much harder to get on shows than it was ten or twenty years ago. At first we thought we'd lost our touch. But it isn't just us; it's an industry-wide enigma. *Publishers Weekly* noted that the bloom is off the rose for author tours: "Supply in excess of demand, too many similar books, and increased local emphasis are making radio and TV stations less receptive than they were." Publicists everywhere are complaining that authors have become a tough sell. Part of the problem is that everybody is competing for the same shows with the same kinds of books—stuff on nutrition, diets, and dollars.

And there's been such a spate of books by film and music celebrities, sports figures, and CEOs lately that the average author has slim pickings.

However, Becky Barker, who wrote and published *Answers*—a three-ring binder full of forms dealing with family, financial, property, insurance, and business issues—struck a vein of gold in national media. Her book came out of a tragedy. Barker's husband was killed, and she didn't know where to find any vital papers or information. She duplicated 20 copies of *Answers* for Christmas gifts, printed 1,000 in November of the next year, and soon went back for printings totaling 50,000.

Barker has appeared on *Good Morning America*, *Hour Magazine*, and *Donahue*. *Good Morning America* had her back for a second time, as the response to her first appearance was one of the largest the show had ever received. What's the secret of her success? "They really liked the book. It was a different concept," she says. Barker had two friends who volunteered to contact the media for her. While they are poised and powerful women, she mainly attributes her acceptance by such top-notch shows to the unusual content of her book. Which goes to prove if you choose your subject carefully, first-rate things can happen!

Funding Your Tour

So if you have a worthy subject, you may decide to put together a package of information that will provide an author tour with expenses prepaid. Impossible? Not really. We did it and you can, too.

After recognizing that we needed to reach people all over the nation through mass-media promotion, a strange sensation set in: fear. How could we afford to go truckin' all over the country to reach the media outlets we needed to promote *Creative Loafing*? Obviously, we would have to sell something. But what? Tom vetoed the house, Marilyn balked at losing her car, and our four teenagers refused to cooperate by working twelve-hour days to fund the operation. This was a time for serious thinking.

What would create funds to offset expenses? Book sales would certainly be a factor. Sure enough, a publicity tour could be paid for by book sales. But one problem becomes immediately apparent. Books are typically sold on credit. While it would be nice to start getting checks after we got home, there is no front money in such an arrangement.

How about selling information? No, not another book—a seminar! After several months of developing a program, securing mailing lists, and designing and printing brochures, we were ready to hit the road. That was the birth of the How to Get Successfully Published conference program. We typically offered a writers' workshop in the evening from seven to ten, then a self-publishing session the next day from ten until four. People could attend one or both. Here again, we offered the option of using credit cards to make it easy to partake.

For the next few months we roared around the country giving eleven sets of seminars and consulting with authors and self-publishers on an individual basis in most cities. At each stop Marilyn plugged *Creative Loafing* on TV, radio, and in newspapers. It was like running for the presidency—a very stressful time! But we were in a hurry; we wanted to get back and write *The Encyclopedia of Self-Publishing*. As it turned out, we became wiser in the process. Things that didn't work were jettisoned for those that did. We reworked and refined the tour and thus shared what was learned.

To be sure, there are other ways to fund author tours besides teaching writing and publishing. You wrote a book; it must be on a subject you're knowledgeable about. As an expert who has authored a book, why not give seminars or lectures to teach others that expertise? (And if you just can't stomach the idea of getting up in front of a bunch of people, you might use your author tour to do article or book research and interview national authorities for a future writing project.)

Some organizations will pick up the tab for travel and accommodations, as well as pay you a fee, in return for your giving presentations to their groups. The previous section gave tips on how to get started in public speaking. As you refine your speaking skills, you'll find the professional lecture circuit exciting and lucrative. One definite advantage of this method over the seminar loop is that *you* don't have to worry about facilities, advertising, scheduling, and coordination. The sponsor is responsible for all the details. You just show up, do your thing, get paid, and go about promoting your book.

There is much to be said for this approach. We presented two seminars at *Folio*'s Face-to-Face Publishing Conference in New York: one on Special Sales Opportunities for Book Publishers; the other on Buying the Right Computer for Book Publishers. It was much easier to just walk in and give a presentation than it would have been to set up and promote the whole thing ourselves. Today we travel all over the country speaking at writers' conferences and publishing events. We're hired by colleges and universities, associations, and regional organizations. Naturally, we always sell our books, too.

Of course, with your own seminar the earning potential is greater. Even after spending up to 50 percent on expenses, a $50 seminar with fifty people nets $1,250. For a $100 admission fee it would cost you about 40 percent for expenses, yielding a net of $3,000. What you can charge depends a lot on your topic. If you have unique information that appeals to the business community, executives will pay hundreds of dollars for it. On the other hand, if your audience is homemakers, the admission fee must be much smaller. There's one consolation, though: America has a lot more homemakers than executives.

And author-publisher Beverly Nye certainly knows how to appeal to this group. To promote *A Family Raised on Sunshine*, Nye bought a thirty-day Greyhound bus ticket and visited the five cities where she had previously lived. Working with Mormon church groups and home-extension classes, she brought audiences together for homemaking lectures. Each time she finished, more than half of those present purchased her book. In a month's time, Nye sold 1,500 books. She also made money from the admission fees.

Self-Sponsored Seminar Strategy

There is no question about seminars being big business. They generate somewhere over $200 million each year in North America. And putting on seminars is a legitimate business expense, so everything is tax-deductible. (But that doesn't mean you can't have a wonderful visit with Aunt Minnie while in Chicago or renew an old friendship with Mark while doing Los Angeles.)

Here are a few specific suggestions: It works well if you have a liaison assisting in each city. You can often find an enthusiastic helper by contacting other members of a national organization to which you belong. Reward this person with a small commission on seminar sales. The local can provide inside information on how to publicize your seminar, help arrange suitable meeting rooms, and assist during the actual function. Another thing we've used to build attendance is setting up referral fees with key people in various cities. If you know others in your field who would have good contacts with people who could benefit from attending your seminar, let them in on the action. Everyone benefits this way. Pay the people finder's fees of so much per head.

Be sure to arrive at least an hour early at the hotel where the seminar is scheduled. Go over everything you need with the meeting coordinator (a list should have been provided by mail earlier). Be sure the lecturn setup is to your liking; that microphones and audiovisual aids are in place. Always ask for water, for both yourself and participants. If the seminar will run long, it's gracious to arrange for coffee, tea, and soft drinks for attendees. Bring name tags with you so people can get acquainted. At some seminars the networking opportunities prove as valuable as the information dispensed. Get your books, ordering literature, and other paraphernalia set up. For display purposes many self-publishers have posters made of blowups of their book covers. Kinko's does this, or check the online companies listed in this chapter's Web Sites, Wisdom, and Whimsey.

Regardless of what tack you take, a PR and advertising campaign is needed to promote your product—you. Seminars are advertised by direct-marketing techniques. (Refer to chapter seventeen for details.) If you choose the lecture circuit, create a package that consists of a cover letter and promotional material, plus testimonials emphasizing your speaking prowess. This can be sent to the list of lecture agents that appears in *LMP*. Or you can create your own specialized list by finding appropriate organizations in *National Trade and Professional Associations of the United States* or *The Encyclopedia of Associations*.

As with most other programs, it's best to start at home and let the ripple of success carry you farther and farther. After the seminars or lectures prove themselves in your own backyard, try neighboring areas. Schedule a couple of sessions in nearby cities within driving distance to keep costs down. Then begin working your way farther from camp. You can eventually cover the country from border to border and coast to coast.

Well, now we have succeeded in designing your program and exploring how you can take the show on the road. But don't forget your most important cargo. The point of this endeavor was to create a big clamor about your book. So let's tend to the matter of setting up the media package for your tour.

In previous chapters we shared how to create marketing plan lists and approach newspapers, radio, and television media—plus the Internet. Those methods hold true for a tour as well as a local area. Check comprehensive radio and television directories that give complete station information, network affiliation, audience profile, and the names of staff and special programs—in short, all the information you could possibly need to select programs for your campaign and tour.

Review all your information sources carefully, and build your mailing lists for the stations and programs you want to hit on your tour. Follow the procedures shared previously. And ask the organizations for which you're speaking if they have lists of media outlets. Many do. (If they are nonprofits, explore working with them on Public Service Announcements.) Or you might contact the phone company to get yellow pages for the cities on your route, or call the chamber of commerce to see if it has a local media list. Assuming you're working at least six weeks out, you may want to start with e-mail, then follow-up via fax and then telephone.

Once you've got your tour set, there are some ways you can make your life easier: In many major cities there are now people who function as publicity escorts. For a couple of hundred dollars a day, they shuttle authors to media appearances. While that may sound like a lot, consider what's involved if you have to rent a car, study maps, wrestle with traffic, allow for getting lost—and still arrive fresh and composed. If you want to use such an escort service, contact the chamber of commerce for referrals in cities you'll be visiting.

As you begin to put the author tour pieces together, leave yourself plenty of time. You'll want to schedule farther in advance than for local coverage. Tours are not for everyone; yet they can be lucrative and fun under the right circumstances.

Working Conventions, Trade Shows, and Book Fairs

A form of advertising that may make sense is to exhibit your book at strategic specialized trade shows and book festivals. The two biggest general conventions of interest to book publishers are BookExpo America, affectionately dubbed the BEA, and the American Library Association (ALA) conference.

The BEA has the largest English-language book show in the world. In addition to featuring some fifteen hundred exhibits, there are daily book and author breakfasts, autographing sessions, and many parties. The convention typically occurs around Memorial Day weekend. If you don't want the expense and commitment of having a booth, which is a huge outlay for a self-publisher, you can learn a great deal by going as a spectator. Nowhere can you put your finger any closer to the pulse of book publishing. Nor are there many places where you can come home with such a haul of free books, catalogs, buttons, tote bags, pens, and any number of invitations to unusual promotional events. It's a wild, giddy whirl—but also a place to make valuable contacts. Editors come out from behind their closed doors for the BEA; so do key marketing people. Using patience and persistence, a self-publisher with a track record could well snag a reprint sale here.

Selling at Special Interest Trade Shows

It might be wise to attend or exhibit at conventions directly related to your product. This is called vertical marketing and can be extremely effective. There are trade associations to match your book subject matter, and most of them sponsor at least one big meeting a year. To find out whom to contact, again consult *National Trade and Professional Associations of the United States* or *Encyclopedia of Associations* or go online and use a search engine to find upcoming shows. Book sales can be brisk when you're in the heart of a large gathering attuned to your subject.

Judy Galbraith of Free Spirit Publishing finds associations a fertile field for selling self-help books for kids. Each year her press attends more than a dozen major meetings of special interest groups that attract teachers, youth counselors, mental health professionals, and others. Two staples in her marketing mix are the National Association for Gifted Children and the National Middle School. Says Galbraith, "People buy on the spot, or they place orders."

Cyndi Duncan and Georgie Patrick have been in publishing for eleven years and have authored six titles. They love topic-specific trade shows because they can find new business avenues, make sales, and get immediate cash flow. Since they specialize in cookbooks, shows in the food/kitchen/gourmet area are their target. Depending on your subject material, the outdoor/sports shows might hold more promise for you. Trade shows can be expensive, so consider sharing a booth if it is allowed. (Having a booth mate also allows you to spell each other and get out and work the show, plus offer each other motivation and encouragement.) Costs include booth fees, furnishings rentals, electricity, meals, hotel or motel, gas, travel, and parking.

Also consider events within your geographic area. Coloradans Duncan and Patrick say, "Shows like Mountains and Plains Booksellers Association or the Colorado Library Conference are excellent for obtaining holiday orders and networking with wholesalers, reps, bookstore owners, and library buyers." These two publishers make it a practice to offer samples made from recipes in their cookbooks to get people to their booth.

Checklist for Trade Shows Exhibitors

- 10′ × 10′ booth (or table and chairs will be provided for smaller shows)
- Rental of furnishings, electricity, and carpet (not needed for small shows)
- Display racks, backboard, or actual booth setup
- Books
- Cover posters
- Promotional materials: business cards, fliers, bookmarks, price sheets, extra covers
- Miscellaneous: wastebasket, paper towels, general office supplies
- Drinking water, refreshments, breath freshener
- Copy of booth rental agreement and furnishings
- Plane tickets or maps
- Hotel reservation

Attending Genre Conferences for Fiction Writers

If you write fiction, you should be attending the genre conferences applicable to the type of novels you write. There are special annual gatherings for mystery writers, those who do romance, and writers of science fiction/fantasy, to mention a few. Find out when yours is, and register early to attend. This is a fabulous place to meet editors who might review your book, to rub elbows with best-selling authors in the genre, and to learn tricks and techniques to make you a better writer and book seller. (If you hope to speak on a panel, throw your hat in the ring early; these assignments are typically made four to six months before the event.)

Connie Shelton is a great believer in genre conferences. She began as a client of ours with her first mystery, *Deadly Gamble*, and it was gung ho from there. A lot of what she learned was from contacts and information gleaned at genre events. Shelton not only published her own subsequent mysteries but brought other good writers under her imprint, Intrigue Press. After she reached almost thirty titles, she sold her successful publishing company to give her more time to write.

Scouting the Book Fairs

Book fairs are less structured, regional events that give you a reasonably priced opportunity to sell books by renting a table. Here you can also get to know other authors and publishers, compare notes on the small-press industry, and hear a diverse group of guest authors talking about their craft and giving readings.

There's the annual New York Is Book Country fair, during which Fifth Avenue is closed to traffic to allow exhibitors to create a generous pedestrian mall. The three-day event features a storytelling area, an auction for such things as book memorabilia, and cooking lessons from a cookbook author. (Some great ideas here for a self-publishing organization to work with.)

Book fairs are not the sole province of New York, however; many flourish in other locales. Some thirty book festivals dot the country from Nashville, Tennessee, to Denver, Colorado. And Canada also has annual or biannual small-press fairs in Toronto, Edinburgh, London, Quebec, and Vancouver.

The Miami Book Fair International has emerged as a world-class literary gathering. For eight days in November, it brings together readers, authors, and publishers for a celebration of all things literary. A virtual city of books takes residence in downtown Miami. More than three hundred exhibitors attract thousands of patrons.

Around the country, festivals are raising the visibility of books. Book fairs have sprung up in Boston, New Orleans, San Francisco, and Milwaukee over the years. Spring 2001 book festivals are scheduled for San Diego (The Latino Book & Family Festival), Oklahoma City (Invitational Cowboy Poetry Gathering), Charlottesville, Virginia (Virginia Festival of the Book), as well as at least seven other locations. So when you are deciding how to allocate your advertising budget, don't overlook exhibits, trade shows, and book fairs. They can be an interesting merchandising tool and provide wonderful networking opportunities.

But suppose you have a book with a great track record. And maybe you need to generate a chunk of cash to do the *next* book. Is there a viable option? You bet. In the next chapter, we scrutinize selling your self-published book to a major publisher.

Web Sites, Wisdom, and Whimsey

Shop at online poster suppliers. While this list isn't intended to be exhaustive, here are three companies who make custom posters. Their prices typically range from $25 (no laminating or mounting) to $60 for a 24″ × 36″ poster made from an electronic file. Check out their prices and specifications for yourself. Contact PostersPLUS at www.wemakeposters.com, (937) 312-9396; Signs and Stripes at www.signsandstripes.com, (800) 406-6553; and Big Color Prints at www.bigcolorprints.com, (800) 697-4670.

* * *

When you're standing in front of a microphone, silence—
unlike the Retriever—is **not** *golden.*

* * *

Take another person to your speeches. It's tough to sell books, autograph them, and visit with members of the audience all at once. Your sales will go up if you have a helper along who can actually sell the products while you are signing them or answering questions relating to your talk.

* * *

Make your trade show booth more appealing. If you can afford it, illumination can increase visual pulling power by 50 percent or more. Of course you not only have to pay for the spotlights but also an extra fee to bring electricity to your booth. Also be aware that square tables and counters can act as barriers that separate you from your prospect.

* * *

Try this unusual promotional ploy for traveling authors. While at the airport, request that an announcement be made for [your name], author of [your book title], call . . ."

* * *

New service matches speakers with libraries. LibraryHQ.com has added a service to its Web site called Speaker Source. Authors listed in the database provide their own brief descriptions of topics, qualifications, and requirements, which include locations (will you travel anywhere?) and costs (do you require just travel expenses or an honorarium, as well?). You can sign up here to share your expertise, and librarians can search for specific topics or browse the whole database. Visit www.libraryhq.com, or call (877) 401-9535 for more information.

Trade show resource is available. For a full list of all U.S. trade shows, consult the *Tradeshow Week Data Book*. Some libraries will carry, it or you can check with the publisher at (800) 375-4212 or investigate online at www.tradeshowweek.com.

PART VII

Propelling Your Business Through the Stratosphere

21 *Bagging the Big Game: Selling Your Self-Published Book to a Goliath Publisher*

Here you are—a self-publisher with a proven book. You don't have to fear getting a rejection that goes something like: "What you've submitted is both good and original. Unfortunately, what's good isn't original, and what's original isn't good." Reviews have been favorable, sales are brisk, and you'd like to turn control of this baby over to someone else.

Or perhaps you're already a trade-published author. You've gotten your rights back on a book that languished under the treatment it received, and you've self-published it and successfully turned it around. What now? In these cases, many authors elect to allow the giants on Publisher's Row to take over their books (again) . . . for a price. They want to cash in by selling out.

Here we explore how to go on safari for the right publisher. Then we'll talk about maximizing that relationship. The fine art of negotiating will be unmasked, as will tips for getting your share—and more—of available marketing dollars. While our comments are directed primarily to self-publishers, authors aspiring to win trade contracts for their manuscripts will find valuable and seldom-disclosed gems here to help them bag real trophy deals.

Insider's Sources for Finding the Right Publisher

If you're like most writers, you have little idea of how to select the most likely publishing houses. A marvelous insider's source available for locating who publishes what is *Publisher's Trade List Annual* (*PTLA*). It is a compilation of catalogs and paid advertising from virtually every major American publisher. Could you ask for a better place to browse for ideal publishing candidates? It's like judging a talent contest. How amazing this prime resource for author-publishers remains such a well-kept secret.

That this book is relatively unknown may be because it is typically housed in the Acquisitions department of libraries rather than out in the public stacks. You will need to request permission to go into the order department and peruse it there. Or perhaps a large bookstore will let you use its copy. By noticing the type of books each publisher puts out, you will soon become sensitive to who produces titles that are in the same category as your work. (Scanning the subject guide to *Books In Print* will also yield this type of information.)

If you find a house that has a book very similar to yours, steer clear. It won't want to compete with itself. On the other hand, if a publisher has books in the same general subject area but none quite like yours, it might be a very good prospect. Clearly, the publisher is interested in the subject and might well be looking for another book to add to its present titles. Also, note the quality of the house's book catalog. Is it professionally designed or hokey? Is it easy to read and well organized? Does the information on each book make it sound appealing and interesting? Overall, does the catalog have, to your eye, that indefinable but necessary quality, *style*? Your book would probably reflect the same level of quality if this company published it. Studying *PTLA* is also a super way to tune into emerging trends. If, page after page, there are titles dealing with the occult, holistic healing, or historical novels, you are finding the pulse of what is currently selling.

If your book is nonfiction, there is another unorthodox place to look for publishing leads. Go to Amazon.com and check the best-seller lists. Notice which publishers have books out in your subject area, and who has recently released titles. Also talk to librarians. They know a lot about various publishers. They can tell you, for example, who keeps books in print the longest and who specializes in what type of books. Independent bookstore owners, managers, and buyers are an additional cherished source of who's who in the publishing industry. And by perusing a large bookstore, you can check out the current crop of books.

Check out *Writer's Market*, *LMP*, and Jeff Herman's *Writer's Guide to Book Editors, Publishers, and Literary Agents*. These are valuable resources. Each of them carries a subject index to publishers, so you can build a further list by researching these sources. After you've squeezed out leads for about a dozen houses, call their toll-free numbers or send notes to Customer Service requesting their most recent catalogs so you can keep abreast of their upcoming titles. Also check listings in the three above references to learn specifics, such as the names of appropriate editors and the numbers of titles their houses publish each year. This pinpoints their size.

And don't overlook the spring and fall "announcement" issues of *Publishers Weekly*. Here you'll find a hefty collection of the titles publishers are proudest of, not to mention page upon page of advertisements that hold more clues. To further help solve the mystery, talk with other authors and self-publishers, and ask for recommendations and past experiences. You can often track down an author via *Contemporary Authors* listings and other writers' directories or by reading their bios and calling information in their cities of residence to get phone numbers.

The five megapublishers are Random House, Simon & Schuster, HarperCollins, Penguin Putnam, and Warner/Little Brown. A selection of mass-market paperback houses includes Bantam Doubleday Dell, Ballantine, Berkley, Tor Books, Zebra Books, and others. Consider what kind of treatment you and your book want. As the large firms are absorbed by conglomerates, they become increasingly preoccupied with "name" authors. They introduce so many titles each season that an unknown writer can easily get left at the starting gate.

Perhaps you'd be happier joining one of the smaller publishing houses. Ten Speed Press, for instance, is an aggressive smaller publisher, yet it has had a book on the national best-seller lists almost half of the years it's been in existence. There are trade-offs either way. You'll usually get more personalized attention at a smaller house, but a big one may have greater national distribution.

There is still another possibility, especially if your book has merit but not much commercial appeal. Literary small presses, publish from two to twenty books a year, encourage artists who write poetry or alternative fiction, or handle avant-garde subjects. You can find their requirements listed in *The International Directory of Little Magazines and Small Presses*.

Let us assume you will be taking the initiative and contacting potential trade publishers yourself, rather than having an agent represent you. Here are some significant pointers.

Launching a Compelling Sales Campaign

OK, you've identified a dozen or so publishers who seem likely targets for your book. Do you approach choice number one, then sit back with your fingers, toes, and eyes crossed? Never! Use a shotgun technique and spread the word to all of them at once. Nothing succeeds like excess.

It is far too costly for a writer-publisher to waste months—or even years—waiting for one publisher after another to pass judgment. If the book deals with a timely subject, this is plain suicide. Seven weeks is the average report time, but three months isn't unusual. Multiple submissions are the only businesslike approach to take. It is a courtesy, however, to tell your prospects you are submitting to more than one publisher.

We recommend sending a proposal with a carefully crafted sales letter to the prospects on your list. Your cover letter had better be gussied up just right if it's to catch the perfect suitor. This must be your *best* writing.

The more precisely and dynamically you communicate, the better your chances of establishing a rewarding relationship. After all, this letter is your sales representative. Its job is to get editors excited about your title. A good proposal will separate you from the deadly "slush pile" or "over the transom" categories. Refresh your writing skills by reviewing chapter five. Speak in specifics. Cut. Tighten. Pare. The idea is to wed you to a very sweet contract. This could be the most profitable thing you ever write! It would be wise to have the whole package professionally edited before it hits the mails.

Before sending it off, call each publisher and get the correct name and spelling for the editor responsible for your type of book. This is important. Otherwise, your material will end up in a slush pile for some junior reader to evaluate. By calling ahead and talking with the appropriate editors, or their secretaries, you make sure your message goes to the right people.

One day a few weeks—or months—later, your phone will ring. It will be so-and-so from XYZ Publishing Company. Bells ring. Whistles toot. Your mouth gets dry. Your eyes mist. It has finally happened! A major trade publisher is interested in your book! There are few natural highs more exhilarating. Somehow you'll muddle through the conversation. Now your really big guns go into action.

Negotiating Contracts in Your *Best Interest*

Chances are if one publisher thinks you have a good book, others will, too. For that reason we feel you should exercise a bit of caution. When one of these publishers comes back and says she or he wants to buy your book, *never, never* agree to anything over the phone. Ask for the offer in writing. And as soon as you've hung up the telephone, get your list of those who haven't already rejected the book and give them a call. You might say something like, "We've had positive reactions from other interested publishers but no response from you regarding our book. Thought we'd just touch base to be sure that wasn't an oversight before we make a final decision on whom to place the book with." This guarantees you won't miss out because the package was inadvertently set aside or misdelivered.

Here are some preliminary questions to ask your potential goliath publisher:

- How many copies do you typically print in the first run of this type book?
- What price would my book sell for?

Reprint Rights Letter

Linda Price
BANTAM BOOKS
666 Fifth Ave.
New York, NY 10103

Dear Ms. Price, RE: REPRINT RIGHTS

Are you aware that six of the ten leading causes of death in the U.S. have been linked to our diet? Yet we have only to learn what, and how, to eat to provide our bodies with all the essential maintenance and repair materials to sustain—or restore—ourselves to good health. This is the theme of a very successful title called *The UnCook Book: Raw Food Adventures to a New Health High*. Originally published in early 1981, this book has gone into three printings with only a limited promotional budget and word-of-mouth recommendations. We are currently accepting bids for reprint rights on this book.

Ironically, the authors of *The UnCook Book* are the "Bakers." Elizabeth and Dr. Elton Baker—both in their seventies—are living testimony that their concepts work! He is a doctor, a trained chemist, and a past advisor to the National Institute of Nutrition in Bogota, Columbia. She cured herself of cancer of the colon and has done extensive nutritional research, writing, consulting, and lecturing. Their unique combination of the academic and the practical yields a detailed and thorough, yet very readable book.

Disregarding the old adage, "Ignorance is bliss," the Bakers set out to educate the public on the potential health hazards in much of the food on the market today. Touching on such topics as what foods to buy and where to buy them, how to learn what things are good for you, combining foods for proper digestion, how to sprout and grow seeds and grains, tips to cut your grocery bill, body language tests to detect personal food allergies, and how to gather foods in the wild, they cover every aspect necessary for implementing a healthy way of life. Additionally, the book describes ways to pack nourishing and satisfying workday lunches and what to do when traveling and eating out.

The last half of this guide is devoted to delicious recipes developed through experimentation and creativity. By feasting on such delectable dishes as Brazil Nut Louie, Raisin Carrot Bread, Asparagus a-la-king, Salad of the Sun, and Banana Date Pudding, a person doesn't even feel like sacrifices have been made by giving up traditional harmful processed foods. But this is more than a cookbook. More than a manual for America's seven million vegetarians. It's a step-by-step guide to well-being and long life . . . complete with charts, tables and extensive vitamin and mineral data.

Should you be the publisher to obtain reprint rights of *The UnCook Book*, you would have two articulate and very promotable authors. Elizabeth and Elton are at home in all media. They've appeared on the Michael Jackson Show and Stacie Hunt's syndicated radio program. Elizabeth's raw food demonstrations delighted audiences on *Sun-Up* in San Diego and *Wake Up Houston* in Texas. This dynamic couple were featured speakers at the National Health Federation's annual convention the last two years and have been invited to participate in a world-wide speaking tour planned for this fall.

In great demand by health food stores, *The UnCook Book* is one of Nutribooks best sellers. This $5.95, 238-page trade paperback is carried in many physician's offices, by catalog houses, small press distributors, and by a worldwide health clinic. One especially rewarding aspect of *The UnCook Book* is its extremely low return history. Virtually everyone who carries this title reorders it.

By no means limited to vegetarians, *The UnCook Book* will appeal to all readers interested in learning more about good health and nutrition. Please contact me for an examination copy if you'd like to be considered as a reprint house for this exciting title.

Sincerely,

Marilyn Ross

Marilyn Ross
MR:sdw
encl.

Here is a sample query letter designed to pitch to paperback publishers who might want to pick up rights to a successfully self-published book.

The Art of Fabulous Proposal Writing

Let's look at how to create a package that really wows editors! This is a formula that has worked for us. This package was sent to thirteen major houses. Four responded, and at one point, we were negotiating with two of these for purchase of reprint rights. Your cover letter goes on the front of a cardboard presentation folder containing the full proposal.

- **A brief cover letter.** While there is no pat formula for successful letters, a good one always gets off to a full gallop with a catchy lead that makes it clear why you are writing. After you've hooked the editor's interest, briefly recount the book's sales history. Include a short paragraph about your special qualifications for writing this book. If you have appeared on strategic TV or radio shows, mention them. Do you give seminars or lecture professionally? Say so. Author promotability is a key factor in signing up books. Also be sure to note why readers are interested in this book. Is the topic timely or the slant unusual? You may want to present it over the signature of the pseudonym you use for promotion so you can more gracefully say favorable things about yourself and your book.
- **The need and potential markets for the book.** Do the work for the editors! By using actual statistics to quantify your market, you build a more dramatic case. "Ten million four hundred thousand farmers" means more than "millions of farmers."
- **A selling handle.** Include twenty to thirty sizzling, benefit-laden words that capture the special essence of your book.
- **Your unique selling proposition.** What sets you apart? Tell about your book's specialness, plus the general tone and scope.
- **Your intended promotional involvement.** Editors know, as well as you do, that *authors* sell books. Describe the participation you will have. Mention any noteworthy personal or professional contacts you have who might be helpful in promoting the book. Perhaps you became friendly with an authority who assisted in the research or wrote the foreword. The publishers' marketing departments would like to know of this. They will also be interested in what channels of distribution you've opened. No doubt you've established contacts they can pick up to add to their own marketing emphasis. It's also a good idea to stress subsidiary rights potential. Are you a speaker who will want to buy thousands of books over a period of time? That will *really* interest them.
- **A powerful author bio.** Parade every credential you have! Now is not the time to be bashful. Make publishers aware of why you are uniquely qualified to address this subject at this time.
- **Special features.** What additional characteristics make this book unique? Are there photos, illustrations, checklists, tables, action tips? (As a way of "branding" our work, we've used the "Web Sites, Wisdom, and Whimsey" technique on our last three books.)
- **Supportive materials.** Include copies of reviews—lots of them—so the editors sense a groundswell of interest about this title. Put the reviews from prime sources on top. Include complimentary fan letters, copies of large orders, articles by and about the author, anything that gives the project credibility.
- **The competition.** Know your competition. What other books are in print on the same subject? How does yours differ? Why is it likely to have long-range sales potential? Research what else is out there, read the top three, and tell how yours is better. Make it easy for them!
- **A copy of the book.**

- Would it be hardcover, trade paperback, or mass-market paperback?
- How long do your books in this genre usually stay in print?
- What amount would you anticipate budgeting to promote my book? (For hardcovers, conventional publishers allocate $1 per book, so if they publish 30,000 copies, expect them to spend $30,000.)
- What royalties are you offering for the manuscript? Standard rates for hardcover are 10 percent on the first 5,000 copies sold, 12½ percent on the next 5,000, and 15 percent thereafter. On mass paperbacks it is 4 to 8 percent on the first 150,000 and a bit more thereafter. These same lower rates are common for children's books and school texts. Trade paperbacks usually bring 10 percent on the first 20,000 copies, 12½ percent up to 40,000, then 15 percent thereafter.) However, we believe you deserve more than a standard rate. You've removed all the risk, done the packaging, and established a market. You're not just an author with hat in hand. You have leverage.
- Are royalties based on the retail price or on the discounted (net) sales price? It's greatly to your advantage to have them based on the full retail price. Unfortunately, this practice is dwindling. You give away a big chunk if they are determined by the discounted amount.

In most cases you will be given an advance against future royalties. The Authors Guild notes that on original manuscript sales (not proven self-published books) the average advance is $5,000. Of course, to arrive at this "average," remember some writers get only a couple of hundred dollars while big names capture advances of several hundred thousand or more.

Advances work this way: Typically, you receive one-half of the advance on acceptance of your book and signing of the contract, the other half when the revised and/or expanded edition is accepted. Another procedure used by some houses pays you in three increments: on signing, upon acceptance of the revised manuscript, and upon publication.

How much might you expect? Carla Emery, who self-published *Old Fashioned Recipe Book*—and sold 70,000 copies herself—allowed Bantam's feisty rooster to take over the book for a cool $115,000 cash advance. That is unusually high. Most such advances run under $10,000. The reason for this? We feel most self-publishers are not knowledgeable on *how* to negotiate a more favorable contract. They take what's offered and are humbly grateful. Hogwash! You sweat blood and tears to turn out a quality book, then market it effectively. You deserve to be justly rewarded. But don't blame the publisher if you settle for too little. In the publisher's shoes you'd handle things the same way.

The advance should cover all the time, work, and financial risk you've borne, plus give you a hefty profit. If it isn't considerably more than you can make continuing to sell the book, why are you doing it? Ask for two or three times the production cost plus 10 percent of projected sales. Insist that it be royalty inclusive. This means you get the money up front instead of months and months after the books are sold. Ideally you'll sell only the North American rights to the *book trade*. That way you retain the ability to work everything else.

Joe Sabah and Judy Sabah have mixed feelings about selling their *How to Get the Job You Really Want—and Get Employers to Call You*. As you may recall, they sold books phenomenally well month in and month out via radio phoner interviews. The $25,000 advance they got from E.P. Dutton was an appealing lump sum, and the fact their book was wanted was indeed flattering. But then they'd have no ongoing cash flow until the advance earned out. And the first royalty statement revealed Dutton's sales were a disappointment.

So be sure you *want* to release the rights to your baby to someone else. Not every author should. A case in point is Bernard Kamoroff and his *Small Time Operator*. "Bear" wouldn't think of parting with his book. It has topped sales of 600,000 copies, has built-in obsolescence, and keeps him in a comfortable lifestyle.

We had an interesting experience concerning a book we wrote, published, and promoted to success. After a long courtship we finally had our chosen publisher committed to wanting the book. Before ever sitting down at the negotiation table, the two of us had discussed the project and determined what we felt would be a fair advance. After talking face-to-face with the editor in chief, however, it seemed our ideas of its value were far apart.

But Tom is an excellent negotiator. He believes that if both parties sincerely want to reach an agreement, something positive is bound to develop. He talked some more, this time including marketing and management personnel, constantly selling them on the idea of the book's track record and potential. They were reminded that we are promotable authors who would participate actively in book marketing. They compromised. We compromised. To make a long story short, he ended up securing the largest five-figure advance the company had ever given—over twice the original offer!

A good mental attitude is paramount to a productive negotiating session. If you go in expecting to sign a contract that is in the best interests of all concerned, that's most likely what will happen. Good negotiators strive to develop rapport; they are open, informed, and flexible communicators.

Remember, as you discuss various points with editors, some things are high priorities for them and some low. Try to match your high priorities with their low ones, and vice versa. That way no one is forced to give up things each considers vitally important. If each side yields on issues of lesser concern, everyone benefits. Know ahead of time what you want . . . and what you *must* have.

Both parties to a negotiation should come out with some needs satisfied. Be open to alternate solutions. We also felt the royalty percentage was unacceptable in the above situation and proposed a different one. This proved unworkable for the publishers. But the publisher in turn suggested another approach—which ultimately met *our* bottom-line goal—and everybody was happy.

Of course, advances and royalties are not the only aspects that warrant mediation. There are many other points—some of great significance—that should be considered.

Let's take a close look at the things you want included in (or omitted from) your book contract. The information we share has been gleaned from personal experience and research, plus interviews with authors who learned after the fact what they should have done to protect themselves. That is not to insinuate that publishers are vultures waiting to pounce on unsuspecting prey. But, as in any business, their standard contracts are slanted toward their own best interests.

One important consideration is the book's actual publication date. The contract should stipulate that the book must be published within one year after acceptance. Otherwise, a sloppy house could take forever to get your work out to the public—and you have only the original one-half of the advance. On a more perverse level, it has happened that a book was bought by a publisher solely to keep it *out* of circulation because it directly competed with one of the house's other titles. Because the unsuspecting author didn't cover this point in the contract, the publisher was able to sit on the manuscript indefinitely.

Insist on getting at *least* a 60 percent discount off the retail price on your own personal book purchases. That way you can continue to profitably sell individual copies, maintain drop-ship arrangements you may have established, take a quantity along when you lecture, and service nontraditional outlets. Reserve for yourself key special sales you may have developed, such as gift shops, health food stores, gourmet stores, or sporting goods outlets.

When Bill Byham sold *Zapp!*, his agent not only negotiated a lofty $275,000 advance from Crown, she also retained a very strategic right for his consulting firm, Development Dimensions International (DDI). She didn't worry about dickering for a good buyback arrangement. Virginia Barber took a different approach to getting books for DDI's resale. It simply pays production costs to join Crown's print runs! That way DDI gets extremely low unit costs on printing and can sell to its customers from its own supply of books. Byham has virtually all the advantages he had as a self-publisher—except he's now $275,000 richer and has the clout of a major publisher to get books in bookstores and generate publicity. This is the savvy way to work this business.

Free copies are another point for consideration. The usual amount is ten. But if you're going to help promote the book and send review copies to important contacts, ten copies won't go anywhere. Twenty-five or fifty is much more like it.

Be sure that book sales on the second (or subsequent) edition start where the previous edition left off. In other words, don't let them reset the counter at zero and thus keep you in the lower royalty range instead of picking up at 10,001 or whatever number is appropriate.

Seek the return of all rights if the book goes out of print and the publisher declines to reprint it within a reasonable period. As you know, excellent books sometimes die because they are not properly marketed. If this should happen to yours, you can always climb on the bandwagon again and breathe fresh life into it—if the rights revert to you. With the e-books and POD of our electronic age, however, that can be tricky. What constitutes "out of print"? Our most recent contract says, "The Work shall not be deemed in print merely because it is stored in a system that can produce hardcover or paperback copies directly from digital form, or because it can be produced through any other print-on-demand method."

Also, should your publisher decide to remainder or destroy the remaining copies of your book, you want the right of first refusal on the remaining stock. What a great way to acquire books for a fraction of what it cost to manufacture them! Also try to add a provision that allows you to have the electronic files so additional books can be printed inexpensively.

Mail-order rights are something else you want to rally for. While few trade houses will grant you these exclusively, most will be happy to let you sell single copies of the new edition of your book through the mail. If you ask. Especially if you're a speaker, it's also important to retain audio and video rights. Don't be surprised if you're expected to refrain from selling copies of an old identical self-published edition once the new trade edition is out.

Electronic rights are an area where publishers are seeking great control and latitude these days. Reserve as much as possible! No one knows what this will encompass a few years from now.

Warranties and indemnities have to do with such things as the work's constituting no infringement of another's copyright, not being libelous, not misrepresenting facts, and so forth. This provision helps protect the publisher from lawsuits and typically puts all the financial responsibility on your shoulders, with little of the say-so. It is a clause that must be read very carefully. You may succeed in winning some changes, such as the author's having to give his consent regarding defense and settlement. Also insist that the clause refer to a "proven" breach. While most publishers won't sit still for much revision here, it is ideal to at least get the wording changed to the effect that "if the defendants do win, the publisher will pay at least half the cost of defense." On that point we simply wish you luck.

Some publishing contracts also stipulate that a reserve to cover returns will be withheld from royalties. Since you are selling a proven book, this seems an unnecessary withholding of money due. Something else you should insist on is that the copyright be in *your* name. Most reputable publishers do this as standard procedure.

Remember, too, that you can negotiate the schedule of payment for the advance. We try to get the bulk of it up front if we're creating a revised product, as that is where all our time is spent. If it is a two-pay advance, suggest a 75/25 split (and be ready to settle for 60/40). In a three-pay go for 50/25/25. One bit of strategy that may help you achieve more front money is to remind the publisher you will supply negatives (or computer disks if this is preferable). By providing these, you cut the production costs dramatically. The publisher should be willing to put part of that money in your pocket.

Many contracts contain a clause stating that the publisher has the first option on your next work. This is called the Right of First Refusal. Think carefully about this. Suppose you run into editorial or promotional snags with this house and find it doesn't give you a fair shake. Wouldn't it be too bad to automatically have to give this company first dibs on your next book? The negotiators may be rather hard-nosed about giving up on this point. If they get a good author under contract, it is sound business practice for them to attach some strings to that author. Try to get out from under this requirement.

In your public library or county law library, there's a volume rich with information. Called *Entertainment, Publishing and the Arts Handbook* and edited by John David Viera, this masterpiece contains sample contracts and explanations of all sorts of legal documents relevant to publishing.

How are publishers going to react to your assertiveness in wanting to modify their contracts? As predictably as fleas in a hot skillet. But after they've hopped around a bit—if our experience is typical—many of the things you want will be accommodated. Don't be afraid to stand up for your rights because you are a fledgling writer-publisher. Use chutzpah! Don't sell out too cheap. If a company wants your book, it will be open to compromise. There is nothing subversive about trying to strike the very best deal possible. Simply use your self-publishing knowledge to work with trade publishers. You're in a much better position than the average author to comprehend publishers' problems and to help find solutions acceptable to both sides.

Getting Your Share of the Marketing Dollar

We're all familiar with the old adage "The squeaky wheel gets the grease." It was never more true than in the publishing industry. According to *Publishers Weekly*, there are some 53,000 books published each year—and many feel the number will more than double with e-publishing. One out of 53,000 isn't very good odds. So it's up to you to make sure your book gets noticed. Oh, we know, that's the publisher's job. But if you want your books to move into people's homes rather than into a remainder dealer's warehouse, you have to squeak often and loudly. You want to keep publicity and sales personnel focusing on your book's case.

You might say this to the publicist: "I know you have many books to work on. I have just my own and I have experience and expertise, so let's work together. I plan to do . . ." Make the publicist your ally rather than your antagonist.

Ironically, one of the things you will probably need to do is hound the publisher to get books into the bookstores. It is especially disappointing when you are giving a lecture, doing a reading, or appearing on television and the local bookstores don't have books. You should alert the publisher in a positive rather than a derogatory way, however. Call and tactfully say that someone inadvertently overlooked stocking the bookstores in such and such town—as opposed to demanding, "Why are there no books available?"

Your publisher's marketing campaign can really be lots of fun. It's simply a matter of being imaginative about getting your book noticed within the house—then within the world. Judith McQuown, author of *Inc. Yourself: How to Profit by Setting Up Your Own Corporation*, decided that a button saying "Inc. Yourself" would be an attention getter. So she called around and got some bids. She then passed the information along to Macmillan, who ordered the buttons. They were such a sensation around the offices—keeping everyone stirred up about her title—that the sub rights people sold the book to five book clubs and ordered another press run before it even reached its official publication date. McQuown was creative. She was also smart. She made it easy for the promoters to go along with her idea by doing the legwork and handing them a ready-made gimmick.

Shortly after signing your contract, you will be sent an Author Questionnaire to fill out. Be as complete as possible and return it promptly. This information is used by the promotion department in several ways. And be sure to point out any new professional or personal contacts you've made in the field who may be willing to say something nice about the book.

But perhaps giving up the rights to Goliath is a deplorable thought. In fact, you want to jump into this publishing adventure with all four feet, be a conquering David, and even publish the works of others. Then read on, friend; advice for enlarging your kingdom awaits.

Web Sites, Wisdom, and Whimsey

Author finds another way to present proposals. When Leslie Morgenstein wanted to gain the attention of publishers for his proposal on a series tentatively titled Gossip Girls, he took to the Internet. Morgenstein sent his proposal via e-mail, then suggested publishers could click his Web site where details of the series are posted. New technology keeps giving us new options.

* * *

Editor: I like your book all except the ending.
Writer: What's wrong with the ending?
Editor: It should be a lot closer to the beginning.

* * *

Do you *really* want to sell out? If you're a niche publisher with a successful book, that book can become a stepping stone to recognition for your company. It helps you get known to your target audience. If you sell the rights, you have money in hand but lose the ability to trade on this success. So if you envision building your presence as a publisher (which we discuss in the next chapter), let your successful book pull others along with it.

* * *

Thank you for sending me a copy of your book. I'll waste no time in reading it.

* * *

A cabby takes poetic license. Marc Anthony Butcher, a Manhattan taxi driver, has a rotating captive audience for selling his book of poetry titled *Before the Divorce, Read This!* When someone jumps into his cab, he asks if he could get the rider's opinion on a poem he wrote, then offers "When You Love Someone . . . Really Love!" which is printed on ivory-colored card stock. Does it work? Last we heard he had sold more than 11,000 copies of his book at $5 each . . . and 10,700 copies of the $2 poetic greeting card. If you want something badly enough, there are amazing ways of getting it!

* * *

Worrying does not empty tomorrow of its troubles,
it empties today of its strength.

22 *Enlarge Your Kingdom: Move Up to "Small Press" Status*

According to a joint study of the Book Industry Study Group and Publishers Marketing Association, 53,000 independent publishers account for $14.3 billion in annual book sales. The role of the small presses is rapidly changing. They are more adventurous, quicker, and more flexible than their large counterparts. And they are on the cutting edge of publishing today, employing tactical marketing techniques and applying the latest technology. Precisely 2,542 presses responded to the fourteen-question survey, revealing that 80.76 percent had annual book sales of under $100,000. While this isn't a fabulous amount, many of these presses are new one- or two-person operations.

Good Growing Pains

Perhaps your destiny lies here: printing revised editions of your title, writing and publishing more books in your niche, or growing from self-publisher status to producing the works of other writers. In all of these cases, there are things to consider.

When you are ready to go back to the printer for a second edition, it's time to celebrate. You've obviously done something, or a lot of somethings, right! You probably weren't lucky, but plucky. Before you turn over your book to the manufacturer, determine whether it should be revised or expanded. Extensive revisions open fresh doors for promotion.

By using the same book manufacturer, you can save part of the initial setup costs. You will want to make some alterations to the copyright page of the book.

It should read: "Second printing" and the year. Perhaps it makes sense to redo the cover to include good reviews.

You might take a leaf out of Greg Godek's book (well, not literally). After his *1001 Ways to Be Romantic* sold 1.5 million copies, the classic book on creating romantic relationships underwent a complete revision, redesign, and expansion. The result is an Author's Annotated Edition that's deeper, funnier, and bigger than the wildly successful original book.

Next he invited readers of *1001 Ways* to submit their favorite romantic ideas and stories. Then he came out with a sequel containing the best of these notions, crediting contributors by name. This technique builds loyalty, gets contributors to buy the book for friends and relatives, and encourages new readers to submit ideas for a *third* book. People love these little gems.

Stephen Covey used the same brilliant method to prolong the life of his franchise: He lets his readers do it for him. *Living the Seven Habits: Stories of Courage and Inspiration* is a collection of stories from readers of his earlier Seven Habits books. Covey simply sandwiches the anecdotes between brief introductory setups and a few paragraphs of closing comments.

Author-speaker Sam Horn says, "One of the best lessons I've learned is the value of adding a page at the back of our book asking readers to get in touch to share success stories. This is a personal note to readers letting them know we enjoy hearing feedback." Horn advises to be sure to include your e-mail address and Web site URL when asking people to submit challenging scenarios they would like to see featured in future books. Besides many U.S. replies, responses came from a fifteen-year-old boy in Singapore, a hotel manager in India, a man from Toronto, and a psychologist from Argentina. Lots of global appeal there for a subsequent book!

Do you perhaps have a sequel in the making? Novelists often end their fiction in such a way as to entice readers into the next books. If you've done a regional travel guide, perhaps you can replicate it in other cities.

Additional books of your own needn't necessarily be on different subjects. The author of *Life Extension*, Durk Pearson, filled his original book with complicated and scientific articles. And it sold over a million copies. Then he did a second edition for the layperson. Adapted for the average reader, it took the same information but slanted it to a less sophisticated reading audience. Same book, two ways. Just another route to experiencing happy growing pains. Also consider disseminating your information in audio, video, or computer formats.

Bottom line: if a subject works, repackage the material and broaden the potential audience. That's one strategy that helped build New Harbinger into a multimillion-dollar business. It likes to "vertically integrate" by publishing a series of books on a topic, each designed for a different segment of the market. On the subject of panic attacks, for instance, New Harbinger did a serious textbook-type book aimed at grad students, a fairly clinical self-help book, then a lighter point-of-sale gift book. The publisher also takes workbook-type information and produces video- or audiotape companions. It's found that audios sell between one-fifth and one-sixth the number of companion books, while videos generate about one-tenth of the book's sales.

A high-priced newsletter may be another natural evolution. After all, you're *the expert* on the subject. With readers clamoring for more information, a quarterly or monthly newsletter to keep them up-to-date might make a lot of sense, especially if you have a good database of previous book buyers. If you are seriously considering launching such a profit center, subscribing to *The Newsletter on Newsletters* will provide you with a world of expert advice on the subject. (Of course, once you have a few titles, you may want to consider a newsletter you *give away* as a promotional tool. That's what Intrigue Press does. It prints a classy four-page, two-color job called *The Web of Intrigue* and uses it to introduce new books to booksellers and to the press's list of mystery fans.)

Various Tips and Techniques for Thriving

There are several things to consider if you plan on enlarging your kingdom. First, you need a block of one hundred ISBNs rather than the smaller list of ten. If your vision is to have several titles, plus produce them in various formats, ten numbers simply won't do. You are also perceived more seriously by the powers that be if you have the one hundred series, which is easily identified from the tens by those in the know.

Once you start publishing books by other authors, you qualify for Cataloging in Publication (CIP). It's a separate Library of Congress service that supplies additional numbers to be printed on the copyright page of the book. These numbers help libraries quickly shelve your books in the correct categories. Here again perception comes into play. You appear more established and bigger when using CIP. Additionally, a whole array of libraries at home and abroad buy sight unseen all books in certain categories after the CIP database is released.

If you've progressed to the point where you're producing three titles a year, get your press listed in *The Book Buyer's Manual*, *LMP*, *Publishers Directory*, *Writer's Market*, and *Publishers, Distributors and Wholesales of the United States*. (Addresses are in *LMP*.)

The *ABA Book Buyer's Handbook* is used by bookstores. The ABA sponsors a program called STOP (Single Title Order Plan). By getting listed in the handbook, you make it easy for bookstores to order single books from you. If you participate, however, expect to give a discount on individual copy orders, perhaps

20 percent. Here's how it works: The bookstore sends you a specially designed order form and a check, typically restricted to a given maximum amount. You complete the check and fill the order; there's no further paperwork involved. The ABA has a new requirement, however, that a publisher must have seven titles to be listed in the handbook, but anyone can participate in STOP.

As you grow, be careful not to get personnel heavy. The Huenefeld Report on independent publishing noted that those publishers that got the most productivity from a small staff were the most profitable. Let machinery and technology do the work wherever possible. Or consider using interns as we discussed previously.

At this point, you may also want to invest in industry-specific software, rather than something like QuickBooks, to handle your accounting functions. As your business builds, the specific publishing needs become increasingly significant. Things like royalty payments, consignment distribution sales and inventory tracing, and sales reps commissions may become considerations. There are three affordable industry-specific programs useful for small presses. They range in price from $199 to $495. Check them out:

- Myrlyn from Fat Boys Software, www.myrlyn.com, (919) 773-2080
- Publishers' Assistant from Upper Access, www.pubassist.com, (800) 310-8716
- Pub123 from Adams-Blake Company, www.adams-blake.com, (916) 962-9296

When you begin to branch out and accept manuscripts from other authors, the playing field tends to skew a bit. You must choose not only a great manuscript but also a promotable author who will be proactive. Grill these supposedly relentless promoters, lest they turn into couch-potato wimps.

And yet independent presses are in an enviable position today. Many good midlist authors who were welcomed at the doors of Publisher's Row in New York only five years ago are now homeless. These people understand the industry, can produce strong books, and recognize they must be involved in promotion. They are ideal candidates for a small press willing to nurture their work and appreciate them personally.

Let us talk a bit about sales reps. With several books on your list, you become much more appealing to them. If you do enter into such an arrangement, treat these people like gold. Get face-to-face and develop a relationship with them. This adds a personal touch to all future communication. Invite them to lunch, find out their birthdays and send personal cards, take a true interest in their lives. And keep them informed about all exciting developments so they can use this as ammunition when making sales calls.

You may want to consider using reading discussion groups as a marketing tool.

These are groups of people who meet in bookstores, living rooms, libraries, and campus unions to discuss books. What books? Usually fiction—including genre fiction, the classics, and short story collections—but also biographies and memoirs, spiritual topics, current affairs, and sociopolitical essays. If your book is selected, you'll sell dozens at a time to each group. Since 1995, Donna Paz and Mark Kaufman have produced an annual publication called *Reading Group Choices: Selections for Lively Book Discussions*. It is a promotional resource you can buy into. For information, call (800) 260-8605 or go to www.readinggroupchoices.com.

On a different front, don't overlook your own mailing list as a money-making possibility. Once it reaches five thousand names, you can rent (not sell) your own in-house list of book purchasers, Web site visitors, e-mail newsletter subscribers, or other valued information. Expect to earn from $70 to $120 per 1,000 names for onetime use. If you're in search of Midas, this is a sure way to turn your list to gold. As we said before, it's a good idea to "seed" it with a name and address that will reach you so it is immediately apparent if someone misuses your trust and tries to recycle the names more than the one time they were rented for.

And if the time should come that you want to sell your company, we suggest you contact Stephen Kerr at Business Marketing Consultants. He knows publishing inside out and specializes in selling publishing houses. Reach him in California at (760) 942-1002 or via the Web at www.bizmark.net.

The Winning Combination: Niche Publishing and Backlist Books

It's a lot easier to be successful in this business if your books center around one or two themes. This is called niche publishing. You do books on parenting, gardening, sex, art, or produce novels in one specific genre, such as mysteries. Then once you've found your market, and how to reach it, you don't have to repeat that process with each new book. Your marketing contacts can be recycled over and over again, and you begin to build relationships, which is the core of strong sales potential.

There is a slogan in independent publishing: "Backlist is where the bucks are." And it's true. So think carefully before you accept a manuscript. Will it be obsolete in a year or two? Perhaps you should pass. You want books that have staying power. You really start making money when you go back to press. There are no editing costs, cover development fees, or typesetting expenses. You pay for the printing, discounts, and author's royalty; the rest is profit.

A perfect example of this is Brenda Ponichtera's *Quick and Healthy Recipes and Ideas*. She originally brought it out eleven years ago. Now there is a Volume II

The Seven Habits of Highly Successful Publishers

1. Own your niche. Decide what major subject area you'll publish in, and concentrate on it exclusively. Know all about it. Join relevant associations, subscribe to all the trade journals and newsletters, get to know the movers and shakers in the subject area. Become *the* authority, the place where others turn for trustworthy information.

2. Select highly promotable authors, and treat them as your partners. No one cares as much as they do, probably not even you. Make sure they can function articulately with the media. Use their contacts, their expertise, their enthusiasm. Give them a deep discount on purchasing their own books so they can resell them at a profit. Keep them in the loop. Tell them promptly about great reviews and important book clubs or special sales. Encourage them not only at the manuscript stage but throughout the life of the book. Their passion and energy make them their books' best salespeople.

3. Cultivate word of mouth. Getting a buzz started—people talking about the book—is the result you desire. Do it by soliciting advance blurbs, getting reviews *everywhere*, tenaciously pursuing feature stories *off* the book pages, giving away tons of free review and reading copies. A complimentary book is your cheapest and most effective advertising.

4. Make it easy. To get people to do what *you* want, make it easy for them to cooperate. Write and typeset a mock review. You'll be amazed how often it comes back as "the" review. Get a toll-free number and merchant status so you can accept credit cards. Put order forms in the back of your books and on your fliers.

5. Ask for what you want. A national magazine contacted us about excerpting our *Big Ideas for Small Service Businesses*. After we negotiated how many words the publication could use and a generous ordering blurb, we asked how much the magazine was offering. The reply? A dollar per word. For years afterward we sold the mag marketing articles based on the book for the same dollar per word—almost $8,000 worth.

6. Apply the 80/20 rule. You'll get 80 percent of your PR results (or orders) from 20 percent of your efforts (or customers). Determine who these biggies are, and concentrate your efforts on them. In 1980, we were helping a client with a raw food cookbook. We determined the book needed to be in health food stores. Yet the distributor's buyer turned it down flat. So we romanced this guy with tearsheets of reviews and copies of large purchase orders stamped "This order could be coming to *you*!" He finally bought a case out of self-defense. That book become the distributor's best-seller and launched a publishing empire for our client.

7. Follow up, follow up, *follow up*. It has been proven to us repeatedly that perseverence equals profits. When we were trying to sell *Country Bound!* to *Mother Earth News* magazine for its back-of-the-book catalog, nothing seemed to move the publication off dead center. Finally—on the fifth phone call—the buyer grabbed the book off a stack, examined it, and gave us a hefty purchase order over the phone. It sold into that market for years afterward.

and both are doing well. Her challenge is to constantly keep coming up with new and different angles on the same subject, something editors and talk show hosts will see as timely and current. She makes sure she doesn't date her book so it remains a backlist all-star.

The Internet is a real blessing for backlist books. Web sites are not nearly as touchy about reviewing older books as are some print media. And there are tons of niche-specific sites looking for content. You might do Internet radio, Webcasts, or online chats. Search for fan sites. There are many ways to reinvent backlist titles and give them new life. Try promoting the authors instead of the books. Or go back to media outlets that initially rejected the books. With typical turnover, there are probably new decision makers in place.

Concentrate on marketing. Today. Tomorrow. Always. Treat your books like soap (a constantly consumed product) not like books (one-shot items). Remember that backlist is where the money is because all the initial production costs are behind you. Keep seeking new review media, virgin opportunities, fresh angles. Moving up to successful small-press status is indeed mission possible!

Web Sites, Wisdom, and Whimsey

When you are young, everybody loves you.
As you grow up and become obnoxious, you must sell yourself.
The same is true for a business. —Ronald K. Law, M.D.

* * *

The sweet taste of success might be yours when you market with chocolate. Now there's a Web site with fifty-five speciality chocolate bars to help you get noticed! The offerings range from chocolate aspirin (tell your prospect/customers how you can give them "relief") to a box of chocolate feet that lend themselves beautifully to "I'm trying to get my foot in the door." What a terrific way to get the attention of a possible premium buyer or key reviewer. Of course, the more traditional "thank-you" bars are ideal for showing your appreciation to a chain buyer, reviewer, or journalist. You can also set up a credit/debit program for $100, which entitles you to twenty-five message bars sent out as you dictate. Then you simply specify the recipient, address, and occasion (congratulations, thank-you, thinking of you, welcome, happy birthday, etc.). And if you want a customized bar, it runs between $150 and $250 to have a mold engraved. For details go to http://chocolatelady.com or call (800) 4-CANDY-3.

* * *

Just when I was getting used to yesterday, along came today.

* * *

Court the major newspapers! The top five U.S. daily newspapers represent a huge circulation. In order, they are *The Wall Street Journal* (1,752,693), *USA Today* (1,671,539), *The New York Times* (1,086,293), *Los Angeles Times* (1,078,186), and *The Washington Post* (763,305).

* * *

Don't you just love shopping carts with attitude? You know, the ones that have one wheel that goes in the opposite direction. We small presses sometimes need 'tude, too. Just make it count when you use it, baby!

* * *

Beware—you could end up with a permanent, lengthy *negative* review at the top of your Amazon.com's book description. As you may know, new reviews push down older ones on this online bookseller's site. There are two exceptions, however: reviews from *The Industry Standard* and *Kirkus Reviews.* Amazon has a contract with both that requires the site to post and leave these reviews at the very top. If you get a good review, great. But what if you are the victim of a lengthy negative review? We know one professional writer who has to live with a commentary of more than a thousand words trashing her book (in spite of a dozen favorable reviews). It's virtually the first thing anyone sees, having pushed the book's description, publisher comments, and author comments to the bottom—even onto another click-through page! This, in spite of the fact all other reviews must be limited to a maximum of *twenty words.* One solution? Maybe not submit your books for review to either *Kirkus* or *Industry Standard.* The chance of catching a grumpy reviewer on an off day might be too dangerous.

* * *

Beginning is half done.

PUTTING IT ALL TOGETHER

Congratulations on sticking with this material to the end. After reading this book, if you've chosen to publish one of your own, you know you're in for a challenge—and lots of work—and lots of fun.

For most of us the process starts out as an idea, then ripens into a dream. It takes hold of our lives, dictates how we spend our time, compels us to capture our thoughts on paper, and tests our ingenuity in a hundred different ways. But dreams are the cartilage and muscle that make humanity strong. Suppose Edison hadn't been dedicated to his purpose? And what if Madame Curie had not been a woman of vision? Capturer of two Nobel Prizes, she is credited with isolating pure radium and discovering radioactivity. Humankind dreamed of orbiting the Earth and landing on the moon. Yury Gagarin and Neil Armstrong made those dreams reality. Big dreams beget big accomplishments.

True, few of us are likely to explore the galaxies . . . or expand the boundaries of scientific knowledge. A different adventure awaits us: birthing a book. And it can be the experience of a lifetime! Who is to say our dreams are less vital than the aspirations of people whose names have become household words?

But a dream without action is like a car with no gasoline. It can't go anywhere. To move your book from inception to completion, you must fuel yourself with education and study to conquer the craft of writing and publishing.

The undertaking is complex. The subject matter must be widely appealing—or tightly focused. A snappy title should be created. Sloppy writing sharpened and honed to a fine edge. A myriad of business procedures need to be mastered: pricing, discounts, invoices, licenses, and taxes all clamor to be reckoned with. Unfamiliar numbers and listings must be conquered. The fine points of design and production seem infinite and incomprehensible. Typesetting decisions, paper weights, and binding options pull you in a dozen different directions. You could feel as though you're drowning in a sea of details.

Then one day it all begins to fall into place and you gain a sense of how the whole process fits together. You feel empowered. The mysteries of advertising and promotion begin to clear up. Your news releases find their mark. Requests for review copies arrive each day. A prestigious national magazine asks about serial rights, and an expert reader gives you a great blurb for the cover.

Finally comes "the day." Your books arrive from the printer. The dream has been given form. The Madame Curies and John Glenns have nothing on you! You had a goal and you reached it. And as your publishing venture matures, you'll mastermind merchandising techniques you never thought possible. Thousands of people have done it successfully. So can you.

Yes, we've traveled a long way together with this dream. We hope you feel we've built a relationship—become friends through this book. And as with any friend, we offer you encouragement, wish you luck, and hope you will triumph!

AFTERWORD

We wrote *The Complete Guide to Self-Publishing* out of a sincere desire to help people put their knowledge and their dreams into print. We wanted to write the most comprehensive manual available on the subject. In writing it, we have withheld nothing as our "special secret." We've shared our victories and our disappointments. Of course, growth is a never-ending process. And as our knowledge deepens, this volume will be updated appropriately. (Meanwhile, visit our Web site at www.About-Books.com for the latest news and strategies.)

We'd be delighted to hear from you, our readers, for these future editions. Share your success stories with us. Tell us what chapters were particularly helpful, and give us feedback on how you put these ideas into action. Offer your suggestions for improvement. Let us know what still perplexes you. Although we can't guarantee success, the principles offered here are tried and proven. They work for those who use them. We do extend this warning, however: Be careful . . . if you follow the guidelines set forth in this manual, you could outgrow the status of self-publisher—just as we did. Best of luck. We delight in your achievements, so please send us an autographed copy of "your baby," won't you?

Marilyn and Tom Ross
425 Cedar St.
P.O. Box 1500-G
Buena Vista, CO 81211
Web site: www.About-Books.com
Book information: www.SPANnet.org/cc

SELF-PUBLISHING TIMETABLE

In *The Complete Guide to Self-Publishing* we've tried to stress that for your self-publishing venture to have a good chance of success, you must plan and execute your actions carefully. This timetable will serve as a checklist to help you use your time wisely and do things in the most effective order. (Some of the steps in this timetable will not be clear before reading the book in its entirety.) Not all items apply to every book; use your own judgment. When you need specific details on any point, refer to the index or check the appropriate appendix.

I. Do Immediately

To set yourself up as a self-publisher, you must first "take care of business"—establish yourself as a commercial entity.

1. Read this book completely to glean an overview of this exciting adventure you've embarked upon. Read it through a second time, taking notes or highlighting sections.
2. Start developing a marketing mind-set now!
3. Subscribe to *Publishers Weekly* magazine.
4. Order a copy of *Literary Market Place* from R.R. Bowker.
5. Review the bibliography in this book. Borrow from the library, or purchase appropriate books.
6. Choose your publishing company name. Remember to research to see if it has already been used.
7. Write the Small Business Administration for its publications.
8. Contact Bowker for ABI information and listing forms, plus ISBN information and log sheet.
9. Contact the Chamber of Commerce and discuss local business license requirements, regulations, and procedures.
10. File a fictitious name statement (if required in your area).
11. Obtain a post office box.
12. Have letterhead, envelopes, mailing labels, and business cards printed.
13. Open a business checking account.
14. Obtain your resale tax permit.
15. Write the Library of Congress to get your LCCN.
16. Join SPAN (Small Publishers Association of North America).
17. Review the chapters "Scoping Out a Marketable Subject" and "Product Development: Writing Your Book or Booklet."

II. Do Just After You've Finished Writing Your Book

With manuscript in hand, you're ready to think about the physical aspects of your book: page count, typeface, design, artwork. Also begin thinking about your specific marketing, PR, and distribution strategy.

1. Research your chosen title to see if it has been used already.
2. Get any needed permissions.
3. Wrap up last-minute research and verifications.
4. Ask competent friends or associates to read/critique/edit the manuscript. Revise accordingly.
5. Have the manuscript *professionally* edited; make changes, proofread them.
6. Plan the interior design, and mark the manuscript for typesetting.
7. Gather any interior artwork, such as photographs or illustrations; size them.
8. Write cutlines for interior art and prepare a keyed list, or incorporate them in computer text.
9. Prepare a castoff to determine preliminary book length and specifications.
10. Get author photo taken.
11. Get *professional help* to design the cover.
12. Request price quotations from manufacturers and typesetters.
13. Determine the tentative retail sales price using our guidelines.
14. Establish your publication date.
15. Photocopy your manuscript and send it out to authorities and key reviewers for advance comments and perhaps a foreword.
16. Assign an ISBN.
17. Complete and submit the ABI form.
18. Complete and submit the LCCN form.
19. Typeset your book or send it to a designer/typesetter.
20. Obtain a Bookland EAN Scanning Symbol.

III. Do These Initial Marketing Strategies

At this point, you set up your promotional campaign and attend to the details of book production.

1. Research your Nationwide Marketing Plan. Track down names of reviewers, syndicated columnists, newsletter editors, associations, wholesalers, bookstores, special sales outlets, librarians, subsidiary rights buyers, local

media people. Think up innovative strategies. Prepare labels or envelopes.

2. Write the following promotional materials: news release, sales letter, mock review, customer sales flier.
3. Contact appropriate book clubs and first serial rights buyers you have identified through market research to interest them in subsidiary rights.
4. Test mail-order ads if you're using direct marketing.
5. Prepare a personal mailing list from holiday card recipients, business associates, club membership directories, your Rolodex, database, or other sources.
6. Carefully proofread typeset galleys and have corrections made.
7. Prepare electronic—or camera-ready—copy according to printer specifications.
8. Double-check that all corrections were made accurately and that all pages, illustrations, and book parts are in the correct places.
9. Prepare the index (if applicable).
10. Typeset and proofread index.
11. Send galleys to sources noted in Appendix E.

IV. What to Do While Your Book Is Being Printed

As you continue your promotional efforts, begin implementing your Nationwide Marketing Plan. Get ready for the arrival of your books.

1. Review bluelines carefully for any final corrections.
2. Set up warehousing space and a shipping area, or arrange for outside fulfillment.
3. Order shipping and office supplies.
4. Prepare the following additional materials: acknowledgment card for reviewers, discount schedule, and return policy statement.
5. Implement your Nationwide Marketing Plan.
6. Follow up on book clubs and first serial rights potential buyers.
7. Mail your prepublication offer to your personal mailing list.
8. Write the copyright office for Form TX.
9. Write Dustbooks for listing in its various directories.
10. Implement full-scale mail-order campaign (if applicable).
11. Coordinate freight delivery of books, making sure you'll be there to receive shipment and have payment ready (if needed).
12. Embellish your book detail page on Amazon.com and barnesandnoble.com.

V. Do When Books Arrive

At last: You have books to sell. Your baby has arrived. Now you can begin filling orders and following up on marketing leads. Rejoice!

1. Take an inventory count and open several random cases to be sure books are not scuffed, bound upside down, or otherwise damaged.
2. Photograph book and order 50 to 100 4″ × 5″ black-and-white prints.
3. Fill complimentary copy requests generated by your Nationwide Marketing Plan.
4. Fill advance orders.
5. Pursue prime wholesalers and distributors who have not yet shown interest.
6. Go after second serial rights sales.
7. Implement special sales and innovative promotional ideas.
8. Request the return of pertinent printing materials from your book manufacturer.
9. Complete your copyright registration on form TX.
10. Send a copy of the book to the CIP office.
11. Send a copy of the book to *Cumulative Book Index*.
12. Send a copy of the book to Baker & Taylor.
13. Always carry a copy of the book with you—in your briefcase, handbag, or backpack—and have a case of books in your vehicle.
14. Contact all bookstores in your area.
15. Set up a "revisions" file for noting corrections and new material for subsequent editions.

VI. Do These Ongoing Promotional Activities

A successful self-publisher's work is never done—you'll always be thinking of new ways to sell books. Now's the time to line up print, radio, TV and Internet interviews.

1. Implement special sales and innovative merchandising techniques.
2. Follow up on prime reviewers to be sure they received books.
3. Develop an Available for Interview sheet.
4. Contact local media for interviews and stories.
5. Expand your media focus to include regional print, radio, and TV.
6. Ask enthusiastic readers to write customer reviews for the book at Amazon .com and barnesandnoble.com.
7. Pursue reviews, excerpts, and book sales on various Internet sites.

8. Be constantly on the lookout for new review sources and sales opportunities.
9. Consider giving lectures and/or seminars as promotional vehicles.

VII. Do After a Successful First Printing

Time to decide whether you want to reprint your book or offer it to a trade publisher.

1. Add favorable reviews to the book cover or first page.
2. Revise the copyright page and correct any typos.
3. Revise, update, and/or expand the book as needed.
4. Review the back-page order form for price or other changes.
5. Get reprinting quotes on a second printing or . . .
6. Offer the book to major trade publishers.

In all you do, much success. You can make it happen!

APPENDIX A

Piloting Your Successful Marketing Plan

We've been asked repeatedly to put on paper a realistic and complete marketing plan, so this new dimension has been added to the fourth edition of *The Complete Guide to Self-Publishing* to help you really fly! We hope you find it helpful. Of course, it will need to be modified and embellished to fit the appropriate months of your schedule and particular title. (Note: This plan will not make sense unless you've first read our book.)

January 1: Early Activities

- Solicit advance blurbs.
- Go after book clubs.
- Seek first serial rights sales in magazines.

February 1: The Galley Stage

- Send galleys to the publications that require early copies: *Library Journal*, *Booklist*, *Publishers Weekly*, and other major review sources appropriate to your topic.
- Set up your Web site.
- Do extensive *research* to determine who should learn about this book nationally:
  - Wholesalers/distributors.
  - Libraries.
  - Schools/colleges.
  - General print media: consumer magazines, trade journals, newsletters.
  - Customized print media: consumer magazines, trade journals, newsletters.
  - Newspapers—sections *off* the book pages.
  - Appropriate associations.

March 1: Hurrah—Printed Books in Hand

- Send out comp copies to reviewers, the media, and trade buyers; fill orders.
- Embellish your book pages on Amazon.com and barnesandnoble.com.
- Implement a campaign to contact all the places you researched above.

- Initiate a local publicity program:
  - Arrange book signings.
  - Contact newspapers—both major and smaller area ones.
  - Get on radio shows.
  - Do television.
  - Investigate area nontraditional retail outlets.

April 1: Time to Roll Out More Big Guns (No Foolin')

- Follow up on previous activity.
- Do additional marketing:
  - Do extensive Internet promotion.
  - Get into catalogs.
  - Go after second serial rights sales.
  - Seek premium sales.
  - Investigate speaking or teaching classes.
  - Look into trade show and book fair participation.

May 1: Your "Official" Publication Date

(Any reviews that are going to appear in *Library Journal*, *Booklist*, *or Publishers Weekly* will have done so.)

- Follow up on all previous activity.
- Recycle publicity to get more bang for your buck.
- Pursue major network or syndicated radio shows slanted to your topic.
- Go after major national TV shows that might be appropriate.
- Court nontraditional retail outlets nationwide.
- Consider foreign rights sales.

APPENDIX B

Organizations and Other Information Sources

About Books, Inc.
Attn: Marilyn and Tom Ross, P.O. Box 1500-G, Buena Vista, CO 81211, (719) 395-2459, www.About-Books.com. Our turnkey professional writing, publishing, and marketing service specializes in working with authors, independent publishers, and professionals with expertise to share. Our services cover manuscript critiquing, editing, interior design/typesetting, cover design, and book production. We also develop and implement nationwide marketing and promotional plans. (Cofounded and operated by the authors of this book.)

American Booksellers Association (ABA)
828 S. Broadway, Tarrytown, NY 10591, (800) 637-0037, (914) 591-2665, www.BookWeb.org. A trade association of some 3,800 retail booksellers. ABA sponsors the Book Sense program.

American Library Association (ALA)
50 E. Huron St., Chicago, IL 60611, (800) 545-2433, www.ala.org. The official organization for all libraries. ALA has over 61,000 members.

American Society of Journalists and Authors (ASJA)
1501 Broadway, Suite 302, New York, NY 10036, (212) 997-0947, www.asja.org. A 955-plus nationwide organization of nonfiction writers. ASJA maintains the Writer Referral Service, a listing of writers for hire, which might be helpful.

The Association for Women in Communications (AWC)
780 Ritchie Hwy., Suite 28-S, Severna Park, MD 21146, (410) 544-7442, www.womcom.org. Seeks to improve women's opportunities in the various communication professions. Approximately 7,500 members belong to this organization.

Association of American Publishers (AAP), Inc.
Attn: Small Publishers Group, 71 5th Ave., 2nd Floor, New York, NY 10003-3004, (212) 255-0200, www.publishers.org. The major trade organization of the

publishing industry. Membership is not required to attend either the Annual Meeting for Small and Independent Publishers or the West Coast seminar for beginning self-publishers and growing independent presses.

The Authors Guild
31 E. 28th St., 10th Floor, New York, NY 10016, (212) 563-5904, www.authorsguild.org. Almost 8,500 published professional writers, most with national reputations. Prospective members must meet certain professional publishing criteria to be admitted.

Book Industry Study Group Inc.
P.O. Box 3629, New York, NY 10168, (212) 929-1393, www.bisg.org. Individuals and firms interested in promoting and supporting publishing industry research.

R.R. Bowker
121 Chanlon Rd., New Providence, NJ 07974, (877) 310-7333, www.bowker.com. Provides ABI forms for listings in *Books In Print* and *Forthcoming Books In Print*. Bowker is also the source of ISBN logs and mailing lists. Easy online registration and update at www.bowkerlink.com.

Christian Booksellers Association (CBA)
P.O. Box 62000, Colorado Springs, CO 80962-2000, (800) 252-1950, www.cbaonline.org. Trade association committed to the development and retail distribution of Christian materials, and ethics in business.

National Association of College Stores (NACS)
500 E. Lorain St., Oberlin, OH 44074-1294, (800) 622-7498, www.nacs.org. Trade association for the college store industry with 3,900 members. NACS rents mailing lists refined by region, sales volume, etc. Its *Book Buyer's Manual* lists publishers' information annually.

National Federation of Press Women (NFPW)
P.O. Box 5556, Arlington, VA 22205, (800) 780-2715, www.nfpw.org. Includes writers, editors, and other communication professionals from across the country. NFPW publishes a bimonthly *Agenda* magazine, and has affiliates in most states.

National Mail Order Association, LLC (NMOA)
2807 Polk St., NE, Minneapolis, MN 55418-2954, (612) 788-1673, www.nmoa.org. Offer discounts on books and printing to members. Those who join the

association receive the group's monthly newsletters, *Mail Order Digest*, and the *Washington Newsletter*.

National Speakers Association (NSA)
1500 S. Priest Dr., Tempe, AZ 85281, (480) 968-2552, www.nsaspeaker.org. An association of professional speakers that offers excellent conferences, monthly magazine, networking opportunities.

PEN American Center
568 Broadway, Suite 401, New York, NY 10012-3225, (212) 334-1660, www.pen .org. A fellowship of writers dedicated to advancing the cause of literature and reading in the United States and defending free expression around the world.

Poets & Writers, Inc.
72 Spring St., New York, NY 10012, (212) 226-3586, www.pw.org. Serves as an information center for the U.S. literary community. Poets & Writers publishes several reference guides and a magazine called *Poets & Writers Magazine*, and subsidizes readings and workshops.

Publishers Marketing Association (PMA)
627 Aviation Way, Manhattan Beach, CA 90266, (310) 372-2732, www.pma-online.org. Specializes in cooperative mailing programs and other marketing venues for small presses.

Small Business Administration (SBA)
409 3rd St., SW, Washington, DC 20416, (800) 827-5722, www.sba.gov. Offers general business guidance. The SBA has many free booklets and other inexpensive ones that are helpful to the new entrepreneur.

Small Publishers Association of North America (SPAN)
P.O. Box 1306, 425 Cedar St., Buena Vista, CO 81211, (719) 395-4790, www.SP ANnet.org. Nonprofit trade association founded by the authors of this book. SPAN welcomes authors, self-publishers, and independent presses, and offers a dynamite monthly newsletter, annual college, and many cost-saving member benefits.

Writer's Digest Books
1507 Dana Ave., Cincinnati, OH 45207, (800) 289-0963, www.writersdigest.c om. Publisher of *Writer's Market* and numerous other books useful to writers.

Note: There are also professional associations that invite writers working on specific subjects to join their groups (Mystery Writers of America, Society of American Travel Writers, Society of Children's Book Writers & Illustrators, and many more). You can find information about these specialized groups in *Encyclopedia of Associations*, in writers' magazines, or through word of mouth.

Many small regional organizations have also sprung up for self-publishers, such as the Bay Area Independent Publishers Association, Colorado Independent Publishers Association, and Arizona Book Publishing Association. Or, talk with other authors and small publishers in your vicinity to see if such a group exists—or start one.

APPENDIX C

Canadian Resources

Association of Canadian Publishers (ACP)
110 Eglinton Ave. W., Suite 401, Toronto, Ontario M4R 1A3, (416) 487-6116. A national trade organization representing over 140 Canadian-owned book publishers across the country. Members must have at least ten books in print, and no more than 25 percent of titles authored by principals, directors, or employees.

Book and Periodical Council
192 Spadina Ave., Suite 107, Toronto, Ontario M5T 2C2, (416) 975-9366. An umbrella organization for national book- and magazine-related associations.

Book Promoters Association of Canada (BPAC)
585 Bloor Street West, Toronto, Ontario M6G 1K5, (416) 534-6125, www.bpacanda.org/index.htm. Newsletter, seminars, and workshops for members. Associate membership category is open to those interested in learning more about book promotion. Directory of BPAC Freelance Promoters is available for those seeking professional help.

The Book Trade in Canada
Quill & Quire, 70 The Esplanade, Suite 210, Toronto, Ontario M5E 1R2, (416) 360-0044, www.quillandquire.com/QQBTIC/btic.htm. Annual directory that includes publishers, distributors, booksellers, agencies, suppliers, awards, associations, printers, binders, plus appropriate government agencies. It is the equivalent to the U.S.'s *LMP* and is the standard reference on the Canadian book industry.

Canada's Business and Consumer Site
www.strategis.gc.ca. A government sponsored site whose mission is to build a growing competitive, knowledge-based economy. Find a plethora of business and consumer information here.

Canadian Authors Association (CAA)
P.O. Box 419, Campbelford, Ontario K0L 1L0, (705) 653-0323. Several branches across Canada. CAA publishes *The Canadian Author and Bookman* (a

quarterly writers' magazine) and *The Canadian Writer's Guide*, which is a directory of writers' markets.

Canadian Book Review Annual
44 Charles St. W., Suite 3205, Toronto, Ontario M4Y 1R8, (416) 961-8537, www.interlog.com/~cbra. An annual compilation of bibliographic data and four-hundred-word reviews for every English-language book published in Canada during a calendar year.

Canadian Books in Print
University of Toronto Press, 10 St. Mary's St., Suite 700, Toronto, Ontario M4Y 2W8, (416) 265-1631, www.utpress.utoronto.ca/publishing/index.html. Listings of books currently available.

Canadian Booksellers Association (CBA)
789 Don Mills Rd., Suite 700, Toronto, Ontario M3C 1T5, (416) 467-7883, www.cbabook.org. Supports booksellers through education and services.

Canadian Cataloguing in Publication Program (CIP)
(819) 994-6881. Program coordinated by the National Library of Canada. See listing National Library of Canada.

The Canadian Children's Book Centre
c/o The Toronto Library, Northern District Branch, Lower Level, 40 Orchard View Blvd., Toronto, Ontario M4R 1B9, (416) 975-0010, www3.sympatico.ca/ccbc. Supports the reading, writing, and illustrating of Canadian children's books.

Canadian Conference of the Arts
189 Laurier Ave. E., Ottawa, Ontario K1N 6P1, (613) 238-3561. Holds regional conferences and meetings throughout the year on arts and cultural topics, such as funding for the arts. Extensive resources and database are available.

Canadian Copyright Institute
Canadian Intellectual Property Office, Copyright Office, 50 Victoria St., 2nd Floor, Hull, Quebec K1A 0C9, (819) 997-1936, www.cipo.gc.ca. Established to promote a better understanding of, and fuller use of, copyrights.

The Canadian Intellectual Property Office (CIPO)
Place Du Portage I, 50 Victoria St., 2nd Floor, Hull, Quebec K1A 0C9, (819) 997-1936, www.cipo.gc.ca. Administers and processes copyrights, trademarks, patents, etc., and offers free copyright kits.

The Canadian ISBN Agency
(819) 994-6872, fax (819) 997-7517. Agency handled by the National Library of Canada. See listing National Library of Canada.

Canadian Library Association
328 Frank St., Ottawa, Ontario K2P 0X8, (613) 232-9625. Represents over 3,000 library organizations and individuals.

Canadian Publishers' Council
250 Merton St., Suite 203, Toronto, Ontario M4S 1B1, (416) 322-7011, www.pub council.ca. Represents the interests of publishing companies that publish books and other media for elementary and secondary schools, colleges, and universities.

Canadian Telebook Agency (CTA)
301 Donald's Ave., Toronto, Ontario M4J 3R8, (416) 467-7887. Bar Code Information Package available. CTA lists Canadian publishers' titles on the Canadian Sourcing Database, which is distributed to over six hundred book buyers. Call or write for a free Publisher's Kit.

The Canadian Writers' Foundation Inc.
One Nakota Way, Nepean, Ontario K2J 4E9, (613) 825-0333. Benevolent trust. It raises money for needy yet distinguished Canadian writers.

Cannon Book Distribution
3710 Nashua Dr., Units 5 and 6, Mississauga, Ontario L4V 1M5, (905) 678-7668. A major distributor of self-published and small-press books.

Centax Books and Distribution
1150 8th Ave., Regina, Saskatchewan, S4R 1C9, Distribution (306) 359-7580, Publishing (306) 525-2304. Both a printer and a distributor. This firm often works with churches, for example, to produce and market their books.

Chapters Inc.
90 Ronson Dr., Toronto, Ontario M9W 1C1, (416) 243-3138, www.chaptersinc .com. The largest bookstore chain in Canada.

Corpus Almanac and Canadian Sourcebook
Southam, 1450 Don Mills Rd., Don Mills, Ontario M3B 2X7, (416) 445-6641. The annual sourcebook for reaching just about any person or organization. The section "Sources Information," includes archives, libraries, publishers, magazines, and associations of special interest to self-publishers.

Doing Business in Canada
(800) 267-5177, www.dbic.com. A helpful online guide that covers the Canadian Goods and Services Tax or Harmonized Sales Tax (GST/HST). To download Canada Customs and Revenue Agency's GST/HST forms, go to www.ccra-adrc.gc.ca.

Editors' Association of Canada
502-27 Carlton St., Toronto, Ontario M5B 1L2, (416) 975-1379, toll-free (866) CAN-EDIT, www.editors.ca/index.htm. Promotes professional editing as key in producing effective communications.

Firefly Books
3680 Victoria Park Ave., Willowdale, Ontario M2H 3K1, (800) 387-6192, www.fireflybooks.com. Publisher and distributor of quality nonfiction and children's books.

Fitzhenry & Whiteside Limited
195 Allstate Pkwy., Markham, Ontario L3R 4T8, (905) 477-9700, www.fitzhenry.ca. Publishing and distribution company specializing in reference, trade, education, and children's books.

General Distribution Services
325 Humber College Blvd, Toronto, Ontario M9W 7C3, (416) 213-1919. A major player in Canadian book distribution.

Hignell Book Printing
488 Burnell St., Minnipeg, Manitoba R3G 2B4, (800) 304-5553. Canadian book manufacturer.

Hushion House Publishing Limited
36 Northline Rd., Toronto, Ontario M4B 3E2, (416) 285-6100, www.hushion.com. Represents over three hundred self-published titles.

Independent Publishers Association of Canada (IPAC)
Bankers Hall, P.O. Box 22184, Calgary, Alberta T2P 4J1, (403) 571-3392. Provides education and resources for self-publishers, small publishers, and those who supply services to them.

The League of Canadian Poets
54 Wolseley St., Toronto, Ontario, M5T 1A5, (416) 504-0096, www.poets.ca. Associate membership category may be open for self-publishers. The annual general meeting includes helpful workshops.

Marginal Distribution
277 George St. N., Unit 102, Peterborough, Ontario K9J 3G9, (705) 754-2326, www.marginalbook.com. A distributor of small-press and self-published titles.

Media Names and Numbers
489 College St., #305, Toronto, Ontario M6G 1A5, (416) 964-7799, www.sources .com/mnnsubs.htm. A directory of Canadian print and broadcast media containing more than six thousand entries.

Milestone Publications
3284 Heather St., Vancouver, British Columbia V5Z 3K5, (604) 875-0611. A distributor specializing in cookbooks and children's books from around the world.

National Library of Canada
395 Wellington St., Ottawa, Ontario K1A 0N4, (613) 995-9481, toll-free in Canada (877) 896-9481, www.nlc-bnc.ca. Handles CIP and ISBN functions. For researching purposes, once your local library staff has exhausted its own resources and other interlibrary loan options, it will access the National Library for information and loan of material.

Pegasus Wholesale
100 Alfred Kuehne Blvd., Brampton, Ontario L6T 4K4, (905) 789-1234, www .pegasuswholesale.com. An independent book and music wholesaler jointly owned by Chapters.

Quill & Quire
70 The Esplanade, Suite 210, Toronto, Ontario M5E 1R2, (416) 360-0044, www.quillandquire.com. Canadian monthly book trade magazine comparable to

Publishers Weekly and also publishes the *Canadian Publishers Directory* and *The Book Trade in Canada*.

Raincoast Books
9050 Shaughnessy St., Vancouver, British Columbia V6P 6E5, (604) 323-7100, www.raincoast.com. Large Canadian distributor.

Sandhill Book Marketing
1270 Ellis St., #99, Kelowna, British Columbia V1Y 1Z4, (205) 763-1406, www.books.bc.ca/members/sandhill.html. A distributor of self-published and small-press books.

Westcan Printing Group
84 Durrand Rd., Winnipeg, Manitoba R2J 3T2, (866) 669-9914. Canadian book manufacturer.

The Writers' Union of Canada (TWUC)
40 Wellington St. E., 3rd Floor, Toronto, Ontario M5E 1C7, (416) 703-8982, www.writersunion.ca. Has publications that cover a variety of topics, including contracts, editing, legal considerations, the publishing process, even taxes.

APPENDIX D

Selected Book Manufacturers

Included here are book manufacturers and some that do POD. For more listings and information, look in *LMP*.

Adams Press
6167 N. Broadway, #236, Chicago, IL 60660 (312) 236-3838

Bang Printing
P.O. Box 587, 1473 Hwy. 18E, Brainerd, MN 56401-0587 (800) 328-0450

B•O•D (Books on Demand)
P.O. Box 4503, 517 S. Main St., Lima, OH 45802-4503 (800) 241-4056

Bookmasters, Inc.
P.O. Box 2139, 2541 Ashland Rd., Mansfield, OH 44905 (800) 537-6727

Central Plains Book Manufacturing
P.O. Box 738, Arkansas City, KS 67005, 22234 "C" St., Strother Field, Winfield, KS 67156 (877) 278-2726

De HART's Printing Services
3265 Scott Blvd., Santa Clara, CA 95054 (888) 982-4763

Documation
1556 International Dr., Eau Claire, WI 54701 (800) 951-6729

Edwards Brothers, Inc.
P.O. Box 1007, 2500 S. State St., Ann Arbor, MI 48106-100, (734) 769-1000

Hignell Book Printing
488 Burnell St., Winnipeg, Manitoba, R3G 2B4, Canada (800) 304-5553

Morgan Printing
900 Old Koenig Lane, Suite 135, Austin, TX 78756 (512) 459-5194

Network Printers, Inc.
1010 S. 70th St., Milwaukee, WI 53214-3103 (414) 443-0530

Pacific Rim International Printing
11726 San Vicente Blvd., Suite 280, Los Angeles, CA 90049 (800) 952-6567

Pneuma Books
22 Sycamore Dr., 1st Floor, North East, MD 21901 (410) 287-1235

The Roberts Group
P.O. Box 10134, Greensboro, NC 27404 (336) 292-1150

Sheridan Books
613 E. Industrial Dr., Chelsea, MI 48118 (800) 999-2665

Thomson-Shore
P.O. Box 305, 7300 W. Joy Rd., Dexter, MI 48130-0305 (734) 426-3939

Vaughan Printing
411 Cowan St., Nashville, TN 37207 (615) 256-2244

Walsworth Publishing Company, Inc.
306 N. Kansas Ave., Marceline, MO 64658 (800) 369-2646

Westcan Printing Group
84 Durrand Rd., Winnipeg, Manitoba, R2J 3T2, Canada (866) 669-9914

Whitehall Printing Company
4244 Corporate Square, Naples, FL 34104 (800) 321-9290

APPENDIX E

Marketing Contacts

Where to Send Galleys

For these prime sources, it's worth a phone call to learn the full name—and spelling—of the correct person and to update any address information. These sources also appear in *LMP.* (Address galleys to the appropriate reviewer.)

Booklist
American Library Association, 50 E. Huron St., Chicago, IL 60611-2795
(800) 545-2433
Phone to receive a fax of submission guidelines.

ForeWord Magazine
Alex Moore, Review Editor, 129½ E. Front St., Traverse City, MI 49684
(231) 933-3699
Phone to receive a fax of submission guidelines.

Kirkus Reviews
770 Broadway, New York, NY 10003 (646) 654-5500
Phone to receive a fax of submission guidelines.

Library Journal
Book Review Editor, Mailing address: 245 W. 17th St.
Messenger address: 232 18th St., New York, NY 10011-5300 (212) 463-6818
Submission guidelines are available online at www.libraryjournal.com/about/submission.asp.

Los Angeles Times Book Review
Steve Wasserman, Book Editor, Mailing address: 202 W. First St.
Messenger address: 130 S. Broadway, Los Angeles, CA 90012 (213) 237-2651
Send one copy with a cover letter.

The New York Times Book Review
229 W. 43rd St., New York, NY 10036 (212) 556-7267
Send one copy with a cover letter (no how-to or self-help).

Publishers Weekly
Mailing address: 245 W. 17h St., New York, NY 10011-5300
Messenger address: 232 W. 18th St., New York, NY 10011 (212) 463-6781

For submission guidelines and correct contact person, see www.publishersweekly.com/about/forecast-guidelines.asp.

Quill & Quire
James Grainger, Review Editor, 70 The Esplanade, Suite 210, Toronto, Ontario, M5E 1R2 Canada (416) 360-4604, ext. 357

This is strictly for Canadian published books.

School Library Journal
Mailing address: 245 W. 17th St.
Messenger address: 232 18th St., New York, NY 10011 (212) 463-6759

Phone to receive a fax of submission guidelines (only if your book is for K–12).

Where to Send Finished Books

Baker & Taylor Company
Publisher Contact Section, P.O. Box 6885, Bridgewater, NJ 08807-0885
(908) 541-7000

Choice
The Association of College and Research Libraries, 100 Riverview Center, Middletown, CT 06457-3445 (860) 347-6933

Send *only finished bound* books appropriate to this academic publication. Phone to receive a fax of submission guidelines.

H.W. Wilson Company
Attn: Indexing Services, 950 University Ave., Bronx, NY 10452 (800) 367-6700

Send one copy; the service will contact you by mail. View the company's list of forty-two journals (including *Book Review Digest*) at www.hwwilson.com/journals/jl.htm.

Note: Don't forget your own local and regional newspaper book review editors!

Major Book Clubs

LMP has an extensive list of book clubs noting areas of specialization. Below are the major ones. All fall under the Bookspan umbrella; all *prefer* hardcover submissions, except Quality Paperback Book Club.

Book-of-the-Month Club
Time & Life Building, 1271 Avenue of the Americas, 3rd Floor, New York, NY 10020-2686 (212) 522-7127

Men's subjects, general fiction and nonfiction, and the genre book clubs: History, Country Homes and Gardens, Crafter's Choice, Children's.

Doubleday Select, Inc.
101 Park Ave., New York, NY 10178 (212) 455-5000

Book club titles: Academic, Literary, Garden, Equestrian, Architecture and Design, Antique Roadshow, Nurse's Society, Library of Science, Astronomy, Natural Science, and Computer.

The Literary Guild
1540 Broadway, 16th Floor, New York, NY 10036 (212) 782-7200

Other book clubs at this location: Mystery Guild, Science Fiction Guild, Military, Outdoorsman's Edge, Black Expressions, Crossings, plus women's subjects.

Quality Paperback Book Club
1271 Avenue of the Americas, New York, NY 10020 (212) 522-4200

General fiction and nonfiction.

Selected Serial and Excerpt Rights Buyers

Writer's Market is a good place to prospect for possible serial rights sales. Our list includes many of the major markets, but several others exist.

Catholic Digest
Articles Editor, 2115 Summit Ave., St. Paul, MN 55105-1081 (651) 962-6725
e-mail: cdigest@stthomas.edu

Globe
Book Editor, 5401 NW Broken Sound Blvd., Boca Raton, FL 33487
(561) 586-1111

The National Enquirer
Joan Cannata-Fox, 5401 NW Broken Sound Blvd., Boca Raton, FL 33487 (561) 989-1355

The New York Review of Books
Editors: Robert Silvers, Barbara Epstein, 1755 Broadway, 5th Floor, New York, NY 10019 (212) 757-8070 Fax: (212) 333-5374

Reader's Digest
Excerpt Editors, Pleasantville, NY 1057 (914) 238-1000 Fax: (914) 238-4559

The Sun
Sun Publishing Company, Editor, 107 N., Roberson St., Chapel Hill, NC 27516 (919) 942-5282 Fax: (919) 932-3101

USA Weekend
Gannett Co., Inc., Editorial Department, 1000 Wilson Blvd., Arlington, VA 22229 (703) 276-6445 Fax: (703) 276-5518

Selected Wholesalers and Distributors

The *American Book Trade Directory* is a great source for more names. Look at it in a large library, where it will be kept in the reference section. You may also want to check *LMP.* Call and get the correct buyer's name. Note that this list does *not* contain exclusive (master) distributors that require you to deal only with them. They are listed in our companion marketing resource, *Jump Start Your Book Sales.*

Anderson News Company
P.O. Box 7771, 5203 Hatcher St., Richmond, VA 23231 (804) 222-7252

Mainly to nontrade markets, such as military bases, drugstores, and airport stores.

Baker & Taylor
Publisher Contact Services, P.O. Box 6885, Bridgewater, NJ 08807-0885 (908) 541-7000

One of two largest wholesalers.

Bookazine Company
75 Hook Rd., Bayonne, NJ 07002 (800) 221-8112

Bookpeople
7900 Edgewater Dr., Oakland, CA 94621 (510) 632-4700

Books West
5757 Arapahoe Ave., Unit D-2, Boulder, CO 80303 (800) 378-4188
Colorado and the West.

Brodart Company
500 Arch St., Williamsport, PA 17705 (800) 233-8467

Coutts Library Services
P.O. Box 1000, 1823 Maryland Ave., Niagara Falls, NY 14302-1000
(800) 772-4304
By the Canadian border.

DeVorss and Company
1046 Princeton Dr., Marina del Rey, CA 90292 (213) 870-7478
Books on metaphysics.

The Distributors
702 S. Michigan, South Bend, IN 46601 (219) 232-8500

Hervey's Booklink
P.O. Box 831870, Richardson, TX 75083 (214) 221-2711
Mainly cookbooks.

Ingram Book Company
P.O. Box 3006, 1 Ingram Blvd., La Vergne, TN 37086-3629 or Nashville, TN 37217 (800) 937-8100

Midwest Library Service
11443 St. Charles Rock Rd., Bridgeton, MO 63044-2789 (314) 739-3100

New Leaf Distributing Company
401 Thornton Rd., Lithia Springs, GA 30057-1557 (770) 948-7845
Metaphysical titles.

Quality Books
1003 W. Pines Rd., Oregon, IL 61061-9680
Library distributor for small presses.

Small Press Distribution
1341 Seventh St., Berkeley, CA 94710-1409 (800) 869-7553
Specializes in independently published literature.

Spring Arbor Distributors
One Ingram Blvd., La Vergne, TN 37086-1986 (800) 395-4340
Leading distributor of Christian books.

Unique Books
5010 Kemper Ave., St. Louis, MO 63139-1106 (800) 533-5446
Library distributor for small presses.

Video Plus
200 Swisher Rd., Lake Dallas, TX 75065 (800) 752-2030
Distributor for personal development, wellness, home-based business, individual finance.

Selected Bookstore Chains

There are many bookstore chains; this is a sampling of some of the largest. Others (and their specialties) can be located in the *American Book Trade Directory*. Address your query to either hardcover or paperback, and either nonfiction or fiction buyer if no contact name is listed.

American Wholesale Book Company (Books-A-Million)
Attn: New Acquisitions, 131 S. 25th St., Irondale, AL 35210 (205) 956-4151
All submissions are nonreturnable. Include a self-addressed postcard with your book so the representative can inform you of her decision. The company makes recommendations to buyers at Books-A-Million, Wal-Mart, and other stores, so send two to four copies. Phone to listen to detailed recorded message.

Barnes & Noble/Doubleday
Small Press Department, 122 5th Ave., New York, NY 10011 (212) 633-3300
Fax: (212) 463-5677 www.barnesandnobleinc.com
Send a finished book, a letter of intent explaining why B&N (and/or Doubleday) should carry your book, any reviews, and a marketing plan. The buyers are the same for both chains. Phone to listen to detailed recorded message.

Borders/Waldenbooks
New Vendor Acquisitions, 100 Phoenix Dr., Ann Arbor, MI 48108
(734) 477-1111 Fax: (734) 477-1313

Send duplicate samples via U.S. Mail. Books will not be returned. You will be informed of the buyer's decision by postcard within ninety days of receipt. Include a cover letter on publishing company letterhead and a list of your book's distributors and wholesalers. To reach specific buyers, address to the appropriate department. Submit questions about the review process in writing via mail or fax only. Phone to listen to detailed recorded message.

Follett Higher Education Group
Evelyn McElroy, General Books & Textbooks, 1818 Swift Dr.,
Oak Brook, IL 60523 (800) 323-4506 (630) 279-2330
EmcElroy@fheg.follett.com www.fheg.follett.com

Buyers review monthly and you can expect a response in six to eight weeks. They will return samples only if you request in your proposal letter and include a FedEx or UPS account number. Phone to listen to detailed recorded message.

Selected Book Review Sources

This is a listing of key newspaper and magazine book reviewers. You will want to choose those publications most suitable to your subject. Additional sources can be found in *LMP*, *Writer's Market*, and the *Standard Periodical Directory*, among other reference guides. Address your query to either hardcover or paperback, and either nonfiction or fiction book review editor if no contact name is listed.

Alternative Press Review
Columbia Alternative Library, P.O. Box 1446, Columbia, MO 65205-1446
(314) 442-4352

American Press Service & Features Syndicate
P.O. Box 917, Van Nuys, CA 91408 (818) 988-4337

Sid Ascher's World
Sidney Ascher Syndicate, 214 Boston Ave., Egg Harbor Township, NJ 08234
(609) 927-1842

The Bloomsbury Review
1553 Platte St., Suite 206, Denver, CO 80202 (303) 455-3123

Book Talk
90 Riverside Dr., Suite 1573, New York, NY 10024 (212) 873-0772

Books
Capital News Service, 530 Bercut Dr., Suite E, Sacramento, CA 95814-0101 (916) 443-5871 (916) 445-6336

The Bookwatch/Midwest Book Reviews
278 Orchard Dr., Oregon, WI 53575 (608) 835-7937

The Christian Science Monitor
One Norway St., Boston, MA 02115-3195 (617) 450-2462

Coast Book Review Service
P.O. Box 4174, Fullerton, CA 92634 (714) 990-0432

Erc Reviews
3955 Denlinger Rd., Dayton, OH 45426-2329 (937) 837-0498

Gannett News Service
Division of Gannett Company, Inc., 1000 Wilson Blvd., 10th Floor, Arlington, VA 22229 (703) 276-5800

The New York Review of Books
1755 Broadway, 5th Floor, New York, NY 10019 (212) 757-8070

Newsday
Times Mirror Company, 2 Park Ave., New York, NY 10016 (212) 251-6625

Parade
711 Third Ave., New York, NY 10017 (212) 450-7284

Patrician Productions
145 W. 58th St., New York, NY 10019-1535 (212) 265-5612

Rainbo Electronic Reviews
8 Duran Court, Pacifica, CA 94044 (650) 359-0221

Ruminator Review
1648 Grand Ave., St. Paul, MN 55105 (651) 699-0587

The San Diego Union-Tribune
Copley Press, Inc., P.O. Box 120191, San Diego, CA 92112-0191
(619) 299-3131

San Francisco Chronicle
901 Mission St., San Francisco, CA 94103 (415) 777-7913

Today's Librarian
P.O. Box 40079, Phoenix, AZ 85067-0079 (480) 990-1101

United Feature Syndicate, Inc.
200 Madison Ave., 4th Floor, New York, NY 10016 (212) 293-8500

United Press International
1510 H St., NW, Suite 600, Washington, DC 20005 (202) 898-8000

Universal Press Syndicate
4520 Main St., Suite 700, Kansas City, MO 64111 (816) 932-6600

The Wall Street Journal
Dow Jones & Company, Inc., 200 Liberty St., 9th Floor, New York, NY
10281-0001 (212) 416-2023

Washington Post Book World
1150 15th St., NW, Washington, DC 20071 (202) 334-6000

Selected Literary Review Sources

Books of poetry, novels, and other literary works will find better reception in these literary review services than in general review sources. To prospect for more possibilities, study the *Small Press Review*.

Amelia Magazine
Amelia Press, 329 E St., Bakersfield, CA 93304

Antioch Review
P.O. Box 148, Yellow Springs, OH 45387

Belles Lettres: A Review of Books by Women
1243 Maple View Dr., Charlottesville, VA 22902

The Bookpress
DeWitt Building, 215 N. Cayuga St., Ithaca, NY 14850

The Boston Book Review
30 Brattle St., 4th Floor, Cambridge, MA 02138

Denver Quarterly
University of Denver, Denver, CO 80208

Fiction International
Department of English, San Diego State University, San Diego, CA 92182

High Plains Literary Review
180 Adams St., Suite 250, Denver, CO 80206

The Hudson Review
684 Park Ave., New York, NY 10021

The Journal
Dept. of English, Ohio State University, 164 W. 17th Ave., Columbus, OH 43210

The Missouri Review
University of Missouri, 1507 Hillcrest Hall, Columbia, MO 65211

New England Review
Middlebury College, Middlebury, VT 05753

New Letters
University of Missouri, Kansas City, MO 64110

The North American Review
University of Northern Iowa, Cedar Falls, IA 50614

Ontario Review
9 Honey Brook Dr., Princeton, NJ 08540

Ploughshares
Emerson College, Dept. M, 100 Beacon St., Boston, MA 02116

Poet Lore
4508 Walsh St., Bethesda, MD 20815

Poetry
60 W. Walton St., Chicago, IL 60610

Prairie Schooner
University of Nebraska, Dept. of English, 201 Andrews Hall, Lincoln, NE 68588-0334

The Virginia Quarterly Review
1 W. Range, Charlottesville, VA 22903

APPENDIX F

Other Helpful Information

Point-of-Purchase (POP) Suppliers

Alpak Industries, Inc.
(845) 457-9100 www.alpak.com

Display International
(800) 600-1919 www.universaldisplays.com

Elwood Packaging
(800) 379-2890 www.elwoodbox.com

Meridian Display
(800) 786-2501 www.meridiandisplay.com

Siegel Display Products
(800) 626-0322 www.siegeldisplay.com

Useful Catalogs

Best Impressions
(800) 635-2378 www.bestimpressions.com
Catalog of imprinted advertising specialties.

U.S. Toy
(800) 255-6124 www.ustoy.com
Catalog of cheap trinkets for PR gimmicks.

Printers for Postcards, Posters, Business Cards, and Fliers

All Color Cards
(888) 788-4028 www.allcolorcards.com

AmericasPrinter.com
(800) 552-1303 www.americasprinter.com

Dynacolor Graphics
(800) 624-8840 www.dynacolor.com

Getz Color Graphics
(800) 562-7052 www.getzcolor.com

Lake Superior Press
(800) 894-0088 www.directpostcards.com

Layton Printing
(800) 655-4858 www.laytonprinting.com

Modern Postcard
(800) 959-8365 www.modernpostcard.com

MWM Dexter
(800) 354-9007 www.mwmdexter.com

Simply Brochures
(800) 770-4102 www.simplybrochures.com

Simply Postcards
(800) 770-4102 www.simplypostcards.com

Tu-Vets Printing
(800) 894-8977 www.tu-vets.com

United Micro Printing
(888) 774-6889 www.unitedmicroprinting.com

U.S. Press
(800) 227-7377 www.uspress.com

BIBLIOGRAPHY/RECOMMENDED READING

Writing and Editing

The Chicago Manual of Style, Fourteenth Edition. University of Chicago Press: 1993. Standard style guide for publishers and editors. Covers fundamentals of printing and typesetting, as well as grammar and style.

The Complete Guide to Editing Your Fiction by Michael Seidman. Writer's Digest Books: 2000. Shows how to use "macro editing," style editing, and market editing to create a polished, publishable piece.

Copyediting: A Practical Guide by Karen Judd. William Kauffman, Inc.: 1982. How it's done from the publisher's point of view. An especially helpful book.

Editing Your Newsletter, Third Edition, by Mark Beach. Coast to Coast Books, distributed by Writer's Digest/North Light Books: 1988. A guide to writing, design, and production of newsletters . . . but also contains good general information.

The Elements of Style, Fourth Edition, by William Strunk Jr. and E.B. White. Macmillan Publishing Co., Inc.: 2000. A small but uniquely comprehensive book on the fundamentals of writing.

Grammatically Correct by Anne Stilman. Writer's Digest Books: 1997. A reference for punctuation, spelling, style usage, and grammar.

How to Write a Cookbook and Get It Published by Sara Pitzer. Writer's Digest Books: 1984. A good step-by-step discussion of the type of cookbook to write and how to make it sell.

How to Write and Sell Your First Novel by Oscar Collier with Frances Spatz Leighton. Writer's Digest Books: 1997. Reveals the keys to writing and publishing a successful novel.

How to Write the Story of Your Life by Frank P. Thomas. Writer's Digest Books: 1989. A step-by-step guide for recording one's life.

Is There a Book Inside You? by Dan Poynter and Mindy Bingham. Para Publishing: 1985. How to pick a topic, break in, do research, etc.

The Marshall Plan Workbook by Evan Marshall. Writer's Digest Books: 2001. A systematic yet creative way to help write a novel, scene by scene.

On Writing: A Memoir of the Craft by Stephen King. Scribner: 2000. What the aspiring writer needs to know, from King's point of view, from idea to execution to sale.

On Writing Well, Fifth Edition, by William K. Zinsser. Harper Resource: 1994. An outstanding book for every nonfiction writer.

Roget's Superthesaurus by Marc McCutcheon. Writer's Digest Books: 1998. New and expanded. Offers more features than any other word reference on the market.

Roget's Thesaurus of Phrases by Barbara Ann Kipfer. Writer's Digest Books: 2001. A reference of 10,000 multiword entries and multiword synonyms.

Speaking and Writing Well by Kathy Alba, Ph.D. Thatch Tree Publications: 2001. An authoritative but wacky guide to improving language skills.

Stet! Tricks of the Trade for Writers and Editors by Bruce O. Boston. Editorial Experts, Inc.: 1986. A remarkable editing tool, plus fun reading for anyone who loves words.

The Twenty-Nine Most Common Writing Mistakes and How To Avoid Them by Judy Delton. Writer's Digest Books: 1985. Will help you improve your writing by avoiding often-made mistakes.

Words Into Type, Third Edition, edited by M. Skillin and R. Gay. Prentice-Hall: 1974. Resource for fine points of grammar, usage, style, and production methods.

The Writer's Digest Flip Dictionary by Barbara Ann Kipfer. Writer's Digest Books: 2000. A huge reference of terms and phrases.

Writing Creative Nonfiction by Theodore A. Rees Cheney. Writer's Digest Books: 1987. Explores the use of fiction techniques to make nonfiction more interesting, dramatic, and vivid.

Writing Nonfiction by Dan Poynter. Para Publishing: 2000. How to write, publish, and promote nonfiction.

Writing the Breakout Novel by Donald Maass. Writer's Digest Books: 2001. Explains the elements that make a novel a best-seller.

Writing the Novel: From Plot to Print by Lawrence Block. Writer's Digest Books: 1985. A perceptive handbook on how to handle the questions that plague prospective novelists.

Writing to Inspire by William Gentz, Lee Roddy, and others. Writer's Digest Books: 1982. A guide to writing and publishing for the expanding religious market.

You Can Write a Memoir by Susan Carol Hauser. Writer's Digest Books: 2001. Guides readers in creating their own memoir as they work through the exercises in each chapter.

You Can Write a Novel by James V. Smith Jr. Writer's Digest Books: 1998. Shows first-time novelists how to create memorable characters, gripping plots, and vivid settings.

Business Procedures

Business and Legal Forms for Authors and Self-Publishers by Tad Crawford. Allworth Press: 1999. Reference book and CD-ROM containing sample contracts and business forms, as well as advice on negotiations.

422 Tax Deductions for Businesses and Self-Employed Individuals by Bernard Kamoroff. Bell Springs Publishing: 2000. Hundreds of deductions that you may not know of or your accountant may have failed to ask you about, and ones that the IRS doesn't list on the tax forms.

Government Giveaways for Entrepreneurs IV by Matthew Lesko. InformationUSA, Inc.: 2000. Over nine thousand sources of money, help, and information.

Inc. Yourself by Judith H. McQuown. Bantam Doubleday Dell Publishing: 2000. How to profit by setting up your own corporation.

Kirsch's Handbook of Publishing Law by Jonathan Kirsch. Acrobat Books: 1996. Explains how the basic principles of publishing law are actually applied in the real world.

Online Operator by Bernard Kamoroff. Bell Springs Publishing: 2001. A business, legal, and tax guide to the Internet.

Psycho-Cybernetics by Maxwell Maltz. Fine Communications: 1999. This is an incredible life-changing book.

Small Time Operator by Bernard Kamoroff. Bell Springs Publishing: 2001. How to start your own business, keep books, pay taxes, and stay out of trouble. The leading book in its field.

Think and Grow Rich by Napolean Hill. Fawcett Books: 1990. A classic to guide you on a path to wealth.

What They Don't Teach You at Harvard Business School by Mark H. McCormack. Bantam Books: 1984. A discussion of the street knowledge that comes from the day-to-day experiences of running a business and managing people.

You Can Negotiate Anything by Herb Cohen. Bantam Books: 1982. The how-to's and whys of negotiating to get what you want.

Internet Information

ePublishing for Dummies by Victoria Rosenborg. Hungry Minds, Inc.: 2000. How to write, format, publish, and market electronic books.

How to Publish and Promote Online by M.J. Rose and Angela Adair-Hoy. Griffin Trade Paperback: 2001. E-books, e-publishing, and Web promotion. Contains over five hundred Web links.

Marketing Online by Marcia Yudkin. Morris Publishing: 1999. Low-cost, high-yield strategies for getting results online.

101 Ways to Promote Your Web Site by Susan Sweeney. Maximum Press: 1999. Hands-on guide for increasing Web site traffic by using hundreds of proven tips, tools, and techniques.

101 Ways to Sell Your Book and Info-Products on the Internet by Raleigh Pinskey.

Brass Ring Publishing: 2001. Dos, don'ts, and other resources for your marketing campaign.

Poor Richard's Creating Books by Chris Van Buren, Matt Wagner, Jeff Cogswell, And Doug Clapp. Top Floor Publishing: 2001. How authors, publishers, and corporations can get into digital print.

Poor Richard's Internet Marketing and Promotions by Peter Kent and Tara Calishain. Top Floor Publishing: 1999. Explains many powerful techniques for getting people's attention on the Internet.

Design and Printing

Getting It Printed by Mark Beach and Eric Kenley. North Light Books: 1999. Offers a fresh, clear explanation of how to work with printers and graphic art services.

Graphics Master by Dean Phillip Lem. Dean Lem Associates, Inc.: 1983. A workbook of planning aids, reference guides, and graphic tools for the design and preparation of printing. A rather technical, but extremely useful, book.

How to Understand and Use Design and Layout by Alan Swann. North Light Books: 1987. A wonderful, easy-to-follow book that helps you produce professional results.

Layout Index by Jim Krause. North Light Books: 2001. Layout ideas that will help designers explore multiple possibilities for visual treatments, from page layout to Web design.

Methods of Book Design by Hugh Williamson. Yale University Press: 1983. A tool for book cover design.

Page Layout, edited by Roger Walton. Writer's Digest Books: 2000. Provides inspiration to graphic artists working on cover designs, page layouts, letterheads, publicity, and more.

Pocket Pal by International Paper. International Paper: 1998. A graphic arts production book with many handy visuals and tips.

Publishing Information

The Complete Idiot's Guide to Getting Published by Sheree Bykofsky and Jennifer Basye Sander. Macmillan Distribution: 1998. Educates the novice in the business of publishing.

Directory Publishing by Russell Perkins. Havestraw Publishers: 2000. A practical guide on how to succeed in this entrepreneurial kind of publishing.

How to Get Happily Published by Judith Appelbaum. HarperCollins: 1998. A classic of ways and resources to get the very best deal for yourself and your writing.

How to Make Big Profits Publishing City & Regional Books by Marilyn and Tom Ross. Communication Creativity: 1987. Everything you need to know to research, write, produce, and sell books with an "area" tie-in.

How to Make Money Publishing From Home by Lisa Rogak. Prima Publishing: 2000. Everything you need to know to successfully publish. Includes updated Internet information.

In Cold Type by Leonard Shatzkin. Houghton Mifflin Company: 1982. An excellent book on the whys and wherefores of book publishing.

One Book/Five Ways. University of Chicago Press: 1994. The publishing procedures of five university presses.

Publish Your Own Novel by Connie Shelton. Intrigue Press: 1996. Takes the reader through the steps of publishing and promoting fiction.

Publishing for Profit by Thomas Woll. Perseus Books: 1998. Sophisticated advice for running a publishing business, no matter how large or small.

Publishing Newsletters by Howard Penn Hudson. H&M Publishers: 1997. A complete guide to markets, editorial content, design, subscriptions, management, and desktop publishing of newsletters.

The Publish-It-Yourself Handbook, edited by Bill Henderson. W.W. Norton & Company: 1998. Good for inspiration; the self-publishing stories of Walt Whitman, Anaïs Nin, Virginia and Leonard Woolf, Alan Swallow, Stewart Brand, and others.

The Self-Publishing Manual by Dan Poynter. Para Publications: 2001. A useful guide on the subject of do-it-yourself publishing.

This Business of Publishing by Richard Curtis. Allworth Press: 1998. A critical look at the changing face of publishing.

Writer's Guide to Book Editors, Publishers, and Literary Agents, 2001-2002 by Jeff Herman. Prima Publishing: 2000. An author's reference tool that gives insights into what editors, publishers, and agents are looking for.

Marketing and Publicity (Many of These Reference Directories Are Also Accessible Online)

All-in-One Media Directory, edited by Mark Gebbie. Gebbie Press: 2001. Annual that lists more than 21,000 daily and weekly newspapers, magazines, TV, and radio.

All TV Publicity Outlets Nationwide. Public Relations Plus. Semiannual directory of outlets for television exposure.

Bulletproof News Releases by Kay Borden. Franklin Sarrett Publishing: 1995. Outlines the best methods to use to the avoid trash can, plus tips on how to write news that will be used.

Burrelles Media Directory. Burrelles Information Services: 2000. Set of six excellent reference resources. Annual.

Cable Contacts Yearbook. Larimi Communications Associates, Ltd.: 1999. An annual listing of cable systems, satellite networks, independent producers, and multisystem operators.

The Catalog of Catalogs, compiled by Edward Palder. Woodbine House: 1999. Lists over 15,000 catalogs in 900 different categories.

Chase's Calendar of Events 2001 by William D. and Helen M. Chase. Contemporary Books, Inc.: 2000. An annual publication listing special days, weeks, and months each year. Useful for promotion.

The Complete Guide to Book Marketing by David Cole. Allworth Press: 1999. A reference for anyone who wants to learn everything about selling books.

The Complete Guide to Book Publishing by Jodeé Blanco Allworth Press: 2000. An effective guide for launching PR and promotion campaigns.

Confessions of Shameless Self Promoters by Debbie Allen. Success Showcase Publications: 2001. A collection of PR strategies applicable to any business.

The Copywriter's Handbook by Robert W. Bly. Henry Holt: 1990. A step-by-step guide to writing copy that sells.

Directory of Literary Magazines. Coordinating Council of Literary Magazines: 2000. Compiled list of magazines that publish literary work.

Encyclopedia of Associations. Gale Research Company: 2001. Annual series that lists societies, associations, and groups representing virtually any subject.

Guerrilla Marketing for Writers by Jay Conrad Levinson, Rick Frishman, and Michael Larsen. Writer's Digest Books, Inc.: 2001. A hundred powerful weapons for selling your work.

Grassroots Marketing by Shel Horowitz. Chelsea Green Publishing Company: 2000. Tips and tricks for getting noticed in a noisy world.

Grumpy's Guide to Global Marketing for Books by Carolyn Mordecai. Nittany Publishers, LLC: 2001. International reference book providing descriptive and contact information for all phases of marketing.

The Home School Market Guide, edited by Jane Williams. Bluestocking Press: 1999. A directory of detailed listings for stores, catalogs, reviewers, conferences, and more.

How to Get on Radio Talk Shows All Across America Without Leaving Your Home or Office by Joe Sabah. Pacesetter Publications: 1989. Unique strategies for how to sell more books on the radio.

Hudson's Subscription Newsletter Directory, compiled by Howard Penn Hudson.

Newsletter Clearing House: 1999. A detailed listing of newsletters from A to Z.

i-Tips 2000 by Kathryn Kleibacker, Linda Winter, and Carol Ann Waugh. Internet Monitor: 2000. For everyone who wants to be successful selling to schools and libraries.

Jump Start Your Book Sales by Marilyn and Tom Ross. Communication Creativity: 2000. The perfect companion for this guide. Twenty-five chapters of PR/ sales strategies by the authors of this book.

Literary Publicity by Joseph Marich Jr. Delmar Publishing: 2001. A step-by-step guide to creating a publicity plan all writers can follow.

LMP (Literary Market Place). R.R. Bowker: 2000. A comprehensive list of prime contacts published annually. A must-have for every self-publisher's library.

Marketing With Newsletters by Elaine Floyd. Writer's Digest Books: 2001. How to boost sales, add members, and raise funds with a print, e-mail, fax, Web site, or postcard newsletter.

National Radio Publicity Outlets. Public Relations Plus, Inc. Semi-annual guide to radio, with separate listings for network shows and syndicated shows.

National Trade and Professional Associations of the United States 2001, edited by Buck Downs. Columbia Books, Inc.: 2001. A useful guide to numerous associations.

101 Ways to Promote Yourself by Raleigh Pinskey. Brass Ring Publishing: 1997. Wonderful compendium of ideas to stimulate a brainstorming session.

101 Ways to Write Foolproof Media Releases by Raleigh Pinskey. Brass Ring Publishing: 2001. Save thousands of dollars in advertising and get new business to come to you.

1001 Ways to Market Your Books by John Kremer. Open Horizons: 2001. Packed with real-life examples showing how authors and publishers have marketed their books.

Poetry Marketing by Lincoln B. Young. Fine Arts Press: 1982. How and where to sell your poetry.

Power Marketing Your Novel by Joyce Spizer. Intercontinental Publishing: 2000. A terrific PR resource for fiction writers.

Promote Like a Pro by Linda Radke. Five Star Publications: 2000. A road map for those who cannot afford (or choose not to hire) public relations and marketing specialists.

Selling Subsidiary Rights by Thomas Woll. Perseus Books: 2000. How to plan your subsidiary rights program and how it functions within your publishing program.

Shameless Marketing for Brazen Hussies by Marilyn Ross. Communication Creativity: 2000. Discusses 307 irreverent moneymaking strategies to boost any entrepreneur's bottom line.

The Standard Periodical Directory. Oxbridge Communications, Inc.: 2000. A great guide to U.S. and Canadian periodicals. Information on over sixty thousand publications.

Successful Direct Marketing Methods by Bob Stone. NTC Business Books: 2001. A masterful book covering all aspects of direct marketing.

Ulrich's International Periodicals Directory. R.R. Bowker: 2001. Information on more than 55,000 magazines listed under some 200-plus subject headings.

Words That Sell by Richard Bayan. Caddylak Systems: 1984. A thesaurus of powerful words, phrases, and slogans.

The Working Press of the Nation. National Register Publishing Company: 2001. A five-volume reference work containing the names and addresses of book reviewers, freelance professional journalists, syndicated columnists, etc.

Writer's Market edited by Kirsten Holm. Writer's Digest Books: 2002. Annual volume that contains excellent marketing sources. Also hints on writing, submitting, trade book publishers, and more.

General Reference and Miscellaneous

American Book Trade Directory. R.R. Bowker: 2001. The most complete list available of individual bookstores and chains, published annually.

The Bookman's Glossary, edited by Jean Peters. R.R. Bowker: 1975. A glossary of terms for the writer-publisher.

Books in Print. R.R. Bowker: 2001. An annual series of reference publications listing all in-print titles from more than seven thousand publishers.

The Complete Guide to Writers Groups, Conferences, and Workshops by Eileen Malone. John Wiley & Sons: 1996. Listings of organizations, resources, and educational groups for writers.

The Dictionary of Publishing by David M. Brownstone and Irene M. Franck. Van Nostrand Reinhold Company: 1982. Reference dictionary of publishing language.

Foundation Grants to Individuals, edited by Phyllis Edelson. The Foundation Center: 2001. The most comprehensive listing available of private U.S. foundations that provide financial assistance to individuals.

Grants and Awards Available to American Writers, edited by John Morrone. PEN American Center: 2000. More than five hundred American and international grants for writers of all kinds.

Merriam-Webster's Collegiate Dictionary. Merriam-Webster: 1998. A comprehensive, useful dictionary.

The Random House Webster's College Dictionary. Random House: 2000. An excellent and easy-to-use dictionary.

Small Press Record of Books in Print, edited by Len Fulton. Dustbooks: 2001. Annual with lists by author, title, publisher, and subject.

A Whack on the Side of the Head by Roger Von Oech, Ph.D. Warner Books: 1998. How to unlock your mind for innovation. A fun book leading to new avenues of creativity.

Words on Tape by Judy Byers. AudioCP Publishing: 1997. Information on how to easily create and sell your own audio products.

The Writer Magazine. Kalmbach Publishing Company. Heavy on how-to articles especially for poets and fiction writers; some marketing tips.

Writer's Digest. Writer's Digest Books Magazine. Has market information, getting-published aids, and how-to articles.

GLOSSARY AND DEFINITIONS OF ACRONYMS

A

AA—author's alterations. Changes by author during the typesetting or printing process and charged to the author. *See also* PE, Printer's error.

ABA—American Booksellers Association. A trade association of major publishers and booksellers.

ABI form—Advance Book Information form. A form filed by publisher with Bowker, which uses the information to list books in its directories, such as *Books In Print*.

Accounts receivable—money owed a company by credit customers.

Acid-free—characteristic of most paper stock now so it will not yellow, has greater strength, and will not deteriorate for two hundred years.

Acknowledgment—the author's expressed appreciation to those who helped in producing the book. Usually a part of a book's front matter.

Acquisition editor—person in a publishing house who is responsible for acquiring new manuscripts.

Acquisition librarian—the librarian who orders new library books.

Adoptions—books accepted for use as textbooks in schools and universities.

Advance—money paid an author before a book's publication. An advance installment against royalties.

Advance Reading Copy (ARC)—a copy of the book issued prior to publication date and sent to reviewers and influential individuals for testimonials or to influential booksellers.

Afterword—part of a book's back matter. The author's parting remarks to the reader.

AKA—also known as. A term referring to another name used for self-promotion or advertising agency business.

ALA—American Library Association. The trade association of libraries.

Anthology—a collection of writings by several authors published as a single work.

Antiquarian bookseller—one who specializes in buying and selling old or rare books.

Appendix—that part of a book's back matter that includes lists of resources or other specialized reference material.

Artwork—a catchall phrase of book production that refers to a photograph, illustration, chart, graph, or ornament—anything other than straight text.

As told to—a book produced by a writer in collaboration with a nonwriter, the platter often a celebrity. Credits the writer as coauthor, e.g., *The Story of My Life* by Famous Person as told to Pro Writer.

ASCII text file—American Standard Code for Information Interchange. The worldwide standard format for text files in computers and on the Internet.

Autograph party—a gathering, usually at a bookstore, where the author signs customers' books.

B

Back flap—the back inner fold of a dust jacket. Often has a continuation of copy from the front flap, as well as a photo and a brief biography of the author.

Back matter—the pages in a book after the main text.

Backlist—previously published books that are still in print and available from a publisher, as contrasted to frontlist (newly published) books.

Backorder—a book order waiting to be filled when a new supply of books becomes available.

Backup—printing the second or reverse side of a sheet or page already printed on one side. Or making a computer disk to store elsewhere for safekeeping.

Bad break—an illogical or unpleasant-looking beginning or end of a page or line of type. Also, an incorrectly broken word at the end of a line.

Bar code—the Bookland EAN scanning symbol that goes on the back book cover.

Bastard title—*See* Half title.

BEA—Book ExpoAmerica. The largest publishing trade show in the United States.

Belt press—an expensive and sophisticated printing press (e.g., Cameron) that prints and binds a book in one pass.

Best-seller—a nationally popular book. Lists compiled weekly by *The New York Times*, as well as by *Publishers Weekly*, *Time*, and others.

Bibliography—the part of a book's back matter listing other books or articles the author either cited or consulted in preparing the book or wishes to bring to the reader's notice.

Binding—the way the leaves or signatures of a book are held together.

Blank—an unprinted page that is part of a signature.

Bleed—printing in which the ink color goes all the way to one or more edges of the paper.

Blue, nonreproducing pencil—a colored pencil or pen whose marks will not photograph and will "wash out" and disappear when printing. Ideal for marking camera-ready copy.

Blue penciling—a term used to refer to correcting or indicating rewrites of copy.

Blueline—a proof the printer provides to catch any errors before a book is actually printed. Consists of white letters on a blue background (or blue letters on a white background). Also called "blues," or sometimes a "brownline," in which case the background is brown.

Blurb—a promotional phrase, announcement, or advertisement.

Boards—the stiff board used to reinforce the covers of a hardcover book.

Boldface—heavy bold type that gives emphasis. *See also* Display type.

Book fair—an event where publishers rent tables to display and sell their wares.

Book handle—a short, strong statement about a book's benefit.

Book manufacturer—a printer that specializes in the printing and binding of books.

Book packager—an individual or company contracting with publishers to handle book functions at least through camera-ready copy, and frequently beyond. Also called a "book producer."

Bookland EAN scanning symbol—*See* Bar code.

Booklet—a small, softcover publication that usually has 16, 24, or 32 pages.

Bookmark—to flag a Web site for quick future reference. Also, a rectangular slip of paper for keeping your place in a book; often used as a promotional piece.

Boxed—a technique for drawing attention to a certain paragraph or feature by enclosing it within a ruled box.

Bulk—the thickness of paper in number of pages per inch (PPI); also the thickness of the pages of the book, not counting the cover. Used as a verb, to make a book appear longer (thicker) than the amount of text would otherwise require by using thicker paper.

Bulletin board—a computer term referring to an electronic communication program allowing the sending and storing of information between computers.

Bullets—small black dots used to set off items in a list and make them easier to read.

C

C1S—coated one side. Refers to book cover stock.

Calligraphy—hand lettering, often ornate, that is sometimes used for poetry and cookbooks in particular.

Camera-ready copy—text or art ready to be shot by the printer's camera. It should be free of smudges and of unclear, broken, or faint type.

Cameron belt press—*See* Belt press.

Caps—short for capitals, or uppercase (uc) letters.

Caption—*See* Cutline.

Captured keystroke—a computer term meaning that information, once entered, is retained by the computer and therefore doesn't need retyping.

Case binding—hardcover.

Castoff—an estimate of the length a manuscript will be when typeset.

Catalog sheet—a promotional page including contents, author, discounts, and a book's vital statistics.

Cataloging in Publication—*See* CIP.
CBA—Christian Bookseller Association. A trade association of religious bookstores and suppliers.
Center spread—the pair of facing pages in the center of a magazine or book.
Chapbook—a small book or pamphlet of popular tales, ballads, or poems.
Chapter head—the chapter title printed before the text in each new chapter.
Character—a letter of the alphabet, numeral, or mark of punctuation.
Chat—an online discussion group or forum.
CIP—Cataloging in Publication. A process that aids librarians in ordering and cataloging a book.
Clean copy—a manuscript or galley free from corrections, deletions, and other unnecessary marks.
Click-through rate—Percentage of Web users who click on a viewed advertisement. This is a good indication of the effectiveness of an ad.
Clip art—inexpensive visuals that can be purchased on the Internet or in book form and added to a book instead of using custom-drawn illustrations.
Clipping service—a firm that, for a fee, collects articles, reviews, and notices about a specific subject.
Cloth—a material used for binding, or casing, of books.
Coated paper—paper stock surfaced with white clay to provide a smooth printing surface. For book covers, enamel-coated glossy papers.
COD—cash on delivery. A form of payment in which money is received when merchandise is delivered.
Collating—gathering sheets together into proper order.
Colophon—a Greek term meaning "finishing touch." A brief listing of production details (typeface, etc.) that occasionally appears in a book's back matter.
Color correction—any method, such as masking, dot etching, re-etching, and scanning, used to improve color rendition.
Color printing—usually any printing color, other than black, on white paper. For instance, three-color printing, is a work with three different colored inks.
Color proof—shows the approximate colors of the cover or artwork.
Color separation—the camera technique of "separating" each of the three primary colors and black for the four necessary printing plates. Prints each color by preparing art on separate acetate overlays.
Comb binding—a plastic multipronged binding that allows a book to lie flat.
Composite film—film composed of the CMYK separations.
Composition—the process of setting type, or the set type itself.
Compositor—another term for typesetter. A person who sets type.
Concordance—the list of primary words, names, etc., that form the foundation of a computerized index.

Condensed—a narrow and more compact version of a given typeface.

Content editing—the process of evaluating a manuscript for style, organization, and large general revisions. *See also* Copyediting.

Co-op advertising—a program in which the publisher and the bookstore share the cost of book advertising, the publisher paying the major share.

Co-op publishing—also called copublishing. Several people—or more than one company—working together to put out a book.

Cooperative publishing—*See* Subsidy publisher.

Copy—the text of a book.

Copyediting—technical editing of a manuscript for spelling, grammar, punctuation, clarity, and overall correctness. *See also* Content editing.

Copyright—the right of persons to retain or to sell copies of artistic works that they have produced. *See also* Copyright notice.

Copyright infringement—unauthorized and illegal use of copyrighted material. Commonly known as, but not identical to, plagiarism.

Copyright notice—a notice that protects publicly distributed information. It must include the symbol © or the word *copyright*; the first year in which the work is published; and the name of the copyright holder. *See also* Copyright.

CPM—Cost Per Thousand Page Views. This is a measure taken from print advertising.

CPU—Central Processing Unit. Generally refers to the microprocessor and memory. A term carried over from the mini computer world.

Credit memo—a statement that shows customers they have credit for returned merchandise.

Cropping—placing pencil (or crayon) marks at the margins and corners to indicate what portion of a photo or illustration is to be reproduced.

Cross reference—a reference made from one part of a book to another.

Cutline—a legend or explanation that identifies an illustration or photograph. Also known as a "caption."

CYMK—the four colors used in printing; includes the three primary colors: cyan, magenta, and yellow, plus black.

D

Database—data stored and managed by a database management system (DBMS). Can be as simple as a mailing list or as complex as needed to provide management of the data for easy access.

DBA—doing business as. Used when a name other than one's own is the business's name.

Deadline—the cutoff date by which a task must be completed.

Dedication—the inscription honoring the person(s) who inspired the work. Part of a book's front matter.

Defamation—a legally actionable attack (either written or spoken) that tends to injure a person's reputation. *See also* Libel.

Delete—a proofreading term directing the removal of certain characters or material.

Demographics—a profile of a group (readers, listeners, viewers, etc.) documenting such things as age, sex, marital status, education, socioeconomic level, and hobbies.

Die-cut—the creation of openings, shapes, or folds by cutting away part of the paper stock.

Direct mail—letters or promotional material mailed directly to potential customers.

Dirty copy—heavily edited or marked-up copy that is difficult to read.

Disk—digital media, either removable disk or CD.

Disk drive—a storage device for holding electronic text.

Display ad—a print advertisement larger than a classified ad.

Display type—larger or bolder type for heads, subheads, etc., as compared with type used in the text as a whole. *See also* Boldface.

Distributor—*See* Wholesaler.

Domain name—the unique name that identifies an Internet site.

Downtime—time when a supplier is not busy and may give better prices. Also the time during which a given piece of equipment is inoperable and/or under repair.

DPI—dots per inch. The more dpi, the sharper the reproduction.

Dummy—a rough layout of how the finished book is to appear.

Dump—a display unit used in bookstores. *See also* Point-of-purchase display.

Dun & Bradstreet rating—a profile of a company's financial stability prepared by Dun & Bradstreet.

Duotone—a process for producing an illustration in two colors from a one-color original. Gives a quality of added depth and texture.

Dust jacket—a protective and attractive cover for hardback books. Provides space for visual display and promotional copy. Also called a "dust cover."

E

Editing—making or suggesting changes in a manuscript.

Edition—a printing of a work that is basically the same as other printings. *See also* Revised edition.

Editor in chief—the top editorial executive in a publishing program, setting policy for that program and directing acquisitions.

Electronic publishing—a general term embracing all forms of computerized publication, particularly those that deliver text or other materials directly to the consumer's computer screen.

Elite type—a common, smaller typewriter face with twelve characters to the inch. *See also* Pica type.

Em—approximately the width of the letter *m* in any given typeface, used to measure such things as indents and dashes. Twice as wide as an en measure, as for dashes.

E-mail—Electronic mail. Mail messages, usually text, sent from one person to another via computer.

Embossing—raising the image above the paper level, such as a title on the cover of a book.

Endpapers—the heavy sheets of paper, one at the beginning and the other at the end, of a hardbound book that fasten the book to its cover.

Engraving—the cutting of a design into a block of material, resulting in a pattern from which a print can be made.

Enlargement—the photographic process of creating an image larger than the original.

Epilogue—a concluding section that rounds out a story and often updates the reader. Part of the text, not of the back matter.

Errata—errors found in printed books. Commonly corrected, prior to the book's next printing, by the insertion of a loose sheet (an "errata sheet") of revised text in each copy of the book.

Estimate—*See* Price estimate.

Evergreen—a book or article that is timeless.

Excerpt—a portion taken from a longer work. Also called an "extract."

Exclusive—a news or feature story, or TV appearance, printed or aired by one media source substantially ahead of its competitors.

Expanded type—a wider-than-usual typeface.

Expert read—a reading of the book done by an authority on the book's subject to determine accuracy and completeness prior to publication. Sometimes called a "peer read."

F

F.O.B.—free on board. Meaning the publisher pays shipping cost to the destination.

Facing page—any page forming a double spread with another.

Fair use—the allowable and legal use of a limited amount of copyrighted material without getting permission.

FAQs—frequently asked questions. Documents that list and answer the most common questions on a particular subject or problem area. A frequently used term on the Internet.

Film lamination—a glossy coating for book covers that protects against scuffing, adds strength, and keeps paperback covers from curling.

First edition—the entire original run of copies of a work from the same plates.

First serial rights—the right to serialize a forthcoming work prior to the publication date. Often sold to only one magazine or one newspaper. *See also* Rights; Second serial rights.

Flap copy—the material describing a book and its author that appears on the inside folds of the dust jacket.

Flat fee—a onetime payment for a job or task, such as the preparation of text or artwork.

Flier—an inexpensive promotional piece often printed on an 8½″ × 11″ sheet of paper.

Flop—to flip a photo negative over so it will be printed facing the opposite way.

Flush—meaning to be even with. Usually refers to the left margin, as in "flush left."

Foil—hot stamping material normally found on the front cover of a book. Can be gold, silver, or standard colors, such as red, blue, green, etc.

Folio—a page number of a book.

Font—complete set of type, including letters, numbers, and punctuation marks, in one typeface.

Font, display—a typeface that is better used for captions, headlines, chapter headings, and the like.

Font, sans serif—an unornamented font, such as Helvetica or Optima. Any type style that does not have cross-strokes or curlicues on the ends of the letters.

Font, text—a typeface that is well suited for the body text of a book. Generally not a sans serif face.

Forecasting—using mathematical computations to predict business trends.

Foreign rights—subsidiary rights allowing a work to be published in other countries and/or translated into other languages.

Foreword—introductory remarks about a book and its author. Often written by an expert (other than the author) to give a book greater promotability and authority. Part of a book's front matter.

Format—designation of typeface, margins, boxing, or any other special treatment of copy. Also used to indicate the trim size and physical layout of the book.

Formatting—the process of designing a publication.

Forum—another name for a newsgroup or chat.

Freelancers—skilled creative people (writers, editors, graphic artists, consultants, etc.) who sell their services as independent contractors.

Front matter—all pages before the main text.

Frontispiece—an illustration preceding and facing the title page. Also called a "front plate." Part of a book's front matter.

FTC—Federal Trade Commission. A governmental regulatory agency.

FTP—File Transfer Protocol. A standard method of sending files between computers over the Internet.

Fulfillment—the filling and shipping of book orders.

G

Galleys—proofs from the typesetter in page format, copies of which may be sent to important book reviewers.

Gang—to run related items (such as photos) together to economize on costs.

Genre—a category or specific kind of writing, such as historical, science fiction, or mystery.

Ghostwriter—a professional writer who produces books attributed to others.

GIF—Graphics Interchange Format. File format commonly used to display graphics and images in HTML documents on the Internet.

Glossary—a body of definitions relevant to the work. Part of the back matter.

Glossy—a photograph with a shiny rather than a matte finish.

Grant—an outright gift of money to subsidize a specific project.

Graphics—the illustrative elements in a work.

Gutter—the inside center margin of a book.

H

Half title—a page on which the title stands alone. Precedes the complete title page. Also known as "bastard title."

Halftone—a photograph or illustration that has been "converted" into a pattern of tiny dots so it can be printed.

Hardcover—a book bound in boards. Also called case-bound or hardback.

Headband—a piece of material affixed to a book's spine for reinforcement.

Headline—a large bold caption appearing at the top of an advertisement or article.

Heads—short for chapter titles.

Hickey—a speck or blotch in a photographic negative.

Home page—the main Web page.

Hot stamping—applying foil to paper using heat and pressure.

House organ—periodical or newsletter issued by a firm or organization for its members, employees, customers, or prospects.

HTML—HyperText Markup Language. Often referred to as HTML. The coding language used to create documents for use on the World Wide Web.

Hyperbole—exaggerated claims intended to sell a product or promote a person. Also known as "hype."

I

Illustrations—visual material, such as photographs, drawings, graphs, and tables.

Image area—the printable area of a page where an image has been, or will be, produced.

Imposition—the positioning of pages for large press sheets so that when cutting and folding is complete the images will be in the correct sequence.

Imprint—the identifying name of a publishing company.

In print—books that are currently available from publishers.

Index—an A to Z list giving the location of specific material in a book. Part of the back matter.

India ink—dense, black ink preferred for drawing artwork.

In-house—those functions performed within a publishing company rather than by outside contractors. Also used to indicate that the finished books have been delivered to the publisher.

Insert—additional material added to a manuscript by an author or editor.

Insertion order—a form advertising agencies use to place advertising in various media.

Inventory—books on hand available for sale.

Invoice—a bill sent with a book order.

ISBN—International Standard Book Number. An essential identifying number used for ordering and cataloging purposes.

ISP—Internet Service Provider. A company that facilitates access to the Internet, usually at a cost to the consumer, although there are still some free community networks.

Italics—type with a right-hand slant like *this*. Often used for quotations, titles, and special emphasis.

J

Jacket—*See* Dust jacket.

Jobber—*See* Wholesaler.

JPEG file—Joint Photographic Experts Group. File format commonly used to display graphics and images in HTML documents on the Internet.

Justify—the setting of type so that the end of each line is flush right and aligned perfectly.

K

Kern—that part of a letter that projects in any direction beyond its own body, or over/under adjacent letters.

Kerning—removing space between letters.

Key—an identifying explanation of coded material, such as a color-coded map and its accompanying key indicating what each color stands for.

Keyboarding—entering data in a computer as opposed to typing a manuscript.

Keyline—essentially the same as a pasteup. The original composite art for offset printing.

Kivar—a proprietary product used for hardcover books.

Kill fee—money paid to a writer in compensation for time spent working on assignment on a piece the publisher decides not to accept.

L

Laminate—to bond a plastic film by heat and pressure to a printed sheet for protection and appearance.

Laser printer—a nonimpact output device that burns an image on paper through the use of a small laser.

Lay-flat binding—a special process that allows a softcover book to fully open and lie flat (so it doesn't snap shut).

Layout—the working template of the proposed design for a printing job.

LCCN—Library of Congress Card Number. An important coding process used by libraries in cataloging.

Leading—(rhymes with "wedding") the amount of space between lines of type.

Letterhead—company stationery that is printed with the name, address, telephone number, URL, e-mail address, and any logo.

Letterpress—printing from raised letters or type, rather than from photographic plates.

Libel—written defamation of character, for which one can be sued. *See also* Defamation.

Light table—a table with a diffused light underneath to facilitate pasteup of text and artwork.

Limited edition—a specified and limited quantity of books, often numbered and signed by the author.

Line art—a black-and-white original illustration that does not require halftone reproduction. Has no in-between tones of gray.

List—all of the titles a publisher has in print and for sale. Or the official or "listed" retail price of a book. *See also* List price.

List broker—someone who handles direct-mail list rentals for use in direct-marketing campaigns.

List price—the full retail price of a book, without discounts. *See also* List.

LMP—Literary Market Place. An important overall publishing reference work. A comprehensive compilation of publishers, agents, book clubs, printers, and everyone else relevant to the book industry.

Logo—a symbol or illustration used as an identifying mark by business.

Lowercase—(lc) small letters as opposed to either uppercase (uc) or small capitals (sc).

Lurker—a person who anonymously observes what everyone else is saying in a Web discussion group.

M

Mail fulfillment house—a company that handles envelope stuffing, addressing, and mailing for a direct-mail campaign.

Mail order—a method of merchandising books directly to the consumer using ads in magazines and newspapers.

Makeready—all preparations for a press to get ready for a specific print run.

Manuscript—the book before it is typeset and printed.

Margin—the edge that surrounds the printed image on a page.

Market research—information gathering and analysis relating to any aspect of marketing.

Marketing plan—a publisher's total advertising and promotional plan to sell books.

Mass-market paperback—the smaller 4″ × 7″ paperbacks designed for the widest possible distribution.

Master—original camera-ready artwork.

Match-print—a proof for four-color process work to show color done properly.

Matte finish—a nonglossy finish.

Measure—the length of a full line of type on a page. Expressed in picas.

Mechanical binding—bindings using wire, staples, or plastic.

Media—all print, TV, radio, and Internet sources for advertising and promotional exposure.

Media kit—a collection of publicity materials used to promote a book or an author to the media. Usually presented in a cardboard presentation folder with pockets.

Microfiche—one of three major microforms (microfilm, microfiche, microfarads) in which information is stored in greatly reduced form on photographic film and read through a special enlarging device.

Midlist—a professional author who has steady, but not strong, sales.

Mock-up—a visual presentation of a proposed page or piece of promotional material.

Model release—a form giving permission to use a photograph of an individual for publication.

Modem—a device used with a microcomputer and a telephone to facilitate telecommunications.

Monitor—a video display unit on which information typed into a computer appears.

Monograph—a short written report covering a single specific subject.

MS—an abbreviation for "manuscript."

Multiple submission—the offering of a work to more than one publisher at the same time.

N

Nationwide marketing plan—*See* Marketing plan.

Negative—a film replica of the original in which the gradations of light and dark are reversed.

Net receipts—moneys received by a publisher on a book's sale after all discounts and returned copies have been deducted. Sometimes, per authors' contracts, used to calculate royalties, rather than using the book's retail (list) price.

News release—a one- or two-page story used for promotion.

Newsgroup—same as forum, an online discussion group.

Nonreturnable—merchandise that may not be returned for credit or a cash refund.

Notch binding—a binding process where the spines are not cut from the signatures but instead notches are cut down each spine and, with signatures still intact, the cover glued on.

Nth name—randomly selected names in a mailing list—often every tenth—used to test the value of the total list.

O

OCR—Optical Character Recognition. A device that reads printed pages into a computer.

Offset printing—any one of several printing processes that print type from a flat, rather than a raised or incised, surface. Also called "offset lithography" and "photo offset."

Opaque—not admitting light. Also, to paint portions of a negative so they will not reproduce.

Operating system—a group of controlling programs that govern the functioning of a whole computer system.

OPM—other people's money. A business term meaning to borrow capital from elsewhere rather than using one's own.

Option—the right to purchase or sell something, such as movie rights, for a specified price and within a certain length of time. Also, the right a publisher may have, by previous contract, to bid on an author's subsequent books.

Ornament—a decorative device in book design, such as a larger initial letter, rule line, or border.

Orphan—the first line of a new paragraph that appears alone at the bottom of a page.

Otabind—a trademarked binding process for trade paperbacks that resembles perfect binding (it has a printable spine) but allows a book to be opened out flat. Ideal for cookbooks or workbooks.

Out of print (OOP)—a book that is no longer available through the publisher. As contrasted with OOS, out of stock.

Out of stock (OOS)—a book not available because its publisher's supply has been temporarily exhausted.

Over the transom—unsolicited material sent to a publisher directly by the author rather than through an agent or at the request of an editor.

Overrun—an extra amount of finished copies of the book the printer may produce above the stipulated order (should never exceed 10 percent). Also, an additional quantity of book covers a publisher may order for promotional purposes.

P

Page proof—a duplicate of the actual layout of the pages exactly as they will appear in the compiled book.

Pagination—the numbering or order of pages in a book.

Paper stock—the paper used for printing a book.

Paperback—A book bound with a flexible paper cover. Also called "paperbound."

Pasteup—the camera-ready original for offset printing. Also, the making of that original.

PC—personal computer.

PDF—Portable Document Format. A self-contained, operating-system-independent file format for distributing digital documents.

PE—a printer's error on typeset galleys. *See also* AA.

Pen name—*See* Pseudonym.

Perfect binding—a flat or squared spine achieved by gluing the sheet ends together. Used for hardcovers, good paperbacks, and some magazines.

Periodical—a magazine, newspaper, or other publication with a fixed interval between issues.

Permission—an authorization from a copyright holder to quote material or reproduce illustrations taken from the copyrighted work. Often requires a fee.

Photo offset—*See* Offset printing.

Photostat—a copy of an illustration, printed page, etc., that is of suitable quality for printing reproduction.

Phototypesetting—a common form of typesetting in which each character and word is a photographic image. Major advantages: crispness, economy, and speed.

Pica—a printer's measurement. Approximately 1/6 inch.

Pica type—the larger typewriter type that runs ten characters to the inch, as contrasted to elite type. *See also* Elite type.

Plagiarism—copying another author's work and passing it off as one's own.

Plate—the final printing master that contains the image to be reproduced. May be metal, plastic, or other material.

Platform—the operating system (e.g., Windows 98, Windows 2000, Windows NT) used by a personal computer.

PMA—Publishers Marketing Association. A nonprofit trade organization that specializes in co-op mailings and other marketing programs.

PMS color—Pantone Matching System. Specially mixed colors used in printing.

POD—print on demand. A current technique of printing only as many books as are needed at the moment.

Point—a unit of vertical measurement. In typesetting, equals 1/72 inch.

Point size—the height of a letter, expressed in point units (e.g., 8-point type, 32-point type).

Point-of-purchase (POP) display—book display racks, posters, bookmarks, and other sales materials given to bookstores or other retail outlets to promote a book. *See also* Dump.

Positioning—strategic placement of an ad where it will get maximum exposure. Also, the place within a list where a book falls in relation to other titles. Also, finding a special niche for your product.

Posting—a message entered into a network communications system, such as a newsgroup submission.

PostScript—a language for controlling printers and imagesetters.

PPI—pages per inch. A term used to measure the thickness of paper stock.

Preface—introductory remarks (usually by the author) telling the reason the book was written and giving its aims and scope. Part of a book's front matter.

Premium—a book that will usually be given away free as part of a promotional campaign for a product or service. Typically bought in large quantities.

Prepack—a point-of-purchase (POP) temporary countertop or floor display unit, often made from cardboard, designed to hold and bring extra attention to merchandise.

Prepublication copies—copies of a book that are circulated or sold prior to the official publication date. Sometimes discounted to stimulate early orders.

Prepublication price—a special lesser price offered on books bought before the official publication date.

Press check—when a customer is at the printing press in order to approve the job as it is printed. Can last a few minutes or several days, depending on the size of the job.

Press proof—a proof drawn just before the press run begins. Sometimes used to check the cover colors, etc., of the printing job.

Press release—*See* News release.

Press run—the number of usable copies produced in a single printing.

Price estimate—an educated guess of how much a job will cost.

Price quote—a firm commitment on how much a job will cost.

Print run—number of ordered copies to be printed.

Printer—another term for a book manufacturer.

Printer's error (PE)—mistake made by the printer (*not* the author) on a typeset galley. *See also* AA.

Production expenses—generally includes typesetting, keylining, printing, and binding.

Promotional material—any printed matter (such as fliers, catalog sheets, letters, review copies) designed to publicize and sell a book.

Proof—a direct impression of type or a photographic reproduction of what the printed job should look like.

Proportion wheel—a small device used to determine enlargements and reductions for artwork.

Proportional spacing—a method of spacing in most typeset copy in which the width of a letter is determined by the actual amount of space it needs.

Proposal—a detailed plan of a proposed new enterprise that is used to sell that project. Also, a package consisting of an outline, sample chapters, author bio, and other supporting materials used by a writer to persuade a publisher to offer a contract for a book.

Pseudonym—an assumed name used to conceal an author's identity. A pen name.

Public domain—material that is not protected by copyright.

Publication date—a date, typically set three to four months after books are actually in-house, when a book is officially launched.

Publicist—one who prepares promotional materials and/or schedules media appearances either as an independent contractor or as part of the staff of a publisher, advertising agency, or PR firm.

Purchase Order (PO)—a document used to order books.

Q

Quality paperback—*See* Trade paperback.

Query letter—a one- or two-page letter created to interest an editor or agent in a book project or magazine article. Displays the author's writing ability and is meant to sell an idea. Also known as a "query."

Quote—a statement, often from a celebrity or key reviewer, used in advertising or for book cover copy. Also, an exact copy of original wording from another source reproduced in one's own writing, enclosed in quotation marks. Also, an offer to do work for a specific sum, as in a price quote.

R

Ragged right—a right-hand margin that does not align evenly.

Rate card—a price sheet giving the costs of media time or space advertising.

Recto—a right-hand page, as opposed to a verso, a left-hand page.

Recto-verso—two-sided printing.

Reduction—the photographic process of creating an image smaller than the original, or scaling an oversize copy for reduction. For example, a half-size image, which is a 50 percent reduction, or "scale 50 percent", or a three-fourths size image, which is "scale 75 percent."

Register—the correct positioning of print on a page or, in color process printing, proper positioning of separations relative to each other so everything appears crisp.

Remaindering—a publisher's selling of the remaining stock of unsuccessful books for a fraction of their list prices.

Remnant space—random advertising space, often in regional editions, that has not been sold when the magazine or newspaper is ready to go to press. Usually available at a reduced rate.

Reprint—a general term used in publishing to describe any new printing of a book.

Repro—reproduction proof. Camera-ready copy on photosensitive paper to be pasted up on mechanicals to be photographed.

Retouching—touch-up of a photograph to correct flaws or improve appearance.

Returns—books that have not been sold and are sent back to a publisher for credit or a cash refund.

Review—a critical evaluation of a work, citing its strengths and weaknesses.

Review copy—a complimentary copy of a book sent to reviewers or potential wholesale purchasers.

Revised edition—a new edition of a previously published book containing updated or supplementary material.

RFQ—request for quotation or bid. The list of specifications of desired items that is sent to a prospective vendor.

Rights—the various rights to reproduce or publish a work in any form, in whole or in part, that its author may sell or retain. *See also* First serial rights; Second serial rights.

Roll-fed press—*See* Web press.

Royalties—the money paid to authors by publishers for the right to use their work, usually computed as an agreed percentage of the price per copy sold.

Rule—a line. Can be made in many different thicknesses, either with a pen, by machine, or with graphic tape.

Run in—proofreader's notation directing that an existing break (such as a paragraph) be ignored and the text continued without break as one paragraph.

Runaround—when typeset words are set to frame artwork. A more costly form of typesetting than straight copy.

Running copy—text, as opposed to headlines.

Running heads—the title and/or chapter headings that often appear on the top of each page in a book.

S

Saddle stitching—binding a booklet or magazine by driving staples through the fold at the very center. Not practical for publications of more than 72 pages.

Sales rep—an individual who represents a publisher's books to retailers, wholesalers, etc., in exchange for a commission. Also called a "traveler."

Sample pages—typeset examples of a book's intended design.

SAN—Standard Account Number. Sometimes used in order fulfillment. A code for identification of book dealers, libraries, schools, and school systems.

Sans serif—refers to typefaces that do not have serifs. *See also* Serif.

SASE—a self-addressed, stamped envelope.

Scale—the percentage of enlargement or reduction based on same size reproduction at 100 percent. For a 4″×6″ piece: if scaled 150 percent, have 6″×9″; if scaled 50 percent, have 2″×3″.

Scaling—using a proportion wheel to determine enlargement or reduction proportions.

Scanner—a piece of equipment that reads and converts pages into a computerized format.

Scoring—creasing or incising paper or card stock in a crisp line in order to facilitate folding or tearing out.

Screen—a masking device used to create various tints of the same color; 10 percent being very pale, 100 percent being the darkest tint possible.

Search and replace—a word processing function that automatically finds and replaces words or text throughout a document.

Search engine—the most popular way to find resources on the Internet. Numerous search engines, each with unique style and capabilities.

Second serial rights—the rights for a magazine excerpt that will appear after the publication date. *See also* First serial rights; Rights.

Self-cover—a cover consisting of the same paper stock as that used for the inside pages.

Serif—the "tails" on typographic characters that make them easier to read. *See also* Sans serif.

Sheetfed press—a press that requires paper cut into separate sheets, rather than a continuous roll. *See also* Web press.

Short rate discount—any discount less than the usual 40 percent, for example, the 20 percent short rate common for schools.

Short rated—when advertising contract obligations are not met and the advertiser is rebilled at the higher actual usage rates.

Short run—small printing jobs of a few hundred (for neighborhood printing) or a few thousand (for book manufacturers) books or booklets.

Shrink-wrap—a clear plastic covering used in shipping from the manufacturer to avoid books' being marred.

Signature—the multiples of pages (8, 16, or 32, depending on the press used) in which books are normally printed. Or a block of information used at the end of every message or online document sent by that user.

Silk-screening—a printing method whereby ink is forced through a stencil, thus creating a design. A more expensive process used for imprinting heavy stock paper.

Simultaneous editions—the printing of hardcover and paperback editions of a book at the same time. *See also* Split runs.

Single-copy order—when only one copy of a book is ordered. Many publishers do not give any discounts on single-copy orders.

Sinkage—the extra white space above a display, such as at a chapter opening.

Slipcase—a protective boxlike container, open at one end, for books.

Slug—spacing between lines of type wider than the usual two or three points of leading.

Small caps—(sc) Proofreader's direction to set material in uppercase letters the same size as the lowercase letters being used.

Smythe sewn—a form of binding used for many hardcover books. Sturdy but costly form of binding in which the signatures are first sewn together then glued into the cover.

Software—individual computer programs, such as word processing or spreadsheets, that make a computer system perform specific functions.

Spamming—an inappropriate attempt to use a mailing list. To send a message to a large number of people who didn't ask for it.

SPAN—Small Publishers Association of North America. A nonprofit trade association for authors, self-publishers, and independent presses.

Special order—on the retail level, an order by a consumer for a book not in stock. On the wholesale level, an order received from a bookseller that requires special handling, such as a rush order.

Specs—an abbreviation of "specifications." The physical details of a publishing project, such as type choice and size, binding, trim size, and number of pages.

Spell out—(sp) a proofreader's mark meaning to spell out, rather than abbreviate or use initials.

Spider—an automated program that indexes and retrieves Web pages and their links.

Spine—that part of a book that connects the front to the back.

Spine out—books placed on shelves so that only the spine shows.

Spiral binding—a continuous wire binding, usually used only on paperbacks.

Split runs—different ads run in regional editions of the same magazine issue; an ideal tool for mail-order testing. Also, an edition of a book printed simultaneously in paperback and hardbound. *See also* Simultaneous editions.

Sponsored book—*See* Premium.

Spreadsheet—a programmable balance sheet commonly used for accounting functions, planning, and forecasts.

SRDS—Standard Rate and Data Services, Inc. A group of reference books designed especially for ad agencies but useful in other marketing efforts, as well.

Stamping—imprinting lettering or a design on a book cover.

Standard trim size—any of a variety of page measurements standard to a particular kind of book: 5½″ × 8½″, 6″ × 9″, and 8½″ × 11″. *See also* Trim size.

Statement—a chronological listing of all charges and credits to date for a specific account.

Stet—from the Latin term "to stand." A mark meaning that a proofreader's symbol should be disregarded and the text left as is.

STOP—Single Title Order Plan. Used by bookstores to order just one book.

Strip in—to combine a photographic negative with one or more others in preparation for making a printing plate.

Stripping—the process of preparing a negative or series of negatives for plate making.

Style sheet—a guide to editorial specifications, or selected typographical details, for a particular book.

Stylebook—also called a handbook of style. A book such as *The Chicago Manual of Style*. Intended to insure consistency within and correct handling of written works.

Subsidiary rights—additional rights, such as book club, serial rights, or paperback rights, that can be sold in addition to the book itself.

Subsidy publisher—a company that charges writers to publish their work. Often retains ownership of the books and does little promotion. Also called a "vanity press" or "cooperative publisher."

Substantive editing—changes to a manuscript to adjust flow and organization and to refine word choices and phrasing.

Subtitle—a second or additional title further explaining a nonfiction book's content and scope.

Syndication—the simultaneous release of written or broadcast material to many outlets.

T

Table of contents—includes the title and beginning page number of each chapter of the book. Sometimes includes descriptive material for each chapter.

Table of illustrations—a list noting illustrations used in the text and their page numbers.

Tailpiece—a small ornament at the end of a chapter.

Tear sheets—newspaper or magazine reviews, ads, or stories cut from the periodicals they appeared in.

Telecommunications—electronic communication between one computer and another using a telephone and a modem.

Terms—the number of days a customer is allowed before paying, as in "net 30."

Text—the main body of type, minus front matter, back matter, and heads.

Thesaurus—a book or electronic program that lists or stores synonyms and antonyms.

TIFF (or TIF) file—Tagged Image File Format. Used for graphics and supported by virtually all paint, image-editing, and page layout software applications.

Tipping in—the insertion of additional material, such as foldout maps, by pasting, into a bound book.

Title—any one of the books a publisher currently has in print. Also, the name of a particular book.

Title page—an early recto page that usually gives the title, author(s) or editor(s), publisher, and place of publication.

Trade paperback—the larger paperback (5″ × 8″ to 7″ × 10″). Used to be called a "quality paperback."
Trade publisher—a conventional publishing house, publishing books for a mass audience, which typically pays authors advances and royalties, as opposed to a self-publisher or a subsidy publisher.
Transpose—to accidentally reverse the order, such as of two letters.
Trim size—the finished size of a book after the signatures have been trimmed and folded. *See also* Standard trim size.
Two-up—pieces printed side by side.
Typeface—the style of the letter or character of the type, what it looks like.

U

Underrun—when a printer manufactures fewer copies than were ordered.
Unit cost—the production cost to print each individual book.
Universal Copyright Convention—an agreement, ratified by ninety nations, to offer the copyrighted works of citizens of other nations the same protections as are extended to those of their own citizens.
Universal discount schedule—a system that gives everyone the same discounts, whether wholesaler, bookstore, individual, or library.
Up-charge—an additional fee incurred over and above a stated price.
Uppercase—(uc) the capital letters of a font.
URL—Uniform Resource Locator. The full name (address) of a Web site.
UV coating—liquid applied to a printed sheet, then bonded and cured with ultraviolet light.

V

Vanity press—*See* Subsidy publisher.
Varnishing—a coating process that results in a hard, glossy surface. Used for protection and eye appeal on book covers.
Vendor—a supplier who sells goods or services.
Verso—a left-hand page, as opposed to a recto, a right-hand page.
Viral marketing—word-of-mouth promotion, especially on the Internet.
Visuals—*See* Artwork.
VOR—Vendor of Record. A term used by distributors and wholesalers to designate one company as the primary source for book returns.

W

Web press—a fast, sophisticated printing press that uses roll-fed paper rather than sheets. *See also* Sheetfed press.
Wholesaler—a person or company who buys from a publisher, then resells to

a bookstore or library. Sometimes referred to as a "jobber" or a "distributor."

Widow—the last line of a paragraph that appears alone at the top of a new page.

Wire service—a news-gathering organization that sells information to its subscribers. UPI and AP are the leading ones.

Word of mouth—an informal, but important, kind of advertising in which a book is praised by one person to another.

Word processing—the electronic manipulation of text that allows a document to be monitored and corrected prior to typesetting.

Work made for hire—work done for a fee in which the author has no copyright or ownership. Under current law, must be covered by a written agreement.

Working title—a preliminary title used while a book is in preparation.

Writer's Market—a publishing reference work important to authors. A comprehensive annual compilation of publishers' and periodicals' names, addresses, current needs, and general policies and contract terms.

Wrong font—(wf) a proofreader's mark indicating that in one or more words, the printer has used the wrong font (face) of type.

Z

Zip disk—file storage disk available in 100MB or 250MB capacity. For Iomega's Zip drive, an external drive added to your computer. Useful for transporting large files (to your printer, for instance) and backing up files on your hard drive.

Zip file—a .zip, or "zipped," file. Has nothing to do with a Zip disk. A file that has been compressed using zip software.

INDEX

Note: Also look in the Glossary and Definitions of Acronyms for descriptions of terms not found here.

More Great Books for Writers!

Too Lazy to Work, Too Nervous to Steal—Learn how to turn your love of writing into a moneymaking business. John Clausen's friendly, funny style—a cross between a pep rally, a writer's workshop, stand-up comedy, and good old-fashioned storytelling—will enable you to live your dream and succeed.
ISBN 0-89879-997-X ✷ hardcover ✷ 256 pages ✷ #10732-K

The Writer's Idea Book—Jump-start your creativity and turn those initial ideas into a completed manuscript. This insightful, invaluable guide makes it fun and easy. You'll find over 400 unique prompts inside, ranging from clustering to role playing, along with encouraging advice that gets—and keeps—your words flowing.
ISBN 0-89879-873-6 ✷ hardcover ✷ 272 pages ✷ #10594-K

Get Organized, Get Published—This lively, inspirational and browsable book provides tips for living the writer's life simply and efficiently. You'll find page after page of useful advice, covering everything from organizing your desk to tracking submissions. You'll generate more ideas, complete more projects, and systematically submit your work to editors and agents.
ISBN 1-58297-003-3 ✷ hardcover ✷ 240 pages ✷ #10689-K

Formatting & Submitting Your Manuscript—This easy-to-use guide provides all the information you need to create effective query letters, proposals, outlines, synopses, and follow-up correspondence. Dozens of charts, lists, models, and sidebars help you to submit your work correctly and enhance your chances of being published.
ISBN 0-89879-921-X ✷ paperback ✷ 208 pages ✷ #10618-K

These books and other fine Writer's Digest titles are available from you local bookstore, online supplier or by calling 1-800-221-5831.

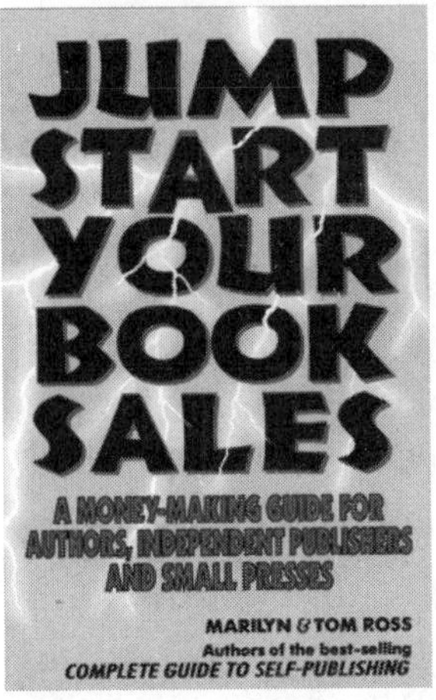

Jump Start Your Book Sales: A Money-Making Guide for Authors, Independent Publishers and Small Presses

by Marilyn and Tom Ross

Turn yourself into a marketing master and make tens of thousands of extra dollars with the ideas in this companion book to *The Complete Guide to Self-Publishing*! Discover more secrets for generating lots of free publicity, then master how to really capitalize on it. Add to that insider information on how to make the Internet a fabulous sales producer, create lucrative strategic alliances, sell to book clubs, get onto QVC Home Shopping Network—and you can't do without this marketing resource.

Fun illustrations, useful checklists, sample forms, *and* the Web sites, Wisdom, and Whimsey chapter endings you've come to love in *The Complete Guide to Self-Publishing*.

Only $19.95. For less than 6¢ a day, you can turn the next year into a wealth-building bonanza!

Here's What the Reviewers Are Saying:

"Demonstrates how energetic authors and publicists can increase revenue by carefully planning a book's marketing strategy on TV, on the Net, in bookstores, through 'buzz,' etc. A particularly helpful section teaches writers how to actually sell their books at those ubiquitous author readings." —*Publishers Weekly*

"Their [Rosses'] advice is up-to-date, specific, and practical, whether the topic is generating publicity, cracking nontraditional markets (home-shopping networks, for example), or 'muscling your way into traditional channels' (wholesalers, the library market, educational sales . . . This guide is an essential reference." —*Booklist*

"Peppered with exciting promotional ideas and filled with real-life examples, *Jump Start Your Book Sales* is an essential reference for publishers."
—Dan Poynter, *The Self-Publishing Manual*

"The information the Rosses have packed into this twenty-five chapter book comes not only from the experience gained in marketing their own books for many years, but from what has been learned from the give-and-take sessions of their highly respected seminars. . . . This is a book for serious people interested in making a serious attempt not to have their books wallow in the basement." —*ForeWord*

"*Jump Start Your Book Sales* is an authoritative kick in the pants. This book thinks of everything you didn't. And then some." —*The Bloomsbury Review*

This book and other fine Writer's Digest titles are available from your local bookseller, online supplier or by calling 1-800-221-5831 or use the order form on the next page.